MAKING

AMERICA

WORK

Jonathan Barry Forman

Also of interest from the Urban Institute Press:

State Tax Policy: A Political Perspective, Second Edition, by David Brunori
The Encyclopedia of Taxation and Tax Policy, Second Edition, edited by
Joseph J. Cordes, Robert D. Ebel, and Jane G. Gravelle
Contemporary U.S. Tax Policy, by C. Eugene Steuerle
Tax Justice: The Ongoing Debate, edited by Joseph J. Thorndike and
Dennis J. Ventry Jr.

MAKING

AMERICA

WORK

Jonathan Barry Forman

THE URBAN INSTITUTE PRESS
Washington, D.C.

THE URBAN INSTITUTE PRESS
2100 M Street, N.W.
Washington, D.C. 20037

Library of Congress Cataloging-in-Publication Data

Forman, Jonathan Barry, 1952-
   Making America work / Jonathan Barry Forman.
      p. cm.
   Includes bibliographical references and index.
   ISBN 0-87766-731-4 (pbk. : alk. paper)
   1. Manpower policy--United States.   2. Labor--United States.   3. United States--
Economic policy.   I. Title.
   HD5724.F67 2006
   331.12'0420973--dc22

                                                                          2006024006

Printed in the United States of America

10 09 08 07 06   1 2 3 4 5

THE URBAN INSTITUTE is a nonprofit, nonpartisan policy research and educational organization established in Washington, D.C., in 1968. Its staff investigates the social, economic, and governance problems confronting the nation and evaluates the public and private means to alleviate them. The Institute disseminates its research findings through publications, its web site, the media, seminars, and forums.

Through work that ranges from broad conceptual studies to administrative and technical assistance, Institute researchers contribute to the stock of knowledge available to guide decisionmaking in the public interest.

Conclusions or opinions expressed in Institute publications are those of the authors and do not necessarily reflect the views of officers or trustees of the Institute, advisory groups, or any organizations that provide financial support to the Institute.

*To my wife, Lani Lee Malysa, and
our children, Neil and Carmen.*

CONTENTS

FOREWORD

Jon Forman is one of a small, but growing, group of analysts who have concluded after years of study that the nation's broken and dysfunctional tax and expenditure systems can be repaired only if they are fixed together. His analysis does not fall easily into the mutually dependent camps of those who attack government or defend it mainly for the sake of a good fight—the type of fight that the media overplay and that camp-based politicians engage in to "appeal to their base." Instead, he understands that the government doesn't do what it is supposed to do for many entwined reasons: it is cumbersome, overrun with programs, poorly integrated, and not well positioned to achieve results, much less efficiently or quickly. Like others in this small, dedicated group, Forman cannot be easily labeled: he urges the nation to pay more attention to and spend more on some things and less on others, and he looks to both conservative and progressive principles for fair and practical ideas.

In *Making America Work*, Forman makes the case for refocusing on two basics: reducing inequality and encouraging greater work effort. At times, these two goals can be mutually incompatible, but he is entirely correct that the current system is so inefficient that a reformed system could do better on both fronts. But a prerequisite, as Forman makes clear, is working through the system as a whole—from taxes to expenditures, from pensions to health care, from family-based subsidies to employment policies. Forman gives us an insight-strewn tour of this vast and complex horizon.

Plain budget arithmetic tells us that proposals like Forman's would set on the right course a country floundering over how to reform such crazy commitments as those increases in health spending so poorly designed that they tend to increase—yes, increase, not decrease—the number of uninsured. Unfortunately, the agencies of the executive branch and of Congress are not organized to conduct the integrated analysis required—a major barrier to reform. No executive branch agency, for instance, does the type of simultaneous research on expenditures and taxes that would carry ideas like Forman's to the next stage.

While you may not agree with some of his proposals, Forman will force you to think on his terrain. He will make you face up to trade-offs directly. He will not let you off the hook by pleading that you don't care about our government's revenue-raising and -spending machinery, at least as long as more spending or lower taxes come your way. And he will remind you of the high costs of ignoring the other side of the balance sheet when it comes to every tax or expenditure change.

If you read *Making America Work*, you'll grasp where the domestic policy debate should and probably must head at the beginning of the 21st century.

C. Eugene Steuerle
Senior Fellow, The Urban Institute
Deputy Assistant Secretary for
Tax Analysis, U.S. Treasury (1987–89)

ACKNOWLEDGMENTS

I am grateful for the academic freedom, collegiality, and financial support that I have found at the University of Oklahoma College of Law. I have had excellent research assistance from Erin Dixon, Nina Jung, and Monica Brewer. I received helpful comments on the entire draft of this book from Kevin Hollenbeck, Joel Newman, and several anonymous referees; Don Bogan, Taiawagi Helton, Kirk Stark, and Ed Zelinsky gave me comments on early chapter drafts. I also benefited from insights and assistance from many others including David Barber, Frances Benson, Adam Carasso, James K. Galbraith, Ron Gebhardts-bauer, Beverly Goldberg, Stephen C. Goss, Janet Holtzblatt, Lawrence Mishel, Robert J. Myers, Patricia L. Scahill, Bruce Schobel, John Karl Scholz, Gene Steuerle, Alice H. Wade, Daniel H. Weinberg, and George Yin. The Urban Institute Press has been easy to work with, and I am especially grateful to my editor, Fiona Blackshaw. She improved the prose and the pace of this book and tolerated my fervor to keep the manuscript up-to-date. Thanks also to the *Journal Record* of Oklahoma City for letting me refine my views and my style in a monthly column.

INTRODUCTION

The purpose of this book is to explain how government policies should be changed to both encourage greater work effort and reduce economic inequality. In a complex society such as ours, the economic rewards from work are determined by a combination of market forces and government policies. Labor markets tend to distribute economic rewards in proportion to productivity. That can be efficient, but it also generates significant inequality.

When the market distribution of economic rewards is unfair, it falls to the government to adopt policies that promote greater economic justice. Governments influence market outcomes through a combination of regulation, spending, and taxation. In a free-market economy, government intervention can and necessarily must be limited. As this book shows, however, government can and should intervene, both to make work more attractive and to promote greater economic justice.

The goal here is not to turn us into a nation of workaholics. On average, Americans probably work hard enough. But we should increase the rewards from work for low-skilled Americans, and we should reduce the work disincentives that so many other workers face.

Chapter 1, *Developing a National Strategy for Work*, explains the centrality of work in American society and shows how market forces and government policies combine to determine the current rewards from work. The chapter also discusses economic inequality in the United States, with particular emphasis on the relatively high level of inequality in the distribution of earnings. Next, the chapter explains how antidiscrimination laws and recent changes in tax, welfare, and elder policy have encouraged greater work and work effort. Finally, this chapter suggests how further improvements in government tax, transfer, and regulatory policies could both encourage work and promote greater economic justice.

Chapter 2, *Working in the U.S.A.*, discusses who is working and who is not. Pay, work patterns, and demographic trends are highlighted. In particular, chapter 2 discusses the relationship of earnings to education, age, gender, race, and other important demographic factors. It also discusses the recent trend of rising earnings inequality.

Chapter 3, *How Labor Markets Reward Work*, uses some of the basic principles of labor economics to explain how labor markets distribute earnings and earnings opportunities. In particular, the chapter explains the standard economic model of labor supply and shows why labor markets inevitably lead to significant inequality in the distribution of earnings and earnings opportunities.

Chapter 4, *How Government Affects the Distribution of Earnings and Income*, explains how government policies can, and should, influence the distribution of earnings and other economic resources. It considers how taxes, transfers, and regulations affect the labor market's initial distribution of earnings and earnings opportunities.

Chapter 5, *Making Government Work*, focuses on the question of just how far the government should go to "correct" the market's unequal distribution of earnings and other economic resources. It also considers how government policies can both promote greater economic justice and encourage greater work effort.

Chapter 6, *Making Taxes Work*, recommends various ways to reform the tax system to minimize work disincentives and promote greater economic justice. The chapter starts by discussing some major problems with the current tax system. Then, the chapter suggests six relatively modest changes that could improve the current system. For example, the chapter recommends that we broaden the tax base and reduce tax rates on earned income, stop taxing low-income workers, restructure the earned income tax credit, replace personal exemptions and standard deductions with refundable personal tax credits, reduce marriage penalties, and simplify the tax system and reduce compliance costs.

Beyond such incremental changes to the tax code, chapter 6 also considers more fundamental changes to the current system. For example, the government could integrate the income and Social Security taxes into a single, comprehensive tax system. That system could be based on earnings, income, consumption, wealth, or some combination of these tax bases. Most important, however, that comprehensive tax system should be designed to both promote greater economic justice and encourage greater work effort.

Chapter 7, *Making Welfare Work*, recommends various ways to make work more rewarding for low-skilled Americans and make the distribution of economic resources fairer. The chapter starts by putting the welfare system in its historical context. Next, the chapter identifies some of the major problems with the current welfare system. The chapter then suggests seven relatively modest changes that could improve the current system. The government should increase earnings subsidies for low-income workers, provide more money to help support the children of low-income parents, provide more child care assistance for low-income parents, and make disability programs work friendly. In connection with those reforms, the government should reduce or eliminate the marriage penalties faced by low-income workers, better coordinate the many overlapping welfare programs, and update the federal measure of poverty.

Beyond such incremental changes, chapter 7 also considers more fundamental restructuring. Ultimately, it would make sense to integrate the tax and transfer systems into a single comprehensive system.

Chapter 8, *Making Social Security Work*, discusses how Social Security influences individual decisions about work and retirement and offers recommendations for improvement. After a brief overview of the current system, the chapter explains the need for reform. The chapter then suggests seven reforms that could increase work incentives and reduce work disincentives. The chapter suggests that we move away from payroll financing, reduce the progressivity of the Social Security benefit formula while concomitantly expanding Supplemental Security Income, increase the Social Security benefit-computation period beyond 35 years, raise the early and full retirement ages, tax Social Security benefits like pensions, replace spousal benefits with earnings sharing, and change the way that benefits accrue and are paid out.

Beyond such modest reforms, chapter 8 also considers replacing the current Social Security system with a two-tiered system. The first tier would provide a basic Social Security benefit to every older American, and these benefits would be financed out of general revenues. The second tier would provide an additional earnings-related benefit based on much-reduced payroll tax contributions made to individual accounts.

Chapter 9, *Making Pensions Work*, discusses how pensions influence individual decisions about work and retirement and offers recommendations for improvement. At the outset, the chapter provides an overview of the current pension system, discusses some recent trends and problems, and explains the work incentives and disincentives created by pension plans. The remainder of the chapter suggests how to make the pension system work. The basic approach is to expand coverage and pay workers in proportion to their productivity. Ultimately, however, we might need to replace the current voluntary system with a mandatory universal pension system.

Chapter 10, *Making Health Care Work*, explains how the American health care system works and suggests a number of improvements. In particular, the chapter recommends ways to expand health care coverage, strengthen the connection between health care and work effort, and restructure health care markets. Ultimately, the goal should be a health care system that provides nearly universal coverage at a reasonable cost and does so with a minimum of work disincentives.

Chapter 11, *Making Labor Markets Work*, discusses how government regulation influences labor markets and offers recommendations for improvement. In particular, the chapter recommends that the government vigorously enforce the laws against employment discrimination, reduce incarceration levels, make education and training work, modestly raise the minimum wage and index it for inflation, expand the unemployment insurance program, promote unionization, and make full employment a reality.

Finally, chapter 12, *Working Together*, pulls together the book's principal recommendations about how to reform the government's tax, transfer, and regulatory policies. The result is a comprehensive system that would generally increase the economic rewards for work and promote greater economic justice. That system would have earnings subsidies and low effective tax rates on earned income. In addition, that system would ensure that workers would not lose their health coverage as a result of changing jobs or as a result of entering or leaving the workforce. That system would also provide government assistance for education, training, child care, and many other social welfare services.

In short, this is a book about how America works and about how to continue making America work in this new millennium.

1

DEVELOPING A NATIONAL STRATEGY FOR WORK

Work. Hard work! And plenty of it. That's what has made the United States into the world's foremost economic superpower. Although the United States has less than 5 percent of the world's population, our economy accounts for more than 28 percent of the world's production.[1] About 149 million Americans are employed in the civilian workforce, and the unemployment rate tends to hover around 5 percent (Bureau of Labor Statistics [BLS] 2006f, table 1). In fact, our unemployment rate is typically lower than that of most other industrialized nations, and our labor force participation rate—66.0 percent in 2005—is higher (BLS 2006c, 2006f).[2]

To be sure, the United States has been blessed with magnificent and abundant resources. But ultimately, the economic success of America is about the hard work of Americans, and about a government that has generally had the good sense to stay out of their way. In just over two centuries, Americans have built a great network of cities and states that would make our founding fathers and mothers proud.

Why does America work? In large part the answer is probably embedded in our cultural values. In particular, we value and respect work. We want to see hard work and creativity rewarded. We love Horatio Alger stories—stories in which our hero triumphs from hard work, honesty, and perseverance.[3] We truly want to have a nation in which any child can grow up to become the president of the United States or, at least, the president of a *Fortune* 500 company. At the same time, however, we respect everyone who works, be they physicians or garbage collectors.

While we value and respect work, we are also concerned about economic justice. In our labor markets, we like to see all American workers earn a fair day's pay for a fair day's work.[4] And we like having a safety net to catch those who, despite their best efforts, cannot compete successfully in our labor markets (Pew Research Center 2003).[5]

In short, America works because it has achieved a balance between our desire to reward work and our concerns about economic justice. But America could work even better. The challenge is to find ways to improve the economic rewards for work and to promote greater economic justice. That challenge is the focus of this book.

THE ROLE OF GOVERNMENT

In a complex society like ours, the economic rewards from work are determined by a combination of market forces and government policies. Markets arise automatically from the economic interactions among people and institutions. Here and there, government policies intervene to influence the operations of those markets and to shape the outcomes that result from market transactions.

Needless to say, policymakers cannot do much about market forces per se. Adam Smith's laws of supply and demand are every bit as immutable as Newton's laws of thermodynamics.[6] But policymakers can change how governments influence market operations and outcomes.

In that regard, governments influence market outcomes through a combination of regulation, spending, and taxation. Government regulation defines and limits the range of markets and so influences the shape of the initial distribution of economic resources. Government taxes and spending also have a significant impact on the distribution of economic resources. Most clearly, government taxes and transfers are the primary tools for the redistribution of economic resources. In addition, taxes and spending change the distribution of economic resources by favoring some sectors of the economy over others and by influencing the behavior of economic actors in the marketplace.

Measuring the Impact of Government on the Distribution of Economic Resources

It is probably impossible to measure the full impact of government on the distribution of economic resources. In particular, it is difficult to estimate the impact of government regulation on the distribution of economic resources. We simply do not start from some theoretical Hobbesian state of nature, only to have government add a regulatory framework to it (Hobbes 1887). Rather, governments define and limit the realms of market competition. These activities both enhance the ability of markets to create wealth and influence the ultimate distribution of that wealth.

For example, government grants of patents not only encourage the creation of tradable property rights in new technologies, but also concentrate the resulting wealth in the hands of the patent owners. Similarly, government-imposed limits on who can practice medicine both protect the public and increase the incomes of physicians over what those salaries might be in a world with completely free competition for medical services. Nobody can really say how excessive the salaries of American physicians are, but it is instructive that there is no shortage of foreign physicians trying to emigrate here, in large part because the average physician in America makes so much more than physicians around the world.[7]

Similar difficulties would arise in trying to estimate the distributional impact of government regulations granting monopolies to utilities, broadcasters, and liquor stores. All in all, it is clear that government regulation significantly affects the distribution of economic resources, but that effect is difficult to measure.

On the other hand, we can get a very good idea about the influence of government tax and spending programs on the relative distribution of economic resources. For example, table 1.1 shows how the current mix of government tax and transfer policies influenced the distribution of household income in 2004. The second column of table 1.1 shows U.S. Census estimates of the market's initial distribution of household income before government taxes and transfers, by quintiles of population ("market income").[8] Before government taxes and transfers, the richest 20 percent of American households received 53.44 percent of

Table 1.1. Share of Aggregate Household Income by Quintiles and Gini Index, 2004

	Market income	Disposable income
Quintiles		
Lowest	1.48	4.68
Second	7.36	10.34
Middle	14.10	16.08
Fourth	23.62	24.02
Highest	53.44	44.88
Gini index	0.496	0.400

Source: U.S. Bureau of the Census (2006), table 2.

household income, while the poorest 20 percent received just 1.48 percent.

That is a rather unequal distribution of income. In that regard, one popular measure of income inequality is the Gini index. Basically, the Gini index is a mathematical measure of income inequality that can range from 0.0, indicating perfect equality (where everyone has the same income), to 1.0, indicating perfect inequality (where one person has all the income and the rest have none). According to table 1.1, the Gini index for the market distribution of household income in the United States in 2004 was a sizeable 0.496.[9]

Table 1.1 also shows how government taxes and transfers reduce economic inequality. More specifically, the third column of table 1.1 shows the "disposable income" shares that households end up with after government taxes and transfers in the year 2004.[10] Taxes and transfers increased the relative share of income held by the bottom four quintiles at the expense of the share of income held by the top quintile, and the Gini index fell to 0.400. All in all, current government tax and transfer policies reduce household income inequality by about 20 percent.[11]

One can get a better sense of economic inequality in America from figure 1.1, which is derived from the numbers in table 1.1. Figure 1.1 also shows how government taxes and transfers reduce economic inequality. The horizontal axis in figure 1.1 shows the cumulative per-

Figure 1.1. How Taxes and Transfers Improved Equity, 2004

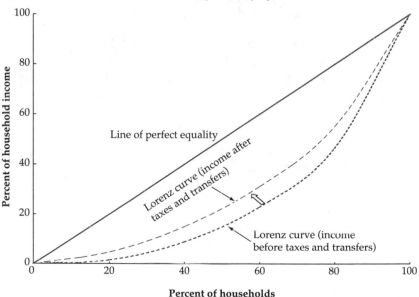

Source: Author's calculations.

centage of households, and the vertical axis shows the cumulative share of income earned by those households. An egalitarian society—that is, one with a perfectly equal distribution of income—is represented by the 45-degree, upward-sloping diagonal line. In such a society, the cumulative share of income would be equal to the cumulative population share. For example, 40 percent of the households would have 40 percent of the income.

The dotted line in figure 1.1 is the Lorenz curve based on the "market income" data from the second column of table 1.1.[12] This curve shows, for example, that the poorest 20 percent of households had just 1.48 percent of market income in 2004 and that the bottom 40 percent of households had just 8.84 percent of cumulative household income.

The higher Lorenz curve in figure 1.1 (the dashed line) is based on the "disposable" income data from the third column of table 1.1. This curve is significantly closer to the diagonal line of perfect equality. After taxes and transfers, the poorest 20 percent of households had 4.68 percent of disposable household income in 2004, and the bottom 40 percent of households had 15.02 percent of household income. The white arrow between the two Lorenz curves in figure 1.1 shows that government taxes and transfers reduced economic inequality by about 20 percent.

The Gini index actually measures the size of the area between the Lorenz curve and the diagonal line of perfect equality. More specifically, the Gini index is the ratio of that area to the entire area of the triangle under the diagonal line. Hence, in an egalitarian society, the Gini index would be 0.0 since the Lorenz curve would match the diagonal line. In a perfectly unequal society in which all the income was held by one person, the Lorenz curve would look like a backwards "L", and the Gini index would have a value of 1.0. Against this background, the 0.496 Gini index for the market distribution of household income in the United States is quite large, and the 0.400 Gini index for the post-tax, post-transfer distribution of household income is still pretty sizeable.

Why Is There So Much Inequality?

Why is the market distribution of household income in the United States so unequal? Much of this inequality is attributable to inequality in the distribution of individual earnings, and much is attributable to inequality in the distribution of investment income. Family structure also significantly affects the pre-tax, pre-transfer distribution of household income.

Earnings Inequality

Earned income is by far the largest component of personal income, making up about three-quarters of all family income.[13] Consequently, any inequality in individual earnings is sure to be reflected in measures of household income inequality. In fact, there is significant inequality of earnings in the United States.

Even among full-time workers, there are vast disparities. Some people just get paid a lot more than others for their 40 hours a week of work. For example, table 1.2 shows the median usual weekly earnings of full-time wage and salary workers for the first quarter of 2006. The median full-time worker made $668 a week in the first quarter of 2006. Table 1.2 also shows median weekly earnings for the top and bottom quartiles of earners and for the top and bottom deciles of earners. For example, a worker in the 90th percentile of full-time workers made $1,535 a week in the first quarter of 2006, while a worker in the 10th percentile made just $318 a week. One common method of measuring earnings inequality is to compare the earnings of workers in various positions in the earnings distribution. For example, dividing $1,535 by $318 gives us a "90/10 ratio" of almost 5 to 1. In short, top earners make almost five times as much as bottom earners.

The Gini index of individual earnings inequality in the United States is also fairly large. For example, the Gini index of individual earnings inequality among full-time workers in the year 2001 was a fairly sizeable 0.409 (U.S. Bureau of the Census 2004b).[14]

Of course, even these measures of inequality mask the truly staggering range of individual earnings in the United States. For example, in 2004, the typical chief executive officer (CEO) in a major U.S. company made more than 400 times as much as the average production worker (Ander-

Table 1.2. Median Usual Weekly Earnings of Full-Time Wage and Salary Workers, First Quarter 2006

	Number of workers (in thousands)	Upper Limit of (in dollars)				
		First decile	First quartile	Second quartile (median)	Third quartile	Ninth decile
All workers age 16 and over	103,469	318	445	668	1,030	1,535

Source: Bureau of Labor Statistics (2006g), table 4.

Note: Ten percent of all full-time wage and salary workers earn less than the upper limit of the first decile; 25 percent earn less than the upper limit of the first quartile; 50 percent earn less than the upper limit of the second quartile, or median; 75 percent earn less than the upper limit of the third quartile; and 90 percent earn less than the upper limit of the ninth decile.

son et al. 2005). And CEOs are by no means the only workers who earn extraordinary compensation. Many movie stars and athletes have seven- or even eight-digit incomes. In 2005, for example, movie actress Reese Witherspoon made $30 million and basketball player Kobe Bryant made $15.9 million.[15] We live in what some have called a "winner-take-all" society in which the top workers in each field of endeavor are likely to earn disproportionately large rewards for their efforts (Frank and Cook 1995; McMahon and Abreu 1999).[16]

Inequality in the Distribution of Investment Income

The second major reason the market's distribution of household income is so unequal has to do with the unequal distribution of investment income and wealth. A significant portion of household income inequality reflects the fact that relatively few well-off households receive most of the nation's investment income.

For example, consider Professor Edward N. Wolff's recent research on wealth holdings in the United States. Wolff found that, in 2001, the top 1 percent of American households controlled 33.4 percent of total household wealth (Wolff 2004, table 2). At the same time, the bottom 80 percent of households held only 15.5 percent of total household wealth. Wolff's estimate of the Gini index for wealth inequality in 2001 was an astonishingly high 0.826. Wolff himself has noted that inequality in wealth holdings is "extreme and substantially greater than income inequality" (Wolff 1999, 27). From Wolff's research, we can surmise that the inequality in the distribution of investment income is also substantial.

In fact, that inequality in investment income shows up quite clearly in Internal Revenue Service reports about individual income tax returns. Of the almost $115 billion in dividends reported by individuals on their 2003 income tax returns, more than 45 percent ($52 billion) was reported by the 2.5 million taxpayers with incomes of $200,000 or more, and another 17 percent ($20 billion) was reported by the 8.9 million taxpayers with incomes between $100,000 and $200,000.[17] On the other hand, less than 21 percent ($24 billion) of dividend income was reported by the 109 million taxpayers with incomes under $50,000.

Family Structure

Normal variations in family structure can also have a considerable impact on the distribution of household income (Karoly 1998). In particular, married-couple families tend to have more income than single-parent families, but marital status is by no means evenly distributed across the income distribution. In 2001, for example, 79.9 percent of households in the top 20 percent of household income were married-couple families, but only 19.6 percent of households in the bottom 20 percent were married-couple families (DeNavas-Walt and Cleveland 2002, table 3). To be sure, human mating behavior is far from random. Rather, there is a tendency toward what sociologists call "assortive mating," in which high-income workers tend to marry other high-income workers, and low-income workers tend to marry other low-income workers.[18]

Also, having a spouse is kind of like having an insurance policy. If a married worker loses her job, her spouse's income acts as a buffer that keeps her household's income from otherwise falling to zero. Additional skewing results from the fact that some households have no earned income and other households have earned income from two workers.

It is worth noting that the breaking apart of American families in recent decades has been one of the primary causes of the increase in household income inequality (Blank 1995; Hoynes, Page, and Stevens 2006). For example, married couples are much less likely to be poor than divorced individuals.[19] Along the same lines, the typical household is smaller today than it was in the past. The average household in 2004 contained 2.57 people, down from 3.35 people per household in 1960 (Census Bureau 2005c).

All in all, such demographic considerations can help us understand why the distribution of household incomes is so much more skewed than the distribution of individual earnings.

What Should the Government Do?

Clearly, there is a significant amount of inequality in the free market's distribution of earnings, income, and wealth. No doubt, much of that economic inequality is justified. For example, most of us would agree that people who work harder than others tend to deserve greater rewards. Similarly, most of us would agree that people who postpone work to gain additional education and skills should be rewarded with extra compensation to make up for their forgone earnings.

The problem is that the amount of economic inequality created by a free market is far greater than what is actually needed to provide reasonable rewards for extra effort and to otherwise ensure adequate production of goods and services. That is where government comes in. One of the central functions of modern governments is to reduce economic inequality, although there is considerable debate as to just how much the government should do to reduce economic inequality.

It is perhaps easiest to articulate the two most extreme sides to that debate: egalitarianism and libertarianism. Pure egalitarians argue that all people are entitled to share equally in the productive output of their society. Consequently, egalitarians favor government tax and transfer policies that would equalize, or at least tend to equalize, the distribution of economic resources. Like latter-day Robin Hoods, egalitarians often favor taking from the rich and giving to the poor. Similarly, egalitarians might argue that everybody who works 40 hours a week should be paid the same.

At the other extreme, libertarians start from the premise that free-market outcomes reflect the free and voluntary trades made by relatively equal market participants. Pure libertarians argue that the market distribution of economic resources is inherently just and that the government has no right to interfere with it. Not surprisingly, libertarians generally argue that individuals should be allowed to keep whatever income and wealth they acquire in the marketplace. Moreover, most libertarians doubt that government intervention would actually make society better.

Almost everybody actually falls somewhere in between these two extreme positions. Those with an egalitarian bent usually concede that differential rewards are needed to ensure adequate productivity, and those with a libertarian bent typically concede that some minimal amount of redistribution is needed to help the truly disadvantaged.

All in all, it seems unlikely that a convincing moral argument can be made for any particular level of redistribution. There is simply no magic Gini index value nor perfect 90/10 ratio that defines the theoretically and morally "correct" level of inequality. Rather, the question of just how much redistribution is appropriate seems to be largely an aesthetic one that turns on individual tastes for redistribution.

Still, there is a fairly strong consensus in favor of at least some government policies to reduce economic inequality. As table 1.1 and figure 1.1 show, current government tax and transfer policies already reduce household income inequality by about 20 percent. Moreover, we are always debating government policies that would involve additional amounts of redistribution. We seem particularly interested in government policies that can both improve the rewards from work *and* promote greater economic justice. Improving the rewards from work would encourage more people to work, and their added productivity would increase the size of the economic pie. Promoting greater economic justice would make the shares of that larger pie more equal.

All in all, improving the rewards from work and promoting greater economic justice would improve society by increasing productivity and individual welfare. The key is to design government policies that encourage work and work effort, and we have already begun to steer in that direction.

RECENT POLICY TRENDS ENCOURAGING WORK

Indeed, four recent policy trends highlight our collective desire to encourage work effort. First, we have changed the focus of social welfare programs to encourage work. Second, we have significantly reduced the income tax rates imposed on earned income. Third, we have outlawed employment discrimination because of an individual's race, color, religion, sex, national origin, age, or disability. Fourth, we have changed Social Security, pension, and labor market policies in order to encourage elderly workers to remain in the workforce.

Social Welfare Policy

The classic example of shifting the focus of social welfare programs to encourage work involves the unemployment compensation program. Created by the Social Security Act of 1935, unemployment compensation was designed to provide temporary and partial wage replacements for laid-off workers.[20] Workers who are unemployed generally receive weekly cash payments for up to six months or until they find employment.

Like most other social welfare benefits, unemployment benefits were not originally subject to income taxation (Forman 1994). By the 1970s, however, many policy analysts argued that the exclusion of unemployment benefits from taxation was inequitable and that it created a disincentive for working.[21] In a seminal paper, Martin Feldstein showed that, on average, unemployment benefits replaced more than 60 percent of lost after-tax income, and he found that such high wage-replacement rates had an adverse impact on the frequency and duration of unemployment (Feldstein 1974). People lingered on unemployment benefits, rather than finding jobs. Accordingly, to make working relatively more attractive than drawing benefits, Feldstein urged that unemployment benefits should be taxed. In a triumph of policy analysis over politics (perhaps coupled with a need for revenues), Congress began taxing a portion of unemployment benefits in 1979; since 1987, unemployment benefits have been fully taxable.[22] Those changes raised the effective tax rate on unemployment benefits and so made work relatively more attractive than unemployment.

More recently, tax and welfare reforms have combined to greatly increase the incentive for welfare recipients to enter the workforce. Government programs now try to reward work. These improved work incentives have contributed to an unprecedented fall in welfare caseloads and a dramatic increase in the employment of former welfare recipients. Only 5.4 million people (2.1 million families) received welfare in an average month of 2001, down from 14.2 million welfare recipients (5.0 million families) in an average month of 1993.[23]

Consider the earned income tax credit. To help low-income working families with children, Congress enacted this credit in 1975 and has expanded the credit many times since then (*Internal Revenue Code* [I.R.C.] § 32; Forman 1988). In 2006, for example, a family with two or more children is entitled to a refundable earned income tax credit of up to $4,536 (Internal Revenue Service [IRS] 2005c). The credit is computed as 40 percent of the first $11,340 of earned income, so a welfare recipient can reap a large reward for working, even at a $5.15-per-hour minimum-wage job.[24]

Similarly, welfare programs have been changed to encourage work. From 1982 until 1996, the Aid to Families with Dependent Children (AFDC) program was characterized by a 100 percent benefit-reduction rate; welfare recipients could also lose Medicaid and housing benefits if they earned "too much." All in all, welfare recipients faced significant work disincentives. It was as if President Lyndon Johnson's War on Poverty had become a "War on Work."

With the passage of the Welfare Reform Act of 1996,[25] Temporary Assistance for Needy Families (TANF) replaced AFDC, and most states have now eliminated those 100 percent benefit-reduction rates. The Welfare Reform Act also increased federal child care assistance for low- and moderate-income families, and Medicaid has also become more work friendly. Not surprisingly, welfare recipients have responded to these financial incentives. For example, according to the Council of Economic Advisers (1999a), the percentage of welfare recipients who were working tripled between 1992 and 1997.

Tax Policy

The income tax rates imposed on the earned income of high-income workers have been significantly reduced over the past 50 years. With the advent of World War II, the income tax became a mass tax, and marginal tax rates soared. Even into the 1960s, marginal tax rates remained as high as 70 percent. To help encourage work effort by high-income taxpayers, Congress added a provision to the Internal Revenue Code that provided a 50 percent maximum tax rate on earned income.[26] To help reduce the tax rates for all taxpayers, the Tax Reform Act of 1986 reduced the maximum income tax rate to just 28 percent.[27] In subsequent years, rates slowly crept up to a 39.6 percent maximum federal income tax rate. More recently, however, the Economic Growth and Tax Relief Reconciliation Act of 2001 (EGTRRA) and the Jobs Relief and Reconciliation Act of 2003 cut tax rates.[28] The maximum income tax rate is now just 35 percent, and many workers face income tax rates of just 10 or 15 percent.

Antidiscrimination Policy

The United States has outlawed employment discrimination because of an individual's race, color, religion, sex, national origin, age, or disability. Discrimination in the labor market against minorities, women, and other groups tends to depress their wages. Those depressed wages tend to discourage those groups from working and result in greater inequality in the distribution of earnings than would result if discrimination were barred. Starting in the 1960s, the injustice of employment discrimination became obvious to federal policymakers.

As an initial response, the Equal Pay Act of 1963 (Public Law 88-38) outlawed the practice of paying women less than men for the same work. Next, the Civil Rights Act of 1964 (Public Law 88-352) generally outlawed employment discrimination because of an individual's race, color, religion, sex, or national origin. Similarly, the Age Discrimination in Employment Act of 1967 (Public Law 90-202, or ADEA) outlawed employment discrimination against individuals who are 40 years of age or older. More recently, the Americans with Disabilities Act of 1990 (Public Law 101-336, or ADA) outlawed employment discrimination against disabled Americans.

These laws were intended to discourage discrimination against the affected groups. In the past few decades, there has been a remarkable increase in the labor force participation of workers in the affected groups and increases in their relative earnings. For example, among women age 16 and older, 59.3 percent were working or seeking work in 2005, up from just 43.4 percent in 1971, and women workers earned an average of 81 percent as much as men, up from just 63 percent in 1979 (BLS 2006f, table 2, and author's computation from table 37).[29]

Aging Policy

The United States has changed Social Security, pension, and labor market policies to encourage the elderly to remain in the workforce. The government has long been concerned about the retirement income needs of the elderly and about the effect of public policy on the timing of retirement. Over the years, Congress has passed several laws expressly to remove impediments to work by the elderly. In addition to banning employment discrimination against workers over the age of 40, the ADEA outlawed mandatory retirement before the age of 65. The limit was raised to 70 in 1978 and finally removed altogether in 1986.[30]

Pension and tax laws have also changed significantly, with traditional pension plans slowly being supplemented or even supplanted by individual retirement accounts and 401(k) plans (Zelinsky 2004; Rajnes 2002). Unlike traditional pension plans that typically impose financial penalties on workers who want to keep working past some arbitrary retirement age, these individual account plans are neutral about the timing of retirement (Forman 2000a, 2004a). Consequently, workers can continue working and accumulating additional retirement assets to support themselves during their ever longer life expectancies. Also of note, the Senior Citizens' Freedom to Work Act of 2000 (Public Law 106-182) repealed the limitation on the amount of outside income that Social Security beneficiaries who have attained full retirement age (e.g., age 65 and 8 months in 2006) may earn without incurring a loss of benefits.

THE NEED FOR FURTHER REFORM

All in all, government policies have become more attuned to the importance of work effort and work incentives, and many changes have been made to promote greater economic justice. But much more still needs to be done.

First, we need to do much more to reduce economic inequality and promote greater economic justice. Second, government programs and combinations of government programs still operate to discourage work effort in some situations. Government programs should instead be designed to encourage work, and taxes should be designed to minimize work disincentives.

Government Intervention Should Promote Greater Economic Justice

When the market distribution of economic rewards is unfair, it falls to the government to adopt policies that promote greater economic justice. In particular, the government should redesign its tax and transfer policies to increase the economic rewards for low-wage workers, and it should do so in a way that minimizes the work disincentives imposed on other workers.

For the most part, the distribution of earned income in America is determined by market forces. Economic "laws" of supply and demand set most prices in America, including the price of labor (wages). Those who have skills in short supply can command higher salaries, and those with low skills must settle for low wages—or none at all.[31] The market is very efficient at generating these differential rewards, and it is clear that differential compensation is needed to assure production.

After all, if everyone got paid the same, who would do the nasty and distasteful jobs?

Still, almost nobody seriously contends that the distribution of earnings that results from the operation of market forces is fair. Labor markets don't miraculously pay people what they "deserve."[32] If they did, preschool teachers might make more than advertising executives, and garbage collectors might make more than lawyers. But they do not.[33]

As table 1.2 shows, even among full-time workers, there are vast disparities. Consider also *Parade* magazine's recent annual report on "What People Earn."[34] *Parade* reported that 12-year-old actress Dakota Fanning made $15 million in 2005, but 66-year-old Senate Minority Leader Harry Reid made just $183,500. Similarly, 34-year-old race car driver Jeff Gordon made $6.9 million, but 39-year-old Iowa firefighter Bobby Wright made just $42,600. Meanwhile, Cathy Wyer, a 42-year-old school secretary in Jackson, Wyoming, made $24,000. Were these the income levels that Plato's philosopher-king would choose?

All in all, it seems fair to conclude that the market's distribution of economic resources, in general, and of earned income, in particular, is far from perfect. Market forces result in a system in which many workers get less than they "deserve" while others get more than they "deserve."[35]

The government should do more to "correct" this situation. In particular, government policies should be redesigned to reduce the inequality of earnings among hard-working Americans. More specifically, it would make sense to redesign government tax, transfer, and regulatory policies to increase the economic rewards for low-wage workers, while minimizing the work disincentives on other workers.

Government Programs Should Encourage Work

There are still some situations in which government programs and combinations of government programs combine and overlap in ways that discourage work effort. No doubt, some work disincentives are inevitable if we are to have a government at all. Taxes, for example, reduce the rewards from work and so tend to make leisure relatively more attractive than work. Similarly, welfare and social insurance programs make it easier to live without working, and so they, too, can undermine the incentive to work.

The problem is that well-intentioned government programs and combinations of programs can often result in extraordinarily large work disincentives. For example, once a worker reaches age 62 and is eligible to receive Social Security benefits, delaying receipt of Social Security by working full-time can be quite costly.[36] Those who delay retirement forgo current benefits, but the increased benefits because of additional work may not adequately compensate for a year of lost benefits. Moreover, those who continue to work must pay Social Security and income taxes on their subsequent earnings, and they may also have to pay income tax on up to 85 percent of their Social Security benefits. Together, these provisions can combine to subject some elderly beneficiaries to confiscatory tax rates on their earned income that can discourage them from working. Not surprisingly, more than 56 percent of the elderly retire as soon as they can—at age 62—and nearly 80 percent of new Social Security beneficiaries claim their benefits by age 65 (U.S. House Committee 2004, table 1-14).

Many low-income workers who are trying to get off welfare face a similar problem. The combination of benefit-reductions and phaseouts in the Food Stamp Program, TANF, and the earned income tax credit can result in extraordinarily high effective marginal tax rates as workers increase their earnings.[27] These high tax rates can discourage individuals from working or improving their work skills.

Along the same lines, the federal tax system often imposes significant "marriage penalties" on married couples in which both husband and wife work (Forman 1996b). These tax penalties can discourage secondary earners (usually wives) from working outside the home at all.

Overall, many government programs and combinations of government programs can discourage individuals from working, and we need to find ways to minimize those explicit and implicit work disincentives.

The United States has already come a long way toward developing a national strategy for work. This book explains how government tax, transfer, and regulatory policies could become even more supportive of individual work and work effort. In sum, this is a book about how America works and about how to make America work even better in this new millennium.

2

WORKING IN THE U.S.A.

M ost Americans work, and they work hard. In 2005, for example,
66 percent of the nation's civilian noninstitutional population age
16 and over participated in the labor force (BLS 2006f, table 1). That is
up from 59.2 percent in 1950, and it is higher than the labor force
participation rates of most industrialized nations (BLS 2006c).[1] Our
employment-population ratio—the ratio of the number of employed
workers to the total population (62.7 percent in 2005)—is also higher
than those in most other industrialized nations, and our unemployment
rate (5.1 percent in 2005) tends to be lower than in those countries (BLS
2006c, 2006f).[2] In addition, American workers tend to work more hours
a year than workers in other industrialized countries. In 2004, for
example, American workers worked an average of 1,824 hours a year,
compared with 1,669 hours for British workers, 1,443 hours for German
workers, and just 1,441 hours for French workers (U.S. Department of
Labor [DOL] 2005, chart 2.8).[3]

Many Americans are working harder than ever (Haveman, Bershadker, and Schwabish 2003; Council of Economic Advisers 1999b;
Mishel, Bernstein, and Allegretto 2005). In 2005, the average American
private-sector worker put in 39.1 hours of work a week; those persons
usually working full-time averaged 42.8 hours a week (BLS 2006f, table
21).[4] In 2004, 77.0 percent of people with work experience worked year
round (either full- or part-time), and 79.9 percent of those who were
employed at some time during 2004 worked full-time (BLS 2005l).
Mothers and married couples are working especially long hours. Nearly
three-quarters of mothers are working outside the home, and the aver-

age married couple, both adults age 25–54, worked 67 hours a week
in 2000, up from 56 hours a week in 1969 (BLS 2002).[5]

Of course, labor force participation and unemployment rates vary
dramatically depending on such demographic factors as age, sex, race,
and education. As shown in table 2.1, labor force participation is greatest among adults age 25 to 54 (82.8 percent). Labor force participation
is also greater among men (73.3 percent) than women (59.3 percent).

Education also has a significant impact on employment. While the
unemployment rate for college graduates was 2.3 percent in 2005, the
unemployment rate for those without a high school diploma was 7.6
percent. That is hardly surprising when you consider how technological
changes in the past few decades have increased the demand for skilled
and educated workers relative to low-skilled and uneducated workers.[6]

Race further affects employment. Unemployment is higher among
blacks (10.0 percent in 2005) and Hispanics (6.0 percent) than it is among
whites (4.4 percent) or Asians (4.0 percent). Similarly, unemployment
among black teenagers is typically more than double that of white teenagers.[7]

Table 2.1. Employment Status of the Civilian Population Age 16 and Older, 2005, by Key Demographic Characteristics (percent)

	Labor force participation rate	Employment-population ratio	Unemployment rate
All	66.0	62.7	5.1
Age			
16 to 19 years	43.7	36.5	16.6
20 to 24 years	74.6	68.0	8.8
25 to 54 years	82.8	79.3	4.1
55 to 64 years	62.9	60.8	3.3
65 years and over	15.1	14.5	3.5
Sex			
Men	73.3	69.6	5.1
Women	59.3	56.2	5.1
Race			
White	66.3	63.4	4.4
Black	64.2	57.7	10.0
Asian	66.1	63.4	4.0
Hispanic-origin	68.0	64.0	6.0
Educational attainment			
Less than a high school diploma	45.5	42.0	7.6
High school graduate, no college	63.2	60.3	4.7
Some college or associate's degree	72.5	69.7	3.9
College graduate	77.9	76.1	2.3

Source: BLS (2006f), tables 3, 4, and 7.

Demographic factors also influence the number of hours that individuals work. For example, men are more likely to work outside the home than women, and employed men work about an hour more a day than employed women (BLS 2005a).[8] Also of note, highly paid workers tend to work more hours than low-paid workers (American Enterprise Institute 2000).

WORKING HARD OR HARDLY WORKING: SOME RECENT LABOR SUPPLY TRENDS

In recent decades, there have been a number of important changes in the nature of the labor force. Perhaps the most significant change has been the remarkable increase in the number of women in the workforce. Another major trend has to do with the aging of America and, until recently, the trend toward earlier and earlier retirement.

A third trend is the decline in men's labor force participation rates. Part of the change is due to earlier retirement by men, but other factors are involved. Of note, there has been an extraordinary increase in the number of American men who are now housed in our nation's prisons and jails. Finally, the nature of work has also changed. There has been a shift away from traditional long-term employment arrangements toward more temporary, part-time, and contingent employment. These trends are discussed in turn.[9]

More Women Are Working Outside the Home

Perhaps the most significant change in the American labor force in the last century was the movement of women into the paid labor force (Ryscavage 1999).[10] For example, among women age 16 and older, 59.3 percent were working or seeking work in 2005, up from just 43.4 percent in 1971, as illustrated in figure 2.1 (BLS 2006f, table 2). All in all, total employment in the United States increased 60 percent from 1975 to 2000, and much of that increase is attributable to rapid increases in the female employment rate.[11] Much of the increase in labor force participation can be explained by a combination of rising real wages for women, a reduction in their childbearing and child-rearing responsibilities, higher education levels, greater marital instability, and changing societal attitudes (Haveman et al. 2003).

Of particular interest, the labor force participation rates for mothers are at record high levels. In 2004, the labor force participation rate for married mothers with children under 18 was 67.8 percent (BLS 2005d). The labor force participation rate of unmarried mothers—those who are single, widowed, divorced, or separated—was 77.1 percent. Even

Figure 2.1. Labor Force Participation Rate, by Sex, 1950–2004 (age 16 and older)

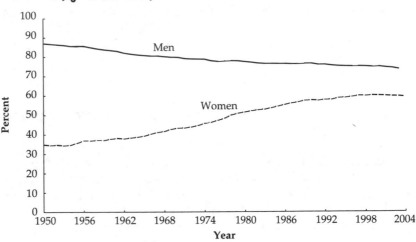

Source: Bureau of Labor Statistics, "Labor Force Statistics from the Current Population Survey," Civilian Labor Force Participation Rate, http://data.bls.gov/labjava/outside.jsp?survey=ln.

among married couples with children under age 18, both parents were working in 60.6 percent of the families, while the father was the sole worker in just 31.2 percent of these families.[12]

All in all, the work and retirement patterns of women and men are becoming more similar. In 1950, for example, women accounted for only about 30 percent of the labor force, but since the 1990s women have account for about 46 percent of the labor force (Ryscavage 1999, 84; author's calculations from BLS 2006f, table 2). Similarly, the average retirement age for women and men is converging, at just over 62 years old according to one study (Munnell 2006).[13] The full implications of this increase in women's labor force participation are still unfolding (Ryscavage 1999). Already, however, the changes in family structure, family income, and income inequality have been immense.

Americans Are Living Longer but Retiring Earlier

Americans are living longer than they were 60 years ago. A male born in 1940 could expect to live 61.4 years, but a male born in 2005 could expect to live to be almost 75 years old (table 2.2).[14] Also, a man reaching age 65 in 1940 could expect to live another 11.9 years, but a man reaching 65 in 2005 could expect to live another 16.3 years.[15]

In addition, as the years go by, an increasing percentage of Americans will survive to old age. Although just 54 percent of men born in 1875

Table 2.2. Life Expectancy for Men and Women, 1940–2060 (years)

Year	Life Expectancy at Birth		Life Expectancy at Age 65	
	Male	*Female*	*Male*	*Female*
Actual				
1940	61.4	65.7	11.9	13.4
1960	66.7	73.2	12.9	15.9
1980	69.9	77.5	14.0	18.1
2000	74.0	79.4	15.9	19.0
2005	74.8	79.6	16.3	19.0
Projected				
2020	76.6	80.7	17.3	19.7
2040	78.5	82.4	18.4	20.8
2060	80.3	83.9	19.5	21.9

Source: Board of Trustees of the Federal Old-Age and Survivors Insurance and Disability Insurance Trust Funds (2006), table V.A3.

Note: The period life expectancy at a given age for a given year represents the average number of years of life remaining if a group of persons at that age were to experience the mortality rates for that year over the course of their remaining lives.

survived from age 21 to age 65 in 1940, almost 83 percent of men born in 1985 are expected to survive from age 21 to age 65 in 2050 (Steuerle and Bakija 1994). In short, there has been a graying of America.[16]

Despite the fact that life expectancies went up throughout the 20th century, there was a trend toward earlier and earlier retirements until about 1985. The labor force participation rate for men over 55 fell dramatically from 1950 to the mid-1980s and has increased modestly since then (figure 2.2).[17] Similarly, one study found that while 49.8 percent of men age 70 in 1950 were still working that year, as were 72 percent of men age 65 and 81 percent of those age 62, by 2003, just 22.6 percent of 70-year-old men were still working, along with just 32 percent of 65-year-old men and 71 percent of 60-year-old men (Quinn 2005).[18] The average age at which workers begin receiving their Social Security retirement benefits also fell from 68.7 years old in 1940 to 63.6 years old in 2002.[19]

The Bureau of Labor Statistics projects that labor force participation rates of older men will continue to increase modestly throughout the coming decade (Quinn 2005; Toossi 2005).[20] For example, the 55-to-64 age group is expected to increase its workforce participation rate from 62.3 percent in 2004 to 65.2 percent by 2014, and the 65-to-74 age group is expected to increase its participation rate from 21.9 percent in 2004 to 26.9 percent by 2014 (Toossi 2005).[21] Also of note, the age of the median worker increased from 35.0 in 1984 to 40.3 in 2004, and it is expected to increase to 41.6 in 2014. Overall, the American workforce has grayed since the mid-1980s.

Figure 2.2. Labor Force Participation of Men Age 55 and Older, 1950–2004

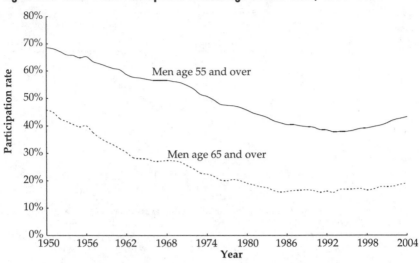

Source: Bureau of Labor Statistics, "Labor Force Statistics from the Current Population Survey," Civilian Labor Force Participation Rate, http://data.bls.gov/labjava/outside.jsp?survey=ln.

Men Are Working Less

While labor force participation rates for women have increased significantly in the past few decades, the labor force participation rates for men have fallen (see figure 2.1). While 79.1 percent of men were in the labor force in 1971, only 73.3 percent of men were in the labor force in 2005 (BLS 2006f, table 2), and 72.7 percent are expected to be in the workforce by 2014 (Toossi 2005). Earlier retirement and longer life expectancies explain part of the fall. Also, as more women have entered the workforce, a significant number of men have become caregivers, a role more traditionally exercised by women.

Another factor is the nature of jobs for low-skilled workers. Basically, relatively fewer jobs are available for low-skilled workers, and the wages associated with those jobs have fallen in real dollar terms. In short, the job situation for low-skilled men has become substantially worse, so they are spending less time working.[22] For example, the unemployment rate for high school dropouts is more than three times higher than the unemployment rate for college graduates (see table 2.1).

Of course, the unemployment rate alone probably understates the problem. Millions of workers have simply left the labor force altogether. In 2005, for example, more than 62 million Americans over the age of 25 were out of the labor force; they were neither employed nor unemployed.[23] And a large proportion of them are low-skilled men and women.[24]

Along the same lines, it is worth noting that the U.S. incarceration rate has increased dramatically in the past two decades, especially among low-skilled men. Figure 2.3 shows that from 1980 to 2004, the number of people in prison or jail increased from 0.5 million to more than 2.1 million. The number of incarcerated men was equal to 2.7 percent of the number of men in the workforce, and the increased incarceration of men reduces the official unemployment rate of men by about 0.3 percentage points.[25]

The United States has the highest incarceration rate in the world—486 adults per 100,000 in 2004.[26] That is five or ten times higher than the rates for most other industrialized nations (Organisation for Economic Co-operation and Development [OECD] 2006b, 221; Western 2001). Almost 90 percent of those incarcerated are men, and almost 56 percent of those men are under the age of 35 (Harrison and Karberg 2004 and author's calculations).

Race is another critical factor. While blacks accounted for just 22 percent of the prison population in 1930, by 2003 they accounted for almost 44 percent (Western 2001; author's calculations from Harrison and Karberg 2004). In 2002, nearly 8 percent of adult black males were incarcerated, and about 32 percent of young black men could expect to spend at least some time in prison or jail (Bonczar 2003; Human Rights Watch 2002).[27]

In addition to the more than 2.1 million persons in jail or prison in 2004, another 4.9 million were on probation or parole.[28] All in all, almost 7 million people were under the supervision of the criminal justice

Figure 2.3. Persons in Jail and Prison, 1980–2004

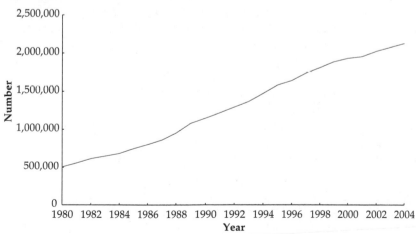

Source: Bureau of Justice Statistics, "Key Crime & Justice Facts at a Glance," Correctional population trend table, http://www.ojp.usdoj.gov/bjs/glance/tables/corr2tab.htm.

system in 2004. These people and many more ex-offenders inevitably have a difficult time fitting into America's job market.

A Shift Away from Long-Term Employment

The nature of work has been changing in recent decades. In particular, there has been a shift away from traditional long-term employment and toward part-time, temporary, and alternative work arrangements.[29] The share of men working in "long-term jobs" (those lasting at least 10 years) fell from 49.8 percent in 1979 to 40 percent in 1996, and to 30.6 percent in 2004 (Mishel, Bernstein, and Boushey 2003, 267; BLS 2004a, table 2).[30] Similarly, a recent BLS study found that the average person born in the later years of the baby boom held 10 jobs from age 18 to age 38 (BLS 2004b). Moreover, while the average length of time that a worker stayed with the same employer increased with the age at which the worker started the job, many younger baby boomers continued to have short-term jobs even as they approached middle age. For example, among jobs started by workers when they were age 33 to 38, 39 percent ended within a year, 54 percent ended within two years, and 70 percent ended within five years.

Like it or not, a large portion of the labor force is now engaged in part-time, contingent, or temporary employment. For example, of the 134.1 million workers in nonagricultural industries in 2005, more than 31.7 million (23.6 percent) worked part-time, or 1 to 34 hours (BLS 2006f, table 21).[31] While the majority of these part-time workers (19.1 million) usually work part-time, 8.3 million of them usually work full-time, and another 4.2 million found themselves working part-time for economic reasons.

Similarly, there were 10.3 million independent contractors in February 2005; that is 7.4 percent of total employment, up from 6.4 percent in February 2001 (BLS 2005c). Also in February 2005, there were 2.5 million on-call workers, 1.2 million temporary help agency workers, and 813,000 workers provided by contract firms. Of note, 55 percent of these contingent workers would have preferred a permanent job, up from 40 percent in February 2001.

All in all, only about 74 percent of workers are working in traditional full-time jobs,[32] and traditional job security has declined, even as unemployment has fallen to some of its lowest levels in decades.

Other Trends

The labor force has also changed in other ways. For example, union membership has dropped significantly in the past few decades. In 2004, just 12.5 percent of wage and salary workers were union members, down from 20.1 percent in 1983, the first year for which comparable union data are available (BLS 2005j).[33]

Also, a larger percentage of our workforce is foreign born. In 2004, 34.2 million U.S. residents were foreign born, representing about 12 percent of the U.S. population.[34] Immigration has been increasing in recent years, and now about 1 million people legally immigrate into the United States each year, and another 350,000 come in illegally or overstay their authorized visas (Homeland Security 2003, 2005). All in all, there were more than 21.4 million foreign-born workers in the United States in 2004, up from 13.1 million in 1994 (CBO 2005e). There were more than 10 million unauthorized immigrants living in the United States at the beginning of 2004, and about 6.3 million of them were in the workforce.[35]

Paying America's Workers

Compensation for services is by far the largest component of personal income, making up about three-quarters of all family income. In 2005, for example, employee compensation and proprietors' income together accounted for 78.7 percent of total personal income in the United States.[36]

Table 2.3 shows the median usual weekly earnings of full-time wage and salary workers by selected characteristics for the first quarter of 2006. Full-time American workers had median earnings of $668 a week; women who worked full-time had median earnings of $600 a week, or 60.6 percent of the $744 median for men. The median earnings for black men working full-time were $577 a week (not shown in table), or 75.6 percent of the $763 median for white men (BLS 2006g). The difference was much less among women, as black women's median earnings ($542) were 89.3 percent of those for their white counterparts ($607, not shown in table). Weekly earnings also varied by educational level. The median wage for someone without a high school diploma was $420 a week, while the median for a college graduate was $1,019 a week.

Table 2.3 also shows average weekly salaries for the top and bottom quartiles of earnings (75th percentile and 25th percentile) and for the top and bottom deciles (90th percentile and 10th percentile). A worker in the 90th percentile of full-time workers earned $1,535 a week in the first quarter of 2006, almost five times as much as a worker in the 10th percentile ($318).

Wage levels tend to vary with age. For example, in the first quarter of 2006, workers age 20 to 24 had median weekly earnings of $417, workers age 25 to 34 had median weekly earnings of $617, workers

Table 2.3. Median Usual Weekly Earnings of Full-Time Wage and Salary Workers by Selected Characteristics, First Quarter 2006

Characteristic	Number of workers (in thousands)	Upper Limit of (in dollars)				
		First decile	First quartile	Second quartile (median)	Third quartile	Ninth decile
Sex, race, and Hispanic origin						
Men	57,950	342	488	744	1,164	1,744
Women	45,519	299	405	600	877	1,262
White	83,710	325	460	688	1,056	1,560
Black	12,536	289	384	560	823	1,198
Asian	4,849	340	492	766	1,290	1,877
Hispanic	15,285	278	351	487	713	1,108
All workers age 16 and over	103,469	318	445	668	1,030	1,535
Educational attainment						
Less than a high school diploma	8,661	259	318	420	580	804
High school graduate, no college	27,725	314	416	592	838	1,159
Some college or associate's degree	25,492	365	492	691	988	1,375
College graduate	31,214	510	705	1,019	1,532	2,171
All workers age 25 and over	93,092	341	483	712	1,084	1,577

Source: Bureau of Labor Statistics (2006g), table 4.

Notes: Quarterly averages, not adjusted. Ten percent of all full-time wage and salary workers earn less than the upper limit of the first decile; 25 percent earn less than the upper limit of the first quartile; 50 percent earn less than the upper limit of the second quartile, or median; 75 percent earn less than the upper limit of the third quartile; and 90 percent earn less than the upper limit of the ninth decile. Detail for the above race and Hispanic-origin groups will not sum to totals because data for the "other races" group are not presented and Hispanics are included in both the white and black population groups.

age 35 to 44 had median weekly earnings of $748, and workers age 45 to 54 had median weekly earnings of $763 (BLS 2006g). After age 54 median earnings can begin to fall, and while workers age 55 to 64 also earned $763 a week, workers age 65 and over earned just $596 a week. Graphically, these numbers would generate what economists call an "age-earnings profile" that is concave, with earnings generally increasing at a progressively slower rate as workers age and eventually declining.[37]

Table 2.4 shows the average annual earnings, average annual hours, and average hourly earnings for various occupations in 2004. The average physician made almost $129,000 that year, while the average hotel

Table 2.4. Annual Earnings, Annual Hours, and Hourly Earnings of Full-Time Workers, 2004

Occupation	Mean annual earnings ($)	Mean annual hours	Mean hourly earnings ($)
Physicians	128,689	2,243	57.90
Airplane pilots and navigators	128,406	1,083	113.82
Lawyers	105,716	2,174	48.60
Managers, marketing, advertising, and public relations	103,704	2,131	48.65
Economics teachers	99,516	1,555	63.98
Law teachers	89,947	1,526	57.05
Dentists	82,437	2,142	42.91
Actuaries	72,088	2,179	33.09
Economists	71,672	2,171	33.02
Registered nurses	53,289	2,002	26.87
Psychologists	51,508	1,776	28.49
Accountants and auditors	50,761	2,073	24.56
Police and detectives, public service	50,063	2,073	24.10
Secondary school teachers	46,038	1,416	32.53
Elementary school teachers	45,296	1,393	32.46
Machinists	40,736	2,078	19.59
Automobile mechanics	38,967	2,097	18.37
Dispatchers	35,115	2,103	16.53
Prekindergarten and kindergarten teachers	33,487	1,672	19.45
Secretaries	32,349	1,994	16.11
Garbage collectors	31,284	2,172	12.96
Transportation ticket and reservation agents	30,044	2,054	14.78
Bank tellers	22,317	2,049	10.65
Nursery workers	21,671	1,937	9.87
Nursing aides, orderlies, and attendants	20,959	2,015	10.20
Cashiers	19,305	2,033	13.23
Hotel clerks	18,255	2,022	8.95
Waiters and waitresses	8,789	1,906	4.44

Sources: Buckley (2005); Bureau of Labor Statistics (2005h), table 2-1.

clerk made about $18,000. Table 2.4 also shows wide variations in hourly wages and in number of hours worked. Airline pilots and navigators earn almost twice as much per hour as physicians ($113.82 versus $57.90), but they work only about half as many hours (1,083 versus 2,243).

Institutional features of the workplace can also make a difference in compensation. For example, the wage structure is more compressed in the public sector than in the private sector; as a result, wage inequality is less pronounced (Fortin and Lemieux 1997).[38]

SOME RECENT TRENDS IN COMPENSATING AMERICA'S WORKERS

In recent decades, we have also seen significant changes in compensation patterns. Most notably, earnings inequality has grown dramatically. Perhaps the most important reason for this increase is the rising premium that employers are willing for pay for educated workers. The result has been to create a chasm between high-skilled and low-skilled workers.

Another trend involves the fall of real wages of men and the increase of real wages of women. The good news is that the historical difference between wages of men and women has shrunk, but the downside has been that fewer families can be supported by a single breadwinner. These trends are discussed in turn.

Overworked and Underpaid: Wage Inequality Is Large and Growing

There is substantial inequality in the distribution of earnings, income, consumption, and wealth in the United States today. To start, figure 2.4 compares the distribution of these resources by quintiles of family units. The distribution of consumption is the least unequal, while the distribution of wealth is the most unequal. Earnings and income fall in the middle.[39]

Consumption is probably the best overall measure of economic well-being at any point in time.[40] To achieve a suitably low level of consumption inequality, however, a society will inevitably have to adopt policies that also reduce inequality in earnings, income, and wealth.

Earnings Inequality

Earnings inequality in America is fairly large, even among year-round, full-time workers. As shown in table 2.3, a worker in the 90th percentile

Figure 2.4. The Distribution of Various Economic Resources, by Quintiles of Families

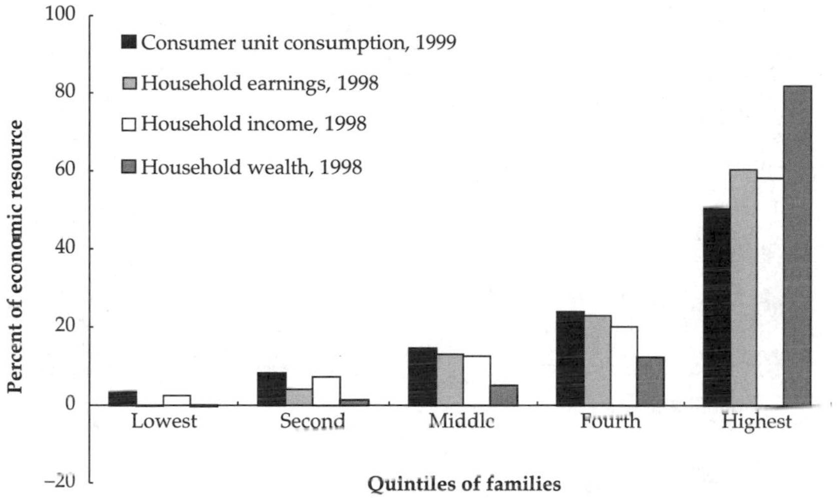

Sources: Rodríguez et al. (2002), tables 5 (earnings), 6 (income), and 7 (wealth); and author's calculations from Bureau of Labor Statistics (2001), table 1.
Note: Consumer units are similar to households.

of full-time workers in the first quarter of 2006 earned almost five times as much as a worker in the 10th percentile, for a "90/10 ratio" of 4.82 to 1. Of note, the earnings ratios for all wage and salary workers are even larger than those for full-time workers. In 2003, for example, the 90/10 earnings ratio for all wage and salary workers was 7.00 to 1 (Mayer 2004).[41]

Similarly, figure 2.5 shows the distribution of earnings of year-round, full-time workers in 2004, by percentile.[42] That year, a worker in the 90th percentile earned $84,000 and a worker in the 10th percentile earned $15,600, for a 90/10 ratio of 5.38 to 1. The earnings distribution in figure 2.5 is skewed strongly to the right because of the extraordinarily high earnings of workers at the top of the pay scale. That skewedness is also apparent from the fact that while the median annual earnings that year was $36,000, the average was more than $47,500.[43]

In fact, the remarkable difference between the pay of average workers and top earners simply cannot be captured in a graph like figure 2.5. In 2004, for example, the typical CEO in a major U.S. company made 431 times as much as the average production worker (Anderson et al. 2005).[44] With roughly 260 work days a year, that means the typical CEO earns more in a day than an average worker earns in a year (Mishel et al. 2005, 214). In 2003, U.S. executives earned more than twice as much as the average of CEOs in the 13 other advanced countries for which there are comparable data; while the ratio of CEO to worker

Figure 2.5. Distribution of Earnings, 2004

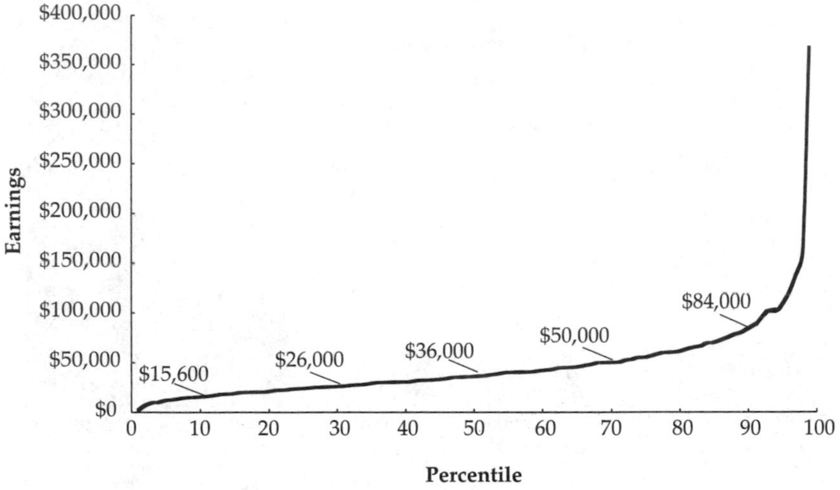

Source: U.S. Census Bureau, Current Population Survey, Annual Demographic Survey, March Supplement, 2005.
Note: Includes all civilian noninstitutionalized year-round, full-time workers.

pay was 44.0 to 1 in the United States, it was just 19.9 to 1 in those other countries (Mishel et al. 2005, 214–16).

Of course, CEOs are by no means the only American workers who earn extraordinary compensation. Movie stars and athletes often have multimillion dollar contracts.[45] All told, more than 150,000 tax returns for the year 2003 reported salaries and wages in excess of $1 million, and more than 5,000 returns showed salaries and wages of more than $10 million.[46] Similarly, one study found that, in 1998, the top 1 percent of households had 158 times as much earnings as the bottom 40 percent of households (Rodríguez et al. 2002). We live in what Robert H. Frank and Philip J. Cook (1995) call a "winner-take-all" society in which the top workers in each pursuit often earn disproportionately large rewards for their work effort.[47] Moreover, the United States generally has much greater wage inequality than other advanced nations (Smeeding and Gottschalk 1998).

Earnings inequality has also increased significantly in recent decades.[48] Table 2.5 shows various measures of earnings inequality for full-time workers from 1970 to 2001. Column 2 of that table shows that the 90/10 earnings ratio of male workers increased from 3.85 to 1 in 1970 to 5.77 to 1 in 2001. In short, a man whose earnings were in the 90th percentile of earnings made almost six times as much as a man whose earnings were in the 10th percentile. Similarly, column 3 shows that top-earning women earned 4.62 times as much as bottom-earning women in 2001, up from just 3.41 times as much in 1970.

Table 2.5. Measures of Individual Earnings Inequality for Full-Time, Year-Round Workers by Sex, 1970–2001

| Year | 90/10 Income Ratios | | Gini Index | | |
	Men	Women	Both sexes	Men	Women
1970	3.85	3.41	0.326	0.305	0.272
1980	4.38	3.27	0.331	0.315	0.265
1990	5.04	4.07	0.359	0.361	0.308
2000	5.67	4.67	0.406	0.420	0.341
2001	5.77	4.62	0.409	0.419	0.362

Source: U.S. Census Bureau (2004b), table IE-2.

Table 2.5 also shows that the Gini index of earnings inequality increased from 0.326 in 1970 to 0.409 in 2001.[49] All in all, inequality of after-tax labor income increased by about 25 percent from 1970 to 2001.[50]

Similarly, figure 2.6 shows how wages for all workers have changed for workers at various points in the earnings distribution from 1973 to 2003.[51] In particular, from 1979 to 2003, the real wages of earners in the 95th percentile of earnings increased by 31.1 percent. On the other hand, workers in the 50th percentile saw their wages grow by 10.2 percent over that period, and workers in the 10th percentile saw an increase of just 0.9 percent.

Income Inequality

Table 2.6 shows various measures of household income inequality for 2004.[52] First, the table shows household incomes at selected percentiles

Figure 2.6. Wages by Percentile, 1973–2003

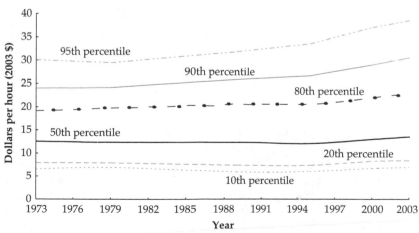

Source: Mishel, Bernstein, and Allegretto (2005), table 2.6.

Table 2.6. Selected Measures of Household Income Dispersion, 2004 (2004 dollars)

Measures of income dispersion	2004
Household income at selected percentiles ($)	
10th percentile upper limit	10,927
20th percentile upper limit	18,500
50th (median)	44,389
80th percentile upper limit	88,029
90th percentile lower limit	120,924
95th percentile lower limit	157,185
Household income ratios of selected percentiles	
90th/10th	11.07
95th/20th	8.50
95th/50th	3.56
80th/50th	2.00
80th/20th	4.76
20th/50th	0.42
Mean household income of quintiles ($)	
Lowest quintile	10,264
Second quintile	26,241
Middle quintile	44,455
Fourth quintile	70,085
Highest quintile	151,593
Shares of household income of quintiles	
Lowest quintile	3.4
Second quintile	8.7
Middle quintile	14.7
Fourth quintile	23.2
Highest quintile	50.1
Gini index of income inequality	0.466

Source: DeNavas-Walt, Proctor, and Lee (2005), table A-3.

and compares the relative incomes of households at those percentiles. For example, households in the 90th percentile had incomes of $120,924, while households in the 10th percentile had incomes of $10,927, for a 90/10 household income ratio of more than 11 to 1.

Next, table 2.6 shows the average household incomes and the relative shares of household income going to households at different income levels. For example, the average income for a household in the top 20 percent of households was $151,593, while the average income of a household in the bottom 20 percent was $10,264. Table 2.6 also shows that the top 20 percent of households received 50.1 percent of household income that year, while the bottom 20 percent got just 3.4 percent; and from those numbers we can compute an 80/20 ratio of household income *shares* of 14.74.[53] Finally, table 2.6 shows that the Gini index of household income inequality was 0.466 in 2004.

All in all, household income is much more unequally distributed than earned income.[54] For example, the Gini index of household income inequality for 2001—0.466 (DeNavas-Walt et al. 2005)[55]—is significantly larger than the Gini index of individual earnings inequality that year— 0.409. The relatively greater inequality of household income can also be seen by comparing household income ratios with earnings ratios. In 2001, for example, the 90/10 ratio of household income was 10.63 to 1, compared with a 90/10 earnings ratio for all wage and salary workers of just 6.83 to 1 (DeNavas-Walt et al. 2005; Mayer 2004).

Much of the reason for greater inequality in household income than in earned income reflects the fact that relatively few well-off households receive most of the investment income. As mentioned in chapter 1, more than 45 percent of the dividends reported on 2003 federal income tax returns was reported by the 2.5 million taxpayers with incomes of $200,000 or more that year, and hardly any was reported by those taxpayers with incomes of less than $50,000. Demography can also help us understand why the distribution of household income is so much more skewed than the distribution of individual earnings. For example, compare the double-income-no-kid families at the top of the household income distribution with the low-income female-headed households that dominate the bottom of the income distribution.[56]

Like earnings inequality, household income inequality has grown significantly in the past few decades. While the Gini index of income inequality was 0.466 in 2004, it was 0.428 in 1990, 0.403 in 1980, and 0.394 in 1970 (DeNavas-Walt et al. 2005). Along the same lines, figure 2.7 shows how family income levels have changed from 1950 to 2003. Similarly, figure 2.8 shows how the ratio of the average incomes of households in the top 5 percent and top 20 percent of households has changed since 1970 relative to the average incomes of households in the bottom 20 percent.[57]

Of particular note, the super-rich have seen an extraordinary increase in their income share in recent years. For example, in 2000, the top 400 individual taxpayers received 1.09 percent of all the income in America, up from just 0.52 percent in 1992 (Parisi and Strudler 2003; Johnston 2003).[58] These top 400 families had an average income of $174 million in 2000 (up from $46.8 million in 1992), and while they paid 1.58 percent of income taxes in 2000 (up from 1.04 percent in 1992), their average income tax rate fell to 22.29 percent in 2000, down from 26.38 percent in 1992.

Changes in family structure, such as the breaking apart of American families, can help explain at least part of the dramatic increase in household income inequality in the past few decades (Blank 1995; Hoynes et al. 2006). In particular, female-headed households are much more likely to be poor than two-parent households. In 2004, for example, while just 5.5 percent of married couples were poor, 28.4 percent of mother-only households were poor (DeNavas-Walt et al. 2005). Also,

Figure 2.7. Family Income by Percentile, 1950–2003

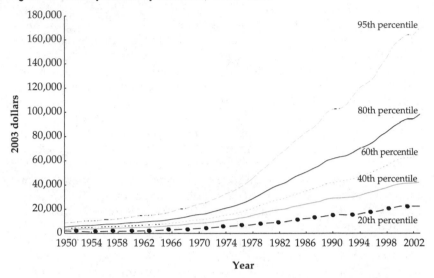

Source: U.S. Census Bureau (2005b), table F-1.

Figure 2.8. Ratio of Average Household Income of the Top 5 and 20 Percent of Households to the Average Household Income of the Bottom 20 Percent of Households, 1970–2000

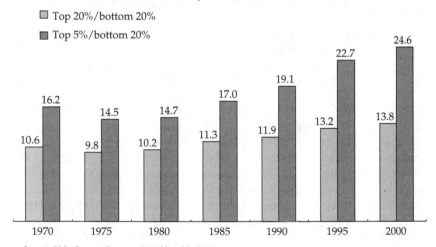

Source: U.S. Census Bureau (2004b), table IE-3.

23 percent of children under the age of 18 lived in mother-only households in 2005 (17 of 74 million children), as opposed to 8 percent in 1960 (5 of 64 million children).[59]

Income inequality in the United States also tends to be larger than in other industrialized nations. Table 2.7 shows how various countries compare on two measures of income inequality: the Gini index and the 90/10 ratio.[60] Not surprisingly, poverty rates also tend to be higher in the United States than in other industrialized nations. One recent study found that, in 2000, relative poverty rates (defined as 50 percent of median income) varied from 5.4 percent in Finland to 17.0 percent in the United States, with an average rate of 10.3 percent among the 11 high-income countries studied (Smeeding 2006b).[61]

Consumption Inequality

Inequality in consumption is not nearly as great as income inequality.[62] In 2001, for example, when the Gini index for household income

Table 2.7. International Comparisons of Income Inequality for Most Recent Year

Country	Gini index	90/10 ratio
Australia	.305	4.1
Austria	.252	3.3
Belgium	.272	3.2
Canada	.301	3.8
Czech Republic	.260	3.0
Denmark	.225	2.7
Finland	.261	3.1
France	.273	3.4
Germany	.277	3.5
Greece	.345	4.8
Hungary	.293	3.6
Ireland	.304	4.4
Italy	.347	4.6
Japan	.314	4.9
Luxembourg	.261	3.2
Mexico	.467	9.3
Netherlands	.251	3.0
New Zealand	.337	4.4
Norway	.261	2.8
Poland	.367	4.2
Portugal	.356	5.0
Spain	.303	4.1
Sweden	.243	2.8
Switzerland	.267	3.2
Turkey	.439	6.5
United Kingdom	.326	4.2
United States	.357	5.4

Source: Förster and d'Ercole (2005), annex table A.3.
Note: Most recent year refers to year around 2000, except for Belgium and Spain (1995).

inequality was 0.466, the Gini index for consumption inequality was just 0.307 (Johnson, Smeeding, and Torrey 2005).[63] Similarly, table 2.8 compares the incomes and expenditures of various consumer units in 2004 (BLS 2006b).[64] It shows, for example, that while the bottom 20 percent of consumer units had an average income of $9,168 before taxes, their average consumption was $17,837. Meanwhile, consumer units in the top 20 percent had an average income of $132,158, but their average consumption was $83,710. Inequality in consumption is smaller than inequality in income because consumers tend to maintain their levels of consumption even when their incomes fluctuate temporarily, because transfer programs increase the consumption levels for low-income households, and because higher-income families save a relatively greater percentage of their income and pay relatively more in taxes. Also of note, the increase in consumption inequality in recent decades has been much less marked than the increases in earnings inequality and in income inequality (Krueger and Perri 2002).

Wealth Inequality

On the other hand, inequality in wealth holdings is "extreme and substantially greater than income inequality" (Wolff 1999).[65] Figure 2.9 shows the size distribution of wealth in 2001 (Wolff 2004).[66] That year, the top 1 percent of wealth holders controlled 33.4 percent of total household wealth, and the top 20 percent controlled 84.4 percent of the wealth. At the same time, the bottom 80 percent of households held less than 16 percent of total household wealth.

In fact, wealth is extraordinarily concentrated in the top 1 percent of households. In 2001, for example, the mean wealth holdings of the top 1 percent were almost $13 million, and more than 338,000 households had a net worth over $10 million (Wolff 2004). Indeed, the top 1 percent of households had more than 1,000 times as much wealth as the entire

Table 2.8. Quintiles of Income before Taxes: Average Annual Expenditures, Consumer Units, 2003 (dollars)

	All consumer units	Lowest quintile	Second quintile	Third quintile	Fourth quintile	Highest quintile
Income before taxes	54,453	9,168	24,102	41,614	65,100	132,158
Average annual expenditures	43,395	17,837	27,410	36,980	50,974	83,710

Source: Bureau of Labor Statistics (2006b), table 1.

Note: A consumer unit generally includes all members of a household related by blood, marriage, adoption, or some other legal arrangement.

Figure 2.9. The Size Distribution of Wealth, 2001: Percentage Share of Wealth Held by . . .

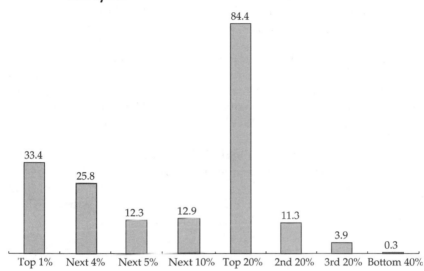

Source: Wolff (2004), table 2.

bottom 40 percent.[67] Also that year, Bill Gates and Warren Buffett topped the *Forbes* list of the 400 richest Americans with net worths of $54 *billion* and $33.2 *billion*, respectively.[68] The distribution of household wealth is also quite skewed: in 2001, for example, median household wealth was $73,500, but average household wealth was $280,100 (Wolff 2004).[69]

Wealth and income are positively correlated (that is, high-income families tend to have greater wealth), but that correlation is tempered somewhat by the fact that older people tend to have accumulated more wealth but have lower earnings (Wolff and Zacharias 2006). All in all, however, wealth is much more unequally distributed than income or earnings. The Gini index for wealth inequality in 2001 was an astonishingly high 0.826 (Wolff 2004). Moreover, wealth inequality tends to be perpetuated through countless generations as a substantial portion of wealth is passed on through inheritance.[70]

Working Smarter: The Rewards for Education Have Grown

Another important trend in the past few decades is the rise in the wage premium for skilled workers.[71] College graduates age 25 and over now earn almost twice as much as workers who stop their education with a high school diploma. For example, table 2.3 shows that the median wage for high school graduates over age 25 with no college was $592 in the first quarter of 2006, while the median wage for college graduates was $1,019 a week.[72] Of note, the gap between the average wages of high school and college graduates has widened significantly in recent years (Kosters 1998). Wages also tend to increase with on-the-job experience and skill development.[73]

Increased wage premiums for skilled and educated workers reflect the underlying shift from a manufacturing economy to a services economy. In the past few decades, in particular, there are far fewer good jobs in the manufacturing sector in the United States, and good jobs in the services sector tend to require high levels of education or experience.[74]

The increased wage premiums are not all bad, however. For example, the increased college wage premiums stimulate more young people to go to college and improve their skills (Welch 1999). More than 60 percent of high school graduates now pursue further education, up from less than 50 percent a couple of decades ago (Kosters 1998).

Working Their Fingers to the Bone: Falling Real Wages for Low-Skilled Workers

On the other hand, the earnings prospects for low-skilled workers have dimmed considerably over the past few decades. For example, while college graduates have seen real (inflation-adjusted) growth in their wages since 1979, high school dropouts have experienced a decline in their real earnings.[75] Life as a low-skilled worker has never been great, but it seems especially hard now.[76]

Moreover, many low-skilled workers face a lifetime of low earnings. For example, of those who started in the lowest quintile of the income distribution in 1974, 42 percent were still in the lowest quintile 17 years later in 1991, and another 23 percent had moved up only to the second lowest quintile (Gottschalk 1997).[77]

In the 1950s, low-skilled workers could easily end up with relatively high-paying factory jobs. Today, however, a low-skilled worker may never have sufficient earnings to bring her family above the federal poverty level.[78] In 2006, for example, the federal poverty level for a family of three is $16,600, and the poverty level for a family of four is $20,000 (U.S. Department of Health and Human Services [HHS] 2006). Table 2.9 shows the disheartening relationship between market earnings and the federal poverty level for families of three and four in 2006.

According to table 2.9, a full-time worker earning the minimum wage would earn just 54 percent of the poverty level for a family of four. The minimum wage is $5.15 an hour in 2006, and it has not been increased since September 1, 1997.[79] Yet millions of workers are paid the minimum wage or less. For example, of the 73.9 million American

Table 2.9. Hourly Wages as a Percentage of the Federal Poverty Level, 2006

Hourly wage ($)	Annual earnings ($)	Salary as a percentage of the three-person federal poverty level	Salary as a percentage of the four-person federal poverty level
5.15	10,712	65	54
7.00	14,560	88	73
8.00	16,640	100	83
9.00	18,720	113	94
10.00	20,800	125	104

Source: Author's calculations.
Note: Based on 2006 federal poverty levels of $16,600 for a family of three and $20,000 for a family of four. All computations are based on 52 weeks of full-time work a year. The minimum wage is $5.15 an hour.

workers who were paid by the hour in 2004, about 2 million (2.7 percent) were paid at or below $5.15 an hour (BLS 2005b).

In fact, a worker would have to work full-time and year-round and make $7.98 an hour to bring a family of three above the poverty level in 2006, and it would take a wage of $9.62 an hour to bring a family of four over its poverty level. Nearly one-quarter of workers earned less than a family-of-four poverty level wage in 2003 ($9.04 an hour in 2003), including 19.6 percent of men, 29.4 percent of women, 20.4 percent of whites, 30.4 percent of blacks, and 39.8 percent of Hispanics (Mishel et al. 2005, 125–34).

Recent increases in immigration may have also contributed to the declining real wages of low-skilled workers. The foreign-born are less educated than natives, and foreign-born workers tend to earn less than natives (Congressional Budget Office [CBO] 2005e; BLS 2005f; Homeland Security 2003). Immigrants compose about 14 percent of U.S. workers but 20 percent of low-wage workers (Capps et al. 2003).[80]

In 2004, almost 40 million Americans (12.7 percent) lived in poverty (DeNavas-Walt et al. 2005). Although most of the poor are children and adults who are not in the labor force, many are among the so-called "working poor," those who spent at least 27 weeks in the labor force (working or looking for work) but whose incomes fell below the poverty level (BLS 2005i). In 2003, for example, 7.4 million individuals (4.2 million families) were classified as working poor, and 3.7 million individuals who were in the labor force for at least 50 weeks and usually worked full-time were classified as working poor.

Poverty rates also vary dramatically depending upon such demographic factors as race, nativity, and family structure. For example, while just 10.8 percent of whites were poor in 2004, 24.7 percent of blacks were poor that year (DeNavas-Walt et al. 2005). Similarly, while just 12.1 percent of natives were poor, 17.1 percent of the foreign-born were poor.

Lower wages and dead-end careers have made work a lot less attractive for low-skilled workers, especially men. One consequence has been a significant reduction in the labor force participation rates of low-skilled men (Welch 1999). At the same time, falling wages may have made alternatives to work—like crime and welfare—more attractive.

Women Are Making More; Men Are Making Less

Over the past two decades, women's real earnings have increased while those of men have stayed about the same. From 1979 through 2004, women's inflation-adjusted earnings increased more than 30 percent, while the real earnings of men increased by just 1.4 percent.[81] The gender pay gap shrank during this period, but in 2004 women, on average, still made only 80.3 percent of what men made (BLS 2005e).[82] Men made more than women at all levels, but the gap was smallest for those age 16 to 25 (women earned 93.7 percent of what men earned).[83]

The Minority/White Wage Gaps Have Also Declined

The gap between the wages of whites and minorities is also fairly large. For example, table 2.3 shows that the median weekly wage for whites was $688 but it was just $560 for black workers and $487 for workers of Hispanic origin.[84]

The good news is that the white/minority wage gaps have shrunk in the past few decades. The black/white wage gap fell by about half from 1963 through 2001 (Welch 2003). Hispanics, too, have seen a narrowing of their wage gap with native whites. In particular, second- and third-generation Hispanic men have higher incomes than their parents, and their economic status is converging toward that of native whites (Smith 2003). Antidiscrimination laws and improvements in education and skill levels both seem to have contributed to these wage gap declines.

Other Trends

Compensation of American workers has also changed in other ways. For example, fringe benefits have grown substantially over the past few decades, and the nature of fringe benefits has changed.[85] While wages and salaries increased by 17.2 percent from 1979 to 2003 (in real dollars), fringe benefits grew by 55.1 percent (DOL 2004). Fringe benefits now make up almost 30 percent of the average employer cost for employee compensation of civilian workers (BLS 2006d).

The most important fringe benefits are health care and retirement plans, and table 2.10 shows the percentage of private-sector workers participating in employer-sponsored health care and retirement plans. The overall coverage rate for retirement plans has held relatively steady in recent years, with about half of private-sector employees participating in an employer-sponsored retirement plan; but, as more fully explained in chapter 9, there has been a shift away from traditional defined benefit pension plans and toward defined contribution plans, especially 401(k) plans. Table 2.10 shows that the probability of having pension and health care coverage is greater for white-collar workers, for full-time workers, for union workers, and for workers at larger firms. The empirical evidence also shows that the probability of fringe benefit coverage is greater for older workers, for whites, for highly educated workers, and for higher-income workers.[86]

Executive compensation packages have also changed in recent years, and stock options have become more widely available to both executives and other employees.[87]

Table 2.10. Percentage of Workers in Private Industry Participating in Health Care and Retirement Benefits, by Selected Characteristics, March 2005

	Retirement Benefits			Health Benefits
	All retirement plans	Defined benefit	Defined contribution	Medical care
Worker characteristics				
White-collar occupations	79	25	64	77
Blue-collar occupations	60	26	50	77
Service occupations	32	7	28	44
Full time	69	25	62	85
Part time	27	10	23	22
Union	88	73	49	92
Nonunion	56	16	54	68
Average wage less than $15/hour	46	12	41	58
Average wage $15/hour or higher	78	35	69	87
Establishment characteristics				
Good-producing	71	33	61	85
Service-producing	56	19	51	66
1–99 workers	44	10	40	59
100 workers or more	78	37	69	84
All workers	60	22	53	70

Source: Bureau of Labor Statistics (2005g), table 1.

SOME KEY IMPLICATIONS

Who works in America? The basic picture here is that high-skilled workers get high earnings, and they are working harder than ever. They have high employment rates and low unemployment rates. On the other hand, low-skilled workers have seen a decline in their real earnings. They have relatively lower employment rates and higher unemployment rates. The labor force participation rates for low-skilled women have gone up, but that is largely due to demographic and economic factors that have swamped the discouraging impact of relatively lower wages for low-skilled workers.

All in all, the United States has a substantially unequal distribution of earned income, and that earnings inequality has increased significantly in the past few decades. The fairness of this distribution of work and of earned income is discussed in greater detail in subsequent chapters. For now, it is perhaps enough to suggest that one cannot help but look at the distribution of earnings and conclude that some Americans are likely paid more than they "deserve," and many other Americans are paid less than they "deserve."

3

HOW LABOR MARKETS REWARD WORK

> The labor market is the primary determinant of living standards for working families. (Mishel et al. 2003)

People work for lots of reasons. The most obvious reason for working is to earn pay that can be used to purchase goods and services in the market. In addition, work can itself be enjoyable and self-fulfilling. Work is also a social institution. There are social pressures to work and a social stigma for not working, and work itself provides many individuals with their most important social interactions outside of family.[1]

All in all, work is central to our understanding of modern society; economics, psychology, and sociology can all offer us insights into the work life of Americans. To be sure, government can influence the way people feel about work and the social structure of work, but this book focuses on the economics of work.

In a complex society such as ours, the economic rewards from work are ultimately determined by a combination of market forces and government policies. Chapter 2 outlined the labor market outcomes that have resulted from the current system of market forces and government policies. The basic picture is one of earnings inequality, and of rising inequality at that. High-skilled workers get high earnings, and they are working harder than ever. Many low-skilled workers are also working hard, but they have seen a decline in their real wages over time. More-over, low-skilled workers have relatively lower employment rates and higher unemployment rates than high-skilled workers. Gender, race, and age are also important demographic factors in our picture of who works and who does not. In sum, the distribution of earnings and earnings opportunities is fairly unequal, and earnings inequality has risen substantially in recent decades.

This chapter explains why labor markets "inevitably" lead to such unequal distributions of earnings and other economic resources (Less-noff 1978, 148). Subsequent chapters explain how government policies can, and should, be used to reduce those inequalities.

WORK EFFORT

Our starting point for understanding how individuals earn economic rewards from work is the standard economic model of labor supply. In the standard model, individuals are assumed to be able to work as many hours as they like at wages that are determined by the market. Pay is assumed to be proportionate to output. Individual decisions about how hard to work depend on each individual weighing the relative benefits of work and leisure; each worker then seeks a combina-tion of market income and non-market leisure that maximizes her satisfaction.[2]

The model assumes that each individual enjoys consuming goods and leisure activities. To be able to buy goods, however, the individual must work, but working cuts into leisure time, which is also a "good."[3] Each individual chooses a level of work that results in a level of income and remaining free time that makes her as happy as possible. The more you work, the more you make, but the less leisure time you have. In short, there is a trade-off between labor and leisure.

Figure 3.1 shows how this simple model works for a hypothetical low-skilled worker who can earn $5.00 an hour in the labor market. Individuals face constraints on the amount of time they can work and, consequently, on the amount of money they can earn at any given wage. The downward-sloping diagonal line in figure 3.1 is the "budget constraint" for this worker. She can earn as much as $350 a week (if she works 70 hours a week) or as little as $0 (if she works 0 hours).

Individuals are thought to have "utility functions" that reflect their preferences for the consumption of goods and leisure time. The curved line in figure 3.1 (with triangles) is a "utility curve."[4] Our hypothetical worker would be equally happy at every point on this utility curve. Given her $5-an-hour wage, the utility curve shown is the highest one she can reach. At the point of tangency (where her utility curve touches

Figure 3.1. The Trade-off between Labor and Leisure

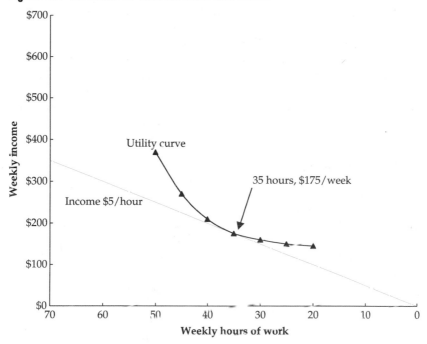

Source: Author's calculations.

her $5-an-hour budget constraint), she will maximize her satisfaction (maximize her utility) by working 35 hours a week and earning $175 a week.[5] She could earn more money if she worked more hours, but then she would lose more leisure time. Alternatively, she could have more leisure time if she worked less, but then she would not be able to buy as many goods.

Of course, different individuals have different sets of preferences between labor and leisure. For example, some people place a higher value on their leisure time than others. For them, a market wage of only $5 an hour will not pull them away from their families, hobbies, and other leisure activities. Economists say these people have a high "reservation wage." Others—we might call them workaholics—have a low reservation wage, and they would be happy to work 70 hours a week even at a low $5-an-hour wage rate.

We can think of the reservation wage as the price of giving up an hour of leisure. Many factors can influence an individual's reservation wage. For example, having a child will increase the reservation wage of adults by increasing the value of spending time at home (Hamermesh and Rees 1988, 11–12). So it is no surprise to see that after the birth of a child, one parent may drop out of the workforce. On the other hand, the availability of inexpensive day care (or grandparents) to watch young children can lower a parent's reservation wage and increase the likelihood that he or she will participate in the workforce.

Reservation wages can also vary with age and experience. For example, the availability of Social Security and pension benefits makes it easier for elderly individuals to live without working. On the other hand, declines in the stock market or increases in inflation may lead older workers to postpone their planned retirements.

The Effects of a Higher Wage Rate

The standard economic model can also help us understand how people will respond to higher wages. According to the model, an individual's response to a wage increase depends on the individual's relative preferences for leisure and other goods. In response to a wage increase, some individuals will end up working more, but some individuals will end up working less.

On the one hand, a higher wage rate will attract more people to the workforce. For example, someone whose reservation wage was $7 an hour would not work at all for $5 an hour but would be thrilled to have a job that paid $10 an hour. On the other hand, some workers who were working 70 hours a week for $5 an hour might choose to spend more time with their families if they suddenly got a raise to $10 an hour.

More specifically, economists say that the effect of a wage increase is hard to predict because an increase in the wage rate results in two separate effects on an individual's labor supply—a *substitution effect* and an *income effect*—and these effects work in opposite directions.

The increase in the wage rate makes working more attractive: it raises the relative cost of leisure time. Consequently, the higher wage will lead individuals to consume less leisure and work more. This is the substitution effect: individuals will "substitute" work for leisure, and the wage increase will lead them to work more.

At the same time, however, the higher wage rate means that the individual will have more total income from the same amount of work effort and so a greater ability to consume all goods, including leisure. This is the income effect: the wage increase will enable individuals to purchase more leisure, and they will work fewer hours.

In response to a wage increase, the income and substitution effects work in opposite directions. Consequently, the net effect on work effort is ambiguous. An increase in the wage rate will result in an increase in the supply of labor if the substitution effect is larger than the income effect, but it will result in a decrease in the supply of labor if the income effect is larger than the substitution effect. Similarly, the net effect of a wage cut on work effort is difficult to predict.

For example, consider what might happen to our hypothetical low-skilled worker if her wage rate suddenly jumped to $10 an hour (figure 3.2). This change would enable her to reach a higher utility curve, so she would clearly be better off. Assuming that the substitution effect for this worker is larger than the income effect, this worker would increase her work effort from 35 to 40 hours a week. Consequently, she would take home $400 a week in pay, more than twice what she initially earned.

Figure 3.2. The Effect of a Wage Increase

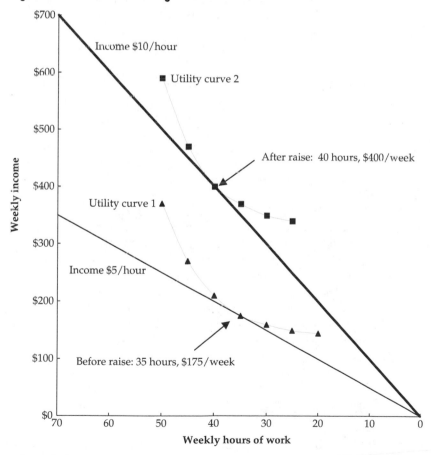

Source: Author's calculations.

Implications of the Standard Model

The foregoing introduction to the standard model of the trade-off between labor and leisure can help us understand a lot about labor force participation in America. Individuals who can command high potential wage rates are more likely to be working, and they are likely to work more hours because of the relatively larger rewards they can get from work as opposed to leisure. That is one reason high-skilled workers are more likely to be working than low-skilled workers.

Low wages just do not offer the same inducement to join the workforce as high wages. It is not that low-skilled workers are lazy or unwilling to work. Every time General Motors posts an advertisement saying that it wants to hire 500 new workers, thousands of applicants show up because the union-backed compensation package is so attractive. But for the $5.15-an-hour minimum wage, surely some people wonder if they should even get out of bed.

Empirical Evidence

Over the years, a fair amount of economic research has evaluated the explanatory power of the standard economic model of the trade-off between labor and leisure. As more fully explained in subsequent chapters, economists often ask how wage changes, taxes, and welfare programs affect the amount of labor supplied by workers.[6] Labor supply responses can include changes in both labor force participation and hours worked, and these responses tend to vary across demographic groups.

Pertinent here, the empirical evidence often suggests that some workers are more responsive to wage, tax, or benefit changes than others. For example, high tax rates seem to have relatively little effect on the time spent working by high-income workers. Executives, for example, seem to work as hard as they can whether they face a 50 percent tax on their earnings or a 35 percent tax on their earnings. On the other hand, high tax rates can have a significant impact on secondary earners in two-earner couples. Faced with a high tax rate, more secondary earners (usually wives) will choose non-taxable housework over taxable work in the labor market.[7]

DIFFERENTIAL WAGE RATES

Although useful to a point, the standard model of the trade-off between labor and leisure does not tell us very much about why there is so much earnings inequality. In fact, relatively little earnings inequality is attributable to differences in the number of hours worked by people with the same hourly wage rate (but different preferences between labor and leisure).[8]

Instead, most earnings inequality can be attributed to the rather significant differentials in wage rates. As we saw in chapter 2, even among full-time, year-round workers, people in the 90th percentile of earnings earn around five times as much as people in the 10th percentile, and CEOs often earn hundreds of times what they pay their rank and file. Most full-time, year-round workers have relatively modest annual earnings, but a few are very nearly off the chart (figure 3.3).[9] According to Derek Bok, such "differences in pay are ubiquitous" (1993, 9).

Fortunately, labor economics can help us understand these remarkable wage disparities. Writing more than 200 years ago, Adam Smith identified most of the reasons for wage inequality:

> The five following are the principal circumstances which, so far as I have been able to observe, make up for a small pecuniary gain in some employments and counterbalance a great one in others: first, the agreeableness or disagreeableness of the employments themselves; secondly, the easiness and cheapness, or the difficulty and expense of learning them; thirdly, the constancy or inconstancy of employment in them; fourthly, the small or great trust which must be reposed in those who exercise them; and fifthly, the probability or improbability of success in them. (Smith 1986, 202)

In Smith's view, perfect competition would always lead to some dispersion in earnings, but most of it was attributable to the "principle of compensation"; that is, pay differentials are needed to compensate for job characteristics. For example, pay variations are needed to make up for the fact that some jobs are more "disagreeable" than others.[10] Similarly, pay variations are needed to encourage workers to acquire skills and education, or to work harder or take on a position of trust, or to compensate for greater risks.[11] For example, there is a large wage premium associated with working in the fairly dangerous mining industry (Mortensen 2003).

Few but pure egalitarians have much objection to such compensating pay differentials. Most of us believe that at least some pay differentials are needed to maintain productivity. After all, if everyone were paid the same, who would do the nasty and distasteful work? Who in their right mind would endure three years of law school, for example, without at least some expectation of greater financial rewards?

That is where compensating pay differentials come in. Increased pay is needed to compensate individuals for greater adversity, forgone

Figure 3.3. Distribution of Workers by Earnings Category, 2004

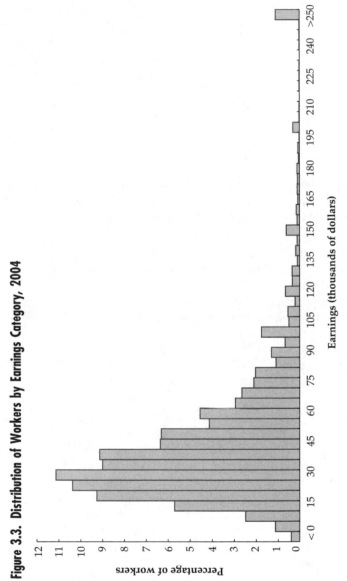

Source: U.S. Census Bureau, *Current Population Survey, Annual Demographic Survey, March Supplement,* 2005.
Note: All civilian noninstitutionalized year-round, full-time workers.

earnings, and greater risks, although there is often considerable disagreement about the appropriate magnitude of those pay differentials. The following example will help us understand how compensating pay differentials can work.

The Economics of Education

Consider the economic payoff from going to college. Assume, for example, that a typical high school graduate can enter the workforce immediately after graduation and work until retiring at age 65. Her salary would start low, but it would increase as she got on-the-job training.

Alternatively, she could go to college for four years and then enter the workforce at a somewhat higher salary. During the four years she is in college, we can assume that she would have no income and that she would, in fact, incur substantial costs for tuition and books. The payoff is that a few years after graduation, she could expect to have a higher salary than if she went to work right after high school, and she could expect to have higher salaries over the remainder of her career until she, too, retires at age 65. These costs and benefits are illustrated in figure 3.4.

More specifically, figure 3.4 shows how a college education can increase the earnings of a typical individual. The figure assumes that a typical high school graduate could join the workforce at age 18 with a salary of $14,000, and, over the course of her career, she could see

Figure 3.4. How Education Can Increase Earnings

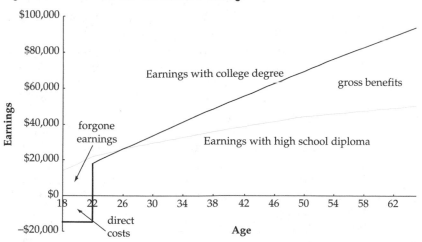

Source: Author's calculations.

modest increases in her salary as she accumulated experience and seniority. If, instead, she goes to college, she would earn nothing for four years and would have to spend, say, $15,000 a year in college expenses from age 18 to age 22. After college, she should be able to start out earning a higher salary, say, $18,000 a year, and she could expect to see more rapid increases in pay as she accumulates experience and seniority. In the figure, her earnings would catch up to those of a high school graduate at age 26, and thereafter her earnings would exceed those of the high school graduate.

Should she go to college? Yes, she should go college if the rewards from college exceed the costs. In the more precise language of economics, she should go to college if the present value of the future benefits exceeds the present value of the forgone earnings and college costs. Factors that will affect her decision about whether the benefits exceed the costs include interest rates, her age, the costs of the education, and the wage differential between high school graduates and college graduates. For example, it makes more economic sense to go to college when you are younger because you can collect the resulting enhancement in earnings over a longer career.[12]

These days there is a particularly large premium for skilled and educated workers. College graduates currently earn nearly twice as much as workers who stop their education with a high school diploma (figure 3.5). One recent study estimated that that difference in earning power for college graduates over high school graduates will amount to more than $1,000,000 over a lifetime (Hill, Hoffman, and Rex 2005).[13]

Labor economists often speak of education as an investment in "human capital." An individual can choose to invest money (capital) in a business or in human capital (i.e., college). Such investments in human capital (i.e., college) "yield a private rate of return that is approximately competitive with rates of return on physical capital" (Hamermesh and Rees 1988, 96).[14] One recent study estimated that the rate of return on a college education is 11.7 percent for men and 11.6 percent for women (Hill et al. 2005). Such high rates of return on college investments have encouraged more people to go to college, and that has been a decidedly good thing for our society (Welch 1999).

Overall, differences in educational attainment and the acquisition of training on the job can account for a significant portion of the observed inequality in earnings (Hamermesh and Rees 1988). According to the principle of compensation, increased pay is appropriate compensation for individuals who invest in education and skill development. Still, there is plenty of room for disagreement about the appropriate magnitude of the resulting pay differentials. For example, one might wonder whether the typical neurosurgeon somehow "deserves" to make 50 to 100 times as much as the typical orderly.[15]

Figure 3.5. Average Annual Earnings by Educational Attainment for All Workers Age 18 and Older, 2003

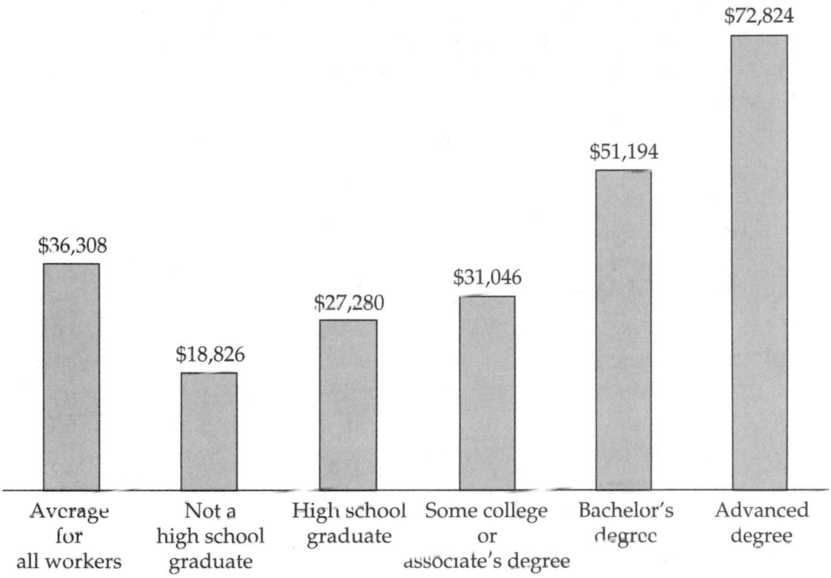

Source: Stoops (2004), table C.

Of note, figure 3.4 also shows how compensation tends to increase with seniority in a typical, concave age-earnings profile. In figure 3.4, it was assumed that the increasing compensation for more senior workers reflected greater skills acquired over time on the job—another form of human capital. In the real world, however, the higher pay of many senior workers may simply be the result of industry-based seniority pay scales that may, or may not, relate to actual increases in productivity.

The Theory of Marginal Productivity

Perhaps even more crucial to our understanding of how labor markets allocate earnings is the economic theory of marginal productivity. According to the theory of marginal productivity, workers are paid in proportion to the value of what they produce.

The bottom line is that people with highly specialized skills that are in short supply can usually demand high salaries, salaries that approach whatever consumers will pay for those services. That is why surgeons make more than family practitioners, why neurosurgeons and heart surgeons make more than run-of-the-mill general surgeons, and why the very best neurosurgeons and heart surgeons can name their own fees.[16] The theory of marginal productivity can also help explain why so many CEOs, top athletes, and movie stars have multimillion-dollar incomes.

Low-skilled workers are also generally paid in proportion to their productivity. Moreover, as low-skilled workers are plentiful, competition keeps their wages low. Pity the poor pizza delivery company that decides to pay its workers a "living wage."[17] That company would have to raise the price of its pizzas and would soon go out of business ("price itself out of the market").

Economists are largely untroubled by the standard supply-and-demand model of wages that results in paying workers in proportion to their productivity. Economics is, after all, not a moral theory but rather a discipline that seeks to explain how markets operate.

Still, when one actually looks closely at the earnings of people at the top of their respective fields, any sense of proportionality between skills and compensation almost certainly breaks down.[18] For example, in *The Winner-Take-All Society*, Robert H. Frank and Philip J. Cook express concern about the dramatically unequal distribution of earnings in the United States:

> It is one thing to say that people who work 10 percent harder or have 10 percent more talent should receive 10 percent more pay. But it is quite another to say that such small differences should cause pay to differ by 10,000 percent or more. (1995, 17)

Similarly, in *The Cost of Talent*, Derek Bok suggests that

> the most vexing moral question posed by professional and executive compensation is why so many people fortunate enough to hold the most interesting, prestigious jobs in society should earn many times the pay of those condemned to work that is much more boring and disagreeable. (1993, 12)[19]

Even that venerable capitalist J. P. Morgan believed that CEOs should not make more than 20 times the compensation of the average worker (Anderson et al. 1999).

THE REST OF THE STORY

To be sure, human capital theory and marginal productivity theory leave unexplained a large portion of the observed inequality in earnings. The factors involved in setting wages in the real world are often quite different from the skill-based equilibrium wages that are supposed to exist in the standard economic theory (Rees 1993; Thurow 1998).[20] Individual wages reflect a variety of factors, not just individual skill levels, supply, and demand. In fact, the observable characteristics of workers (e.g., age and education) only explain about 30 percent of the variation in compensation across workers (Mortensen 2003).

No doubt, a portion of the remaining 70 percent of wage dispersion is due to unmeasured differences in ability, and some is due to the fact that individuals working for a productive firm are paid more than those working for an unproductive firm or in an unproductive sector of the economy (Mortensen 2003; Thurow 1998). There is also a wage premium associated with working for large firms compared with small firms (Mortensen 2003).[21]

Luck, too, seems almost a super factor.[22] All in all, people with equivalent talents are often paid widely different amounts, even when they work in the same company or locale.

The bottom line is that pay is, at best, only loosely proportionate to productivity and skills. According to James K. Galbraith,

the notion that wages depend on personal skill, as expressed in the value of output, makes no sense in any organization where production is interdependent and joint—which is to say it makes no sense in virtually any organization. The image holds together only because of the power of that supply-and-demand model. (1998, 265)

Indeed, Galbraith believes that what economics needs is "a rebellion against the idea that people are actually paid in proportion to the value of what they produce."

For that matter, even if pay were directly proportionate to productivity, many of us would still be troubled by the magnitude of the resulting inequality in earnings, income, and wealth.

That is where the government comes in. One of the central functions of government is to "correct" the market's unequal distribution of earnings and other economic resources. Just how much the government should redistribute is, of course, a matter of considerable debate. To start, chapter 4 explains how government policies currently influence the distribution of income, in general, and earnings, in particular. Chapter 4 also begins our consideration of some of the redistributive tools that governments can, and should, use to increase the rewards from work and to reduce economic inequality.

4

HOW GOVERNMENT AFFECTS THE DISTRIBUTION OF EARNINGS AND INCOME

Governments influence the market's distribution of earnings and income through regulation, spending, and taxation. Government regulation defines and limits the range of markets and so influences the shape of the initial distribution of earnings and income, and taxes and transfers are the primary tools for achieving redistribution. Because taxes and spending influence the behavior of economic actors in the marketplace and favor some sectors of the economy over others, they, too, have a significant regulatory impact on the distribution of earnings and other income.

HOW TAXES AFFECT THE DISTRIBUTION OF EARNINGS AND INCOME

First and foremost, taxes reduce the incomes of those who are taxed; while much of the revenue collected is spent for defense and routine government operations, at least a portion of the revenue collected from well-to-do taxpayers is redistributed to help those who are less fortunate.

Taxes also influence how individuals and businesses behave and so indirectly influence the distribution of economic resources.

An Overview of the U.S. Tax System

The federal government raises virtually all of its revenue from the individual income tax, Social Security payroll taxes, the corporate income tax, estate and gift taxes, and excise taxes on selected goods and services. State and local governments raise most of their revenue from income taxes, sales taxes, and property taxes. All in all, taxes take about 30 percent of the United States gross domestic product (GDP), and federal taxes take about two-thirds of that. For example, in 2002, when the gross domestic product of the United States was just over $10 trillion, the federal government collected around $2 trillion in taxes, and state and local governments collected around $1 trillion in taxes.[1]

Table 4.1 shows the various sources of federal revenues since 1940, and figure 4.1 shows the relative portion of federal revenues coming from each source. What is most striking is that the federal government has increased its reliance on individual income taxes and payroll taxes and decreased its reliance on corporate income taxes, excise taxes, and other sources of revenue.

In fiscal year 2002–03, state and local governments collected $297 billion in property taxes, $338 billion in sales taxes, $199 billion in individual income taxes, $31 billion in corporate income taxes, $390 billion in revenue from the federal government, and $508 billion from all other sources, yielding total general revenues that year of $1.763 trillion (Council of Economic Advisers 2006, table B-86).

The remainder of this section explains how the principal federal taxes work.

Table 4.1. Federal Revenues by Source, 1940–2011 (millions of dollars)

Fiscal year	Individual income taxes	Corporate income taxes	Social insurance and retirement receipts	Excise taxes	Other	Total receipts
1940	892	1,197	1,785	1,977	698	6,548
1960	40,715	21,494	14,683	11,676	3,923	92,492
1980	244,069	64,600	157,803	24,329	26,311	517,112
2000	1,004,462	207,289	652,852	68,865	91,750	2,025,218
2005	927,222	278,282	794,125	73,094	81,136	2,153,859
2011 estimate	1,466,869	292,012	1,096,698	83,124	96,158	3,034,861

Source: Executive Office of the President and Office of Management and Budget (2006b), table 2.1.
Note: Numbers may not add to totals because of rounding.

Figure 4.1. Percentage Composition of Federal Receipts by Source, 1940–2005

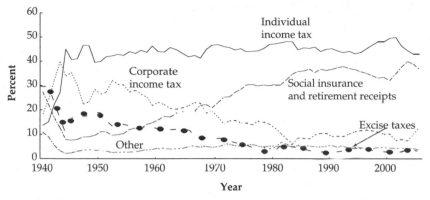

Source: Executive Office of the President and Office of Management and Budget (2006b), table 2.2

The Income Tax on Individuals

The largest of the federal taxes is the income tax imposed on individuals. As shown in table 4.1, the individual income tax raised more than $927 billion in 2005. About 130 million individual income tax returns are filed each year.[2]

The federal income tax is imposed on a taxpayer's *taxable income*.[3] Taxpayers file returns as unmarried individuals, heads of household, married couples filing joint returns, or married couples filing separate returns.

As a starting point, taxpayers first determine the amount of their *gross income*.[4] Gross income includes all income from whatever source derived, including (but not limited to) the wages, salary, tips, gains, dividends, interest, rents, and royalties received by taxpayers during the taxable year. The United States Supreme Court has interpreted the term "gross income" broadly to include all "undeniable accessions to wealth, clearly realized, and over which the taxpayers have complete dominion."[5]

At the same time, however, there are numerous statutory *exclusions* from gross income. For example, gifts, inheritances, and life insurance proceeds received by a taxpayer are expressly excluded from gross income, as are certain scholarships, fringe benefits, interest earned on state and local bonds, welfare benefits, and most Social Security benefits (Forman 1994; I.R.C. §§ 86, 101, 102, 103, 106, 117, 119, and 132). Also of note, economic gains are not taxed until the underlying property has been sold and the gain is "realized."[6]

From gross income, taxpayers subtract certain *deductions* to get to taxable income. Most taxpayers simply claim a standard deduction and personal exemptions. Many taxpayers, however, claim certain itemized deductions in lieu of the standard deduction. Also, certain other deductions are allowed without regard to whether the taxpayer chooses to itemize.

Each year, the U.S. Department of Treasury indexes the standard deduction amounts, the personal exemption amounts, and the income tax rate tables to reflect the prior year's change in the Consumer Price Index; table 4.2 shows the basic standard deductions, personal exemptions, and simple income tax thresholds for various taxpayers in 2006. For example, a married couple with two children can claim a standard deduction of $10,300 and four $3,300 personal exemptions. Consequently, the couple will not have any taxable income unless its gross income exceeds $23,500.

Table 4.2 also shows the tax rate schedules for 2006. For a taxpayer with gross income in excess of her simple income tax threshold, her regular tax liability would be determined by applying the 10, 15, 25, 28, 33, and 35 percent rates to taxable income. The maximum tax rate on dividends and net long-term capital gains, however, is just 15 percent.[7]

By historical standards, the present income tax rates are relatively low. Rates were quite low in the early part of the 20th century after the 16th Amendment to the Constitution first authorized Congress to enact an income tax. To raise the revenue needed for World War II,

Table 4.2. Standard Deductions, Personal Exemptions, and Simple Income Tax Thresholds, and Tax Rate Schedules for Various Taxpayers, 2006

	Unmarried individuals	Married couples filing joint returns with two children	Heads of household with two children
Standard deduction	$5,150	$10,300	$ 7,550
Personal exemptions	$3,300	$13,200 (4 × $3,300)	$ 9,900 (3 × $3,300)
Simple income tax threshold	$8,450	$23,500	$17,450

Tax rate (imposed on taxable income)		Rate bracket	
10	$0 to $7,550	$0 to $15,100	$0 to $10,750
15	$7,551 to $30,650	$15,101 to $61,300	$10,751 to $41,050
25	$30,651 to $74,200	$61,301 to $123,700	$41,051 to $106,000
28	$74,201 to $154,800	$123,701 to $188,450	$106,001 to $171,650
33	$154,801 to $336,550	$188,451 to $336,550	$171,651 to $336,550
35	Over $336,550	Over $336,550	Over $336,550

Source: Internal Revenue Service (2005c).

however, Congress expanded the reach of the income tax to more households, and marginal tax rates soared. Even into the 1960s, marginal tax rates remained as high as 70 percent. To help encourage work effort by high-income taxpayers, Congress added a provision to the Internal Revenue Code that provided a 50 percent maximum tax rate on earned income.[8] And to help reduce the tax rates for all taxpayers, the Tax Reform Act of 1986 reduced the maximum income tax rate to 28 percent.[9] In subsequent years, the maximum federal income tax rate crept up to 39.6 percent. More recently, however, the Economic Growth and Tax Relief Reconciliation Act of 2001 and the Jobs Relief and Reconciliation Act of 2003 cut income tax rates.[10] The maximum income tax rate is now 35 percent, and many workers now face income tax rates of just 10 or 15 percent.[11]

Income Tax Credits. The amount that a taxpayer must actually pay (or will receive as a refund) is equal to the taxpayer's regular tax liability minus her allowable tax credits. Pertinent here, certain low-income taxpayers are entitled to claim the refundable earned income tax credit, the partially refundable child tax credit, and the nonrefundable dependent care credit.[12]

The earned income tax credit. The earned income tax credit is a refundable tax credit for certain low-income workers. In 2006, for example, a family with two or more qualifying children is entitled to a refundable earned income tax credit of up to $4,536.[13] The credit is computed as 40 percent of the first $11,340 of earned income (figure 4.2). For married

Figure 4.2. Earned Income Credit Amounts Available to Married Couples in 2006

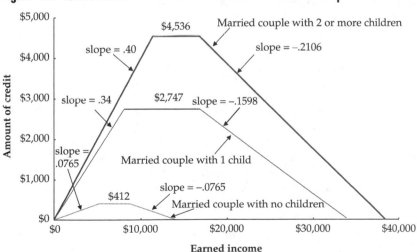

Source: Author's calculations.

couples filing joint returns, the maximum credit is reduced by 21.06 percent of earned income (or adjusted gross income, if greater) in excess of $16,810 and is entirely phased out at $38,348 of income. For heads of household, the maximum credit phases out over the range from $14,810 to $36,348. Also, families with one child are entitled to an earned income credit of up to $2,747 in 2006, and childless individuals are entitled to an earned income credit of up to $412.[14] Over 22 million taxpayers claimed a total of $38.7 billion in earned income tax credits for 2003, of which $19.2 billion was refundable (Parisi and Hollenbeck 2005). Of note, 19 states have adopted their own earned income tax credits that provide additional benefits for working families (Nagle and Johnson 2006).[15]

The child tax credit. Taxpayers with children under the age of 17 can claim a tax credit of up to $1,000 per child. The child tax credit is first applied to offset a taxpayer's income tax liability (if any), and, for taxpayers with earned income in excess of $11,300 in 2006, a portion of the credit is refundable.[16] For example, a married couple with two children and $15,000 of earned income in 2006 would be entitled to a refundable child tax credit of $555, but married couples with two children and at least $24,180 of earned income can generally claim the full $2,000 worth of child tax credits.[17]

Child tax credits phase out once a taxpayer's adjusted gross income reaches $110,000 for married couples filing joint returns, $55,000 for married individuals filing separately, and $75,000 for all other taxpayers. For example, a married couple with two qualifying children would see their two child tax credits phase out as their adjusted gross income increases from $110,000 to $150,000.[18] Some 25.7 million taxpayers claimed a total of $31.9 billion of child tax credits for 2003, of which $9.1 billion was refundable (Parisi and Hollenbeck 2005).

The dependent care credit. The federal income tax system also provides a dependent care credit to certain taxpayers who incur employment-related expenses to care for children under the age of 13.[19] A taxpayer can claim a tax credit of up to $1,050 (35 percent of $3,000) a year for one qualifying child, or up to $2,100 (35 percent of $6,000) a year for two or more qualifying children. The credit is reduced for taxpayers whose adjusted gross income exceeds $15,000 until it levels off at $600 (20 percent of $3,000) for one qualifying child and $1,200 (20 percent of $6,000) for two or more qualifying children for taxpayers with adjusted gross income over $45,000. Over 6.3 million taxpayers claimed a total of $3.2 billion in dependent care credits for 2003 (Parisi and Hollenbeck 2005). Perhaps the biggest limitation is that the dependent care credit is not refundable.[20] That means it is of no value to low-income Americans who are exempt from income taxation.

The Alternative Minimum Tax. Some individuals must also pay the *alternative minimum tax,* which is payable when it exceeds the individual's regular income tax liability.[21] The tax is imposed at rates of 26 and

28 percent on "alternative minimum taxable income" in excess of an exemption amount.[22] In 2006, the exemption amounts are $58,000 for married couples filing joint returns, $40,250 for single individuals and heads of household, and $29,000 for married individuals filing separate returns.

State Income Taxes. More than 40 states and numerous local governments also levy income taxes on individuals.[23] These state income taxes are typically imposed on a variation of federal taxable income, albeit at lower rates. In 2006, for example, the tax rates in Washington, D.C., range from 5 to 9 percent.

Social Insurance Taxes

Federal and state governments also collect payroll taxes to help fund the social insurance safety net.

Social Security Taxes. Social Security taxes are levied on earnings in employment and self-employment covered by Social Security, with portions of the total tax allocated by law to the Old-Age and Survivors Insurance trust fund (OASI), the Disability Insurance trust fund (DI), and the Medicare Hospital Insurance trust fund.[24] For 2006, employees pay Social Security taxes of 7.65 percent on the first $94,200 of wages and 1.45 percent of wages over $94,200 (Social Security Administration 2005c). The lion's share of these payroll taxes is used to finance the OASI program (5.30 percent of wages), and the rest pay for DI (0.9 percent) and Medicare (1.45 percent).

Employers pay a matching Social Security tax of 7.65 percent of up to $94,200 of wages for each covered employee. Employees are not allowed to deduct their portion of Social Security taxes for income tax purposes.[25] On the other hand, the employer's portion of Social Security taxes is excluded from the employee's income for income tax purposes.[26]

Similarly, self-employed workers pay an equivalent Social Security tax of 15.3 percent on the first $94,200 of self-employment earnings and 2.9 percent of self-employment earnings over that amount. To put self-employed individuals in an approximately equivalent position as employees, self-employed individuals can deduct half these taxes for both Social Security and income tax purposes.[27]

Social Security and Medicare taxes have grown over the years. In 1940, for example, an employee and her employer each paid a Social Security payroll tax equal to 1 percent on the first $3,000 in wages, for a total of 2 percent of wages. In 2006, however, an employee and her employer each must pay 7.65 percent of the first $94,200 of wages, and 1.45 percent on wages over $94,200 (figure 4.3). Not surprisingly, social insurance taxes rose from just 19 percent of federal revenues in 1965

Figure 4.3. U.S. Payroll Tax Rates, Selected Years

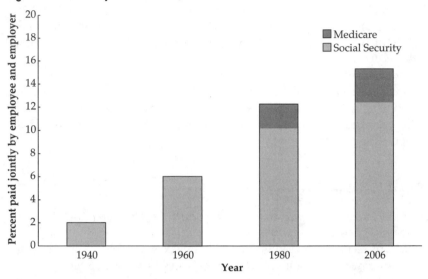

Source: U.S. House Committee (2004), table 1-1.

to 36.9 percent of federal revenues in 2005—and from just 3.2 percent of GDP in 1965 to 6.5 percent of GDP in 2005 (Executive Office of the President and Office of Management and Budget [OMB] 2006b, tables 2.2 and 2.3).[28]

Unemployment Compensation Taxes. Unemployment compensation is a joint federal-state program that provides cash benefits to individuals who have recently become unemployed.[29] Benefits are financed through Federal Unemployment Tax Act (FUTA) taxes, a gross tax of 6.2 percent on the first $7,000 paid annually by covered employers to each employee.

The Corporate Income Tax

The federal government also imposes an income tax on corporations.[30] The taxable income of a corporation generally is made up of gross income less allowable deductions. Allowable deductions include ordinary and necessary business expenditures, such as salaries, wages, interest expense, depreciation, certain losses, selling expenses, and other expenses. Most large corporations pay tax at a 35 percent marginal tax rate.

Some corporations are also subject to an alternative minimum tax, which is payable, in addition to all other tax liabilities, to the extent that it exceeds the corporation's regular income tax liability.[31] The alternative minimum tax is imposed at a flat rate of 20 percent on "alternative minimum taxable income" in excess of a $40,000 exemption amount.

Many states also have corporate income taxes.

Estate and Gift Taxes

The federal government also imposes estate and gift taxes on lifetime transfers and transfers at death.[32] In 2006, each taxpayer can give away up to $2 million of property tax free over her lifetime or at death. Transfers in excess of $2 million are generally subject to an estate tax or a gift tax of up to 46 percent. Transfers to a spouse and gifts of up to $12,000 to others each year are exempt from tax (IRS 2005c). Of note, the estate tax is scheduled to disappear in 2010, but it will bounce back into existence in 2011 unless Congress acts.[33]

Many states also impose modest taxes on estates or inheritances.

Other Taxes

In addition, the federal government collects excise taxes on various consumer products and services, including alcoholic beverages, tobacco products, motor fuels, and air transportation; and the government collects customs duties. State and local governments also collect a significant share of their revenues from sales taxes and from real and personal property taxes.

Earned Income and the Federal Tax Code

Congress has fashioned numerous special rules relating to earned income into the Internal Revenue Code.[34] Most notably, the Social Security payroll taxes apply only to covered wages and self-employment earnings. For example, investment income and welfare benefits are both exempt. Also, the earned income credit and the refundable portion of the child tax credit are expressly conditioned on the taxpayer having "earned income," and the dependent care credit requires the taxpayer to have "employment-related expenses."[35]

At times, Congress has also tried to use the tax code to discourage excessive compensation packages. For example, businesses are only allowed to claim a deduction for "reasonable compensation."[36] In addition, corporations generally cannot deduct more than $1 million a year of cash compensation paid to their directors, nor can they deduct extraordinary "golden parachute" payments made to former executives.[37]

Congress also uses the tax code to try to help low-income workers. In addition to the earned income tax credit, the "work opportunity tax credit" provides employers with an incentive to hire individuals from certain targeted groups that tend to have high unemployment rates (Hamersma 2003; I.R.C. § 51; IRS 2004b).[38] The credit is equal to 40 percent of up to $6,000 of wages paid to a targeted group member during the first year of employment, for a maximum credit per worker of $2,400. The "welfare-to-work credit" provides businesses with a similar incentive to hire long-term welfare recipients.[39]

Redistribution and Marginal Tax Rates

Taxes are one of the primary ways that the government redistributes economic resources. Government operations and transfer programs are largely financed by taxes imposed on higher-income Americans, and overall, the federal tax system is decidedly progressive.[40] Table 4.3 shows the Congressional Budget Office's recent estimates of the shares of federal tax liabilities and effective federal tax rates for all households for 2003.[41]

The individual income tax is particularly progressive. The top 1 percent of taxpayers paid 34.6 percent of all federal income taxes in 2003, and the top 5 percent paid 56.6 percent (CBO 2004b, table 2).[42] At the other extreme, Americans with incomes below the poverty level generally do not pay any federal income tax at all (Forman and Jung 2004).

Corporate income taxes are also quite progressive. From an economic point of view, corporations are fictional entities, and the burden of the corporate income tax must be borne by individuals. In that regard, economists generally believe that much of the burden of the corporate

Table 4.3. Shares of Federal Tax Liabilities and Effective Federal Tax Rate, for All Households, by Household Income Category, 2003

Income category	Share of federal tax liabilities	Total effective federal tax rate
Lowest quintile	1.0	4.8
Second quintile	4.5	9.8
Third quintile	9.9	13.6
Fourth quintile	18.6	17.7
Highest quintile	65.7	25.0
All quintiles	**100.0**	**19.8**
Top 10 percent	50.2	26.8
Top 5 percent	38.7	28.4
Top 1 percent	22.6	31.4

Source: Congressional Budget Office (2005c), summary tables 1 and 2.

Note: Shares do not total 100 because of rounding.

income tax is borne by the shareholders in the form of lower net profits, and the rest is borne by corporate employees (in the form of lower wages) and customers (in the form of higher prices). The net effect is that corporate income taxes have a progressive impact on individual incomes.

On the other hand, social insurance payroll taxes are regressive.

Marginal Tax Rates under the Income Tax

The current federal income tax system imposes relatively high effective marginal tax rates on earned income, and the highest rates are often imposed on low-income taxpayers in the phaseout range of the earned income tax credit.[43] Figure 4.4 shows the effective marginal income tax rates imposed on a typical married couple with two dependent children and with varying amounts of earned income.[44] Taxpayers in states with an income tax would generally face even higher effective marginal tax rates.

Marginal Tax Rates under the Social Security Payroll Tax

Figure 4.5 shows the marginal Social Security payroll tax rates imposed on workers with varying levels of earned income. Most economists believe that the burden of most payroll taxes paid by employers falls on the employees themselves.[45] In effect, workers bear the brunt of the

Figure 4.4. Effective Marginal Income Tax Rates on Married Couples with Two Children and Earned Income Only, 2006

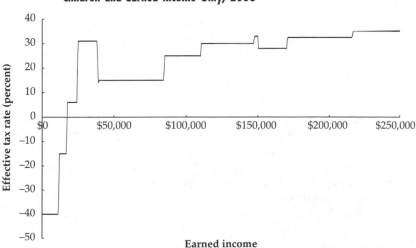

Source: Author's calculations.

Figure 4.5. Social Security: Effective Marginal Tax Rates on Earned Income, 2006

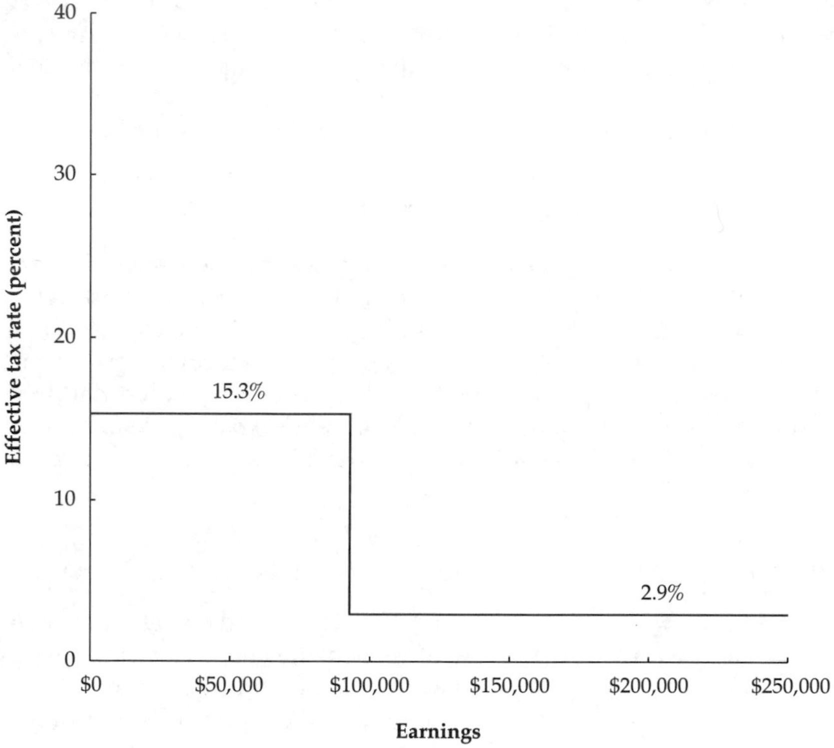

Source: Author's calculations.

employment taxes paid by their employers. Overall, the payroll tax is regressive, with workers paying roughly 15.3 percent of their first $94,200 of earned income and 2.9 percent on earnings in excess of $94,200 (in 2006).[46] As is common in this type of analysis, figure 4.5 ignores the value of any future Social Security and Medicare benefits that might result from these payroll taxes.[47]

Of note, most households pay more Social Security payroll taxes than income taxes. For example, 70.6 percent of households paid more payroll taxes than income taxes in 2000—41.3 percent if just the employee share is considered (CBO 2003b, table 2).[48] Moreover, low-income households are much more likely than high-income households to pay more payroll taxes than income taxes. In 2000, almost 98 percent of households in the lowest income quintile paid more payroll than income taxes, while just over 26 percent in the top quintile paid more payroll taxes than income taxes. This relationship is not all that surprising given the lack of a tax threshold before the Social Security payroll tax kicks in, the $94,200 cap on the OASI and DI taxes, and the progressivity of the income tax rate structure.[49]

Marginal Tax Rates under the Income and Payroll Taxes Combined

When both income and payroll taxes are considered, the effective marginal tax rates on earned income can be extraordinarily high, especially on low-income workers with children. For example, figure 4.6 shows the effective marginal tax rates imposed on married couples with two children and earned income only.[50] Once again, effective marginal tax rates bounce all over the place, rather than increasing monotonically as earned income increases, and some of the very highest marginal effective tax rates are imposed on couples earning around $30,000 a year. Figure 4.6 also includes a linear trend line, so the reader can imagine what a more rational, progressive tax rate structure might look like. Figure 4.7 shows similar results for heads of household with two children.[51]

Marginal Tax Rates on Earned Income versus Investment Income

Obviously, the kind of income a taxpayer receives can also affect her effective marginal tax rate. For example, while earned income is taxed at rates as high as 35 percent under the income tax and roughly 15.3 percent under the Social Security payroll tax, investment income is often taxed at much lower rates. Interest earned on state and local bonds is tax-exempt.[52] Also, dividends and net capital gains are generally taxed at no more than 15 percent, although most large businesses are subject to the corporate income tax rates of up to 35 percent. All

Figure 4.6. Combined Effective Marginal Tax Rates (Income and Payroll Taxes), Married Couples with Two Children and Earned Income Only, 2006

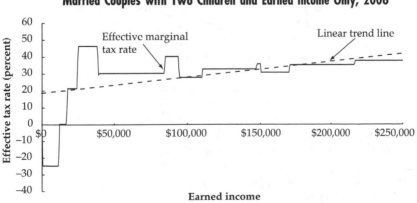

Source: Author's calculations.

Figure 4.7. Combined Effective Marginal Tax Rates (Income and Payroll Taxes), Heads of Household with Two Children and Earned Income Only, 2006

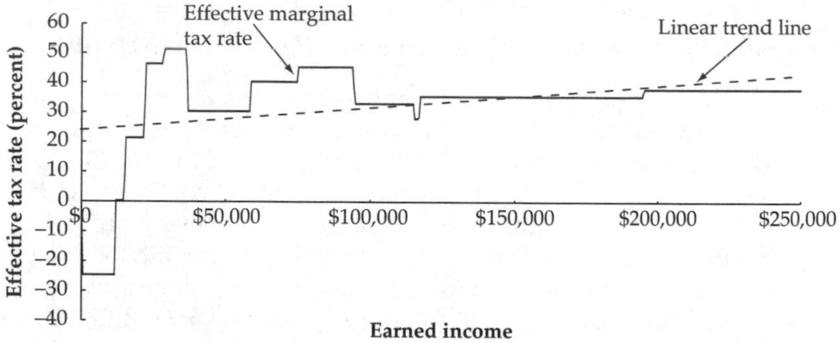

Source: Author's calculations.

in all, however, recent tax policy changes, such as cutting the tax rate on dividends and capital gains from 20 to 15 percent and cutting the estate tax, have shifted a large share of taxation away from investment income and onto earned income.[53]

How Taxes Influence Work Behavior

Taxes influence the behavior of economic actors and so indirectly influence the distribution of earnings and other economic resources. In particular, changes in tax rates will lead individuals to change their behavior to minimize their tax liabilities. These behavioral changes will include changes in labor supply, savings, and investment.[54]

For example, because a tax on earnings reduces our ability to purchase goods, it may encourage us to work harder to make more money. This is an example of the "income effect." On the other hand, because a tax on earnings makes leisure relatively more attractive, we may work less and consume more leisure. This is an example of the "substitution effect." Because the income and substitution effects often work in opposite directions, the net effect of an earnings tax on work effort is ambiguous and will depend heavily on individual preferences. Some people will want to work more to restore their income to its pre-tax level. Others will work less because leisure has become relatively more attractive.

On the whole, however, a fair amount of empirical evidence suggests that imposing high taxes on earned income tends to discourage work effort and reduce labor supply.[55] In particular, the evidence shows that high tax rates tend to discourage low-skilled workers and secondary earners in two-earner couples from working.[56]

Figure 4.8 shows how an individual might reduce her work effort in response to a 30 percent payroll tax. The worker in figure 4.8 earns $10 an hour and, in the absence of a payroll tax, she would like to work 2,000 hours a year and earn $20,000 a year. Faced with a 30 percent payroll tax, however, she would work just 1,750 hours a year and take home just $12,250 a year after tax. In short, payroll taxes can reduce work effort.[57]

All in all, the empirical research suggests that increases in the marginal tax rate on earned income tend to reduce labor supply, while decreases in marginal tax rates tend to increase labor supply. For example, the Congressional Budget Office has estimated that recent tax cuts reduced the average marginal tax rate on wages from 25.6 percent in 2000 to 22.7 percent in 2004; as a result, the overall labor supply increased by 0.72 percent (CBO 2004a, 8–9). On the other hand, the Congressional Budget Office predicts that future increases in marginal tax rates on wages will reduce overall labor supply.[58]

The bottom line is that high marginal tax rates on earned income discourage people from working. Consider Nobel prize–winning economist Edward C. Prescott's recent research on why Americans work

Figure 4.8. How a 30 Percent Payroll Tax Can Reduce Work Effort

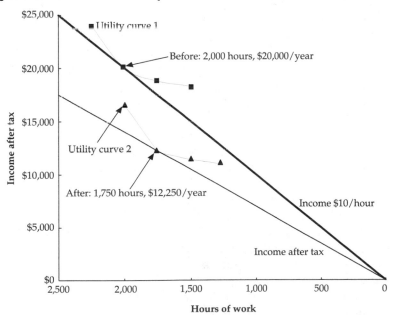

Source: Author's calculations.

more than Europeans (Prescott 2004).[59] Using labor market statistics from the Organisation for Economic Co-operation and Development, he noted that on a per-person basis, Americans age 15–64 work about 50 percent more than the French and Italians and a third more than the Germans. His analysis of historical tax-rate data in the United States and Europe led him to conclude that these differences in work effort are largely attributable to differences in marginal tax rates rather than "cultural" differences or other factors.[60] Again, the message is that low marginal tax rates will encourage greater work effort (perhaps, even by Europeans).

Taxes on earned income do more than just influence labor supply. For example, taxes on earnings influence worker decisions about developing human capital. In that regard, research suggests that progressive taxes on earned income reduce the incentive to accumulate skills that would promote earnings growth, as accumulation of those skills would move workers into discouragingly higher tax brackets (Heckman, Lochner, and Taber 1998, 4). Taxes on earned income can also encourage some individuals to *evade* taxes, for example, by working in the underground economy or underreporting their earnings (Fehr et al. 2005; Schneider and Enste 2002). High tax rates also encourage individuals to *avoid* taxes, for example, by shifting their compensation toward untaxed forms such as health insurance, traditional pensions, and 401(k) plans (Slemrod 2003; Feldstein 1995, 1999). High tax rates can also lead individuals to find other ways to reduce their taxable income, for example, by shifting investments to tax-exempt bonds and growth stocks and by increasing their deductions for mortgage interest, investment interest, and charitable contributions (Feldstein 1995, 554–55).[61]

How about other types of taxes? The federal income tax is basically a tax on earned income and investment income (e.g., interest, dividends, and gains), and it has progressive rates and low exemptions.[62] Because the income tax is imposed on both earned income and investment income, it will have lower rates and so distort work incentives less than an equal-yielding payroll tax. Of course, taxing investment income raises its own concerns, as taxes on investment income can distort the behavior of investors.

How about a consumption tax, like a 10 percent national sales tax? For most wage earners, this type of tax has the same effect as a tax on wages.[63] That is because most workers save little and spend almost everything they earn. Consequently, taxing everything a typical worker spends is economically equivalent to taxing everything that the worker earns.

All in all, for most workers, income taxes and consumption taxes will have pretty much the same effects as a payroll tax. Some workers will decrease their work effort as leisure becomes relatively more attractive, while other workers will increase their work effort in order to buy almost as many goods as if there were no tax.

Estate and gift taxes can also have an adverse effect on work effort. These taxes can lead wealthy individuals to favor leisure over work and consumption over savings (McCaffery 1994, 320).[64]

In short, taxes on labor income tend to discourage work effort, and high tax rates tend to discourage work effort exponentially more. Consequently, if government wants to minimize the work disincentives inherent in any system of taxation, it should try to keep the effective marginal tax rates on earned income as low as possible.

How Transfers Affect the Distribution of Earnings and Income

Government spending is the second major way that governments influence the distribution of earnings and income. In particular, the federal government operates a number of transfer programs specifically intended to redistribute economic resources and reduce inequality. Government spending and transfer programs can also influence the economic behavior of individuals and other economic actors and so indirectly influence the distribution of economic resources.[65]

The federal government spends money for defense and numerous other governmental functions. That spending only indirectly influences the distribution of economic resources. The federal government also operates numerous transfer programs, some of which are designed to reduce poverty and inequality. All told, the federal government spent almost $2.5 trillion in fiscal year 2005 (Executive Office and OMB 2006b, table 8.1).[66]

In addition, the states spent around $1.2 trillion in fiscal year 2004, including $262.6 billion (22.3 percent) for Medicaid, $24.8 billion (2.1 percent) for public assistance, and much of the rest for education, transportation, and corrections (National Association of State Budget Officers 2005).[67]

The Major Federal Transfer Programs

Dozens of federal transfer programs provide assistance to individuals for retirement, disability, health, education, housing, public assistance, employment, and other needs. The vast majority of these programs transfer cash or in-kind benefits (e.g., food or medical care) directly to individuals. Social welfare analysts generally differentiate between transfer programs that are "means-tested" and those that are not. For means-tested programs (e.g., family support, Medicaid, and food stamps), eligibility and benefits depend upon an individual's need, as measured by the individual's income and assets. For non-means-tested programs (e.g., social insurance programs like Social Security and Medicare), eligibility is based on other criteria such as age and work history. Table 4.4 shows the federal government's outlays for the principal federal transfer programs, and the remainder of this part summarizes how some of the key programs work.

Means-Tested Programs

Several federal programs are distributed based on a family's need. These programs include Supplemental Security Income (SSI), Temporary Assistance for Needy Families, the earned income and child tax credits, Medicaid, and the Food Stamp Program.

Supplemental Security Income. Supplemental Security Income is a federally administered program that provides monthly cash benefits to certain low-income elderly, disabled, or blind Americans (U.S. House Committee 2004, section 3). Benefits are indexed for inflation and, in 2006, the maximum federal benefit is $603 a month for individuals and $904 a month for couples (Social Security Administration [SSA] 2005c). In December 2004, about 7 million Americans received SSI benefits, and the average benefit was about $449 a month (SSA 2006b, tables 7.A1 and 7.A5). Of these, almost 5.8 million recipients were blind or disabled and about 1.2 million were elderly (table 7.A1).

Family Support. The Personal Responsibility and Work Opportunity Reconciliation Act of 1996 (PRWORA) replaced the old Aid to Families with Dependent Children program with Temporary Assistance for Needy Families.[68] Under the TANF program, the federal government

Table 4.4. Outlays for the Principal Federal Benefit Programs (billions of dollars)

	2005 actual	2011 estimate
Social Security	519	780
Medicare	294	489
Medicaid	182	264
Unemployment compensation	32	47
Supplemental Security Income	35	47
Earned income tax credit	35	40
Food assistance	45	54
Family support	24	24
Housing assistance	38	35
Retirement and disability programs for civilians, the military, and veterans	139	182

Sources: Executive Office of the President and Office of Management and Budget (2006b), table 3.2 for housing assistance, table 8.5 for all other entries.

provides block grants to the states, and the states use their family assistance grants to provide cash assistance and other support to needy families. TANF set a five-year limit on federally funded aid and generally requires recipients to work after a maximum of two years of benefits. The states set all the remaining eligibility criteria, including income eligibility thresholds, resource limits, disregards, and benefit levels. About 1.9 million families (4.5 million persons) received TANF benefits in December 2005.[69]

The work requirements under TANF were designed to ensure that at least 50 percent of TANF participants are involved in "countable work activities," such as paid or unpaid work, vocational training, job search, or providing child care for other participants.[70] The expected level of effort is 30 hours a week for a parent with a child over the age of 6 and 20 hours a week for a parent with a child under the age of 6. By 2002, states had achieved an average work participation rate of 33 percent, and almost two-thirds of TANF recipients who met their work requirements did so by working in unsubsidized jobs (Pavetti 2004).

Earned Income and Child Tax Credits. As more fully explained above, certain low-income taxpayers are entitled to claim the refundable earned income tax credit and partially refundable child tax credits on their federal income tax returns. Because these credits can exceed a taxpayer's income tax liabilities, many observers view the excess credits as a part of the federal government's transfer system, albeit administered by the Internal Revenue Service. Indeed, the earned income tax credit is one of the largest federal welfare programs, and according to one study it now lifts more children out of poverty than any other government program (Nagle and Johnson 2006, 12).

Medicaid. Medicaid is a federal-state matching entitlement program that provides medical assistance for needy persons who are elderly, blind, disabled, members of families with dependent children, and certain other pregnant women and children. Total federal and state outlays for the Medicaid program were $276.8 billion in fiscal year 2004 (Hoffman, Klees, and Curtis 2005, 22). The program served 51.6 million people in fiscal year 2002, and the average expenditure was about $4,140 per person.[71]

Food Assistance. Several federal programs provide food assistance to needy households. The largest of these, the Food Stamp Program, is administered by state agencies operating under the supervision of the U.S. Department of Agriculture (U.S. House Committee 2004, section 15; U.S. Department of Agriculture 2005; Lerman and Wiseman 2002). The federal government fully finances food stamp benefits and reimburses one-half of state administrative expenses. Food stamp benefits are a function of a household's size, its counted monthly income, and a maximum monthly benefit level. In 2005, the Food Stamp Program served almost 26 million Americans, and the average monthly food stamp benefit was $93 per person.[72]

Historically, food stamp benefits were issued as booklets of coupons that participating households used to buy food items for home preparation and consumption. These days, however, some 80 percent of food stamp benefits are delivered through electronic benefit transfer systems, in which recipients use debit-like cards to pay for their food at the checkout counters of authorized retail stores (U.S. General Accounting Office [GAO] 2002a).

Other Means-Tested Programs. The federal government also provides Child Care and Development Block Grants to the states for child care, and some states also use a portion of their TANF funding to pay for child care assistance. In fiscal year 2004, federal and state funds for child care totaled almost $9.4 billion.[73] Child care subsidies usually come in the form of vouchers that can be used to pay willing child care providers.[74]

Head Start provides comprehensive child development programs for poor children from birth to age 5, but it serves less than half of eligible children (Currie 2001).[75] In fiscal year 2005, the program served 906,993 poor children at a total cost of about $6.8 billion.[76]

A number of federal programs also provide housing assistance to low-income families (U.S. House Committee 2004, section 15 and appendix K). Housing aid typically comes in the form of rental subsidies or mortgage interest subsidies. In 2002, for example, the U.S. Department of Housing and Urban Development spent nearly $32 billion to provide housing assistance to about 5 million households. There are also several programs designed specifically to help the homeless.

The Low-Income Home Energy Assistance Program (LIHEAP) provides energy assistance for the poor (U.S. House Committee 2004, section 15). LIHEAP is a block grant program that provides grants to states to run home energy assistance programs for needy families. In 2003, the federal government spent almost $2 billion on the program.

Non-Means-Tested Programs

The major non-means-tested programs are Social Security, Medicare, and unemployment compensation.

Social Security. The Old-Age and Survivors Insurance program provides monthly cash benefits to retired workers and their dependents and to survivors of insured workers (U.S. House Committee 2004, section 1). The Disability Insurance program provides monthly cash benefits for disabled workers under age 65 and their dependents. A worker builds protection under these programs by working in employment that is covered by the Social Security system and paying the applicable payroll taxes. At present, roughly 96 percent of the workforce is in covered employment (U.S. House Committee 2004, 1-4).

At retirement, disability, or death, monthly Social Security benefits are paid to insured workers and to their eligible dependents and survivors. In general, OASI and DI benefits are related to the earnings history of the insured worker. In December 2004, there were 47.7 million beneficiaries of the OASI and DI programs (SSA 2006b, table 5.A1). The average payment to a retired worker was $955 a month, and the average payment to a disabled worker was $894 a month. Additional amounts were paid on behalf of dependents of these covered workers.

Medicare. The Medicare program provides nearly universal health care coverage for elderly Americans and for certain people with disabilities (U.S. House Committee 2004, section 2; Hoffman et al. 2005).[77] Medicare Part A provides hospital insurance coverage for almost everyone over age 65 and for certain disabled persons under age 65. Medicare Part B is a voluntary program that generally pays 80 percent of the doctor bills and laboratory tests for those elderly and disabled individuals who choose to enroll and pay the monthly premium ($88.50 in 2006) (HHS 2005). The Medicare Prescription Drug, Improvement, and Modernization Act of 2003 (Public Law 108-173) added a prescription drug benefit to the program (i.e., "Medicare Part D"). In 2005, some 42.5 million people were covered by Medicare, and total program outlays that year were $336.4 billion (Boards of Trustees 2006, table II.B1).

Unemployment Compensation. Unemployment compensation is a joint federal-state program that provides cash benefits to individuals who have recently become unemployed (U.S. House Committee 2004, section 4). States administer their programs within federal guidelines. Some 99.7 percent of all wage and salary workers and 89 percent of the civilian labor force are covered by unemployment compensation, about 128 million individuals in all. Benefits are financed through FUTA taxes, a gross tax of 6.2 percent on the first $7,000 paid annually by covered employers to each employee.

States set the benefit amounts as a fraction of the individual's weekly wage up to some state-determined maximum. Unemployed persons usually receive unemployment benefits for 26 weeks; the federal-state extended benefits program, however, provides up to 13 additional weeks. In 2004, the average weekly benefit amount was $262.50, and the average duration was 16.1 weeks (SSA 2006b, table 9A2).

Other Programs

A variety of programs also provide education, training, and other services to low-income families. In particular, many states provide a whole range of work-support services to their welfare recipients, including job search, job placement, and job readiness services; transportation assistance; and short-term loans for work-related supplies (GAO 2002c, 8).

Spending and Redistribution

Most government spending has only a slight or indirect impact on the distribution of earnings and income. Spending on the military and other government operations, for example, probably has relatively little impact on economic inequality. The typical government worker or contractor presumably makes a little more than the average American worker, but that small difference probably has little effect on the overall distribution of economic resources. Similarly, it seems unlikely that government spending on a new aircraft carrier, Amtrak, or the bailout of a failing airline will do much to reduce economic inequality.

Moreover, even among federal transfer programs, relatively few programs are actually designed to reduce inequality in earnings or income. Agricultural subsidies, for example, involve redistribution, but as most recipients are the enviable owners of valuable agricultural land, this kind of redistribution is unlikely to reduce economic inequality. Even among entitlement programs, relatively few programs are means-tested, and only about 10 to 15 percent of the federal budget is spent for such explicit redistribution. To be sure, the larger non-means-tested programs like Social Security and Medicare probably reduce income inequality. All in all, however, only a relatively small portion of federal government spending is specifically intended to "correct" the market's maldistribution of economic resources.

How Transfers Influence Work Behavior

Transfers also influence the behavior of economic actors and so indirectly influence the distribution of earnings and other economic resources. In particular, traditional welfare programs tend to reduce work effort. On the other hand, earnings subsidies can increase work effort. These two approaches are discussed in turn.

How Traditional Welfare Tends to Reduce Work Effort

It is widely understood that traditional welfare programs tend to reduce work effort.[78] For example, consider the standard economic analysis of a simple cash transfer program like today's TANF program and its predecessor, AFDC. These types of cash transfer programs operate like a negative income tax. A negative income tax is a system of cash transfers in which the amount of the cash transfer varies inversely with the individual's income: the lower the individual's pre-transfer income, the greater the amount of the government's net transfer to her.

Generally, two policy variables can define a simple negative income tax.[79] The *target* or *break-even income level* is the income level at which an individual becomes ineligible for benefits and the government transfer equals zero. The *benefit-reduction rate* (sometimes called the marginal tax rate) determines the rate of reduction of an individual's transfer as the individual's pre-transfer income increases.

For example, consider a simple negative income tax that guarantees everyone at least $5,000 a year and phases out that benefit as income increases to $10,000.[80] Under such a system, individuals with zero income would receive a maximum benefit of $5,000 a year. This is sometimes called the *guarantee* or *guaranteed benefit*. Individuals with more income would receive smaller benefits, and individuals with $10,000 of income would receive no benefits. Finally, some or all of those making more than $10,000 a year would have to pay positive taxes to pay for the transfers to those making less than $10,000 a year. Table 4.5 shows how this simple income tax would work for selected individuals making from $0 to $20,000, and figure 4.9 illustrates how this system would affect post-transfer income.

According to the standard labor-leisure analysis, negative income tax–type welfare programs almost invariably lead to a reduction in work effort.[81] In that regard, cash transfers to individuals have two types of effects on individual decisions about labor supply. First, an income effect will arise any time an individual receives a cash transfer. Generally, any cash transfer to an individual will increase her demand for leisure relative to her desire to work, and induce her to work less.

Table 4.5. A Simple Negative Income Tax System (dollars)

Pre-transfer income	Negative income tax transfer amount	Post-transfer income
0	5,000	5,000
2,000	4,000	6,000
4,000	3,000	7,000
6,000	2,000	8,000
8,000	1,000	9,000
10,000	0	10,000
12,000	0	12,000
14,000	0	14,000
16,000	0	16,000
18,000	0	18,000
20,000	0	20,000

Source: Author's calculations.

Figure 4.9. A Simple Negative Income Tax

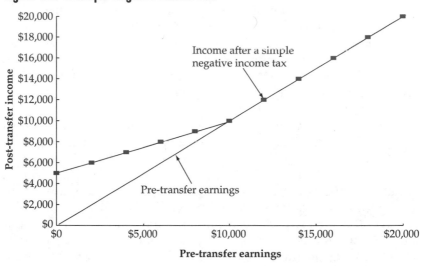

Source: Author's calculations.

Thus, the income effect is expected to cause welfare recipients to reduce their hours of work.

Second, there is a substitution effect because the relative prices of an hour of leisure versus an hour of work change as a result of a welfare program. For example, the benefit-reduction rate of the negative income tax reduces the value of earnings, and so makes leisure more attractive.

All in all, the income and substitution effects operate together as work disincentives, and hours of work will fall. Figure 4.10 shows how a simple negative income tax could reduce the work effort of a low-skilled worker with a $5-an-hour wage rate. In the absence of a negative income tax, this worker would choose to work 1,500 hours a year and make $7,500. With a simple negative income tax, however, this worker would reduce her work effort to just 1,250 hours a year and see her post-transfer income rise to $8,125.[82]

Before the 1996 welfare reform act, AFDC operated a lot like a negative income tax, and it is estimated that AFDC resulted in "nontrivial work disincentives" for welfare recipients of around 5.4 hours a week, implying a 30 percent reduction in their work effort (Moffitt 1992, 16).

How Earnings Subsidies Tend to Encourage Work Effort

On the other hand, earnings subsidies like the current earned income tax credit can increase the work effort of recipients. Basically, an earnings subsidy is a transfer program that provides cash benefits to supple-

Figure 4.10. How a Negative Income Tax Reduces Work Effort

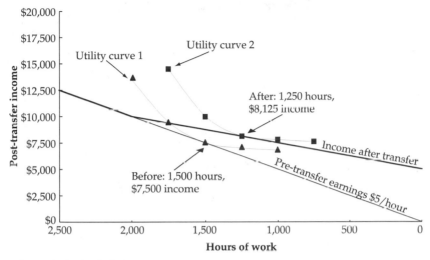

Source: Author's calculations.

ment the low market wages paid to low-skilled workers. Those cash benefits raise the financial return from work and so tend to provide strong work incentives for low-income individuals.[83] In that regard, the earned income tax credit has shown itself a great tool for encouraging work effort and alleviating poverty (Berube 2003; Forman 1988; Hoffman and Seidman 2002). Similarly, research has shown that welfare programs that supplement the earnings of low-income adults are an effective way to increase their employment, earnings, and income (Michalopoulous 2005).

Three policy variables define a simple earnings subsidy system. First, the *subsidy rate* is the rate at which earnings are subsidized. Second, the *target earnings level* is the earnings level at which a worker will no longer receive a subsidy. Finally, the *benefit-reduction rate* determines the amount of reduction in the subsidy as the pre-transfer earnings level increases beyond a certain wage.

In that regard, figure 4.2 shows how the earned income tax credit subsidizes the earnings of low-income married couples in 2006. A married couple with two children will get a subsidy of 40 percent on up to $11,340 of earnings (40 percent subsidy rate). Once the couple's earnings exceed $16,810, the credit is phased out at a 21.06 percent benefit-reduction rate and is entirely phased out at $38,348.

Figure 4.11 shows how the credit can increase the income of a married couple with two children by as much as $4,536 in 2006.[84] The earned income credit provides the largest transfers to those with moderate

**Figure 4.11. Income after Earned Income Credit, 2006
Married Couple and Two Children**

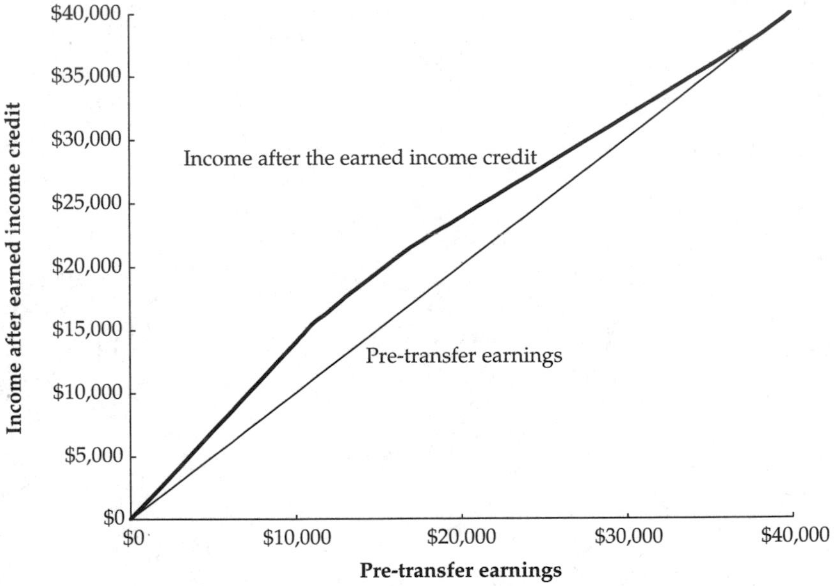

Source: Author's calculations.

hourly wages and the smallest transfers to those with either no income or high income.

Most analysts believe that earnings subsidies increase work effort, at least in the phase-in range of the subsidy. We have seen that under a negative income tax, the income and substitution effects both operate as work disincentives. Under an earnings subsidy, however, the standard labor-leisure model tells us that the income and substitution effects work in opposite directions. For low-skilled workers, it seems likely that the substitution effect will dominate; consequently, recipients of an earnings subsidy are likely to increase their labor supply.[85]

For example, figure 4.12 shows how a simple 50-percent-of-earnings subsidy could increase the work effort of a low-skilled worker who had a market wage of, say, $5 an hour. In the absence of this simple earnings subsidy, this worker would choose to work 1,500 hours a year and make $7,500. With this simple earnings subsidy, however, this worker would increase her work effort to 1,750 hours and see her post-subsidy income rise to $13,125.[86] In short, at least in the phase-in range of an earnings subsidy, low-skilled workers are expected to increase their work effort. Not surprisingly, recent research has found that

Figure 4.12. How a Simple 50 Percent Earnings Subsidy Can Increase Work Effort

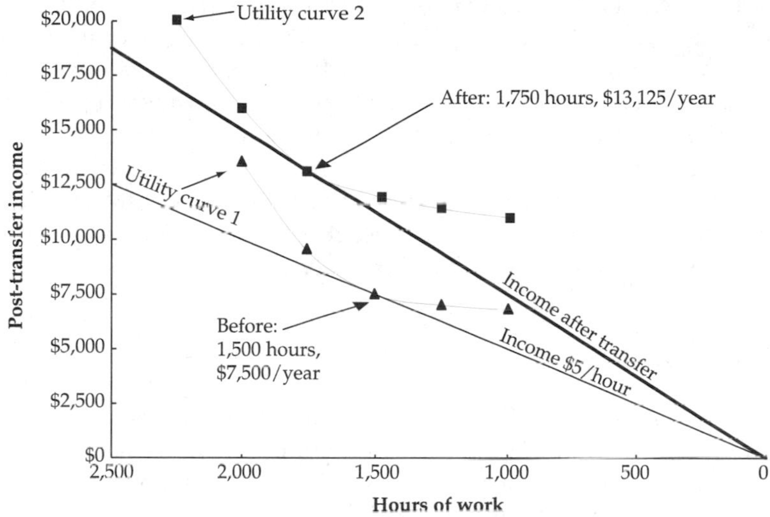

Source: Author's calculations.

the earned income tax credit significantly increased the labor supplied by low-skilled single mothers—typically, in the phase-in range of the credit (Hoynes 1997).[87]

Moreover, an earnings subsidy can increase employment opportunities for low-wage workers. By increasing the compensation paid to low-wage workers at no cost to employers, an earnings subsidy should increase the demand for low-wage labor.[88] Earnings subsidies can also cost less to administer than means-tested transfer programs and can be more effective in reaching targeted beneficiaries. For example, while 86 percent of eligible households with children claimed the earned income tax credit in 1999, the TANF participation rate was just 52 percent (Burman and Kobes 2003). All in all, the type of subsidy provided to low-income Americans can significantly affect their work effort, and there is a lot to be said for earnings subsidies.

HOW REGULATION AFFECTS THE DISTRIBUTION OF EARNINGS AND INCOME

Regulation is the third major way that governments influence the distribution of earnings and income. Government regulation defines and limits the range of markets and so influences the shape of the initial distribution of economic resources.

To be sure, most government regulation probably has relatively little direct or even indirect effect on the distribution of earnings and income. For example, it is wonderful when the Food and Drug Administration keeps a dangerous drug out of the marketplace, and it is great when the Justice Department busts up monopolies, but these regulatory efforts have relatively little impact on how economic resources are distributed.[89]

On the other hand, several government interventions into the labor market have a direct impact on the distribution of earnings and income. For example, consider the minimum wage.

The Minimum Wage

Under the Fair Labor Standards Act, most hourly workers are entitled to a minimum wage of at least $5.15 an hour.[90] In 2004, about 2 million American workers (2.7 percent of those paid by the hour) were paid at, or below, the minimum wage (BLS 2005b).

Of note, the minimum wage rate is not automatically adjusted for inflation, and it has not been increased since 1997. In that regard, the real value of the minimum wage has fallen in recent years. More specifically, figure 4.13 compares the total annual earnings of full-time, year-round workers earning the minimum wage with the inflation-adjusted poverty levels from 1960 through 2006.[91] The real value of the minimum wage peaked in 1968 at the equivalent of $7.54 an hour in 2005 dollars (Bernstein and Shapiro 2005, figure 2).[92] The bottom line is that full-time, year-round workers earning the minimum wage do not earn enough to bring their families out of poverty.[93] Also of note, the decline in the real value of the minimum wage has contributed to an increase in wage dispersion and, consequently, a rise in earnings inequality (Fortin and Lemieux 1997).[94]

Nevertheless, the labor economics literature has not been kind to minimum wage laws.[95] The most common objection is that raising the minimum wage can lead to a decrease in employment for the low-skilled workers affected by the hike. Because a higher minimum wage raises the cost of low-skilled workers, employers tend to substitute more skilled workers and equipment for the relatively more expensive low-skilled workers. Indeed, according to one recent summary of the literature, a 10 percent increase in the minimum wage would lead to a 2 percent decrease in employment of workers affected by the hike (Macphearson 2004, 46–47). In short, raising the minimum wage could have deleterious effects on the employment levels of low-skilled workers. Those who keep their jobs would earn more, but at least some low-skilled workers would lose their jobs if the minimum wage were raised.

Figure 4.13. Minimum-Wage Earnings versus Poverty Levels, 1960–2006

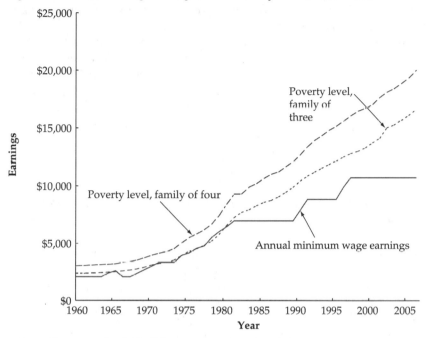

Sources: For poverty thresholds: U.S. Department of Health and Human Services, "Poverty Guidelines, Research, and Measurement," http://aspe.hhs.gov/poverty/poverty.shtml, and *Social Security Bulletin, Annual Statistical Supplement: 2004*, table 3.E8; for minimum wage: U.S. Department of Labor, "History of Federal Minimum Wage Rates under the Fair Labor Standards Act, 1938–1996," http://www.dol.gov/esa/minwage/chart.htm.

Instead, labor economists tend to favor earnings subsidies such as the earned income tax credit. Of particular importance, while minimum wage laws reduce employment opportunities for low-skilled workers, earnings subsidies increase the demand for low-skilled workers by making it relatively cheaper to employ them. The earned income tax credit is also better targeted to help low-income working families than the minimum wage (Hotz, Mullin, and Scholz 2001).

Other Labor Market Programs and Regulations

Many other government programs also affect the distribution of earnings and earnings opportunities. For example, equal pay and antidiscrimination laws regulate pay and hiring practices of employers in ways that almost certainly tend to reduce earnings inequality. Similarly, the Fair Labor Standards Act rules that require employers to pay time-and-one-half wages to employees working more than 40 hours a week push employers to spread work out among more employees and so improve the earnings distribution.[96] Pension and health care laws also have a considerable effect on the structure of employee benefit plans and, consequently, on worker decisions about work and retirement. In addition, unemployment compensation laws and disability insurance laws tend to preserve the incomes of unemployed and disabled workers and so reduce income inequality. Child care assistance, education and training programs, and worker safety laws also have a positive impact on the distribution of earnings and incomes. As more fully discussed in later chapters, many of these programs can provide significant work incentives.

MEASURING THE IMPACT OF GOVERNMENT ON THE INCOME DISTRIBUTION

Governments can influence the distribution of economic resources through taxes, spending, and regulation. As we saw in chapter 1, it is probably impossible to measure the full impact of government policies on the distribution of economic resources. In particular, it is difficult to estimate the effect of government regulation on the distribution of economic resources, as nobody can really say what that distribution would look like in the absence of government.

On the other hand, we can get a very good idea about how much influence government tax and spending programs have on the relative distribution of economic resources. For example, table 1.1 and figure 1.1 showed that the current mix of government tax and transfer policies reduce household income inequality by about 20 percent. More specifically, transfers reduce household income inequality much more than taxes. According to a recent Census Bureau report, subtracting taxes and including the earned income tax credit lowered the Gini index of household income inequality by just 4.6 percent in 2003 (from 0.498 to 0.475), while including transfers lowered the Gini index by 17.0 percent (from 0.475 to 0.394) (Cleveland 2005, 4–5).[97]

As to how the United States tax and transfer system affects poverty levels, there is some dispute. Using the "official" estimate of poverty (based on "money income"), some 40 million Americans (12.7 percent) were poor in 2004 (DeNavas-Walt et al. 2005, tables 3 and B1). A recent report by the Census Bureau used alternative definitions of resources to estimate the effect of taxes and transfers on poverty levels. Based on "market income" alone, that report estimated that 19.3 percent of Americans were poor in 2004. After taxes and transfers, however, just 10.4 percent of Americans had "disposable income" that left them in poverty (Census Bureau 2006, table 3).[98]

On the other hand, a recent comparative study found much more modest effects for the U.S. tax and transfer system. That study estimated that our current tax and transfer system reduced the poverty rate of two-parent families by just 0.5 percentage points in 2000, from 13.7 to 13.2 percent (Smeeding 2006b, table 5). That was a mere 3.6 percent reduction in two-parent poverty rates, compared with an average reduction of 44 percent across all 11 high-income countries studied (including the United States).[99]

SOME FINAL THOUGHTS

The Constitution of the United States created a new American government to, among other things, "establish Justice" and "promote the general Welfare."[100] The American experiment has worked because it has encouraged its citizens to be productive and because it has promoted economic equality. But America could work even better. The way to make America work better is to make the government work better, and the remaining chapters explain how government tax, transfer, and regulatory policies should be redesigned to both promote even greater economic justice and maintain high levels of production.

5

MAKING GOVERNMENT WORK

To have no government programs for redistributing income is simply to certify de facto that the existing market distribution of incomes is equitable. (Thurow 1973, 57)

What matters is . . . whether the totality of government's treatment of its subjects, its expenditures along with its taxes, is just. (Murphy and Nagel 2002, 31)

The last two chapters explained how the free market distributes earnings and other economic resources and how government taxes, transfer programs, and regulation influence the market's initial distribution of resources. This chapter focuses on the question of just how far the government should go to "correct" the market's unequal distribution of earnings and other economic resources.

At the outset, this chapter considers what a just distribution of economic resources would look like. Next, this chapter discusses how government policies can promote greater economic justice without significantly undermining the incentives to work and produce. In particular, government tax and transfer policies should be redesigned to increase the economic rewards for low-skilled workers. At the same time, however, government policies should be redesigned to minimize the work disincentives imposed on other workers.

WHAT WOULD A JUST DISTRIBUTION OF ECONOMIC RESOURCES LOOK LIKE?

What would a just distribution of economic resources look like? This question has plagued political philosophers from Plato to Rawls. It is perhaps easiest to articulate the two most extreme answers to this question: egalitarianism and libertarianism.[1]

Egalitarians believe that all people are entitled to share equally in the productive output of their society. Consequently, egalitarians favor government tax and transfer policies that would equalize, or at least tend to equalize, the distribution of economic resources. For example, egalitarians favor taxing the rich to support the poor. Similarly, egalitarians might argue that everyone who works 40 hours a week should be paid the same.[2]

At the other extreme, libertarians start from the premise that free-market transactions reflect the free and voluntary trades made by relatively equal market participants. Accordingly, libertarians believe that the market distribution of economic resources is inherently just and that the government has no right to interfere with it. Consequently, libertarians tend to argue that individuals should be allowed to keep whatever income they acquire in the marketplace. In any event, most libertarians doubt that government intervention would actually make things fairer.

Almost everybody actually falls somewhere in between these two extreme positions.[3] Those with an egalitarian bent usually concede that differential rewards are needed to ensure adequate productivity. After all, if you can eat without working, why work? And if all the jobs paid the same, why would anyone do the dirty and unpleasant jobs?

At the same time, those with a libertarian bent typically concede that some minimal amount of redistribution is needed to help the truly disadvantaged. Liam Murphy and Thomas Nagel put it this way:

> Very few people are consciously committed to the libertarian theory of justice. Hardly anyone really believes that market outcomes are presumptively just and that justice does not require government to provide welfare support of those of its subjects who are destitute, without access to food, shelter, or health care. (2002, 33)

In the United States, market forces are the primary determinant of the distribution of economic resources. Because most of us agree that the market's distribution is not inherently fair, however, we have called upon our government to intervene and temper the market's unequal distribution of economic resources, and table 1.1 showed that the government's tax and transfer programs currently reduce household income inequality by about 20 percent.

Is the post-tax, post-transfer distribution of economic resources in the United States just? If not, is more redistribution called for? In what Murphy and Nagel lament as "everyday libertarianism," the prevailing ideology of our time is a belief that pre-tax, pre-transfer market outcomes are presumptively just (2002, 15). We know that we have a full *legal* right to the money we earn in the marketplace, and we are inclined to believe that we have a moral right to it as well.[4] Invariably, this ideology has put the burden on government to justify any redistributive tax, transfer, and regulatory policies, and redistribution has been constrained. This chapter challenges that prevailing ideology and shows why additional redistribution is needed and desirable.

A Simple Model of the Economy

As a starting point, it is worth considering a very simple model of our economy. Figure 5.1 portrays a hypothetical society consisting of just

Figure 5.1. A Simple Five-Family Model Economy

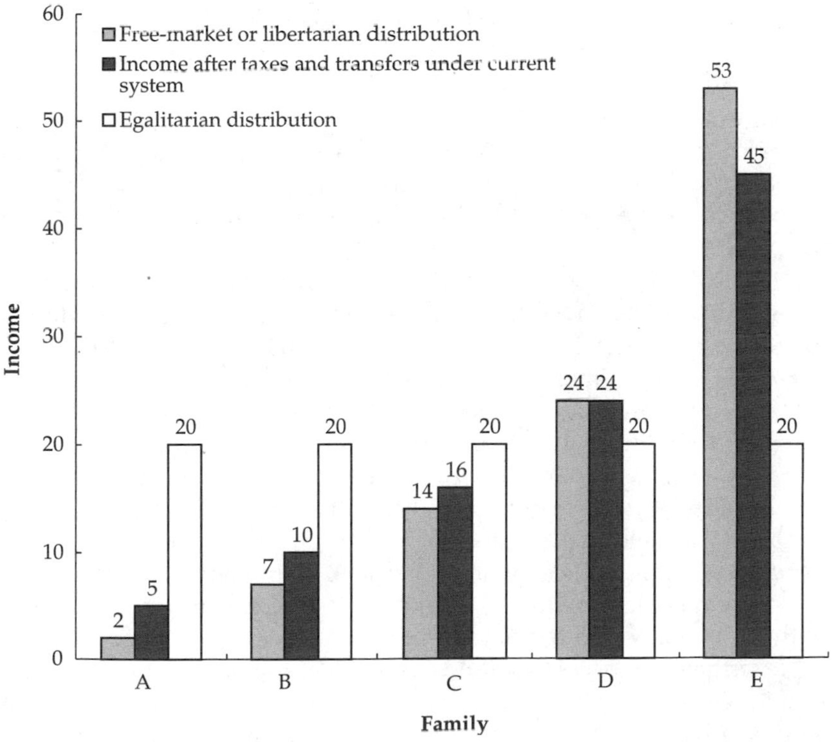

Source: Author's calculations.

five families: A, B, C, D, and E. The light gray bars of figure 5.1 show the hypothetical incomes that might be earned by these five representative families in a free-market or libertarian society. The family incomes in these light gray bars were derived by rounding the pre-tax, pre-transfer income shares of the five quintiles of families identified in column 2 of table 1.1.[5] The total output of this model economy is assumed to be 100 units and, consequently, the average income is 20 units. The Gini index for this model economy is around 0.496, and the 80/20 ratio is about 27 to 1 (53 ÷ 2).[6] In short, the light gray bars in figure 5.1 approximate the basic distribution of income that would result from the operation of our free-market economy under libertarian or laissez-faire conditions.[7]

The dark gray bars in figure 5.1 approximate how the current mix of taxes and transfer programs reduces household income inequality. The numbers in the dark gray bars were derived by rounding the post-tax, post-transfer income shares of the five quintiles of households identified in column 3 of table 1.1. The total output of this model economy is still assumed to be 100 units, and the average income is still 20 units. Here, however, taxes have reduced the income of the top family, and transfers have increased the incomes of the bottom three families. The net effect is that household inequality has been reduced by about 20 percent. The Gini index falls to around 0.400, and the 80/20 ratio falls to 9 to 1 (45 ÷ 5).

At the opposite extreme from the free market's distribution, the white bars in figure 5.1 show what an egalitarian distribution of income would look like in a five-family world. Here, each family would receive 20 percent of the income. The Gini index would fall to 0, and the 80/20 ratio would fall to 1 to 1 (20 ÷ 20).

Of course, with an egalitarian distribution, there would be absolutely no individual incentives for production. Consequently, it would no longer be realistic to assume that output could remain at 100 units, nor could average income remain at 20. Therein lies the crux of the problem for those who are interested in promoting greater economic equality. Individuals will change their behavior in response to taxes, transfers, and regulation. The trick is to try to maximize both output and equality in the face of what is typically a trade-off between them. Arthur Okun eloquently describes this problem as the trade-off between equality and efficiency (Okun 1975). In general, we can have a more equal distribution of economic resources but, perhaps, not without at least some reduction in the incentives to produce.

Nevertheless, most of us would agree that the simple society reflected in the light gray bars in figure 5.1 is disturbingly unequal. There just seems to be something wrong with a society in which top-quintile families have 27 times as much income as bottom-quintile families.

That is why we have already adopted tax and transfer systems that shift the distribution of household incomes toward the incomes in the dark gray bars in figure 5.1.

Of course, most Americans are unhappy about the current high level of economic inequality even after taxes and transfers. For example, in a 1996 survey, two-thirds of Americans agreed with the statement that "Differences in income in America are too large."[8] At the same time, however, nobody reasonably believes that we have much chance of getting anywhere close to the egalitarian society shown in the white bars in figure 5.1.

Still, we should be able to achieve a much fairer distribution than we currently have. With care, we should be able to reduce economic inequality without unduly affecting the incentives to produce. We might, for example, strive to achieve a post-tax, post-transfer household income distribution with an 80/20 ratio of, say, 5 to 1.

To be sure, it seems unlikely that a convincing moral argument can be made for any *particular* distribution of economic resources. There is simply no magic Gini index value or 80/20 ratio that defines the theoretically and morally "correct" level of inequality. Rather, the question of just how much economic inequality is appropriate seems to be largely an aesthetic question that turns on our individual tastes. The proposed 80/20 ratio of 5 to 1 is offered merely as a kind of aspirational target, not as *the* theoretically correct level of inequality.

All in all, it is worthwhile to contemplate what a just distribution of economic resources would look like. The usual way of getting at this question is to ask whether a given system gives people what they "deserve." A system that gives people the economic rewards that they deserve would be an economically just system.

Justice in the Distribution of Earnings

As a starting point, it would make sense to simplify the question of "just deserts" by focusing on economic justice in the distribution of earnings. As we saw in chapter 2, earned income constitutes roughly three-quarters of all personal income. To be sure, capital and returns to capital are important to any real-world society, but as an initial matter, capital can be ignored. Instead, we can start by assuming that the total economic product of a society is the result of the combined productivity of its workers. We can bring savings, investment, and capital back into the analysis later. For now, however, we can conduct a thought experiment about *just wages*. In short, how much do individual workers "deserve" to earn?

Criteria of Desert

One might start with the egalitarian presumption that individuals deserve to share equally in the total output of their society. This equal-share principle is the one that children (and adults) use to divide a pie or cake amongst themselves, and an equal-share system has some inherent appeal even for dividing the economic rewards of a productive society. Sharing equally also comports with notions that, all other things being equal, individuals can be assumed to have equal needs and desires.

When it comes to dividing the economic rewards that result from the productive efforts of individual workers, however, rewards must invariably be more closely tied to incentives. As many communist, fascist, and utopian societies have discovered the hard way, compensation systems must be designed to encourage work.[9] A society simply cannot succeed if there are no incentives to work.

Consequently, the egalitarian principle cannot be the only criterion used to determine whether a given distribution of earnings is just. Most analysts suggest four additional criteria for determining the rewards that workers deserve: ability, effort, contribution, and compensation.[10] First, rewards might be proportional to ability. For example, smarter and more talented people could be paid more than others.

Second, rewards might be proportional to effort. For example, people working 40 hours a week could be paid twice as much as people working just 20 hours a week.

Third, rewards might be proportional to contributions. For example, a worker who produced 10 times as much as another could be paid 10 times as much to reflect the greater value of that contribution.

Fourth and finally, under the compensation principle, economic rewards might compensate for the nonmonetary differences in jobs. For example, dangerous and unattractive jobs could pay more than safe and interesting jobs. Such "equalizing differences are relatively easy to understand and account for, and offer no special problem from a normative point of view" (Dick 1975, 266).[11]

We have seen already that free-market systems do not miraculously pay people what they "deserve" in accordance with any of these criteria. The free-market system, perhaps, comes closest to distributing the economic rewards from work in accordance with the principle of contribution. When markets work well, the rewards from work do, indeed, bear a rough relationship to the value of each worker's contribution.

In our economy, however, pay is, at best, only loosely proportionate to productivity. Individual wages reflect a variety of factors, not just individual skill levels and productivity. People with equivalent talents are often paid widely different amounts, even when they work in the same company or locale. There is also an element of "economic rent" in the current rates of remuneration of many workers: those workers whose skills are in short supply can earn compensation that is out of all proportion to their "merit," however defined.[12] Moreover, one should never underestimate the importance of luck, particularly in our winner-take-all society.[13]

Further, even if pay were directly proportionate to productivity, many of us would still be troubled by an economic system that resulted in such wide disparities in earnings and income. Free markets generate differential rewards that encourage productivity, but there is simply "no necessary correlation . . . between economic justice and economic efficiency" (Vickers 1997, 141).

For most of us, a just distribution of earnings would probably involve several of these criteria of desert. All other things being equal, we do divide things equally. We also like to reward ability, although we are at least somewhat concerned when those abilities reflect mere genetic accidents of birth. We value hard work, and so we like to see effort rewarded. We also value output, and so we like to see contributions and achievements rewarded. Finally, we value choice, and so we have little difficulty in justifying differential rewards according to the compensation principle, for example, higher pay for those who have chosen more dangerous or demanding careers.

In the end, most of us would probably agree that workers deserve to be rewarded according to their "merit," with merit loosely defined to include a number of these criteria of desert.[14] Still, most of us share fairly similar ideas about what is meritorious. Consequently, most of us share somewhat similar ideas about what a just distribution of earnings might look like. An example or two will help show how much we share a common conception about merit and economic justice.

How Much Do Workers Deserve?

Consider, for example, a simple farming society consisting of five workers who plant a single crop that meets all their needs. Assume that the workers have identical abilities and tastes, that they all work equally hard growing the crop, and that each worker produces the same amount of food. In this egalitarian utopia, all of us would conclude that the crop should be divided equally among the workers. As all have worked equally hard and are equally productive, all "deserve" to share equally in the rewards of that work.

Of course, this egalitarian utopia is nothing at all like the real world. In the real world, some workers work harder than others, and, presumably, they "deserve" to be rewarded for it. Also, people do not have equal abilities in the real world, nor do they contribute equally. Some people are vastly more productive than others. On the other hand, some people are not even capable of working, perhaps because of age or infirmity. Almost all of us would favor providing at least some minimal level of economic support for those who are incapable of working.

From a moral point of view, however, the really interesting questions have to do with how to distribute earned income among those who can work but who are not equally productive. For example, should someone who is 100 times as productive as the average worker get paid 100 times as much? In a free-market economy, that is exactly what would happen. But should that be the rule for our post-tax, post-transfer society?

On closer examination, it is clear that various factors result in differences in productivity. From a moral standpoint, some factors deserve to be rewarded but others, perhaps, do not. At first, it is perhaps easiest to see which factors should be rewarded. For example, differences in productivity can be the result of differences in effort, and most of us would agree that workers putting forth greater efforts deserve greater rewards. All other things equal, someone who works twice as many hours should get paid more, perhaps even twice as much.[15]

Adam Smith's "compensation principle" should also lead to appropriate pay differentials. People who choose more difficult or more demanding jobs are rightly entitled to greater compensation. For example, in order to make up for the greater dangers inherent in their jobs, police officers should be paid more than dispatchers. Similarly, individuals who postpone work to gain needed education and skills should be rewarded with additional compensation to make up for their forgone earnings. For example, to compensate for the years of training required to get the needed medical education and skills, physicians should, indeed, be paid more than orderlies.

As to differences in achievement that arise because of differences in innate abilities or "endowments," however, there is much dispute. For example, consider an innate ability like intelligence. Intelligent people tend to get better jobs and make more money than those who are less intelligent. Should a just distribution of earnings reward greater intelligence, or might society instead demand greater productivity from those with greater intelligence?[16]

There is also a lack of consensus about what to do about the differences in productivity that are attributable to advantages provided by one's family. Some children have parents who pay for their college and graduate education, extracurricular activities, and travel; and these children tend to have higher incomes as adults. Other children come from broken homes and have lesser opportunities, and they tend to have lower incomes as adults. One study found a strong correlation ($r = 0.4$) between the earnings of children and those of their parents (Burtless and Jencks 2003, 30).[17]

All in all, in the economic race of life, we simply do not all start with an equal chance of winning. Instead of a race that starts afresh with each generation, many believe that our economic race is really more like an "intergenerational relay race" in which "children born to wealthy parents start at or near the finish line, while children born in poverty start behind everyone else" (McNamee and Miller 2004, 13, 49).[18] As former president John F. Kennedy said, "Life is unfair."[19]

Still, few actually believe that individuals somehow "deserve" more income and wealth just because they are innately intelligent or because their parents are wealthy. Murphy and Nagel put it this way:

The notion of desert entails that of responsibility; we cannot be said to deserve outcomes for which we are not in any way responsible. Thus, to the extent that market outcomes are determined by genetic or medical or social luck (including inheritance), they are not, on anyone's account, morally deserved. (2002, 32)

Similarly, Stephen Nathanson has this to say:

Much of what people possess is undeserved—either because it came to them through processes (such as inheritance) that have nothing to do with effort or contribution, or because, even where their efforts were required, they do not deserve the specific holdings that they have acquired through the market system. To return to our baseball example, a good player may deserve a high salary, but he does not deserve a salary that is one hundred times larger than that of a school teacher. (1998, 65)

Finally, there are differences in tastes and needs. Would a just distribution of earnings take tastes and needs into account? In the world of philosophy, we might ask whether people with expensive tastes should be paid more than people with simple tastes—so they can both become equally happy. For example, should gourmands be paid more than others because they need to spend more on food? Similarly, we might ask whether workers with families should get greater compensation than single workers. In the real world, such additional compensation comes from employers that provide subsidies for family health care benefits, and it comes from government in tax reductions for taxpayers with children. The issue involved is precisely how much a just society should take into account individual differences in tastes and needs.[20]

What Is the Right Amount of Earnings Inequality?

The problem is that the distribution of earnings in the real world is much more unequal than it needs to be or "should" be. Labor markets tend to distribute earnings in accordance with the laws of supply and demand, but the resulting distribution bears relatively little resemblance to anyone's notion of just deserts. Even a cursory examination of labor-market outcomes suggests that the labor market tends to pay low-skilled workers less than they "deserve" and high-skilled workers more than they "deserve."

It does not have to be that way. As James K. Galbraith has noted:

> The economy is a managed beast. It was managed in such a way that this was the result. It could have been done differently. (1998, 167)

In large part, the distribution of earnings is what we choose it to be.

Ultimately, the question of just deserts boils down to a question of just how large the economic rewards for work have to be to secure the productive efforts of high-skilled workers and how much we can "get away with" redistributing to lower-skilled workers. Most everyone agrees that physicians should be paid more than orderlies, but how much more? And most everyone agrees that CEOs should be paid more than line workers, but again, the question is: how much more? It is one thing to say that physicians and CEOs should make more than orderlies and line workers, but it is quite another to say that they should make 100 or even 1,000 times more.[21]

To be sure, we need talented physicians and CEOs, and we should compensate them fairly. But we pay economic rents to these high-skilled workers that are far in excess of what would be necessary to secure their valuable services. At the same time, we often pay low-skilled workers too little for their hard work. As we saw in chapter 2, the net effect is that we have encouraged high-skilled workers to work harder than ever, and we have discouraged many lower-skilled workers from even bothering to look for a job.

Society as a Monopoly in the Labor Market. Consider how compensation would be determined if society could act as an all-powerful monopoly in the labor market. When there is only one all-powerful buyer of labor in a particular labor market, that monopoly buyer is referred to as a "monopsonist." Rather than being forced by competition to pay each worker a competitive wage based on the market value of that worker's output, a monopsonist can exercise considerable control over the wages paid to individual workers. The net effect is that a monopsonist can pay workers less than they would earn in a competitive market.[22]

Theoretically, a monopsonist society could set almost whatever wage levels it wanted for each and every job.[23] Admittedly, many communist, fascist, and utopian societies have tried this type of command-economy experiment, and the usual result is that their economies failed miserably. Central planning just does not work very well. All that is proposed here, however, is a thought experiment designed to get at our sense of what a just distribution of wages would look like and at how government policies might be able to move us in that direction.

Just Wages in a Five-Worker World. Reconsider the five-family model economy in figure 5.1. Rather than being the incomes of five separate families, assume instead that the numbers in the light gray bars reflect the productive output from five full-time, year-round workers. Worker A produces 2 units, worker B produces 7 units, worker C produces 14 units, worker D produces 24 units, and worker E produces 53 units.[24] In a free-market economy, these five individual workers would be paid in direct proportion to their productivity: A would earn 2 units, B would earn 7 units, and so on. The 80/20 ratio would be almost 27 to 1, and the Gini index would be around 0.496.

Using its monopoly power, however, society could use desert criteria other than pay proportional to productivity to determine compensation.[25] For example, a society might want to provide greater rewards for work effort by formally setting pay levels at, say, 5, 10, 16, 24, and 45, as in the dark gray bars in figure 5.1, with its 80/20 ratio of 9 to 1. For that matter, if effort is thought to be an even more important criterion of desert, society might set wage levels at, say, 8, 12, 18, 22, and 40, with a resulting 80/20 ratio of just 5 to 1. Figure 5.2 compares our hypothetical free-market wage levels with this last set of hypothetically just wage levels.

Ultimately, the key question is whether the monopsonistic society can "get away with" having a wage structure that is not strictly proportional to productivity. In our hypothetical five-worker society, for example, we would need to know whether our five workers would still produce 100 units of output with a wage structure of 8, 12, 18, 22, and 40, instead of a pay-proportional-to-output wage structure of 2, 7, 14, 24, and 53.

In that regard, the critical question is whether key worker E would still produce 53 units of output if she received just 40 units of compensation. The answer to that question may well depend on the mechanisms used to break the connection between productivity and pay. For example, Lester Thurow notes that, "people react differently to having tax-free earnings of $100 per week and to having earnings of $150 per

Figure 5.2. Market Wages and Hypothetical Just Wages in a Five-Worker World

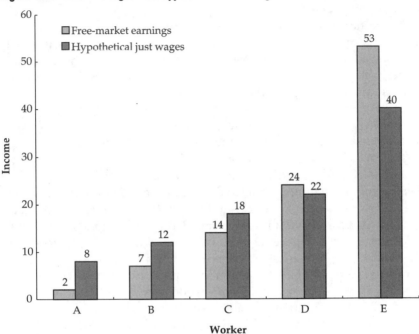

Source: Author's calculations.

week with a tax bill of $50 per week" (1973, 73). In short, different tax, transfer, and regulatory mechanisms can be expected to have quite different impacts on the work efforts of workers. No doubt some redistributive approaches would significantly reduce the output of high-skilled workers.

Yet there is every reason to believe that some redistributive approaches might have relatively little impact on the output of highly productive workers like worker E. Whether worker E is willing to produce 53 units of output in exchange for 40 units of pay may depend on her alternatives and on her feelings about the fairness of the deal. Lacking economic power, individual workers are essentially "price-takers," and wages are the price that individuals are paid for their labor. As a "wage-taker," worker E's alternatives would consist of choices about which job to choose and how hard to work on that job. Depending on the opportunities available in her society, this job, effort level, and 40-unit wage could still be her best alternative. As to her feelings about the fairness of her 40-unit employment package, she would still be the highest paid worker, and she would make five times as much as the lowest paid worker, so she could still see herself as quite handsomely rewarded.

At the same time, however, worker A, for example, would probably feel under-rewarded in a free market economy that paid her just 2 units for her full-time work, but she could easily feel adequately rewarded in a post-government system that paid her 8 units for her work. Depending on the mechanisms that connected her work effort to her rewards, she might even choose to work harder.

Just Wages in the Real World. The question of just wages in the real world raises all the same questions as in our hypothetical five-worker world. The key questions are, first, whether the economic rewards for work are "right" for high- and low-skilled workers; and, second, whether high levels of production could still be maintained if additional criteria of economic justice are used to temper the market's inherently unequal distribution of earnings.

For example, consider the appropriate level of compensation for Bill Gates, the founder of Microsoft Corporation. Obviously, Mr. Gates and the Microsoft Corporation have added enormous value to our economy. But does Bill Gates "deserve" the billions of dollars he has "earned" as a reward for his work? Does he really deserve to make 100,000 times as much as a waitress? Would he have worked as hard to create a valuable software system and company if his economic rewards had been smaller? If so, how much smaller could and should those rewards have been?

Perhaps more fundamentally, we should consider the typical range of earnings in the U.S. economy. For example, the average physician made $128,689 in 2004, the average registered nurse made just $53,289, and the average orderly made just $20,959 (see table 2.4). Within these categories, however, there is often a wide variation in earnings. According to a 2004 survey of physicians with at least three years of experience, the average pediatrician made $175,000 a year, the average general surgeon made $291,000, and the average neurosurgeon made $541,000.[26] Should the average physician make six times as much as the average orderly? Should the average neurosurgeon make more than 26 times as much? Would those neurosurgeons be as productive if they only earned 10 or 15 times as much as orderlies?

Could our society get away with paying physicians less? Probably. Presumably, government could intervene to achieve a post-tax earnings structure with lower rewards for physicians. For example, the government could intervene to increase the supply of physicians, perhaps by building more medical schools or making it easier for foreign-trained doctors to become licensed in the United States.[27] Similarly, government could intervene to reduce the demand for medical services by reducing its health care spending and tax expenditures.

Faced with a given wage structure, however it is created, individuals are "wage takers" who endeavor to make the best choices that they can—the ones that maximize their satisfaction. When it comes to work, individuals can choose a career direction from among the available alternatives, and they can choose how hard to work. Given the current wage structure, it is no surprise that the typical physician is highly motivated, intelligent, and hard-working; and it is no surprise that there is a good deal of student competition for the relatively few available slots in our nation's medical schools.

If society were to reduce the amount of compensation paid to physicians, fewer individuals might want to become physicians. After a few years, we might find that the average physician was not quite as motivated, intelligent, or hard-working. Presumably, however, society could afford to have more of them. Indeed, it seems quite likely that a concerted effort to control the compensation paid to physicians could actually result in both a better and less expensive health care system and also in less inequality in the distribution of earnings.[28]

All in all, if the government could exercise more control over compensation throughout the economy, it should be able to both maintain high levels of productivity and achieve a much lower level of earnings inequality than we presently have. For example, the wage structure in the public sector is much more compressed than in the private sector, and, consequently, wage inequality is much less pronounced (Fortin and Lemieux 1997).

To be sure, given our political aversion to the kind of central planning found in command economies, it would be more realistic for us to imagine how government could reduce earnings inequality indirectly—for example, through taxes and transfer programs. As Henry David Thoreau said, "That government is best which governs least" (1849/1906, 356). For example, we should be able to tax away much of the economic rent that is built into the compensation of high-skilled workers and still elicit a reasonable amount of work effort from those workers (Dick 1975; Van Parijs 1995; Fried 1995).

To summarize, it is clear that the market distribution of earnings is not per se just. Instead, markets distribute earnings in accordance with laws of supply and demand, and the result is significant inequality in the distribution of earnings. From a moral point of view, various criteria of desert should be involved in the determination of a just wage; if more of those criteria were taken into account, the resulting distribution of earnings would be much more equal. While it seems unlikely that a convincing moral argument can be made for any particular distribution of earnings, it does seem that the current system tends to undercompensate low-skilled workers and overcompensate high-skilled workers. Accordingly, it would make sense to adopt policies that would increase the economic rewards earned by low-skilled workers, even if those policies also required modest reductions in the rewards earned by high-skilled workers.

A Just Distribution of Economic Resources

A just distribution of economic resources involves more than a fair distribution of earned income. Given that earned income is the largest component of income, achieving a just distribution of earnings would take us a long way toward a just distribution of economic resources. To achieve a just distribution of economic resources, however, we would also need to consider what, if anything, should be done about the even more skewed distributions of investment income and of wealth. Of course, government policies that affect the distribution of investment income and wealth also raise important questions of economic justice and influence individual decisions about working, spending, and saving.

At its core, however, the question of justice in the distribution of economic resources is very similar to the question of justice in the distribution of earnings. We again see a divergence of opinion between libertarians and egalitarians, we again find that most of us come out somewhere in between, and we are again unlikely to find that a convincing moral argument can be made for any particular distribution of economic resources. Still, many of us can agree that there is simply too much economic inequality in our current system.

In fact, virtually all of us favor some distribution based on need and some based on merit. That is, we tend to favor some version of the modern welfare state—a welfare capitalist system in which most rewards are distributed by the free market but where the government taxes the winners and redistributes at least a social minimum to the losers.

John Rawls suggests that decisions about what a just society would look like should be made from an "original position" behind a "veil of ignorance" (1971, 12). That is, we should decide the rules governing our society without knowing our own class position, social status, or natural abilities. From that vantage point, Rawls suggests that economic inequalities "are just only if they result in compensating benefits for everyone, and in particular for the least advantaged members of society" (14–15). Rawls calls this the "maximin rule," and he uses it to justify significant redistribution by the government, for example, through progressive income taxes and taxes on inheritances.

Similarly, M. H. Lessnoff has argued that economic inequality can be considered just only if "(1) it is to the advantage of the less well-off; or (2) it is deserved (where advantage is due to harder work, for example)" (1978, 147–48). Lessnoff's conception of economic justice

implies state intervention to provide a social minimum both for those who work and for those who are unable to work, which should be as high as possible. . . . Ideally, transfers to those who would otherwise fall below the minimum should be financed only out of *undeserved* extra earnings of those favored by the luck of the market. (1978, 148)

Many other philosophers have also criticized the economic inequality inherent in the current system and offered various justifications for additional redistribution.[29]

What these theories of economic justice have in common is an understanding that the free market's distribution of economic resources is not per se just and a belief that it falls to the government to adopt policies that would achieve greater economic justice. For example, Kenneth Cauthen notes that

the productive capacities of the economic system are the product of many persons, groups, and classes over a long period of time. Hence, to isolate present operations and individual transactions as the sole object of moral consideration is pure folly. (1987, 140)

Similarly, Stephen Nathanson remarks that

The distribution of resources in a purely capitalist economy is determined in large part by factors that have nothing to do with what people deserve: supply and demand and inheritance. (1998, 56)[30]

Nathanson doubts that it would be possible or desirable to implement a desert-based distribution system, but he believes that the modern-day welfare state can get us at least part of the way toward a world in which people get what they deserve. The welfare state can achieve this result by providing larger rewards for "personal effort and contribution" and by providing some resources to people "outside of the market system" based on their needs (Nathanson 1998, 67).

In the end, we are unlikely to reach unanimity as to what *the* ideal distribution of economic resources should look like, but we do not need to. Given how unequal the present distribution of economic resources in the United States is, it is clear which direction we should move to reduce economic inequality, and it is clear that additional government intervention will be needed to achieve that result.

Mechanisms for Achieving a Just Distribution of Economic Resources

The primary tools for achieving a just distribution of economic resources are the tax and transfer systems. This section illustrates some simple tax and transfer mechanisms that could be used.

Taxes and Transfers in a Hypothetical Five-Family World

Table 5.1 portrays a hypothetical society consisting of five families: F, G, H, I, and J. Column 2 shows the hypothetical incomes that might be earned by those families in a free-market economy. The incomes in column 2 represent the average pre-tax, pre-transfer income for the five quintiles of households in 2004. That year, average household income was around $60,528 (DeNavas-Walt et al. 2005). Consequently, five households had around $300,000 of income; 1 percentage point of income was about $3,000. To reflect the overall distribution of market incomes that year, the numbers in column 2 were derived by multiplying the numbers in column 2 of table 1.1 by $3,000 and then rounding. The Gini index for this simple system is about 0.496, and the 80/20 ratio for this simple system is 32 to 1 ($160,000 ÷ $5,000).

In the interests of economic justice, society might want to move toward a system with a much lower 80/20 ratio—say, 5 to 1 (and with a much lower Gini index). Column 3 of table 5.1 suggests one possible set of after-tax, after-transfer incomes with an 80/20 ratio of 5 to 1.[31] Column 4 of table 5.1 then shows the transfers and taxes that would be required to achieve that after-tax, after-transfer distribution: that is, transfers of $19,000 to F, $14,000 to G, and $12,000 to H, paid for with taxes of $5,000 on I and $40,000 on J.

What tax and transfer systems could achieve this kind of redistribution?

A Negative Income Tax. One simple approach would be to have a negative income tax system make transfers to low-income families and use a flat income tax to pay for it. For example, column 5 of table 5.1 shows the after-tax, after-transfer income of these five families under a negative income tax that guaranteed every family at least $15,000, and paid for it with a flat tax on those families with incomes over $50,000 a year. The negative income tax would have a 50 percent benefit-reduction rate and a $30,000 break-even point. Under that system, family F would receive a transfer of $12,500, and family G would receive a transfer of $4,000.[32] Then, a flat tax with an exemption amount of $50,000 would need to have a tax rate of around 13 percent.[33]

A Universal Grant. Another simple approach would be to have a system of universal grants paid for with a flat income tax. Basically, a universal grant is a cash transfer paid to every person without regard to income level.[34] For example, column 6 of table 5.1 shows the after-tax, after-transfer income of these five families under a scheme that gave every family a universal grant of $15,000 and paid for it with a 25 percent flat tax on all pre-tax income.[35] Under this tax and transfer system, F would receive a $15,000 universal grant and pay tax of $1,250 on its $5,000 of pre-tax, pre-transfer income, for an after-tax, after-

Table 5.1. Taxes and Transfers in a Simple Five-Family Model Economy (dollars)

Family	Market income	A more just distribution of income (i.e., 80/20 ratio of 5 to 1)	Difference: transfer or (net tax)	Income after a simple negative income tax funded by a flat tax	Income after a $15,000 universal grant funded by a flat tax	Income after an earnings subsidy funded by a flat tax
F	5,000	24,000	19,000	17,500	18,750	10,000
G	22,000	36,000	14,000	26,000	31,500	27,000
H	42,000	54,000	12,000	42,000	46,500	47,000
I	71,000	66,000	(5,000)	68,350	68,250	72,000
J	160,000	120,000	(40,000)	146,150	135,000	144,000

Source: Author's calculations.

transfer income of $18,750. Unlike the negative-income-tax-plus-flat-tax system in the prior paragraph with its 50 percent benefit-reduction rate on low-income families and 13 percent tax on high-income families, this universal-grant-and-flat-tax system would impose a 25-percent rate on all five families.

An Earnings Subsidy. Finally, another approach would be to have an earnings subsidy paid for with a flat tax. For example, column 7 of table 5.1 shows the after-tax, after-transfer income of these five families under a simple system that provided a universal earnings subsidy equal to 100 percent of the first $5,000 of earnings and paid for it with a flat tax on families with incomes over $50,000 a year. Under this simple earnings subsidy system, all five families would receive the $5,000 earnings subsidy, and those subsidies would be paid for with a 19 percent flat tax on the two families with earnings over $50,000 a year.[36]

Taxes and Transfers in the Real World

Because the real world is more complicated than our hypothetical five-family world, designing an ideal tax and transfer system presents more challenges. First and foremost, because real-world governments do much more than just redistribute revenue, real-world governments must collect more taxes. Additional revenues are needed to pay for a broad range of public goods such as roads, defense, and government operations. As a result, overall tax rates would have to be higher in the real world than in our hypothetical five-family world.

Unfortunately, however, those higher tax rates will result in more distortion and economic inefficiency. As more fully discussed below, that means there are limits on how much redistribution a real-world tax and transfer system can accomplish, and a real-world tax and transfer system will have a hard time achieving anyone's vision of "true" economic justice. For example, while we can imagine having a $15,000 per family universal grant in a hypothetical five-family world, it would be a struggle to imagine a universal grant that generous in the real world (let alone the hypothetical $19,000 transfer to F that was postulated in column 4 of table 5.1). To be sure, the actual cost to the government of family assistance, Medicaid, housing assistance, and child care benefits for at least some low-income families can certainly exceed $15,000 a year, but the average benefit per low-income family is much less than $15,000.

Second, the dispersions of earnings, income, and wealth are much greater in the real world than in our hypothetical five-family world. For example, as we saw in chapter 2, while the 90/10 earnings ratio for wage and salary workers is around 7 to 1, the typical CEO of a major U.S. company makes more than 400 times what the average line worker makes. Also, while our hypothetical five-family world contemplated no wealth, in the real world, wealth matters; as figure 2.9 showed, the top 1 percent of households hold about 33 percent of household wealth, while the bottom 40 percent of households hold less than 1 percent of household wealth. All in all, the greater dispersion of economic resources in the real world makes it much harder to design tax and transfer mechanisms that could achieve as much redistribution as we might be able to achieve in a hypothetical five-family world.

In short, the need for more revenue and the greater dispersion of economic resources in the real world will push us to favor somewhat different real-world tax and transfer solutions than we might select in a hypothetical five-family world, but we can still move in the direction of greater equality.

How Far Should the Government Go to Promote Economic Equality?

How strongly should the government promote economic justice? Murphy and Nagel suggest that

> if the distribution produced by the market is not presumptively just, then government should employ whatever overall package of taxation and expenditure policies best satisfies the correct criteria of justice. (2002, 30)[37]

In short, the government should do as much as it possibly can to achieve greater economic justice.

The Trade-off between Equality and Efficiency

What matters in terms of economic justice is the shape of the post-tax, post-transfer distribution of economic rewards. If economic justice was all that mattered, however, government could achieve perfect equality by simply expropriating the wealth of the rich and giving it to the poor. As we well know, however, individuals will change their behavior in response to taxes, transfers, and regulation. If we all got equal shares whether we worked or not, who would work? A simple expropriate-and-redistribute scheme would devastate the economy. The trick is to try to maximize both production and equality in the face of what is typically a trade-off between them.

In short, our ability to divide the economic pie more equally is limited. In general, we can have a bigger pie or more equal slices, but not both. Redistribution—that is, taking money from one person and giving it to another—typically involves efficiency costs that reduce overall productivity and output. Moreover, collecting taxes from the rich and delivering benefits to the poor both incur bureaucratic costs. According to Arthur Okun, redistribution is a "leaky bucket" (1975, 91). When we try to carry money from the rich to the poor in a leaky bucket, some of that money "will simply disappear in transit, so the poor will not receive all of the money that is taken from the rich."[38]

All in all, taxing the rich to provide benefits for the poor can increase economic equality, but it is likely to decrease the productivity of both the rich and the poor, and it will produce bureaucratic costs in both collecting the taxes and distributing the benefits. For example, chapter 4 showed how traditional welfare programs reduce the work effort of beneficiaries and how taxes on earned income tend to reduce the work effort of taxpayers. Consequently, while greater equality could be achieved by taking money from the rich and giving it to the poor, both the recipients of that largesse and the taxpayers who pay for it may reduce their work effort. Many forms of redistribution will reduce the size of the economic pie.

Some Government Policies Can Both Increase the Size of the Pie and Make the Shares More Equal

On the other hand, many forms of redistribution can actually increase the size of the economic pie.[39] In particular, some forms of redistribution can act as investments that generate long-term gains far exceeding the present costs of redistribution. Education and health transfers to children, for example, are likely to have substantial long-term benefits that far outweigh their costs.[40] Research has shown that public health programs to immunize children result in significant reductions in future direct medical costs and indirect social costs (Blank 2002a). The Head Start program for low-income children also achieves significant long-term benefits (Blank 2002a, Currie 2001). Public education, too, has significant long-term benefits.

Other forms of government redistribution can also generate significant long-term economic gains. Consider, for example, the recent emphasis on the earned income tax credit and welfare-to-work programs for low-skilled workers. Such programs have significantly increased the labor force participation of single mothers and significantly improved their skill levels in the long term.

Moreover, even if we acknowledge that many redistributive mechanisms can reduce economic growth, from where we stand today, there is every reason to believe that we can both increase our economic output *and* promote greater economic justice. We simply do not live in a country ruled by the standard economic model.

Instead, we live in a country in which current government interventions are almost as likely to discourage work effort as to encourage it. After all, we still pay farmers *not* to grow crops.[41] And we live in a country in which redistribution is at least as likely to favor special interests as it is to favor the disadvantaged. Just think about the hundreds of special-interest tax breaks in the Internal Revenue Code.[42]

The gains from refocusing government policies to encourage productivity could easily generate more than enough efficiency gains to offset any efficiency losses that might occur from reorienting and increasing redistribution to promote greater economic justice. As Lester Thurow has noted, "current inequalities are much larger than those necessary to produce and expand the current gross national product" (1973, 77).[43] James K. Galbraith puts it this way:

> No dreadful loss of efficiency will follow a concerted political program of inequality reduction. Quite to the contrary. We will discover that efficiency improves when a larger number of people feel they have a fair shot at being middle class.... We will find that people work harder under these conditions, that they are happier, that families are more stable, and that patterns of investment, consumption, and even technological change will accommodate themselves to more equality in the nation at large. (1998, 266)

In short, with the right set of government policies, we should be able to achieve greater reductions in economic inequality without sacrificing much, if anything at all, in the way of productivity.

The Basic Approach: Increasing the Rewards for Work

The key is to focus on work and work incentives. To achieve greater economic justice without sacrificing much, if anything, in the way of productivity, government needs to follow two overarching policies. First, government policies should be designed to increase the economic rewards for work for low-skilled workers. Increasing the economic rewards for low-skilled workers will increase their participation in the workforce, their productivity, and their incomes. Second, government policies and combinations of policies should be designed to keep the effective tax rates on earned income as low as possible. Keeping effective tax rates on earned income as low as possible will minimize the work disincentives that can result from taxes and benefit reductions.

These two policies are at the core of many reforms discussed throughout the remainder of this book.

Increase the Economic Rewards for Low-Skilled Workers

Government policies should enhance the economic rewards for low-skilled workers. Increasing the economic rewards for low-skilled workers will tend to make work more attractive than "nonemployment,"[44] work more attractive than retirement, and honest work more attractive than criminal endeavors. With greater economic rewards for low-skilled workers, society would see increased productivity and greater economic equality, not to mention such indirect benefits as reduced crime and greater social cohesiveness.[45]

Earnings subsidies are a particularly effective way to increase the economic rewards for low-skilled workers.[46] According to Edmund S. Phelps,

> low-wage employment subsidies, their imperfections notwithstanding, are the most effective instrument we have available to re-create lost opportunities for work and self-support, to restore inclusion and cohesion, and to reclaim responsibility for oneself and others. (1997, 7)[47]

For example, it could make sense to expand the earned income tax credit, employment subsidies, and the various subsidy programs for employers of low-skilled workers. Child care subsidies for low-income parents also raise their incomes and increase their productivity. Modestly expanding these programs would promote greater economic equality by providing even greater rewards for low-skilled workers, yet those expansions could be achieved without having too adverse of an impact on the productivity of higher-income taxpayers.[48]

Keep Effective Tax Rates on Earned Income Low

Government policies and combinations of policies should keep the effective tax rates on earned income as low as possible. Keeping effective tax rates on earned income as low as possible will minimize the work disincentives that can result from taxes, from benefit reductions, and from combinations of the two.

In the positive income tax system, for example, it would make sense to keep effective marginal tax rates on earned income as low as possible, perhaps no more than 30 or 35 percent. In order to have low tax rates, a tax system must have a broad base. Unfortunately, the current federal tax system is replete with special tax breaks for everything from chicken farms to oil wells.[49] We have known since Stanley S. Surrey was the assistant secretary of the Treasury in the 1960s that the more of these so-called "tax expenditures" that we can repeal, the lower tax rates can be (Surrey 1973).

Similarly, it would make sense to keep the benefit-reduction rates in the transfer system as low as possible. For example, it could make sense to increase the amount of earned income that is ignored in computing various welfare benefits.

Finally, in areas where both the tax and transfer systems overlap, it would be especially important to coordinate these programs to keep effective tax rates low, for example, by extending the phaseout range of the earned income tax credit. Since Milton Friedman proposed the negative income tax, we have known that a single integrated benefit program would have lower effective tax rates and be more efficient than multiple overlapping welfare programs (1962, 192).

6

MAKING TAXES WORK

With a better, more efficient, tax system, we can have more guns *and* butter. (Slemrod 2003, 623)

Taxation . . . does not usually deprive people of their just deserts because most of what they possess is not justly deserved. (Nathanson 1998, 65)

Taxes are one of the most important tools that governments can use to shape the economy. First, taxes provide governments the revenue that they need to fund redistributive transfer programs and other government operations. Second, taxes are one of the primary tools that governments use to redistribute economic resources. Third, taxes have a regulatory impact on the structure of the underlying economic system—for example, by favoring some sectors of the economy over others and by influencing individual choices between labor and leisure. Pertinent here, if the government wants to minimize work disincentives, it should strive to keep the effective marginal tax rates on earned income as low as possible.

This chapter offers several recommendations about how to reform the tax system to minimize work disincentives and promote greater economic justice. Tax reforms can, of course, raise or lower the overall burden of taxation. The focus of this chapter, however, is on revenue-neutral tax reforms. The goal is to design a better tax system that would raise about the same amount of revenue as the current system.[1] The focus is primarily on how to improve the federal tax system, but many of the same principles and recommendations could also be applied to improve state and local tax systems.

To start, this chapter discusses some of the major problems with the current tax system. Next, this chapter suggests six relatively modest changes that could improve the current system. Beyond such incremental changes, this chapter also considers seven more fundamental changes to the current system. In particular, it could make sense to integrate the current income and Social Security tax systems into a single, comprehensive system. That comprehensive system could be based on earnings, income, consumption, wealth, or some combination of these. Most important, however, that comprehensive tax system should be designed to both minimize work disincentives and promote greater economic justice.

PROBLEMS WITH THE CURRENT SYSTEM

The current system has four major problems: it can discourage work, it interferes with choices about marriage, it is too complicated, and it is unfair.

The Current System Can Discourage Work

As we saw in chapter 4, taxes influence individual choices between labor and leisure, and high tax rates on earned income tend to discourage work. The implication is clear: the government should keep tax rates on earned income as low as possible, especially on low- and moderate-income workers, as they tend to have the largest behavioral responses to high rates.

Indeed, one of the most fundamental problems with the current federal tax system is that tax rates imposed on many moderate-income taxpayers are too high. For example, many married couples with children and with incomes around $30,000 face effective marginal tax rates above 40 percent (see figure 4.6). Those high rates inevitably discourage secondary earners (usually wives) from even bothering to enter the workforce. Similarly, many heads of households with children and with incomes around $30,000 face effective marginal tax rates above 50 percent (see figure 4.7). Those high rates inevitably discourage those heads of household (usually women) from working more hours or improving their skills.

Worse still, those high effective marginal tax rates in the federal tax system often combine with state income tax rates and even higher benefit-reduction rates in the welfare system to result in virtually confiscatory effective marginal tax rates on the earned income of many low- and moderate-income taxpayers. Dan R. Mastromarco puts it this way:

> Such steeply progressive marginal tax rates punish lower-middle-class workers. Once state taxes are considered, many lower-middle-income single parents keep only 40 cents of each dollar they earn. Once the costs of commuting, child care, and other work-related expenses are considered, choosing to work makes very little economic sense for single-parent families. (1999, 235)[2]

The Current System Interferes with Choices about Marriage

Marital status also plays far too significant a role in the federal tax system. The current system subjects many couples to "marriage penalties" and subjects many individuals to "single penalties." Such penalties lead many analysts to question the fairness of the tax system.[3]

To be sure, fairness is in the eye of the beholder. Still, when it comes to marital status, most analysts agree that there are two major principles against which we can measure the fairness of a tax system. One principle is that different couples with the same combined income should pay the same amount of tax, regardless of the distribution of income between husband and wife. This is known as the principle of *couples neutrality*.

The other principle is that the decision to marry or divorce should not change the total tax liabilities of the two individuals involved; that is, a tax system should avoid marriage penalties and bonuses. This is known as the principle of *marriage neutrality*. If either of these two principles is violated, somebody is sure to cry foul.

A tax system could satisfy these two principles if they were the only ones we held dear, but many other principles govern the design of tax systems. For example, most analysts believe that individuals with a greater ability to pay taxes should pay more taxes than those with a lesser ability to pay taxes.[4] And many believe that progressively higher tax rates should be applied to those with a greater ability to pay taxes. Simplicity and efficiency are also important principles that govern the design of a tax system.

Unfortunately, when all these many principles come into conflict, the principles of couples neutrality and marriage neutrality can be violated and inequities created. As more fully explained below, the income and Social Security taxes both create inequities for various individuals and couples.

Marriage and the Federal Income Tax

Basically, it is impossible for an income tax system to have progressive marginal tax rates, couples neutrality, and marriage neutrality (Bittker

1975; Chirelstein 2002).[5] The current federal income tax achieves a form of couples neutrality, but only at the expense of marriage neutrality. In particular, the income tax frequently results in "marriage penalties" on two-earner couples and "single penalties" on unmarried individuals.

The basic problem is the inevitable result of allowing married couples to file joint returns. For example, consider the tax liabilities of the various taxpayers in table 6.1. Individuals A, B, C, and D are individuals with earned income of $40,000, $40,000, $80,000, and $0, respectively. If each is an unmarried individual, A and B will each pay $4,445 in federal income taxes for 2006, C will pay $14,445, and D will pay no federal income tax.[6]

Until recently, if A and B married and filed a joint tax return, they would have seen their total tax liability increase as a result of marriage. Tax legislation in 2001 eliminated two primary sources of that marriage penalty, although marriage penalties persist at higher income levels. First, the basic standard deduction for married couples is now twice that available to unmarried individuals ($10,300 and $5,150 in 2006, respectively); second, the marriage penalties associated with the 10 and 15 percent tax rate brackets were eliminated. Consequently, there is no longer a marriage penalty if A and B choose to get married. Before marriage, A and B paid total taxes of $8,890 ($4,445 + $4,445); if they marry, their total tax liability will still be just $8,890.[7]

On the other hand, the current system still has significant marriage bonuses. For example, as an unmarried couple, C and D would owe total taxes of $14,445. If they get married, however, their total tax will fall to just $8,890, just like when A and B got married. That is a marriage bonus for C and D together of $5,555. Of course, viewed from the perspective of unmarried individuals, a marriage bonus is just another

Table 6.1. Hypothetical Income and Taxes for Various Households before and after Marriage, 2006 (dollars)

	Income	Tax
A (a single individual)	40,000	4,445
B (a single individual)	40,000	4,445
C (a single individual)	80,000	14,445
D (a single individual)	0	0
A and B (an unmarried couple)	80,000	8,890
A and B (a married couple)	80,000	8,890
C and D (an unmarried couple)	80,000	14,445
C and D (a married couple)	80,000	8,890
A and D (an unmarried couple)	40,000	4,445
A and D (a married couple)	40,000	2,710

Source: Author's calculations.

way of saying "singles penalty." For example, before C married D, C paid $14,445 in tax, while married co-workers with the same $80,000 income paid just $8,890 in tax. From unmarried C's point of view, that was a singles penalty of $5,555.

Similarly, consider what would happen if A and D marry. Before marriage, A paid $4,445 in tax and D paid no tax. If they marry, however, their total tax will fall to $2,710.[8] That is a marriage bonus for A and D together of $1,735, or it could be viewed as a singles penalty on unmarried A of $1,735.

All in all, the current federal income tax system has progressive tax rates and couples neutrality (to ensure that couples with equal incomes pay the same amount of income tax, via the income sharing on joint returns). As a result, marriage neutrality is impossible, and there are significant marriage bonuses and singles penalties.[9]

In addition to the marriage bonuses and single penalties in the rate tables, numerous other federal income tax provisions can operate to generate or compound marriage penalties and bonuses. Some of the largest marriage bonuses and penalties in the federal income tax system are those associated with the earned income tax credit. In 2006, for example, if a woman with no income and two children marries a man with $15,000 of earned income, the couple will receive a marriage bonus of $5,746.[10] On the other hand, if a single father with two children and $15,000 of earnings marries a single mother with two children and $15,000 of earnings, the couple will face a hefty marriage penalty of $5,539.[11]

Significant marriage penalties and bonuses also result from the fact that many other tax breaks phase out as income increases.[12] Similarly, while unmarried elderly or blind individuals can claim additional standard deductions of $1,250 for each eligibility, these drop to just $1,000 for each person in a married couple (IRS 2005c).

Marriage and the Payroll Tax

Marriage per se does not affect the Social Security payroll tax liabilities of individual workers who marry, but it can greatly affect their benefits. Consequently, viewed as a whole, the Social Security system fails to achieve either couples neutrality or marriage neutrality. As this topic is more fully addressed in chapter 8, it is sufficient to note here that the Social Security system tends to impose penalties on two-earner couples, in general, and on secondary workers in those couples, in particular.

Medicare also engenders significant marriage penalties and bonuses. Medicare benefits are available to workers who have paid Medicare payroll taxes and their spouses, regardless of whether those spouses have ever worked and paid Medicare taxes. Consequently, the Medicare system tends to result in large bonuses for one-earner couples. In effect, the Medicare taxes paid by a one-earner couple secure twice as much health care coverage as the taxes paid by an unmarried worker. Also, a two-earner couple could easily pay twice as much in Medicare taxes as a one-earner couple for the same amount of Medicare coverage.

All in all, the income tax and the payroll tax both result in significant marriage penalties and bonuses that can push up effective marginal tax rates on certain workers and so discourage them from working.

The Current System Is Too Complicated

Another problem with the current federal tax system is that it is just too complicated. According to a 2001 study by the Joint Committee on Taxation (JCT), the Internal Revenue Code contains more than 1 million words; the applicable Treasury regulations contain more than 8 million words; and a taxpayer filing an individual income tax return could face a return with some 79 lines, 144 pages of instructions, 11 schedules, 19 separate worksheets embedded in the instructions, and the possibility of filing at least 18 other forms (JCT 2001, 4).[13] The resultant costs of compliance and administration are borne by taxpayers and operate like a rate increase on them. Like any rate increase, it distorts taxpayer decisions and discourages work effort.

Our complicated tax system results in high administrative compliance costs and in great uncertainty about the tax consequences of even the simplest transactions. A simpler tax system could save taxpayers some of or all the money that they now spend paying tax professionals to prepare their tax returns; save taxpayers hours of time they now spend gathering records and filling out paperwork to comply with the current system; and reduce the government's cost to administer the tax system. In addition, making the tax system more stable would make it easier for taxpayers to efficiently plan their future business and personal transactions.

Compliance Costs Are Too High

Most of the burden of administering and complying with the federal tax system is the result of the individual and corporate income tax systems. For example, a recent study estimated that for the 2000 tax year, some 125.9 million individual taxpayers spent more than 3 billion hours and more than $18.8 billion complying with the federal income tax system (Guyton et al. 2003). That translated into an average compliance burden of 25.5 hours and $149 per taxpayer. Assuming a taxpayer's time was worth $20 an hour, the study estimated the average monetized compliance costs for each taxpayer at $532 a year. The study also noted that the budget of the Internal Revenue Service runs about $10 billion a year.[14]

All in all, about 60 percent of Americans use paid preparers to help them with their income tax returns. Out of 130 million returns filed for 2003, almost 79 million returns had a paid preparer's help (President's Advisory Panel 2005b, 3; IRS 2005d, tables 1 and 23). Worse still, more low-income taxpayers are paying for tax preparation, electronic filing, and refund anticipation loans. For example, nearly three-quarters of low-income workers claiming the earned income credit for 2003 used paid preparers (President's Advisory Panel 2005b, 3).[15]

Wage Earners Pay a Disproportionate Share of Taxes

Research on compliance also suggests that wage earners pay a dispro-portionately large share of federal tax liabilities. Because of wage with-holding, wage earners report virtually all their income. Businesses, on the other hand, fail to report a significant share of their income.

For example, for the 2001 tax year, taxpayers paid about $1.78 trillion in taxes on time, or about 85 percent of the total amount due for all types of taxes (GAO 2006b; IRS 2006).[16] The tax gap that year—the difference between taxes owed and taxes paid on time—was more than $345 billion. Underreporting of income is the largest component of the tax gap, and most underreporting came from business activities, rather than wages or investment income. Not surprising, compliance rates are the highest where there is withholding or third-party reporting. As there is relatively little third-party reporting in the business sector, compliance rates there are relatively low. The net effect is that wage earners pay tax on almost all their income, but the business sector does not. All in all, improving compliance in the business sector should result in additional revenues that could be used to reduce tax rates.[17]

The System Is Unstable

Another problem with the tax system is that it changes so frequently. This greatly complicates compliance and administration, and it contri-butes to great uncertainty for taxpayers trying to plan their affairs. For example, there have been more than 14,000 changes to the Internal Revenue Code since 1986 (President's Advisory Panel 2005a).[18]

Of course, even without legislative changes, the tax rules change every year. Many provisions are temporary; that is, they are scheduled to phase out or expire (Gale and Orszag 2003b; JCT 2004a). While some of these provisions were enacted on a temporary basis because Congress had concerns about the underlying policy of the provision, most were enacted on a temporary basis to meet short-term revenue constraints. In both cases, the future of those provisions creates uncertainty for taxpayers and complexity for the system. For example, the estate and gift taxes are scheduled to disappear in 2010 but will bounce back into existence in 2011 unless Congress acts. Indeed, virtually all the tax cuts made by the Economic Growth and Tax Relief Reconciliation Act of 2001 and the Jobs Relief and Reconciliation Act of 2003 are scheduled to expire in 2011 unless new legislation is enacted.

The System Is Fraught with Special Tax Breaks

To have low tax rates, a tax system must have a broad base. Unfortunately, the present federal tax system is replete with special tax breaks for everything from chicken farms to oil wells. In effect, these special tax provisions are spending programs channeled through the tax system. We have known since Stanley S. Surrey was the assistant secretary of the Treasury in the 1960s that the more of these so-called "tax expenditures" that we can repeal, the lower, and less distortionary, tax rates can be.[19]

Under a theoretically pure income tax, individuals would pay tax on the sum of the wages, interest, dividends, and other forms of economic income that they earn.[20] Of course, the federal income tax deviates from this pure income tax ideal in a number of ways. For example, under an ideal income tax, employer contributions to pension plans and the investment income earned by those plans would be taxed currently to the covered workers. Instead, none of this income is taxed until these workers retire and begin receiving their pension benefits.

The Congressional Budget and Impoundment Act of 1974 (Public Law 93-344) requires the federal government to keep track of the revenue "lost" as a result of deviations from an ideal income tax through tax expenditure budgets prepared annually by the Office of Management and Budget and the Joint Committee on Taxation (Executive Office and OMB 2006a, chapter 19; JCT 2006a).[21] The Congressional Budget Act of 1974 does not, however, actually specify the ideal structure of a tax law, so deciding which provisions are special or preferential is necessarily a matter of judgment, over which there is often much debate.[22] Table 6.2 shows OMB's list of the 25 largest tax expenditures in the federal income tax system.

This author's favorite tax expenditure is a little-known tax credit added to the tax code in 1999 by the late Senator William V. Roth of Delaware. Then chair of the Senate Finance Committee, Senator Roth was able to expand the tax code's renewable energy production tax credit to include energy produced from poultry waste. This chicken-

Table 6.2. Top 25 Income Tax Expenditures, Ranked by Total 2007–11 Projected Revenue Effect (millions of dollars)

Provision	2007	2007–11
Exclusion of employer contributions for medical insurance premiums and medical care	146,780	888,990
Deductibility of mortgage interest on owner-occupied homes	79,860	471,430
Accelerated depreciation of machinery and equipment	52,230	357,200
Capital gains exclusion on home sales	43,900	318,250
401(k) plans	39,800	232,870
Employer plans	52,470	228,000
Exclusion of net imputed rental income	33,210	204,849
Child credit	42,120	199,620
Deductibility of charitable contributions, other than education and health	34,430	198,120
Step-up basis of capital gains at death	32,460	177,210
Exclusion of interest on public purpose state and local bonds	29,640	168,330
Deductibility of nonbusiness state and local taxes other than on owner-occupied homes	27,210	161,710
Exclusion of interest on life insurance savings	20,770	129,810
Capital gains (except agriculture, timber, iron ore, and coal)	26,760	121,370
Social Security benefits for retired workers	19,590	104,870
Deduction for U.S. production activities	10,670	78,560
Deductibility of state and local property tax on owner-occupied homes	12,810	74,200
Deferral of income from controlled foreign corporations	11,940	68,580
Keogh plans	10,670	63,810
Deductibility of medical expenses	5,310	41,000
Individual retirement accounts	5,970	38,500
Exclusion of workers' compensation benefits	6,180	33,150
Exception from passive loss rules for $25,000 of rental loss	6,230	29,380
Expensing of research and experimentation expenditures	6,990	28,250
Earned income tax credit	5,147	28,104

Source: Executive Office of the President and Office of Management and Budget (2006a), table 19-3.

shit tax credit costs the taxpayers about $135 million a year (Forman 1999a).

It is also worth noting that many tax expenditures operate like "upside-down subsidies," benefiting high-income taxpayers more than low- and moderate-income taxpayers. High-income taxpayers are more likely to itemize their deductions and structure their affairs in order to take advantage of such tax breaks as the home mortgage interest deduction, the exclusion for pension contributions, and other investment incentives. For example, one study found that the top 5 percent of individual income taxpayers—those with incomes over $100,000—receive over half the benefits from the largest tax expenditures (Burman 2003, 624).[23]

The Current System Is Unfair

Another problem with the current tax system has to do with fairness. First, the current system imposes relatively high effective marginal tax rates on earned income, as opposed to investment income. Second, the current system does not do enough to reduce economic inequality.

High Tax Rates on Earned Income

First of all, the current system imposes relatively high tax rates on earned income, as opposed to investment income.

At the outset, compare the tax liability of a young married couple with $50,000 of wage income with the tax liability of a middle-aged couple with $50,000 of income from dividends. For 2006, the working couple will owe more than $8,000 in federal taxes and face a marginal tax rate on additional wages of more than 22 percent, while the investor couple would owe less than $2,000 in taxes and face a marginal tax rate of just 5 percent on additional dividend income.

More specifically, the working couple would owe $4,210 in federal income taxes and $3,825 in Social Security taxes ($7,650 if both the employer's 7.65 percent of wages and the employee's 7.65 percent of wages are counted).[24] The working couple would face a marginal tax rate of 22.65 percent on any additional wages (15 percent income tax rate plus 7.65 percent Social Security tax rate) or 30.3 percent (15 percent income tax rate plus 15.3 Social Security tax rate) if the employer share is also counted.

Yet the investor couple would owe just $1,655 in federal income taxes and no Social Security taxes,[25] and it would face a marginal tax rate of just 5 percent on any additional dividend income. Their investment income is not subject to Social Security taxation, and a special rule provides that the capital gains and dividends received by moderate-income taxpayers are taxed at no more than a 5 percent rate, as opposed to the usual 15 percent rate. In general most stock is held by high-income households, and, consequently, most of the benefits of the low rates on capital gains and dividends go to those households (Friedman and Richards 2006).

Let us also compare the tax liability of a young married couple with $30,000 in wage income with the tax liability of an elderly retired couple with $18,000 of pension income and $12,000 of Social Security benefits.

For 2006, the working couple would owe $3,605 in federal taxes, while the retired couple would pay no federal taxes whatsoever.

More specifically, the working couple with $30,000 of earned income in 2006 would owe $3,605 in taxes ($1,310 in income taxes and $2,295 in Social Security taxes [$4,590 if both the employer and employee shares are counted]).[26] The retired couple, however, would pay no Social Security taxes because it has no wages or earned income, and the retired couple would pay no income taxes either. That is because Americans over the age of 65 are entitled to additional standard deductions of $1,000 each, which will raise this couple's simple income tax threshold to $18,900, and Social Security benefits are excluded from gross income unless a couple's income exceeds $32,000 (IRS 2005c).[27]

Together, the individual income tax and the payroll tax impose relatively high tax rates on earned income and fairly low rates on investment income. In that regard, *New York Times* reporter David Cay Johnston argues that "our tax system now levies the poor, the middle class and even the upper middle class to subsidize the rich" (2003, 2).[28]

The 2003 legislation that reduced the tax rate on net capital gains and dividends to no more than 15 percent significantly reduced the overall effective tax rates on high-income taxpayers. For the year 2000, the effective tax rate on the highest quintile of households was 28 percent, and it was 33.2 percent on the highest 1 percent of households (CBO 2003b, table B1-A). After the 2001 and 2003 tax cuts, the effective tax rates fell to 25.0 percent for the highest quintile of households and to 31.4 percent for the top 1 percent of households (see table 4.3).

The Current System Is Not Progressive Enough

Another problem with the current tax system is that it simply does not do enough to reduce economic inequality. To be sure, the current system is quite progressive. For example, the bottom 40 percent of households paid just 5.5 percent of federal taxes in 2003, the next 40 percent paid just 28.5 percent of federal taxes, and the top 20 percent paid 65.7 percent of federal taxes (see table 4.3). But if we truly want to achieve a just distribution of economic resources, we probably need our tax system to be even more progressive.

It is simply not enough to have a fair tax system, we need to have a fair distribution of economic resources after all taxes and transfers. According to Liam Murphy and Thomas Nagel,

> taxes must be evaluated as part of the overall system of property rights that they help to create. Justice or injustice in taxation can only mean justice or injustice in the system of property rights and entitlements that result from a particular tax regime. (2002, 8)

Similarly, Barbara Fried puts it this way:

> Once we recognize the redistribution of income for social welfarist
> ends as a legitimate role for the government, isolating the tax side
> from the transfer/expenditure side of the fiscal ledger becomes a
> morally incoherent stance. (2002, 173)[29]

In short, when we talk about achieving a fair tax system, we must
talk about taxes as a tool that can help us achieve a just distribution
of economic resources after taxes and transfers. Measured against that
standard, the current system does not seem progressive enough.

MODEST CHANGES THAT COULD IMPROVE THE TAX SYSTEM

This part considers seven modest tax reforms that could help encourage
greater work effort and promote greater economic justice. More specifically, we could broaden the tax base and reduce tax rates on earned
income; stop taxing low-income workers; restructure the earned income
tax credit; replace personal exemptions and standard deductions with
refundable personal tax credits; reduce marriage penalties; and simplify
the tax system and reduce compliance costs.

Broaden the Tax Base and Reduce Tax Rates on Earned Income

In order to have low tax rates, a tax system must have a broad base.
Unfortunately, the present federal tax system is replete with special
tax breaks and tax expenditures for everything from chicken farms to
oil wells. The more of these special tax breaks that are repealed, the
lower tax rates on earned income can be. At the extreme, one recent
study suggests that if we get rid of virtually all deductions and exemptions, we could replace the federal personal and corporate income taxes
with a single 11 percent tax on all income (Fehr et al. 2005, 13–17).

Repeal Costly and Inefficient Income Tax Expenditures

The amount of tax raised by a tax system depends on its base and the
applicable tax rates applied to that tax base. Because high tax rates
tend to discourage work, it would make sense to reduce tax rates. This
can easily be done by broadening the tax base and eliminating costly
and inefficient tax expenditures. The U.S. Government Accountability
Office (2005b, 1) recently described the problem as follows:

Tax expenditures have a significant effect on overall tax rates—in that, for any given level of revenue, overall tax rates must be higher to offset the revenue foregone through tax expenditures— as well as the budget and fiscal flexibility. They also contribute to the growing complexity of the federal tax system.

Of note, the Tax Reform Act of 1986 dramatically broadened the income tax base and lowered tax rates. That act reduced the maximum individual income tax rate from 50 percent to around 28 percent. By all accounts, that act had a positive impact on both labor supply and economic growth.[30]

Unfortunately, tax legislation enacted since 1986 has generally added more tax breaks to the income tax system and, therefore, required rate increases.[31] Consequently, even after the recent spate of tax cuts, the maximum individual income tax rate is 35 percent. Broadening the tax base would enable the government to lower tax rates even more.

In particular, it might make sense to repeal many of the existing tax expenditures for various kinds of investment income. Raising the taxes imposed on investment income would enable us to lower the taxes imposed on earned income.[32] For example, the exclusion of interest on life insurance savings is a tax expenditure that costs about $21 billion a year, the exclusion of interest on state and local bonds is a tax expenditure that costs about $30 billion a year, and the partial exclusion of Social Security benefits for retired workers is a tax expenditure that costs about $20 billion a year (see table 6.2). Repealing these tax breaks could raise billions of dollars in new tax revenues and so allow us to lower overall tax rates.

Similarly, repealing the preferences for capital gain and dividend income could raise more than $94 billion a year (JCT 2006a, table 1). For that matter, it could make sense to tax many gains annually, rather than waiting until the property is sold (and the gain is "realized"). There is no reason publicly traded stocks and bonds could not be valued at the end of the year. Taxpayers could then report their gains and losses annually, and the Treasury would collect billions more in taxes.[33] The built-in gains on stock options and other forms of so-called "nonqualified" deferred compensation could also be taxed annually.[34]

An alternative approach for taxing gains would be to tax built-in gains at death.[35] Under current law, if a taxpayer holds property until death, the gain is completely forgiven: there is no tax on the unrealized gain at death, and the taxpayer's heirs treat the property as if they purchased it for its fair-market value at the time of death. In tax parlance, the current-law approach is referred to as the "step-up" in basis at death; it is a tax expenditure that costs over $32 billion a year (table 6.2).

Current law also provides extraordinarily generous deductions for the purchase of new machinery and equipment. For example, small businesses can deduct up to $100,000 of such purchases each year, and all businesses can take accelerated depreciation deductions far in excess of what could be justified by the actual economic decline in the value of those assets. These extraordinary investment incentives are major revenue-losers. Worse still, they encourage businesses to invest in machinery and equipment (capital) rather than, say, employees and training (labor). Consequently, repealing these extraordinary investment incentives would raise revenue and have the added benefit of encouraging businesses to shift more of their spending from capital to labor.

Current law also permits taxpayers to deduct the mortgage interest and real property taxes that they pay on the homes they own; the capital gains from the sale of homes are also generally excluded from gross income. These tax expenditures cost about $80 billion a year, $13 billion a year, and $44 billion a year, respectively (table 6.2).[36] If these provisions were repealed, tax rates could be reduced. Moreover, tax returns could be greatly simplified: without a deduction for mortgage interest and real property taxes, few individuals would itemize their deductions.

It could also make sense to require taxpayers to include gifts and inheritances in income.[37] Although the receipt of gifts and inheritances clearly enhance one's economic well-being, these transfers are currently excluded from the gross income of recipients. The exclusion of gifts and inheritances is not typically identified as a tax expenditure in government-prepared tax expenditure budgets, so a precise estimate of the potential revenue gains is unavailable, but it would be in the billions. Consequently, broadening the income tax base to include the value of gifts and inheritances in income would permit a significant reduction in tax rates on income, in general, and on earned income, in particular.

All in all, the more chickenshit tax expenditures that we can get rid of, the more we can lower marginal tax rates on earned income and reduce economic inequality. Moreover, getting rid of most tax expenditures and shifting to an ideal income tax or consumption tax system could increase economic output by as much as 5 or 10 percent (Auerbach and Hassett 2005, 150).

Expand the Tax Base for Social Insurance Taxes

Some of the provisions identified as income tax expenditures are also tax expenditures for the Social Security payroll tax.[38] For example, employer contributions to employee pension plans and health care plans are excluded from both the income tax base and the payroll tax base. Consequently, repealing those tax expenditures would permit both income and payroll tax rate cuts.

Also, the current Old-Age, Survivors, and Disability Insurance (OASDI) tax is capped at $94,200 (in 2006). Some have suggested that removing the cap could generate revenues that could lead to a reduction in payroll tax rates.[39]

For that matter, one has to wonder why Social Security and Medicare benefits are financed with payroll taxes at all. Both programs involve significant redistribution from some workers to other workers and their families. For example, the 2.9 percent Hospital Insurance payroll tax is used to pay for health care benefits for virtually all elderly and disabled Americans. But why use a payroll tax to pay for such redistribution? If redistribution is called for, why not use an income tax or, perhaps even a wealth tax? Shouldn't high-income investors, as well as high earners, be called upon to help pay for health care coverage for the elderly and disabled? In that regard, the tax rates on earned income could be reduced if more of the costs of social insurance programs were paid for with the broader-based income tax rather than with the current payroll tax (Center for American Progress 2005).

Improve Compliance

Improving compliance with existing tax laws could also result in additional revenues that could be used to reduce tax rates, in general, and the tax rates on earned income, in particular. Research on tax compliance shows that compliance rates are the highest where there is withholding or third-party reporting.[40] Because of wage withholding, wage earners report virtually all of their income. Many businesses, however, fail to report a significant share of their income. The U.S. Government Accountability Office recently suggested such compliance reforms as requiring tax withholding and more or better information return reporting on payments made to independent contractors and requiring information return reporting on payments made to corporations (GAO 2005f, 18). It would also help if the IRS were given additional resources for audits and other enforcement activities. In short, improving compliance would be a step toward "enhancing fairness for those citizens who meet their tax obligations" (GAO 2005f, 16).

Stop Taxing Low-Income Workers

Low-income families with children generally do not owe any federal taxes. Some low-income unmarried individuals and families without children, however, do owe federal taxes. Also, many low-income individuals and families must pay state income, sales, and property taxes. If we are serious about increasing the rewards for low-skilled workers, it would make sense to stop taxing them.[41] Workers earning less than the poverty level just should not have to pay taxes.

Federal Income and Payroll Tax Thresholds

Table 6.3 compares the 2006 federal tax thresholds and poverty income guidelines for selected households.[42] Consider a family of four consisting of a married couple and two children. This family unit's poverty income guideline for 2006 is $20,000 (HHS 2006) and its simple income tax threshold is $23,500.[43] After taking into account the earned income and child tax credits, the couple will not actually owe any income tax until its income exceeds $41,867.[44] Because the Social Security tax system has no standard deductions or personal exemptions, the couple's Social Security tax threshold is zero. Finally, this married couple with two children will not actually have a net federal tax liability for 2006 unless its income exceeds $32,101.[45]

On the other hand, many poor childless individuals and couples must pay federal taxes. We should restructure the federal tax system so it no longer taxes any low-income workers. As more fully explained below, this could largely be achieved, for example, by adding standard deductions and personal exemptions to the Social Security payroll tax.

State Income Tax Thresholds

Many low-income workers are also required to pay state income taxes. In 2005, for example, two-parent families of four with incomes below

Table 6.3. Poverty Levels and Net Federal Tax Thresholds after Tax Credits in 2006, for Selected Households (dollars)

	Unmarried individual	Married couple with no children	Single parent with two children	Married couple with two children
Poverty level	9,800	13,200	16,600	20,000
Simple income tax threshold (before credits)	8,450	16,900	17,450	23,500
Income tax threshold after the earned income and child tax credits	10,043	16,900	35,524	41,867
Social Security tax threshold	0	0	0	0
Combined income and Social Security tax threshold (i.e., net federal tax threshold)	5,380	5,380	24,590	32,101

Source: Author's calculations

the poverty level owed state income taxes in 19 of the 42 states with an income tax (Levitis and Johnson 2006). In addition, in 16 of those states, single-parent families of three also paid state income taxes. Low-income individual workers can face even heavier burdens. States, too, should raise their income tax thresholds to ensure that low-income workers are not subject to tax, for example, by raising their standard deductions and personal exemption amounts and indexing them for inflation.[46]

Restructure the Earned Income Tax Credit

A particularly effective way to reduce effective marginal tax rates on low-income workers would be to restructure the earned income tax credit. As figure 4.2 showed, the $4,536 earned income tax credit for a married couple with two or more children currently phases out at a 21.06 percent rate as income goes from $16,810 to $38,348. It would make sense to restructure the earned income credit to reduce the negative impact of such high phaseout rates.

A Social Security Payroll Tax Exemption and a Child Tax Credit

One approach would be to replace the earned income tax credit with a $10,000 exemption from Social Security taxes and a fully refundable $1,000 per child tax credit—a work benefit and a child benefit.[47] Consider a single mother with two children. Under current law she can claim an earned income credit of up to $4,536, but that credit phases out at the rate of 21.06 percent of her income in excess of $14,810. Replacing the current earned income tax credit with a $10,000 per worker exemption and a $1,000 per child tax credit, our hypothetical mother would receive up to $2,765 worth of tax benefits, and her benefits would not phase out as her income increased. A $10,000 exemption from Social Security payroll taxes would be worth $765 per worker, and the two child tax credits would be worth $2,000.[48] As there would be no reason to phase out either the $10,000 per worker exemption or the $1,000 per child tax credits, millions of low-income workers would no longer face the extraordinarily high effective marginal tax rates that result from the current phaseout of the earned income tax credit.[49]

Alternatively, Congress could allow taxpayers to claim standard deductions and personal exemptions under the Social Security tax system, as well as under the income tax system. For example, in 2006, a single mother with two children can claim a $7,550 standard deduction and three $3,300 personal exemptions under the income tax, for a simple income tax threshold of $17,450 (see table 4.2). If she were allowed to claim a $17,450 tax threshold for the Social Security payroll tax as well, she would save $1,335 in employee Social Security taxes, and the earned income credit could be reduced accordingly.[50] Refundable child tax credits could again be used to give her $1,000 per child. As above, taxpayers would no longer face extraordinarily high marginal effective tax rates like those that result from the phaseout of the current earned income tax credit.

A $2,000 per Worker Earned Income Credit

Another approach for keeping marginal effective tax rates low would be to replace the current earned income tax credit with a universal $2,000 per worker earned income tax credit and $1,000 per child refundable tax credits.[51] The $2,000 per worker earned income tax credit could be computed as, say, 20 percent of the first $10,000 of earned income, and it might not phase out at all, or phase out only very slowly, say, at the rate of 5 percent of income from $30,000 to $70,000.[52] Figure 6.1 shows how such a $2,000 per worker earned income tax credit would work with, or without, a phaseout.

Under this approach, many single mothers with at least two children would get more benefits than under the current earned income credit. They could claim two $1,000 refundable child tax credits, and if they

Figure 6.1. Hypothetical $2,000 per Worker Earned Income Tax Credit, With or Without a Phaseout

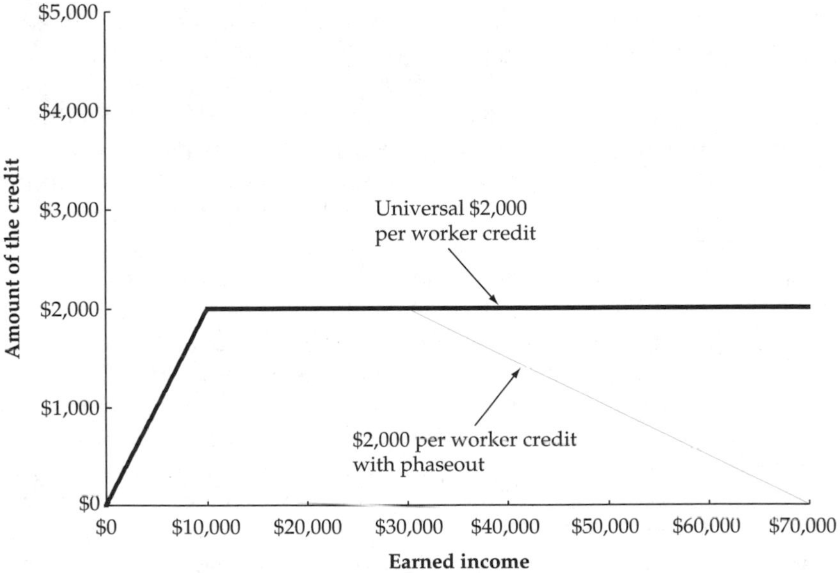

Source: Author's calculations.

worked full-time year-round at the minimum wage they could pick up another $2,000 from the $2,000 per worker earned income credit, for a total of $4,000. There would be no particular reason for either of these tax credits to phase out.

A universal $2,000 per worker earned income tax credit would increase the rewards for work for all low-income workers and help reduce the hardships faced by all low-income families with children.[53] Marriage penalties would also disappear in a system of $2,000 per worker earned income tax credits. If two workers married, each would still be entitled to an earned income credit of up to $2,000, and depending on how the phaseout (if any) worked, they might lose little or no credit by getting married.[54]

Replace Personal Exemptions and Standard Deductions with Refundable Personal Tax Credits or Universal Grants

Another approach that could simplify the tax system and achieve greater economic justice would be to replace personal exemptions, standard deductions, and other child and family tax benefits with refundable personal tax credits or universal grants. For example, it could make sense to provide every person with a simple universal grant that guaranteed every person $1,000 or even $2,000 a year.[55]

Universal Grants Would Provide Income Assistance yet Leave Beneficiaries with the Incentive to Work

Universal grants are universal benefits that would be especially helpful to low-income beneficiaries. For example, consider a simple universal grant that guaranteed every person $2,000 a year. Under such a system, an unmarried individual would receive $2,000, a parent with two children would receive $6,000, and a married couple with two children would receive $8,000. These universal grants could be paid out in the form of refundable personal tax credits; and these personal tax credits could replace personal exemptions, standard deductions, child tax credits, and the child-related component of the earned income credit.

There would be no revenue loss associated with replacing personal exemptions, standard deductions, and the other child and family tax benefits with a system of $1,680 per person universal grants, if we also got rid of most other deductions and credits (Forman, Carasso, and Saleem 2005). As more fully explained in chapter 7, some of the revenue needed to pay for $2,000 per person universal grants could come from cashing out food stamps and other means-tested and non-means-tested transfer programs.

By providing needed income assistance to low-income individuals, universal grants would help promote economic justice. Universal grants paid in the form of refundable tax credits have an equal value for all individuals, whereas deductions are more valuable to individuals facing higher tax brackets. For example, the current personal exemption ($3,300 in 2006) is worth $924 to taxpayers in the 28 percent tax bracket but just $330 to taxpayers in the 10 percent bracket.[56] On the other hand, a $2,000 refundable personal tax credit would have the same value for all individuals.

Like most other transfer programs, universal grants would tend to reduce work effort by beneficiaries, but the reduction in work effort would be much less than under a negative income tax transfer. That is because negative income tax systems subject workers to high benefit-reduction rates, but universal grants do not have to be phased out.

Figure 6.2 shows how a simple tax and transfer system with $2,000 per person universal grants could modestly reduce the work effort of a hypothetical working mother with two children earning, say, $5.00 an hour. In the absence of universal grants, she would work 1,500 hours and make $7,500. With universal grants, however, she would reduce her work effort slightly, to 1,400 hours a year, but she would see her post-transfer, post-tax income rise to $13,000. In short, as long as there is no phaseout, individuals should still have great

Figure 6.2. Universal Grants Result in Only Modest Reductions in Work Effort: Parent with Two Children ($2,000 per Person Universal Grants)

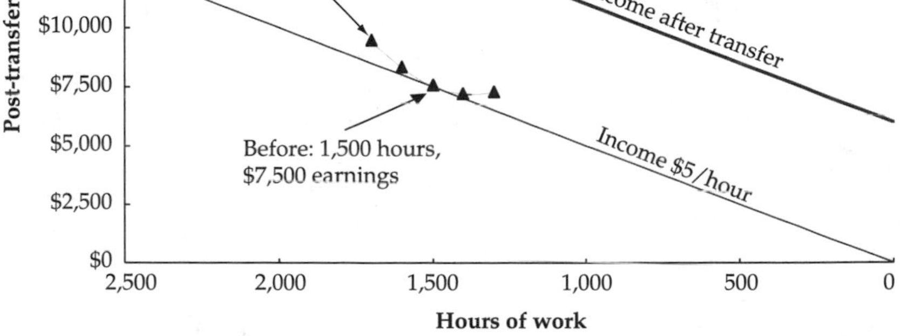

Source: Author's calculations.

incentives to get out and work to earn money to support themselves and their families.

It is also worth noting that refundable personal tax credits could help bring rationality to the tax rate structure.[57] For example, imagine a simple, progressive income tax system with $2,000 personal tax credits and a tax rate schedule with three rates: 10 percent of the first $20,000 of income and 20 percent of income from $20,000 to $50,000, and 30 percent on income in excess of $50,000. Figure 6.3 shows how this simple tax and universal grant system would affect the post-transfer income for a single parent with two children, and figure 6.4 shows the effective marginal tax rates imposed on those families.

Together, figures 6.3 and 6.4 show how this simple tax and universal grant system could help meet the income needs of single mothers without undermining their incentives to work. In sharp contrast to the current tax system (as portrayed in figure 4.7), marginal tax rates would not bounce all over the place under this simple tax and universal grant system, nor would the highest effective marginal tax rates be imposed on low-income taxpayers.

Universal Grants Would Be Easy to Administer

As more fully explained in chapter 7, a system of universal grants in the form of personal income tax credits could greatly simplify the

Figure 6.3. How a Simple Tax and Universal Grant System Would Affect a Single Parent with Two Children ($2,000 Universal Grants and 10, 20, and 30 Percent Tax Rates)

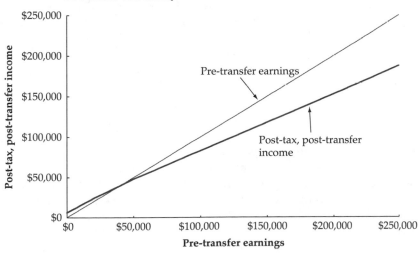

Source: Author's calculations.

Figure 6.4. Effective Marginal Tax Rates for a Parent with Two Children and Earned Income Only in a World of Universal Grants ($2,000 Universal Grants and 10, 20, and 30 Percent Tax Rates)

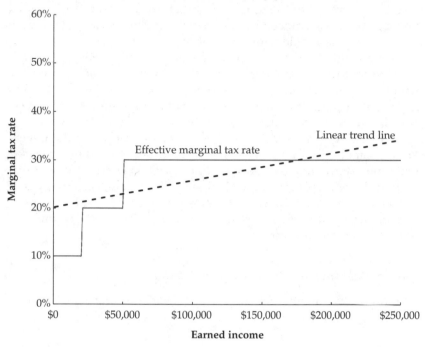

Source: Author's calculations.

administration of both the tax and social welfare systems. Refundable personal income tax credits could be claimed on an individual's income tax return in much the same way that personal exemptions are claimed. Families subject to income taxation could reduce their withholding to account for their credits, rather than simply receiving a large annual lump-sum refund.

For low-income taxpayers, a mechanism similar to the advance payment feature of the current earned income tax credit or the direct deposit program for Social Security benefits could be developed. For example, a qualifying taxpayer could present something like the current IRS Form W-2, Wage and Tax Statement, to her employer, bank, or social service agency. Employees would then receive advance payment of their personal income tax credits from their employers, while other claimants would have their monthly payments directly deposited with their designated banks or social service agencies. Such an advance payment system would help provide timely assistance to low-income families. For example, a parent with two children would be eligible for three refundable personal tax credits. Assuming a credit amount of, say, $2,000 a year, she could have $500 a month directly deposited into her bank account.[58]

Reduce Marriage Penalties

Another way to help encourage work would be to reduce the effective marginal tax rates imposed on secondary earners in two earner couples. Under current law, secondary earners face relatively high tax rates, as their earnings are stacked on top of the income of the primary earner. For example, instead of facing low 0, 10, 15, and 25 percent income tax rates on her modest earnings, the spouse of a high-income worker can see all her earnings taxed at the 35 percent rate. Together with the Social Security payroll tax, state income taxes, and the costs of commuting, work clothes, and child care; many secondary earners face confiscatory tax rates on their earned incomes. Much as they might want to work, it just does not pay.

By raising the standard deduction for married couples, increasing the size of the 10 and 15 percent rate brackets, increasing the amount of the dependent care credit, and reducing maximum tax rates, recent tax legislation has diminished the marriage penalties faced by many two-earner couples. Nevertheless, many secondary earners continue to face high effective marginal tax rates if they choose to work. If we want to stop discouraging secondary earners from working, various changes could be made.

Create a Deduction for Two-Earner Couples

One approach would be to add some kind of deduction for two-earner couples. Back when the maximum tax rate on earned income was 50 percent, the Economic Recovery Tax Act of 1981 added such a deduction for two-earner couples.[59] Under former I.R.C. § 221, married couples filing jointly could deduct 10 percent of the earnings of the lower-earning spouse up to $30,000, for a maximum deduction of $3,000 a year. That deduction was repealed by the Tax Reform Act of 1986, presumably to help offset the costs of reducing the maximum tax rate to 28 percent.

In raising the maximum tax rate to 39.6 percent, President Bill Clinton's Revenue Act of 1993 significantly increased the "marriage penalty" imposed on many two-earner couples (Feenberg and Rosen 1994). The recent tax cuts have reduced the maximum tax rate to just 35 percent, but that still leaves many secondary earners facing high marginal tax rates if they choose to work. It could make sense to restore and expand that old deduction for two-earner couples, for example, by allowing secondary earners to deduct up to 20 percent of their first $50,000 of earned income.

Expand the Dependent Care Credit and Make It Refundable

Expanding the dependent care credit could help encourage secondary earners with children to work. Under current law, the dependent care credit offsets up to $1,050 (35 percent of up to $3,000 of employment-related expenses) per year for one qualifying child or up to $2,100 (35 percent of up to $6,000 of employment-related expenses) per year for two or more qualifying children; these credit amounts are reduced to $600 and $1,200, respectively (20 percent of applicable employment-related expenses), for taxpayers with adjusted gross income over $45,000. Raising the applicable employment-related expenses or the credit percentages would help make it easier for secondary earners with children to work.

Also, as more fully discussed in chapter 7, it would make sense to make the dependent care credit refundable. This change would make it easier for low-income workers with children to enter the workforce.[60]

Flatten the Rate Structure

Another way to reduce the effective marginal tax rates on secondary earners would be to move toward a flatter rate structure. For example, consider a tax system that provided a basic exemption of $10,000 *per worker*, and then taxed all income above $10,000 at a 25 percent rate. Such a flat tax system would virtually eliminate marriage penalties and bonuses.[61] For example, a man making $210,000 a year would owe $50,000 in taxes, and a woman making $30,000 a year would owe $5,000 in taxes, for a total of $55,000. If they got married, together they would still owe $55,000 in taxes. Under this kind of system, each worker would earn $10,000 tax free, and the rest of her earned income would be taxed at the 25 percent rate, regardless of her marital status or the amount of her spouse's income.

Similarly, in a progressive tax system, broadening the tax rate brackets could eliminate most marriage penalties and bonuses. For example, consider a system that provided a $2,000 universal grant to each person and then taxed the first $100,000 of income at a 20 percent rate and income over $100,000 at a 35 percent rate. Under this a system, marriage penalties would be confined to those few couples whose combined income exceeded $100,000. The rest would pay tax at that "flat" 20 percent rate.

Replace Joint Returns with Individual Filing

Perhaps the best approach for reducing the effective marginal tax rates on secondary earners would be to replace joint returns with a system of individual filing. This would be accomplished by having each individual, married or unmarried, file as an individual under a single tax rate schedule.[62] Under this approach, both primary and secondary earners would face the 0, 10, 15, 25, 28, 33, and 35 percent rates on their earned income. This individual-filing approach would virtually eliminate marriage penalties and bonuses from the current system.[63] To keep tax returns simple, spouses could be allowed to file separately on the same return, as, for example, on the Arkansas state income tax return.

Other Possible Changes

Assuming the current joint return system is retained, a number of other changes could help reduce the high effective marginal tax rates and marriage penalties that can deter secondary earners from marrying and working. For example, it would be appropriate to amend virtually all the specific tax code provisions that cause marriage penalties and bonuses.

Simplify the Tax System and Reduce Compliance Costs

Another way to reduce effective marginal tax rates on earned income would be to simplify the tax system (Forman 1996a, 2001c). Our complicated tax system imposes high costs of compliance and administration. These costs operate like a surtax on taxpayers' money and time. Consequently, reducing the tax compliance burden on taxpayers would raise their after-tax incomes and restore lost time to them. Moreover, the savings that would result from reducing the costs of administering the tax system could be returned to taxpayers in the form of lower tax rates. This section offers five recommendations for simplifying the tax system.

Increase Tax Thresholds and Repeal Itemized Deductions

Raising the standard deduction and/or personal exemption amounts would raise the income tax thresholds. That would mean that fewer taxpayers would be required to file income tax returns, and that would greatly simplify the tax system for individuals and for the IRS.

Raising the standard deduction would also reduce the number of taxpayers who itemize their deductions. Typically, about 65 percent of Americans claim the standard deduction and 35 percent itemize their deductions.[64] Consequently, raising the standard deduction would mean millions fewer complicated tax returns for taxpayers to file and for the IRS to process.

Also, repealing any of the many itemized deductions would reduce the number of individuals who itemize their deductions and simplify their returns. Indeed, if the deductions for mortgage interest, state and local taxes, and charitable contributions were repealed, hardly any taxpayers would end up itemizing their deductions.

Similarly, adding a floor to any of the itemized deductions would reduce the number of itemizers and so simplify their returns. For example, it might be appropriate to allow charitable contribution deductions only to the extent that the taxpayer's contributions exceed 1, 2, or 5 percent of the taxpayer's adjusted gross income.[65]

All in all, reducing the number of taxpayers who itemize their deductions would simplify the tax system for individuals and for the IRS. Indeed, with enough simplification, most individuals would be able to file their tax returns on postcards.

Create a $1,000 per Year Exclusion for Interest, Dividends, Gains, and Other Miscellaneous Income

Another way to simplify income tax returns would be to add an exclusion for some modest amount of unearned income. It just does not make sense to require millions of individuals to report negligible amounts of interest, dividends, gains, state tax refunds, and other miscellaneous items of income and then make the IRS dispute returns that miss a few dollars of that income. One option would be to let taxpayers exclude from gross income up to $1,000 a year of interest, dividends, gains, state tax refunds, and other miscellaneous items of income. Allowing an exclusion for up to $1,000 of such unearned income would reduce the record-keeping and filing burdens on these taxpayers and on the IRS.

Repeal the Presidential Election Campaign Checkoff

Another way to help simplify income tax returns would be to repeal the Presidential Election Campaign Fund checkoff. The checkoff clutters up individual income returns.[66] Consequently, repealing the checkoff would simplify tax returns for both taxpayers and the IRS. If Congress remains committed to public financing of presidential election campaigns, it could replace the checkoff with direct appropriations to the presidential campaign election fund and pay for those appropriations out of general revenues.

Move to a Return-Free Tax System

A major simplification would be to move toward a return-free tax system. Under this approach, most Form 1040EZ and Form 1040A filers and a few Form 1040 filers could elect to have the IRS compute their tax liabilities and prepare their returns—some 55 million taxpayers in all (U.S. Department of Treasury 2003; IRS 1987).[67]

Another alternative would be to move to a "final withholding" tax system. Final withholding tax systems are similar to return-free systems, except that they rely even more heavily on withholding. Under a final withholding system, the amounts withheld from employers and other income sources *are* the tax, thus eliminating the need for most taxpayers to file tax returns. Over 35 foreign countries use some form of final withholding, including the United Kingdom, Japan, Germany, and Argentina (Turnier 2003; GAO 1992).

For example, in the United Kingdom, the income tax is withheld by employers under the PAYE (Pay As You Earn) final withholding system. When an individual first becomes potentially subject to tax, an initial return must be filed so the Inland Revenue can determine how much the employer should withhold. Thereafter, individuals with simple incomes and modest earnings are normally required to file a return only about once every five years. In 1999–2000, about two-thirds of British taxpayers were able to avoid filing returns (Burman 2000).

Would a final withholding system work in the United States? A final withholding system could significantly reduce burdens on both taxpayers and the IRS. In its analysis of the issue, the General Accounting Office concluded that most taxpayers who now file 1040EZ returns (about 20 million in 2003) and many of those who now file 1040A returns (about 30 million in 2003) could be served by a final withholding system (GAO 1992).[68] Most of these people no longer would have to gather information, become familiar with tax laws, or prepare and file returns. The burden on the IRS also would be greatly reduced.

Repeal the Alternative Minimum Taxes

The individual and corporate alternative minimum taxes also create enormous complexity. Many taxpayers are required to compute their tax liability twice, once for the regular income tax and another time to see if they are subject to the alternative minimum tax. Moreover, because the alternative minimum tax exemption amounts are not indexed for inflation, more taxpayers will be affected as the years go on. For example, by 2010, more than 20 percent of individual taxpayers will get hit by the alternative minimum tax (JCT 2005c). Accordingly, many analysts recommend that we repeal the alternative minimum taxes, perhaps making up the lost revenue by getting rid of tax expenditures under the regular income tax.[69]

A MORE COMPREHENSIVE PROPOSAL

Beyond the incremental changes to the tax code described above, the government could instead fundamentally restructure the current tax system. For example, the government might integrate the current income and Social Security taxes into a single, comprehensive tax system. That comprehensive tax system could be based on income, earnings, consumption, wealth, or some combination of these. Most important, however, this comprehensive tax system should be designed to both promote greater economic justice and encourage greater work effort.

Integrating the Income and Payroll Taxes

Many problems of the current tax system are attributable to the fact that there are two major taxes imposed on individuals: income taxes and Social Security payroll taxes. Under current law, Social Security taxes are collected on every dollar of earned income, and the income tax system uses the earned income tax credit and a portion of the child tax credit to refund at least part of those taxes to millions of low-income workers. As already discussed, it would be a lot simpler if the federal tax system did not collect Social Security taxes from low-income individuals in the first place, and one approach would be to add a $10,000 per worker exemption to the Social Security system. Another approach would be to use universal earned income tax credits to offset those payroll taxes. For example, a $1,530 per worker earned income tax credit could exactly offset both the employer and employee portions of the Social Security payroll taxes on the first $10,000 of wages.

A broader approach would be to combine the individual income and Social Security taxes into a single, comprehensive tax system. That comprehensive tax system could be based on income, earnings, consumption, wealth, or some combination of these.

A Comprehensive Income Tax

As a starting point, consider how the individual income tax and the Social Security payroll tax could be combined into a comprehensive *income* tax system.[70] Individuals with incomes below some poverty threshold would be exempt from tax, and tax rates could be increased to raise the same amount of revenue as the current system. In effect, there would be a single, higher-yield income tax instead of the current bifurcated tax system. Such an integrated system would be simpler to administer than the current system. Literally millions of low-income individuals would no longer have to file tax returns simply to recover overwithheld taxes.

Moreover, such an integrated tax system could have a logical tax rate structure, as opposed to the roller-coaster rate structure of the current tax system. Now, an individual's effective marginal tax rate depends upon an almost random combination of income tax rates, Social Security tax rates, and phaseouts of the earned income credit, dependent care credit, personal exemptions, and many other tax benefits. An integrated tax system could be designed to impose, say, no tax on income below some poverty threshold; a 20 percent tax rate on income from that threshold up to, say, $50,000 of income; and a 30 percent tax rate on income over $50,000. Alternatively, such a system might be designed to impose no tax on income up to some poverty threshold and a 25 percent "flat" tax rate on income above that threshold. Either of these alternatives would be modestly progressive, but in a logical, easy-to-understand way (Bankman and Griffith 1987).

Moreover, an integrated tax system could easily accommodate a few refundable tax credits. For example, one could easily imagine an integrated tax system with $1,000 or $2,000 refundable personal tax credits, $2,000 per worker refundable earned income credits, and two tax rates: 20 percent of the first $50,000 of income and 30 percent on income in excess of $50,000.

Also, to avoid marriage penalties and bonuses, it would make sense for this comprehensive income tax system to have individual filing. Each worker could claim her own universal grant and her own worker credit and face the 20 percent rate before hitting the 30 percent maximum tax rate. Also, a comprehensive income tax system could be designed as a final withholding system. The amounts withheld from employers and other income sources would be the tax. Consequently, few taxpayers would ever need to file tax returns.

All in all, an integrated, comprehensive income tax system would be simpler and fairer than the current system, it would lower the tax rate on earned income, and it would rationalize the rate structure for all workers. As a result, it would promote greater economic justice and minimize work disincentives.

Corporate Tax Integration

Of note, the corporate income tax could also be folded into a comprehensive income tax system. Since people ultimately bear the burden of the corporate income tax, it is not necessary to tax corporations. We can instead tax their shareholders.

Indeed, over the years, many economists and politicians have called for integration of the individual income and corporate income tax systems.[71] Theoretically, this integration could be accomplished either by eliminating the corporate tax or by excluding dividends received from shareholder income. Either approach would eliminate the so-called "double tax" on corporate earnings that comes from taxing both corporate income and the dividends that corporations pay to their shareholders. In that regard, the Jobs Relief and Reconciliation Act of 2003 achieved a degree of partial integration by cutting the maximum tax rate imposed on dividends received by shareholders to just 15 percent.

Full corporate tax integration could be accomplished, for example, by repealing the corporate income tax and taxing the dividends received by shareholders at the ordinary progressive tax rates.[72] More specifically, we could repeal the corporate income tax and tax shareholders on their proportionate share of corporate earnings each year, whether those earnings were distributed in the form of dividends or retained as corporate investments.

An alternative way to achieve full corporate tax integration would be to tax all corporate income at a flat rate—say, 30 percent—and exclude 100 percent of dividends received by individual shareholders. Adjustments could be made for shareholders who are in tax brackets lower than 30 percent.

Presumably, individual income tax rates would need to be increased somewhat to make up for the loss of about $200 billion a year in corporate income tax revenues. For example, the integrated, comprehensive income tax system described above contemplated a top individual income tax rate of 30 percent. To accommodate full corporate tax integration, we might need to raise that top rate to 35 percent or lower the entry point for that top 30 percent bracket to $40,000.

A Comprehensive Earnings Tax Alternative

Another comprehensive tax reform alternative would be to integrate the income and payroll taxes into a single tax on *earned income*. In effect, there would be a single, higher-yield payroll tax instead of the current bifurcated tax system. Like the integrated, comprehensive income tax approach, this approach could also result in substantial simplification. After all, it takes only a handful of tax code sections to explain the Social Security wage and self-employment taxes, yet it takes hundreds of sections to explain the individual and corporate income taxes. Granted it would become more important to differentiate between earned income and investment income, but almost all the income tax rules that determine depreciation, capital gains, and the timing of investment income would disappear.

On the other hand, many would view an earnings tax as inequitable. Theoretically, a progressive rate structure could make an earnings tax progressive. In reality, however, many high-income investors would completely avoid paying any earnings tax, and that would not set well with low- and middle-income workers, nor would it comport with the view of economic justice developed in earlier chapters.

Also, because earned income is just one form of income, to raise the same amount of revenue, tax rates under an earnings tax would have to be higher than under an income tax. In that regard, personal income in the United States in 2005 was $10.2 trillion, but personal earnings that year were just $8.1 trillion (Council of Economic Advisers 2006, tables B-30 and B-28). Consequently, to raise the roughly $2.5 trillion that the federal government spent that year, the average tax rate of an earnings tax would have to be at least 31 percent, compared with an average income tax rate of just 25 percent (Council of Economic Advisers 2006, table B-82).[73] Needless to say, this author opposes high tax rates on earned income.

A Comprehensive Consumption Tax Alternative

Another comprehensive tax reform alternative would be to replace the current income and payroll tax systems with a comprehensive consumption tax. For a variety of reasons, a number of analysts have argued for moving to a consumption tax base instead of an income tax base.[74] In particular, many analysts believe that consumption taxes can encourage savings and investment and so promote growth. Moreover, consumption may actually be a better measure of well-being than income.[75] Consumption taxes come in a variety of forms.

A National Sales Tax

We could, for example, replace the current tax system with a national sales tax.[76] For example, a 20 percent national sales tax similar to state retail sales taxes could be imposed on all retail sales of goods and services.

In that regard, the staff of President George Bush's Advisory Panel on Federal Tax Reform recently modeled a broad-based national retail sales tax.[77] Unlike the typical state retail sales tax, the panel's proposal would tax sales of both goods and services. More specifically, all retail sales of goods and services to individuals would be taxed, except for educational services, expenditures abroad by U.S. residents, food produced and consumed on farms, and imputed rent on owner-occupied and farm housing. To raise as much money as the current income tax system, the national sales tax rate would have to be somewhere between 22 and 27 percent, depending upon compliance levels.[78] For example, if a microwave costs $100, expect to pay around $125 for it.

Of course, there are a number of problems with a national sales tax. First, some are concerned that it would apply to both goods and *services*. If a person gets a $10 haircut, that person will have to pay $12.50 (before the tip). But what about the doctor's bill? Will a patient have to pay $125 for a $100 check-up? Will a client have to pay $1,250 for $1,000 of legal services? Yes, if we want a national sales tax with a broad base. Otherwise, the national sales tax rate would have to be much higher. Indeed, if a national sales tax applied only to the typical U.S. state sales tax base (with exemptions for prescription drugs, food, clothing, and services), the revenue-neutral tax rate would have to be 64 to 87 percent!

Second, many are concerned that a national sales tax would crowd out state and local revenues. In Norman, Oklahoma, where this author lives, the sales tax is 8 percent (4.5 percent for the state and 3.5 percent for the city). That means a $10 item already costs $10.80. With a 25 percent national sales tax, every $10 item would cost $13.30 ($10.00 + $2.50 + $0.80). Compliance would clearly be a problem, as under-the-table sales would be a very attractive way to avoid the 33 percent cumulative sales tax rate. There would also be downward pressure on state and local sales tax rates and on the government services that they pay for. Sales of goods and service might also fall with these higher prices, even if the national sales tax replaced the income tax and left us with more money to spend.

Finally, sales taxes are regressive. That is, the burden falls more heavily on low-income families than on higher income families (the latter save a greater portion of their income). To be sure, a national sales tax could be made more progressive by giving rebates to low-income families, for example, to offset the amount of sales taxes due on a poverty-level income. With a large enough rebate (or "prebate" if paid ahead of time), a national sales tax could be roughly as progressive as the current income tax system—but the national sales tax rate would jump to between 34 and 49 percent.

We will probably never see a national sales tax. State and local politicians do not want the federal government to encroach on their traditional retail sales tax base, and doctors and lawyers will balk at having their services taxed.

A Value-Added Tax

Alternatively, we could replace all or a portion of the current tax system with some form of value-added tax (VAT). Under a value-added tax, a low-rate tax would be imposed on the value added at each stage of production, distribution, and retail sale of a given product.[79] Each firm would pay the tax on the value it added to the ultimate product, as measured by the difference between its costs and the sales price of its output.[80]

Would it make sense to replace the current tax system with a value-added tax? Opponents often argue that value-added taxes are regressive. With the right design, however, it is possible to design a progressive value-added tax. For example, a value-added tax can be made progressive by coupling it with rebates paid out in refundable tax credits (Seidman 2004). Modest rebates would protect low-income families from any value-added tax burden and reduce the burden on middle-income taxpayers.

Similarly, Yale Law School professor Michael Graetz recently proposed a two-tier system that would replace much of the tax system with a value-added tax (Graetz 1997, 2002; Field 2003). His proposal calls for a $100,000 per family exemption under the individual income tax together with a value-added tax of 14 or 15 percent. Professor Graetz believes that his proposal would eliminate the need for as many as 100 million individual income tax returns. Under his approach, only those relatively few families with incomes over $100,000 would have to file individual income tax returns.

A Personal Consumption Tax

Finally, we could replace the current tax system with some type of consumed income tax or personal consumption tax. Basically, under a personal consumption tax, each individual would add up all her wages, dividends, interest, gains, and other income; subtract her net savings; and pay tax on the balance. Pertinent here, it is worth considering whether it would make sense to replace the current income and payroll tax systems with a progressive personal consumption tax along the lines of the cash flow tax described in the U.S. Department of Treasury's *Blueprints for Tax Reform* (Andrews 1974; Bradford and the U.S. Treasury 1984; Engler 2003; Frank and Cook 1995; Graetz 1979; MacGuineas 2004; McCaffery 2002a, 2003; Pechman 1980; Shaviro 2004a).

Theoretically, an income tax is imposed on all income, whether that income is saved or consumed. A consumption tax is imposed only on that portion of income that is consumed and not on the portion of income that is saved. Dissavings (borrowings), however, must be included in a consumption tax base, while they are not taxed at all under an income tax.

The current federal income tax system is really a hybrid income-consumption tax system in which some investments are taxed on the income tax model and others are taxed on the consumption tax model (Goldberg 2003; Aaron, Galper, and Pechman 1988; McCaffery 1992). In general, wages, interest, dividends, and other forms of income are taxed when received, whether saved or not. On the other hand, pension benefits are taxed under the consumption tax model. For example, employer contributions to a pension plan are excluded from employee income; the earnings on those contributions are tax exempt; and employees are only taxed when their pension benefits are distributed at retirement.

Under a personal consumption tax, all forms of savings would be entitled to the tax-deferred status currently available for retirement savings. Basically, each individual would total her income from wages, dividends, interest, gains, and other sources; and subtract her net savings to get to taxable consumption. In short, all types of savings would be tax-favored.[81]

Like the income tax, a consumed income tax could be designed with a "flat" or progressive rate schedule. For example, Hoover Institution fellows Robert E. Hall and Alvin Rabushka have long been proponents of a flat personal consumption tax (Hall and Rabushka 1995).[82]

On the other hand, a number of analysts argue in favor of progressive personal consumption taxes. For example, University of Southern California Law Professor Edward J. McCaffery recommends that we replace most of the current tax system with a two-tiered progressive consumption tax system (McCaffery 2002a).[83] The first tier would consist of a 10 percent value-added tax or national sales tax on all sales of goods and services. The second tier would consist of a supplemental progressive consumption tax on taxpayers with consumed incomes over $80,000 a year. For example, the typical family of four with $20,000 of earned income would get a rebate of $2,000 to offset the value-added tax or national sales taxes it paid. Families with consumed incomes between $80,000 and $160,000 would pay a supplemental personal consumption tax equal to 10 percent of their consumption, and families with higher levels of consumed income would pay tax at rates going up to 40 percent on consumed income in excess of $1,000,000.

Alternatively, the late David F. Bradford proposed replacing the current system with what he called the "X tax" (Bradford 2005). The X tax consists of two parts: a flat-rate *business tax* paid by all businesses on all sales less all purchases from other businesses and less compensation paid to workers (including contributions to pension); and a progressive *compensation tax* on payments for work, including pensions. The rates for these two taxes would be set to meet both revenue and distributional objectives, and the final result could be as progressive as desired.

The Merits of Consumption Taxes

Supporters of consumption taxes usually argue that relative to income taxes, consumption taxes would encourage investment and so promote growth. Supporters also argue that consumption taxes hold the promise of collecting taxes from those who currently can evade personal taxes. For example, drug dealers are not known to properly report and pay their income taxes, but their purchases of cars and goods do get snared by sales taxes and could get snared by many other types of consumption taxes. Also, many types of consumption tax can avoid the complicated income tax rules needed to determine depreciation, capital gains, and the timing of investment income. Also of note, consumption taxes currently raise a much smaller proportion of revenue in the United States than they do in other industrialized countries. In 2002, for example, sales taxes and other consumption taxes raised 2.2 percent of GDP in the United States, compared with more than 7 percent for all other OECD countries (Gale and Stephens-Davidowitz 2005).

Opponents of consumption taxes usually object that consumption taxes tend to be more regressive than income taxes.[84] Of course, that is the reason to consider a progressive personal consumption tax.

Opponents also note that because a consumption tax base is theoretically smaller than an income tax base, tax rates would have to be higher under a consumption tax than under an income tax. While personal income in the United States in 2005 was $10.2 trillion, personal consumption expenditures that year totaled $8.7 trillion (Council of Economic Advisers 2006, table B-30). Consequently, to raise the roughly $2.5 trillion that the federal government spent that year, the average consumption tax rate would need to be at least 29 percent, compared with an average income tax rate of just 25 percent.[85]

In addition, opponents of consumption taxes are quick to point out that consumption taxes in the real world are every bit as complicated as the current federal income tax, and that a pure income tax would stack up pretty well against anybody's idea of a pure consumption tax. In that regard, for example, moving to a consumption tax base does not automatically simplify the tax system for low-income individuals. Just as an income tax can be either simple or complicated, a consumption tax can also be either simple or complicated. Simplifications such as flat rates, high exemptions, limited itemized deductions, and refundable tax credits would fit as well in an income tax as in a personal consumption tax.

Still, to the extent that the income tax could be replaced by a national sales tax or VAT that collects taxes from just 10 to 20 million producers and sellers, there would certainly be an opportunity to simplify the federal tax system for individual taxpayers, even though some new complexities would result from adding refundable personal tax credits or some other mechanism to help offset the impact of those taxes on low-income individuals.

Taxing Economic Resources

So far this chapter has focused on taxing individuals on their income, wages, or consumption. Each of these tax bases could offer a rough measure of people's ability to pay tax, but other important components of well-being should also be considered. In particular, should we tax individuals on their wealth or on their consumption of leisure?

Is There a Role for Taxing Wealth?

Wealth per se is not taxed by the federal tax system. Much of the income from wealth, however, is taxed under the income tax, and certain transfers of wealth are taxed by the estate, gift, and generation-skipping taxes. For example, interest, rents, dividends, and royalties are subjected to the income tax; estates of $2,000,000 or more (in 2006) may be subject to the federal estate tax; gifts of more than $12,000 (in 2006) may be subject to the gift tax; and certain generation-skipping transfers are also subject to tax.[86]

Over the years, many analysts have called for toughening the estate and gift taxes.[87] Alternatively, some analysts have suggested the adoption of an inheritance tax or an accessions tax as an alternative to the taxation of wealth transfers. An estate tax is based on the amount of property left to heirs by the deceased, while an inheritance tax is imposed on each heir by reference to the value of property received from a deceased. An accessions tax is an excise tax imposed on the transfer of property by gift or at death.[88] While any of these approaches to taxing the transfer of wealth could help equalize the distribution of resources, none of them directly measure a taxpayer's wealth on a regular basis as would seem appropriate under a tax system that tries to tax individuals based on their ability to pay.

An Annual Wealth Tax. Many analysts have suggested the adoption of a direct annual wealth tax,[89] and a number of European countries already have annual wealth taxes.[90] The typical European wealth tax is imposed on the value of assets less liabilities of an individual or family, but many assets are excluded from the tax base. High exemptions are provided to exclude taxpayers with few economic resources. The tax rates are graduated, but the maximum tax rates are 3 percent or less.

Wealth taxes can be powerful revenue raisers. For example, according to New York University economics professor Edward N. Wolff, even a very modest wealth tax system would have raised $45 billion in 1995 (1999, 41).[91] Wolff bases his estimate on a wealth tax system like the Swiss have, with marginal tax rates of 0.05 percent to 0.30 percent and an exclusion of about $50,000.

Moreover, because their burden falls heaviest on those with greater economic resources, wealth taxes might more accurately measure the ability to pay of taxpayers and so help achieve greater economic justice. After all, taxpayers with greater wealth have a greater ability to pay taxes. In that regard, the distribution of wealth is far more skewed than the distribution of income or consumption (see figure 2.4).[92] Consequently, taxing wealth could be a powerful tool for promoting greater economic justice.

On the other hand, wealth taxes inevitably raise numerous valuation questions. Also, opponents of wealth taxation have expressed the concern that they would impose further burdens on capital and so might reduce savings and investment.[93] There are also significant timing questions because people tend to accumulate wealth in their working years in order to support themselves in their retirement years. Moreover, there may also be constitutional problems with a direct annual federal wealth tax.[94]

Income plus Wealth. Another possible tax base would be income plus wealth. After all, the sum of one's income plus wealth is the total amount that a person can spend in a year (without borrowing). Thus, income-plus-wealth could be a respectable measure of one's control over economic resources and the ability to pay taxes. Moreover, according to one estimate, a flat 4 percent tax rate applied to an income-plus-wealth tax base would yield about as much revenue as the current income tax (Davies 1984, 889). Given our concerns about work disincentives, a tax rate that low would certainly be attractive, especially for low- and moderate-income workers with lots of earned income and relatively little wealth.

What about Taxing Leisure?

Leisure and the ability to work are other possible targets for federal taxes (Stark 2005; Shaviro 2000). According to the standard economic theory, an optimal tax system would tax all goods including leisure. Income and consumption taxes can reach all goods except leisure. Indeed, that is where much of the distortion and work disincentives of income and consumption taxes comes from.

Unfortunately, nobody has yet suggested a plausible approach for taxing leisure, and no new approach is offered here. To be sure, excise taxes on sporting events and other leisure activities could raise some revenue and make work relatively more attractive than those leisure activities, but there is no realistic way to tax leisure directly.

Designing a Work-Friendly Tax System

All in all, the federal tax system needs to raise about $2.5 trillion a year, and most of that will come from high-income individuals. The key to a work-friendly tax system is to have a system that promotes greater economic justice with a minimum of work disincentives.

Eventually, the federal government is likely to adopt a VAT system for a large portion of its revenue needs, while retaining some form of progressive income, consumption, or wealth tax on high-income individuals.[95] Such a system would collect all its value-added tax revenues from just 10 or 20 million producers and sellers, and it would collect additional revenues from progressive income, consumption, and/or wealth taxes imposed on just 20 or 30 million high-income families.

In the near term, however, it is more realistic to think about restructuring the existing tax system, rather than replacing whole portions of it with new and untried taxes. This approach follows that old maxim of tax design, "an old tax is a good tax."[96] This chapter has already sketched out how such a restructured tax system could work.

We could, for example, integrate the individual income tax, Social Security payroll tax, corporate income tax, and estate and gift taxes into a single, comprehensive income tax system. That integrated tax system could have $1,000 or $2,000 refundable personal tax credits and just two tax rates: 20 percent of the first $50,000 of income and 30 or 35 percent on income in excess of $50,000. To encourage work, that system could also have a $2,000 per worker refundable earned income credit (computed as 20 percent of the first $10,000 of earned income), and there would be no need to phase out either the personal tax credits or the worker credits.

To achieve a rate structure like this, the tax system could not afford to have many special deductions and credits. Virtually all those tax expenditures would have to be repealed, including the deductions for home mortgage interest, state and local taxes, and, perhaps, even charitable contributions. Moreover, gains should be taxed annually, and gifts and inheritances should be included in income.

Finally, joint returns should be replaced with a system of individual filing. Hardly any individuals would actually have to file tax returns, however, as final withholding could be achieved through withholding from employers and other income sources.

All in all, such a restructured tax system would be simpler to administer than the current system, and it would both minimize work disincentives and promote greater economic justice. Low- and moderate-income individuals would have every incentive to get out there and work, and even high-income individuals would face smaller work disincentives than under the current tax system. In short, this approach would make taxes work.

7

MAKING WELFARE WORK

Families need help bridging the gap between the incomes they earn in the labor market and the income they need to meet their basic needs. (Boushey et al. 2001)

Effective poverty reduction depends [on] both market forces and redistribution of economic resources. (Mishel et al. 2003)

Previous chapters showed that the market distribution of earnings and economic resources tends to underreward low-skilled workers and those who are unable to participate in the market system because of age or disability. This chapter recommends a variety of welfare reforms that would make work more rewarding for those who can work and make the distribution of economic resources fairer for all low-income Americans.

At the outset, this chapter puts the development of the welfare system into its historical context (Forman 1988; Ventry 2001). Next, this chapter identifies some of the major problems with the current welfare system. The chapter then suggests several relatively modest changes that could improve the current system. Beyond such incremental changes, this chapter considers more fundamental restructuring. Ultimately, it would make sense to integrate the tax and transfer systems into a single comprehensive system.

A Brief History of the Welfare System

It can be argued that the American government has always favored work. Even the New Deal antipoverty programs were largely designed as "wage-replacement" programs. Only those Americans who had a work history could qualify for benefits. For example, Social Security replaces the wages of workers who are "too old" to work, the unemployment compensation program replaces the wages of laid-off workers, and the Aid to Families with Dependent Children program was designed to replace the lost wages of a deceased or otherwise absent father.

From the Great Depression until the 1970s, however, the government's focus seemed to shift away from work and toward concerns about economic justice, in general, and the alleviation of poverty, in particular. The Social Security program and the welfare system both steadily expanded during this period. Moreover, with the publication of Michael Harrington's *The Other America* in 1962, Americans slowly came to realize that there was another America—an America that included poor whites in Appalachia, poor blacks in the South, and poor Native Americans living on reservations. Poverty increasingly came to be viewed as a social problem and as a social and governmental responsibility. Also in 1962, Milton Friedman proposed replacing the existing welfare system with a negative income tax.[1]

The War on Poverty

As concern about poverty in America grew, President Lyndon B. Johnson even went so far as to declare a "War on Poverty."[2] Medicare and many other "Great Society" programs were created during the Johnson administration. Also, in January 1968, President Johnson appointed a blue-ribbon Commission on Income Maintenance Programs to study the income needs of all Americans, to examine all existing government programs designed to meet those needs, and to make recommendations for constructive improvements (President's Commission on Income Maintenance 1969). The Commission concluded that the welfare system was badly in need of reform, and it recommended the adoption of what was essentially a federal negative income tax—cash payments to poor families because they are poor.[3]

President Richard M. Nixon also favored welfare reform. President Nixon outlined a plan to ensure an adequate income for all American families.[4] His plan, known as the Family Assistance Plan, was also essentially a negative income tax for families. In 1970, a modified version of the plan passed the House of Representatives but was rejected in conference with the Senate.[5]

The high point of the antipoverty movement came in 1972 when Democratic presidential candidate George S. McGovern proposed giving $1,000 universal grants to every American.[6] Under his proposal, every American would have been given $1,000 a year from the federal government; however, the grants would have been taxable income, and higher proposed income tax rates would have recovered all the benefits provided to those with moderate and high incomes. In response, President Nixon abandoned his family assistance plan proposal and soon thereafter defeated McGovern resoundingly in the presidential race.

From Welfare to Work

Since the early 1970s, the government has been much less concerned with economic justice and much more concerned with promoting work incentives for low-income Americans. The goal has been to combat poverty by getting low-income Americans into the workforce and off traditional welfare. In particular, various tax and welfare reforms have combined to increase work incentives for low-skilled Americans. The two most important reforms have been the creation and expansion of the earned income tax credit and the welfare reforms of the 1990s.

The Earned Income Tax Credit

Congress created the earned income tax credit in 1975 and has expanded it many times since then. In the Tax Reduction Act of 1975 (Public Law 94-12), the earned income tax credit was a small, one-time "work bonus" for low-income taxpayers with children. Intended primarily to offset the Social Security taxes paid by low-income workers with children, the credit was a refundable tax credit equal to 10 percent of a taxpayer's annual earned income up to $4,000. The $400 maximum credit was reduced $1 for each $10 of income above $4,000, and was completely phased out at an income level of $8,000.

Various tax laws extended the earned income tax credit through 1978, and it was finally made a permanent part of the Internal Revenue Code by the Revenue Act of 1978 (Public Law 95-600). The Revenue Act of 1978 also extended the credit to 10 percent of the first $5,000 of earned income (a maximum credit of $500), and raised the income range over which the credit phased out.

President Ronald Reagan saw the credit as an important tool for rewarding low-income workers with children, and during his presidency the credit was expanded significantly. The Deficit Reduction Act of 1984 (Public Law 98-369) increased the rate of the credit to 11 percent of the first $5,000 of earned income, thus raising the maximum credit to $550 a year; that Act also raised the income range over which the credit phased out. In addition, the Tax Reform Act of 1986 (Public Law 99-514) increased the credit to 14 percent of the first $5,714 of earned income (thus raising the maximum credit to $800), further raised the income phaseout levels, and indexed the credit for inflation.

The earned income credit was further expanded in 1990 and especially in 1993.[7] The federal government now spends more on the earned income credit than it does on any other federal transfer program. In 2006, for example, a low-income working family with two or more children is entitled to a refundable earned income tax credit of up to $4,536 (IRS 2005c). In addition, the earned income credit reaches more families than TANF or food stamps (Burman and Kobes 2003).

Along the same lines, Congress created a new child tax credit in 1997, and expanded it in 2001 and 2003.[8] Families can now claim a $1,000 per child tax credit for children under the age of 17, and the credit is partially refundable for those taxpayers that have earnings in excess of $11,300 a year in 2006 (IRS 2005c).

Welfare Reform

So far, the high point of the welfare-to-work movement came with the passage of the bipartisan welfare reform act of 1996—the Personal Responsibility and Work Opportunity Reconciliation Act of 1996.[9] The welfare reform act of 1996 replaced the traditional Aid to Families with Dependent Children anti-poverty program with a pro-work system of Temporary Assistance for Needy Families. With relatively few exceptions, recipients must work after two years on assistance, and families that have received assistance for five years are ineligible for additional cash assistance.

From 1982 through 1996, the AFDC program had a 100 percent effective tax rate. The typical welfare recipient lost a dollar of benefits for each additional dollar she earned, and families typically lost Medicaid and housing benefits if they earned "too much."

High cumulative effective tax rates on earned income were the norm. One study of AFDC recipients in California in 1993 found that AFDC recipients going from no work to part-time work faced an average effective tax rate of 52.9 percent, those going from part-time to full-time work faced an average rate of 75.8 percent, and those going from no work to full-time work faced an average rate of 64.3 percent (Hoynes 1997, 109–10).

It was as if the War on Poverty had become a "War on Work."[10] Not surprisingly, hardly any welfare recipients even tried to work. One study of 1988–93 Census data found that only about 20 percent of single mothers who were on AFDC continuously during the year had any labor earnings (Blank, Card, and Robins 1999, 6–7).[11]

States began experimenting with welfare-to-work reforms in the 1980s, and that experimentation increased after the passage of the Family Support Act of 1988 (Public Law 100-485). In 1992, presidential candidate Bill Clinton promised to "end welfare as we know it,"[12] and after his election, the pace of welfare reform increased dramatically.[13]

The 1996 welfare reform act was the culmination of the welfare-to-work reform movement. The 1996 welfare reform act replaced AFDC with time-limited and work-related TANF. Under TANF, each state receives a block grant, and each designs its own welfare program. The states have great freedom in designing their programs to meet the work-related goals of the welfare reform act of 1996, and most states have now eliminated the 100 percent earnings "tax" that was built into the AFDC benefit structure.

The welfare reform act also increased federal child care assistance for low- and moderate-income families. In addition, Congress has greatly expanded the health care benefits available to low-income working families. For example, Medicaid was expanded to cover the children of former welfare recipients, and, in 1997, Congress created the State Children's Health Insurance Program (SCHIP) to provide health care coverage to working families whose income exceeds the Medicaid eligibility thresholds (U.S. House Committee 2004, section 15).

The Net Effect

All in all, the tax and welfare reforms in recent decades have helped "make work pay" for welfare recipients. Since 1984, the government supports for low-income working families—from such programs as the earned income credit, the child tax credit, expanded Medicaid coverage, SCHIP, and child care assistance—have increased almost tenfold (Sawhill 1999).[14] In 1999, for example, low- and moderate-income families received almost $52 billion, compared with just $6 billion (in 1999 dollars) if these welfare-to-work changes had not been enacted (Sawhill and Haskins 2002).

TANF work requirements and restrictions on the number of years that families can receive benefits have further increased the incentives for beneficiaries to find work, and the focus of welfare spending shifted away from monthly cash payments and toward spending on work support services. Writing in 2001, David Ellwood noted

> average benefits received by those with zero earnings have fallen precipitously in recent years, moving from an average of over $7,000 to less than $5,000. By contrast, aid for those in the

$7,500–$15,000 category after falling in the early '80s during Reagan-era cuts have grown dramatically in recent years from roughly $1,500 in the mid-'80s to $3,500 today. (2001, 32)[15]

Needless to say, the financial incentives resulting from these changes made it very attractive for families to enter the workforce, even at low wage levels. For example, a typical single mother who moved from being a nonworking welfare recipient to working full-time at the minimum wage in 1986 saw her net income increase by $2,005 (24 percent); making that transition in 1997, however, would net her a $7,129 (95 percent) increase (Ellwood 2000a).[16]

The net effect of these welfare-to-work changes has been to dramatically increase the number of low-income families that are working and decrease the number of low-income families on welfare. The percentage of welfare recipients that was working tripled between 1992 and 1997, and the number of people receiving welfare dropped by almost half from 1993 until 1999 (Council of Economic Advisers 1999c).[17] According to the Council of Economic Advisers, "The fall in welfare caseloads has been unprecedented, widespread, and continuous, and employment of welfare recipients has increased" (1999c, 1).

Even women with less than a high school diploma have found work: their employment rates jumped from 33 percent to 53 percent between 1994 and 2001 (Sawhill and Haskins 2002).[18] And the number of welfare recipients has continued to drop. In June 2003, for example, about 5 million people (2 million families) received welfare benefits.[19] To a large extent, the welfare-to-work movement has been a huge success.[20]

PROBLEMS WITH THE CURRENT SYSTEM

Compared with the welfare system of the 1970s and 1980s, the current system provides a number of incentives for low-income families to choose work over welfare. Unfortunately, the current system still has significant work disincentives and disincentives for improving work skills, can still discourage marriage, is unnecessarily complicated, and fails to bring all low-income Americans out of poverty. These four problems are discussed in turn.

The Current System Can Discourage Work

While the current system of financial rewards and welfare work requirements has been fairly effective in encouraging families to enter the workforce, there are still significant work disincentives for some workers (Moffitt 2002). Moreover, the rapid phaseouts in government-provided benefits, together with income and payroll taxes, leave most workers with little incentive to improve their skills.

For example, according to a 1998 study by researchers at the Urban Institute, a mother with two children could bring her family's income to almost 120 percent of the poverty level by working full-time at the minimum wage and supplementing her earnings with tax credits, food stamps, and other public assistance (Coe et al. 1998).[21] Her income would increase 51 percent just by going from no work to working 20 hours a week at the $5.15 minimum wage. Unfortunately, however, because she would lose benefits as her income further increased, the rewards from additional work or from a wage increase would be quite small. For example, if she moved from part-time work (20 hours a week) to full-time work (35 hours a week) at minimum wage—a 75 percent increase her work effort—her family's income would grow just 20 percent. Similarly, if she moved from full-time work at the minimum wage to full-time work at $9 an hour—a 75 percent increase in hourly earnings—her family's income would grow just 16 percent. In short, the typical welfare recipient will receive a large financial reward for going to work at least part-time, but there is relatively little incentive for her to work full-time at the minimum wage or to develop skills that would lead to a higher-paying job.[22]

The problem is that to keep costs manageable, most transfer programs phase out benefits as family income increases. In the pertinent income range, these phaseouts often combine with income and payroll taxes to subject recipients to extraordinarily high effective tax rates as they work more hours or at higher wage rates. Indeed, moderate-income workers can face high effective tax rates as a result of the combination of federal income tax rates; within the federal income tax, the phasing out of the earned income tax credit; federal payroll taxes; state and local income, sales, excise, and property taxes; the phasing out of TANF benefits; the phasing out of food stamps; the phasing out of federal housing subsidies; and the loss of Medicaid benefits. Indeed, at some points between $10,000 and $25,000 of income, the effective marginal tax rate can reach or even exceed 100 percent (Shaviro 1997, 1999).

The resulting high effective marginal tax rates discourage low-skilled Americans from working or improving their skills.[23] The complicated work incentive effects of transfer programs, taxes, and phaseouts are perhaps best understood by considering the wealth of recent research relating to the earned income tax credit.[24] Because the credit is only available to taxpayers with earned income, the standard economic theory predicts that the credit will encourage taxpayers without earnings to enter the workforce, and there is a good deal of evidence that the credit encourages labor force participation among single parents. For example, in 2006, a nonworking mother with two children can collect up to $4,536 if she goes to work.

On the other hand, the standard economic theory also predicts that the credit will discourage work effort by those in the phaseout range of the credit. For example, in 2006, a married couple with two children will see its earned income tax credit fall by 21.06 percent of earnings in excess of $16,810 (see figure 4.2).[25] Not surprisingly, the earned income tax credit tends to encourage married mothers to stay home. One study found that women in the phaseout range of the earned income credit were 5 percent less likely to work, and if they were already working, the phaseout of the credit led them to work as much as 20 percent fewer hours a year (Eissa and Hoynes 1999).[26]

Another problem is that the current system has financial incentives that discourage individuals with disabilities from working. More specifically, the current system provides individuals with financial incentives to exaggerate their disabilities so they can draw disability benefits rather than work; the loss of cash and health care benefits upon reentering the workforce also acts as a work disincentive.[27] According to the Census Bureau, 49.7 million Americans had some type of long-lasting condition or disability in 2000—19.3 percent of the 257.2 million people age 5 and older in the civilian noninstitutionalized population (Waldrop and Stern 2003). Another 33.2 million Americans age 16 to 64 were classified as disabled that year (18.6 percent), and 21.3 million of those had a condition that affected their ability to work at a job or business (11.9 percent of the 178.7 million people this age).

Pertinent here, relatively few working-age disabled individuals are in the workforce. Only 52 percent of adults age 21 through 64 years with disabilities were employed in 1994–95, compared with 82 percent of those without disabilities (HHS 2000, vol. 1, 6-18). Those with a nonsevere disability had an employment rate of 77 percent, but those with a severe disability had a rate of just 26 percent. Moreover, in the past few decades there has been a "stunning" decline in the employment rates of individuals with disabilities (Burkhauser and Stapleton 2003).[28]

The Current System Can Discourage Marriage

The interaction of benefit programs, the tax system, and marriage is complex. Because marriage results in a pooling of income by a husband and wife, marriage often results in "marriage penalties" and "bonuses" that can affect marriage incentives and family well-being.[29]

There is little need overall to worry about the occasional marriage bonus for low-income welfare recipients. Marriage is often a way to improve income and well-being. We should be concerned, however, about marriage penalties. Promoting marriage—or, at least, not discouraging it—could help reduce poverty and promote greater economic justice.[30]

On this topic, chapter 6 showed rather considerable marriage penalties and bonuses associated with the earned income tax credit.[31] All in all, the impact of the earned income tax credit marriage penalties and bonuses alone seems fairly small (Dickert-Conlin and Houser 2002). But it is worth remembering that the earned income tax credit is not the only part of the tax and transfer system that is affected by marriage. TANF benefits, Medicaid, food stamps, child care assistance, and housing benefits all phase out as family income increases. Together, the combination of phaseouts in these transfer programs and the income and payroll tax rates are cumulative. The net effect is that many low-income parents face confiscatory effective tax rates on the increased earnings associated with marriage.[32]

The Current System Is Too Complicated

A third major problem with the current welfare system is that it is unnecessarily complicated. Dozens of transfer programs distribute cash, food, health care, and other benefits to low-income Americans. In addition, numerous benefits are administered through the federal income tax system. The House Committee on Ways and Means recently identified 85 different programs providing everything from cash aid to energy assistance (U.S. House Committee 2004, K-10–K-12).[33] In fact, there are so many different and overlapping programs that "an unduplicated count of welfare beneficiaries is not available" (K-2).[34]

This welfare "system" developed with almost no regard for coordination among these various tax and welfare programs. There is a dizzying array of programs, and each has its own eligibility criteria and administrative system. The application processes for all these different benefits can be quite burdensome, particularly for applicants who are not native English speakers (Holcomb et al. 2003; Sawhill and Haskins 2002; GAO 2001a). Not surprisingly, many low-income Americans never receive the benefits to which they are entitled. For example, less than 60 percent of those eligible for food stamps actually receive them (U.S. Department of Agriculture 2003).

In sum, the current system of transfer and tax programs for low-income workers is unnecessarily complicated, inequitable, and expensive to administer.

The Current System Has Not Solved the Problem of Poverty

In 2004, almost 12.7 percent of Americans (40 million people) lived in poverty, up from 11.1 percent (23 million people) in 1973 (DeNavas-

Walt et al. 2005, tables 3 and B1). Clearly, the current system has not solved the problem of poverty (Hoynes et al. 2006; Handler and Hasenfeld 1997). Market earnings alone often do not provide enough income for families to escape poverty, let alone economic hardship. These days, about one-quarter of workers simply do not earn an hourly wage that would be sufficient to support a family of four at the poverty level.[35] Education and training opportunities for low-skilled workers can help, but these opportunities alone are not likely to move many families out of poverty (Boushey 2002, 9). That is why work supports—such as the earned income tax credit, child care assistance, and health care coverage—are so important.[36]

It is also worth noting that a significant portion of welfare recipients are hard to employ. According to one estimate, somewhere between one-third and one-half of welfare recipients seem not to be employable (Louray 1998, 48). Table 7.1 shows the prevalence of selected characteristics among welfare recipients that can act as barriers to employment.[37] Faced with such barriers, this hard-to-employ group is likely to experience significant hardships from the recent welfare reforms, especially from such provisions as the TANF work requirements and the five-year limit on benefits (Danziger et al. 2002). In particular, because the safety net is no longer designed to catch everyone, there is a danger that more families and children will fall into extreme poverty (defined as income below 50 percent of the federal poverty level). Some increase in extreme poverty has already been documented (Zedlewski et al. 2001, 2003).

MODEST CHANGES THAT COULD IMPROVE THE WELFARE SYSTEM

The recent expansions of the earned income tax credit and other supports for low-income workers have gone a long way toward reducing

Table 7.1. Prevalence of Selected Characteristics among TANF Recipients Based on Selected Studies

Characteristic	Estimated range of TANF recipients with characteristic (percent)
Health problems or disabilities	20–40
Lack of high school diploma	30–45
Current domestic violence	10–30
Lack of job skills	20–30
Substance abuse	3–12
English as a second language	7–13
Multiple barriers	44–64

Source: GAO (2001b), 16.

poverty among working families. According to Isabel Sawhill, "we are within striking distance of eliminating poverty through work" (1999, 30). But there is still much more to be done.

If we are serious about making the welfare system work, we should make sure that all low-income families have the financial incentive to work. In particular, many analysts favor increasing the work supports for low-income families that can work.[38] Chapter 6 already discussed mechanisms to ensure that we stop imposing taxes on taxpayers with incomes below the poverty level. Discussed below are some additional recommendations for helping low-income workers. Specifically, the government should increase earnings subsidies for low income workers, provide more money to help support the children of low-income parents, provide more child care assistance for low-income parents, and make disability programs work friendly. In connection with these reforms, the government should reduce or eliminate the marriage penalties faced by low-income workers, better coordinate the many overlapping welfare programs, and update the federal measure of poverty. Also, chapter 10 offers recommendations to provide health care coverage for all low income workers and their families, and chapter 11 offers recommendations to improve training opportunities for welfare recipients and other low-skilled workers and retraining opportunities for workers who lose their jobs.

Increase Earnings Subsidies for Low-Income Workers

In the absence of generous government assistance, most low-skilled workers would remain poor even if they worked full-time year-round. Their skill levels are often low, and, even with work or training programs, they are unlikely to improve their skills enough to earn their way out of poverty.[39] As already noted, a worker would have to work full-time year-round and make $7.98 an hour to bring a family of three above the poverty level in 2006, and it would take $9.62 an hour to bring a family of four over the poverty level.

As we saw in chapter 4, earnings subsidies can encourage work effort and increase the demand for low-skilled workers, and they are relatively inexpensive to administer. The federal government currently provides earned income tax credits to workers and welfare-to-work tax credits to employers, and many states use their TANF funds to subsidize wages directly or through an employer.[40] Expanding these earnings subsidy programs would increase the economic rewards for low-skilled workers and so promote work effort and reduce economic inequality.

Expand the Earned Income Credit and Extend It to More Workers

In particular, it would make sense to expand the earned income credit so it provides greater economic benefits to more low-skilled workers. A larger credit would provide even greater rewards for work and have an even greater antipoverty impact. For example, for married couples with two or more children, we could increase the credit by raising the credit's phase-in percentage from 40 percent to, say, 50 percent of earnings and/or by raising the phase-in floor from $11,340 to, say, $15,000. One study found that the efficiency cost of increasing progressivity by expanding the earned income tax credit can be quite low, perhaps less than 20 cents per dollar transferred from upper-income groups to lower-income groups (Triest 1996a).

We should also think about restructuring the credit so it is more directly tied to work and work effort, and less dependent on the presence of dependent children. The current credit reflects a nearly universal consensus that the government should do something to help working poor *families*. Credits of up to $4,536 are available for families with two or more children in 2006, but no more than $412 is available to childless individuals and couples.

Given the extraordinarily unequal distribution of earned income, however, the government should provide earnings subsidies for nearly all low-income workers. On this topic, chapter 6 suggested replacing the current earned income credit with a universal $2,000 per worker earned income credit (computed as 20 percent of the first $10,000 of earned income) and a universal $1,000 per child tax credit. Under that approach, a low-income parent with two children would still be entitled to $4,000 in refundable tax credits,[41] and low-skilled workers without children would be entitled to up to $2,000 in credits. With more than 2 million, mostly low-skilled, Americans in jail or prison, we should be interested in an approach like this that would encourage individuals to choose work over crime.[42]

Reduce the Work Disincentives in the Phaseout Range of the Credit

Whatever earned income credit amounts and coverage policymakers decide on, it is important to keep marginal effective tax rates low, either by eliminating the phaseout or extending the phaseout range. There is a good deal of evidence that the earned income tax credit encourages low-skilled individuals in the phase-in range of the credit to enter the workforce or work more hours (Hoynes 1997; Browning 1995). On the other hand, the higher effective tax rates imposed on workers in the phaseout range of the earned income credit may cause certain individuals to reduce their work effort. Given that some 60 percent of current earned income tax credit recipients (9 million families in 1994) are in the phaseout range (GAO 1996, 2–3), lowering or eliminating the earned income tax credit phaseouts should help encourage recipients to work and to improve their skills. For example, it could make sense to raise the current credit's phaseout floor to $20,000 and/or lower the current credit's phaseout percentage from 21.06 percent to 10 percent.

Minimize Marriage Penalties

Also, whatever earned income credit amounts we decide on, it is important to minimize marriage penalties. As we saw in chapter 6, the current earned income tax credit can result in some pretty hefty marriage penalties. It would make sense to restructure the earned income tax credit to minimize or eliminate such marriage penalties (Ellwood and Sawhill 2000; Cancian et al. 1999; Sawhill and Thomas 2001; CBO 1997, chapter 5).

One approach would be to extend the phaseout range for married couples, for example, by raising the starting point of the phaseout by $10,000 or by lowering the phaseout rate from 21.06 percent to 10 percent.[43] Another approach would be to allow each spouse to claim the credit based on individual earnings rather than family earnings. As we saw in chapter 6, marriage penalties would disappear in a system of $2,000 per worker earned income tax credits.

Convert the Earned Income Credit into a Wage Subsidy

Finally, it is worth considering whether the earned income tax credit could be restructured to make it even more effective in encouraging work effort and skill improvement. The short answer is yes. Unfortunately, tying the credit more closely to work effort could make it more difficult to administer.

In general, the more directly a reward is tied to the desired behavior, the more effective the reward is. Pertinent here, wage subsidies are more closely tied to work effort than are earnings subsidies, let alone income subsidies. Basically, a wage subsidy is a transfer program that provides cash benefits to supplement the low market wages paid to low-skilled employees.[44] Typically, the amount of the wage subsidy an individual receives is based on the number of hours she works and her hourly wage level.[45]

Three policy variables define a simple wage subsidy system. First, the *subsidy rate* is the rate at which wages are subsidized. Second, the *target wage level* is the wage level at which a worker will no longer receive a subsidy. Third, the *benefit-reduction rate* determines the amount of reduction in the subsidy as the pre-transfer wage level increases beyond a certain wage.[46] For example, consider a simple wage subsidy of up to $2.50 an hour that phases out at a 50 percent benefit-reduction rate as wages go over the target wage of $5.00 an hour. As shown in table 7.2, the largest subsidy is provided to people earning the target wage, and lower subsidies are provided to those earning either higher or lower wages.

Under a wage subsidy system, a wage earner's net annual (post-transfer) income will equal the sum of her pre-transfer earned income and the total wage subsidy she receives for the year.[47] Figure 7.1 translates the data in table 7.2 into an annualized subsidy based on the assumption that each worker works full-time (2,000 hours a year).[48] At the target wage of $5.00 an hour under the wage subsidy system set forth in table 7.2, that worker would earn $10,000 a year and be entitled to a total annual subsidy of $5,000 a year ($2.50 an hour × 2,000 hours), for a total post-transfer income of $15,000 a year. At higher or lower annual wages, the subsidy is smaller.[49]

In general, wage subsidies are more effective motivators than earnings subsidies or income subsidies (Allgood 2003; Bartik 2001; Forman 1988). For example, consider two unmarried workers in 2006, each with $6,000 of earned income. One works 1,000 hours at $6.00 an hour, while the other works just 100 hours at $60 an hour. Under a $1.00 an hour wage subsidy, the first worker would get $1,000 subsidy, and the second worker would get a subsidy of $100. Under an earnings subsidy, however, they would both get the same benefit. Each could claim an earned income tax credit of $412 in 2006. In effect, a simple wage subsidy can be targeted to help low-skilled workers, while a simple earnings subsidy cannot. On the other hand, earnings subsidies do not require employees (and employers) to report the number of hours worked.

Table 7.2. A Simple Wage Subsidy System (dollars)

Pre-transfer hourly wage	Wage subsidy amount	Net hourly wage
0	0	0
1.00	0.50	1.50
2.00	1.00	3.00
3.00	1.50	4.50
4.00	2.00	6.00
5.00	2.50	7.50
6.00	2.00	8.00
7.00	1.50	8.50
8.00	1.00	9.00
9.00	0.50	9.50
10.00	0	10.00

Source: Author's calculations.

Figure 7.1. A Simple Wage Subsidy

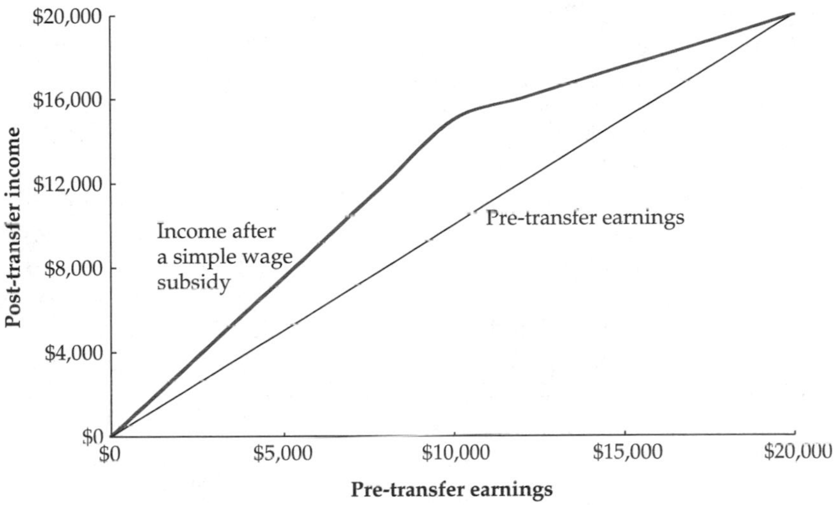

Source: Author's calculations.

Other Wage Subsidies

Other approaches to subsidizing the wages of employees are also worth considering, including earnings supplements and employer wage subsidies.

Earnings Supplements. Several welfare programs already use specially designed earnings supplements. Milwaukee's New Hope Project provided a monthly earnings supplement to low-income parents who worked at least 30 hours a week (Michalopoulous 2005; Fishman 2004). The supplement was designed to bring the family's income up to the poverty level. New Hope also provided health insurance and child care assistance to parents that worked full-time. Benefits were available for up to three years.

Similarly, Canada has recently experimented with a financial incentive program that rewards welfare recipients, but only if they work full-time.[50] Under Canada's Self-Sufficiency Project (SSP), long-term welfare recipients who take and keep full-time jobs are eligible to receive a substantial earnings supplement for up to three years. The program has been quite successful, with full-time employment among the program group more than double that of the control group—29 percent versus 14 percent.[51]

These kinds of employment subsidies are a very effective way to increase the employment, earnings, and income of low-income parents in the short term.[52] Unfortunately, the effects diminish over time, both because of the time limits and because the programs did not lead to lasting wage gains. Of note, however, combining earnings supplements with employment services designed to help recipients find and keep jobs did produce larger and longer-lasting effects on employment and earnings.

Employer Subsidies. Another approach for subsidizing wages would be to provide subsidies to employers instead of, or in addition to, the subsidies provided to employees.

The federal government currently provides modest work opportunity and welfare-to-work tax credits to the employers of certain low-income workers, and it could make sense to expand these credits.[53] Before these, the federal government experimented with the New Jobs Tax Credit and the Targeted Jobs Tax Credit (Blassi 1995).

Many analysts believe that a more universal program of wage subsidies for employers could increase both the demand for low-skilled workers and the incomes of those workers.[54] For example, Edmund S. Phelps recommends wage subsidies paid to the employers of low-wage workers (1997). Under his approach, all qualifying jobs that have a net hourly cost to the employer of $4 an hour would be eligible for a wage subsidy of, say, $3 an hour. For jobs that cost the employer more than $4 an hour, the subsidy would gradually decline to zero once wage cost an hour reached, say, $12 an hour. Phelps believes that these employer subsidies would pass through to workers and thereby increase employment opportunities among low-wage workers and decrease economic inequality.

Finally, it is worth noting that cash subsidies to supplement the wages or earnings of low-income workers are just one form of employment subsidy. As more fully described below, child care subsidies and health care subsidies can also help raise the real compensation of workers (Ellwood et al. 2000, 118).

Help Support the Children of Low-Income Parents

Low-income families with children need income assistance.[55] A plethora of overlapping social welfare programs and tax benefits now provide some assistance to some families. It would make sense to integrate those benefits into a single, universal benefit for children. Chapter 6 suggested two very straightforward approaches that would provide income assistance to families with children. One approach would be to provide fully refundable child tax credits of, say, $1,000, or even $2,000 per child a year. Alternatively, we might replace the current system of personal exemptions, standard deductions, child tax credits, and the child-related component of the earned income credit with a new system of $1,000 or even $2,000 per *person* refundable tax credits or universal grants. Either way, individuals would claim these credits annually by filing a tax return, but an advance payment mechanism could be designed so low-income individuals could have their payments directly deposited into their bank accounts.

Another way that governments currently help support children is by enforcing child support orders that collect money from noncustodial parents and transfer it to the custodial parents. In principle, this system makes sense in that it requires parents to be responsible for supporting their own children. In practice, however, the child support system "is a regressive system that places a greater burden on noncustodial parents at the bottom of the economic ladder than those further up" (Edelman, Holzer, and Offner 2006, 100). Some 3.5 million noncustodial parents are poor, and 1 million of them pay child support (with one-quarter of those paying out more than half their income in child support).

A big part of the problem is that the noncustodial parent's obligation to pay child support operates like an additional tax on earnings that can virtually eliminate the incentive to work in the legitimate economy. Marginal tax rates due to child support alone run around 20 to 35 percent; together with federal and state taxes and food stamp benefit-reductions, effective marginal tax rates on low-income noncustodial parents can become confiscatory (Edelman et al. 2006, 25–26, 101). For example, a typical noncustodial parent making court-ordered child support payments in Maryland would face an effective marginal tax rate of 83.3 percent as his earned income went from $5,000 to $15,000.[56] Similarly, the effective marginal tax rate is 85.8 percent in California and 65.2 percent in Texas. Not surprisingly, the recent toughening of child support enforcement has depressed employment and labor force activity among young black men.

A universal $2,000 per worker earned income tax credit could help offset the work disincentives inherent in the current child support system, and universal child tax credits or universal grants would reduce the need for as much child support. Similarly, it could make sense for the federal government to impose limits on the child support orders imposed on low-wage noncustodial parents. Peter Edelman and colleagues (2006) recently suggested making sure that noncustodial parents earning less than $5,000 pay no more than 5 percent of income in child support, those earning between $5,000 and $10,000 pay no more than 15 percent (for one child) or 25 percent (for two children), and those earning between $10,000 and $20,000 pay no more than 23 percent (for one child) or 35 percent (for two children). Also, as more than 40 percent of low-income noncustodial parents are high school dropouts, it would make sense to target this group for education, training, and work supports that would improve their earnings capacity.

Provide Child Care Assistance for Low-Income Parents

Child care is one of the most significant work-related expenses. In 2004, 70.4 percent of women with children were in the workforce, including 52.9 percent of mothers with children under the age of 1 (BLS 2005d).[57] While many have relatives to help care for their children, millions more must pay for child care. In the winter of 2002, more than 9 million mothers with at least one child under the age of 15 made cash payments for child care averaging $92 a week (Johnson 2005, table 6).

Helping families pay for child care can help parents stay employed. One study found that single mothers with young children are 40 percent more likely to still be employed after two years if they receive child care assistance, and former welfare recipients with children are 60 percent more likely to still be employed if they receive assistance (Boushey 2002, 2, 9–13).

Child care costs can present particular challenges for low-income parents trying to work. According to one recent study, costs range from $204 to $222 a month for working poor families that pay for care (Hartmann and Spalter-Roth 2004, 57).[58] Unfortunately, the cost of child care is often beyond the means of low-income workers. For poor families with preschool-age children in child care, child care costs consumed an average of 28.5 percent of their incomes in 1999 (U.S. House Committee 2004, 9-16).[59] Yet in the winter of 2002, government agencies provided assistance to just 12.5 percent of families with income below the poverty level and to just 10.2 percent of families with income between 100 and 200 percent of the poverty level (Johnson 2005, table 7).[60]

All in all, the government should provide more child care assistance to low-income families.[61] Funding for child care needs to be increased, and the availability of subsidies needs to be expanded. These results could be achieved by expanding such existing transfer programs as the Child Care and Development Block Grant program. In addition, as more fully explained in chapter 11, it would make sense to expand the Head Start program so all low-income children can participate, and to make full-day public kindergarten and prekindergarten universally available throughout the United States.

We should also expand the child and dependent care tax credit and make it refundable (Burman, Maag, and Rohaly 2005; Danziger and Reed 1999; Forman 1989; Maag 2003).[62] Under current law, a taxpayer can claim a credit of up to 30 percent of employment-related child care expenses—up to $1,050 a year for one child under the age of 13 or up to $2,100 a year for two or more qualifying children. Because the credit is not refundable, however, it is of little or no value to low-income families with children. To help low-income families with their child care expenses, the applicable percentages of employment-related child care expenses should be increased so the credit reimburses low-income families for 50 percent, or even 80 percent, of their child care expenses, up to, say, $4,000 a child.[63]

However it is accomplished, providing greater child care assistance could significantly increase parental work and work effort. One recent study found large increases in the labor force participation of married mothers with young children after Quebec moved to a nearly universal, heavily subsidized child care system in the late 1990s (Baker, Gruber, and Milligan 2005). In response to the new child care subsidies, the employment of Quebecois married women with children 0 to 4 years old, relative to the rest of Canada, rose 7.7 percentage points (14.5 percent of baseline participation), and average weeks of work rose by 3.5 percent (13 percent of baseline).[64] Generous child care subsidies should lead to even larger labor supply increases for single mothers as they often cannot afford to work unless they receive adequate child care assistance.

Reduce or Eliminate Marriage Penalties

We have seen how easy it is for marriage penalties to develop in tax systems and transfer programs. In that regard, Professor Edward J. McCaffery argues, "it's inexcusable that there should be marriage penalties among the poor, the very income class that is most fragile in any event" (2002b, 21).

The key to avoiding marriage penalties is to base taxes and transfers on individuals rather than on couples. That is why chapter 6 recommended individual filing rather than joint returns for married couples and recommended restructuring the earned income tax credit so it is based on the earnings of individual workers rather than on family earnings.

When it comes to such other benefits as TANF and medical assistance, however, it is probably much harder to get away from using the family unit as the basis for determining eligibility for benefits. Still, if benefits are paid out as individual or child benefits instead of family benefits, marriage penalties would be reduced. For example, shifting money from family-based TANF to refundable child tax credits or universal grants would reduce marriage penalties: while TANF benefits can easily fall if a single parent marries, refundable child tax credits and universal grants need not.

All in all, government transfer programs need to be sensitive to the impact of marriage on the overall benefit package available to low-income individuals. At the very least, it would be appropriate to coordinate the phaseouts of those benefits in order to minimize marriage penalties.

Better Coordinate and Consolidate Welfare Programs

The government also needs to better coordinate and consolidate its many disparate and overlapping welfare programs. We simply do not need 85 different income-tested programs and dozens of different universal benefit programs and tax benefits. One of our principal goals should be to combine, or at least integrate, these many different programs (Forman 1993a; Weisbach and Nussim 2003).

Admittedly, there are tremendous obstacles to achieving coordination, let alone integration, among current social welfare programs and tax provisions. At present, the sheer number of agencies, organizations, and congressional committees involved in administering and overseeing the social welfare system makes even simple coordination efforts difficult. At best, improving coordination within the current social welfare system is a time-consuming process. Moreover, there are few rewards for such efforts: the benefits of successful coordination may be realized in the future or by some other agency or committee.

Synchronization and integration efforts seem likely to fare even worse. Most such efforts require both executive branch leadership and congressional action, and "the goal of simplicity has been singularly without appeal to the framers of our tax and welfare laws" (Aaron 1982, 214). Instead, protecting one's turf and power and catering to organized special interests often seems more important than improving the delivery of services to constituents. In short, politics will generally work against coordination, synchronization, and integration efforts, and such efforts, at times, seem almost quixotic.

Nevertheless, in the short term, it should be possible to achieve some modicum of program integration at the state level, given that states have a good deal of flexibility in designing their welfare programs. For example, states should be able to develop a single application process to cover as many different welfare benefits as possible (Sawhill and Haskins 2002).

In the long term, policymakers should be able to identify overlapping programs and work to achieve better coordination among them.[65] Eventually, however, we should develop a more comprehensive approach to welfare reform.

Update the Official Federal Measure of Poverty

The official measure of poverty in the United States is the Census Bureau's poverty income thresholds.[66] The very similar U.S. Department of Health and Human Services' poverty income guidelines are used to determine eligibility for various benefits, from food stamps to the school lunch program (HHS 2006). In 2006, the poverty income guidelines are $9,800 for an individual, $13,200 for a for a family of two, $16,600 for a family of three, $20,000 for a family of four, and so on for larger families.

Developed in the 1960s as a provisional measure of poverty, the original poverty income thresholds were based on three times the family unit's cost for the U.S. Department of Agriculture's "economy food plan," and there have been only relatively minor changes in the way that the thresholds have been calculated since then (Fisher 1992). Each year, the Census Bureau and the Department of Health and Human Services update their respective poverty levels for inflation as measured by the consumer price index.

Much has changed since the 1960s, and the official measure of poverty has come under increasing criticism.[67] Many analysts believe that the measure is out of date and may result in a significant understatement of the actual amount of poverty. For example, today food costs are less than one-fifth of the typical family budget, suggesting that poverty levels should be set higher.[68]

One of the most important questions is whether poverty levels should be defined "absolutely" or "relatively." The current levels are defined in absolute terms (based on three times the standard food plan). Yet most cross-national studies of poverty instead define the poverty levels in relative terms—typically, as one-half of national median income (Smeeding 2006b).[69] In that regard, the official U.S. poverty threshold for a family of four was around 48 percent of median family income in 1960, but it fell to just 29.2 percent in 2004 (Smeeding 2006b).

While a better definition of poverty will not, per se, reduce the amount of economic inequality or otherwise make welfare work, a better definition of poverty would help us better keep track of how well (or badly) we are doing. That would enable policymakers to make improvements and keep on target. Accordingly, it would make sense to revise our decades-old poverty income levels.

Make Disability Programs Work Friendly

Changes in federal disability policies are also needed. Historically, government policies assumed that individuals with disabilities could not work and so were in need of cash benefits and medical assistance. Recent legislation such as the Americans with Disabilities Act of 1990 (Public Law 90-202) and the Ticket to Work and Work Incentives Improvement Act of 1999 (Public Law 106-170) reflect a more pro-work approach. Nevertheless, employment for individuals with disabilities is quite low, and further initiatives are needed to encourage the disabled to work, to increase their work skills, and to break down institutional and physical barriers to their employment. In particular, adults with severe disabilities face a "staggering nonemployment rate hovering around 70 percent" (Presidential Task Force 1998).[70] Similarly, in 2002, just 13.8 percent of Social Security disability insurance beneficiaries were working along with just 6.1 percent of disabled SSI beneficiaries (SSA 2004b, 133–34).

No doubt, these low employment rates occur for several reasons. For example, many adults with severe disabilities simply cannot work, and others face employment discrimination. Pertinent here, however, are the many disincentives for work in the existing disability programs. In particular, there are financial incentives to draw disability benefits rather than work, and the loss of cash and health care benefits upon reentering the workforce acts as a work disincentive (Social Security Advisory Board 2003).

Government policies should instead encourage adults with disabilities to work. To start, the federal government's *Healthy People 2010* project recently set as one of its goals the elimination of disparities in employment rates between working-age adults with and without disabilities (HHS 2000, vol. 1, 6–18).[71] Richard V. Burkhauser and David C. Stapleton also recently offered a three-part strategy to help increase work effort by the disabled. They suggest that the government provide more assistance to help persons with disabilities find jobs and keep them, offer financial incentives that will make work pay, and expect persons with disabilities to "do whatever they reasonably can to support themselves" (2003, 5–6).

The federal government tries to be a model employer for persons with disabilities. Nevertheless, while almost 20 percent of Americans age 21–64 are disabled, only about 7 percent of executive branch employees are persons with disabilities—120,525 out of almost 1.8 million employees in 2000 (Presidential Task Force 2002, 3).

After a brief explanation of disability benefits, the remainder of this section offers some recommendations about how the federal government could restructure its disability benefit programs to provide financial incentives to encourage disabled individuals to work and to provide health care assistance to them.

Disability Benefits

Social Security's Disability Insurance program and Supplemental Security Income are the principal cash benefit programs for disabled Americans (U.S. House Committee 2004, sections 1 and 3). To qualify for benefits under these programs, individuals must be unable to engage in any "substantial gainful activity" by reason of a medically determined physical or mental impairment that is expected to last for at least 12 months or result in death. Generally, the individual must be unable to do any kind of work that exists in the national economy, considering their age, education, and work experience. Workers can lose benefits if they regain the ability to work (Social Security Advisory Board 2003).

Workers build protection under the DI program by working in employment that is covered by the Social Security system and paying the applicable payroll taxes, and benefits are related to the earnings history of the insured worker. An initial five-month waiting period is required before disability benefits are paid. DI benefits are based on the same formula as retirement benefits, and additional benefits are available for disabled workers with families. Unlike retirement benefits, however, DI benefits are not reduced for fewer years of computation, nor are they actuarially reduced for receipt before the Social Security full retirement age. In December 2004, there were 6.2 million disabled beneficiaries in the DI program, and the average payment to a disabled worker was $894 a month (SSA 2006b, tables 7.A1 and 7.A5). Recipients of DI also qualify for Medicare after a two-year wait (U.S. House Committee 2004, 2-5). Also of note, the Ticket to Work and Work Incentives Improvement Act provides a 45-month period for DI beneficiaries to test their ability to work without losing their entitlement to DI and Medicare benefits (U.S. House Committee 2004, 1-30).

Similarly, SSI is a means-tested, federally administered program that provides monthly cash benefits to certain low-income elderly, disabled, or blind Americans. Benefits are indexed for inflation; in 2006, the maximum federal benefit for an individual is $603 a month, and the maximum federal benefit for a couple is $904 a month (SSA 2005c). Some states also provide small additional supplements (U.S. House Committee 2004, 3-27–3-35). In December 2004, about 5.8 million blind or disabled Americans received SSI benefits (SSA 2006b, tables 7.A1 and 7.A5).

Restructure the Programs that Provide Cash Benefits for Disabled Individuals

Some analysts believe that the benefits provided by Disability Insurance are too generous and so provide perverse incentives for workers to try to get benefits, whether or not they are truly disabled (Ippolito 1997, 196). Benefits as a percentage of pre-award earnings are relatively high—up to 80 percent for disability recipients with families and up to 55 percent for single recipients. Consequently, the DI program encourages individuals who can qualify for benefits to leave the workforce in exchange for relatively generous benefits. At its worst, the program seems to "reward those who are disinclined to work for exaggerating their physical or mental shortcomings so they can leave the workforce early" (Ippolito 1997, 197–98).

To reduce these perverse incentives, it could make sense to tie benefits more directly to contributions.[72] For example, it could make sense to eliminate family benefits. If that leaves family income below the poverty level, then universal grants or other parts of the welfare system could provide needed assistance.

Also, it might make sense to lower the benefit amounts available to workers who claim disability benefits. Under the current system, an individual who qualifies for disability benefits at age 55 is entitled to a higher benefit than a worker who waits until full retirement age to claim a retirement benefit, and the temptation to try to get higher benefits by exaggerating one's disability can be great. To combat this abuse, it might make sense to actuarially reduce those disability benefits to reflect their early receipt.[73]

Another approach would be to break away from the all-or-nothing benefit structure of the DI and SSI benefit programs and move to a "continuum of disability" approach like that used in other programs.[74] For example, in December 2005, veteran disability compensation benefits varied from $112 to $2,393 a month, depending upon the extent of the disability.[75]

All in all, restructuring the financial incentives associated with the DI and SSI programs could increase the work efforts of disabled individuals and reduce the DI and SSI beneficiary rolls (Hoynes and Moffitt 1999).[76]

Improve Access to Health Care

Inadequate access to health care is another barrier that keeps Americans with disabilities from living independently and entering or rejoining the workforce. In particular, people with disabilities who enter or re-enter the workforce face the potential loss of health benefits under Medicare and Medicaid (Wiener 2003). The Ticket to Work and Work Incentives Improvement Act increased Medicaid options and state resources for people with disabilities and allowed more Americans receiving DI to retain Medicare coverage when they return to work. Nevertheless, further legislation is needed to ensure that persons with disabilities who work have adequate health care coverage. Government policies should also be aimed at preventive care and otherwise promoting good health among the disabled.[77]

A MORE COMPREHENSIVE APPROACH TO WELFARE REFORM

Ultimately, what is needed is a comprehensive approach to social welfare reform. After all, we do not need 85 separate federal programs to provide income-tested benefits. In that regard, many analysts have concluded that social welfare reform should proceed by combining as many social welfare transfer programs and tax provisions as possible into a single rational and unified program.[78] For example, we might combine most social welfare transfer programs and tax expenditures into an integrated system of refundable tax credits and a few related programs.[79] Such an integrated social welfare program would achieve significant administrative savings by eliminating much of the complexity and duplication in the current social welfare system.

An integrated system would also have a rational effective marginal rate structure. In that regard, New York University law professor Daniel Shaviro recently concluded:

> the income phaseouts of such programs as AFDC, Food Stamps, and the EITC are irrational—mainly because they create unduly high marginal tax rates in low-income brackets, although secondarily because they cause marginal rates to bounce up and down for no apparent reason. (1997, 409)

Perhaps more important, an integrated social welfare system could help ensure that low-income families would get the benefits they need. Under the current system, coverage and participation rates vary dramatically from program to program. For example, as noted in chapter 4, the Food Stamp Program typically covers around 20 million recipients; TANF, 5 million; SSI, 6 million; the earned income tax credit, 22 million; and Medicaid, 40 million. Participation rates also vary dramatically. For example, while 86 percent of eligible households with children claimed the earned income tax credit in 1999, food stamp participation that year was 62 percent of those eligible, and TANF participation was just 52 percent (Burman and Kobes 2003).[80]

The bottom line is that we are unlikely to achieve any meaningful reform of the welfare system by simply "trying to patch up each one of the innumerable and uncountable programs" (Browning 1977, 209). Instead, we need to think about ways to combine these programs into a more comprehensive welfare system.

A Negative Income Tax

Of course, the classic way to integrate social welfare transfer programs and tax expenditures is to replace them all with a negative income tax.

Milton Friedman and many others suggested this approach back in the early 1960s (Friedman 1962).[81] Replacing most welfare programs with a negative income tax would decrease administrative costs and increase participation.

To be sure, benefit costs would unequivocally increase if a generous negative income tax were adopted. For example, a generous negative income tax would surely cover more beneficiaries and have greater total benefit costs than the current social welfare system. For that matter, even a modest negative income tax system could have greater total benefit costs than the current system, depending upon the number and amount of benefits provided to additional beneficiaries.

Perhaps more troubling, many of the additional beneficiaries brought in by a negative income tax would be people that the public generally expects to work, whereas any offsetting benefit-reductions would likely be faced by those most in need of public assistance. For all its faults, the current categorical system at least tries to differentiate between those who are expected to work (able-bodied individuals) and those who are not (the elderly, the disabled, children, and, perhaps, mothers with small children). This distinction between those who are expected to work and those who are not is an important one, rooted in basic American values toward labor force participation (Gueron 1990). Worse still, as we saw in chapter 4, a generous negative income tax could discourage work by able-bodied individuals. The current categorical system at least tries to restrict generous means-tested welfare benefits to those who are not expected to work and thereby concentrates the adverse work incentives on the population least likely to be affected by them (Burtless 1990, 65).

With all these problems, it is hardly surprising that negative income taxes have not been given serious political consideration for years. According to economist Gary Burtless, "it is safe to say that the negative income tax has had only one major constituency—economists" (1990, 64).

A System of Universal Grants and Earnings Subsidies

Alternatively, it could make sense to replace most welfare programs with a system of universal grants and earnings subsidies.[82] As more fully explained in chapter 6, universal grants would reduce work effort, but the reduction in work effort would be much less than under a negative-income-tax system. That is because a negative income tax would subject workers to a high benefit-reduction rate, but a universal grant would not need to be phased out. Moreover, if we combined universal grants with earnings subsidies and child care assistance, it should be possible to have a system that actually increases work effort by low-income individuals.

This country has been trying for years to avoid the costs of a universal grant by restricting most transfer payments to individuals who are not expected to work.[83] Unfortunately, the current categorical social welfare system has run into the formidable problems of inequity, inefficiency, complexity, and high administrative expense. Universal grants could help avoid these problems.[84]

First, universal grants would be inherently fair in that they would be universally available. Second, universal grants would be efficient. In particular, working would not subject individuals to the high cumulative tax rates of current means-tested programs, and the relatively low-level universal grants proposed here would leave individuals with virtually every incentive to work to supplement their incomes. Third, universal grants would be simple to understand and distribute. Finally, universal grants would result in tremendous administrative savings as they would not require means-testing, and they would replace numerous overlapping and duplicative programs.

The general idea is to replace as many welfare programs as possible with a system of universal grants. These universal grants could replace the current personal exemptions, standard deductions, and many other child and family tax benefits. For example, there would be no revenue losses associated with replacing personal exemptions, standard deductions, and the other child and family tax benefits with a system of $1,680 per person universal grants, if we also got rid of most other deductions and credits (Forman et al. 2005).

Cashing out means-tested and non-means-tested transfer programs would provide additional revenue that could be used for even larger universal grants. For example, these universal grants could replace all or a portion of TANF, food stamps, SSI, energy assistance, and housing assistance; they could even replace all or a portion of the transfer components in such social insurance programs as Social Security, unemployment compensation, and workers' compensation, as well as the benefits for veterans, Native Americans, and other special groups. The money generated as a result of administrative savings from integrating these tax expenditures and social welfare programs could also be used for financing.

A Simple, Integrated Tax and Transfer System. Such universal grants could form the basis for a basic safety net for all Americans. For example, imagine a simple integrated tax and transfer system with $2,000 per person refundable tax credits, $2,000 per worker refundable earned income credits (computed as 20 percent of the first $10,000 of earned income), and two tax rates: 20 percent of the first $50,000 of income and 35 percent on income above $50,000. Assume further that there is no phaseout of either the personal tax credits or the worker credits. To keep tax rates this low, the system would not have many other credits or deductions.

Table 7.3 shows how such an integrated tax and transfer system would work for single parents making from $0 to $200,000 with two children, and figure 7.2 illustrates how this system would affect those families' post-tax, post-transfer incomes. For example, a single parent earning $10,000 a year would be entitled to three $2,000 universal grants and a $2,000 worker credit. She would owe $2,000 in taxes on her $10,000 of pre-transfer earnings, and that would leave her with a $16,000 disposable income after taxes and transfers.

An Initial Step: Cashing Out Food Stamps. As an initial step toward an integrated tax and transfer system, it would make sense to cash out the Food Stamp Program (Forman 1993b; Weisbach and Nussim 2003; Lerman and Wiseman 2002). In 2005, the Food Stamp Program served almost 26 million Americans at a cost to the federal government of about $31 billion, and the average monthly food stamp benefit was about $93 a person.[85]

Unfortunately, the Food Stamp Program is beset with all three major problems of the welfare system—complexity, inequity, and high administrative costs. First, the Food Stamp Program is extraordinarily complicated. Like most welfare programs, the Food Stamp Program has arcane eligibility criteria and baffling administrative procedures.[86]

Second, the Food Stamp Program is inequitable. For example, in 2003, only 54 percent of those eligible for food stamps actually received them (U.S. Department of Agriculture 2005, 9).

Table 7.3. How an Integrated Tax and Transfer System Would Affect a Single Parent with Two Children ($2,000 Universal Grants, $2,000 per Worker Credits, and 20 and 35 Percent Tax Rates) (dollars)

Pre-transfer earnings	Plus universal grants	Plus worker credit	Less tax imposed	After-tax income
0	6,000	0	0	6,000
5,000	6,000	1,000	1,000	11,000
10,000	6,000	2,000	2,000	16,000
20,000	6,000	2,000	4,000	24,000
30,000	6,000	2,000	6,000	32,000
40,000	6,000	2,000	8,000	40,000
50,000	6,000	2,000	10,000	48,000
100,000	6,000	2,000	27,500	80,500
150,000	6,000	2,000	45,000	113,000
200,000	6,000	2,000	62,500	145,500

Source: Author's calculations.

Figure 7.2. How an Integrated Tax and Transfer System Would Affect a Single Parent with Two Children ($2,000 Universal Grants, $2,000 per Worker Credits, and 20 and 35 Percent Tax Rates)

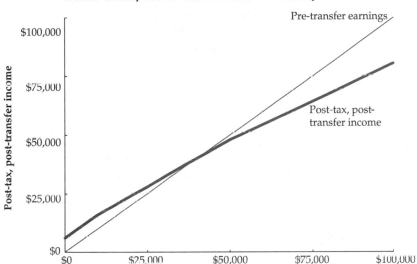

Source: Author's calculations.

Third, the Food Stamp Program has high administrative costs. In fiscal year 2005, some $28.5 billion in food stamps were distributed, and the combination of federal and state administrative expenses came to $2.4 billion, about 8 percent of total expenditures.[87] In sharp contrast, the Social Security system's administrative costs are less than 1 percent of total expenditures (Board of Trustees 2006, 5). Food stamps are simply more expensive to distribute than cash benefits.[88]

Tinkering with the Food Stamp Program will not solve these problems. Instead, we should repeal the program and use its $31 billion-a-year appropriation to help pay for universal grants. This "cashing out" of the Food Stamp Program would make the welfare system simpler, fairer, and less expensive to administer.

Additional Steps. Next, we should integrate as many other transfer programs as is possible into a single, comprehensive tax and transfer system. For example, we should take the money that we currently spent on housing assistance for low-income families and use it for universal grants rather than for rental subsidies and mortgage interest subsidies. Table 4.4 showed how much the federal government currently spends on these and most other transfer programs.

To be sure, it would take more than just universal grants and worker credits to solve the problem of poverty in America. We would need to provide additional benefits to individuals who are not able to work. For example, many elderly and disabled individuals would need additional cash benefits. The additional benefits that these recipients need could continue to come in the form of SSI benefits, or they could be distributed through additional refundable tax credits.

To the extent possible, it would make sense to have the relevant determinations of employability and need made by a single agency at the local level. For example, caseworkers could classify beneficiaries into a variety of employability categories and subcategories and develop a coherent program of cash benefits for them. Employability categories could include the elderly; the totally disabled; the partially disabled; single parents with young children; and the unemployed.

Finally, an effective welfare system would also need to provide other services to beneficiaries. Health care coverage, education, training, job search and placement, counseling, and child support collection are but a few that come to mind. To the extent possible, however, many of these services could also be provided at the local level through a single social welfare agency.

All in all, a comprehensive system of universal grants, earnings subsidies, and other work supports would help make the welfare system work.

8

MAKING SOCIAL SECURITY WORK

The great innovation of the twentieth century was the democratization of retirement and the substitution of broad-based retirement systems for the historical pattern of work and poverty in the elderly working population coupled with retirement only for the well-off. (Dilley 2004, 250)

Early retirement may seem like a worthy individual goal, but it is a socially expensive one, and, as far as public pensions are concerned, quite unsustainable. (Leibfritz 2002)

Social Security is the largest social welfare program in the United States. In 2004, for example, Social Security's Old-Age and Survivors Insurance program alone collected some $473 billion in payroll taxes and distributed more than $415 billion in benefits to elderly Americans and their dependents (SSA 2006b, table 4.A1). These Social Security benefits are incredibly important for the population age 65 and older. In 2002, Social Security provided all the income for 22 percent of elderly households and more than half the income for another 44 percent of elderly households (SSA 2004a, 4).[1] Social Security has been especially successful in reducing the level of poverty among the elderly. With Social Security, only 9 percent of beneficiaries in 2000 were poor; without it, 48 percent would have been poor (SSA 2002, 9).[2]

Three aspects of Social Security benefits are critical. First, benefits are paid in the form of an annuity that lasts the rest of a retiree's life; second, benefits are adjusted for inflation so the real benefits do not decline as the retiree grows older. As a result, Social Security benefits are designed to provide real benefits as long as the retiree lives. Third, additional spousal and dependent benefits help support the retiree's family during life and even after the death of the retiree.

Unfortunately, however, many features of the current Social Security system tend to discourage individuals from working just when the system should encourage them to stay in the workforce so they can accumulate additional economic resources to support themselves over ever-longer lives and ever-longer retirements.

The current Social Security system discourages work in two principal ways. First, because the system redistributes economic resources from certain workers to other workers and their families, it sometimes acts like a tax and other times acts like a welfare program. Such taxes and transfers inevitably influence individual decisions about work and retirement; as it turns out, the net taxes and the net transfers both tend to discourage work effort. Second, particular features of how Social Security benefits are financed, accrue, and are paid out tend to compound these work disincentives.

This chapter explains how the Social Security system should be redesigned to make it more work friendly.[3] More specifically, this chapter considers how Social Security should be structured to encourage work and counter the trend toward early retirement. After a brief overview of the current Social Security system, this chapter explains the need for reform. Finally, this chapter offers various recommendations about how to restructure the current system in order to increase work incentives and reduce work disincentives.

OVERVIEW OF THE SOCIAL SECURITY SYSTEM

The current Social Security system includes two programs that provide monthly cash benefits to workers and their families. The Old-Age and Survivors Insurance program provides monthly cash benefits to retired workers and their dependents and to survivors of insured workers, and the Disability Insurance program provides monthly cash benefits for disabled workers under full retirement age and their dependents.[4] A worker builds protection under these programs by working in employment covered by Social Security and paying the applicable payroll taxes. At present, about 96 percent of workers are working in covered employment (U.S. House Committee 2004, 1-4). At retirement, disability, or death, monthly Social Security benefits are paid to insured workers and to their eligible dependents and survivors.

The Old-Age and Survivors Insurance program is by far the larger of these two programs, and it is usually what people mean when they talk about Social Security. In 2004, OASI paid more than $415 billion in benefits to almost 40 million retired workers and their families, and the average monthly benefit paid to a retired worker was about $955 (SSA 2006b, tables 4.A1 and 5.A1). Consequently, for the remainder of this chapter, "Social Security retirement taxes" will refer to OASI taxes, and "Social Security retirement benefits" will refer to OASI benefits.

In addition, a separate Supplemental Security Income program provides monthly cash benefits to certain low-income elderly, disabled, or blind Americans (U.S. House Committee 2004, section 3). In December 2004, about 1.2 million elderly Americans received SSI benefits from the federal government, and the average monthly benefit was about $357 (SSA 2006b, tables 7.A1 and 7.A5).

Social Security Taxes

As more fully explained in chapter 4, Social Security benefits are financed primarily through payroll taxes imposed on individuals working in employment or self-employment that is covered by the Social Security system. For 2006, employees and employers each pay a Social Security retirement tax of 5.3 percent on up to $94,200 of wages, for a combined OASI rate of 10.6 percent—the lion's share of the total 15.3 percent collected for OASI, DI, and Medicare (SSA 2005c). Self-employed workers pay an equivalent OASI tax of 10.6 percent on up to $94,200 of net earnings. Of note, however, the earned income tax credit in the individual income tax system offsets a large portion of the Social Security payroll taxes paid by low-income workers.

Additional revenue for the Social Security system comes from the income taxation of as much as 85 percent of a beneficiary's Social Security benefits. The actual amount to be included is determined by applying a complicated two-tier formula. Basically, single taxpayers with incomes over $25,000 and married couples with incomes over $32,000 must include as much as half their Social Security benefits in income, and single taxpayers with incomes over $34,000 and married couples with incomes over $44,000 must include as much as 85 percent of their Social Security benefits in income. For 2003, an estimated 13.2 million OASI and DI beneficiaries paid tax on at least some of their benefits (39 percent of all beneficiaries), and the federal government collected about $19.5 billion in taxes from those beneficiaries (U.S. House Committee 2004, table 1-25).

Social Security Benefits

Social Security benefits are for workers and also for the families and survivors of workers.

Worker Benefits

Workers over the age of 62 generally are entitled to Social Security retirement benefits if they have worked in covered employment for at least 10 years, or 40 "quarters" (42 U.S.C. §§ 402, 414(a)(2); U.S. House Committee 2004, 1-14). Benefits are based on a measure of the worker's earnings history in covered employment known as the average indexed monthly earnings (AIME). The AIME measures the worker's career-average monthly earnings in covered employment. The AIME considers only covered earnings up to the maximum applicable annual earnings cap. For example, no more than $94,200 of 2006 earnings could count toward a Social Security retirement benefit.[5]

The starting point for determining the worker's AIME is to determine how much the worker earned each year through age 60. Once those "benefit computation years" and covered earnings for those years have been identified, the worker's earnings are indexed for wage inflation, using the year the worker turns 60 to index the earnings of prior years. This indexing ensures that the same relative value is given to wages no matter when they are earned and makes earnings early in the worker's career comparable to earnings in later years.[6] Earnings in and after age 60 are not indexed but can enter into the benefit computation formula.

The highest 35 years of earnings are then selected, and the other years are dropped out. The AIME is then computed as the average earnings for the remaining 35 years. More specifically, the sum of the indexed earnings in the worker's highest 35 years is divided by the 420 months in that 35-year computation period.

The AIME is then linked by a formula to the monthly retirement benefit payable to the worker at full retirement age, a benefit known as the "primary insurance amount" (PIA). For a worker turning 62 in 2006, the PIA equals 90 percent of the first $656 of the worker's AIME, plus 32 percent of the AIME over $656 and through $3,955 (if any), plus 15 percent of the AIME over $3,955 (if any), as shown in figure 8.1.[7]

Historically, "full retirement age" was age 65, but it is gradually increasing to age 67 for workers born after 1959 (reaching age 62 in or after 2022 and reaching 67 in or after 2027).[8] For workers born in 1941 and turning 65 in 2006, full retirement age is 65 and eight months.

The benefit formula is highly progressive—that is, it is designed to favor workers with relatively low lifetime earnings. For example, figure

Figure 8.1. Primary Insurance Amount Formula for Adults Turning Age 62 in 2006

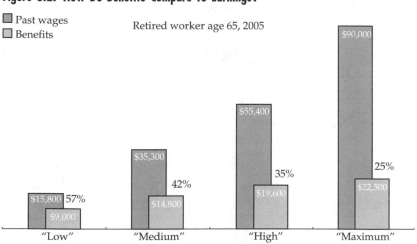

Source: Author's calculations.

8.2 shows how a worker's benefits compare to her final pre-retirement earnings. In addition, for workers with very low AIMEs, a special minimum benefit provides supplemental benefits to those who worked in covered employment for many years but had low earnings.

Figure 8.2. How Do Benefits Compare to Earnings?

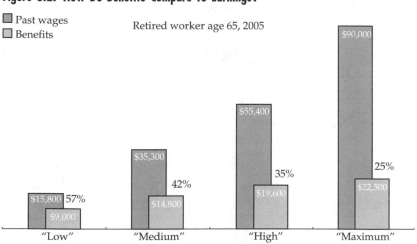

Source: National Academy of Social Insurance (2005a), 7.

A worker's benefits may be increased or decreased for several reasons. Most important, benefits are indexed each year for inflation as measured by the increase in the consumer price index. Also, workers who retire before their full retirement age have their benefits actuarially reduced. For example, a worker who turned 62 in 2006 and had yearly earnings throughout her career equal to the average wage would be entitled to a worker benefit starting at her full retirement age of 66 of $1,334 a month.[9] If she instead started to draw her benefit at age 62, that benefit would be actuarially reduced to about $1,000 a month. As the full retirement age slowly increases to age 67, the actuarial reduction from the full retirement age of 67 to the early retirement age of 62 will also increase up to 30 percent (U.S. House Committee 2004, table 1-20).

On the other hand, benefits payable to workers who choose to retire after their full retirement age are actuarially increased through the delayed retirement credit. The credit increases the monthly benefit paid to a worker who delays receipt of benefits until after full retirement age by 8 percent a year.

Finally, the "retirement earnings test" can reduce the benefits of individuals who have not yet reached full retirement age and who continue to work after starting to draw Social Security retirement benefits. In 2006, for example, workers who have not yet reached full retirement age lose $1 of benefits for every $2 of annual earnings over $12,480 (SSA 2005c).

Family Benefits

Spouses, dependents, and survivors of the worker may also receive additional monthly benefits.[10] These family benefits are also based on the worker's primary insurance amount. In particular, a retirement-age wife or husband of a retired worker is entitled to a monthly spousal benefit equal to 50 percent of the worker's PIA. Consequently, a retired worker and retirement-age spouse generally can claim a monthly benefit equal to 150 percent of what the retired worker alone could claim. For example, if a retired worker could claim a benefit equal to $1,000 a month, a retired couple could claim a benefit of $1,500 a month. In December 2004, almost 2.6 million spouses of retired workers were collecting benefits averaging $464 a month (SSA 2006b, table 5.A1.3).

In addition, a retirement-age widow or widower of the worker is entitled to a monthly surviving spouse benefit equal to 100 percent of the worker's PIA. For example, if a retired worker could claim a benefit of $1,000 a month (and a retired couple benefit of $1,500 a month), the surviving spouse could claim a benefit of $1,000 a month.

Like worker benefits, family benefits are subject to the retirement earnings test. In addition, under the "dual entitlement rule," when an individual can claim both a worker benefit and a benefit as a spouse, survivor, or dependent of another worker, only the larger of the two benefits is paid to the individual. For example, if our hypothetical spouse is entitled to a spousal benefit of $500 a month and is also entitled to her own worker benefit of $300 a month, she will get just $500 a month, not $800 a month.[11]

Supplemental Security Income

Supplemental Security Income is a means-tested, federally administered program that provides monthly cash benefits to certain low-income elderly, disabled, or blind Americans (U.S. House Committee 2004, section 3). Benefits are indexed for inflation; in 2006, the maximum federal benefit for an individual is $603 a month, and the maximum federal benefit for a married couple is $904 a month (SSA 2005c). Some states provide small additional supplements.[12] As currently structured, however, SSI benefits alone are insufficient to pull recipients out of poverty. For example, in 2006, the maximum federal benefit for an individual is just 74 percent of the poverty level, and the maximum federal benefit for couples is just 82 percent of the poverty level.[13] Unlike Social Security, the SSI program is financed by general revenues— individual income taxes, corporate income taxes, and other taxes.

The total number of recipients on SSI has increased from around 4 million in 1975 to nearly 7 million in December 2004 (U.S. House Committee 2004, 3-54; SSA 2006b, tables 7.A1 and 7.A3). Most are under age 65 and disabled. Still, in December 2004, more than 1.2 million elderly Americans received SSI benefits, and their average benefit was about $357 a month (SSA 2006b, tables 7.A1 and 7.A5). By long-standing administrative policy, public assistance payments such as SSI are not subject to income taxation (IRS 2004c, 26–27; U.S. House Committee 2004, 13-4–13-6, 13-42).[14]

Eligible recipients do not have to be totally without income to receive SSI benefits. Eligible recipients receive the maximum benefits if they have no other "countable" income in that particular month. If an individual or couple has "countable" income, however, there is a dollar-for-dollar reduction against the maximum payment. Just over half of SSI beneficiaries have another source of income, and the largest fraction of these received modest Social Security benefits (U.S. House Committee 2004, table 3-1). For example, in December 2004, 35.5 percent of SSI beneficiaries also received Social Security benefits, and the average amount of those Social Security benefits was almost $435 a month (SSA 2006b, table 7.D1). SSI beneficiaries are also typically covered by Medicaid (U.S. House Committee 2004, 3-15–3-16). Also of note, various special rules enable disabled SSI beneficiaries to test their ability to work without losing their entitlement to benefits (3-48–3-50).

THE NEED FOR REFORM

Social Security needs to be reformed for two principal reasons. First, Social Security is in financial trouble and will not be able to meet its future benefit commitments. Second, Social Security discourages people from working just when it should encourage them to stay in the workforce so they can accumulate additional economic resources to support themselves over longer lives and retirements.

The Social Security System Is Vastly Underfunded

Perhaps the most obvious problem with Social Security is that it is in financial trouble. The Social Security system operates largely on a pay-as-you-go basis.[15] Social Security benefits are primarily paid out of current-year Social Security payroll taxes, and the Social Security Trust Funds maintain only enough reserves to cover a few years of benefits. In 2004, the OASI Trust Fund received $473 billion in payroll tax contributions, paid out $415 billion in benefits, and had $1.5 trillion on hand at the close of the year (SSA 2006b, table 4.A1). Similarly, in 2004, the DI Trust Fund received $80 billion in payroll tax contributions, paid out $78 billion in benefits, and had almost $186 billion on hand at the close of the year (SSA 2006b, table 4.A2).

Although the trust funds are currently operating at a surplus, the long-term picture is bleak. Social Security retirement and disability benefits will exceed trust fund income starting around 2017, and the Social Security system will be unable to pay full benefits after about 2040 (Board of Trustees 2006, 2). The Trustees of the Social Security Trust Funds estimate that the deficit over the traditional 75-year projection period is about 2.02 percent of payroll, and the unfunded liability of the system is $4.6 trillion.[16] All in all, a funded system would be preferable, because insolvency would be less of a problem and because a funded system would require lower contribution levels (Modigliani and Muranlidhar 2004, 48).

The primary reason that Social Security is in financial trouble is that people are living longer and retiring earlier.[17] As a result, there are a lot of Social Security beneficiaries, and there are fewer workers to support them.[18] That is not necessarily bad. After all, it is great that we are living longer, and it is great that we can expect to have long and leisurely retirements. But it has led to the current financing problem. Social Security must either find new sources of revenue or cut benefits.

The Social Security System Discourages People from Working

A second major problem with the current Social Security system is that it tends to discourage people from working. Because the system redistributes economic resources from some workers to other workers and their families, it acts like a tax on some workers and like a welfare transfer program for other workers. Such taxes and transfers inevitably distort individual decisions about work and retirement; the net taxes and the net transfers both tend to discourage work effort. The way Social Security retirement benefits are financed, accrue, and are paid out tends to compound these work disincentives.

How Social Security Redistributes Economic Resources

A casual observer of Social Security would see that it is a pay-as-you go social welfare system that takes payroll taxes from current workers and redistributes those funds to current retirees and their families. On closer inspection, however, most experts agree that the best way to understand Social Security's distributional features is to evaluate the program's impact over the course of a worker's lifetime.[19] This lifetime perspective leads to a comparison between the Social Security taxes paid by a worker and the expected benefits.[20]

Numerous studies have made just such comparisons.[21] Those studies clearly show that the link between the Social Security taxes paid by a worker and her expected benefits is quite loose and can vary dramatically depending on such factors as family status, income, and age.

In fact, the current Social Security system is wildly redistributive, and not everyone gets his or her "money's worth." In effect, the system takes money from some workers and gives it to other workers and their families. The current Social Security system particularly favors early generations of retirees over later generations, workers with low lifetime earnings over workers with high lifetime earnings, married couples over single individuals, one-earner couples over two-earner couples, larger families over smaller families, and elderly retirees over elderly workers. These pairs are discussed in turn.

Early Generations versus Later Generations. Early generations of Social Security beneficiaries receive disproportionately greater benefits than their meager tax contributions might otherwise justify. Their rich rewards are the inevitable consequence of two facts: early participants paid relatively low taxes over relatively short coverage periods, yet they received relatively generous benefits over relatively long periods. Thus, Social Security favors early generations of beneficiaries over later generations.

This redistribution in favor of early generations of retirees can be most easily understood by considering the very first Social Security beneficiary, Ida May Fuller of Ludlow, Vermont (DeWitt 1996).[22] Miss Fuller was a legal secretary who retired in November 1939. She started collecting benefits in January 1940 at age 65 and eventually lived to be 100 years old, dying in 1975. Miss Fuller worked for just three years under the Social Security retirement program. The accumulated payroll taxes on her salary during those three years totaled $24.75. Her initial monthly check was $22.54. During her lifetime she collected $22,888.92 in Social Security benefits.

Another way to see how various generations have fared under the Social Security system is to compare their "internal rates of return" on their respective Social Security payroll tax contributions. Internal rates of return are estimates of the real annual yield that would be earned by various groups of workers if their payroll tax contributions were invested to fund the future benefits of those workers and their dependents. Table 8.1 shows recent estimates of the internal rates of return for various groups of workers, based on the contributions and benefits scheduled in present law (Nichols, Clingman, and Wade 2005, 6).[23] Pertinent here, the rate of return for workers retiring in 1985 (born in 1920) is higher than the rates of return for later generations. For example, the rate of return for a single male worker with low lifetime earnings who retired in 1985 was 4.35 percent, versus 2.87 percent for a low-earning man who retires in 2008.

Fortunately, the Social Security system is now mature, with most workers in covered employment or self-employment throughout their careers. Additionally, the Social Security tax rate and tax base have both been increased. Accordingly, studies project that by the time the baby boomers retire (starting around 2010), the value of the Social Security benefits they will receive should roughly equal the value of the Social Security taxes they paid.[24] Generations retiring before 2010 will continue to receive more favorable treatment, but the size of these intergenerational transfers will diminish over time.

Low Earners versus High Earners. Because of the progressive formula used to compute Social Security benefits, workers with low earnings over their careers tend to receive disproportionately greater benefits than workers with high earnings. In that regard, the net losses for middle- and high-wage workers can be especially large. The net loss for a high-wage married couple, for example, can be as much as $200,000 (Joint Economic Committee 1997, 5). Similarly, the internal rates of return are much higher for workers with low lifetime earnings

Table 8.1. Internal Real Rates of Return for Various Workers (percent)

Earnings level	Year of birth	Year attains age 65	Single male	Single female	One-earner couple	Two-earner couple
Very low	1920	1985	5.30	6.07	9.02	6.37
	1943	2008	4.00	4.42	6.59	4.57
	1973	2038	4.08	4.48	6.15	4.46
	2004	2069	4.48	4.71	6.31	4.72
Low	1920	1985	4.35	5.19	7.91	5.29
	1943	2008	2.87	3.35	5.42	3.39
	1973	2038	2.99	3.41	5.10	3.36
	2004	2069	3.39	3.65	5.29	3.65
Medium	1920	1985	2.82	3.73	6.36	3.62
	1943	2008	1.82	2.35	4.40	2.31
	1973	2038	1.96	2.41	4.13	2.32
	2004	2069	2.35	2.65	4.31	2.62
High	1920	1985	2.52	3.45	6.00	3.30
	1943	2008	1.18	1.74	3.73	1.64
	1973	2038	1.33	1.79	3.50	1.68
	2004	2069	1.72	2.05	3.70	1.99
Maximum	1920	1985	2.26	3.21	5.78	. . .
	1943	2008	0.57	1.19	3.25	. . .
	1973	2038	0.39	0.88	2.55	. . .
	2004	2069	0.78	1.13	2.74	. . .

Source: Nichols, Clingman, and Wade (2005), table 1.
Note: Based on the contributions and benefits scheduled in present law.

than for workers with higher lifetime earnings (see table 8.1). For example, the rate of return for a single male worker with very low lifetime earnings who retires in 2008 is 4.00 percent, but the rate of return for a single male with the maximum earnings is just 0.57 percent. Figure 8.2 also shows the much higher relative returns received by workers with low lifetime earnings.

Of note, however, this redistribution from high earners to low earners occurs only within the limited range of covered earnings (i.e., up to $94,200 in 2006); above the cap, earnings are not redistributed. For example, a worker earning $1,000,000 a year pays no more Social Security retirement taxes than a worker earning $94,200 a year.[25] Also, the progressive redistribution (from high earners to low earners) may be somewhat offset by the relatively longer life expectancies of high-income workers and their spouses and by the greater likelihood that spousal and surviving spouse benefits will be paid to spouses of high earners.[26]

Married Couples versus Single Individuals and Larger Families versus Smaller Families. Because of spousal and surviving spouse benefits, married couples tend to receive relatively more benefits than single individuals.[27] To illustrate this inequity, consider that a single worker with no dependents will receive a benefit at full retirement age of just 100 percent of the worker's PIA, while a worker with a spouse will receive 150 percent of the worker's PIA, and a surviving spouse can receive 100 percent of a worker's benefit long after that worker's death. The internal rate of return for a single male worker with very low lifetime earnings who retires in 2008 is just 4.00 percent, while the rate of return for a one-earner couple with very low lifetime earnings is 6.59 percent (table 8.1).

The redistribution that results from spousal benefits can be most easily understood when one considers how long surviving spouse benefits can last. For example, consider Gertrude Janeway, the last widow of a Union veteran from the Civil War.[28] Ms. Janeway married her husband in 1927, and when she died in January 2003 at the age of 93—more than 137 years after the Civil War—she was still collecting a $70-a-month pension from the Veterans Administration.[29]

In addition, providing family benefits for other dependents favors larger families over smaller families and single individuals. A retiree with a spouse and additional dependents could receive a monthly benefit of as high as 188 percent of the worker's PIA (U.S. House Committee 2004, 1-21). In contrast, a worker with a spouse and no other dependents would receive a monthly benefit of just 150 percent of the worker's PIA, and a single retiree would receive a monthly benefit of just 100 percent of her PIA.

One-Earner versus Two-Earner Couples. Two additional problems result from providing spousal and surviving spouse benefits based on the earnings of a retired worker. First, two-earner couples generally receive lower total benefits than one-earner couples with the same earnings. Second, because married women with earnings usually earn less and work a shorter time than their husbands, they often receive little or no additional Social Security retirement benefits from their Social Security tax payments.

The following example helps illustrate the penalty on two-earner couples:

The Greens and the Whites each earn twice the average wage. But while Tom Green is the sole breadwinner, Ted and Becky White each earn the same amount. When Tom Green retires in 2032, the couple receives a Social Security benefit of $37,769—Tom's retired worker benefit of $25,179 plus Beth Green's spousal benefit of half that amount, $12,590. When Ted and Becky White retire in 2032, each spouse gets a retired worker benefit of $17,358, a family total of only $34,716. That's $3,053 less than Tom and Beth's benefit.

Tom Green dies. Beth Green moves up from spousal benefit to survivor benefit and receives $25,179. But when Ted White dies, Becky White continues to get only her retired worker benefit of $17,358. Taking into account life expectancy, Tom and Beth can anticipate lifetime benefits of $549,694, while Ted and Becky are likely to receive $100,103 less—only $449,561. (Stanfield 2000, 9)

Similarly, table 8.1 shows that two-earner couples earn much lower rates of return than one-earner couples at each earnings level.

In fact, the inequity really falls on the secondary earners themselves—married individuals (primarily wives) who earn less than their spouses. When a secondary earner is entitled to Social Security benefits as both a retired worker and a spouse (or surviving spouse) of a primary earner, the dual entitlement rule prevents the secondary earner from receiving the full worker benefit and the full spousal (or surviving spouse) benefit. Instead, only the larger of the two benefits is paid. As a result, the secondary earner gets no return on the Social Security retirement taxes she paid unless her worker benefit exceeds the spousal (or surviving spouse) benefit to which she is entitled. Consider this example:

Jorge Rodriguez earns $40,000 a year, entitling him to a retired worker's benefit of $14,758 when he retires in 2000. His wife, Inez, earns $15,000 a year, which yields a retired worker's benefit of $7,967. Granted that's more than the spousal benefit of $7,379—but not much more, only $588 a year. In fact, if instead of Inez working at all, Jorge earned that $15,000 on top of his current salary, he would be entitled to $17,008 a year at retirement and Inez would get $8,504 in spousal benefits. . . . When either Jorge or Inez dies, the survivor gets $2,250 more if Jorge, rather than Inez, had earned the extra $15,000. (Stanfield 2000, 11)

Indeed, for many secondary earners in two-earner couples, the additional Social Security retirement taxes they paid will produce absolutely no more retirement benefits than if they had not worked at all and paid no retirement taxes. For spousal benefits, this inequity will occur any time the worker benefit earned by the primary earner is more than twice the worker benefit earned by the secondary earner. The secondary earner would then receive a greater Social Security retirement benefit as a spouse than as a retired worker.[30]

Elderly Retirees versus Elderly Workers. The current Social Security retirement program also favors elderly retirees over elderly workers (Forman 1998a). Monthly Social Security retirement benefits are paid as a matter of right to a qualified individual who retires at age 62 or older. If the individual continues to work, however, she must continue to pay Social Security and income taxes on her subsequent earnings, and she may well die before she collects any benefits. To be sure, the benefits to which she is entitled will be actuarially adjusted to account for her postponing retirement, but if she dies before retiring, she will get nothing. And if she dies without a surviving spouse or other dependents, her heirs will get nothing.

Continuing to work can also subject certain elderly individuals to confiscatory tax rates. For example, a self-employed worker who faces the 25 percent income tax rate, the inclusion of 85 percent of her Social Security benefits in income, and the 15.3 percent Social Security tax rate can face an effective marginal tax rate of more than 60 percent. Worse still, elderly workers who are also subject to the Social Security retirement earnings test can face even higher effective marginal tax rates.

How Redistribution in Social Security Discourages Work and Encourages Early Retirement

The net effect of redistribution within the Social Security retirement program is that the program operates like a net tax on some workers and a net transfer in favor of other workers and their families. These net taxes and transfers inevitably distort individual decisions about work and retirement. As it turns out, both tend to discourage work effort.

Low-Skilled Workers. For example, consider how the Social Security retirement program might influence a low-skilled individual's decisions about work at various points in her career. In the early part of her career, Social Security's progressive benefit formula and generous minimum benefits should encourage the worker to qualify for Social Security benefits, as these features provide disproportionate rewards for workers with low lifetime earnings.

Once a worker has completed the 10 years of service needed to qualify for benefits, however, these subsidies becomes less valuable. Moreover, as a worker completes more years of service and achieves a higher AIME, additional Social Security contributions will purchase fewer additional benefits. Once a worker has 35 years of covered earnings, each additional year of work simply replaces some earlier year of covered earnings in the benefit computation formula, and the rate of return on additional payroll taxes paid drops precipitously.

In addition, once benefits become available at age 62, the disproportionately generous benefits available to low-income workers can make early retirement relatively more attractive than working.

How do low-income individuals respond to such transfers? They reduce their work effort. More than 56 percent of the elderly retire as soon as they can—at age 62—and nearly 80 percent of new beneficiaries claim their benefits by age 65 (U.S. House Committee 2004, 1-47). And, low-skilled workers are more likely to leave the labor force than high-skilled workers (Besl and Kale 1996; Haider and Loughran 2001; Munnell and Soto 2005; Purcell 2005a; Stewart 1995; Williamson and McNamara 2001). Why work for low wages, when Social Security pays almost as much?

The Supplemental Security Income program creates additional work disincentives for its eligible beneficiaries. This occurs largely because SSI imposes a confiscatory, dollar-for-dollar benefit-reduction rate on earned income beyond some very small income disregards. There is also some evidence that features of SSI and Social Security interact to create incentives for prospective SSI recipients to take early retirement under Social Security as a way of maximizing their total lifetime benefits.[31]

Secondary Earners. Similarly, consider how the presence of spousal and surviving spouse benefits tends to undermine the work effort of secondary earners (primarily wives). First, the availability of generous spousal benefits means that at full retirement age, most secondary earners in two-earner couples can claim a benefit equal to half the primary earner's worker benefit; after the primary earner's death, the secondary worker can claim a benefit equal to 100 percent of the primary earner's worker benefit. The availability of these generous benefits makes it easier for secondary workers to leave the workforce at full retirement age or even earlier. Like other welfare transfers, the provision of these benefits is expected to reduce work effort.

Second, because of the dual entitlement rule, Social Security retirement taxes will operate like real taxes on many secondary earners, and these taxes will discourage them from working. For many secondary earners in two-earner couples, the additional Social Security taxes they pay will produce absolutely no more retirement benefits than if they had not worked at all and had not paid retirement taxes.

All in all, generous spousal benefits and payroll-tax financing discourage secondary earners from working. In that regard, there is a good deal of evidence that women—who make up the bulk of secondary earners—spend much less time in the workforce than men. Of workers retiring in 1996, for example, the median woman had worked 27 years over her lifetime, while the median man had worked 39 years (National Economic Council 1998, 8–9). Similarly, while 33.6 percent of men age 65 through 69 remained in the workforce in 2005, 23.7 percent of women that age were still in the workforce that year (BLS 2006f, table 3).

Elderly Workers. Consider also how the current Social Security system generally discourages elderly individuals from working. Here, the availability of reduced benefits at Social Security's early retirement age of 62 and the availability of full benefits at full retirement age are powerful inducements to retire (OECD 2004, 6–9; Gruber and Wise 2003; Gustman and Steinmeier 2005). Moreover, once a worker has completed 35 years of covered service, she is unlikely to see much increase in benefits resulting from working more years and paying more Social Security retirement taxes. Indeed, few workers who have reached the Social Security early retirement age will see much increase in their benefits resulting from additional payroll taxes paid on additional years of work.

These financial incentives help explain why labor force participation has fallen so dramatically among the elderly. For example, the average age at which workers begin receiving their Social Security retirement benefits fell from 68.7 years old in 1940 to 63.6 years old in 2002 (table 8.2).[32] Older men leaving the workforce today can anticipate 18 years in retirement, up from just 13 years in retirement 30 years ago (Committee for Economic Development 1999, 6).[33]

Of course, it is great that we are living longer and healthier lives.[34] And it is wonderful that most of us can look forward to decades of retirement. But it is doubtful that either individuals or the nation can continue to afford ever-longer retirements. There were seven working-age persons for every elderly person in the United States in 1950 (Lahey 2005). By 2030, that ratio will shrink to less than 3 to 1. With fewer workers relative to retirees, we will see increasing burdens placed on younger generations to support the elderly. Social Security and Medicare are already in financial trouble, and in 30 years they will be all but bankrupt (Board of Trustees 2006). Medicaid, SSI, food stamps, and the private pension system will also be stretched to the limit. Meanwhile, the rate of economic growth is expected to fall significantly (Committee for Economic Development 1999, 11).

Table 8.2. Percentage of Workers Electing Social Security Retirement Benefits at Various Ages, Selected Years

Year	Age 62	Age 63–64	Age 65	Age 66+	Average age (years)
1940	NA	NA	8.3	91.7	68.7
1960	10.0	7.9	35.3	46.7	66.2
1980	40.5	22.2	30.7	6.6	63.7
2000	51.7	17.2	19.6	11.5	64.0
2002	56.1	22.7	16.9	16.9	63.6

Source: U.S. House Committee (2004), table 1-14.
NA = not applicable
Notes: The age distribution excludes conversions at age 65 from disability to retirement rolls. Retirement before age 65 was not available in 1940. Some rows do not total 100.

Individual resources will also be stretched by longer retirements. Pertinent here, delaying retirement can increase retirement income substantially, through both earnings and investments. Each additional year increases Social Security benefits by 5 to 8 percent and reduces the number of years over which private pension benefits and other retirement wealth needs to be spread (Munnell 2006). One recent study found that working another year would increase the average annuity income at retirement of workers in the lowest quintile by 16 percent, while working another five years would increase average income 98 percent (Butrica, Smith, and Steuerle 2006, figure 2).[35]

All in all, it is striking that so many Americans retire while they are still productive. No doubt, many retirees will have the resources to enjoy all their golden years. Unfortunately, many others may face economic hardships after they have exhausted their own resources but have become too frail to return to work.

Some Recent Proposals to Reform Social Security

Given the current problems with the Social Security system, it is no surprise that Social Security reform has been a hot topic for the past few years.[36]

Maintaining Benefits

Historically, the simplest way to fix the Social Security system has been to raise payroll taxes. Indeed, the Social Security payroll tax has been increased more than 20 times since the program began in 1937 (Executive Office of the President 2001). Benefit cuts have also been used to help restore financial solvency to the Social Security trust funds. In 1983, for example, Congress passed legislation (Public Law 98-121) that is gradually increasing the normal retirement age from 65 to age 67 in 2022. Other possible ways to cut benefits include reducing future cost-of-living adjustments and reducing the replacement percentages in the primary insurance amount formula.[37]

Toward an Individual Account System

More recently, a number of analysts have called for replacing all (or a portion of) the current Social Security system with a system of individual retirement savings accounts—accounts that would operate pretty much like today's employer-sponsored 401(k) plans or individual retirement accounts.[38] These individual account proposals typically recommend that the government maintain much of the current Social Security system, but "add on" or "carve out" 2, 3, or even 5 percent of payroll for a system of individual accounts. For example, model 1 in President Bush's *Strengthening Social Security and Creating Personal Wealth for All Americans* called for the creation of voluntary personal accounts that would carve 2 percent of taxable payroll out of the current Social Security system (President's Commission 2001).[39]

Over the years, several proposals have suggested adding mandatory individual accounts on top of the current Social Security system. In 1981, for example, the President's Commission on Pension Policy recommended adoption of a Mandatory Universal Pension System that would have required all employers to contribute at least 3 percent of wages to private pensions for their workers (President's Commission on Pension Policy 1981). That proposal drew little interest at the time, but there has recently been renewed interest in such mandatory add-on accounts.[40] Pertinent here, Carasso and Forman estimate that, in the long run, 3 percent add-on individual accounts could provide an annual retirement benefit equal to 14.5 percent of final wages for men, 13.3 percent of final wages for women, 14.5 percent of final wages for one-earner couples, and 13.9 percent of final wages for two-earner couples (Carasso and Forman 2006).

Replacing all, or a portion of, the current Social Security system with individual accounts could help improve the funding of the Social Security system. Perhaps even more important, individual account proposals would strengthen the relationship between contributions and benefits and reduce the work disincentives that pervade the current system (Prescott 2005). With individual accounts, there would be no redistribution at all. Contributions and the earnings on them would remain in individual accounts, and no money would ever be taken from a worker's individual account to provide benefits for other workers or their families.

Individual account systems also tend to be neutral on the timing of retirement. Individuals who choose to work past normal retirement age would continue to have additional contributions made to their individual accounts, and they would continue to earn income on the growing balances in those accounts. Consequently, individuals would not face financial penalties for staying in the workforce.

MODEST CHANGES THAT COULD IMPROVE THE SOCIAL SECURITY SYSTEM

The analysis so far suggests that various improvements could make the current Social Security retirement system more work friendly. To begin, this section offers seven modest recommendations that could help reduce the system's work disincentives. The next section takes a broader look at what we want the Social Security system to do and offers a more comprehensive solution to the current system's work-disincentive problems.[41]

Move Away from Payroll Tax Financing

To pay for retirement benefits, a source of revenue is needed. One approach would be to have a straight "forced savings" system in which individual workers are required to set aside a portion of their earnings in exchange for actuarially fair benefits paid to them at retirement. Social Security looks a little like that, but as this chapter has shown, benefits are not directly proportional to Social Security retirement tax "contributions." Individuals do pay a flat Social Security retirement payroll tax, but the benefits paid out are not directly proportional to those taxes. Instead, taxes paid by some workers are redistributed to other workers and their families. The net effect is that Social Security payroll taxes operate like real taxes on the earned income of many workers, and faced with those taxes, many workers reduce their work effort.

Pertinent here, the government bears the burden of justifying its redistributive taxation. To be sure, it can make sense to redistribute economic resources from rich to poor—from those with a greater ability to pay tax to those with a lesser ability to pay tax. And some analysts are concerned that Americans would not be willing to support the redistribution built in to the current Social Security system if that redistribution were more transparent.[42] These analysts like that the current Social Security system is a "black box" that hides massive amounts of redistribution. People may grumble about paying into the system, but almost everyone believes that they deserve the benefits they get out of the system, and that has led to overwhelming public support for a system that achieves a great deal of redistribution. Those analysts would be willing to tinker with the current system to improve the targeting of that redistribution, but they believe it is necessary to retain its opaqueness.

Still, if redistribution is called for, the payroll tax seems a particularly poor choice as the redistributive mechanism.[43] Wages taxed for Social Security purposes constitute just 39 percent of the nation's gross domestic product (National Academy of Social Insurance 2005a, 30–31). That means that 61 percent of GDP is not taxed to help pay for Social Security, including earned income above the earnings cap ($94,200 in 2006); non-taxable fringe benefits and other tax-exempt compensation; the wages of state, local, and other workers that are not covered by Social Security; and investment income. If the Social Security tax base were broadened to include these other sources of income, tax rates could be slashed.

Admittedly, the earned income tax credit offsets the Social Security taxes paid by many low-income workers, particularly those with children. Consequently, the credit tempers the regressivity of the Social Security payroll tax and moves the Social Security program closer to an ability-to-pay tax base. And, as already discussed in chapters 6 and 7, it could make sense to expand the credit or otherwise further integrate the payroll and income tax systems.

For that matter, simply doing nothing about Social Security's impending financial problems is likely to result in greater reliance on income tax revenues and relatively less reliance on payroll-tax financing. The political power of the elderly and elderly lobbies such as the AARP makes it unlikely that future Social Security retirement benefits will actually ever be cut by much.[44] At the same time, however, it also seems unlikely that Congress will ever again find the political will to increase Social Security payroll taxes to pay for retirement benefits. Consequently, once the Social Security trust funds are exhausted, the government will have to use general revenues to make up any shortfalls in promised benefits. Unless some new source of revenue is found, most of the increased burden will fall on the individual income tax, currently the largest source of federal revenue.

Reduce the Progressivity of the Social Security Benefit Formula, but Expand Supplemental Security Income

An alternative way of reducing the work disincentives implicit in our payroll tax–financed Social Security retirement system would be to make Social Security retirement benefits more proportional to taxes paid. This could be accomplished by reducing the progressivity of the benefit computation formula. For example, instead of computing a worker's PIA as 90 percent of her first $656 of average indexed monthly earnings, plus 32 percent of the next $3,239 of AIME, plus 15 percent of AIME over $3,955; a worker's PIA might be set at, say, a flat 50 percent of her AIME.[45] That would make each worker's benefits more directly proportional to her payroll tax contributions.

To protect workers with low lifetime earnings, any reduction in benefits that resulted from decreasing the progressivity of the Social Security benefit formula could be offset by increasing Supplemental Security Income benefits. Of note, SSI benefits are funded out of general revenues, not out of regressive payroll taxes.

Increase the Benefit Computation Period beyond 35 Years

Another way to strengthen the relationship between a worker's payroll tax contributions and her resulting benefits—and so reduce work disincentives—would be to increase the benefit computation period beyond 35 years. Under current law, an individual worker's AIME and, consequently, her PIA, is based on her highest 35 years of indexed earnings. In effect, individuals who work more than 35 years get no return on the payroll taxes they paid in those additional years that they worked. Hence, this benefit computation rule operates to discourage elderly workers from continuing to work beyond 35 years. The rule also operates to subsidize the benefits of those who are able to take time out of the workforce to go to college or to stay home to care for young children or elderly parents.

To understand the unfairness of this 35-year benefit computation rule, consider two individuals, Alice and Beth. At age 18, Alice goes to work and pays payroll taxes continuously until age 62 (44 years). Beth goes to college and graduate school until she is age 27, when she too joins the workforce and works and pays payroll taxes continuously until age 62 (35 years). Both will compute their benefits based on their highest 35 years of earnings, but Alice will get absolutely nothing back for her additional nine years of payroll tax "contributions."[46]

Moreover, neither Alice nor Beth will have much incentive to keep working beyond age 61. Only their 35 highest years of indexed earnings will enter into the computation of benefits. In all likelihood, that means that working another year will knock out an earlier year of relatively lower indexed earnings. Still, whether an earlier year or the additional year gets knocked out of the computation, the payroll taxes paid in that drop-out year will result in absolutely no additional retirement benefits for Alice or Beth.[47]

In short, capping the benefit computation period at 35 years operates as a work disincentive and one that seems to have had an especially powerful impact on elderly workers. Consequently, extending the benefit computation period should be a powerful work incentive. The 1994–96 Social Security Advisory Council favored computing average indexed monthly earnings on a worker's highest 38 years of earnings, and some analysts would compute the AIME on a worker's highest 40 years of earnings (Advisory Council on Social Security 1997, vol. 1, 20; Committee for Economic Development 1997, 39).[48] Better still, we should change the AIME formula so every year of work counts in determining benefits.[49]

Raise the Early and Full Retirement Ages

Another change that would encourage elderly workers to remain in the workforce would be to raise the early and the full retirement ages. The modest increases in Social Security's full retirement age have not kept up with the rather dramatic increases in the life expectancies of men and women since the Social Security system was created (figure 8.3). Under current law, the early retirement age is age 62. The full retirement age is currently 65 and eight months (for those born in 1941 and turning 65 in 2006), but it is slowly increasing to age 67.

Raising the early or full retirement ages would almost certainly encourage workers to stay in the workforce longer. Indeed, the empirical evidence shows that the age of initial eligibility for benefits "appears to be the most powerful influence" on the timing of retirement (Aaron 1999b).[50] For example, there has long been a "spike" in retirement levels at Social Security's early retirement age (Advisory Council 1997, vol. 2, 21; Burtless 1999; Leonesio 1996).

Pertinent here, a majority of the members of the 1994–96 Social Security Advisory Council favored accelerating the increase in the full retirement age to 67 and continuing to increase the full retirement age thereafter to keep pace with increases in life expectancy (Advisory Council 1997, vol. 1, 21).[51] Still other analysts have recommended raising the full retirement age to 70 (Committee for Economic Development 1997, 39; Burtless and Quinn 2001, 402–406). In addition, many analysts have recommended gradually increasing the early retirement age from 62 to 65.[52]

Figure 8.3. Life Expectancies at Birth versus Social Security Full Retirement Age

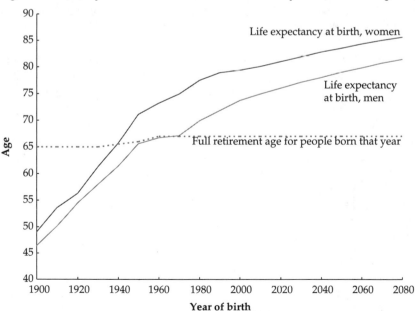

Sources: U.S. House Committee (2004), table A-2; Board of Trustees of the Federal Old-Age and Survivors Insurance and Disability Insurance Trust Funds (2006), tables V.A3 and V.C3

All in all, it seems likely that raising the early and full retirement ages would keep many older Americans working longer. At the same time, however, we would probably need to expand the DI and SSI programs to help elderly Americans who can no longer work but are still too young to claim Social Security retirement benefits.[53]

Tax Social Security Benefits Like Private Pensions

Another change that could encourage at least some elderly individuals to remain in the workforce would be to change the way we tax Social Security benefits. Under current law, single taxpayers with incomes over $25,000 and married couples with incomes over $32,000 must include as much as half their Social Security benefits in income, and single taxpayers with incomes over $34,000 and married couples with incomes over $44,000 must include as much as 85 percent of their Social Security benefits in income. Largely because of the interaction between these floors and the income and payroll taxes imposed on individuals who continue to work past age 62, some workers can face confiscatory tax rates that will discourage them from working.

There would be much smaller work disincentives if the floors were repealed. For example, we might tax Social Security benefits like private pensions.[54] Pension benefits are fully taxable except when those benefits reflect previously taxed employee contributions.

Replace Spousal Benefits with Earnings Sharing

Replacing Social Security spousal benefits with an earnings sharing system would further strengthen work incentives (CBO 1986; Forman 1999b; HHS 1985; House Committee 1985). Under earnings sharing, the current Social Security system's spouse and surviving spouse benefits would be eliminated. Instead, each spouse in a married couple would be credited with half the couple's combined earnings during marriage.

For example, consider a two-earner couple in which the primary earner makes $40,000 in a given year and the secondary earner makes $10,000. Under the current Social Security system, each earner is credited with his or her own earnings. Under earnings sharing, each would be credited with $25,000 of earnings for that year for purposes of computing their benefits.

Social Security's generous spousal benefits were added to the Social Security system in the 1930s when most families followed the traditional model of working husband and stay-at-home mother. Redistribution based on marital status may have appeared to make sense back then—as a proxy for need—but it makes little sense today (Forman 1996b). In particular, spousal benefits are poorly targeted. The largest spousal benefits go to the spouses of primary earners with the highest lifetime earnings (Steuerle, Spiro, and Carasso 1999a). Relatively low benefits go to the elderly who need them most: octogenarian widows, divorcees, and other unmarried women who had low lifetime earnings. Moreover, even though women at age 62 tend to live about three years longer than men, the availability of generous spousal benefits actually encourages women to retire early. In 2003, for example, 58.6 percent of women claimed actuarially reduced benefits at age 62, compared with just 53.3 percent of men (Munnell and Soto 2005, table 2).

Replacing spousal benefits with an earnings sharing system would encourage work in two ways. First, strengthening the relationship between payroll taxes paid by workers and their retirement benefits would encourage greater work effort by current workers. A worker's payroll tax contributions would still be shared with his or her own spouse, but those taxes would no longer be redistributed to some other worker's spouse or dependents.

Second, replacing spousal benefits with earnings sharing would increase work incentives for secondary earners (primarily wives). No longer would so many secondary earners see absolutely no return from their payroll tax contributions. With the repeal of spousal benefits, the dual entitlement rule would also disappear. Consequently, secondary earners would always see their payroll taxes lead to increased benefits, and making those workers' benefits proportional to their payroll taxes would encourage them to work harder and longer.

All in all, replacing spousal benefits with earnings sharing would get rid of the current system's marriage penalties and bonuses, both of which can discourage secondary earners from working. With earnings sharing, there would be no marriage penalties or bonuses, and work would be encouraged.

Change the Way Benefits Accrue and Are Paid Out

We should also change the way that benefits accrue and are paid out, especially once a worker becomes eligible for benefits. Under current law, an eligible worker can start drawing reduced benefits at age 62. If that individual keeps working, however, the retirement earnings test can take those benefits away. If the individual does not live until full retirement age, she may never draw any benefits.

Workers tend to decide the timing of retirement a little bit myopically; that is, they tend to underestimate their life expectancies and overvalue in-hand benefits.[55] The life expectancy tables may say that a 62-year-old will live another 20 or more years, but many people think they will only make it 10 or 15 years, so they want to get the full value of their benefits, and that means retiring early. To the extent that the fear of losing benefits is driving people to retire early, there are several better approaches.

One possibility would be to repeal the retirement earnings test, even for those who have not yet reached full retirement age (Burtless and Quinn 2002; Gustman and Steinmeier 2002, 2004; Ippolito 1997; Kaplan 2002). Then, starting at age 62, workers could start drawing benefits whether they were working or not. The retirement earnings test currently reduces the benefits that certain individuals who work past age 62 receive. An actuarial adjustment restores any lost benefits to the worker's subsequent benefit stream, but most analysts believe that the earnings test nevertheless operates as a work disincentive (Gustman and Steinmeier 2002; Loughran and Haider 2005).[56] In that regard, the Senior Citizens' Freedom to Work Act of 2000 (Public Law 106-182) recently repealed the limitation on the amount of outside income Social Security beneficiaries who have attained full retirement age may earn without incurring a loss of benefits (Burke 2000). Consequently, workers can start taking benefits at full retirement age, and they will not lose benefits even if they keep working.[57]

Alternatively, we could allow workers who have reached age 62 to set up "deferred retirement option plans" (DROPs), like those used with many state and local government pension plans.[58] Under a DROP plan, once a worker reaches age 62, she could elect to have her benefit payments set aside in an individual retirement savings account until she retires.

Another approach would be to create individual Social Security retirement savings accounts for each worker at age 62 (Forman 1998a). The starting balance in each worker's account would equal the cost for an inflation-indexed annuity equal in value to the worker's Social Security benefit entitlement at that time. Thereafter, workers would earn investment income on the balance in their accounts, and they would see their subsequent Social Security retirement taxes contributed into their accounts. When workers eventually retire, the balance in their accounts would be reconverted into a larger lifetime annuity. Alternatively, if workers die before retiring, the balance in their accounts could be transferred to their heirs.

Also pertinent here, Social Security reform plans that would create individual retirement accounts for workers would be more neutral on the timing of retirement than the current system. Hence, proposals to replace all or a portion of Social Security with individual accounts should result in significantly more elderly individuals remaining in the workforce than under the current system (Forman 1998a, 2000a).

A MORE COMPREHENSIVE SOLUTION

The Social Security system was designed in the 1930s, and it is time to reconsider its structure with an eye on what we want the system to do today and into the future. Once we know what we want from the Social Security system, it should be relatively easy to design a system that can achieve those results.

What do we want the Social Security retirement system to do? It would make sense for the Social Security system to satisfy three principal goals. First, the system should ensure that every elderly American has an adequate income throughout her retirement years. Second, the system should have a minimum of work disincentives. Finally, the system should have a minimum of marriage penalties and bonuses.

One way to achieve these goals would be to have a two-tiered Social Security system to provide benefits to individuals. The first tier would provide a basic Social Security benefit to every older American. These benefits would be financed out of general revenues. The second tier would provide an additional earnings-related benefit based on payroll tax contributions made to individual accounts. Finally, married couples would share their earnings.[59]

The Basic Social Security Benefit

The first tier of this new Social Security system would provide a basic Social Security benefit to every older American. For example, at full retirement age, the government might guarantee every retiree a first-tier benefit equal to 100 percent of the poverty level. In 2006, for example, the poverty level for a single individual is $9,800, yielding a monthly benefit of about $817 (HHS 2006).

That benefit, $817 a month, would be the benefit payable to every individual at full retirement age. In that regard, there is every reason to think about raising the full retirement age to age 70, or at least to 68, but perhaps allowing individuals as young as 65 to receive actuarially reduced benefits. For example, if full benefits were payable at age 70, the first-tier benefit at age 65 would be about 30 percent less, or $572 a month.

First-tier benefits paid in subsequent years would be increased for inflation, as measured by the consumer price index. In any event, first-tier benefits would terminate at death.

This first-tier benefit would replace the current SSI program and all the redistributive features of the current Social Security system.[60] Like the current SSI program, the first-tier benefits would be paid for out of general revenues. Unlike SSI, however, these first-tier benefits would be universally available and would not be subject to any income or asset test.[61] Benefits would not phase out if the recipient had other income or wealth.

On the other hand, unlike current SSI benefits, these first-tier benefits would be taxable for income tax purposes. The standard deductions and personal exemptions of the current income tax system are large enough to ensure that few individuals with income below the poverty level would pay any federal income tax.

There would also be no retirement earnings test. Individuals could work and begin drawing actuarially reduced benefits at the early retirement age. Alternatively, they could wait and claim larger benefits, and it would probably make sense to just go ahead and pay full benefits starting at full retirement age to those who had not already claimed them.

In addition, there would be no marriage penalties or bonuses for first-tier benefits. Each individual would be entitled to $9,800 a year at age 70, regardless of marital status. Consequently, a married couple, both age 70, could claim a combined family benefit of $19,600 a year ($1,633 a month).

If these first-tier benefit levels seem too generous, then an alternative approach might be to provide each individual with a first-tier Social Security benefit equal to half the poverty level for a married couple. In 2006, for example, the poverty level for a married couple is $13,200 (HHS 2006). That would suggest a first-tier benefit of $6,600 for each individual, starting at age 70, or about $550 a month. With an actuarial reduction of 30 percent, that would yield a benefit of $385 a month starting at age 65.

An Additional Earnings-Related Benefit

In addition to these first-tier benefits, every worker would earn retirement benefits based on earnings. These second-tier benefits would be financed with a much-reduced system of payroll taxes. In effect, each worker would have an individual retirement savings account, and the reduced payroll taxes they paid would be credited to those accounts, along with investment income on the balance in those accounts.

The individual retirement savings accounts could be funded, defined contribution accounts, or hypothetical cash balance accounts (Forman 2000b, 2001b).[62] The government would simply establish an individual account for each worker and keep track of the payroll tax contributions and investment returns on those accounts.[63] A number of countries—including Sweden and Poland—have recently replaced all or a portion of their traditional Social Security systems with hypothetical account systems—"notional defined contribution plans"—that look a lot like cash balance plans (Brooks and Weaver 2005; Forman 2001b; Williamson 2004).

In order to make the transition from the current system to this new two-tier system, participants in the current system could be given large starting balances in their second-tier accounts to reflect their already-accrued earnings-related benefit entitlements. From then on, each worker's payroll tax contributions would be added to her individual account, and each year the starting balance in the account would be credited with interest.

At retirement, the balance in a worker's account would typically be used to purchase an additional inflation-adjusted annuity over and above the individual's first-tier benefit, although in some cases workers with large accounts might be allowed to make larger withdrawals (National Academy of Social Insurance 2005b; SSA 2005b). In the case of a worker who died before withdrawing her benefits, the balance in her account would go to her heirs.

For example, the government might want to require that individuals take monthly distributions that, with their first-tier benefits, would provide them with the equivalent of an inflation-indexed annuity targeted to, say, 200 percent of the poverty level for a single individual (i.e., $19,600 in 2006). If workers wait until full retirement age to retire, their first-tier benefits would provide half the required amount, and their second-tier individual accounts would pay the other half for those with large enough account balances (and smaller amounts for those with smaller account balances). Beyond that 200-percent-of-the-poverty-level combined first- and second-tier annuity, however, more relaxed distribution rules could apply. Finally, at death, any remaining balance in worker account would go to spouses or other heirs.

Because first-tier benefits would be used to ensure that every elderly American has income sufficient to keep him or her out of poverty, the second-tier individual accounts would not have to be all that large, and payroll tax rates could be reduced. For example, the second-tier individual accounts might be funded by a combined payroll tax contribution by employers and employees of just 6 or 7 percent of compensation, as opposed to the 10.6 percent level paid under the current Social Security retirement system.[64]

Replace Spousal Benefits with Earnings Sharing

Finally, these second-tier individual accounts of husbands and wives should be subject to earnings sharing annually according to the standard approach. Basically, each spouse in a married couple would be credited with half the couple's combined earnings during each year of marriage, and the current Social Security system's spouse and surviving spouse benefits would be eliminated. At retirement, each spouse's second-tier benefit would be based on half the married couple's earnings credits during marriage plus whatever earnings credits that spouse accrued before or after the marriage.

Some Final Thoughts

Replacing the Social Security retirement system and the Supplemental Security Income program with the proposed two-tier system would meet all three of our articulated goals. First, the system would ensure that every elderly American had an adequate income throughout her retirement years. Indeed, first-tier benefits should be designed to ensure that every American who works until full retirement age is entitled to a benefit at least equal to the poverty level.

Second, the system would have minimal work disincentives. The new system would be much more neutral about the timing of retirement than the current system. In particular, redistributive first-tier benefits would be paid for with income taxes and other general revenues, not with regressive payroll taxes. Second-tier benefits would be paid for with much-reduced proportional payroll taxes. All in all, marginal tax rates on earned income would go down, and workers would have greater incentives to work harder and longer.

Third, the system would not have marriage penalties or bonuses. Replacing spousal benefits and surviving spouse benefits with earnings sharing would eliminate those distortions.

Although tinkering with the Social Security retirement system could certainly reduce its work disincentives, a more comprehensive approach could solve all the current system's work disincentive problems. In short, the two-tiered system described here would make Social Security work.

9

MAKING PENSIONS WORK

Ideally, every employer would have a plan covering all their employees. Employees would all earn a pension that, when combined with Social Security, would replace their final earnings, and this pension would be indexed for inflation. (Halperin 2003, 42)

The current pension system is failing American workers and their families. Only about half of American workers have pension plans, and few can be confident they will have enough income to meet their economic needs throughout retirement. Moreover, the current pension system often has an adverse impact on individual decisions about work and retirement. For example, traditional pension plans often push older workers into retirement when those workers should instead be encouraged to keep working and accumulating assets to fund later retirements. In short, the current system is not working.

This chapter considers how to reform the pension system so that it better meets the retirement income needs of American workers and their families and helps make American workers as productive as possible.[1] To reform the pension system, pension policy should be redesigned to strengthen the connection between pension benefits and work effort and to help ensure that all American workers and their families have adequate retirement incomes.

The basic approach is to pay workers in proportion to their productivity. Under the current system, pension plans regularly create cross-subsidies that, in effect, take money from some workers and give it to other workers and their families. Like taxes and transfers, these cross-subsidies distort the relationship between a worker's productivity and her compensation. As a result, pension plans can have an adverse impact on workforce selection, retention, retirement behavior, and worker effort (Even and Macpherson 2003; Burman, Johnson, and Kobes 2004). Redesigning the pension system so workers are paid in proportion to their productivity will help minimize work disincentives and maximize worker productivity.

This chapter provides an overview of the current pension system, discusses some recent trends and problems, and explains the work incentives and disincentives created by pension plans. The remainder of the chapter offers suggestions about how to make the pension system work better. In that regard, it offers modest proposals that could help reduce work disincentives in the current system and help meet the retirement income needs of workers and their families. Finally, this chapter offers more comprehensive solutions.

OVERVIEW OF THE PENSION SYSTEM

American workers now receive more than one-quarter of their compensation in the form of fringe benefits. Fringe benefits made up 29.8 percent of the average employer cost for employee compensation of civilian workers in March 2006 (BLS 2006e). Employers are generally required to provide legally mandated benefits for such programs as Social Security, unemployment compensation, and workers' compensation, and these now account for about 8.0 percent of compensation. In addition, many employers provide such other benefits as pensions, health benefits, paid leave, educational assistance, and dependent care assistance. The structure of these fringe benefit programs can have a significant impact on Americans' work and retirement behavior. In particular, this chapter explains how the pension system influences individual decisions about work and retirement.

It is important to note that the United States has a "voluntary" pension system. Employers are not required to have pensions, but if they do, they are subject to regulation. The Employee Retirement Income Security Act of 1974 (ERISA) governs most private retirement plans.[2]

Most pension plans qualify for favorable tax treatment. Basically, an employer's contributions to a tax-qualified retirement plan on behalf of an employee are not taxable to the employee. Moreover, the pension fund's earnings on those contributions are tax-exempt. Workers pay tax only when they receive distributions of their pension benefits, and, at that point, the usual rules for taxing annuities apply.[3] Nevertheless, the employer is allowed a current deduction for its contributions (within limits). The federal government routinely identifies these deviations from normal income tax rules as tax expenditures in the tax expenditure budgets it prepares annually. For example, the *2007 Federal Budget* estimates the exclusion of pension contributions and earnings costs almost $102 billion in fiscal year 2006 (Executive Office and OMB 2006a, table 19-1).[4]

Types of Pension Plans

Pension plans generally fall into two broad categories based on the nature of the benefits provided: defined benefit plans and defined contribution plans.

Defined Benefit Plans

In a defined benefit plan, an employer promises employees a specific benefit at retirement. To provide that benefit, the employer makes payments into a trust fund and makes withdrawals from the trust fund. Employer contributions are based on actuarial valuations, and the employer bears all of the investment risks and responsibilities. Benefits are typically guaranteed by the Pension Benefit Guaranty Corporation.

Defined benefit plans typically provide each worker with a specific annual retirement benefit tied to the worker's final average compensation and number of years of service. For example, a plan might provide that a worker's annual retirement benefit is equal to 2 percent times years of service times final average compensation ($B = 2$ percent $\times$ *yos* $\times$ *fac*). Under this final-average-pay formula, a worker with 30 years of service would receive a retirement benefit equal to 60 percent of her pre-retirement earnings ($B = 60$ percent $\times$ *fac* $= 2$ percent $\times$ 30 *yos* $\times$ *fac*). Final average compensation is typically computed by averaging the worker's salary over the three or five years prior to retirement.

Defined Contribution Plans

Under a typical defined contribution plan, the employer simply contributes a specified percentage of the worker's compensation to an individual investment account for the worker. For example, contributions might be set at 6 percent of annual compensation. Under such a plan, a worker who earned $30,000 in a given year would have $1,800 contributed to an individual investment account for her ($1,800 = 6 percent × $30,000). Her benefit at retirement would be based on all such contributions plus investment earnings. Defined contribution plans are also known as "individual account" plans because each worker has her own account, as opposed to defined benefit plans, where the plan's assets are pooled for the benefit of all of the employees.

There are a variety of different types of defined contribution plans, including money purchase pension plans, target benefit plans, profit-sharing plans, stock bonus plans, and employee stock ownership plans ("ESOPs").

Profit-sharing and stock bonus plans may include a feature that allows workers to choose between receiving cash currently or deferring taxation by placing the money in a retirement account according to Internal Revenue Code § 401(k). Consequently, these plans are sometimes called "401(k) plans." The maximum annual amount of such elective deferrals that can be made by an individual in 2006 is $15,000, although workers over the age of 50 can contribute up to $20,000 (IRS 2005c).

"Hybrid" Retirement Plans

Alternatively, many employers rely on hybrid retirement plans that mix the features of defined benefit and defined contribution plans. For example, a cash balance plan is a defined benefit plan that looks like a defined contribution plan (Forman and Nixon 2000; Campbell 1996). Like other defined benefit plans, employer contributions are based on actuarial valuations, and the employer bears all of the investment risks and responsibilities. Like defined contribution plans, however, cash balance plans provide workers with individual accounts (albeit hypothetical). A simple cash balance plan might allocate 6 percent of salary to each worker's account each year and credit the account with 5 percent interest on the balance in the account. Under such a plan, a worker who earned $30,000 in a given year would get an annual cash balance credit of $1,800 ($1,800 = 6 percent × $30,000), plus an interest credit equal to 5 percent of the balance in her hypothetical account as of the beginning of the year.

Individual Retirement Accounts and Keoghs

Favorable tax rules are also available for certain individual retirement accounts (IRAs). Almost any worker can set up an IRA with a bank or other financial institution. In 2006, individuals without pension plans can contribute and deduct up to $4,000 to an IRA (individuals over age 50 can contribute and deduct up to $5,000), and spouses can contribute and deduct similar amounts.[5] If a worker is covered by another retirement plan, however, the deduction may be reduced or eliminated if the worker's income exceeds $50,000 for a single individual or $75,000 for a married couple (in 2006). Like private pensions, IRA earnings are tax-exempt, and distributions are taxable.

Also, since 1998, individuals have been permitted to set up Roth IRAs.[6] Unlike regular IRAs, contributions to Roth IRAs are not deductible. Instead, withdrawals are tax-free. Like regular IRAs, however, Roth IRA earnings are tax-exempt.

Also, Keogh plans give self-employed workers an ability to save for retirement that is similar to plans that employers sponsor, and Keogh plans allow self-employed workers to contribute more than they could otherwise contribute to an IRA.[7]

The Regulation of Employment-Based Retirement Plans

In the more than 30 years since it was enacted, the Employee Retirement Income Security Act has been amended numerous times, and a whole regulatory system has grown up to enforce its provisions. The key agencies charged with the administration of ERISA are the U.S. Department of Labor, the IRS, and the Pension Benefit Guaranty Corporation (PBGC).

Pension plans must be operated for the exclusive benefit of employees or their beneficiaries, and plan assets generally must be held in a trust. To protect the interests of plan participants, ERISA requires significant reporting and disclosure in the administration and operation of employee benefit plans. In addition, ERISA and the Internal Revenue Code impose many other requirements on retirement plans, including rules governing participation, coverage, vesting, benefit accrual, contributions and benefits, and funding.

Participation

A pension plan generally may not require, as a condition of participation, that an employee complete a period of service extending beyond the later of age 21 or one year of service. Also, a plan may not exclude employees from participation just because they have reached a certain age (e.g., age 65). Employees can be excluded for other reasons, however. For example, a plan might be able to cover only those employees working at a particular location or in a particular job category.

Coverage

Under the minimum coverage rules, a pension plan must usually cover a significant percentage of the employer's workforce. Alternatively, a plan may be able to satisfy the minimum coverage rules if it benefits a certain class of employees, as long as it does not discriminate in favor of the employer's highly compensated employees.

Vesting

Pension plans must also meet certain minimum vesting requirements. A worker's retirement benefit is said to be vested when the worker has a nonforfeitable right to receive the benefit. Under the five-year, cliff-vesting schedule, an employee who has completed at least five years of service must have a nonforfeitable right to 100 percent of her accrued benefits. ERISA only imposes minimum vesting requirements, and plans are free to use a faster vesting schedule. Nevertheless, most plans use five-year cliff vesting. In 2003, for example, 77 percent of employees in private industry defined benefit plans faced the five-year cliff-vesting schedule, and hardly any plans provide for immediate vesting or for 100-percent vesting after one year of service (BLS 2005g, table 55).

Benefit Accrual

In keeping with the voluntary nature of our pension system, employers have relatively great freedom in the design of their pension plans. ERISA does not mandate any specific benefit levels, nor does it require that benefits accrue evenly over time.

When it comes to benefit accrual, there are just a few rules about how benefits must accrue. These rules help ensure that pension benefits accrue at certain minimum rates, and these rules limit the extent to which employers can skew or "backload" benefits in favor of their long-service employees. A typical plan must comply with at least one of three alternative minimum benefit accrual rules. For example, under the "3 percent rule," a worker must accrue, for each year of participation (up to 33⅓ years) at least 3 percent of the normal retirement benefit that she would receive if she stayed with the employer until age 65.

Another benefit accrual rule bars employers from reducing or ceasing an employee's benefit accruals just because they have reached a certain age (e.g., age 65), but employers are permitted to design their plans in ways that result in benefit reductions that correlate with age, for example, by restricting the number of years of benefit accrual (e.g., 30 years).

Contributions and Benefits

The Internal Revenue Code also imposes limits on contributions and benefits. In 2006, for example, generally no more than the lesser of

$44,000 or 25 percent of compensation can be added to the individual account of a participant in a defined contribution plan (IRS 2005c). Also, the maximum annual amount of elective deferrals that can be made by an individual to a 401(k)-type plan in 2006 is $15,000, although workers over the age of 50 can contribute up to another $5,000. With defined benefit plans, the highest annual benefit that can be paid to a retiree in 2006 is $175,000 or 100 percent of compensation. The highest amount of compensation that can be considered in determining contributions or benefits in 2006 is $220,000.

Funding

Retirement plans must also meet certain minimum funding standards. These rules help ensure that the money needed to pay the promised benefits is set aside in a trust fund where it can earn income until it is used to pay benefits when the employee retires.

Other Requirements

ERISA imposes extensive fiduciary responsibilities on employers and administrators of employee benefit plans. In addition, prohibited transaction rules prevent parties in interest from engaging in certain transactions with the plan. For example, an employer usually cannot sell, exchange, or lease any property to the plan.

ERISA also created the Pension Benefit Guaranty Corporation to administer a new plan termination insurance program. Defined benefit plans generally pay annual termination insurance premiums to the PBGC. In the event an underfunded plan terminates (for example, because the employer went out of business), the PBGC guarantees payment of pension benefits to the participants, up to $47,659 per participant in 2006 (PBGC 2005).

Retirement Plan Trends and Problems

Our pension system should be designed to meet the retirement needs of American workers and their families, and it should be designed to help make American workers as productive as possible. This section considers just how well the current pension system meets those goals.

Only About Half of American Workers Have Pensions

As Harvard Law professor Daniel Halperin suggested in the quote at the beginning of this chapter, "ideally, every employer would have a plan covering all their employees" (2003, 42). Measured against this standard, the current pension system must be viewed as a failure. The overall coverage rate for retirement plans has held relatively steady in recent years, with only about half of private-sector employees participating in an employer-sponsored retirement plan. Just 48.3 percent of all wage and salary workers age 21 to 64 were participating in an employment-based retirement plan in 2004, up only slightly from the 46.1 percent participating in 1987 (Copeland 2005b, figure 15).[8]

Similarly, of the 152.7 million Americans workers in 2004, just 81.2 million (53.2 percent) worked for an employer (or union) that sponsored a retirement plan, and just 63.9 million (41.9 percent) participated in that plan (Copeland 2005b, figure 1).[9] Table 9.1 provides more details about employer sponsorship of retirement plans in 2004 and worker participation in those plans. For example, the probability of pension coverage is greater for older workers, for whites, for highly educated workers, for higher-income workers, for full-time workers, and for workers at larger firms. Participation rates increased through age 55 and then declined. But even among older workers age 55 to 64, only 53 percent participated in a pension plan in 2004.[10]

Table 9.1 also shows that the probability of participating in a pension plan increases significantly with income level. While 69.5 percent of workers with annual earnings of $50,000 or more participated in a plan in 2004, only 18.2 percent of workers earning between $10,000 and $14,999 participated that year.[11] Similarly, while 52.8 percent of full-time workers participated in a pension plan, just 28.5 percent of part-time workers participated.[12]

Table 9.1 also shows that the probability of a worker participating in an employment-based retirement plan increases significantly with the size of her employer. Workers in small businesses are particularly hard hit: while 53.8 percent of employees at large private firms (1,000 or more employees) participated in a pension plans in 2004, only 23.9 percent of workers at firms with 10 to 24 workers participated in a plan that year.[13]

Gender no longer bears much relationship to plan participation rates for current workers. There is, however, a large gender gap concerning the private pension income of retired persons. While 44.7 percent of men over age 65 received income from employer pensions in 2004, only 27.9 percent of women over age 65 received pension income that year (Purcell 2005a, table 5).[14] Moreover, women age 50 or over are more likely to receive a pension benefit through their husbands (as spouses or survivors) than through their own savings or employment.

Participation in individual retirement accounts is even lower than participation in employment-based plans. For example, only 16.7 percent of American workers over the age of 16 had an IRA or Keogh in

Table 9.1. Share of Workers with an Employer that Sponsored a Retirement Plan and Share Participating in the Plan, by Various Characteristics, 2004

Worker characteristic	Sponsorship rate	Percent participating
Age		
20 or younger	24.9	4.1
21–24	41.0	19.4
25–34	52.8	39.7
35–44	57.3	48.3
45–54	61.2	53.9
55–64	60.3	53.0
65 and older	38.4	25.8
Gender		
Male	52.3	42.5
Female	54.2	41.2
Race/Ethnicity		
White	56.3	45.0
Black	54.9	41.5
Hispanic	35.1	25.6
Other	51.8	40.7
Education		
No high school diploma	26.3	14.7
High school diploma	48.5	37.1
Some college	55.2	41.8
Bachelor's degree	65.8	55.9
Graduate/professional degree	73.0	65.5
Annual earnings		
< $5,000	24.5	6.1
$5,000–$9,999	30.7	11.5
$10,000–$14,999	34.5	18.2
$15,000–$19,999	42.2	27.6
$20,000–$29,999	53.0	41.0
$30,000–$39,999	64.4	55.7
$40,000–$49,999	72.1	65.3
$50,000 or more	73.9	69.5
Work status		
Full-time, full-year	61.0	52.8
Part-time, full-year	43.8	28.5
Employer size		
Fewer than 10 employees	15.8	12.3
10–24 employees	31.4	23.9
25–99 employees	48.2	36.2
100–499 employees	60.3	46.8
500–999 employees	66.8	51.2
1,000 or more employees	71.1	53.8
Public	83.4	72.9

Source: Copeland (2005b), figure 2.

2002 (Copeland 2006a). Moreover, only 3.4 million tax returns for 2003 showed deductible IRA contributions that year, and their deductible contributions totaled just over $10 billion. Another 1.2 million returns showed Keogh/self-employed contributions totaling almost $18 billion. As with employment-based plans, participation in IRAs and Keoghs tends to be highest among those who are older, those who have attained a higher educational level, and those who have a higher income level.

Americans Are Living Longer but Retiring Earlier

As more fully discussed in chapter 8, an important demographic trend is that Americans are living longer but retiring earlier. The life expectancy for a male born in 2005 is 74.8 years, up from 61.4 years in 1940 (see table 2.2). Meanwhile, the average age at which workers begin receiving their Social Security retirement benefits fell from 66.2 years old in 1960 to 63.6 years old in 2002 (see table 8.2). All in all, older men leaving the workforce today can anticipate 18 years in retirement, up from just 13 years in retirement 30 years ago (Committee for Economic Development 1999, 5).[15]

The Current System Will Not Provide Adequate Retirement Incomes

The combination of earlier retirements and longer life expectancies has led a number of analysts to express concern about the financial prospects of elderly retirees in the 21st century.[16] The United States already has 36 million residents who are age 65 and over and 4.7 million who are age 85 and over (He et al. 2005, 6). By 2030, however, the United States will have 72 million residents age 65 and over, and it will have 9.6 million residents age 85 and over.

The economic problems of these elderly citizens will be of paramount importance to the nation in the 21st century. According to Lawrence Thompson (1998), the economic cost of supporting the elderly is best understood in terms of the fraction of society's goods and services that are consumed by them. Specifically, "the cost of supporting the retired is simply the product of three different economic and demographic ratios:

the *aggregate consumption ratio*, which is the fraction of total economic activity devoted to producing consumer goods and services;

the *retiree dependency ratio*, which is the fraction of the population that is retired (which is going to be very similar to the aged dependency ratio); and the *living standards ratio*, which is the ratio of the average consumption of a retired person to the average consumption of all persons." (Thompson 1998, 40)

The importance of this formulation is that it can be used to illustrate some rather direct and simple relationships between the ratios and the cost of supporting the elderly (Thompson 1998, 41). For example, a 10 percent increase in the fraction of the population that is retired will result in a 10 percent increase in the cost of supporting the retired. Only 12.4 percent of the U.S. population consisted of persons age 65 or over in the year 2000, but by 2030, 19.6 percent of the population will be 65 or older (He et al. 2005, figure 2-6).[17] That is about a 60 percent increase.

There Are Fewer Traditional Defined Benefit Plans

In recent years, there has been a marked shift away from traditional defined benefit plans and toward defined contribution plans and their cash balance cousins. Many medium and large private establishments have switched from defined benefit plans to defined contribution plans (table 9.2).[18] Among the reasons for the shift toward defined contribution plans are the higher administrative costs associated with defined benefit plans, employment shifts from large to small firms, the decline in unionism, the rise of 401(k) plans, workers' interests in having more portable pensions, and firms' interests in attracting younger workers

Table 9.2. Full-Time Employees in Medium and Large Private Establishments Participating in Defined Benefit and Defined Contribution Retirement Plans, Selected Years (percent)

Year	Defined benefit plans	Defined contribution plans	All retirement plans
1985	80	41	91
1986	76	47	89
1988	63	45	80
1989	63	48	81
1991	59	48	78
1993	56	49	78
1995	52	55	80
1997	50	57	79
1999	42	52	72
2000	36	50	70

Source: Bryandt Rose Dickerson, "Employee Participation in Defined Benefit and Defined Contribution Plans, 1985–2000," revised June 14, 2004, http://www.bls.gov/opub/cwc/cm20030325tb01.htm.

and in having pensions encourage later retirement (Even and Macpherson 2003).[19]

Lately, even economically healthy employers have been freezing or abandoning their traditional defined benefit plans (Munnell et al. 2006; VanDerhei 2006). At the same time, the nature of the remaining defined benefit plans has been changing: defined benefit plans have been moving away from the traditional final-average-pay model. In 2003, 43 percent of employees in private industry defined benefit plans were in plans with a final-average-pay formula (BLS 2005g, table 55).[20] Employee activists have been outraged at what at times seems like a "race to the bottom for the defined benefit system."[21]

In sum, Edward A. Zelinsky concludes that the era of the traditional defined benefit plan is largely behind us (1999, 2004).

The Trend toward Phased Retirement and Bridge Jobs

As America ages, the workforce has also begun to change. Since the Age Discrimination in Employment Act's elimination of age-65 mandatory retirement, phased or gradual retirement has started to replace the traditional "cliff" retirement pattern in which older workers would leave the workforce and never return.[22] Many older Americans stay in or reenter the workforce, especially in part-time and contingent work situations.[23] According to one estimate, roughly one-third of older workers leave their long-held career jobs in favor of new jobs that serve as a bridge to full retirement (Committee for Economic Development 1999, 9).[24]

The Decline of Annuitization

Another significant retirement plan trend is the general decline of annuitization among American workers.[25] The shift to defined contribution plans is part of the story, but defined benefit plans are also changing (GAO 1997, 49). For example, 48 percent of participants in medium and large defined benefit plans were permitted to take a lump-sum distribution in 2003, up from 14 percent in 1991 (BLS 2005g, table 47).[26] Moreover, among defined contribution plans, lump-sum payouts are increasingly prevalent, and a declining fraction of participants even have access to a life annuity as a payout option. One study of the plans of medium and large firms found that just 27 percent of those with 401(k) plans could take their funds as a life annuity (Mitchell with Dykes 2003).[27]

THE FINANCIAL INCENTIVES CREATED BY PENSION PLANS

Pension plan designs can create powerful financial incentives that influence individual decisions about work and retirement (Forman 1999c; Gustman and Steinmeier 1995; Munnell, Triest, and Jivan 2004; Ippolito 1986; Leonesio 1996; Quinn, Burkhauser, and Myers 1990). At the outset, the tax preferences for pension savings reduce the work disincentives inherent in the taxation of earned income.

In addition, private pension plans can significantly affect the timing of retirement. First, along with Social Security and other public benefits, private pensions help provide additional income and wealth that is needed for retirement. Second, traditional defined benefit plans are typically designed to have financial incentives that induce most workers to retire during "windows" of opportunity that range from the plan's early retirement age through the normal retirement age.[28] These plans provide large financial incentives for workers to stay with a firm at least until they are eligible for early retirement, but they impose large financial penalties on workers who stay past the plan's normal retirement age. Moreover, many traditional defined benefit plans provide early retirement incentives that push older workers out of the workforce at even earlier ages.

Defined contribution plans can also influence the timing of the decision to retire, but their effects are typically less dramatic (Ippolito 1997, 10–17).

Tax Preferences for Pension Savings Reduce the Work Disincentives Inherent in the Taxation of Earned Income

The favorable tax treatment for retirement savings generally reduces the work disincentives that can come from taxing earned income. Under current law, earned income is typically subject to federal income tax rates of up to 35 percent and payroll tax rates of up to 15.3 percent. But contributions to retirement plans are typically exempt from taxation, and benefits are typically not taxed until after retirement.[29] The net effect of this tax regime is to reduce the effective marginal tax rates imposed on earned income and so reduce the work disincentives that result from the taxation of earned income.[30]

Also, the favorable tax treatment of pensions reduces the price of pension benefits for employers and employees and can be expected to increase the demand for pensions by workers, especially workers in higher tax brackets.[31] As a result, workers in higher tax brackets are more inclined to seek employers that provide tax-favored pension benefits than workers in lower brackets (Fronstin 2000; Pesando and Turner

2000; Reagan and Turner 2000). Similarly, workers in higher brackets are likely to voluntarily contribute a greater proportion of their income to 401(k) plans and IRAs than workers in lower tax brackets.[32]

In short, exempting pension contributions and earnings from taxation tends to encourage people to work.[33]

The Accumulation of Pension Wealth Encourages Early Retirement

On the other hand, the accumulation of pension wealth enables pension plan participants to retire earlier than they would in a no-pension world. Along with Social Security and Medicare, pensions provide a big chunk of the income and wealth that enable elderly Americans to choose retirement over work. Dora Costa argues that the decline in the average age of retirement is largely attributable to the increasing income and wealth of American families (Costa 1999).[34] From 1962 to 1995, the average net worth of American families increased from $114,000 to $206,000 (Committee for Economic Development 1999, 6). A large part of that increase is attributable to the rapid expansion of the private pension system after World War II. One study estimated that the growth of pensions could account for as much as one-quarter of the decline in labor force participation in the early postwar period (Samwick 1998), and numerous studies have found that workers with access to pension income are more likely to retire than workers without such coverage (Munnell et al. 2004; Uccello 1998; Samwick 1998).

Moreover, these income and wealth effects have an impact on people at all income levels (Committee for Economic Development 1999, 6). In particular, generous Social Security benefits and the health security provided by Medicare and Medicaid have made early retirement possible for virtually all Americans. Most analysts believe that the availability of full Social Security benefits at age 65 and the availability of reduced benefits at age 62 have greatly contributed to the trend toward earlier retirement (Advisory Council on Social Security 1997, vol. 2, 21; Leonesio 1993).

Of course, the income and wealth effects of pension plans probably have their greatest impact on the older workers in the upper half of the income distribution. While 69.5 percent of workers with annual earnings of $50,000 participated in a pension plan in 2004, only 18.2 percent of workers earning between $10,000 and $14,999 participated that year (see table 9.1). Similarly, while pensions accounted for 21 percent of the aggregate income of elderly Americans in the highest income quintile in 2002, pensions accounted for 4 percent of the income of elderly Americans in the lowest quintile (SSA 2004a, 22).[35]

Benefit Accrual Patterns Influence Decisions about Work and Retirement

Pension benefits typically accrue differently under defined benefit plans and defined contribution plans. In particular, under a traditional defined benefit plan (that is, a final-average-pay plan), benefit accruals increase significantly the closer a worker gets to retirement.

Indeed, one of the most obvious features of traditional plans is that they are "backloaded." That is, traditional plans tend to disproportionately favor older workers who have stayed with an employer for 25 or 30 years. The primary reason for this backloading is that the value of benefit accruals typically increases as a percentage of pay as workers approach retirement age. In fact, well over half the value of a worker's pension can accrue in the last 5 or 10 years of service (Ippolito 1997). In short, traditional plans provide relatively larger benefit accruals to older workers and relatively smaller benefit accruals for younger workers.

On the other hand, defined contribution plans (and cash balance plans) typically provide more uniform accruals over a worker's career. Of course, that means that defined contribution plans provide larger benefit accruals than final-average-pay plans for younger workers and smaller benefit accruals for older employees.

Figure 9.1 provides a graphic comparison between a typical defined contribution plan and a traditional defined benefit plan. The figure compares the contributions made on behalf of an individual for the following two hypothetical pension plans. The first is a simple defined contribution plan with a flat contribution rate of 6 percent of salary and interest accruing at 5 percent per year. The second is a traditional defined benefit plan that pays a pension benefit at age 65 of 1 percent times years of service times final average compensation ($B = 1$ percent $\times$ yos $\times$ fac)—that is, a final-average-pay plan.

As shown in figure 9.1, the defined contribution plan has a level contribution rate at all ages. It provides relatively larger benefit accruals than a final-average-pay plan for younger employees and relatively smaller benefit accruals for older employees. The traditional final-average-pay plan, on the other hand, is backloaded. It has severe financial penalties for leaving too early and for working past the normal retirement age.

The differing rates of benefit accrual under traditional final-average-pay plans versus typical defined contribution plans result in different incentives that can affect employee decisions about work and retirement. In particular, traditional final-average-pay plans penalize workers who change jobs frequently. Traditional final-average-pay plans also create large financial incentives for workers to stay on the job at least until they are eligible for early retirement. Traditional plans also

Figure 9.1. Annual Contribution Rates

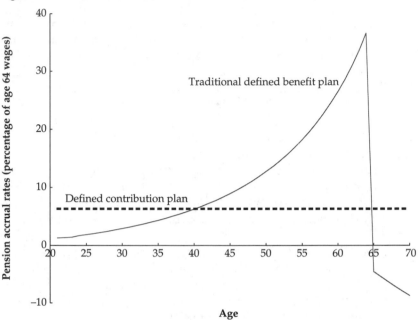

Source: Based on Gebhardtsbauer (1999).

impose large financial penalties on older workers that tend to push them out of the workforce once they have reached the plan's early or normal retirement age.[36]

Traditional Pensions Penalize Mobile Workers

Traditional final-average-pay plans also penalize workers who change jobs frequently. Table 9.3 shows the magnitude of these financial penalties by comparing the retirement benefits of four workers.[37] These workers all have identical 30-year pay histories (6 percent annual pay increases starting at $20,000 and ending at $108,370), and all their employers have identical final-average-pay plans (1.5 percent times years of service times final pay). The only difference among these workers is that the first worker spent her entire career with one employer, while the other workers divided their careers over two or more employers. The long-tenure worker would receive a pension of $49,000 a year at retirement, but the worker who held five jobs would receive pensions totaling just $27,000 a year.

Mobile workers covered by a traditional final-average-pay plan can suffer large benefit losses every time they change jobs, and even greater

Table 9.3. Non-portability of Final-Average-Pay Plans

Worker no.	Employer no.	Yearly accrual rate (percent)	Years of service	Final pay ($)	Total pension ($)
1	1	1.5	30	108,370	**49,000**
2	1	1.5	15	45,219	10,174
	2	1.5	15	108,370	24,383
					35,000
3	1	1.5	10	33,791	5,069
	2	1.5	10 .	60,513	9,077
	3	1.5	10	108,370	16,256
					30,000
4	1	1.5	6	26,765	2,409
	2	1.5	6	37,967	3,417
	3	1.5	6	53,856	4,847
	4	1.5	6	76,396	6,876
	5	1.5	6	108,370	9,753
					27,000

Source: Falivena (1990), 15.

financial penalties can occur when workers change jobs without vesting (it usually takes five years to vest). All in all, traditional final-average-pay plans penalize workers who change jobs frequently.

At the same time, however, traditional final-average-pay plans create large financial incentives for workers to stay with a single employer at least until they are eligible for early retirement (Gustman and Steinmeier 1995, 13–14).[38] This is an example of the "golden handcuffs" phenomenon.

Traditional Pensions Push Workers into Retirement

Traditional final-average-pay plans also typically push older workers out of the workforce once they reach normal retirement age (often between age 60 and 65). Once a worker reaches normal retirement age and is eligible to receive full retirement benefits, delaying retirement can be quite costly.[39] Those who delay retirement lose current benefits, but the increase in benefits that can result from an additional year of work rarely compensates for the benefits lost. And those who work until they die may leave nothing behind for their survivors.

Numerous studies of real-world pension plans have found that particular plan designs can result in a significant loss in pension wealth for employees who work past age 65 (Kotlikoff and Wise 1985, 1987, 1989). Moreover, employers can significantly influence the timing of retirement by offering subsidized benefits for workers who elect to retire early (Fronstin 1997; Lumsdaine, Stock, and Wise 1997). Indeed, the structure of private pensions may have a greater influence than Social Security on decisions about the timing of retirement (Dulitzky 1999; Lumsdaine et al. 1997).[40]

Explicit early retirement incentives are common among firms with traditional defined benefit plans. At least 80 percent of *Fortune* 500 companies have used early retirement incentive plans (Committee for Economic Development 1999, 24–25).[41] It is also common for employers to design their plans in such a way that benefit accrual rates turn negative at a relatively early age.[42]

For example, because early retirees will receive benefits for a longer period, an actuarial reduction in monthly benefits should be required, and it is often suggested that an accrual reduction of at least 6 percent a year is required for actuarial neutrality (Mitchell with Dykes 2003, 122).[43] However, traditional final-average-pay plans often encourage workers to take their benefits prior to normal retirement age by providing enhanced early retirement benefits.[44] Current law permits employers to offer generous early retirement incentives and Social Security supplements. Current law also permits employers to design their plans in ways that impose financial penalties on those who work past the plan's normal retirement age—for example, by not requiring that additional years of service (e.g., beyond 30 years) count toward the accrual of benefits.

In short, "early retirement has been institutionalized" (Casey 1997, 20). Traditional defined benefit plans provide incentives for workers to retire during "windows" of retirement opportunity that typically range from the early retirement age through the normal retirement age. The trend in recent decades has been toward a decline in the normal retirement age and toward incentives for early retirement.

Ultimately, the problem may boil down to the fact that employers often have economic incentives to rid themselves of older workers. Workers generally cost more to employ as they get older (Committee for Economic Development 1999; Munnell 2006; Minda 1994).[45] One large company saw an increase in total compensation costs of 13 percent from 1990 to 1995 due to aging alone, and that company expected its total compensation costs due to an aging workforce would increase by 24 percent over the entire decade (Watson Wyatt 1999). As a result, the compensation of workers nearing the end of their careers can exceed their productivity (Minda 1994; Kotlikoff and Gokhale 1992). When that happens, employers will have an economic incentive to avoid hiring or retaining older workers (Leibfritz 2002; Scott, Berger, and Garen 1995). An employer might also find it advantageous to tap its traditional defined benefit plan or otherwise create financial incentives for early retirement.[46]

Defined Contribution Plans and Cash Balance Plans Tend to Be Neutral about the Age of Retirement

Defined contribution plans (and their cash balance cousins) can also be designed to influence the timing of a worker's decision about when to retire, but usually these plans have significantly less impact on those decisions. For example, a recent study by Leora Friedberg and Anthony Webb found that the absence of age-related incentives in defined contribution plans leads workers to retire an average of almost two years later than workers with traditional defined benefit plans (Friedberg and Webb 2004).

To be sure, defined contribution plans have large income and wealth effects. Access to pension income, whether from a defined benefit plan or a defined contribution plan, just makes retirement more attractive, but defined contribution plans typically do not incorporate plan design provisions that are intended to encourage early retirement.[47] Because these plans are not typically backloaded, vested workers do not suffer benefit losses from changing jobs or retiring too early.[48] Nor do workers face financial penalties for working past the plans' normal or earlier retirement ages. All in all, defined contribution plans (and cash balance plans) tend to be neutral about the age of retirement (Johnson and Steuerle 2003; Diamond 2005).

Modest Changes that Could Improve the Pension System

This part offers some modest changes that could help the current pension system better meet the retirement income needs of American workers and their families and that could help reduce the work disincentives in the current system. The basic approach is to expand coverage and pay workers in proportion to their productivity. Expanding coverage would ensure that more workers and their families have adequate pensions, and paying workers in proportion to their productively would minimize work disincentives and maximize worker productivity.

Society and individuals both have an interest in strengthening the relationship between benefits and productivity. The recent trend in benefits is the unbundled approach, under which workers tend to "get what they pay for" (Mitchell 2003, 12). For example, in lieu of a traditional pension, an employer might offer a defined contribution plan in which each worker gets, say, 10 percent of compensation contributed to her individual account. Similarly, an employer might have a cafeteria plan that gives each employee a fixed amount of benefit "dollars" that can be used to purchase fringe benefits from health insurance to day care. These plans can minimize work disincentives and maximize worker productivity.[49]

Proposals to Expand the Pension System

This section suggests several ways to expand the current pension system, including expanding coverage and increasing portability, moving toward automatic enrollment, expanding the saver's credit, and requiring employers without pensions to offer payroll-deduction IRAs.

Expand Coverage and Increase Portability

At the outset, it would make sense to make retirement plans universal and portable. Our goal should be to ensure that virtually every worker has the opportunity to participate in a meaningful retirement plan that can travel with her when she moves from job to job. For example, federal pension policy should not permit employers to use onerous coverage and vesting requirements to limit or backload benefits in favor of their long-service workers. Instead, pension rules should be changed to toughen coverage and participation requirements and to shorten minimum vesting schedules. Pension policy should also be designed to enhance investment returns on retirement savings and to preserve those savings until retirement.

Toughen Coverage and Participation Requirements. Toughening coverage and participation requirements should help ensure that more workers earn adequate pensions. Employers should be required to cover virtually all their workers, even those who work part-time. Certainly, some employers might abandon their plans rather than comply with tougher coverage and participation requirements. That can happen in a voluntary pension system like ours. On the whole, however, most employers need to offer a competitive compensation package to attract and retain workers, and a desirable pension plan is an important part of that package.

Shorten Vesting Periods. Vesting periods should also be shortened. For example, it would make sense for workers to be 100 percent vested after they complete no more than one year of service. That way, workers who change jobs frequently or move in and out of the labor market would still earn significant retirement benefits along the way.[50]

Enhance Investment Returns. Employees tend to be pretty poor investors. One recent study found that defined benefit plans managed by investment professionals tend to get annual returns 1.9 percentage points higher than defined contribution plans where individuals tend to choose the investments (Goodman 2004). In addition, employees tend to invest too heavily in the stock of their employers, as the recent

Enron scandal showed.[51] High and hidden administrative costs and management fees can also reduce investment returns, particularly on individual accounts. To help boost investment returns, it could make sense to let employers encourage employees to put more of their investments into premixed, balanced stock/bond portfolios.

Moreover, there is a desperate need for more financial education of all kinds—from elementary school through retirement. In particular, it would make sense to give employers greater freedom to provide unbiased third-party investment advice to their workers.

Preserve Benefits until Retirement. Another major problem with pension plans and IRAs is that they are leaky. While defined benefit plans typically provide lifetime annuities for retirees and their spouses, defined contribution plans typically allow participants to withdraw all or a portion of their individual accounts, and many plans allow participants to borrow against their accounts. In 1997, 52 percent of the savings and thrift plans of medium and large businesses permitted withdrawals, and 54 percent permitted loans (BLS 1999, table 146).[52] Dissipation of retirement savings is also a problem for IRAs, as pre-retirement distributions may be used for education, health, and first-time homebuyer expenses.[53]

Unfortunately, a significant portion of these distributions and loans may end up dissipating before retirement. One study suggests that 60 percent of the lump-sum distributions made to job changers from large plans are not rolled over into IRAs or other retirement savings plans (Yakoboski 1997).[54] It would make sense to prohibit cash-outs, distributions, or loans from pension plans and IRAs.[55]

Another problem has to do with the treatment of pensions under the asset tests used in such means-tested programs as Medicaid, food stamps, and SSI (Orszag and Hall 2003; Ippolito 1997, 200; SSA 2006a). The stringent asset tests under those programs often require low-income workers to withdraw the balances in their defined contribution plans and IRAs (but not from defined benefit plans) and "spend down" those assets before they can qualify for benefits. Consequently, these asset tests dissipate retirement savings and may reduce saving by low-income families. While actual withdrawals from retirement accounts should count as "income" in determining eligibility for means-tested benefits, the amounts held in retirement accounts should be excluded from asset tests.

Automatic Enrollment and Minimum Contributions

For employers with 401(k) plans, we should move to the negative election approach under which all employees are automatically enrolled in the plan unless they execute a rejection form opting out.[56]

Financial planners usually suggest that the easiest way to save is through a payroll-deduction mechanism: "If you don't see the money, you won't spend it." The plan could also set an initial minimum contribution rate of, say, 5 percent of income, unless the employee specifically opts for a smaller amount.

Expand the Saver's Tax Credit and Make It Refundable

Another way to help increase the number of Americans with pensions would be to expand the saver's tax credit and make it refundable.[57] Since 2002, certain low- and moderate-income individuals have been able to claim a tax credit of up to $1,000 for certain qualified retirement savings contributions. The credit equals a percentage (50 percent, 20 percent, or 10 percent) of up to $2,000 of contributions. In effect, the credit acts like an employer match: the government matches a portion of the employee's contributions. Employer matches encourage workers to contribute, at least up to the match level, and the saver's tax credit should have similar pro-savings effects.[58]

Because the saver's tax credit is not refundable, it provides little benefit to low-income workers. According to one study, some 57 million returns in 2003 had income low enough to qualify for the credit; because the credit is not refundable, however, only one-fifth of those could actually benefit from the credit if they made qualifying retirement savings contributions, and only 64,000 (or slightly more than one out of every 1,000) could receive the maximum possible credit of $1,000 (Orszag and Hall 2003; Gale, Iwry, and Orszag 2005).[59]

Accordingly, it would make sense to expand and extend the saver's tax credit. More specifically, we should make the credit refundable and extend the 50 percent credit rate further up the income distribution.

Require Employers without Pension Plans to Offer Payroll-Deduction IRAs

Employers without a retirement plan should be required to offer payroll-deduction IRAs to interested employees. Under current law, an employer can establish a payroll-deduction IRA program to help employees save for retirement through their own IRAs.[60] These work much like the federal savings bond program. Under a payroll-deduction program, an employee may contribute to an IRA by electing to have the employer withhold amounts from her paycheck and forward those amounts to her IRA. Payroll deduction contributions are included in the employee's wages for the taxable year, but (in the case of contributions to traditional IRAs) the employee may deduct the contributions on her tax return, subject to the usual limits.

Requiring employers without other pension plans to offer payroll-deduction IRAs would dramatically increase coverage. Also, these employers should be required to adopt an automatic-enrollment arrangement. It would also help if participating employees were allowed to *exclude* allowable contributions from their income, as opposed to deducting them at the end of the year.

Proposals to Reduce Work Disincentives

This section suggests seven ways to reduce the work disincentives associated with the current pension system. This section recommends toughening the penalty on premature withdrawals, raising the normal retirement age, raising the minimum distribution age, repealing the age discrimination exceptions, changing the limits on benefits and contributions, requiring that benefits be paid as indexed annuities, and making phased retirement easier.

Toughen the Penalty on Premature Withdrawals

Internal Revenue Code § 72(t) generally imposes a 10 percent tax on pension distributions made before an individual reaches age 59½. Toughening this penalty could significantly affect the timing of retirement. In particular, it would make sense to raise the eligibility age to 62 and keep it tied to Social Security's early retirement age, even if that age is increased. As we saw in chapter 8, raising the age of initial eligibility for Social Security benefits would increase the average age of retirement, and so would raising the age of eligibility for pension distributions.

In addition, we should eliminate virtually all exceptions to the premature distribution penalty and significantly increase the penalty rate.[61] An alternative approach would be to significantly limit, or completely eliminate, the right to receive withdrawals before the age of initial eligibility.[62] We should also require that most lump-sum distributions from pension plans be rolled over into another plan or into an IRA.

Raise the Normal Retirement Age

Along the same lines, we should raise the normal retirement age for pensions. ERISA generally defines "normal retirement age" as the earlier of the time specified in the plan or age 65.[63] On the other hand, "full retirement age" under the Social Security system is already 65 and 8 months (in 2006) and is gradually increasing to 67. It would make sense to gradually increase the normal retirement age for pension plans to 67 and keep it tied to the Social Security's full retirement age, even if that full retirement age is increased. Increasing the normal retirement for pensions would encourage workers to stay in the workforce longer (Aaron 1999b; Polapink 2006). Moreover, delaying retirement should lead to higher benefit levels when workers eventually retire.

Raise the Minimum Distribution Age or Repeal the Rule

Internal Revenue Code § 401(a)(9) generally requires participants in retirement plans to begin taking distributions soon after they reach age 70½.[64] An exception allows older workers with a pension plan from their current employer to delay distributions until they retire, but workers with pensions from prior employers and IRA holders must begin taking distributions from those plans soon after they reach age 70½. Failure to take the required minimum distribution can result in a 50 percent excise tax penalty on the excess of the amount required to have been distributed over the amount that actually was distributed.[65] In addition, a plan that fails to make the required minimum distributions can be disqualified.

Admittedly, most elderly Americans retire long before they reach age 70½. Nevertheless, by compelling many of the remaining elderly American workers to take retirement distributions soon after age 70½, these rules invariably prod still more elderly workers into retirement. Consequently, repealing these rules or raising the minimum distribution age to say, 75 or 80, could help encourage elderly workers to remain in the workforce.[66]

Repeal the Age Discrimination Exceptions

The Age Discrimination in Employment Act of 1967 outlawed mandatory retirement before the age of 65. The limit was raised to 70 in 1978 and finally removed altogether in 1986. The Act generally prohibits employers from discriminating against workers over the age of 40. Since 1988, employers have been prohibited from ceasing benefit accruals for employees who work beyond age 64 and from excluding participants who are hired within five years of normal retirement age.[67]

These statutes clearly forbid a cessation of benefit accruals or a reduction in the rate of benefit accruals because of age, but they do not automatically prohibit benefit reductions that correlate with age. In fact, various exceptions expressly allow retirement plans to limit the total amount of benefits or the total number of years used to compute benefits.

For example, consider a traditional final-average-pay plan that provides workers with a pension benefit at age 65 equal to 2 percent times years of service times final average pay. Under current law, that plan may also provide that no more than 30 years of service count in computing a worker's retirement benefits. Final average pay might go up if a worker remained on the job for more than 30 years, but a worker with 35 years of service would still receive a benefit of just 60 percent of her then-final average pay (60 percent = 2 percent × not more than 30 years of service). With this type of plan design, the employer is able to significantly reduce the rate of benefit accruals for workers who stay past 30 years and so induce them to retire. According to one study of medium and large firms some 31 percent of the defined benefit plan participants studied faced a maximum limit on years of service in 1997 (Mitchell with Dykes 2003).[68]

Still other exceptions to the age discrimination laws allow plans to provide subsidized early retirement benefits and Social Security supplements.[69] Thus, despite the general prohibition on age discrimination, firms are still allowed to use pension incentives to encourage older workers to leave their jobs (Burkhauser and Quinn 1997; Mitchell with Dykes 2003, table 2).

Pertinent here, it is not at all clear why federal retirement policy should allow employers to use tax-preferred retirement savings to push their older workers into early retirements (Goodman 2004). Accordingly, Congress should repeal virtually all these exceptions to the age discrimination rules (Rix 2005; Meyers 1991).

For example, Congress should repeal the exception that allows plans to limit the number of years used to compute benefits. If the years-of-service exception to the age discrimination rules were repealed, the hypothetical worker described above would be entitled to a retirement benefit of 70 percent of her final average pay after 35 years of service, not 60 percent. That benefit enhancement would significantly reduce her incentive to retire after just 30 years of service.

All in all, repealing these pension exceptions to the age discrimination laws would curtail the ability of employers to design plans to provide explicit financial incentives for early retirement. As a result, more older workers would remain at work, and that would be good for them and society as a whole.[70]

Change the Limits on Benefits and Contributions

Congress should also simplify and consolidate the limits on contributions. Current law provides a rather arbitrary mix of limits on contributions, depending upon the type of plan involved. In 2006 some workers are able to put up to $44,000 in a defined contribution plan, while others can put no more than $15,000 into a 401(k) plan, or $4,000 into an IRA. It would be better to have a single, uniform annual limit for all retirement savings (Goodman 2004).

Congress should also relax the I.R.C. § 415(b) limit on the amount of benefits that can be paid to retirees by defined benefit plans (Scahill 1999). That provision limits the annual benefit that can be paid at the Social Security retirement age to the lesser of $175,000 (in 2006) or 100 percent of the participant's compensation; actuarial reductions are required for earlier retirement. The provision is unnecessarily complicated, and its stingy limits may actually discourage the formation of pension plans that could help expand pension coverage. Pertinent here, however, is section 415's impact on the timing of retirement. By limiting the maximum annual benefit that can be paid to a retiree, section 415 can push some elderly workers into retirement.[71]

One solution would be to increase the normal retirement age dollar limit, at least for older workers who face the cap because of already long years of service. In particular, a worker with 25 or 30 years of service should not be prevented from earning additional retirement benefits merely because she has already accrued a benefit equal to 100 percent of her final average pay (albeit under a rather generous plan).[72]

Require that Benefits Be Paid as Indexed Annuities

Government policy should also encourage or even require that pension benefits be paid as annuities, perhaps even indexed-for-inflation annuities. Annuities help ensure that workers and their families will not outlive their retirement savings, and inflation-adjusted annuities keep benefits from eroding because of inflation (GAO 1997, 49).

Defined benefit plans are typically designed to pay benefits in the form of a lifetime annuity, and for married couples, joint and survivor annuities and pre-retirement survivor annuities are the default form of distribution.[73] In recent years, however, defined benefit plans have been moving away from paying annuities, with more plans offering installment and lump-sum distribution alternatives (Mitchell with Dykes 2003). Defined contribution plans typically make lump-sum distributions.[74]

Inflation after retirement almost invariably erodes the value of accrued pension benefits. Post-retirement inflation is always a problem for defined contribution plans, and very few defined benefit plans are indexed for inflation.[75] Moreover, older workers often fail to consider how their benefits and needs will change over the course of their retirement (Steuerle, Spiro, and Carasso 1999b).

This trend away from annuitization and toward lump-sum distributions is quite troublesome, because older Americans tend to be so myopic in their decisions about when to retire. They underestimate their life expectancies, overestimate their financial ability to meet their future retirement income needs, and fail to understand the deleterious effects of inflation; consequently, they choose to retire too early.[76] What looks like an adequate retirement income at age 55, 62, or even 65 may not be enough to live on at age 80 when work is not a likely option and savings have been depleted. Poverty statistics already show that Americans age 80 and older are 40 percent more likely to live in poverty than those age 65 to 69 (U.S. House Committee 2004, table A-7).[77]

The government could combat this myopic decisionmaking by requiring retirement plans to pay benefits in the form of annuities, perhaps even indexed-for-inflation annuities. Such annuities keep the purchasing power of benefits constant over time by lowering initial benefits enough to pay for higher benefits later on (Steuerle et al. 1999b). Alternatively, Congress could require that all plans at least offer participants the option of taking benefits in the form of an inflation-adjusted annuity.

For example, the government might want to require that individuals take a basic pension distribution that, together with Social Security, would provide them with the equivalent of an indexed annuity that is targeted to, say, 200 percent of the poverty level. Beyond that basic annuity, however, more relaxed distribution rules might apply.

In 2006, for example, the poverty level for a single individual is $9,800 (HHS 2006). Consequently, assuming a 200-percent-of-the-poverty-level target, a single individual retiring in 2006 would need the equivalent of an indexed annuity that paid $19,600 that year and appropriately inflation-adjusted amounts in future years.[78] For most retirees, Social Security would provide a good chunk of this minimum 200-percent-of-the-poverty-level benefit, leaving only the balance to be made up from the worker's indexed-for-inflation pension.

Make Phased Retirement Easier

Pension plans are generally prohibited from making distributions to active employees. For example, a Treasury regulation says that defined benefit plans can make distributions only in the event of retirement, death, disability, or other severance from employment.[79] Somewhat less restrictive withdrawal rules apply to profit-sharing, stock bonus plans, and 401(k) plans (Treasury Regulation § 1.401-1(b)(ii); VanDerhei and McDonnell 2000).[80] These rules make phased retirement difficult for workers and push them to take full retirement when some would prefer to keep working, albeit on a reduced basis. It is worth considering whether we should make it easier for workers to tap their pensions to help them finance a phased retirement.[81] In that regard, the Treasury

Department recently offered proposed regulations that would make it easier for pensions to provide phased retirement options (IRS 2004a).

More Comprehensive Proposals

This section offers some comprehensive proposals that could help reduce work disincentives in the current pension system and help meet the retirement income needs of workers and their families.

Mandate Age Neutrality

One approach would be for the government to encourage, or even mandate, age-neutral pension policies. Current pension rules permit employers to design pension plans in which pension benefit accruals vary dramatically over a worker's career, and employers use those rules to manipulate their workers' choices about work and retirement. With five-year cliff vesting, for example, employers can encourage some workers to stay for at least five years but keep shorter-term workers from earning any pension benefits. With a traditional final-average-pay plan, employers can backload benefits in favor of long-service workers and embed financial penalties that push expensive, older workers into premature retirement once they have reached some arbitrary retirement age (see figure 9.1). The current pension system permits retirement plans to be non-neutral on age, and employers use that permission to promote their own rather parochial interests (Goodman 2004).

The government, however, has much broader goals for pension policy. The government wants workers to earn pensions that are adequate to support them throughout their retirement years, and the government wants to encourage Americans to be as productive as possible. Measured against these goals, the current pension system must be viewed as a failure.

A big part of the solution would be to move toward a pension system that is age neutral. Under an age-neutral approach, workers would earn meaningful retirement benefits virtually every year that they worked. Employers would not be allowed to impose onerous vesting rules, backload benefits in favor of long-service workers, or impose financial penalties on workers who continue to work beyond some arbitrary retirement age.

The previous section of this chapter offered a number of recommendations that would help make the current pension system more age neutral. For example, toughening the coverage and participation rules would help ensure that more workers are covered by retirement plans, and shortening the vesting periods would help ensure that more workers actually earned benefits. Moreover, repealing the rules permitting retirement plans to limit the number of years that count for benefit accrual purposes and repealing the exceptions to ADEA that permit early retirement subsidies would help encourage older workers to stay on the job.

The government should also adopt policies that require pensions to achieve actuarial neutrality, at least beyond some minimum retirement age. Put simply, the government should mandate policies that ensure "that the present value of benefits accrued at a particular point in time is identical, whether those benefits are drawn early, late, or at the normal time" (Casey 1997, 18). An age-neutrality requirement would require plans to ensure that the value of accrued benefits would be actuarially adjusted for any delay in their receipt.

A more comprehensive approach, however, would be to expressly mandate age neutrality in all retirement plans for workers of all ages. Presumably, benefits would accrue at a constant annual rate, like they do now in the typical defined contribution plan. Indeed, the typical defined contribution plan could easily satisfy an age-neutrality mandate. For example, a simple defined contribution plan might provide that an employee is entitled to a contribution of 6 percent of salary each year and that accumulations earn a market rate of return. Such a plan does not penalize workers who change from job to job, nor does it impose financial penalties on those who keep working past some arbitrary retirement age. In short, defined contribution plans are age-neutral.[82]

On the other hand, most defined benefit plans would clearly flunk an age-neutrality requirement. For example, traditional final-average-pay plans have backloaded benefit-accrual formulas and typically cease benefit accruals after 30 years of service.

Indeed, among defined benefit plans, only cash balance plans could easily meet an age-neutrality requirement. Like defined contribution plans, cash balance plans have individual accounts, albeit hypothetical. For example, a simple cash balance plan that provided wage credits of 6 percent of a salary and market-rate interest credits would clearly be age neutral.

All in all, an age neutrality policy would be a major step forward. Benefit accruals would be tied to productivity, not age or years of service. Workers could be expected to respond by being more productive, and no worker would be pushed into retirement by financial penalties.

The net effect of mandating age neutrality would be to move the current pension system toward a world of individual accounts, both real (defined contribution plans) and hypothetical (cash balance plans).

In an age-neutral world, virtually all workers would see a flat percentage of pay contributed to individual accounts on their behalf, and those workers would earn interest on their accumulations at the market rate. Workers would no longer be locked into particular jobs, nor would they have any incentive to retire during arbitrarily created retirement "windows." Consequently, more workers would remain in the workforce, accumulating assets for their eventual retirement or for their survivors.[83]

A Mandatory Universal Pension System

In the end, a voluntary pension system cannot be counted on to meet the retirement income needs of American workers and their families.[84] However, we could meet those needs with a mandatory universal pension system.[85] Under this approach, workers and their employers would be required to set aside a large enough share of their earnings over their careers to fund adequate retirement benefits. A mandatory universal pension system could also be designed to minimize work disincentives.

As mentioned in chapter 8, The President's Commission on Pension Policy recommended adoption of a mandatory universal pension system (MUPS) that would have required all employers to contribute at least 3 percent of wages to private pensions for their workers (President's Commission on Pension Policy 1981). Although that proposal drew little interest at the time, there has recently been renewed interest in mandated pensions.[86]

The simplest design for a mandatory pension system would be to piggyback a system of individual retirement savings accounts (IRSAs) onto the existing Social Security withholding system. For example, employers and employees could both be required to contribute 1.5 percent of payroll to these IRSAs (and the self-employed would be required to contribute 3 percent). These accounts could be held by the government and invested in secure equity funds and annuitized on retirement. Alternatively, these individual accounts could be held by financial institutions and their investment could be directed by individual workers.[87] All in all, this type of mandatory universal pension system could help ensure that all American workers and their families have adequate retirement incomes (Carasso and Forman 2006). At the same time, a mandatory universal pension system would have a minimum of work disincentives.

10

MAKING HEALTH CARE WORK

The most obvious way to make life better for low-income workers is to improve their access to health care. It is unconscionable
that more than 40 million Americans don't have health insurance, most of them in working families. (Rivlin 2002, 8)

T he structure of the American health care system significantly affects
the work and retirement patterns of Americans. Most Americans
are covered by a health insurance plan related to employment. In
general, having health care tied to employment encourages individuals
to enter and remain in the workforce.

On the other hand, working does not guarantee health care coverage.
Employers are not required to provide health care coverage to their
employees, yet people who work typically earn too much to be covered
by Medicaid. Of the 45.8 million (15.7 percent of) Americans without
health care coverage in 2004, 27.3 million were between 18 and 64 and
worked during the year, and 21.1 million of them worked full-time
(DeNavas-Walt et al. 2005, tables 7 and C-1).

All in all, our predominantly employment-based health care system
has a considerable influence on work and retirement behavior, but not
all of that influence is positive. This chapter explains how the current
health care system works and offers recommendations about how to
make it work better.

Overview of the Health Care System

In 2003, national health expenditures totaled $1,679.9 billion, about 15.3 percent of the gross domestic product (National Center for Health Statistics 2005, table 119).[1] The per capita health care expenditure was $5,671. The United States currently spends about twice as much, per capita, on health care as other industrialized nations (OECD 2006b, 209).

The principal coverage mechanisms are employment-based health insurance, Medicare, and Medicaid. In 2004, 174 million Americans (59.8 percent) were covered by employment-based private health insurance, and 26.9 million (9.3 percent) bought their own private insurance. Another 79.1 million (27.2 percent) had government health insurance (i.e., Medicare, Medicaid, or military health care), and 45.8 million (15.7 percent) had no coverage (DeNavas-Walt et al. 2005, table C-1).[2]

Most nonelderly Americans receive their health care coverage through employment-based coverage provided to workers and their families. In 2004, for example, 161.2 million nonelderly Americans (63.2 percent) received their health care coverage through an employment-based plan (table 10.1).[3] Another 34.2 million (13.4 percent) were covered by Medicaid, and 6.2 million (2.5 percent) were covered by Medicare. All in all, some 210.4 million nonelderly Americans (82.2 percent) had health coverage in 2004, while 45.5 million (17.8 percent) had no coverage.

The Medicare program provides nearly universal coverage for elderly Americans. For example, 95 percent of the elderly were covered by Medicare in 2004, and only 0.8 percent of the elderly were without health care coverage that year (table 10.2). In addition to Medicare, many elderly Americans are covered by employment-based retiree health insurance and/or individually purchased Medigap policies.

All in all, the federal government is heavily involved in providing health care assistance through Medicare, Medicaid, SCHIP, veterans

Table 10.1. Health Care Coverage of the Nonelderly, 2004

Source of coverage	Millions	Percentage
Total population	255.9	100.0
Employment-based coverage	161.2	63.2
Individually purchased	17.0	6.6
Public	45.5	17.8
Medicare	6.2	2.5
Medicaid	34.2	13.4
Military health care	8.1	3.2
No health insurance	45.5	17.8

Source: Author's calculations from U.S. Census Bureau, *Historical Health Insurance Tables* (2005), table HI-2.

Table 10.2. Health Care Coverage of the Elderly, 2004

Source of coverage	Millions	Percentage
Total population	35.2	100.0
Employment-based coverage	12.5	35.5
Individually purchased	10.0	28.3
Public	33.6	95.4
Medicare	33.5	95.0
Medicaid	3.3	9.4
Military health care	2.5	7.1
No health insurance	0.3	0.8

Source: Author's calculations from U.S. Census Bureau, *Historical Health Insurance Tables* (2005), table III-2.

benefits, the exclusion for employer-provided health insurance premiums, the deduction of health care costs, federal employee benefits, and other mechanisms. In 2001, the federal government accounted for 32.9 percent ($406.6 billion) of all health spending, and state and local governments picked up another 10.6 percent ($130.4 billion) (U.S. House Committee 2004, appendix C, C-9).

Employment-Based Health Care Coverage

Employers are not required to provide health care coverage for their workers. Nevertheless, many employers provide coverage to attract and retain workers and to promote worker health and productivity. Nearly two-thirds of nonelderly individuals receive health care benefits through employment-based plans, and surveys show that health insurance is the fringe benefit that is most valued by workers and their families (Blakely 1999, xviii).

Employment-based coverage peaked at 69.2 percent of the nonelderly population in 1987 and has declined in recent years (Fronstin 1999). Coverage also varies dramatically depending on such factors as firm size, industry, and earnings. For example, while 78.1 percent of employees at large private firms (1,000 or more employees) had health care coverage from their employers in 2004, only 27.5 percent of workers at firms with 10 to 24 workers received health care coverage from their employers that year (Fronstin 1999).[4] Similarly, while 82.1 percent of workers with annual earnings of $50,000 or more had employment-based coverage in 2004, only 12.8 percent of workers earning less than $5,000 had employment-based coverage that year (Fronstin 2005c).[5]

Also of note, individuals typically have to work full-time to obtain a job with health insurance. In 2004, for example, 72.7 percent of nonelderly full-year, full-time workers had employment-based health care coverage, compared with just 39.8 percent of other nonelderly workers (Fronstin 2005d).

Before World War II, relatively few workers had health insurance coverage. When wages were frozen during World War II, some employers began offering health insurance as a way of getting around government wage controls (Fronstin 1999). Union support of health insurance and favorable tax treatment were also significant factors in the expansion of the employment-based health care system. Employers also find that they can purchase group health insurance coverage at better rates than individual employees.

Many employees are required to pay for at least a portion of their family health care coverage. Many employers, however, provide "cafeteria plans," which give employees a choice among fringe benefits and enable them to exclude their premiums from income.[6] Also, many employers allow their employees to set up "flexible spending accounts" to tax shelter their out-of-pocket co-pays and other health care expenses.

Under the health care continuation rules provided by the Consolidated Omnibus Budget Reconciliation Act of 1986 (COBRA), former employees of firms with 20 or more workers are typically entitled to continue their health care coverage for up to 18 months after leaving the firm, although the worker is responsible for 102 percent of the employer's premium cost during that period.[7]

Some employers also provide health care coverage for their retired workers, but such coverage is on the decline. Only 28.7 percent of retirees age 55–64 had health care coverage from a former employer in 2002, down from 39.2 percent in 1997 (Fronstin 2005b).[8] Similarly, only 13 percent of private employers offered health benefits to their retirees in 2003, down from 22 percent in 1997.

Tax Advantages

The tax advantages connected with employment-based health care plans are significant, and these advantages are one reason employment-based plans dominate the provision of health care to working-age Americans and their families. Workers generally must pay income tax on the compensation that they receive from an employer. To encourage employment-based health care coverage, however, employer contributions to health care plans are excluded from income (I.R.C. § 106; JCT 2006b; Fronstin 2006). The exclusion covers employees, former employees, and their families. Also, many employers provide cafeteria and flexible spending plans that enable employees to shelter their share of premiums and other health care costs. Self-employed individuals are also permitted to deduct 100 percent of their health insurance costs, but there is no similar tax benefit for employees whose employers do not provide health care coverage.[9]

The tax savings from being able to shelter $5,000 or $10,000 a year per family from the income tax makes employment-based health care coverage much more valuable than taxable cash compensation. For example, an employee in the 25 percent income tax rate bracket would not be taxed if her employer contributed $5,000 on her behalf to an employer-sponsored health care plan. On the other hand, that employee would have to pay $1,250 in income tax on the receipt of $5,000 in cash compensation ($1,250 = $5,000 × 25 percent), leaving just $3,750 after tax—hardly enough to buy an individual health insurance policy.[10]

In short, the tax system provides significant incentives for employers to provide compensation in the form of tax-free health care coverage rather than taxable wages. All in all, $561.9 billion in employer contributions for health care escaped tax in 2003 (U.S. House Committee 2004, table 13-2),[11] and the revenue lost by not taxing these health care contributions exceeds $100 billion a year (Executive Office and OMB 2006a, table 19-1).

Federal Preemption of State Laws

Another reason employment-based plans dominate the provision of health care to working-age Americans and their families is that federal law generally makes it extremely difficult for states to experiment with more universal systems for the provision of health care benefits. The Employee Retirement Income Security Act of 1974 preempts "any and all State laws insofar . . . . as they relate to any employee benefit plan."[12] Although ERISA was largely intended to federalize pension law and had little to say about health care plans, this preemption rule enables employers to avoid state regulation by setting up "self-insured" plans. State governments can dictate how health *insurance* plans work, but they are prevented from telling *self-insured* employment-based plans what to do. The resulting inability of states to regulate all health care plans makes it difficult for the states to act as "laboratories of democracy" that could experiment with the whole range of approaches for expanding coverage.[13]

Medicare

The Medicare program provides nearly universal coverage for elderly Americans and for certain disabled persons (U.S. House Committee 2004, section 2). Medicare Part A provides hospital insurance coverage for almost everyone over age 65 and for certain disabled persons under age 65. Medicare Part B is a voluntary program that generally pays 80 percent of the doctor bills and laboratory tests for elderly and disabled individuals who choose to enroll and pay the monthly premium, which is $88.50 in 2006 (HHS 2005). In 2005, 42.5 million people were covered by Medicare, and total program outlays that year were $336.4 billion (Boards of Trustees 2006, table II.B1).

Medicare Part A is financed primarily through Social Security payroll taxes. Employees pay a Medicare payroll tax rate equal to 1.45 percent of wages, and employers pay a matching amount. Self-employed individuals pay a Medicare tax equal to 2.9 percent of net earnings from self-employment. About 75 percent of the financing for Medicare Part B comes from general revenues, and the rest comes from the monthly premiums collected from participants.

Benefits under Medicare are excluded from income. Consequently, almost $279 billion in Medicare benefits escaped tax in 2003 (U.S. House Committee 2004, table 13-2), and the estimated revenue lost by not taxing Medicare benefits is about $27 billion a year (JCT 2006a, table 1).

Medicaid and the State Children's Health Insurance Program

Medicaid is a federal-state matching entitlement program that provides medical assistance for needy persons who are elderly, blind, disabled, members of families with dependent children, and certain other pregnant women and children (U.S. House Committee 2004, section 15). The program is means-tested; that is, eligible recipients must have relatively low income and relatively few assets. The program is financed by general revenues from federal and state governments. States design and administer their programs within federal guidelines, and the federal government reimburses them for 50 to 83 percent of their costs.

Total federal and state outlays for the Medicaid program were $276.8 billion in fiscal year 2004 (Hoffman et al. 2005). The program served 51.6 million people in fiscal year 2002, and the average expenditure was about $4,140 per person. The average annual expenditure for elderly persons was $11,450, and the average annual expenditure for the blind or disabled was $12,015, but the average annual expenditure for nondisabled children and adults was relatively low ($1,865 per adult and $1,470 per child).

Transitional Medicaid assistance provides certain families who would otherwise lose their coverage as a result of employment with up to one year of additional Medicaid coverage (GAO 2002b). In addition, the State Children's Health Insurance Program was enacted by Congress in 1997 to expand health care coverage for children in low-income families. The program provides block grants to states in order to provide health care benefits for uninsured children, ineligible for Medicaid, whose families have incomes below 200 percent of the federal poverty level. SCHIP covered more than 4.6 million children in fiscal year 2001 (GAO 2003, 7).

Despite Medicaid and SCHIP, 8.3 million children (11.2 percent) lacked health care coverage in 2004 (DeNavas-Walt et al. 2005). Some 18.9 percent of children living in families with incomes below the poverty level had no medical coverage that year.[14]

PROBLEMS WITH THE HEALTH CARE SYSTEM

Two of the major problems with the health care system are that it does not cover all Americans and that it distorts individual decisions about work and retirement.

Millions of Americans Lack Health Care Coverage

Far and away the biggest problem with the American health care system has to do with coverage. In 2004, for example, while 245.3 million Americans (84.2 percent) had some type of health care coverage, 45.8 million (15.7 percent) were without coverage (DeNavas-Walt et al. 2005, table C-1).[15] Clusters of individuals that tend to lack coverage include employees of small business, workers who lose their jobs, workers who decline employer coverage, low-income parents, low-income childless adults, the near-elderly, young adults, children, and immigrants (Dorn 2004; Pollack and Kronebusch 2004).

Of particular concern, many of those without insurance are workers. Of the 37.3 million uninsured Americans between 18 and 64 years old in 2004, 27.3 million worked during the year, and 21.1 million worked full time (DeNavas-Walt et al. 2005, 18).[16] Contingent and part-time workers are especially at risk. For example, in February 2005 only 18 percent of contingent workers were covered by health insurance from their employer, although 59 percent had insurance from some source (BLS 2005c, 4).

Pertinent here, a recent study by the Employee Benefit Research Institute explored the reasons wage and salary workers age 18 to 64 lacked coverage in 2002 (Fronstin 2005a).[17] That study found that 41.9 percent of those workers reported that they worked for an employer that did not offer health insurance, another 17 percent worked for an employer that offered benefits but were ineligible for those benefits, and another 27 percent were offered benefits but chose not to participate. Of those who were not eligible for their employer's benefits, 57 percent worked part-time, 30 percent had not completed the required waiting period, and almost 9 percent were temporary or contract workers. Of those who chose not to participate, 75.4 percent reported that they were covered by someone else's plan, and 22 percent said the employer's plan was too costly.

Part and parcel of the growing coverage problem is the fact that health care costs are spiraling out of control. Spending on health care has grown from under 6 percent of GDP in 1965 to 16 percent of GDP in 2004 and is expected to reach 19 percent by 2014 and 22 percent by 2025 (Council of Economic Advisers 2006, 85–86). These ever-increasing costs have put pressure on employers, employees, and governments. For example, health insurance premiums rose by 73 percent from 2000 through 2005, compared with inflation growth of 14 percent and wage growth of 15 percent (Kaiser Family Foundation 2005, 1).[18] The average annual premiums for employment-based coverage rose to $4,024 for single coverage in 2005 and $10,880 for family coverage. Moreover, Medicare and Medicaid spending are both on "unsustainable" growth paths (Walker 2005).[19]

Of particular concern, the administrative costs associated with the American health care system are "enormous," with estimates ranging anywhere from $90 billion to $294 billion a year (Haase 2005, 25). Every health care plan has a different set of rules, and it seems like every insurance company, every employer, every hospital, and every doctor has a different set of claim forms.

Another significant problem has to do with risk segmentation in the small-group and individual insurance market (Wicks 2003). In a free market, insurance companies will offer their best premium rates to healthy individuals and make older and sicker individuals pay much more for identical coverage. That way, the premiums will cover the anticipated health care costs (leaving a little extra for profits). Large employers can spread the anticipated health care costs of a few higher-risk employees over a much larger number of low-risk employees; consequently, large employers can secure relatively low group-term health insurance rates. On the other hand, insurance companies will charge individuals and small employers much higher rates for the same coverage, and those higher rates will effectively price many individuals and small businesses out of the market.

The Health Care System Distorts Individual Decisions about Work and Retirement

Another problem with the American health care system is that it distorts individual decisions about work and retirement (Aaron 1999a; Gruber and Madrian 2004; Cutler 1997; Even and Macpherson 2003). In general, the employment-based health care system encourages individuals to enter and remain in the workforce. By working for employers that provide health care coverage, individuals who value health care coverage can share in the lower price for health care that comes with a group health plan and the extra savings that come from the associated tax benefits. On the other hand, providing health insurance through employers can distort the work and retirement decisions of employees. The categorical eligibility requirements for Medicare and Medicaid also influence individual decisions about work and retirement.

Employment-Based Health Insurance Can Encourage Individuals to Enter and Remain in the Workforce

The availability of employment-based health insurance clearly encourages many workers to enter and remain in the workforce (Aaron 1999a). Individual health insurance policies can be hard to get and, in any event, are more expensive than group policies. Providing group coverage through employment avoids the risk segmentation issues that exist in individual markets (Cutler 1997). The empirical research suggests that employment-based health insurance is likely to be especially attractive to particular types of workers, such as those with health problems and those who are "risk-averse" (Even and Macpherson 2003, 51).[20]

The availability of employment-based health insurance also has a significant impact on individual and family decisions about work. For example, when their husbands lacked health insurance, married working women were more likely to secure jobs that provided health insurance (Olson 2000). On the other hand, women whose husbands have health insurance tend to work fewer hours: these women are more willing to shift from full-time jobs with insurance to nonemployment or part-time employment without coverage (Buchmueller and Valletta 1999).

The rising costs of employment-based health insurance are putting strains on the system (Cutler 1997; Baicker and Chandra 2005). The percentage of workers with health care coverage has been falling for decades, and the share of health care costs borne by employees (and retirees) has been increasing. Employers and employees have both responded to these higher costs by changing their behavior.

Employers often respond to these higher costs by trying to pass the costs on to their employees, for example, by decreasing wages, by converting full-time jobs with coverage to part-time positions without coverage, or by dropping coverage altogether. One recent study found that for workers with health insurance coverage, a 10 percent increase in health insurance premiums was offset by a 2.3 percent decrease in wages and a 3.8 percent decrease in the probability of being offered coverage (Baicker and Chandra 2005).

Also, as employee health insurance premiums have increased, more employees have responded by choosing plans that provide less cover-

age or by declining coverage altogether.[21] For example, of those uninsured workers who declined coverage in 2002, 64.4 percent reported
that they declined coverage because it was too costly (Fronstin 2005a).
Workers in general, and low-wage workers in particular, are just not all
that willing to accept wage reductions to pay for health care coverage.[22]

Job Lock

The current employment-based health care system also has an adverse
impact on job mobility. Workers often find themselves locked into
working for a particular employer to keep their health care coverage.
One study found that employer-provided health insurance cut voluntary turnover by 25 percent (Even and Macpherson 2003). The usual
suggestion for reducing the problem of job lock is to make health care
coverage more "portable," and the COBRA health care continuation
rules are, at least, a first step in that direction.

Transition from Welfare to Work

Another problem with the current structure of the health care system
is how it interferes with the transition from welfare to work. Welfare
recipients and individuals with disabilities who enter or reenter the
workforce often face the loss of health benefits under Medicaid. This
loss of health benefits can be a strong disincentive for working, at least
on the books (Handler and Hasenfeld 1997). One recent study found
that former welfare recipients were 2.6 times as likely to still be
employed two years later if they were covered by employer-provided
health insurance (Boushey 2002).

Retiree Health Insurance

Retirees—at least those over age 65—typically pay for their health care
expenses with a combination of Medicare Part A, Medicare Part B, and
a supplemental insurance policy from their employer or otherwise.
Retirees also inevitably incur additional out-of-pocket expenses. All in
all, it has been estimated that an individual who retires at age 65 in
2005 and lives to age 80 will need $112,000 in savings to pay for
Medicare Part B premiums, an employment-based health insurance
policy to supplement Medicare, and $1,800 a year for out-of-pocket
expenses (Fronstin and Yakoboski 2005).[23]

Not surprisingly, the availability—or unavailability—of health
insurance after retirement also has "a powerful effect" on the timing
of retirement (Aaron 1999a, 53).[24] Workers who have retiree health
coverage are likely to retire much earlier than those who do not. One

study estimated that the availability of retiree health insurance increased retirement rates by 26 percent for men and 31 percent for women (Johnson, Davidoff, and Perese 2003).

On the other hand, workers without retiree health benefits have an incentive to remain on their current job at least until they are eligible for Medicare. In that regard, studies suggest that universal health care coverage or lowering the Medicare eligibility age would almost certainly encourage some workers to retire earlier. One study estimated that lowering the Medicare eligibility age to 62 would increase overall retirement rates among full-time workers age 51 to 61 by about 7 percent (Johnson 2003).[25] On the other hand, increasing the Medicare eligibility age to 67 would reduce annual retirement rates for workers age 55 to 64 by about 5 percent.

Age Discrimination

Another problem with the health care system is that it costs employers more to provide health care coverage for older workers than for younger workers. In 2004, health care cost $1,519 for the average person age 25–34, $2,263 for those age 35–44, $2,695 for those age 45–54, $3,262 for those age 55–64, and $3,899 for those age 65 and older (BLS 2006b, table 4).[26] The costs of life insurance coverage also increase as workers age, as do the costs associated with work injury and disability (Committee for Economic Development 1999, 31).[27] Workers generally cost more to employ as they get older (Watson Wyatt 1999; Minda 1994; Kotlikoff and Gokhale 1992).

Theoretically, employers could pass those higher benefit costs on to their older workers, but few do. Instead, the typical employer charges all its workers the same health care premiums, regardless of age. In effect, younger workers cross-subsidize the health care benefits for older workers. All in all, the compensation of workers nearing the end of their careers can exceed their productivity, while the compensation of younger workers can lag behind. When that happens, employers will have an economic incentive to avoid hiring or retaining older workers, and younger workers will have an economic incentive to work elsewhere.[28]

MODEST CHANGES THAT COULD IMPROVE THE HEALTH CARE SYSTEM

The health care system should be designed to meet the needs of workers, retirees, and their families. First and foremost, the health care system should provide affordable coverage for workers, retirees, and their families. Second, the health care system should strengthen the relationship between individual work effort and health care coverage. Finally, the health care system should be designed to make coverage affordable and widely available.

Expand Coverage

While universal coverage should almost certainly be our ultimate goal, we might want to start with a more incremental approach that focuses on designing and expanding health care programs for particular groups of the uninsured (Dorn 2004). For example, the government might want to expand coverage for low-income working families.

One way to help low-income working families would be to expand the Medicaid and SCHIP programs to cover virtually all low-income children. Of the 8.9 million children who were uninsured in 1999, some 4.6 million were actually eligible for Medicaid, and another 2.3 million were eligible for SCHIP (Dubay, Hill, and Kenney 2002). The government needs to develop policies to get those children covered. In addition, the federal government could expand its Medicaid and SCHIP programs so they cover all children in families with incomes up to, say, 300 percent of the poverty income guidelines.[29]

The government might also expand Medicaid or develop other programs to ensure seamless coverage for individuals making the transition from welfare to work (Handler and Hasenfeld 1997). For example, it could make sense to simplify transitional medical assistance by allowing former welfare recipients to continue their Medicaid coverage for months or even years after they start working, regardless of income level. Another approach would be to create a new earnings subsidy that would provide health care vouchers for low-income workers (Haveman 1995). Together, these kinds of programs could help ensure that virtually all low-income working families have adequate health care coverage.

Similarly, the government could extend health care coverage to more unemployed workers by expanding the recently created health care coverage tax credits. Created by the Trade Reform Act of 2002, these credits pay up to 65 percent of the health care premiums of qualifying workers who lost their jobs because of foreign trade.[30] Another approach would be to extend COBRA health care continuation coverage to 36 or more months or until eligibility for Medicare at age 65 (Nichols 2001). The government might also be able to expand coverage for employees of small businesses by providing tax credits to employers that provide health insurance to their employees (Garrett, Nichols, and Greenman 2001; Gruber 2005).

Strengthen the Relationship between Work Effort and Benefits

While health care coverage costs more for older workers than for younger workers, under traditional employment-based health care plans, young and old workers both pay the same premiums. In short, benefits are not tied to productivity. That gives younger workers the incentive to find employment where compensation *is* tied to their productivity, and it gives employers the incentive to replace older workers with younger workers. These are perverse incentives.

Consequently, both society and individuals have an interest in strengthening the relationship between benefits and productivity. As more fully discussed in chapter 9, the recent trend in benefits is the "unbundled approach," under which benefits are paid in proportion to compensation (Mitchell 2003). For example, in lieu of a traditional pension, an employer might offer a defined contribution pension plan in which each worker gets, say, 10 percent of compensation contributed to her individual retirement account. Or an employer might have a cafeteria plan that gives each employee a fixed amount of benefit "dollars" that can be used to purchase various fringe benefits, from health insurance to day care.

Pertinent here, one recent trend in employment-based health care coverage has been the emergence of "consumer-driven" health plans (MacDonald 2006; Fronstin 2001). Consumer-driven health care plans tend to shift the responsibility for the payment and selection of health care benefits from employers to employees. For example, an employer might provide each employee $300 a month for health care coverage and leave it to the employee to choose among various health plans to pay for coverage. Key here is the fact that individual employees might face different premiums based on such factors as their age, personal health risk, or geographic location.

Along the same lines, the federal government has recently let employers experiment with a range of defined contribution health plans and medical savings accounts. For example, the Medicare Prescription Drug, Improvement, and Modernization Act of 2003 (Public Law 108-173) authorized new health savings accounts (Fronstin and Collins 2005; Fronstin 2004; Kaplan 2005; Monahan 2006; Aaron 2004). In 2006, people covered by high-deductible health care plans can contribute up to $5,450 per family ($2,700 per individual) to these tax-favored accounts, and withdrawals are excluded from income if they are used for qualified health expenses (Council of Economic Advisers 2006, 100–104).

It could make sense to move further in the direction of consumer-driven health care plans and other mechanisms that strengthen the relationship between employee productivity and benefits. On the other hand, unless the government somehow steps in and provides subsidies to help older and higher-risk individuals pay their higher premiums, moving toward consumer-driven health care plans could actually *decrease* coverage as more older and higher-risk individuals are priced out of the market. Health outcomes are also a concern with consumer-driven plans, as there is evidence that individuals with these plans are more likely than those with traditional health care plans to avoid, skip, or delay treatment because of costs (MacDonald 2006; Monahan 2006).

Along the same lines, many have suggested that we should make Medicare, rather than employment-based health insurance, the primary source of health care coverage for workers age 65 and over (Burkhauser and Quinn 1997). This change would increase Medicare expenses, but it would lower a major barrier to the employment of older workers.

Restructure Health Care Coverage Markets

On the other hand, many observers believe that the solution to many of the labor market distortions that result from the current health care system is to remove the link between health care and employment (Cutler 1997; Haase 2005). As a starting point, we might encourage community groups and nonprofit organizations to offer health care plans and give them the same tax and regulatory advantages that are now available only to employment-based plans. For example, President Bush recently called for the creation of "association health plans" for small businesses that would allow insurance to be more portable and purchased more easily across state lines (Council of Economic Advisers 2006, 100; DOL 2002).

We might also think about modifying ERISA so federal preemption no longer prevents state efforts to expand coverage. The state of Maryland recently flexed its muscles and enacted legislation that would require companies with at least 10,000 employees (i.e., Wal-Mart) to spend at least 8 percent of payroll on health care or give the difference to the state. In July 2006, however, a federal district court struck down that law, ruling that it was preempted by ERISA.[31] Perhaps now there will be more interest in relaxing ERISA's overly broad preemption rule so states *can* experiment with a broader approaches for expanding coverage.

Government could also adopt rules to counter insurance industry policies that drive up premium costs in the individual and small-group market. In general, government can reduce such insurance industry risk segmentation practices by preventing it from occurring in the first place or by allowing it but offsetting its effects (Wicks 2003). Community rating is an example of the first approach. Under a community rating system, insurance companies are required to take all comers and charge them all the same rate. Alternatively, under the second approach, the government could allow wide variation in premiums based on risk but provide subsidies to help older and higher-risk individuals pay their higher premiums.

Finally, the current tax advantages associated with employment-based health care plans have come under scrutiny. In particular, the current $100 billion-a-year exclusion for employment-based health care has helped fuel inflation in health care costs (Steuerle 2003, 2004). Consequently, capping the current exclusion at a fixed-dollar amount could help bring health care costs under control and make coverage more affordable.

An alternative approach would be to replace the current exclusion with a refundable health care tax credit (Burman and Gruber 2005). Like deductions, exclusions are the most valuable to high-income taxpayers in the highest tax brackets, while refundable tax credits are equally valuable to all taxpayers. Consequently, replacing the exclusion with a refundable tax credit would shift the health care subsidy toward low-income individuals and families that have the greatest need for government assistance. One recent study found that a refundable health tax credit of $1,000 for a single person and $2,000 for a family would reduce the number of uninsured by between 17.5 and 28 percent at a cost of between $16.6 and $44 billion (Emmons, Madly, and Woodbury 2005).[32]

More Comprehensive Proposals

Ultimately, however, the government will need to develop programs that provide a way to achieve nearly universal health care coverage. Universal coverage would certainly promote greater economic justice, as most of the uninsured have low income levels. In addition, with universal coverage, we should finally be able to reduce our health care system's burdensome administrative costs, and we should also be able to get medical treatment costs under control.

Universal coverage would also solve much of the distortion in labor markets that results from the current structure of the health care system. In particular, universal coverage would solve job lock, as workers would no longer lose their health insurance benefits just because they changed jobs. Universal coverage would also solve the problems relating to the transition from welfare to work and the transition from disability to work. Today, recipients of welfare or disability benefits can lose Medicaid or Medicare coverage if they enter or reenter the workforce. With universal coverage, however, they would not lose their coverage.

On the other hand, making health care universally available could result in earlier retirements. Today many workers delay their retirement until they are eligible for Medicare at age 65. With universal health care coverage, however, older workers would have less reason to postpone their retirements.

Making health care universally available might also reduce the labor supply of younger workers. In particular, people who currently work full-time to qualify for health care benefits would find it easier to shift from full-time jobs to part-time jobs or nonemployment.

Over the years, there have been countless suggestions about how to achieve universal coverage. Some have argued for a single-payer national health insurance system.[33] That could be as simple as expanding Medicare to cover everyone,[34] or as complicated as President Clinton's 1993 health care reform proposal.[35]

Many proposals call for employer mandates—requiring employers to either provide health care coverage for their workers or pay a payroll tax so the government can provide coverage. This is sometimes referred to as the "play or pay" approach. Alternatively, many proposals call for individual mandates—requiring individuals to secure coverage from their employers or otherwise.[36] Many proposals would also create tax credits or other financial incentives to help employers or individuals secure coverage. Still other proposals call for the establishment of purchasing pools in every state, and some proposals call for other insurance market reforms.

A Universal Coverage/Universal Responsibility Approach

One of the more promising approaches for universal health care coverage is typified by a recent proposal by the New America Foundation (Calabrese and Rubiner 2004).[37] Under this approach, the government would guarantee access to adequate and affordable health insurance for everyone. In exchange, each person would be required to maintain health insurance and to pay for that insurance with a combination of employer and employee contributions and government assistance based on ability to pay. An adequate but basic level of health care coverage would be required, and community insurance pools would be established in each state to offer individuals a choice among alternative health care plans. Government assistance would be provided in the form of refundable tax credits calculated on a sliding scale based on need.

Similarly, the state of Massachusetts recently enacted major legislation designed to achieve nearly universal coverage.[38] The new law requires individuals to have health insurance and redeploys state funds to help pay for it. Within three years, the law is expected to provide health insurance coverage to 95 percent of the 550,000 uninsured Massachusetts residents. Everyone "plays their part": individuals, government, health care providers, and employers.

The law creates a new agency—the Massachusetts Health Insurance Connector—to connect individuals and small businesses with health insurance products and to ensure that individuals continue to have insurance when they change jobs. There are also insurance market reforms. For example, the law will merge the individual and small-group markets in July 2007, a provision that will produce an estimated drop of 24 percent in non-group premium costs.

The Massachusetts law also provides health care subsidies for low-income residents through a new Commonwealth Care Health Insurance Program. Under that program, sliding-scale subsidies will be available to individuals with incomes below 300 percent of the federal poverty level ($49,600 for a family of three in 2006), and there will be no premiums for people with incomes below 100 percent of the poverty level ($9,800 for an individual in 2006). There are also no deductibles. Medicaid will also be expanded, for example, to cover children in families with incomes up to 300 percent of the poverty level.

Under the individual mandate, individuals must have health insurance by July 1, 2007. The penalty for not having insurance in 2007 is the loss of the personal exemption. In subsequent years, the penalty will be a fine equal to 50 percent of the monthly cost of health insurance for each month without insurance. Those who cannot afford insurance, however, will not be penalized.

Employers who do not make "fair and reasonable" contributions will be required to make per-worker "fair share" contributions. These contributions will be capped at $295 per full-time-equivalent worker, per year, but businesses with 10 or fewer employees will not have to make these contributions.

A Universal Coverage/Wage Subsidy Approach

Another promising approach would be to combine an *employer* mandate with targeted health care subsidies.[39] Under this approach, all employers would be required to either provide health care coverage for their workers or pay a payroll tax so the government could provide coverage ("play or pay"). In addition, the government would provide targeted subsidies to help pay the health care costs of low-income workers and their families.

To be sure, an employer mandate—without more—would likely decrease employment opportunities for low-skilled workers (Wolaver, McBride, and Wolfe 2003). On the other hand, an employer mandate combined with government subsidies could be designed to increase employment opportunities.

According to standard economic theory, employee compensation is tied to productivity, and employers only care about total compensation, not about the mix between wages and health benefits. Consequently, employers would respond to an employer mandate by providing health care coverage and offsetting those costs by decreasing cash wages. But there are two problems with making that kind of dollar-for-dollar offset.

First, the minimum wage would prevent some employers from reducing cash wages by enough to cover their costs. Consider a firm that pays its workers $7.00 an hour but does not provide any health insurance. Under an employer mandate, that firm would have to provide health care coverage for its workers. If that health coverage costs the equivalent of $3.00 an hour, the firm would want to cut wages to $4.00 an hour, but the $5.15 minimum wage would make that impossible. To the extent that the employer mandate raises the labor costs of workers above the market value of their labor, some workers would lose their jobs.[40]

Second, an employer mandate would also result in changes in the supply of labor, depending on the value that workers put on receiving health insurance. If workers value health insurance over its cost, they would increase their labor supply. If workers would rather have cash, however, then they would decrease their labor supply.[41]

The net effect of an employer mandate on employment is ambiguous, but the empirical evidence suggests that a decline in the employment levels of low-skilled workers is likely (Wolaver et al. 2003).

To be sure, a well-designed system of government subsidies could more than offset the adverse impacts of an employer mandate. Those subsidies could be provided either to employers or to workers, perhaps in the form of an earnings subsidy. For example, the federal government could provide a tax credit to the employers of low-wage workers to help offset the increased costs of providing health insurance. Alternatively, the federal government could provide health care vouchers to workers that could be used to purchase health care from authorized providers.

Transition to Universal Health Care

We can and we should make the transition from the current system to a system of nearly universal coverage. For example, the elements of such a transition could include tax changes, an employer mandate, and an individual mandate (Steuerle 2003).

- **Tax changes.** The exclusion for employer-paid health insurance premiums should be capped at a fixed-dollar amount and gradually replaced with a refundable tax credit.
- **An employer mandate.** Employers should be required to offer, but not necessarily pay for, at least one state-approved health insurance plan for employees. Employers should be encouraged to adopt the practice of automatically enrolling employees in the employer's health plan unless the employees specifically choose to opt out.
- **An individual mandate.** Individuals should be required to get health insurance or lose tax benefits like the personal exemption and standard deduction.

All in all, we should be able to redesign the current health care system so it provides universal coverage, and we should be able to redesign the system so it minimizes work disincentives. In short, we can make universal health care work.

11

MAKING LABOR
MARKETS WORK

Labor market policies designed to improve the employment
and earnings prospects of workers could serve as an important
adjunct to welfare policy. (Bassi 1995, 137)

Efforts to address the labor market opportunities of the least
skilled members of the labor force should not only improve
wages at the bottom of the wage distribution, but should also
have spillover benefits in terms of improvements in family
incomes through higher rates of family formation, greater
family stability, and higher rates of labor force participation.
(Karoly 1998, 256)

The previous chapters generally discussed how the government's tax
and transfer policies could be changed to improve work incentives
and promote greater economic justice. In particular, several chapters
touted the power of earnings subsidies to improve work incentives for
low-skilled workers and reduce earnings and income inequality. This
chapter explains how improving the government's regulation of labor
markets could also help encourage work effort and promote greater
economic justice.

Specifically, this chapter offers a number of recommendations for
improvements in labor market policies, including suggestions that the

government vigorously enforce the laws against employment discrimination; reduce incarceration levels; make education and training work; modestly raise the minimum wage and index it for inflation; expand the unemployment insurance program; promote unionization; and make full employment a reality.

VIGOROUSLY ENFORCE THE LAWS AGAINST EMPLOYMENT DISCRIMINATION

Discrimination in the labor market against minorities, women, and other groups tends to depress their wages. Those depressed wages tend to discourage members of those groups from working. The result is greater inequality in the distribution of earnings than if there were no discrimination in employment.[1] Consequently, laws prohibiting employment discrimination tend to equalize the distribution of earnings and so reduce economic inequality (Hamermesh and Rees 1988).

Over the past 40 years, four major laws have addressed employment discrimination. The Equal Pay Act of 1963 outlawed the practice of paying women less than men for the same work. The Civil Rights Act of 1964 outlawed employment discrimination because of an individual's race, color, religion, sex, or national origin. Similarly, the Age Discrimination in Employment Act of 1967 outlawed employment discrimination against individuals who are 40 years of age or older. More recently, the Americans with Disabilities Act of 1990 outlawed employment discrimination against disabled Americans. These laws have significantly reduced discrimination against the affected groups.

Partially as a result of these antidiscrimination laws, the earnings of whites and blacks and the earnings of men and women have converged markedly over the past few decades. For example, the black/white wage gap fell by about half from 1963 to 2001 (Welch 2003). Similarly, in 2004, women workers earned 80 percent as much as men, up from just 63 percent in 1979 (BLS 2005e).

Vigorously Enforce the Existing Laws against Employment Discrimination

Despite the gains that have already been achieved by antidiscrimination laws, it seems clear that more rigorous enforcement of antidiscrimination laws is needed. Because at least a portion of gaps between the wages of whites and minorities and between men and women are attributable to discrimination, it is important for the government to continue and intensify its enforcement of laws against discrimination in employment. In addition, as education is foundational to developing worker skills, the government needs to vigorously enforce the antidiscrimination laws pertaining to education. The government also needs to expand programs like Head Start that help equalize the educational opportunities for low-income children, especially minority children.

States also need to combat discrimination in employment. Federal laws generally apply only to enterprises in interstate commerce with a minimum number of employees. For example, the Age Discrimination in Employment Act applies only to firms with 20 or more employees and so excludes a not insignificant proportion of the labor force. That is where state enforcement should take over. All in all, it would make sense to vigorously enforce the current laws against discrimination in employment.[2]

Toughen the Laws against Employment Discrimination

It would also make sense to toughen our laws against employment discrimination. As the American workforce ages, it will become especially important to augment our efforts to combat age discrimination and the other barriers that keep elderly Americans from working. To be sure, older workers tend to have higher earnings and lower unemployment rates that younger workers.[3] Nevertheless, it seems clear that older workers face substantial barriers to job change, and age discrimination in employment is rampant. Indeed, many workers report that they have witnessed or experienced age discrimination on the job (Rix 2004),[4] and 16,585 charges of age discrimination were filed with the Equal Employment Opportunity Commission in fiscal year 2005 (22.0 percent of all discrimination charges filed).[5]

Older workers also seem to have a much harder time finding a job when they become unemployed. In 2005, for example, the median duration of an unemployment spell for workers age 55 to 64 was 11.7 weeks, compared with 9.6 weeks for workers age 25 to 34 (BLS 2006f, table 31).[6] Also, while surveys routinely report that many elderly workers would prefer cutting back their work hours or otherwise changing the type of work that they do rather than fully retiring, a surprisingly large fraction of those workers stop working entirely (Abraham and Houseman 2004; Ehrenreich 2005a). All in all, it would seem that tougher age discrimination laws may well be needed to combat what appears to be widespread discrimination against older workers.[7] Along the same lines, the U.S. Government Accountability Office recently recommended that the Department of Labor should do more to encourage employers to find ways to recruit and retain older workers and to assist older workers in finding opportunities to continue to work (GAO 2006a).

In addition, despite the Americans with Disabilities Act, discrimination against the disabled seems pervasive. For example, 14,893 charges of disability discrimination were filed with the Equal Employment Opportunity Commission in fiscal year 2005 (19.7 percent of all discrimination charges filed).[8] All in all, just 52 percent of adults age 21 through 64 with disabilities were employed in 1994–95, compared with 82 percent of those without disabilities (HHS 2000, section 6-8). While employment discrimination is by no means the only reason for the low employment rate for individuals with disabilities, no one doubts that discrimination is a problem. Here again tougher antidiscrimination laws are needed (Weber 1998).

REDUCE INCARCERATION LEVELS

From 1980 to 2004, the number of people in prison or jail increased from 0.5 million to more than 2.1 million people (see figure 2.3). Clearly, having so many people incarcerated has significant impacts on the U.S. labor market in general and on the affected demographic groups in particular. For example, because people who are incarcerated do not show up in either the numerator or the denominator of the official unemployment rate, the official estimates of unemployment are too low. In 2004, the number of incarcerated men was equal to 2.4 percent of the number of men in the workforce, and the increased incarceration of men since 1985 has reduced the official unemployment rate of men by about 0.3 percentage points (see chapter 2).

Other studies suggest that unemployment and wage rates may influence crime rates (Council of Economic Advisers 2005). It seems that young men respond to wage incentives. In that regard, it has been estimated that the decline in wages of less-skilled men between 1979 and 1995 resulted in a 10 to 13 percent increase in property crimes and an increase in violent crimes by about half as much. In short, when legitimate wages fall, the "wages of crime" become relatively more attractive. When wages rise and unemployment falls, crime becomes less attractive. For example, the crime rates for robbery, burglary, larceny, and motor vehicle theft all fell during the economic boom of the late 1990s (Saving and Cox 2000).

Economists since Gary S. Becker have noted this trade-off between legitimate wages and the wages of crime (Becker 1968; Bernstein and Houston 2000). According to the standard economic analysis, criminals are rational actors who weigh their legitimate earnings opportunities against their criminal earnings opportunities, taking into account such factors as the likelihood that the crime will succeed and the penalties that they will pay if caught. In short, labor market incentives can influence the supply of criminals, and when real wages for unskilled workers are low, young men may come to believe that crime pays. When justice is swift and certain, a life of crime should be less attractive.[9]

Although good for the prison-industrial complex, high incarceration rates have an adverse effect on labor markets and on specific demographic groups. Most significantly, incarceration has negative effects on the future labor market prospects of the individuals so incarcerated (Clear 1996). Richard B. Freeman argues that finding ways to improve the legitimate job market for unskilled workers "is *the problem* of our times, with implications both for crime and many other social ills" (1996, 24).

Various policies could be used to help encourage low-skilled workers to choose legitimate work rather than a life of crime. Chapters 6 and 7 noted that earnings subsidies could be used to increase the rewards for work for all low-skilled workers (i.e., a $2,000 per worker earned income tax credit). In addition, raising the minimum wage and trying to achieve low unemployment rates could benefit low-skilled workers.

The government also needs to think about expanding programs that provide alternatives to incarceration. In particular, it would make sense to expand community-based mental health and drug treatment alternatives to incarceration. About one-quarter of those in prison are there because of drug offenses (458,131 in 2000) (Beatty, Holman, and Schiraldi 2000). In addition, drug abuse and driving under the influence are the two top categories of arrests in the United States. For example, of the 14,004,300 people arrested in 2004, 1,745,700 people were arrested for drug abuse violations and 1,432,500 were arrested for driving under the influence.[10] We cannot, and should not, put them all in jail or prison.

Instead of incarceration, we should think about treatment alternatives. For example, certain alcohol- or drug-addicted defendants in Brooklyn, New York, that plead guilty to a crime are allowed to enter a residential, therapeutic community treatment program that can last for up to two years (McVay, Schiraldi, and Ziedenburg 2004). Along the same lines, many communities now have drug and mental health courts that try to provide treatment instead of jail for nonviolent offenders with substance abuse and mental health problems (Bailey 2003; Berman and Feinblatt 2003; Fox and Wolf 2004).

Expanding restitution, suspended sentences, diversion, day-reporting, and probation alternatives to incarceration would also help keep offenders working in their communities rather than languishing in jail or prison.[11] Day reporting centers, for example, are community-based facilities that require offenders to report to the center daily and file written itineraries about their daily movements. At the same time, however, these centers provide offenders with treatment and counseling services.

We should also do more to help offenders who are imprisoned. For example, we should expand the reentry programs that help inmates make the transition from incarceration to employment, reestablish family ties, and fit into their communities.[12] Something like 600,000 prisoners are released each year, but about two-thirds are rearrested and about half are re-incarcerated within three years (Freeman 2003).[13] In particular, it would make sense to expand prison inmate work programs. More than 90 percent of all correctional facilities have some type of work program, ranging from prison industries and farms to public works projects such as road and park maintenance (U.S. Department of Justice, Bureau of Justice Statistics 2003, 10). Although some worry that these programs can be exploitative and some fear that prison labor might displace civilian business and labor, the bottom line is that prison labor programs can increase worker skills, reduce inmate recidivism, and produce "profits" that can help offset the costs of incarceration.[14]

Finally, we should do more to help ex-offenders. Almost 5 million people were on parole or probation in 2004.[15] Inevitably, these ex-offenders have a tougher time finding jobs than non-offenders. Ex-offenders tend to have less education and less work experience than non-offenders, and many ex-offenders have medical problems or addictions that impair their ability to work (Freeman 2003). Moreover, employers generally prefer to hire non-offenders. The criminal justice system could help these ex-offenders by providing more education and training along with treatment and counseling services.

MAKE EDUCATION AND TRAINING WORK

The acquisition of job skills and education clearly tends to benefit private individuals in terms of higher market wages. In that regard, chapter 3 showed that a college degree can be worth more than $1,000,000 in additional earnings over a high school diploma. More generally, education at all levels can help increase U.S. productivity and competitiveness, and education can play an important role in reducing poverty and income inequality. In particular, increasing the job skills of low-skilled workers should make them more productive and more attractive to employers. In addition, many people believe that education also produces positive externalities that can benefit society as a whole (Council of Economic Advisers 2006). For example, increasing support for education and training should lead to lower crime rates (Lochner 2004).

All in all, it makes sense for the government to subsidize education (Waldron, Roberts, and Reamer 2004; Heckman and Krueger 2003).

There is a much higher rate of return on investments in early childhood education than on remedial investments later on in the life cycle (figure 11.1) (University of Wisconsin–Madison Institute for Research on Poverty 2005; Heckman and Lochner 2000). Consequently, some of the most efficient government policies should involve trying to improve the basic educational opportunities available to children, particularly children in low-income families.[16] Of course, the government should also play a significant role in expanding the opportunities for postsecondary education: college, vocational education, and lifelong learning.

Expand Opportunities for Preschool Education

There is simply "no substitution for high-quality education from the earliest years of child development and preschool and beyond" (Kochran 2004, 71). In that regard, it would make sense to expand the Head

Figure 11.1. Rate of Return to Investment in Education as a Function of Age

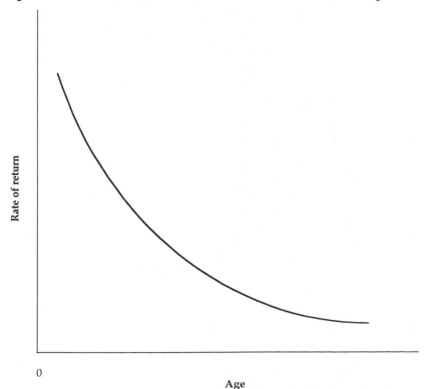

Source: Author's calculations.

Start program so virtually all low-income children can participate. Head Start provides some comprehensive child development programs for poor children from birth to age 5, but it serves less than half of all eligible children (Currie 2001).

Along the same lines, we should make full-day public kindergarten and prekindergarten universally available throughout the United States.[17] To the same effect, a recent report of the American Assembly notes that

> preschool programs have expanded in recent years, but coverage is far from complete and should be expanded further. No child should for reason of income be denied a strong preschool experience. (1999, 10)

In particular, a well-designed early education program serving low-income children could generate "exceptional returns" for the affected children, government, and society as a whole. Such a program would improve the skills of a large fraction of the U.S. workforce and so eventually lead to increases in employment and productivity and to reductions in poverty, welfare dependency, and crime. For example, one study estimated that a high-quality early childhood education program for poor 3- and 4-year-old children would cost about $19 billion a year, would start paying for itself in 17 years, would reap budgetary benefits of more than double the costs within 30 years, and would produce additional saving from lower crime rates (Lynch 2004).

Improve Primary and Secondary Education

Additional government resources should also be devoted to improving the quality of primary and secondary public education.[18] In particular, every effort should be made to reduce the high school dropout rate. In 2000, 9.8 percent of individuals age 16 to 19 were high school dropouts (Day with Jamieson 2003).[19] As education has such a large effect on earnings and income, lowering the dropout rate could help raise the earnings of low-skilled workers and so help reduce economic inequality.[20] Among other changes, we might raise the age for compulsory schooling to 18.[21]

We also need to bolster the mathematics and science skills of America's primary and secondary students. A recent study by the Organisation for Economic Co-operation and Development found that American 15-year-olds ranked 24th out of 29 industrialized countries in mathematical literacy in 2003 (OECD 2006b, 163).[22] Most workers in the 21st century will need basic math, science, and technology skills, and we need to do a better job of providing that education. Improvements could result from raising teacher salaries to attract better trained teachers, reducing class sizes, and lengthening the school year.[23]

Increase the Opportunities for Postsecondary Education

Federal and state governments also have an important role to play in providing assistance with college and other postsecondary education.[24] For one thing, the market for financing college education and other postsecondary training is inefficient (Heckman and Carneiro 2003). While a home buyer can pledge her future home as security in order to borrow money, a student cannot generally pledge her future earnings as security for a loan to pay for college or other training designed to increase her future earnings potential. Consequently, it makes sense for the government to provide or guarantee financial assistance, especially for low-income individuals who cannot otherwise secure adequate financing for advanced education.

Numerous programs already provide assistance for college education and other postsecondary training. In fiscal year 2004, for example, the federal government provided $14 billion in Pell and similar grants, $56 billion in student loan assistance, and $10 billion in Hope and Lifetime Learning tax credits and other tax preferences (GAO 2005e, 5).[25] Unfortunately, that federal assistance is inadequate, and the assistance provided is not all that well targeted to help low-income students (Dynarski 2004; Ellwood and Kane 2000). For example, because the Hope and Lifetime Learning tax credits are not refundable, they are rarely of use to low-income students and their families (Dickert-Conlin et al. 2005).

Moreover, generic subsidies for college education, such as state support of public institutions and Lifetime Learning and Hope credits, may even exacerbate income inequality, as the children of higher income parents are more likely to go to college than the children of low-income parents.[26] All in all, federal assistance should be designed to increase college attendance and performance, and that assistance should be better targeted to help low- and moderate-income students, parents trying to work their way out of the welfare system, and dislocated workers.

Government policies should also be designed to improve opportunities for vocational education. Vocational education at both the secondary and postsecondary level has a substantial positive effect on earnings for most recipients. At the secondary level, for example, one study found that high school graduates who had taken vocational education courses made more money seven years after graduation than those who did not—about 2 percent for each extra high school occupational course they took (Silverberg et al. 2004, 3–4). At the postsecondary level, the greatest benefits go to those who earn a credential. For example, men who earn a vocational associate degree make an average of 30 percent more than those who stop with a high school diploma, and female associate degree holders earn 47 percent more (Silverberg et al. 2004, 12). Along the same lines, the government could work with private industry to develop more employer-provided apprenticeships and internships (Edelman et al. 2006, 126–28).

Of particular importance, the government should provide training opportunities for low-skilled workers and retraining opportunities for workers who lose their jobs. To be sure, traditional public training programs for adults tend to produce only modest incremental increases in employment and earnings, but those impacts are lasting (King 2004). Given the importance of education and skills in today's labor market, however, the government should expand and improve its training efforts and encourage private employers to provide more and better training as well (Barnow and King 1999; Lerman, McKernan, and Rigg 2004). Successful training efforts need to be designed to provide occupational training that will prepare participants for occupations that are in demand in their local labor markets (Barnow and King 1999). Employers, too, can play a critical role in providing various types of training and other assistance to their low-wage workers.

Finally, government policies should be designed to encourage lifelong learning (Kochran 2005, 60–66; Levine 1998, 104–33). For example, government policies could be designed to encourage employers to provide general training to their workers, as well as firm-specific training. Internal Revenue Code § 127 already provides tax incentives for employers to set up educational assistance programs to help pay tuition for their employees, but perhaps additional incentives are needed.[27] Other possible tools for promoting lifelong learning include expanding opportunities for adult public education, extending minimum education and continuing education requirements to more professions and occupations, and encouraging more joint union-management training programs (Lynch 2005).

RAISE THE MINIMUM WAGE

The standard economic model generally suggests that wage or earnings subsidies are likely to be more effective than minimum wage mandates at helping low-skilled workers. Nevertheless, it could make sense to set a modest minimum wage level and to index that level for inflation. Combining a modest minimum wage with a comprehensive system of wage or earnings subsidies could help guarantee that virtually every low-skilled worker would earn enough to bring her family above the poverty level.

Under the Fair Labor Standards Act, most hourly workers are entitled to a minimum wage of at least $5.15 an hour. For example, of the 73.9 million American workers who were paid by the hour in 2004, about 2 million (2.7 percent) were paid at, or below, $5.15 an hour (BLS 2005b). Most of those workers (1 million) were under the age of 25, and 497,000 were 16 to 19 years old.

Modestly Raise the Minimum Wage and Index It for Inflation

The minimum wage rate is not automatically adjusted for inflation, and it has not been increased since 1997. As a result, the real value of the minimum wage has fallen in recent years relative to the inflation-adjusted poverty levels (see figure 4.13). Moreover, the brunt of that decline in real wages is felt by low-skilled workers. Consequently, it could make sense to raise the minimum wage and index it for inflation.[28]

As we saw in chapter 4, the economics literature tends to prefer earnings subsidies like the earned income tax credit over hikes in the minimum wage. Most economists believe that minimum wage laws tend to reduce employment opportunities for low-skilled workers, while earnings subsidies can actually increase the demand for low-skilled workers by making it relatively cheaper to employ them. Earnings subsidies are also better targeted to help low-income families. For example, while most of the benefits of an increase in the current earned income tax credit would go to families in the lowest quintile of income, much of the benefits of an increase in the minimum wage would go to teenagers and other secondary workers in high-income households (Turner and Barnow 2003; Shaviro 1997).

Still, in order to prevent exploitation of low-skilled workers and to bring a certain stability to labor markets, it would make sense to set a modest minimum wage level and to index that level for inflation. By January 2006, 17 states and the District of Columbia had minimum wages set higher than the federal minimum wage (Bernstein, McNichol, and Lyons 2005). Combining a modest minimum wage with a comprehensive system of earnings subsidies would guarantee that virtually every low-skilled worker would earn enough to bring her family out of poverty.

What about Paying Living Wages?

Recently, there has been a movement for legislation to require government and private employers to pay so-called "living wages," typically defined as "what a family would need to earn in order to support itself at the poverty level" (Boushey et al. 2001, 44).[29] To bring a family of three above the poverty level in 2006, a worker would have to make $7.98 an hour and work full-time and year-round, and it would take a wage of $9.62 an hour to bring a family of four over the poverty level (see table 2.9 and accompanying text). Approximately 100 communities around the country have already adopted living wage ordinances (Adams and Neumark 2005).[30]

Some living wage advocates suggest that we go beyond regional living wage laws. Instead, they would amend the U.S. Constitution to give everyone the right to a job that pays a living wage (Quigley 2003).[31] Congress would then have the obligation to enact legislation to implement those rights. Presumably, Congress would fulfill that obligation with a combination of legislative initiatives including, perhaps, increasing and indexing the minimum wage, providing new tax incentives and earnings subsidies for employers and employees, and creating a guaranteed government job program.

Much as we want workers to earn enough to support their families, regional living wage laws are not likely to achieve that result. Like setting the minimum wage rate too high, living wage laws can actually reduce wage opportunities for low-skilled workers. One recent study estimated that a 50 percent boost in the living wage would increase the wages of those in the bottom 10 percent of the wage distribution by about 3 percent but would also reduce employment of those workers by about 6 percent (Adams and Neumark 2005).[32] Moreover, living wage laws can adversely affect the local economies of the communities that adopt them (Macphearson 2004).

Also, like minimum wage laws, living wage laws are poorly targeted to help low-income working families. One study estimated that a broad-based living wage law would benefit just 39 percent of the poorest working families (those with incomes below 60 percent of the federal poverty level), whereas the earned income tax credit already benefits 92 percent of those families (Turner and Barnow 2003). Similarly, that study also found that only about 12 percent of the families that would benefit from a broad-based living wage law are poor, while 44 percent of those benefiting from the earned income tax credit are poor.

All in all, living wage laws are not very well targeted to help low-income working families and are likely to have disemployment effects on the least skilled as employers seek to replace them with higher-skilled workers. Accordingly, we would be better off combining a modest minimum wage with expanded earnings subsidies.

EXPAND THE UNEMPLOYMENT INSURANCE PROGRAM

Unemployment compensation is a joint federal-state program that provides cash benefits to individuals who have recently become unemployed. States administer their programs within federal guidelines. Some 99.7 percent of all wage and salary workers and 89 percent of the civilian labor force are covered by unemployment compensation, about 128 million individuals in all (U.S. House Committee 2004, section 4).

Benefits are financed through Federal Unemployment Tax Act taxes, a gross tax of 6.2 percent on the first $7,000 or so paid annually by covered employers to each employee. States set the benefit amounts as a fraction of the individual's weekly wage up to some state-determined maximum. Unemployed persons usually receive unemployment benefits for 26 weeks; the federal-state extended benefits program, however, provides for up to another 13 additional weeks. In 2004, approximately 8.8 million workers received unemployment benefits, totaling more than $41 billion (GAO 2005h). The average weekly benefit amount that year was $262.50, and the average duration was 16.1 weeks (SSA 2006b, table 9A2).

To qualify for benefits, an unemployed person usually must meet eligibility criteria that vary from state to state. In general, the unemployed person must have worked recently for a covered employer for a certain period and earned a minimum amount of wages. In 2003, for example, in order to qualify for a minimum monthly benefit, the typical worker would have had to have worked in two of the four calendar quarters before claiming benefits and earned $1,770 in the prior year (U.S. House Committee 2004, section 4). The unemployed person must also demonstrate the ability and willingness to seek and accept suitable employment, and usually this means full-time employment. Finally, the unemployed person must not have left her most recent employment for the wrong reason, including voluntarily quitting without "good cause," being fired for "misconduct," or going on strike.

All in all, the unemployment insurance payroll tax is regressive, but benefits tend to be paid out progressively (Anderson and Meyer 2003).[33]

Problems and Recommendations

Perhaps the biggest problem with unemployment insurance is its stringent eligibility rules. Even though the unemployment compensation system covers 99.7 percent of wage and salary workers, relatively few unemployed persons receive benefits at any point in time. For example, only 44 percent of unemployed persons received benefits in 2002 (U.S. House Committee 2004, section 4).[34]

Of particular concern, unemployed low-income workers are much less likely to receive unemployment benefits than other unemployed workers, even though low-income workers are twice as likely to be unemployed. In March 1995, only about 18 percent of low-income unemployed workers were receiving benefits, as opposed to some 40 percent of higher-wage unemployed workers (GAO 2000c, 5, 13).[35] Similarly, less than 20 percent of those leaving welfare for work are likely to become eligible for unemployment insurance through their new jobs (Committee for Economic Development 2000, 6–7, 40–42).

To help low-income workers, states should relax their eligibility criteria, particularly the criteria that make it hard for low-wage, part-time, and short-term workers to qualify for benefits (Committee for Economic Development 2000; Advisory Council on Unemployment 1996; Handler and Hasenfeld 1997).[36] In 2000, for example, half-time, half-year workers earning the minimum wage failed to qualify for unemployment benefits in 13 states (GAO 2000c). Similarly, in some 30 states, an otherwise qualified claimant is disqualified from receiving benefits if the worker is only looking for part-time work.

All in all, it would make sense for states to relax their eligibility criteria so more low-income and part-time workers qualify for benefits, and so claimants who are seeking part-time work are not disqualified. Economists generally believe that the burden of payroll taxation ultimately falls on the employees whose employers pay them. Consequently, if the employers of part-time, part-year workers are paying unemployment taxes, it would only seem fair to let their part-time, part-year workers share in the benefits.

It could also make sense to decouple benefit eligibility from earnings level. For example, in Washington State, eligibility is based on working 680 hours in the base year, regardless of earnings level (GAO 2000c).

Other factors can also help explain why low-income workers are so much less likely to receive unemployment benefits (GAO 2000c). For example, low-income workers may be more likely to voluntarily quit work to look for a better job or because child care is temporarily unavailable. Unfortunately, voluntarily quitting usually disqualifies a worker from claiming benefits. Relaxing the rules disqualifying workers who voluntarily quit would help low-income workers maintain their incomes. At the same time, however, relaxing the rules too much could undermine the work ethic by making it too easy to get benefits.[37] In any event, states should not disqualify claimants who quit a job to care for a dependent.

Another problem has to do with the lag time in qualifying for benefits. Under current law, a worker's most recent earnings typically do not count toward eligibility because of the three- or six-month lag time allowed to process wage records. One study found that only 11 states will look at a worker's most recent earnings if those are needed to qualify the worker for benefits (GAO 2000c). More states should shorten the lag time in qualifying earnings.

It would also make sense to raise minimum benefits so unemployed workers do not have to live in poverty while they are looking for jobs.

The average unemployment insurance benefit was just $257 a week in 2002, and the minimum benefit (in 2003) ranged from $1 in Vermont to $107 in Washington (U.S. House Committee 2004, table 4-5). Additional revenue to pay for enhanced benefits should probably come from general revenue sources like the progressive income tax, rather than from any increase in the regressive federal unemployment payroll tax. It could also make sense to extend the period over which benefits are paid (Vroman 2003).

Another possibility would be to incorporate reemployment bonuses into the unemployment insurance program (Bassi 1995). With reemployment bonuses, an unemployed worker would get a lump-sum payment when she found a new job. To encourage unemployed workers to intensify their job search efforts, the bonus amount might decline the longer an individual is unemployed.

Another approach to the problem of unemployment is to offer incentives for employers to hire the unemployed. These incentives could come in the form of training tax credits, grants, or wage subsidies to employers that hire the unemployed (Bassi 1995). For example, the Internal Revenue Code § 51 work opportunity tax credit provides employers with wage subsidies for hiring individuals from certain targeted groups that tend to have high unemployment rates. It could make sense to extend and increase the work opportunity tax credit so it benefits more unemployed individuals.[38]

PROMOTE UNIONIZATION

Enhancing the power of unions could also help reduce wage inequality and increase labor's share of the gross domestic product to the advantage of all workers. Many analysts decry the waning strength of unions in the workplace and call for changes to make it easier to form and join unions. For example, we could strengthen the collective bargaining protections in the National Labor Relations Act.[39] At the same time, however, we need policies that will move us away from the adversarial labor-management relations of the industrial era and toward the greater cooperation between labor and management that will be needed to sustain the knowledge-based and human-capital work systems of the future (Kochran 2005).

The empirical evidence suggests that having strong unions helps both unionized and nonunionized workers. Unions have successfully raised the wages of unionized workers about 20 percent and have raised total compensation (including both wages and benefits) about 28 percent (Mishel and Walters 2003).[40] Unions also reduce overall earnings inequality because they raise wages more for blue-collar workers than for generally higher-paid, white-collar workers. Moreover, union efforts to secure pension, health care, and vacation benefits for their members have led to a prevalence of those benefits throughout the workplace.

Historically, unions have also been instrumental in securing such legislated labor law protections as child safety laws, workplace safety laws, the minimum wage, overtime pay, Medicare, and Social Security. Indeed, many believe that unions play a crucial role in modern political democracies. For example, Paula B. Voos recently suggested that unions are "essential vehicles of democracy in contemporary society and that when they are weak democracy suffers" (Voos 2004).

Conversely, we need to appreciate that the low level of unionization in the United States may have increased our economy's flexibility and enhanced our ability to achieve low unemployment rates. Europe is far more unionized than the United States. According to one study, just 18 percent of workers in the United States were covered by a collective bargaining agreement in 2004, compared with more than 90 percent of workers in France and Germany (Alesina, Glaeser, and Sacerdote 2005). That study argues that unions in Europe have promoted "work less, work all" labor market policies that have led to more vacation time, lower average hours per week, and higher unemployment rates for European workers. Similarly, another study found that those countries that have high barriers to job loss (i.e., Germany, France, Italy, and Spain) have unemployment rates about double those of low-barrier countries like the United States (Labonte 2004).[41] And recall how the French government's early 2006 proposal to modestly cut back on job protections for young workers led to nationwide demonstrations by French students and their supporters.[42]

All in all, it would make sense to adopt policies that make it easier for American workers to form or join a union. For example, the proposed "Employee Free Choice Act," would make it easier for employees to choose whether to form unions by signing cards authorizing union representation, would provide mediation and arbitration for first contract disputes, and would establish tougher penalties for violation of employee rights when workers seek to form a union and during first contract negotiations.[43] At the same time, however, we need to be cautious about expanding worker rights and protections so much that we end up with the kind of high levels of youth unemployment and discontent we see in Europe.

MAKE FULL EMPLOYMENT A REALITY

One of the best ways to make work pay and reduce economic inequality would be to achieve full employment (Galbraith 1998; Bernstein and

Baker 2003; Shulman 2005). With full employment—an unemployment rate of at most 4 percent or as little as 2.5 percent—everybody who wants a job could have one. There would be fewer discouraged workers, and there would be pressure on employers to provide higher wages and benefits, even for low-skilled workers.

When labor markets are tight, real wages tend to go up, particularly for those at the lower end of the wage scale. With more jobs and higher wages, low-skilled workers see their incomes rise and poverty rates fall. For example, in the go-go years of the late 1990s, the labor market achieved full employment for the first time in 30 years, and that tight labor market led employers to raise wages and expand their workforce. From 1995 to 2000, the unemployment rate fell 1.6 percentage points, and the poverty rate fell 2.5 percentage points (Mishel et al. 2003). Real wages grew by an average of 7.8 percent, but by 11 percent for low-skilled workers in the 20th percentile of earnings. Full employment was especially helpful for minorities: their poverty rates fell quickly, and their incomes grew quickly, both in historical terms and relative to whites. Finally, although economic inequality continued to grow during the 1990s, it grew more slowly.

In short, full employment is a boon to low-skilled workers, and it can be a powerful force for ameliorating economic inequality. Moreover, creating employment opportunities for unemployed and discouraged workers can help them improve their work habits and skills, boost their self-esteem, and generally reduce social malcontent.

Several policies can help the government achieve full employment. For example, expanding the earned income tax credit and providing additional health care and child care subsidies to working families should help increase the demand for low-skilled workers. Expanding education and training opportunities can make workers more productive and so more attractive to employers. Toughening antidiscrimination policies and reforming unemployment and incarceration policies could also contribute to a lower unemployment rate and move us toward full employment.

Monetary policy can also be used as a tool to keep unemployment rates low. In that regard, James K. Galbraith believes that the causes of rising inequality are mainly *macroeconomic*, and he argues that the Federal Reserve Board should focus its monetary policy on achieving full employment rather than, say, low interest rates or low inflation. According to Galbraith:

> If we want a more equal wage structure, we need a low rate of unemployment. Other conditions would help: a still higher minimum wage, a more competitive value of the dollar, general price stability. Nevertheless, a low unemployment rate—say, 4

percent or lower, and sustained for a long period of time—is the essential thing. This is the principal way to equalize the playing field between sellers of technology and those who must buy it, and so turn the American wage structure from a bloody battle-ground back toward a model of middle-class solidarity. (1998, 171)

In the final analysis, many believe that full employment can only be achieved by having the government create jobs for all Americans who need them, either through public-service employment or through government subsidies to private-sector employers.[44] In effect, the government would act as the employer of last resort.[45] The federal government could institute a guaranteed job program similar to the New Deal's Works Projects Administration, Civilian Conservation Corps, and National Youth Administration programs (Bell and Wray 2004). Programs like today's Vista and Peace Corps programs could also serve as a model for the new government jobs program.[46]

For example, Stephanie A. Bell and L. Randall Wray recommend that the federal government create a public service job opportunity program (2004).[47] Under this approach, the government would announce the wage at which it would offer employment and then provide jobs for all who want to work at that wage, either in the public sector or at designated nonprofit organizations.

Although such a guaranteed jobs program would be costly, those costs could largely be offset by eliminating much of the social spending that is currently targeted to the unemployed and by the increased productivity of these new public workers, not to mention the intangible benefits from the reduction in the social and psychological costs of unemployment. Indeed, Bell and Wray argue that a guaranteed jobs program would easily pay for itself:

Using Minsky's 2.5 percent unemployment rate as a benchmark, this would be about 3.3 percent less than the actual 5.8 percent reported for 2002. By Okun's Law, a reduction of unemployment by 3.3 percentage points would raise GDP by 9.9 percent. Multiplying this percentage by 2002 GDP of $10.481 trillion, we obtain $1.038 trillion. In 2002 there were 7,229,000 families living below the official poverty line, with an average deficit of $7,205 per family required to bring each up to the poverty line. . . . In addition, another 9,618,000 individuals were living below the poverty line, with an average deficit of $4,798. . . . The total cost of eliminating poverty in 2002 would have been just under $100 billion, or about 10 percent of the extra GDP that would have been generated by reducing the unemployment rate to 2.5 percent. (2004, 22)

Moreover, because many of those who would accept jobs under a public service job opportunity program are not currently counted as unemployed, the increases in employment and GDP from a guaranteed jobs program could be even larger.

All in all, a guaranteed jobs program may be a necessary tool for achieving full employment and the benefits associated with it.

SOME OTHER IDEAS FOR IMPROVING LABOR MARKETS

Four other ideas for improving labor markets are regulating executive compensation, reducing the workweek, restricting immigration, and promoting worker safety.

Regulate Executive Compensation

Another approach for reducing earnings inequality would involve imposing additional regulatory limits on the compensation paid by businesses to top executives. A few limits are imposed by current tax laws. For example, under the Internal Revenue Code, corporations cannot generally deduct more than $1 million a year of cash compensation paid to their directors, and they cannot deduct extraordinary "golden parachute" payments made to former executives.[48] The Securities and Exchange Commission recently toughened the disclosure rules that relate to executive compensation (U.S. Securities and Exchange Commission 2006). Some argue that we should impose even more limits on executive compensation.

For example, it could make sense to toughen the limits on the deductibility of executive salaries (Anderson et al. 2005). Along the same lines, James K. Galbraith recently suggested that an "inequality surcharge" could be imposed on corporations that pay their top executive more than 50 times as much as their line workers, perhaps falling to a target ratio of, say, 30 to 1 over time (1998).[49] Other reform options include proposals to further improve the accounting and securities law disclosure standards of executive compensation; require shareholder approval of extraordinary executive severance and retirement packages; ban companies from offering executive perks that are not broadly available to employees; and increase the penalties for selling company stock based on insider information (Anderson et al. 2004).

Reduce the Workweek to 35 Hours

In addition to setting the minimum wage, the Fair Labor Standards Act guarantees millions of workers the right to overtime pay, or time-

and-one-half wages for every hour worked beyond the normal 40-hour workweek.[50] These rules tend to push employers to spread work out among more employees and so may have a modest impact on the earnings distribution.[51] Along similar lines, some policymakers argue that shortening the workweek would spread the work around, giving jobs to the unemployed and reducing earnings inequality. This kind of "work less, work all" strategy has been tried in France (35-hour workweek) and other European countries, but there is little evidence to suggest that reducing the workweek would increase the number of workers. Instead, it is likely that reducing the workweek would have adverse effects on output, inflation, the balance of trade, and individual choice regarding the work-leisure allocation.[52]

Restrict Immigration

Immigration policy can also have a large impact on the U.S. economy, in general, and the labor market, in particular. Under the standard neoclassical model of labor supply, a rise in immigration translates into an increase in labor supply that will tend to reduce wages of native workers, particularly the wages of low-skilled workers who most likely have to compete with immigrants for jobs. Theoretically, then, reducing immigration could benefit native workers, forcing employers to hire more native workers, pay them higher wages, and provide them with additional training to upgrade their skills.

Empirical studies, however, have generally found only a small impact of immigration on the wages of native workers (CBO 2005e). An exception is a recent study by George J. Borjas. He finds that immigration increased labor supply by about 11 percent between 1980 and 2000 and that the increase reduced the wage of the average native worker by 3.2 percent. He also finds that "the wage impact differed dramatically across education groups, with the wage falling by 8.9 percent for high school dropouts, 4.9 percent for college graduates, 2.6 percent for high school graduates, and barely changing for workers with some college" (Borjas 2003, 36).

As chapter 2 showed, there were more than 21.4 million foreign-born workers in the United States in 2004, up from just 13.1 million in 1994. These immigrants tend to be less educated and earn less than natives. For example, immigrants compose about 14 percent of U.S. workers but 20 percent of low-wage workers.

All in all, it seems likely that immigration does generate pressure to lower wages on low-skilled workers (Mishel et al. 2005). Nevertheless, immigration may contribute to the economy in other ways that may offset our concerns about the wage pressures generated by immigration. For example, immigration accounts for 37 percent of current U.S.

population growth, and immigrants were responsible for more than 40 percent of the labor force growth in the mid- to late 1990s (The Century Foundation 2000; Orrenius 2004). Also, in the long run, the work effort of immigrants may have a beneficial impact on the fiscal health of such pay-as-you-go government programs as Social Security and Medicare.

Immigration policy has long been a critical labor market policy. Indeed, until World War II, the Immigration and Naturalization Service was housed in the Department of Labor (Smith 1998).[53] More recently, the Welfare Reform Act of 1996 made most immigrants ineligible for such welfare programs as food stamps and SSI.[54] Also, a number of recent proposals to permit more "guest" agricultural workers or more high-tech workers (i.e., Specialty Occupation Workers with H-1B visas) are intended to alleviate purported labor supply shortages in those areas.[55]

Recent immigration policy has focused on reuniting families, rather than on acquiring workers.[56] In 2004, for example, of the 946,142 legal immigrants, 406,074 came in as immediate relatives of U.S. citizens, 214,355 came in as family-sponsored immigrants, but just 155,330 came in on employment preferences (Homeland Security 2005, table 4). Instead, it could make sense to reorient immigration policy to favor economic growth rather than family considerations, perhaps by shifting admissions from family-based to skill-based categories and toward policies that favor highly skilled immigrants over low-skilled immigrants.[57] Also, implementing a legalization program for illegal immigrants could help foreign-born persons and their children better assimilate into the U.S. economy and culture (The Century Foundation 2000).

Promote Worker Safety

Government also needs to do more to guarantee workers a safe and healthy workplace (Levine 1998). In the decades since the passage of the Occupational Safety and Health Act of 1970, workplace injuries and illnesses have declined significantly (Conaway 2003). Unfortunately, many workers continue to face unsafe and unhealthy working conditions.

The Occupational Safety and Health Administration (OSHA) needs to toughen safety standards in the workplace and be more aggressive in its enforcement efforts. For example, the government needs to strengthen whistle-blower protections for those who cooperate with OSHA or otherwise speak out about hazardous conditions (Shulman 2005). Developing safety and health programs in each workplace that provide for employee participation could also help (U.S. Commission on the Future of Worker-Management Relations 1994, section 7).

12

WORKING TOGETHER

The goals for the nation should be straightforward and ambitious: to sufficiently reward work, to strengthen policies that make economic advancement and security possible, and to promote the creation of jobs that pay well. (Waldron et al. 2004, i)

If we honor work, we must reward it. For generations, Americans shared a tacit understanding that if you worked hard, a livable income and basic securities were to be yours. That promise has been broken and as a nation, we are living a lie. (Shulman 2005, 13)

In a complex society like ours, the economic rewards from work are determined by a combination of market forces and government policies. As we have seen, the free market alone can never achieve economic justice, nor has our present market-plus-government system yet achieved economic justice. While taxes and transfers reduce household income inequality by about 20 percent, in our post-tax, post-transfer society, the top 20 percent of households still have almost 25 times as much income as the bottom 20 percent and hundreds of times as much wealth.

To be sure, it is unlikely that a convincing moral argument can be made for any particular level of redistribution. There is no magic Gini index value or perfect 90/10 ratio that defines the theoretically and morally "correct" level of inequality. But we do not need to identify *the* theoretically correct distribution of economic resources. Given how unequal the present distribution of economic resources in the United States is, we know which direction to go.

In particular, this book has suggested several changes in government tax, transfer, and regulatory policies that could promote greater economic equality. The key is to design government policies that encourage work and work effort. Such changes can increase the size of the economic pie and enable us to divide it more equally.

This chapter pulls together the principal recommendations about how to reform the government's tax, transfer, and regulatory policies. The result is a comprehensive proposal that would generally increase the economic rewards for work and promote greater economic justice. First, we should replace most of the current tax system with a comprehensive progressive tax system that imposes low tax rates on earned income. Second, we should replace most of the current welfare system with a system of earnings subsidies, universal grants, and child care assistance. Third, we should replace the current Social Security system with a two-tiered system designed to ensure that every elderly American has an adequate income throughout her retirement years. Fourth, we should restructure the pension system so it no longer pushes older workers into premature retirements. Fifth, we should restructure the health care system so it provides nearly universal coverage and does so with a minimum of work disincentives. Finally, we should improve the operation of labor markets and move toward full employment.

A COMPREHENSIVE PROGRESSIVE TAX SYSTEM

We should create a broad progressive tax system that imposes low tax rates on earned income. For example, it would make sense to integrate the individual income tax, Social Security payroll tax, corporate income tax, and estate and gift taxes into a comprehensive, progressive income tax system. That integrated tax system could have a logical tax rate structure, as opposed to the roller-coaster rate structure of the current system, and it could easily accommodate a few refundable tax credits targeted toward low-income workers and their families. In addition, hardly any individuals would have to file tax returns, as final withholding could be achieved through exact withholding from employers and other income sources.

EARNINGS SUBSIDIES, UNIVERSAL GRANTS, AND CHILD CARE ASSISTANCE

Most of the current welfare system should be replaced with a system of universal grants, earnings subsidies, and child care assistance. The general idea is to "cash out" as many social welfare programs as possible and use the savings to pay for such benefits as $2,000 per person universal grants, $2,000 per worker earned income tax credits, and child care assistance, and to pay these benefits out monthly. This restructured welfare system should be integrated with the tax system.

For example, we might replace the current tax system and most of the current transfer system with a comprehensive tax and transfer system. That system could have two tax rates, say, 20 percent of the first $50,000 of income and 35 percent on income in excess of $50,000; $2,000 per person refundable personal tax credits; $2,000 per worker refundable earned income credits; and hardly any other deductions or credits. Table 7.3 and figure 7.2 showed how such an integrated tax and transfer system could work. This system would be simpler than the current system, it would encourage low-skilled workers to enter and remain in the workforce, and it would minimize the work disincentives on higher-income workers.

Presumably, each individual would present something like the current IRS Form W-2, Wage and Tax Statement, to her employer, bank, or social service agency. Employees would then receive advance payment of their tax credits from their employers in the form of reduced withholding, while other claimants would have their monthly payments directly deposited with their designated banks or social service agencies.

Disabled individuals, retired individuals, and others with greater needs could receive additional monthly benefit payments, but most Americans would receive only their $2,000 per person universal grants and their $2,000 per worker earned income credits.

A Two-Tiered Social Security System

We should replace the current Social Security system with a two-tiered system. The first tier would provide a basic Social Security benefit to every older American, and would be financed out of general revenues. At full retirement age, the government might guarantee every retiree a first-tier benefit equal to 100 percent of the poverty level. In 2006, for example, the poverty level for a single individual is $9,800, yielding a benefit of about $817 a month (a portion of which would come from those $2,000 per person universal grants).

In addition to these first-tier benefits, every worker would earn retirement benefits based on earnings. These second-tier benefits would be financed with a much-reduced system of payroll taxes. In effect, each worker would have an individual retirement savings account, and the reduced payroll taxes that he or she paid would be credited to those accounts, along with investment income on the balance in those accounts. At retirement, the balance in a worker's account would typically be used to purchase an inflation-adjusted annuity over and above the individual's first-tier benefit, although in some cases workers with large accounts might be allowed to withdraw part of their benefits in a lump sum.

A RESTRUCTURED PENSION SYSTEM

We should restructure the pension system so it no longer pushes older workers into premature retirements. Pension policy should instead be redesigned to strengthen the connection between pension benefits and work effort and to help ensure that all American workers and their families have adequate retirement incomes.

Right now, only about half of American workers have pensions; in the end, a voluntary pension system simply cannot be counted on to meet the retirement income needs of American workers and their families. We need to move to some type of mandatory universal pension system. The simplest design would be to piggyback a system of individual retirement savings accounts onto the existing Social Security withholding system, like the second tier of the Social Security system described above. This type of mandatory individual retirement savings account system would help ensure that all American workers and their families would have adequate retirement incomes, and it would help ensure that American workers would face a minimum of work disincentives.

UNIVERSAL HEALTH CARE COVERAGE

We should restructure the health care system so it provides nearly universal coverage and does so with a minimum of work disincentives. Today, we are spending about 16 percent of our GDP on health care, yet some 46 million Americans lack coverage. Most working-age Americans get their health care coverage through their employers, but employers face increasing pressures to try to shift the costs of health care to their workers or to the government. For example, many employers are abandoning their retiree health care plans, and they are restructuring their workforces to shift work to part-time and contingent workers with no health care coverage.

America's health care system needs to be redesigned to recognize the complex economic incentives that influence employer and employee decisions about health care. One of the most promising approaches would be to require every individual to have health care coverage, and we would pay for that universal coverage with a combination of employer contributions, employee contributions, and government assistance based on ability to pay.

Move Toward Full Employment

Finally, we should improve the operation of our labor markets. We should vigorously enforce policies against employment discrimination, reduce incarceration levels, and improve education and training opportunities. We should also modestly raise the minimum wage and index it for inflation, expand the unemployment insurance program, and make every effort to achieve full employment.

Like Clockwork

Government can, and should, intervene in the free market to encourage work and promote greater economic equality. We simply do not have to settle for a society with so much economic inequality. We should not be content to live in a society where the top 20 percent of households have almost 25 times as much income as the bottom 20 percent and hundreds of times as much wealth.

Adopting the proposals offered in this book would go a long way toward improving the rewards for work and toward promoting greater economic justice. These proposals are generally designed to encourage low-skilled workers to enter and remain in the workforce. At the same time, the proposals offered in this book endeavor to minimize the work disincentives on higher-income workers. Consequently, these proposals should increase overall productivity. Together, these proposals should increase the size of the economic pie *and* enable us to divide it more equally. Together, these proposals would help make America work even better than it already does.

To be sure, it will be impossible to achieve anyone's utopian vision of economic justice, but we certainly know which direction to go. Over time, we should be able to build on these proposals and achieve even larger reductions in economic inequality. For example, we should be able to provide larger and larger earning subsidies and larger and larger universal grants. The clock is ticking, but we can, and we should, work toward a better future. That is the way to make America work in this new millennium.

NOTES

Chapter 1. Developing a National Strategy for Work

1. Author's computations from World Bank, "Quick Reference Tables," http://www.worldbank.org/data/quickreference/quickref.html (Total GDP 2004 and Population 2004). See also Organisation for Economic Co-operation and Development (OECD) (2006b), 13 (Population and Migration, Total Population, Evolution of the population), 31 (Macroeconomic Trends, Gross Domestic Product [GDP], Size of GDP).

2. Similarly, our employment-population ratio, 62.7 percent in 2005, is higher than those in most industrialized nations.

3. See, for example, Alger (1986); Pew Research Center for People and the Press (2003), a public opinion survey finding that since 1992, at least 87 percent of Americans agree that "they admire people who have gotten rich through hard work"; and Alesina and Angeletos (2005), discussing *World Values Survey* results showing that "Americans perceive wealth and success as the outcome of individual talent, effort, and entrepreneurship" while "Europeans attribute a large role to luck, corruption, and connections."

4. See, for example, President Franklin Delano Roosevelt, *Public Papers*, VI (May 24, 1937): 209–14 (sending what would become the Fair Labor Standards Act of 1938 to Congress). See also Sheet Metal Workers' International Association, *Mission*, available at http://www.smwia.org/about: "To establish and maintain desirable working conditions and thus provide for themselves and their families that measure of comfort, happiness, and security to which every citizen is entitled in return for his labor, from a deep sense of pride in our trade, to give a fair day's work for a fair day's pay." See also Engels (1881).

5. According to the survey, 66 percent of Americans say that "it is the responsibility of the government to take care of people who can't care for themselves."

6. See, for example, Smith (1986).

7. For example, physicians in Canada and Germany earn about half as much; physicians in Austria, France, and Britain earn less than one-third as much; and physicians in Finland, Norway, and Sweden earn just one-quarter as much (Herrick 2001).

8. A quintile is 20 percent of the population. Market income includes money income except government cash transfers, includes imputed realized capital gains and losses, includes the imputed rate of return on home equity, and subtracts imputed work expenses (U.S. Bureau of the Census 2006, 1–2).

9. For some international comparisons of household income inequality, see table 2.7 and accompanying text. The "official measure" of the Gini index for household income inequality in 2004 was 0.466 (DeNavas-Walt et al. 2005, table A-3). See also U.S. Bureau of the Census (2004a), table RDI-7 (Share of Aggregate Income by Each Fifth of Households, by Selected Definition of Income: 1979 to 2001); and DeNavas-Walt and Cleveland (2002), table 6, explaining a wide range of census definitions of income.

10. Disposable income includes money income, the value of noncash transfers (food stamps, public or subsidized housing, and free or reduced-price school lunches), imputed realized capital gains and losses, and the imputed rate of return on home equity; it subtracts imputed work expenses, federal payroll taxes, federal and state income taxes, and property taxes on owner-occupied homes (Census Bureau 2006, 2). Unfortunately, however, this definition fails to take into account the expenses for travel to work and for child care (Erik Eckholm, "Report on Impact of Federal Benefits on Curbing Poverty Reignites a Debate," *New York Times*, 18 February 2006, A10).

11. To the same effect, Yellon (1998, 13–14) notes that "taxes and transfers eliminate about one-fifth of pre-government inequality, as measured by the Gini index, and more than one-half of pre-government poverty."

12. The Lorenz curves in figure 1.1 are only close approximations of the true Lorenz curves for households in 2004. The curves in figure 1.1 are based on the summary information in table 1.1, rather than on the Census Bureau's underlying household income files.

13. In 2005, for example, total personal income in the United States was $10,238.2 billion (Council of Economic Advisers 2006, table B-29). Of that, $7,113.6 billion was attributable to compensation of employees, and proprietor's income accounted for another $937.8 billion, for a total of $8,051.4 billion; and $8,051.4 billion divided by $10,232.2 billion equals 78.7 percent. See also Mishel, Bernstein, and Allegretto (2005), table 1.24, estimating labor's share of national income at 71.6 percent in 2000.

14. See also Mayer (2004), table 2, showing Gini coefficients for workers from 1994 to 2003.

15. "What People Earn: Our Annual Report on the Economy and You," *Parade: The Sunday Newspaper Magazine* (in *The Sunday Oklahoman*, 12 March 2006).

16. See also Bok (1993).

17. Author's calculation from Internal Revenue Service (IRS) (2005b), table 1.4.

18. Sociologists call this tendency to marry within one's social circle "class endogamy." See, for example, McNamee and Miller (2004), 65.

19. For example, while just 5.5 percent of married couples were poor in 2004, 28.4 percent of female-headed households (with no husband present) were poor that year (DeNavas-Walt et al. 2005, table 3).

20. Public Law 74-271. See, for example, U.S. House Committee (2004), section 4.

21. See, for example, Sunley (1977), 100; and Bradford and the U.S. Treasury Tax Policy Staff (1984), 56. The exclusion of unemployment compensation benefits from gross income was thought to be inequitable because it resulted in people with equal spending power owing differing amounts of income taxes.

22. Revenue Act of 1978, Public Law 95-600; Tax Reform Act of 1986, Public Law 99-514; I.R.C. § 85.

23. U.S. Department of Health and Human Services, Administration for Children and Families, "Cash assistance for needy families—Aid to Families with Dependent Children (AFDC) and Temporary Assistance for Needy Families (TANF) Average Monthly Families and Recipients for Calendar Years 1936–2001," http://www.acf.dhhs.gov/news/stats/3697.htm.

24. 29 *United States Code* (U.S.C.) § 206. See also U.S. Department of Labor, "History of Federal Minimum Wage Rates under the Fair Labor Standards Act, 1938–1996," http://www.dol.gov/esa/minwage/chart.htm. Working 40 hours a week, 52 weeks a year, at $5.15 an hour, a worker would earn an annual income of $10,712, and she would be entitled to an earned income tax credit up to $4,285 ($4,284.80 = .40 × $10,712, assuming that she had two qualifying children).

25. Personal Responsibility and Work Opportunity Reconciliation Act of 1996 (PRWORA), Public Law 104-193.

26. Former I.R.C. § 1348 was added by the Tax Reform Act of 1969, Public Law 91-172.

27. Public Law 99-514. A 5 percent surtax pushed marginal tax rates up to 33 percent for some taxpayers.

28. Public Law 107-16; Public Law 108-27; I.R.C. § 1.

29. See also BLS (2005e).

30. 29 U.S.C. §§ 621–634.

31. Barbara Ehrenreich cautions against thinking of low-wage work and low-skilled work as almost identical. She points out that many low-wage jobs take effort, intelligence, and concentration; she has vowed never to use the word "unskilled" again (Ehrenreich 2005b).

32. See, for example, Dick (1975), Sher (1987), Gilbert (1991), and Nathanson (1998).

33. In 2004, for example, prekindergarten and kindergarten teachers made an average of $19.45 an hour, while marketing, advertising, and public relations managers made an average of $48.65 an hour. Similarly, garbage collectors made $12.96 an hour, while lawyers made $48.60 an hour (BLS 2005h, table 2.1). See also table 2.4.

34. "What People Earn: Our Annual Report on the Economy and You," *Parade: The Sunday Newspaper Magazine.*

35. As more fully discussed in chapter 5, most of us would probably agree that workers deserve to be rewarded according to their "merit," and most of us probably share fairly similar ideas about what is meritorious.

36. See, for example, Forman (1998a) and "Report of the Technical Panel on Trends and Issues in Retirement Savings," in Advisory Council on Social Security (1997), vol. 2, 15–20.

37. See, for example, Carasso and Steuerle (2005) and Forman (1996a).

Chapter 2. Working in the U.S.A.

1. See also U.S. Department of Labor (2005) and BLS (2006a).

2. See also Freeman (1997).

3. See also OECD (2006b), 117 (Labour Market, Hours worked); Mishel et al. (2005), table 7.18; DOL (2004); Karoly and Panis (2004), 53–54, showing relatively high levels of "labor utilization" (i.e., a combination of workforce participation, [lack of] unemployment, and annual hours worked per worker) in the United States compared with other industrial nations; and Alesina, Glaeser, and Sacerdote (2005).

4. See also BLS (2005a), showing that employed persons worked an average of 7.6 hours on the days that they worked.

5. See also Waldron, Roberts, and Reamer (2004), 8, noting that the average low-income family worked 2,500 hours a year, equivalent to 1.2 full-time jobs. Of note, from 1975 to 2000, women dramatically reduced the amount of time they spent doing housework; this reduction swamped the modest increase in the amount of time men spent on housework during that period. See, for example, Haveman et al. (2003) and BLS (2005a).

6. See also Haveman et al. (2003), 133–38, showing lower utilization of the earning capacity of less-educated workers.

7. In 2005, for example, 33.3 percent of black teenagers (age 16 to 19) were unemployed, compared with just 14.2 percent of white teenagers (BLS 2006f, table 3). See also Haveman et al. (2003), showing lower utilization of the earning capacity of minority workers; Wilson (1996), documenting the disappearance of jobs from poor, black inner-city neighborhoods like the South Side of Chicago; and Edelman, Holzer, and Offner (2006), discussing the characteristics of "disconnected" young men.

8. On the other hand, employed women spend an hour more a day doing household activities and caring for household members.

9. See also Karoly and Panis (2004).

10. See also BLS (2005k).

11. See, for example, Haveman et al. (2003). At the same time, the economic dependency ratio in the United States has declined. The economic dependency ratio is the number of people in the total population who are not in the labor force per 100 of those who are in the labor force. For every 100 people in the labor force in 2004, for example, about 98.3 were not, down from 126.3 in 1975 and headed toward just 96.3 in 2014 (Toossi 2005, table 10).

12. Indeed, the United States has "the world's highest ratio of two-income households, with its hidden, de facto tax on time and families" (Phillips 2002, 113).

13. Average retirement is the age at which more than 50 percent of the cohort is out of the labor force. See also Haveman et al. (2003), showing a convergence in the labor force participation rates of men and women.

14. Life expectancies also vary by race. For example, the life expectancy of a white male born in 1999 was 74.7 years, while the life expectancy for a black male born that year was just 68.4 years (Census Bureau 2000).

15. See also figure 8.3 (comparing life expectancies at birth with the Social Security full retirement age).

16. See, for example, Aaron, Bosworth, and Burtless (1989) and Budetti et al. (2001). For international comparisons, see World Bank (1994) and OECD (2006a).

17. See also Committee for Economic Development (1999); Samwick (1998); Haveman el al. (2003, 106), finding that early retirement "is the most rapidly growing reason why working-age people fail to fully use their human capital in market activities"; and Burtless and Quinn (2002).

The trend for women has been going in somewhat the opposite direction. As more women enter and remain in the workforce, their average retirement age has increased from about age 53 in 1961 to about age 62 in 2004 (Munnell 2006).

18. See also Purcell (2005a), table 2; and Haveman el al. (2003), 138–43. Nevertheless, older Americans stay busy. Eight out of 10 adults age 65 to 74 engage in at least one of four types of productive activity: paid work, formal or informal volunteering, or family caregiving (Zedlewski and Schaner 2005).

19. See table 8.2. See also Purcell (2005a), table 7.

20. See also Purcell (2005a), table 3; and U.S. Government Accountability Office (2005d).

21. Also of note, the United States has one of the developed world's highest labor force participation rates for persons age 65 and older (Rix 2004).

22. According to Rebecca M. Blank, for example, "Since the mid-1970s . . . falling wages for less-skilled workers can explain most of the decline in work effort, assuming reasonable elasticity responses among men to earnings opportunities" (1995, 56). See also Blank (1997) and Haveman et al. (2003).

23. Author's calculation from BLS (2006f), table 35. In that regard, rather than focusing on employment-population ratios, some economists prefer to calculate the obverse "nonemployment" ratio. See, for example, Steuerle and Spiro (1999).

24. See, for example, Pigeon and Wray (1999).

25. Author's calculation (2.7 percent = 2,135,901 incarcerated men in 2004 ÷ 78,980,000 civilians in the labor force), based on data from Bureau of Justice Statistics, "Key Crime & Justice Facts at a Glance" correctional population table, http://www.ojp.usdoj.gov/bjs/glance/tables/corr2tab.htm; BLS (2006f), table 2; and Katz and Krueger (1999). See also Western (2001) and Freeman (2003).

26. Bureau of Justice Statistics, "Key Crime & Justice Facts at a Glance," incarceration rate, 1980–2004 table, http://www.ojp.usdoj.gov/bjs/glance/tables/incrttab.htm.

27. See also Edelman et al. (2006); Raphael (2006); Oliver (2001); and Holzer, Offner, and Sorenson (2004).

28. Bureau of Justice Statistics, "Key Crime & Justice Facts at a Glance," correctional population table.

29. See, for example, Mishel et al. (2005), 256–76.

30. See also Friedberg and Owyang (2004), noting that the average job tenure of male full-time employees age 22–59 in the Survey of Consumer Finances fell from 9.2 years in 1983 to 8.6 years in 1998; and Copeland (2005a).

31. See also BLS (2006f), table 19.

32. Author's calculation from BLS (2005c), table 5 (0.7405 = 102,889 thousand noncontingent full-time workers ÷ 138,952 thousand employed).

33. See also Mishel et al. (2005), 189–98.

34. U.S. Census Bureau, "Foreign-Born Population of the United States Current Population Survey—March 2004, Detailed Tables (PPL-176)," table 2.1, available at http://www.census.gov/population/www/socdemo/foreign/ppl-176.html. See also Larsen (2004)—33.5 million foreign born in 2003 (11.7 percent of the population).

35. See also BLS (2005f).

36. Author's calculation from Council of Economic Advisers (2006), table B-29. In 2005, total personal income in the United States was $10,238.2 billion. Of that, $7,113.6 billion was attributable to compensation of employees, and another $937.8 billion to proprietor's income, for a total of $8,051.4 billion; and $8,051.4 billion ÷ $10,232.2 billion = 78.7 percent. See also Mishel et al. (2005).

37. An age-earnings profile shows the average hourly or annual earnings of a cross-section of people of different ages who have had the same amount of schooling.

38. See also Borjas (2002). According to the U.S. Office of Personnel Management, "2006-GS" web page, http://www.opm.gov/oca/06tables/html/gs.asp, an employee at GS level 1, step 1 makes $16,352 in 2006, and an employee at GS level 15, step 1 makes $91,507. The ratio between these two numbers is 5.6 to 1.

39. Of note, because the lowest quintile of households includes so many retirees, it has close to zero earnings (Rodríguez et al. 2002).

40. See, for example, Johnson et al. (2005); Wolff, Zacharias, and Caner (2004); and Garner and Short (2005).

41. Also of note, the top 20 percent of all wage and salary workers received 45.3 percent of all earnings in 2003, but the bottom 20 percent received just 5.2 percent of earnings, for an 80/20 ratio of earnings *shares* of 8.71 to 1. The second quintile received 10.7 percent of earnings, the third quintile received 15.8 percent, and the fourth quintile received 23.0 percent.

42. Following Daniel H. Weinberg, "Evidence from Census 2000 about Earnings by Detailed Occupation for Men and Women" (Washington, DC: U.S. Census Bureau Census 2000 Special Report No. CENSR-15, 2004), figure 1.

43. Author's calculations from U.S. Census Bureau, *Current Population Survey, Annual Demographic Survey, March Supplement,* 2005.

44. See also Burtless and Jencks (2003); Mishel et al. (2005); and Piketty and Saez (2006).

45. For example, movie actress Angelina Jolie made $30 million in 2005, and baseball player Alex Rodriguez made $25 million. "What People Earn: Our Annual Report on the Economy and You," *Parade: The Sunday Newspaper Magazine.*

46. Author's calculation from IRS (2005b), table 1.4. As returns include joint returns of husbands and wives, in many cases these numbers reflect the combined earnings of both a husband and a wife.

47. See also Bok (1993); McMahon and Abreu (1999); and Paul Krugman, "For Richer," *New York Times Magazine,* 20 October 2002, 62. Similarly, Paul Samuelson notes:

> If we made an income pyramid out of child's blocks, with each layer portraying $1,000, the peak would be far higher than the Eiffel Tower, but most of us would be within a yard of the ground. (1980, 80)

See also figure 2.5, which shows a similar distribution of earnings.

48. See, for example, Gottschalk and Danziger (2003); Gottschalk (1997); and Piketty and Saez (2003).

Of note, wages alone are a poor measure of compensation because today's workers receive so many fringe benefits. Wage inequality tends to understate compensation inequality because fringe benefits, such as pensions and health insurance, are less common among low-income workers than high-income workers. Consequently, proper measures of earnings inequality look at differences in compensation, not wages (Pierce 1999).

49. See also U.S. Census Bureau, *Current Population Survey, Annual Demographic Survey, March Supplement*, 2002, table PINC-10, http://ferret.bls.census.gov/macro/032002/perinc/new10_001.htm (showing a Gini index of .475 in 2001 for wage and salary workers 15 years and older) and table PINC-08, http://ferret.bls.census.gov/macro/032002/perinc/new10_001.htm (showing a Gini index of .483 in 2001 for earnings of people 15 years and older); and Mayer (2004), table 2 (showing Gini indices for wage and salary workers from 1994 to 2003; for example, 0.396 in 2001 and 0.399 in 2003).

50. See also Krueger and Perri (2002), estimating that inequality of after-tax labor income increased by 25 percent from 1972 to 1998; and Aronson (2002).

It is worth acknowledging, however, that at least some of the increases in earnings inequality over the past few decades may be attributable to aging of America and the normal age-earnings increases of the disproportionately large baby-boom generation. See, for example, Fennell and Stark (2004), discussing the need to develop statistical measures that remove age-related inequality from annual measures of inequality; and Paglin (1975), suggesting that about one-third of income inequality in 1972 was attributable to the normal age-income profile and not related to long-run or lifetime inequality. It is also worth noting that the age-earnings curve is becoming flatter as the crowding effect that depressed the wages of baby boomers when they were young continues to depress their wages in near-old-age relative to younger cohorts (Triest, Sapozhnikov, and Sass 2006).

51. See also Saez (2006), finding "an unprecedented surge in top-wage incomes" in the United States over the past 30 years.

52. See also Census Bureau (2004b), table IE-1; and Aizcorbe, Kennickell, and Moore (2003).

53. See also Rodríguez et al. (2002), table 1 (finding that, in 1998, the top 1 percent of households had 73 times as much earnings as the bottom 40 percent of households).

54. Of note, gross money income is widely used to measure the level and distribution of economic inequality. The Levy Economics Institute of Bard College, however, is working to develop a more comprehensive measure of economic well-being. See, for example, Wolff et al. (2004). In addition to household money income, the Levy Institute measure of economic well-being (LIMEW) includes the value of employer contributions for health insurance, income from wealth, transfers and public consumption, and the value of household production. This broader measure of economic well-being generally increases household incomes and results in less inequality (e.g., a lower Gini index) than the usual measure of gross money income. For example, for the year 2000, Wolff and colleagues estimate that the Gini index of gross money income plus employer contributions for health insurance was 0.51, but the Gini

index for LIMEW was just 0.42 (2004, figure 3). See also Wolff and Zacharias (2006).

55. Coincidentally, that is the same as it was in 2004, as reflected in table 2.6.

56. Also of note, income inequality is greater among elderly households (age 65 and older) than among nonelderly households, but the gap between elderly and nonelderly households narrowed from 1967 to 1997 (Rubin, White-Means, and Daniel 2000).

57. Author's analysis of Census Bureau (2004b), table IE-3. For example, in 2000, the top quintile's share of aggregate household income was 49.8 percent and the bottom quintile's share was 3.6 percent. Consequently, the top 20 percent/bottom 20 percent ratio is 13.8 ($13.8 = 49.8 \div 3.6$). Similarly, in 2000, the top 5 percent/bottom 20 percent ratio is 24.6 ($24.6 = [4 \times 22.1] \div 3.6$). See also Mishel et al. (2005), figure 1J; and Bernstein, McNichol, and Lyons (2005).

58. See also David Cay Johnston, "Big Gain for Rich Seen in Tax Cuts for Investments," *New York Times*, 5 April 2006, A1; McMahon (2004); and Geier (2003).

59. U.S. Census Bureau, table CH-1 (Living Arrangements of Children under 18 Years Old: 1960 to Present) (May 25, 2006), available at http://www.census.gov/population/socdemo/hh-fam/ch1.pdf.

60. See also Burtless and Jencks (2003); OECD (2005b); and Jencks (2002).

61. Using the official poverty level, the United States fell to second worst, behind the United Kingdom.

62. The most common way to measure inequality in consumption is to compare various households' current outlays.

63. See also Census Bureau (2005d).

64. A consumer unit generally includes all members of a household related by blood, marriage, adoption, or some other legal arrangement.

65. See also Cagetti and De Nardi (2005); Kopszuk and Saez (2004); and Rodríguez et al. (2002).

66. See also Kennickell (2003); Aizcorbe et al. (2003); and Caner and Wolff (2004).

67. $1,113.33 = 33.4 \div .03$. See also Rodríguez et al. (2002).

68. *Forbes*, "The Forbes Four Hundred" (September 27, 2001), http://www.forbes.com/lists/forbes400/2001/09/27/400.html. See also Matthew Miller and Peter Newcomb, eds., "The 400 Richest Americans" (September 22, 2005), http://www.forbes.com/400richest, showing Gates and Buffett topping the lists again in 2005 with $51 billion and $40 billion, respectively.

69. Wealth holdings also vary with such demographic variables as age, race, gender, and marital status. See, for example, Schmidt and Sevak (2005); and Cagetti and De Nardi (2005).

70. See, for example, McNamee and Miller (2004): "The advantages of being born wealthy are cumulative and substantial." (13)

71. See, for example, Mishel et al. (2005); Topel (1997); Johnson (1997); and Stoops (2004).

72. See also Census Bureau (2005a); Day and Newberger (2002); BLS (2002); Census Bureau (2005b), table F-18; Hill, Hoffman, and Rex (2005); and Kosters (1998).

73. See, for example, Mishel et al. (2005), table 2.21.

74. See, for example, Council of Economic Advisers (1999a).

75. See, for example, Danziger and Reed (1999) and Karoly (1998). See also figure 2.6, showing that workers in the 10th percentile of earnings saw only a 0.9 percent increase in real wages from 1973 to 2003.

76. See, for example, Acs and Loprest (2005); Johnson (2002); Ehrenreich (2001); Shipler (2004); BLS (2005i); and Terkel (1985).

77. See also Bradbury and Katz (2002), 2–5, showing that during the 1990s, less than half of low-wage families advanced into the middle class; and Aaronson and Mazumber (2005), finding that intergenerational mobility increased from 1940 to 1980 but has declined sharply since 1980.

78. To the same effect, see, for example, Blank (1997); Waldron et al. (2004, i), noting that "one out of four American working families now earn wages so low that they have difficulty surviving financially"; and Bowles, Gintis, and Osborne (2005).

79. 29 *United States Code* § 206. See also U.S. Department of Labor, "History of Federal Minimum Wage Rates under the Fair Labor Standards Act, 1938–1996," http://www.dol.gov/esa/minwage/chart.htm.

80. See also Mosisa (2002) and Orrenius (2003).

81. Author's calculations from BLS (2005e). See also Bowler (1999) and Mishel et al. (2005).

82. See also Bowler (1999); Borass and Rogers (2003); and Haveman et al. (2003).

83. See also Bowler (1999); O'Neill (2003); Blau and Kahn (2000); and Ferrell (2005).

84. See also Mishel et al. (2005).

85. See, for example, Schwenk and Pfuntner (2001); Mitchell (2003); and McDonnell (2005a).

86. See, for example, Schwabish (2004). See also table 9.1 (pensions) and the text accompanying tables 10.1 and 10.2 (health care).

87. See, for example, Crimmel and Schildkraut (2001); and McClendon (2004), noting that from 1985 to 2001, equity-based CEO pay increased from 1 percent to 66 percent of total compensation.

Chapter 3. How Labor Markets Reward Work

1. See, for example, Lea, Tarpy, and Webley (1987), 135–71; and Fehr and Falk (2002).

2. In the language of economics, individuals are said to be utility-maximizers, and each individual chooses a level of work (and so leisure) that maximizes her overall utility.

3. Leisure is considered a "normal" good. If you have more money, you will buy (consume) more of it.

4. Utility curves are commonly used by economists to show an individual's choices between two goods, like pretzels and potato chips. These are sometimes also called "indifference curves," as individuals are said to be indifferent between the choice of any point on the curve. Here the choice is between *wages*, which can be used to buy goods, and *leisure*, a good that reflects the time spent on all activities other than market work.

5. She will be happier at this point of tangency than she would be at any point on any lower utility curve that crosses her budget constraint line, and given her budget constraint, she cannot attain points on any higher utility curve.

6. This research enables economists to estimate the "elasticity of labor supply"—basically a measure of how responsive individuals are to changes in the wage rate. The elasticity of labor supply equals the ratio of the percentage change in the quantity of labor supplied to a percentage change in the wage rate.

7. See, for example, CBO (1996a); and Eissa, Kleven, and Kreiner (2004), noting that labor supply responses from the earned income tax credit can come along both the extensive (participation) and intensive (hours worked) margins.

8. Graphically, the utility curves of workaholics would touch the budget line to the left of the average worker, and the utility curves of the indolent would touch to the right of the average worker.

9. Following Daniel H. Weinberg, "Evidence from Census 2000 about Earnings by Detailed Occupation for Men and Women" (Washington, DC: U.S. Census Bureau Census 2000 Special Report No. CENSR-15, 2004), figure 2.

10. See, for example, Jencks, Perman, and Rainwater (1988).

11. Smith also saw that workers whose skills were in short supply could command large economic rents. The culprit for Smith, however, was the government, which at the time was the enforcer of most guilds and monopolies that limited the supply of talent. See also Neal and Rosen (1998), 19–20.

12. In addition to higher expected earnings, the benefits of going to college can include more pleasant jobs, lower expected unemployment rates, and the pleasure that can come from attending college.

13. See also tables 2.1 and 2.3; Census Bureau (2005a); and BLS (2002).

14. See also Jaeger (2003).

15. James K. Galbraith, for example, argues that

in an unequal meritocracy, education becomes, in effect, the purchase of tickets to a lottery, with high stakes and, as the investment in education grows, a larger proportion of losing tickets. Meritocracy and egalitarianism are distinct values, both with their proper place. In the discussion of the inequality crisis and the role of education, they have become tragically confused, and in the rush of concern over access to lottery tickets, the structure of the prizes has slipped from view.

Galbraith also argues that "investment in education" may be nothing more than a liberal "mantra," and he doubts whether efforts to promote more equal educational opportunity can have much impact on the overall level of economic inequality (Galbraith 1998, 264–65).

16. According to a 2004 survey of physicians with at least three years of experience, the average pediatrician made $175,000 a year, the average internist made $176,000, the average general surgeon made $291,000, the average heart surgeon made $515,000, and the average neurosurgeon made $541,000. Allied Physicians, "Physicians Salaries and Salary Surveys," http://www.allied-physicians.com/salary_surveys/physician-salaries.htm, updated January 2004.

17. A "living wage" is typically defined as "what a family would need to earn in order to support itself at the poverty level" (Boushey et al. 2001). For more on living wages, see chapter 11.

18. To be sure, since many firms and government agencies use categorical pay schedules, some low-skilled workers probably also earn more than the value of what they produce.

19. Bok laments that it is "grossly unfair that such favored individuals should earn first, one hundred, even two hundred times the average pay of

working people who toil away at much less interesting jobs" (1993, 227). Similarly, Dale T. Mortensen wonders why "job amenities, both benefits and creature comforts on the job, are positively associated with wages received across jobs, not negatively correlated as the pure theory of compensation differentials suggests" (2003, 26).

20. According to Derek Bok, "no effective competitive market regulates professional compensation in this country" (1993, 246).

21. Firms may also pay higher than market wages to secure and retain higher-quality workers. See, for example, Weiss (1990).

22. See, for example, McNamee and Miller (2004), 117–35.

Chapter 4. How Government Affects the Distribution of Earnings and Income

1. Author's calculation from Council of Economic Advisers (2006), tables B-1, B-82, and B-85. The GDP in 2002 was $10,469.6 billion, federal government receipts were $1,853.2 billion, and state and local government tax receipts were $1,047.6 billion. See also Citizens for Tax Justice (2005), finding that total federal, state and local taxes in the United States were 24.2 percent of GDP in 2003 and that the United States ranked 29th out of the 30 OECD countries.

2. See, for example, IRS (2005b), table A.

3. I.R.C. §§ 1, 63.

4. I.R.C. § 61.

5. *Commissioner v. Glenshaw Glass Co.*, 348 U.S. 426 (1955).

6. I.R.C. § 1001(a).

7. I.R.C. § 1(h). In addition, the maximum tax rate on capital gains and dividends received by moderate-income taxpayers (those in the 10 and 15 percent income brackets) is just 5 percent, and this rate is scheduled to fall to 0 percent in 2008.

8. Former I.R.C. § 1348 was added by the Tax Reform Act of 1969, Public Law 91-172.

9. Public Law 99-514. A 5 percent surtax pushed marginal tax rates up to 33 percent for some taxpayers.

10. Public Law 107-16; Public Law 108-27.

11. I.R.C. § 1.

12. Non-refundable tax credits reduce the amount of income taxes owed, but if the total of these credits is more than the amount owed, the taxpayer does not get a refund for the difference. With refundable tax credits, the difference is paid out as a tax refund.

13. I.R.C. § 32; IRS (2005c). The term "qualifying child" generally includes a child under the age of 19, a child under the age of 24 who is in college, or a child of any age who is permanently and totally disabled (I.R.C. § 32(c)(3)).

14. A family with one child is entitled to an earned income credit of up to $2,747, computed as 34 percent of the first $8,080 of earned income. For married couples filing joint returns, the maximum credit is reduced by 15.98 percent of earned income (or adjusted gross income, if greater) in excess of $16,810 and is entirely phased out at $34,001 of income. For heads of household, the maximum credit phases out from $14,810 to $32,001.

A childless individual between age 25 and 65 is entitled to an earned income credit of up to $412, computed as 7.65 percent of the first $5,380 of earned income. For married couples filing joint returns, the maximum credit is reduced by 7.65 percent of earned income (or adjusted gross income, if greater) in excess of $8,740 and is entirely phased out at $14,120 of income. For heads of household, the maximum credit phases out from $6,740 to $12,120.

15. These state earned income tax credits are typically set as a percentage of the federal credit, and, like the federal credit, they are typically refundable.

16. I.R.C. § 24; IRS (2005c).

17. $555 = .15 × ($15,000 − $11,300). A married couple with two children and $24,280 of earned income in 2006 can claim the full $2,000 worth of child tax credits: $68 would offset the couple's income tax liability, and $1,932 would be refundable. This couple has a simple income tax threshold of $23,500 and pays tax at a 10 percent rate on its first $15,100 of taxable income; in 2006 the couple's child tax credit is refundable to the extent of 15 percent of the couple's earned income in excess of $11,300. Consequently, the formula to solve for the income level (I) at which this couple gets to first claim all of its $2,000 child tax credits is: $2,000 = .10 × (I − $23,500) + .15 × (I − $11,300). Solving for I, I = $24,180.

18. I.R.C. § 24(b). Although the statute itself is ambiguous, the applicable IRS publication suggests that the couple's two child tax credits are phased out sequentially rather than simultaneously. The result is that the amount of a taxpayer's child tax credits is phased out at a 5 percent rate on income over the taxpayer's threshold amount (IRS 2005a, 4; Schmalbeck and Zelenak 2004, 9).

19. I.R.C. § 21. Employment-related expenses include expenses for household services and expenses for the care of a qualifying individual, but only if such expenses are incurred to enable the taxpayer to be gainfully employed. A qualifying individual is a dependent of the taxpayer who is under the age of 13 or a dependent or spouse of the taxpayer who is physically or mentally incapable of caring for herself.

20. I.R.C. § 26. Another limitation on the credit is that the amount of the employment-related expenses taken into account by a taxpayer in computing the credit may not exceed the lower of the earned income of the taxpayer or the earned income of the taxpayer's spouse (I.R.C. § 21(d)(1)).

21. I.R.C. § 55. The individual alternative minimum tax (AMT) operates parallel to the regular income tax system. The AMT imposes a slightly lower rate of tax on a broader tax base than the regular income tax base. The AMT was added to the tax code in the 1970s to help make sure millionaires could not use tax shelters to escape the bite of income taxation. See, for example, Burman, Gale, and Rohaly (2003).

22. Alternative minimum taxable income is determined by starting with a taxpayer's regular taxable income and adding back in such items as personal exemptions, the standard deduction, and the itemized deductions for state and local taxes and for miscellaneous expenses. That is why taxpayers with lots of children, or those who live in high-tax states like California or New York, are more likely to pay the AMT. The AMT rules also limit depreciation deductions and other investment preferences. Once a taxpayer adds back all those deductions and preferences and subtracts her AMT exemption, the result is alternative minimum taxable income. The first $175,000 is taxed at 26 percent, and the rest is taxed at 28 percent. The AMT exemption itself phases out for those with higher incomes, so the effective AMT tax rate can be as high as 35 percent.

23. "State Individual Income Tax Rates," http://www.taxadmin.org/fta/rate/tax_stru.html. See also Dubay and Hodge (2006).

24. I.R.C. §§ 1401, 3101, 3111.

25. I.R.C. §§ 275(a)(1)(A), 3502(a); Treasury Regulations § 1.164-2(a).

26. House Report No. 47, 98th Cong., 1st sess. 125–26 (1983), reprinted in 1983 *U.S. Code and Congressional and Administrative News Service* 404, 414–15.

27. I.R.C. §§ 164(f), 1402(a)(12).

28. See also U.S. House Committee (2004) appendix I, tables I-11 and I-12; and Graetz (1997), 21.

29. See, for example, U.S. House Committee (2004), section 4.

30. I.R.C. § 11.

31. I.R.C. § 55.

32. I.R.C. §§ 2001 et seq. and 2501 et seq.

33. See, for example, Gale and Orszag (2003b). See also Graetz and Shapiro (2005).

34. See, for example, Snyder (1998). Snyder notes that it is not always easy to differentiate between earned and investment income, particularly for taxpayers that "earn their incomes from a *combination* of invested capital and work effort, such as computer software, auto body shops, and natural resource activity" (244–45).

35. I.R.C. §§ 24(d), 32(a), 21.

36. I.R.C. § 162(a)(1).

37. I.R.C. §§ 162(m), 280G.

38. A targeted group employee is any employee who has been certified by a state employment security agency (SESA) as a recipient of assistance under TANF; veteran; ex-felon; high-risk youth; vocational rehabilitation referral; summer youth employee; food stamp recipient; or Supplemental Security Income recipient. Economists tend to believe that most of the benefits of these employer wage subsidies pass through to employees themselves. Technically, this credit expired on December 31, 2005; however, most observers expect that it will once again be reauthorized retroactively.

39. The credit generally equals 35 percent of the first $10,000 of eligible wages in the first year of employment and 50 percent of the first $10,000 of eligible wages in the second year of employment, for a maximum credit per worker of $8,500 (I.R.C. § 51A; see also IRS 2004b and Hamersma 2003). Technically, this credit expired on December 31, 2005; however, most observers expect that it will once again be reauthorized retroactively.

40. A progressive tax is one in which individuals with higher incomes pay a higher percentage of their income in taxes than those with lower incomes. On the other hand, a regressive tax is one whose rate increases as the taxpayer's income decreases. Finally, a proportional tax is one in which the tax rate stays the same as income rises.

41. The Congressional Budget Office's analysis assumed that households bear the burden of the income and payroll taxes they pay directly and the payroll taxes paid by their employers; excise taxes were generally assumed to be borne by households according to their consumption; and corporate taxes were assumed to be borne by all the owners of capital in proportion to their income from interest, dividends, rents, and capital gains. The analysis omitted the 5 percent of revenues that come from estate and gift taxes, customs duties, and other miscellaneous sources. Effective tax rates measure the effective liability for taxes as a percentage of household income (CBO 2004b, 2005c).

Of note, however, even though the 2001 and 2003 tax cuts disproportionately benefited high-income taxpayers, the overall federal tax system continues to be quite progressive in 2006 and beyond. See, for example, Gale, Orszag, and Shapiro (2004); Citizens for Tax Justice (2003); and Penner (2004).

42. See also Hoffman (2002).

43. See, for example, CBO (2005b); Geisler (2003); Burman and Saleem (2003); and Browne (2003).

44. Some explanation is in order. The couple in figure 4.4 initially has income below its $23,500 simple income tax threshold and receives an earned income tax credit equal to 40 percent of its first $11,340 of earned income. Once its earned income exceeds $11,340, the couple is entitled to the maximum earned income tax credit of $4,536; once its income exceeds $16,810, it starts to lose that credit at the rate of 21.06 percent, until the credit is fully phased out at $38,348. Also, once its earned income reaches $11,300, the couple's two $1,000 child tax credits become refundable on 15 percent of their earned income in excess of $11,300, until the full amount is attained at $24,180 of income. Once the couple's income reaches its simple income tax threshold of $23,500, the couple is subject to positive income tax rates, initially at the 10 percent rate and then at the 15, 25, 28, 33, and 35 percent rates. Also, once the couple's income exceeds $110,000, it will begin to lose its two $1,000 child tax credits; those credits will be completely taken away when its income reaches $150,000. Further, once its income exceeds $225,750, it will lose its four $3,300 personal exemptions; those exemptions will be completely taken away when its income reaches $348,250. Finally, some couples will have to pay the AMT if it exceeds the couple's regular individual income tax liability. The first $175,000 of alternative minimum taxable income is taxed at 26 percent, and the rest is taxed at 28 percent.

45. See, for example, CBO (2005b), box 1.

46. For simplicity, the 15.3 and 2.9 percent stated payroll tax rates are used. It is worth noting, however, that because the half of the payroll tax paid by the employer is excluded from the individual's taxable income, the effective marginal tax rates are generally slightly less than 15.3 and 2.9 percent. For example, for someone in a 25 percent income tax bracket, the effective tax rate increase because of the employer's share of the payroll tax is 5.74 percent, not 7.65 percent (5.7375 = 7.65 × [1 − 0.25]). See, for example, Feldstein (2005b), 17; and CBO (2005b), box 1.

47. See, for example, CBO (2003b), 5. As more fully explained in chapter 8, however, because social insurance benefits (e.g., Social Security, Medicare, and unemployment benefits) tend to favor low-income Americans, the combination of social insurance taxes and benefits may actually end up slightly progressive. See, for example, Fullerton and Mast (2005) and Cushing (2005), showing, inter alia, that net tax rates are considerably lower when Social Security benefits are taken into account.

48. See also Mitrusi and Poterba (2001), 95, 99–103; Mastromarco (1999), 228; and Gale and Rohaly (2003).

49. Also of note, 54 percent of families with labor income face higher marginal tax rates under the payroll tax rate than under the income tax (Mitrusi and Poterba 2001). If the present discounted value of incremental Social Security benefits is subtracted from the 15.3 percent payroll tax rate, however, only about 9 percent of families have a payroll tax rate that exceeds their income tax rate.

50. Figure 4.6 is the result of combining the income tax and payroll tax data underlying figures 4.4 and 4.5. The figure assumes that all the income is earned

by one worker; consequently, marginal tax rates fall when earned income exceeds the $94,200 ceiling on OASI payroll taxes (in 2006). If both spouses work, marginal tax rates would be higher for couples with incomes in at least some of the range over $94,200.

51. For an international comparison of effective marginal tax rates, see OECD (2005b), table I.1.2, showing effective marginal tax rates on average production workers in 2002 ranging from 17.4 percent in Korea to 34.3 percent in the United States to 66.4 percent in Belgium.

52. I.R.C. § 103.

53. See, for example, Center for American Progress (2005), 768.

54. See, for example, Rosen (2002), 20–22, 374–76; and Slemrod and Bakija (2000), 105–13. Tax changes will also lead taxpayers to change the timing of their economic activity and to restructure their activities to obtain more favorable tax treatment. Moreover, recent research suggests that timing and restructuring choices are even more responsive to tax changes than are such real economic variables as labor supply, savings, and investment. See, for example, Slemrod (2003), 623; Feldstein (1995), 553–54, finding a substantial response of taxable income to changes in marginal tax rates (estimating an elasticity of taxable income with respect to the marginal net-of-tax rate that is at least one); Gruber and Saez (2002); and Giertz (2005).

55. See, for example, Richards (1999), finding that if the Social Security payroll tax had not been raised from 1984 onward GDP would have been higher by more than $80 billion; labor supply would have been higher by roughly 800,000; and employment would have been higher by roughly 1 million. See also Prescott (2005); Liu and Rettenmaier (2002); Triest (1996b); Eissa (1996); and Hausman (1981).

56. See, for example, Rosen (2002); Eissa (1996); Edelman et al. (2006); and Eissa and Hoynes (2005).

57. We also know that the distortions that result from taxes increase as effective marginal tax rates increase. Indeed, economists suggest that the distortions increase exponentially with increases in the effective tax rate (Feldstein 2005b; Shaviro 1999, 1198).

So-called "optimal tax" theory also suggests that it is important to keep marginal tax rates low (Mirlees 1971). Interestingly, much of the optimal tax literature suggests that there would be efficiency gains from having marginal tax rates that *fall* at higher income levels. This approach could "induce greater labor supply from the most productive segment of society, with the increased tax revenue used to lower the tax burden of the least productive segment" (Slemrod et al. 1994, 285–86). See also Sillamaa (1999) and Kaplow (2006).

58. The Congressional Budget Office's microsimulation model applied estimated elasticities of labor supply averaging 0.07 for men and 0.5 for women, implying an elasticity of 0.15 for the total labor force. See also Feldstein (2005b), summarizing research suggesting that a reasonable estimate of the elasticity of labor supply is 0.5.

59. See also Edward C. Prescott, "Why Do Americans Work More than Europeans?" *Wall Street Journal*, 21 October 2004, A18; and Davis and Henrekson (2004).

60. On the other hand, Alesina and coauthors (2005) suggest that the lower levels of work effort in Europe than the United States are the result of Europe's more extensive labor regulations and higher levels of unionization, rather than Europe's relatively higher tax rates.

61. High tax rates can also influence the distribution of income. See, for example, Altig and Carlstrom (1999).

62. The current federal tax system is really a hybrid income-consumption tax system in which some investments are taxed on the income tax model and others are taxed on the consumption tax model. In general, wages, interest, dividends, and other forms of income are taxed when received, whether or not saved. On the other hand, pension benefits are taxed under the consumption tax model. For example, employer contributions to a pension plan are excluded from employee income, the earnings on those contributions are tax-exempt, and employees are only taxed when their pension benefits are distributed at retirement. See, for example, Aaron, Galper, and Pechman (1988) and McCaffery (1992).

63. See, for example, Slemrod and Bakija (2000), 174–75.

64. McCaffery also notes that the anti-work incentives of an estate tax regime can extend down to the donee level. By encouraging lifetime gifts, the estate tax leads the "wealthy young" to receive their wealth earlier in life, and that "may undercut their incentives to work and save." See also Slemrod (2002).

65. Government loans and loan guarantees can also influence the distribution of earnings and income. For example, in fiscal year 2003, the federal government guaranteed $365 billion in new loans (two-thirds for home mortgages), and extended $36 billion in direct loans. The total value of all federal direct and guaranteed loans that were outstanding that year was $1.4 trillion (CBO 2004c).

66. The federal government spent $2,472.2 billion in fiscal year 2005: $968.5 billion on defense and nondefense discretionary spending and $1,503.8 billion on entitlements, other mandatory spending, and net interest. Federal expenditures are projected to grow to $3,239.8 billion in fiscal year 2011.

67. See also Council of Economic Advisers (2006), table B-86, showing state expenditures from 1927 to 2003.

68. Public Law 104-193. See, for example, U.S. House Committee (2004), section 7.

69. U.S. Department of Health and Human Services, Administration for Children and Families, Office of Family Assistance, "Temporary Assistance for Needy Families Separate State Program-Maintenance of Effort Aid to Families with Dependant Children Caseload Data," http://www.acf.hhs.gov/programs/ofa/caseload/monthly/200512tanf.htm.

70. See, for example, Pavetti (2004). A caseload reduction credit of 1 percentage point for every percentage point reduction in their TANF caseload rewards those states that help welfare recipients leave the rolls.

71. See also U.S. House Committee 2004, section 15; and U.S. General Accounting Office (GAO) (2003). Of note, transitional Medicaid assistance provides certain families who would otherwise lose their coverage as a result of employment with up to one year of additional Medicaid coverage. See, for example, GAO (2002b).

72. U.S. Department of Agriculture, Food and Nutrition Service, "Food Stamp Program and Participation Costs," http://www.fns.usda.gov/pd/fssummar.htm.

73. U.S. Department of Health and Human Services, Administration for Children and Families, Child Care Bureau, "Announcements, Data Sets & Reports" (2004 CCDF Expenditure Data), http://www.acf.hhs.gov/programs/ccb/research/index.htm.

74. The Child Care and Development Block Grant program alone provided subsidies to some 1.9 million low-income children under age 13 in fiscal year 2000, up from 1 million in 1996 (Adams and Rohacek 2003, 3). Still, only a fraction of those children potentially eligible for these child care subsidies are receiving them (ibid., 4–5; Sawhill and Haskins 2002, 6; HHS 1999, showing that in an average month in 1998, only 15 percent of eligible children actually received help from the Child Care and Development Fund).

75. See also U.S. House Committee (2004), section 15.

76. U.S. Department of Health and Human Services, Administration for Children and Families, Head Start Bureau, "Research and Statistics," http://www.acf.hhs.gov/programs/hsb/research/factsheets.htm, click on "2006."

77. People under age 65 who are receiving monthly DI benefits are eligible for Medicare after a two-year wait.

78. See, for example, Moffitt (2002).

79. See, for example, Moffitt (2003) and Forman (1988).

80. This simple negative income tax system could be expressed algebraically as follows:

$T = .50 \times (\$10,000 - I)$, for $I < \$10,000$, and

$T = 0$, for $I \geq \$10,000$

where T is the amount of the negative income transfer to the person and I is the pre-transfer income of the person.

81. See, for example, Moffitt (1992), 15–16; and Hoynes (1997), 121.

82. $\$8,125 = 1,250 \times \$5.00 + .50 \times (\$10,000 - [1,250 \times \$5.00])$.

83. See, for example, Allgood (2003), finding that wage subsidies tend to increase labor supply and have lower efficiency costs than negative income taxes; and Eissa and Hoynes (2005), suggesting that the earned income tax credit is preferable to a negative income tax.

To be sure, earnings subsidies do not always have to be paid in cash. For example, an earnings subsidy could be paid in the form of a health care voucher that could be used to purchase care from authorized providers. See, for example, Haveman (1995), 200.

84. Figure 4.11 ignores child tax credits and other aspects of the current tax system.

85. Moreover, to the extent that effective higher wages act as a work incentive to those receiving an earnings subsidy and so result in them working more hours, earnings subsidies can equalize the distribution of pre-transfer ("market") earnings. By contrast, because a negative income tax tends to reduce the work incentives of recipients and so results in them working fewer hours, a negative income tax makes pre-transfer earnings more disperse. See, for example, Blinder (1974), 153.

There is also reason to believe that an earnings subsidy is a much more powerful redistributor of income than a negative income tax (Blinder 1974, 149–56; Phelps 1997).

86. $\$13,125 = 1,750 \times \$5.00 + .50 \times (1,750 \times \$5.00)$.

87. On the other hand, however, that research also found decreases in the labor supplied by mothers in two-earner couples (who tend to face higher effective tax rates in the phaseout range of the credit). See also Hotz and Scholz (2003) and Moffitt (2003), 132.

88. Another advantage of an earnings subsidy relative to a negative income tax is that the poorest workers would gain by reporting rather than hiding

their wages. On the other hand, workers in the phaseout range of an earnings subsidy would still have an incentive to underreport earnings. Another difficulty is that an earnings subsidy provides a perverse incentive for employers and employees to collude in reporting lower wages and greater hours than actually worked by the employee in order to obtain greater government subsidies (Joint Economic Committee 1974, 145).

89. Other laws can also affect the distribution of economic resources. For example, a legal rule that increases the liability of manufacturers of a product for harms to buyers would seem to favor low-income buyers over higher-income shareholders. At best, however, the distributional effects of this legal rule would be diffuse, as victims would be a diverse group. Moreover, the distributional effects of this legal rule would largely be offset by manufacturers raising their prices on potentially harmful goods and passing their expected liability costs on to consumers. Given that we can always use the tax and transfer system to achieve our distributional goals, most analysts believe that we generally should not choose legal rules on the basis of their distributional consequences. See, for example, Shavell (2004), 654. Consequently, this book generally ignores legal rules, except for those that directly affect labor market earnings.

90. 29 *United States Code* § 206. See also U.S. Department of Labor, "Minimum Wage," http://www.bls.gov/cps/minwage2003.htm.

91. See also table 2.9 and Mishel et al. (2005), estimating that the real value of the minimum wage fell 22.9 percent from 1967 to 2003.

92. Bernstein and Shapiro also note that, as of September 1, 2005, the minimum wage equaled just 32 percent of the average wage for the private sector, the lowest share since 1949.

93. Working a 40-hour week, 52 weeks a year at the minimum wage ($5.15 an hour), a worker would earn $10,712 a year ($10,712 = 40 × 52 × $5.15). See also Mishel et al. (2005), noting that the erosion of the minimum wage value hits low-skilled women the hardest.

94. This study showed that the real value of the minimum wage decreased by more than 30 percent during the 1980s from $2.90 in 1979 to $2.01 (in 1979 dollars) in 1989, with the proportion of workers at or below the minimum wage in the Current Population Survey (CPS) falling from 12 percent in 1979 to 4 percent in 1988. The study suggests that 20 to 30 percent of the rise in wage dispersion in the 1980s could be attributed to the decline in the real value of the minimum wage. But Autor, Katz, and Kearney (2005) question the extent of the impact of changes in the minimum wage on wage inequality.

95. See, for example, Neumark, Schweitzer, and Wascher (2000); and Gregg (2000). But also see Card and Krueger (1995).

96. See generally "Compliance Assistance–Fair Labor Standards Act (FLSA)," http://www.dol.gov/esa/whd/flsa/.

97. See also Census Bureau (2006), table 2, showing the Gini index declined 9.5 percent between market income and post-social insurance income in 2004 and declined another 10.9 percent going from post-social insurance to disposable income; and Strudler, Petska, and Petska (2004), showing a Gini index of 0.555 for income before tax in 2002 and a Gini index of 0.525 after tax, a difference of just over 5 percent.

98. But see Erik Eckholm, "Report on Impact of Federal Benefits on Curbing Poverty Reignites a Debate," *New York Times*, 18 February, 2006, A10 (questioning the report's definitions).

99. That study also found that our tax and transfer system reduced the poverty rate of one-parent families by just 4.6 percentage points, from 46.0 to 41.4 percent. That was a net 10 percent reduction in one-parent poverty rates compared to average reduction of 46.3 percent across all 11 high-income countries studied. See also Hoynes et al. (2006), 61–64, discussing the relative effectiveness of various transfer programs.

100. Preamble to the U.S. Constitution (1787).

Chapter 5. Making Government Work

1. See, for example, Nathanson (1998).

2. See, for example, Kranich (1994), exploring how this "equal-division-for-equal-work" principle would affect efficiency.

3. See, for example, Rivlin (2002).

4. On the other hand, Murphy and Nagel argue that "the wage for which you agree to sell your labor, and which your employer agrees to pay you, is merely a bookkeeping figure. . . and what it legally entitles you to is morally legitimate only by virtue of the legitimacy of the system" (2002, 75).

5. To reach 100 units, the entries for the third (14.10), second (7.36) and highest (53.44) quintiles were rounded down to 14, 7, and 53; and the entries for the fourth (23.62) and lowest (1.48) quintile were rounded up to 24 and 2. This approach seemed the most logical, even though it somewhat under states the relative poverty of the poorest family.

6. The actual Gini index for this five-family world would be very close to Census Bureau's 0.496 estimate of the Gini index for household income inequality in the United States in table 1.1, but it is less confusing to just reuse that Census Bureau estimate. The actual 80/20 ratio for household income before taxes and transfers is closer to 36 to 1 (36.108 = 53.44 percent income share for the highest quintile ÷ 1.48 income share for the lowest quintile).

7. In fairness to libertarians, however, it should be admitted that in the absence of government interference, the pre-tax, pre-transfer distribution of income might not be as unequal as it now is. According to the public choice theorists, a fair amount of government intervention is at the behest of special interests whose goals are to boost their own income shares (e.g., agricultural subsidies and competition-limiting licensing). On this view, a reduction in government intervention could actually result in a reduction in pre-tax, pre-transfer inequality.

8. 1996 General Social Survey (Subject: Inequality; Income Differences in U.S., INCGAP, Question 802), available at http://webapp.icpsr.umich.edu/GSS/.

9. One of the most famous workers in Joseph Stalin's Soviet Union was Alexei Stakhanov, a 30-year-old miner who, on August 31, 1935, hewed 102 tons of coal during his six-hour shift—14 times his quota. To encourage such production achievements, the Communist party launched the Stakhanovite movement, which provided such hard workers with party recognition and, perhaps more important, with increased earnings through a progressive piece-rate system. See, for example, "Year of the Stakhanovite, Seventeen Moments in Soviet History," http://www.soviethistory.org/index.php (click on "1936").

10. See, for example, Dick (1975), 258; and Nathanson (1998), 52–67.

11. As we saw in chapter 3, the compensation principle has been recognized by economists going back at least as far as Adam Smith.

12. The "economic rent" earned by a factor of production is defined as "that portion of total payments to the factor which is in excess of what is needed to keep the factor in its current occupation" (Nicholson 1978, 403).

13. See, for example, Frank and Cook (1995); Thurow (1975); and McNamee and Miller (2004).

14. For example, Norman Daniels sees "merit" as a combination of "ability plus effort" (1978, 207). See also Young (1958).

15. Some philosophers object to strict proportionality between income and productive effort as a specification of distributive justice. See, for example, Van Parijs (1995), 160–69.

16. According to the Bible, for example, "To whom much is given, much is also required" (Luke 12:48). To be sure, "It is clear that virtually unsurmountable obstacles would stand in the way of effecting redistributions of initial endowments" (Vickers 1997, 128).

Moreover, anyone serious about achieving equality in the distribution of endowments would do well to read the short story by Kurt Vonnegut Jr., "Harrison Bergeron," in *Welcome to the Monkey House* (New York: Dell Publishing, 1988). Vonnegut contemplates a futuristic dystopia in which government officials use handicapping devices to bring everybody "down to an equal level." The story starts out like this:

> The Year was 2081, and everybody was finally equal. They weren't only equal before God and the Law. They were equal every which way. Nobody was smarter than anybody else. Nobody was better looking than anybody else. Nobody was stronger or quicker than anybody else. All this equality was due to the 211th, 212th, and 213th Amendments to the Constitution, and to the unceasing vigilance of agents of the United States Handicapper General.

George Bergeron, for example, whose "intelligence was way above normal, had a little mental handicap radio in his ear" that emitted painful and distracting noises.

17. See also Mazumder (2004), finding a correlation in earnings and family incomes of around 0.5, suggesting that family background accounts for about half of all inequality in America; Mazumder (2005); Solon (1992); and Zimmerman (1992).

18. "The most important determinant of where people end up in the economic pecking order of society is where they started in the first place" (ibid., 13).

19. "The President's News Conference of March 21, 1962," *Public Papers* 259 (March 21, 1962). See also President Jimmy Carter, "The President's News Conference of July 12, 1977," *Public Papers*, II 1237 ("Well, as you know, there are many things in life that are not fair, that wealthy people can afford and poor people can't.").

20. The distribution approach most frequently attributed to Karl Marx relies heavily on the criterion of needs: "From each according to his abilities to each according to his needs."

21. See Frank and Cook (1995), 17.

22. See, for example, Ehrenberg and Smith (1996), 78–84. According to economic theory, in a competitive market, employers would hire labor until the marginal revenue product of labor equaled the wage. On the other hand, in a labor market that is monopsonized, wages can be set at a level lower than the value of the marginal product.

23. Similarly, Murphy and Nagel believe that the government should operate like a price-discriminating monopoly that figures out how much each public good is worth to each individual and charges each of them accordingly (2002, 83).

24. These numbers are not far from the actual share of earnings for households by quintiles. Using data from the 1998 Survey of Consumer Finance, one study found that the bottom quintile had 0.2 percent of earnings, the second quintile had 4.0 percent, the middle quintile had 13.0 percent, the fourth quintile had 22.9 percent, and the top quintile had 60.2 percent (Rodriguez et al. 2002, table 5). The negative earnings for the bottom quintile reflected a combination of zero earnings for many retiree households and actual losses for some small businesses. Similarly, Mayer estimates the share of weekly total earnings of all wage and salary workers by quintile in 2003 as follows: lowest quintile, 5.2 percent; second quintile, 10.7 percent; third quintile, 15.8 percent; fourth quintile, 23.0 percent; highest quintile, 45.3 percent (Mayer 2004, table 7).

25. At first, of course, a monopsonistic society would need to have some conception of a just distribution of wages, or at least some conception of the appropriate criteria of desert for determining just wages. Then, given that conception, the monopsonistic society could set that ideal wage structure or at least set up appropriate reward mechanisms to achieve that ideal wage structure.

26. Allied Physicians, "Physicians Salaries and Salary Surveys."

27. For more about the supply of physicians, see U.S. House Committee (2004), appendix C, C-27–C-33. It is also worth noting that physicians in the United States earn far more than their counterparts around the world. Physicians in Canada and Germany earn about half as much; physicians in Austria, France, and Britain earn less than one-third as much; and physicians in Finland, Norway, and Sweden earn just one-quarter as much (Herrick 2001).

28. In fact, we are in the midst of large changes to the health care system that have significantly affected physician pay. In recent years, the federal government has kept tight controls on Medicare and Medicaid reimbursement levels. Also, because of changes in the nature of health care systems, more physicians find themselves working in salary or per capita arrangements with hospitals and health maintenance organizations rather than earning their livelihood from traditional fee-for-service arrangements. Overall, these changes have modestly reduced the earnings of physicians—or, at least, the growth rate of their earnings.

29. See, for example, Feinberg (1970, 1973); Miller (1999); Roemer (1996, 1998b); Sher (1987); and Dworkin (1981a, 1981b). See also Lardner and Smith (2005).

30. See also Van Parijs (1995) and Fried (2002), 173.

31. 5.0 = $120,000 ÷ $24,000. The entries in column 3 of table 5.1 are based on multiplying each entry for the hypothetically just distribution of wages shown in the dark gray bars in figure 5.2 by $3,000.

32. $12,500 = .5 × ($30,000 − $5,000). $4,000 = .5 × ($30,000 − $22,000).

33. 12.59541 percent tax rate = $16,500 ÷ $131,000; $131,000 total income subject to the flat tax = (J's $160,000 income − $50,000 exemption) + (I's $71,000 income − $50,000 exemption); $16,500 total transfers = $12,500 to F + $4,000 to G.

34. These are sometimes called "demogrants." See, for example, Shaviro (1997), 470; Bankman and Griffith (1987); Okner (1975); Tobin (1977); and Van

Parijs (2000), 8, suggesting that every adult member of society should be paid a "universal basic income" at a level "sufficient for subsistence."

35. Five $15,000 universal grants would cost $75,000, which could be raised by a 25 percent flat tax on all $300,000 of income ($300,000 = $3,000 + $21,000 + $42,000 + $69,000 + $165,000; $75,000 = .25 × $300,000).

36. 19.08396 = $25,000 ÷ $131,000; $131,000 total income subject to the flat tax = (J's $160,000 income − $50,000 exemption) + (I's $71,000 income − $50,000 exemption); $25,000 = 5 × $5,000.

37. Murphy and Nagel go on to conclude:

> A capitalist market economy is the best method we have for creating employment, generating wealth, allocating capital to production, and distributing goods and services. But it also inevitably generates large economic and social inequalities, often hereditary, that leave a significant segment of society not only relatively but also absolutely deprived, unless special measures are taken to combat those effects. Our view is that while every government has the fundamental duty against coercion and violence, both foreign and domestic, and to provide the legal order that makes prosperity possible, it is almost as important to find ways of limiting the damage to the inevitable losers in market competition without undermining the productive power of the system. (2002, 181)

38. See also Browning (1987).

39. See, for example, Blank (2002a) and Pressman (2005), 96 ("for countries like the U.S., it appears that equity efforts can be increased substantially without any serious negative efficiency effects").

40. For example, Burtless and Jencks (2003, 28), suggest that "programs that improve the health, education, and work readiness of low-income children and young adults seem to have the most promise for success" in reducing income inequality without having too adverse an impact on output or efficiency.

41. The U.S. Department of Agriculture's Conservation Reserve Program is a voluntary program under which agricultural landowners receive annual rental payments and cost-share assistance to plant grasses and trees on eligible farmland instead of cash crops. See, for example, "Conservation Reserve Program," http://www.fsa.usda.gov/dafp/cepd/crp.htm.

42. See, for example, table 6.2.

43. To the same effect, Thurow (1976) argues that substantial equalization could occur without adversely affecting growth; Nathanson (1998) argues that it is possible to limit rewards—through taxation—without undermining production.

44. See, for example, Steuerle and Spiro (1999).

45. See, for example, Murphy and Nagel (2002), 87. Increasing the labor supplied by low-skilled workers will also improve their future retirement security, as those earnings will help fund larger Social Security, pension, and retiree health benefits (Johnson, Favreault, and Goldwyn 2003).

46. See, for example, Haveman and Palmer (1982); U.S. Departments of Labor and Treasury (1986); Kesselman (1969); Papadimitriou (1998); and Roemer (1998a), providing a detailed model of a possible wage subsidy program.

47. Similarly, James K. Galbraith suggests that "the direct approach to wage inequality is to raise wages and improve the employment prospects of the comparatively low-skilled" (1998, 20). Galbraith also notes that

reducing wage inequality will not by itself solve the larger rise in inequality that stems from changing employment patterns, family structures, and the distribution of profits, interest, and wealth. But the measures leading to more equal wages will sure help. (1998, 269)

48. One study estimates that increasing redistribution by expanding the earned income tax credit costs less than 20 cents per dollar transferred from upper-income groups to lower-income groups (Triest 1996a).

49. See table 6.2 and accompanying text.

Chapter 6. Making Taxes Work

1. That was the goal of President Reagan's Tax Reform Act of 1986, and it really worked. That marvelous piece of legislation lowered the maximum federal individual income tax rates from 50 percent to around 28 percent. A 5 percent surtax pushed marginal tax rates up to 33 percent for some taxpayers, but it was revenue neutral. We got a better tax system that raised about the same amount of revenue.

2. See also Carasso and Steuerle (2005); Shaviro (1997), 422; Coe et al. (1998); Danziger et al. (2002); Holt (2005), detailing tax and transfer program participation and effective marginal tax rates for welfare recipients in Wisconsin in 2000; Hassett and Moore (2005); and Romich (2006).

3. See, for example, CBO (1997) and Forman (1996b, 1999c). Fairness generally requires that equals be treated equally. In tax parlance this is known as horizontal equity. Hence, all other things being equal, couples with equal incomes should pay the same amount of tax. Of course, if the couples have different distributions of income between husband and wife, an argument can be made that all other things are not equal.

4. In tax parlance, this is called vertical equity.

5. For international comparisons of the tax treatment of one-earner versus two-earner couples, see OECD (2005b), 55–60.

6. A and B can each claim a personal exemption of $3,300 and a standard deduction of $5,150, so each will have taxable income of $31,550. Of that $31,550, the first $7,550 will be taxed at the 10 percent rate, the next $23,100 will be taxed at 15 percent, and the balance will be taxed at 25 percent ($4,445 = $755 + $3,465 + $225).

C can claim a personal exemption of $3,300 and a standard deduction of $5,150, so C's taxable income will be $71,550. Of that $71,550, the first $7,550 will be taxed at the 10 percent rate, the next $23,100 will be taxed at 15 percent, and the rest will be taxed at 25 percent ($14,445 = $755 + $3,465 + $10,225).

D will have zero taxable income and owe zero dollars of tax.

7. Gross income of $80,000 less two $3,300 personal exemptions and a standard deduction of $10,300 leaves taxable income of $63,100. Of that $63,100, the first $15,100 will be taxed at the 10 percent rate, the next $46,200 will be taxed at the 15 percent rate, and the balance will be taxed at the 25 percent rate ($8,890 = $1,510 + $6,930 + $450).

Marriage penalties are still common at higher income levels, for example, because the upper rate brackets for married couples filing jointly are not double the rate brackets for unmarried individuals.

8. Gross income of $40,000 less two $3,300 personal exemptions and a standard deduction of $10,300 leaves taxable income of $23,100. Of that $23,100,

the first $15,100 will be taxed at the 10 percent rate, and the rest will be taxed at the 15 percent rate ($2,710 = $1,510 + $1,200).

9. On closer inspection, however, one might question whether even couples neutrality has been achieved. For example, consider whether the two-earner married couple A-B and the one-earner married couple C-D really have the same amount of economic income. Admittedly, they have the same amount of gross income ($80,000). On the other hand, because of their two jobs, A and B will have little time for the household chores that D may routinely perform for the C-D household. After they pay for housecleaners and take-out food, the two-earner married couple A-B will have much less disposable income than the one-earner married couple C-D. Nor is the value of D's household services included in the C-D couple's gross income. In the parlance of economists, this kind of income is called "imputed income," but it is not taxed by the income tax system (see, for example, Chirelstein 2002, 23–26). In short, two-earner couples can argue that even the couples neutrality principle is violated because the income tax system fails to tax the imputed value of extra household services provided by nonworking spouses in one-earner couples.

10. Before the marriage, neither would qualify for the earned income tax credit, and the man would owe $655 in federal income taxes. He would be entitled to a standard deduction of $5,150 and a personal exemption of $3,300, leaving him with a taxable income of $6,550. The tax on $6,550 is $655 ($655 = .10 × $6,550). After the marriage, however, the couple would have $15,000 of income and two children; so, together they would qualify for the maximum earned income tax credit of $4,536 and a refundable child tax credit of $555. $555 = .15 × ($15,000 − $11,300). In addition, as their income would not exceed the income tax threshold for a married couple with two children, the man would no longer owe $655 in income tax. All in all, that is a marriage bonus of $5,746 ($5,746 = $4,536 + $555 + $655).

11. Before the marriage, each would be entitled to an earned income credit of $4,496 and a refundable child tax credit of $555, and their combined refunds would be about $10,102. $10,102 = 2 × $5,051; $5,051 = $4,496 + $555; $4,496 = $4,536 − .2106 ($15,000 − $14,810).

After the marriage, however, the couple would get a single refund of just $4,563, largely because their income pushes them far into the phaseout range for the earned income tax credit. Their total marriage penalty would be a little smaller, as the couple would now be entitled to claim a larger portion of their child tax credits. Together, they would be entitled to a refund of $4,563.19. $4,563.19 = $1,758.19 earned income credit + $2,805 refundable child tax credit. They would be entitled to a single earned income tax credit of just $1,758.19. $1,758.19 = $4,536 − .2106 ($30,000 − $16,810). The couple would now be eligible for four child tax credits, of which $2,805 would be refundable, up from just $1,110 before the marriage. After marriage: $2,805 = .15 × ($30,000 − $11,300). Before marriage: $1,110 = 2 × $555; $555 = .15 × ($15,000 − $11,300). The couple would get a refund of $4,379.52, computed as follows: the couple would have taxable income of $0 (−$100 = $30,000 − $10,300 − [6 × $3,300]); its regular tax liability would be $0; its earned income tax credit would be $1,758.19; and its child tax credit would be $2,805. Moreover, the couple's $30,000 income is likely to disqualify them for any Medicaid or welfare benefits they might have been receiving before marriage. See also Renshaw and Milani (2004); and Holtzblatt and Rebelein (2001).

12. For example, there is a marriage penalty associated with the partial exclusion of Social Security benefits from gross income (I.R.C. § 86). Under current law, Social Security benefits are excluded from gross income unless an individual has more than $25,000 of income, but married couples must begin to pay tax on their Social Security benefits if they make more than $32,000. Consequently, there would be a significant marriage penalty if a widow with $16,000 of investment income and $5,000 of Social Security income marries a widower in the same situation. Before marriage, neither would pay tax on their Social Security benefits, but if they married, a significant share of their combined Social Security benefits would be subject to tax.

Other provisions that can result in marriage penalties include the medical expense deduction (I.R.C. § 213, because of the interaction of the incomes and medical expenses of two spouses and the 7.5 percent floor), the moving expense deduction (I.R.C. § 217 provides dollar limits for each tax unit, and a married couple filing a joint return is a single tax unit), and the exclusion of up to $5,000 of employer-provided child care (I.R.C. § 129 also provides a dollar limit for each tax unit, and a married couple is treated as a single unit).

13. See also The President's Advisory Panel on Federal Tax Reform (2005b), recommending simplification; *National Taxpayer Advocate 2004 Report to Congress* (Washington, DC: Internal Revenue Service, 2005), 2–7, advising that the complexity of the Internal Revenue Code is the most serious problem facing taxpayers and the IRS; and The President's Advisory Panel on Federal Tax Reform (2005a), 4, noting that "there are 15 common tax benefits available to families—including provisions that relate to children, education, and retirement savings—that provide 14 different phase-out provisions to reduce benefits above specified income levels that, in turn, contain nine different definitions of income."

14. Other studies have reached similar estimates of the time and money spent by taxpayers to comply with the federal tax system. For example, Slemrod (1996) estimates that the total costs of compliance and administration for the individual and corporate income taxes in 1996 was around $75 billion, or about 10 percent of the revenue then raised by those taxes; and Wrcholik, Moody, and Hodge (2006) estimate that in 2005 individuals, businesses, and nonprofits would spend 6 billion hours to comply with federal tax laws and compliance costs would total over $265.1 billion. See also President's Advisory Panel (2005b), 2, noting that Americans spent 3.5 billion hours doing their taxes in 2004; GAO (2005g); JCT (2001), 103–108; Blumenthal and Slemrod (1992); Slemrod and Bakija (2000), 134–37; and Donaldson (2003), 698–704.

15. See also Holtzblatt and McCubbin (2004), noting that 64 percent of low-income workers claiming the earned income tax credit in 2000 used paid preparers; Maag (2005), noting that 66.8 percent of low-income parents received help with their tax returns in 2002; Berube et al. (2002); Lipman (2003b), noting literacy limitations on many low-income taxpayers; and Nightingale (1995).

Also of note, an increasing share of the IRS enforcement burden has fallen on low-income working taxpayers, particularly those claiming the earned income tax credit. For example, in 2002, the working poor had one chance in 47 of having their returns audited, compared to one in 145 for affluent taxpayers (Book 2003; Johnston 2003, 166).

16. See also Internal Revenue Service, "The Tax Gap," http://www.irs.gov/pub/irs-utl/tax_gap_facts-figures.pdf; and Ledbetter (2005), estimating a 14.4 percent tax gap for 2003—a $1,041.7 billion gap in adjusted gross income.

17. Of course the IRS should aggressively pursue tax evaders, particularly high-income individuals who hide their income in tax shelters or offshore. If the IRS could collect more from those tax evaders, Congress could reduce the tax burden on honest taxpayers. In short, "Congress needs to unshackle the tax police" (Johnston 2003, 316).

18. Similarly, according to that 2001 study of tax simplification by the Joint Committee on Taxation, over 500 public laws made changes to the tax code from 1954 to 2001. While many changes were minor, others were major, and the pace of change is like a steady drumbeat. There were 9 public laws changing the tax code in the 106th Congress, 12 in the 105th Congress, 14 in the 104th Congress, and so on. In addition, the IRS issues thousands of pages of regulations and other guidance every year, and there are new court decisions interpreting federal tax law decided almost every day.

19. See, for example, Surrey (1973); The Century Foundation (2002); and GAO (2005b), 7.

20. The classic economic definition of income (also known as the Haig-Simons definition of income) is as follows:

> Personal income may be defined as the algebraic sum of (1) the market value of rights exercised in consumption and (2) the change in the value of the store of property rights between the beginning and end of the period in question. In other words, it is merely the result obtained by adding consumption during the period to "wealth" at the beginning of the period. The sine qua non of income is gain, as our courts have recognized in their more lucid moments, and gain to someone during a specified time interval. Moreover, this gain may be measured and defined most easily by positing a dual objective or purpose, consumption and accumulation, each of which may be estimated in a common unit by appeal to market prices. (Simons 1938; Haig 1921, 7)

See generally Pechman (1977, 1980); Aaron (1969); and Bradford and U.S. Treasury (1984).

21. For a historical analysis, see Forman (1986) and Wooten (1999). See also JCT (2005a), presenting dozens of proposals to reduce various tax expenditures.

The Congressional Budget and Impoundment Act of 1974 defines tax expenditures as follows:

> those revenue losses attributable to provisions of the Federal tax laws which allow a special exclusion, exemption, or deduction from gross income or which provide a special credit, a preferential rate of tax, or a deferral of tax liability. (Public Law 93-344, § 3(a)(3)).

Thus, the definition of a tax expenditure draws a distinction between the ideal provisions of an income tax and the special or preferential provisions that are exceptions to that ideal structure.

22. See, for example, Bittker (1969a, 1969b) and Surrey and Hellmuth (1969).

For example, most tax expenditure budgets treat the deduction for state and local taxes as a federal tax expenditure; however, a pure income tax should allow taxpayers to deduct their state and local taxes, at least to the extent that those state and local taxes exceed the value of any benefits received. Most tax expenditure budgets also fail to properly account for both Social Security taxes and benefits. See, for example, Forman (2001a).

For that matter, many tax experts would prefer if tax expenditure estimates were based on a consumption tax ideal rather than an income tax ideal. Under a consumption tax, savings are not supposed to be taxed until consumed. Consequently, using a consumption tax ideal would lead to quite different tax expenditure estimates. For example, under a consumption tax, the tax expenditure associated with pensions would be zero (or, to the extent of any "over-taxation" of pension savings, negative). See, for example, Executive Office and OMB (2006a), 321–25, comparing current tax expenditures with those implied by a comprehensive consumption tax; and Forman (1997a, 1997b).

Still, whether one sees an income tax or a consumption tax as the ideal, even a casual look at the current tax code and list of tax expenditures reveals many tax expenditures of questionable merit.

23. See also JCT (2006a), table 3; Mann (2000), 1361; Stark (2004); and Roger Lowenstein, "Who Needs the Mortgage-Interest Deduction?" *New York Times Magazine*, 5 March 2006.

24. Against its $50,000 of income, the couple could claim a $10,300 standard deduction and two $3,300 personal exemptions, leaving a taxable income of $33,100; the first $15,100 would be taxed at the 10 percent rate and the balance would be taxed at the 15 percent rate ($4,210 = .10 × $15,100 + .15 × [$33,100 $15,100]).

25. Against its $50,000 of income, the couple could claim a $10,300 standard deduction and two $3,300 personal exemptions, leaving a taxable income of $33,100, all of which would be taxed at the special 5 percent capital gains rate ($1,655 = .05 × $33,100).

26. Against its $30,000 of income, the couple could claim a $10,300 standard deduction and two $3,300 personal exemptions, leaving a taxable income of $13,100, all of which would be taxed at the 10 percent rate ($1,310 = .10 × $13,100).

27. $18,900 = standard deduction ($10,300 + $1,000 + $1,000) + personal exemptions ($3,300 + $3,300). See I.R.C. § 86.

28. To be sure, the examples so far have ignored the impact of the corporate income tax. Still, even if one believes that the burden of the corporate income tax falls entirely on investment income, the typical tax rates imposed on investment income would not come close to the rates often imposed on earned income.

29. See also Penner (2004).

30. See, for example, Auten and Carroll (1999); Feldstein (1995); and Hausman and Poterba (1987).

31. The number of tax expenditures doubled from 1974 to 2004 (from 67 to 146), and revenue losses, adjusted for inflation, tripled (from $240 billion to nearly $730 billion) (GAO 2005b, 4).

32. See, for example, Center for American Progress (2005).

33. This is the "mark-to-market" approach to taxing accrued gains. See, for example, Cunningham and Schenk (1993); Shakow (1986); Strnad (1990); and Miller (2005).

34. See, for example, Halperin (1993).

35. See, for example, Zelenak (1993) and Kaplan (2002), 37–41.

36. In addition, the exclusion of net imputed rental income on owner-occupied homes costs $33 billion a year.

37. See, for example, Kornhauser (1992); Dodge (1978); Murphy and Nagel (2002), 187; and Gac and Brougham (1988).

If there is any constitutional problem with taxing gifts and inheritances as income, then the identical tax treatment could be achieved with an accessions tax. An accessions tax is an excise tax imposed on the transfer of property by gift or at death. As an accessions tax is an excise tax, it is not subject to the Constitution's limit on "direct" taxes. See generally Andrews (1967).

38. See, for example, JCT (2006a), 3; and Forman (1993c).

39. See, for example, Geier (2002).

40. See, for example, Internal Revenue Service, "The Tax Gap" web page.

41. See, for example, Committee for Economic Development (2000), 7–8, 19.

42. The table reflects the assumptions that all family income consists of wages or salaries earned by a single worker, that all family members are under age 65 and not blind, that all family units are eligible for the earned income credit, and that all children qualify for the child tax credit. Also, only the employee's portion of Social Security taxes is considered.

43. For 2006, a married couple with two children can file a joint tax return and claim a $10,300 standard deduction and four $3,300 personal exemptions (see table 4.2).

44. Algebraically, each computation in row 3 involved determining the appropriate equation for computing each family unit's income tax liability after its earned income and child tax credits and solving for the income level at which that income tax liability is equal to zero.

For example, for 2006, for a married couple with two children with income (I) in excess of the $38,600 level at which the taxpayer enters the 15 percent tax bracket, the couple's income tax liability (T) can be determined by the following formula:

$$T = \$1,510 + .15 \times (I - \$38,600) - (2 \times \$1,000).$$

Setting T to zero and solving for I shows that the couple's income tax threshold after the earned income and child tax credits is $41,866.66.

45. Algebraically, each computation in row 5 involved determining the appropriate equation for computing each family unit's combined income and Social Security tax liability after its earned income and child tax credits and solving for the income level at which that tax liability is equal to zero.

For example, for 2006, for a married couple with two children with income (I) in excess of its $23,500 simple income tax threshold and in excess of $24,180 (the point at which the couple can claim the full $2,000 worth of child tax credits) but less than the $38,348 level at which the taxpayer's earned income tax credit disappears, the couple's combined income and Social Security tax liability (T) can be determined by the following formula:

$$T = .10 \times (I - \$23,500) + .0765 \times I - (\$4,536 - .2106 \times [I - \$16,810]) - (2 \times \$1,000).$$

Setting T to zero and solving for I shows that the couple's combined income and Social Security tax threshold after the earned income and child tax credits is $32,100.71.

46. Also, if states broadened the sales tax base to include more services consumed by high-income families, sales tax rates could be lowered, and that could help reduce the generally regressive impact of sales taxes (Bernstein et al. 2005).

47. See, for example, Forman (1996a), 182–86; Yin and Forman (1993); Yin et al. (1994); and Carasso, Rohaly, and Steuerle (2005). But see Sullivan (2003). Of note, many industrialized nations provide universal cash transfers for children (OECD 2005b, table I.2.14; Corak, Lietz, and Sutherland 2005).

48. The benefit could be twice as large if the employer portion of Social Security taxes were also exempt from tax and the employer passed the savings on to the worker as additional compensation. Similarly, self-employed workers would save $1,530 from a $10,000 exemption ($1,530 = .153 × $10,000).

49. My research estimates that there would be no revenue loss if we replaced the current earned income and child tax credits with a $6,800 payroll tax exemption and $1,000 per child refundable tax credits (Forman, Carasso, and Saleem 2005).

50. $1,334.93 = .0765 × $17,450. Again, the benefit could be twice as large if the tax threshold also applied to the employer portion of the Social Security tax.

51. Along the same lines, The President's Advisory Panel on Federal Tax Reform recently called for consolidating standard deductions, personal exemptions, child tax credits, and head of household filing status into a new Family Credit and consolidating the earned income tax credit and refundable child tax credit into a single Work Credit (President's Advisory Panel 2005b, 63–69). Similarly, some have suggested replacing the earned income tax credit with a $1,530 payroll tax credit, to offset the payroll taxes incurred on the first $10,000 of earnings, and with a $2,000 per child "simplified family credit." See, for example, Catts (2003); Sawicky (2003); H.R. 3655, 108th Cong., 1st sess., introduced by Dennis J. Kucinich, Barbara Lee, and Bernie Sanders; and Marguerite Casey Foundation (2005).

Also of note, current law limits the earned income tax credit for taxpayers without children to taxpayers who are between age 25 and 65. Consequently, the credit is not available to many elderly workers with modest income. On the other hand, a universal $2,000 per worker credit would be available to workers age 65 and older without qualifying children. This would make some low-income older workers eligible for this credit and, hence, more willing to work at low wages. See, for example, Burkhauser and Quinn (1997), 17. See also Rix (2005), 10–11, suggesting reducing the tax rates on earned income to encourage the elderly to work and suggesting wage and other subsidies to make older workers attractive.

52. Along similar lines, Edelman, Holzer, and Offner also suggest expanding the current earned income tax credit for low-wage workers. Under their proposal, the credit would equal 20 percent of the first $7,500 of annual earnings, for a maximum credit of $1,500, and would phase out at 15.98 percent of income over $10,000. They also suggest providing noncustodial fathers a larger earned income credit if they are making their child support payments. They estimate that their basic earned income tax credit for low-wage workers would cost $9.8 billion a year, and the extra credit for noncustodial parents would cost $1 to $2 billion a year (Edelman et al. 2006, 87–99). "Millions of disadvantaged youth have little incentive to work in the above-ground economy. If we can improve their employment rates by subsidizing their wages, the benefits to their children, their communities, and the economy would make this modest public expense a wise investment" (ibid., 91–92).

53. Alternatively, we might limit the availability of the $2,000 per worker earned income tax credits to working parents with children under age 18. Such "working parent tax credits" would be less costly than universal $2,000 per worker tax credits, but, of course, they would not provide any work incentives for taxpayers without children.

A $2,000 per worker earned income tax credit could also be justified as a way of offsetting the costs of commuting, business clothing, meals away from home, and similar expenses that result from working, as well as being a way to mitigate the work disincentives inherent in the income tax. See, for example, Vickrey (1992), 262, suggesting a deduction from income of 40 percent of the first $10,000 of earnings of each individual, plus 20 percent of the next $5,000.

54. Another approach would be to replace the current earned income tax credit with a system of refundable child tax credits and parent tax credits. For example, we might provide a $2,000 refundable tax credit to every *parent* with a child under the age of 18. Then, a typical single mother with two children would get one $2,000 parent tax credit and two $1,000 child tax credits, for a total of $4,000. Similarly, a typical married couple with two children would get two $2,000 parent tax credits and two $1,000 child tax credits, for a total of $6,000. Again, there would be no reason to phase out any of these credits, so marginal effective tax rates could be low. Also, with parent tax credits, there would be no marriage penalties. For example, if two single parents married, they would each retain their parent tax credits and combine their child tax credits. On the other hand, there would still be marriage bonuses. For example, if a single parent married a childless individual, together they could claim two $2,000 parent tax credits, while before only the single parent could claim a single $2,000 parent tax credit. That is a $2,000 marriage bonus. Then again, as marriage is often one of the best ways for single parents to escape poverty, it may well be appropriate for the tax system to provide such a marriage bonus. See, for example, Jon Forman, "Maybe a Tax Credit for Parents Instead of Kids," *Washington Times*, 26 July 1995, A23; and Alstott (2004), 171–95, recommending $5,000 annual caretaker grants to help parents support their children.

55. See also Murphy and Nagel (2002), 141.

56. $924 = .28 \times \$3,300$; $330 = .10 \times \$3,300$.

57. In that regard, Professor Daniel Shaviro has noted,

> the reason for starting with a universal grant, that then is reduced through the application of an explicit positive tax rate, is that one thereby makes conscious and explicit the marginal tax rates that are actually applying as income increases, and one can therefore make explicit, deliberate, and (one hopes) sensible choices. (1997, 470)

58. $500 = 3 \times \$2,000$ per year ÷ 12 months. See, for example, Forman (1989), 687–88, 694. Alternatively the Social Security Administration could distribute the benefits. It already deals with poor SSI recipients, and its offices are more decentralized than those of the IRS. See, for example, Roddis and Tzannatos (1999), explaining that European nations typically provide their "family allowances" through social welfare agencies.

59. Former I.R.C. § 221 (1984) (enacted as Economic Recovery Tax Act of 1981, Public Law 97-34, *repealed by* Public Law 99-514). See also OECD (2005b), 55–60, noting that most OECD countries provide incentives for nonworking spouses to enter the workforce.

60. See, for example, Danziger and Reed (1999); and Forman (1989). Another alternative would be to allow taxpayers to deduct the costs of employment-related child care.

61. Most so-called "flat" tax system cannot manage to satisfy both the couples neutrality and marriage neutrality principles. Flat tax systems are not really flat: they tend to be moderately progressive with effective tax rates going up as income goes up. See, for example, Bankman and Griffith (1987). For example, consider a simple flat tax that provides a basic exemption of $10,000

per person, and then taxes all income above $10,000 per person at a "flat" 25 percent rate. Such a tax system would actually be moderately progressive, not flat: someone making $20,000 would pay only $2,500 in taxes (12.5 percent average rate); someone making $100,000 would pay $22,500 in taxes (22.5 percent average rate); and so on. Consequently, even a "flat" tax system would invariably end up violating the couples neutrality principle, or the marriage neutrality principle, or both. Still, while a "flat" tax system would not eliminate marriage penalties and bonuses, a flat tax system with few deductions and a low rate would have fewer marriage penalties and bonuses than the current system.

62. Head of household filing status would also disappear. For investment income, the tax rules might allocate that income 50-50 between them, allocate it based on who owns the underlying investment assets, or permit the spouses to allocate that income any way that they want. See generally, Forman (1996b); Zelenak (1994); Dodge (1995); Kornhauser (1993); and Gann (1980). For a discussion of how joint and individual filing influences the distribution of work effort between spouses, see, for example, Schroyen (2003).

As explained in the earlier text discussion of marriage penalties and bonuses, there is no way to design a progressive income tax that achieves marriage neutrality and couples neutrality. The argument for the present income tax system is that progressivity and couples neutrality are the most important goals, and if a goal must be sacrificed, it should be marriage neutrality. In short, a joint return system with progressive tax rates cannot be marriage neutral: it will invariably have marriage penalties and/or marriage bonuses for some couples. Moreover, the more progressive the rate structure, the larger the marriage penalties and bonuses. On the other hand, a progressive tax system could eliminate marriage penalties and bonuses, but only at the expense of abandoning the principle of couples neutrality. The easiest way would be to replace the current joint filing system with individual filing.

63. Depending on how income would be allocated between spouses, there still could be differing tax liabilities for some married and unmarried couples.

64. For example, some 44 million tax returns showed itemized deductions for 2003, out of some 130 million returns filed that year (44 million ÷ 130 million = 34 percent) (IRS 2005b, table A).

65. See, for example, President's Advisory Panel (2005b), 75–78, recommending a 1 percent floor.

66. Under current law, every individual who has an income tax liability can check a tax return box to designate three dollars to be paid to the Presidential Election Campaign Fund (up to six dollars for married couples). The funds so designated are made available to various presidential election campaigns (I.R.C. §§ 6096, 9004). The checkoff was apparently designed to provide each taxpayer with a choice about whether to help finance presidential election campaigns.

67. For various reasons, the IRS decided not to implement its proposed system. In truth, the IRS system was not really "return-free." Rather, at a taxpayer's election, the burden of preparing the return would shift from the taxpayer to the IRS. Taxpayers would save some time filing their returns, but many would have to wait longer to get their refunds. Also, the return-free system would increase the burdens on the IRS and on employers and other filers of information documents. To generate tax returns, the IRS then estimated that it would need to timely receive, verify, and post more than 970 million wage and information documents. And the IRS estimated it would cost over

$1 billion and require about 17,000 additional staff to implement the return-free system.

68. The number of 1040A and 1040EZ forms filed in 2003 is from Internal Revenue Service, *Individual Income Tax Returns 2003*, table A. To the same effect, the Treasury estimates that up to 52 million taxpayers (41 percent) could be freed from having to file income tax returns with a final withholding system (U.S. Department of Treasury 2003). Even more taxpayers could be freed from having to file returns if Congress were to restructure the tax system. In that regard, the Treasury notes that final withholding would work best if we had fewer tax rates; fewer deductions, allowances, and credits; and if interest and dividend income were taxed at a flat rate and withheld at the source. It would also make sense to get rid of joint tax returns and instead have the unit of taxation be the individual, not the family.

69. See, for example, Committee for Economic Development (2005b), 26–27.

70. See, for example, Forman (1992, 2001c); and Geier (2002). Along similar lines, the Center for American Progress recently suggested that we replace the revenue from the employee portion of the Social Security payroll tax with a combination of general revenues and removal of the earnings cap on the employer share of Social Security payroll taxes (Center for American Progress 2005, 771).

71. See generally Bradford and the U.S. Treasury (1984), 63–69; American Law Institute (1993); U.S. Department of Treasury (1992a, 1992b); Esenwein and Gravelle (2003); and Yin (1992).

72. The dividend exclusion approach turns out to be cheaper, since lots of dividends are received by tax-exempt pensions and charities, and lots of earnings are retained by corporations and never paid out as dividends.

73. 24.88 percent average income tax rate = $2,547.5 billion federal spending ÷ $10,238.2 billion personal income. 31.64 percent average earnings tax rate = $2,547.5 billion federal spending ÷ $8,051.4 billion personal earnings.

74. See, for example, McCaffery (2002a); Hall and Rabushka (1995); and Feldman (2002).

75. See, for example, Census Bureau (2003) and Wolff et al. (2004).

76. See, for example, Boortz and Linder (2005) on replacing the income tax with a 23 percent national retail sales tax; President's Advisory Panel (2005b), chapter 9; and Fehr et al. (2005), 5, 19, on replacing the current income tax with a 16 percent national retail sales tax.

77. President's Advisory Panel on Federal Tax Reform, "Understanding Tax Bases: Staff Presentation" http://www.taxreformpanel.gov/meetings/docs/understanding_tax_bases.ppt.

78. Ibid.; see also Gale (1999, 2005); and Fehr et al. (2005), suggesting that a 16 percent rate would be high enough.

79. See, for example, President's Advisory Panel (2005b), chapter 8; Fehr et al. (2005), 5, 18–19, who suggest replacing the current income tax with a 14 percent VAT; American Bar Association (1989); U.S. Department of Treasury (1984), vol. 3; and Westin (2004).

80. For example, consider a multistage VAT of 10 percent. A mining company would pay that VAT on the difference between the amount it receives for the mineral it sells and the cost of supplies needed to recover that mineral, perhaps adding $90 of value to each $100 of mineral sold. A manufacturing company that buys $100 of that mineral from the mining company and makes a widget that

it then sells for $150 adds $50 of value. Finally, a retailer that buys that widget for $150 and sells it for $250 adds another $100 of value. The mining company would pay $9 of tax on the $90 of value it added, the manufacturing company would pay $5 of tax on the $50 of value it added, and the retailer would pay $10 of tax on the $100 of value it added, for a total tax of $24 on the widget. Alternatively, a 10 percent single-stage retail sales tax would raise $25 on the single retail sale.

It can be seen that the multistage VAT is roughly equivalent to a national sales tax of the same rate imposed only on retail sales to ultimate consumers. The advantage is that roughly two-thirds of the revenue of a VAT could be collected before the retail stage. Proponents of VATs also note that a value-added tax would be a particularly good alternative to the income tax with respect to international trade, since export goods could be exempted from the tax.

81. Most investments would be kept in "qualified accounts" that would be handled in much the same way that individual retirement accounts (IRAs) are used under current law. A taxpayer would deduct any amount deposited into a qualified account, the earnings on deposits would be tax exempt, and the taxpayer would include the amount of any withdrawals in the tax base. To capture consumption out of borrowed funds, taxpayers would also include loan proceeds in the tax base, but they could deduct payments of loan principal and interest.

The "tax prepayment" approach would apply to investments in housing and other consumer durables. Under this approach, investments would not be deductible, but the investment proceeds would not be included in the tax base when consumed. For example, the purchase price of an automobile would not be deductible, but the subsequent sales receipts would be excluded from the tax base. Also, if a loan were used to help buy the car, the loan proceeds would be excluded from the tax base, but no deduction would be allowed for repayment of the loan principal and interest.

82. See also Fehr et al. (2005), who suggest replacing the income tax with a 14 percent personal consumption tax; and Forbes (2005).

83. See also Frank and Cook (1995).

84. In that regard, consumption is a much larger share of income for lower-income households than for higher-income households. See, for example, table 2.8 and Burman and Kravitz (2004).

85. 29.13 percent consumption tax rate = $2,547.5 billion federal spending ÷ $8,745.9 billion personal consumption expenditures; 24.88 percent average income tax rate = $2,547.5 billion federal spending ÷ $10,238.2 billion personal income. See also Slemrod and Bakija (2000), 209–12; and Fehr et al. (2005), suggesting that we could replace current income and corporate taxes with either an 11 percent flat-rate income tax or a 14 percent flat-rate tax on personal consumption.

86. I.R.C. §§ 61, 2001 et seq., 2501 et seq., 2601 et seq.; IRS (2005c).

87. See, for example, Graetz (1983) and Surrey (1950). To be sure, the most recent trend has been toward getting rid of these taxes altogether. Indeed, under EGTRRA, the estate and gift taxes are scheduled to disappear in 2010 but reappear in 2011. This indeterminate situation is likely to compel Congress to reconsider the future of estate and gift taxes fairly soon.

88. Most likely an accessions tax would be adopted as an alternative to the estate and gift taxes. Unlike the estate and gift taxes, however, the tax is

imposed on the recipient of gifts and inheritances rather than on the donor or estate. The tax is based on the total of taxable accessions received from all sources by a recipient. Assuming that the accessions tax rate structure is progressive, then an accessions tax will impose a greater burden than the estate and gift taxes on a single person inheriting from several sources, but it would impose less burden than the estate tax on a single estate divided among a number of recipients. Accordingly, a progressive accessions tax should promote a greater dispersion of economic resources than the current transfer tax system. See, for example, Andrews (1967); Kirshberg (1966); and Rudnick (1945, 1950).

89. See, for example, Wolff (1999); Shakow and Schuldiner (2000); Chester (1976, 1982); Institute for Fiscal Studies (1978); Sanford (1971); Cooper (1979); and Thurow (1972). For a survey of ways to tax wealth, see, for example, Cremer and Pestieau (2003).

90. See, for example, Lehner (2000) and Thuronyi (2000).

91. See also Executive Office and OMB (2006a), table 13-4, showing that the net national wealth for the United States in 2005 was $101.4 trillion.

92. Chapter 2 also showed that the Gini index for wealth inequality in 2001 was an astonishingly high 0.826, while the Gini index for income inequality was 0.466, and the Gini index for consumption inequality was 0.307.

93. See, generally, Slemrod (2002).

94. U.S. Constitution, Article I, § 2, cl. 3; § 9, cl. 4 requires that direct taxes be apportioned among the states on the basis of population. License Tax Cases, 5 Wall (72 U.S.) 462, 471 (1866). Accordingly, a constitutional amendment might be needed. See, for example, Isaacs (1977).

95. See, for example, Committee for Economic Development (2005b), 24–26 (calling for a broad-based 10 percent value-added tax to supplement the income tax); and Avi-Yonah (2005), arguing that we need both an income tax and a value-added tax.

96. See, for example, Turnier (2003), 208.

Chapter 7. Making Welfare Work

1. Basically, a negative income tax is a system of cash grants to families in which the amount of a family's grant varies inversely with the amount of that family's income (Friedman 1962, 192). See also Lampman (1965); Tobin (1965); and Tobin, Pechman, and Mieszkowski (1967).

2. "Annual Message to the Congress on the State of the Union," *Public Papers* 112 (January 8, 1964); "Special Message to the Congress Proposing a Nationwide War on the Sources of Poverty," *Public Papers* 375 (March 16, 1964). See Bell and Wray (2004), arguing that Johnson's War on Poverty was doomed to fail because it failed to include a program of direct job creation.

3. There was also a good deal of social science research on welfare reform during this period, most notably the negative income tax experiments. See, for example, Rees (1974); and Burtless and Greenberg (1983). See also such important sociological works as Elliot Liebow's *Tally's Corner* (Boston: Little, Brown and Company, 1967).

4. "Address to the Nation on Domestic Programs," *Public Papers* 637 (August 8, 1969); "Special Message to Congress on Welfare Reform," *Public Papers* 647 (August 11, 1969).

5. The details are discussed in Moynihan (1973).

6. *Congressional Record* 143 (1972): 11,799–801. These are sometimes called "demogrants."

7. Omnibus Reconciliation Act of 1990, Public Law 101-508; Omnibus Reconciliation Act of 1993, Public Law 103-66.

8. Taxpayer Relief Act of 1997, Public Law 105-34; EGTRRA, Public Law 107-16; Jobs Relief and Reconciliation Act of 2003, Public Law 108-27.

9. See, for example, Weaver (2000).

10. The late Senator Daniel Patrick Moynihan used to say that the welfare system would have worked better if it had been placed in the Department of Labor, rather than in the Department of Health, Education, and Welfare (author's personal recollection from having been tax counsel to Senator Moynihan, 1983–84).

11. See also Meyer and Rosenbaum (2000).

12. "In Their Own Words; Transcript of Speech by Clinton Accepting Democratic Nomination," *New York Times*, 17 July 1992, A-14.

13. In particular, from 1993 to 1996, the Department of Health and Human Services granted waivers of the federal AFDC rules to more than 40 states, enabling them to impose tougher work requirements and even time limits on the receipt of cash benefits. See, for example, Bloom and Michalopoulos (2001).

14. See also Meyer and Rosenbaum (2000).

15. The General Accounting Office found that in fiscal year 1995, spending on AFDC accounted for 71 percent of welfare spending; by fiscal year 2000, only 43 percent of welfare spending went for monthly cash payments (GAO 2002c, 6).

16. See also Danziger et al. (2002) and Cancian et al. (1999). In particular, expanding the earned income tax credit and enhancing earnings disregards in state TANF programs have both encouraged increased work effort by single parents. See, for example, Blank et al. (1999), 40–41.

17. See also GAO (2002c), finding that the number of families receiving cash welfare payments dropped from 4.4 million in August 1996 to 2.1 million in July 2001—a 53 percent drop; Haveman et al. (2003), reviewing the level of earnings capacity and its utilization for "vulnerable groups" from 1975 to 2000; Council of Economic Advisers (1999a), noting that as much as 60 percent of the increase in employment of single mothers was attributable to the expansions of the earned income tax credit; Blank (2002b); and Grogger, Karoly, and Klerman (2002).

18. Also of note, between 1996 and 2000, the employment rates of single-mother heads of households with low incomes (less than 200 percent of the federal poverty level) increased from 51 to 61 percent (Thompson 2003). Similarly, from 1979 to 2000, for single mothers with income below the median, labor market earnings as a share of income increased from 41 to 73 percent (Mishel et al. 2003, 12).

19. "TANF Caseloads Reported as of 12/02/03," http://www.acf.hhs.gov/news/press/2003/mar03_jun03.htm. See also "Cash assistance for needy families: Aid to Families with Dependent Children (AFDC) and Temporary Assistance for Needy Families (TANF) Average Monthly Families and Recipients for Calendar Years 1936–2001," http://www.acf.dhhs.gov/news/stats/3697.htm.

20. See, for example, Committee for Economic Development (2000), 1–2, 19–26.

21. See also Carasso and Steuerle (2005); Shaviro (1997, 1999); and Danziger et al. (2002).

22. See also Sawhill and Thomas (2001).

23. In addition, the disincentives that result from high effective marginal tax rates increase exponentially as rates increase (Shaviro 1997, 422). For example, if a 10 percent effective marginal tax rate leads a worker to reduce the time she works by 5 percent, a 20 percent rate might lead her to reduce her work effort by 15 or 20 percent.

24. See, for example, Eissa et al. (2004); Eissa and Hoynes (1999); Hotz and Scholz (2003); Hoynes (1997); and Cancian et al. (1999).

25. These losses can be somewhat offset by small increases in the amount of the couple's child tax credits that is refundable.

26. In effect, the earned income credit subsidized married mothers to stay at home.

27. See also Social Security Advisory Board (2003), 14, identifying various work disincentives resulting from the DI program. Of note, the increased availability of disability benefits has led to a reduction in the labor force participation of older males, although it is not the main factor (Haveman et al. 2003, 9).

28. See also McNeil (2001).

29. See, for example, CBO (1997); Carasso and Steuerle (2005); Ellwood and Sawhill (2000); and Dickert-Conlin and Houser (1998).

30. See, for example, Horn (2001); Sawhill and Thomas (2001); and Hoynes et al. (2006), finding that changes in family structure over the past 40 years (i.e., an increase in female-headed households) would have led to a rise in the poverty rate from 13.3 percent in 1967 to 17 percent in 2003, holding everything else constant.

31. There is reason to believe that more low-income couples face marriage penalties than bonuses (Ellwood 2000b).

32. Chapter 1 showed that marital status is not evenly distributed across the income distribution. Another way of looking at the problem is to recognize that married couples are rarely poor, while single parents often are. In 2004, for example, only 5.5 percent of married-couple families were poor, but 28.4 percent of female-headed households with no husband present were poor (DeNavas-Walt et al. 2005, table B3).

33. The total spent on income-tested benefit programs in fiscal year 2002 came to $522.2 billion: $373.2 billion in federal funds and $149 billion in state and local funds.

34. Similarly, a 1986 study by President Reagan's Domestic Policy Council found there were 59 major welfare programs, from AFDC to the earned income tax credit (Domestic Policy Council 1986). See also Forman (1993a).

35. See table 2.9 and accompanying text. Similarly, Rebecca Blank notes that only about three-quarters of less-skilled men in 1997 could earn enough to assure that their families would escape poverty (1997, 79–80). See also BLS (2005i).

36. See, for example, Stoker and Wilson (2006); and Danziger and Reed (1999), emphasizing the importance of wage supplements and refundable child care tax credits. See also Ellwood (2001); and Smeeding (2006b), 87–88 ("If the United States is to reduce poverty substantially, it will need to do a better job of combining incentives to work with an increase in benefits targeted to low-wage workers in low-income families.").

37. See also Urban and Olson (2005).

38. See, for example, Sawhill (1999); Handler and Hasenfeld (1997), 213; Ellwood et al. (2000), 118; American Assembly (1999), 13; Boushey et al. (2001); and Committee for Economic Development (2000).

39. See, for example, Burtless (1995, 1998); and Haveman and Berkshadker (1998), discussing the low "net earnings capacity" of low-skilled workers.

40. I.R.C. §§ 32, 51A; U.S. Department of Health and Human Services, Administration for Children and Families, "Helping Families Achieve Self-Sufficiency: A Guide on Funding Services for Children and Families through the TANF Program," http://www.acf.hhs.gov/programs/ofa/funds2. htm#introduction. Technically, the welfare-to-work credit expired on December 31, 2005, but most observers expect that it will once again be reauthorized retroactively.

41. She would automatically be entitled to $2,000 in refundable child tax credits, and if she worked full-time year-round at the minimum wage she would pick up another $2,000 earned income credit, for a total of $4,000. As her income grew from additional work or a higher wage, she would lose that $2,000 per worker earned income credit only if there was a phaseout; even then, she would only lose the credit very gradually.

42. This proposed system of universal worker and child tax credits could be expanded to further reduce economic inequality. For example, the refundable child tax credits could be set at $1,200 or even $2,400 a year ($100 or $200 a month), and the universal worker credits could be set at $3,000 or even $4,000 per worker a year.

43. In fact, EGTRRA made the phaseout range for married couples higher than it is for other taxpayers. In 2006, for example, the earned income tax credit for a married couple with two children phases out from $16,810 to $38,348, as opposed to from $14,810 to $36,348 for other taxpayers.

44. See, for example, Haveman (1995), 197–98.

45. Most workers are, in fact, paid by the hour or in a manner easily translatable into hours of work (e.g., weekly salary).

46. Algebraically, the per hour wage subsidy received by a worker can be expressed as follows:

$s = r \times w$, for $w \leq W$

$s = r \times W - m(w - W)$, for $W < w < (r + m)W/m$, and

$s = 0$, for $w \geq (r + m)W/m$

where s is the amount of the subsidy an hour to the wage earner, r is the subsidy rate expressed as a fraction, w is the pre-transfer wage level received by the worker, m is the benefit-reduction rate, and W is the target wage rate.

For example, a simple wage subsidy with a target wage of $5.00, a 50 percent subsidy rate, and a 50 percent benefit-reduction rate could be expressed algebraically as follows:

$s = 0.50w$, for $w \leq \$5.00$

$s = \$2.50 - 0.50(w - \$5.00)$, for $\$5.00 < w < \$10.00$, and

$s = 0$, for $w \geq \$10.00$.

47. Algebraically, the wage earner's net annual income, I', can be expressed as follows:

$I' = I + S$

where I is the pre-transfer income of the household and S is the total annual amount of the wage subsidy.

48. In the absence of a wage subsidy, an earner whose only income is from work will have income precisely equal to the product of her hourly wage and the number of hours she works during the year. The total annual subsidy resulting from a wage subsidy is equal to the product of the number of hours worked during the year and the amount of the subsidy an hour. Algebraically, the total annual subsidy, S, can be expressed as follows:

$$S = h \times s$$

where h is the number of hours worked and s is the amount of the wage subsidy an hour.

49. Compare figure 7.1 with figure 4.11 (showing income after the earned income credit for a married couple with two children).

50. Because unskilled workers can rarely become self-sufficient while working part-time, it would make sense to design earnings subsidies so they encourage full-time work. See, for example, Bloom and Michalopoulos (2001), 26–36; Michalopoulos and Berlin (2001); and Robins and Michalopoulos (2001), 108–109.

51. Such a program would likely generate similar effects in the United States (Robins and Michalopoulos 2001). Earnings subsidies work better than earnings disregards. Robins and Michalopoulos also believe that an SSP-type program—in place of the enhanced earnings disregards currently used—could significantly increase full-time employment for long-term welfare recipients at only a modest additional cost to the government.

52. See Michalopoulous (2005), ES-2, 25–27.

53. So far, however, participation rates for these employer credits have been "shockingly low" (Dickert-Conlin, Fitzpatrick, and Hanson 2005, 765).

54. See, for example, Haveman (1995), 197–98; and Bartik (2001), suggesting a revised version of the New Jobs Tax Credit.

55. Children in low-income families fare worse than children in higher-income households on a host of social welfare indicators. About one-quarter of American children (19 million) live in low-income families, and, of those, 59 percent have at least one parent who worked full-time all year ("Low-Income Working Families: Facts and Figures," http://www.urban.org/url.cfm?ID=900832).

56. His disposable income (total earnings minus federal and state taxes, work expenses, and child support, plus food stamps) would go from $4,805 out of $5,000 to just $6,472 out of $15,000.

57. For unmarried mothers, the labor force participation rate was 77.1 percent; for married mothers it was 67.8 percent.

58. See also Sawhill and Haskins (2002).

59. See also HHS (1999) and GAO (2005a).

60. According to another recent study, 39 percent of low-income working families with a child under age 13 received nontax child care assistance in 1999. About 16 percent received help from relatives, and 21 percent received help from a government or other organization. Of the 61 percent that did not receive assistance, many did not ask about government assistance. Of those that did, many were ineligible or could not obtain assistance because of a waiting list or other limits on its availability (Giannarelli, Adelman, and Schmidt 2003).

61. See, for example, Maynard (1995), 121; Handler and Hasenfeld (1997), 213; and Boushey et al. (2001), 77. According to one study, if child care costs

were fully subsidized for families that would otherwise have been poor in 1996, the poverty rate would have fallen from 12.2 percent of families to just 2.3 percent (Sawhill 1999).

62. One study estimates that 490,000 more urban households would benefit from making the current child and dependent care tax credit refundable (Berube, Gale, and Kornblatt 2005).

63. It would also make sense to adopt an advance payment mechanism so the credit could be paid to eligible families throughout the year, rather than in a large annual lump-sum refund. Such an advance payment system would help provide timely child care assistance to low-income families and so provide an important work incentive. It would also make sense to index the credit for inflation and to extend the credit to single parents who are full-time students.

64. In subsidy terms, each 10 percent subsidy raises maternal work by 2.4 percent (elasticity = 0.236). On the downside, the authors also find evidence that Quebec's new child care program had negative effects on young children's behavior and health, on parental health, and on parent-child relationships.

65. For example, recent tax legislation better coordinated the earned income tax credit and the child tax credit. In 2006, a married couple with two or more children will see its earned income tax credit increase up to $4,536 as its earnings increase up to $11,340, but the credit starts to decline once the couple's income exceeds $16,810. Starting at $11,300, however, the couple begins to earn the refundable portion of its child tax credits. Even after the couple moves into the phaseout range of the earned income tax credit, the couple continues to earn more of its refundable child tax credits. In effect, the increase in the refundable child tax credit helps to temper the phaseout of the couple's earned income tax credit.

66. U.S. Census Bureau, "Poverty Thresholds," http://www.census.gov/hhes/www/poverty/threshld.html. See also Census Bureau (2006), table 3, showing poverty estimates based on market income, money income, post-social insurance income, and disposable income.

67. See, for example, Citro and Michael (1995); Dalaker (2005); Short (2001); and Boushey et al. (2001), 5–7.

68. "Poverty and Family Budgets," http://www.epi.org/content.cfm/issueguides_poverty_poverty. The poverty measure may also understate poverty because it does not take into account child care and other employment-related expenses. On the other hand, the current measure may overstate poverty because it does not take into account food stamps, housing subsidies, or the earned income tax credit. See, for example, Shapiro and Parrott (2003), 14.

69. See also Smeeding (2006a), 151–57; and Fisher (1996).

70. All in all, "adults with severe disabilities are one of the largest minorities in the nation without jobs" (Presidential Task Force 1998).

71. See also Mashaw and Reno (1996), offering recommendations to promote work and reduce reliance on cash benefit programs; and Levine (1998), outlining a disability policy that "makes work pay."

72. Disability benefits are not closely tied to contributions. As with Social Security's retirement program, a "money's worth" analysis would show redistribution from high earners to low earners and from single workers to those with families. See, for example, GAO (2004), 15–17.

73. Professor Ippolito has suggested the hypothetical benefit at full retirement age could still be calculated as under current law (counting service as

though retirement occurred at full retirement age), but these benefits would then be actuarially reduced to be economically equivalent to the full retirement benefit (Ippolito 1997, 198). Consequently, those who claim disability benefits at an early age would not receive a higher present value than those who claim their retirement benefits at the full retirement age.

74. See, for example, Wittenburg and Loprest (2003); and Social Security Advisory Board (2003), 14, 24.

75. U.S. Department of Veteran Affairs, "Disability Compensation Benefits," http://www.vba.va.gov/bln/21/Milsvc/Docs/Compeg.doc.

76. But see Moffitt (2002), suggesting that disabled SSI recipients appear to be relatively unresponsive to financial incentives.

It might also make sense to restructure the work opportunity tax credit and better coordinate it with the earned income tax credit and the other cash benefit programs for disabled workers. See, for example, Lipman (2003a).

77. See, for example, National Rehabilitation Hospital (2003).

78. See, for example, Friedman (1962); and Karger and Stoesz (1992). Basically, Karger and Stoesz would collapse AFDC, SSI, the earned income tax credit, and the income support components of all other social welfare programs (including food stamps, WIC, LIHEAP, and Section 8 housing benefits) into a single income-maintenance program—the Stable Incomes Program—that would be under one administrative unit. Each beneficiary would receive a single benefit package developed with a case manager. Money would go from the IRS to the appropriate welfare agency and on to the beneficiary.

79. See, for example, Brazer (1969); Cohen (1969); and Surrey (1969). An income transfer program provides cash benefits to the poor. An income transfer program can be called "comprehensive" if it replaces or incorporates other programs.

80. See also Currie (2006); Lugalia (2005); and Hoynes (2005), 14, noting that in 2003 the earned income tax credit cost $33.4 billion and reached 19.6 million families, TANF cost $24.5 billion and reached 2.1 million families, and food stamps cost $21 billion and reached 7.4 million families.

81. See also Lampman (1965); and Tobin et al. (1967).

82. To the same effect, professor Daniel Shaviro concludes "income transfer to the poor should rely on two basic tools: (1) a universal lump-sum payment (which for most taxpayers could simply reduce their positive tax liability) and possibly (2) negative marginal tax rates at low levels of earned or total income" (1997, 410).

83. This point was made by James Tobin decades ago, and it is even more true now (Tobin 1977).

84. See also Haveman (1988), 149–71, proposing a universal grant to ensure that every family has income of at least one-half to two-thirds of the poverty income guideline; Danziger (1987); Garfinkel and Haveman (1983); Lerman (1985); and Murray (2006).

85. U.S. Department of Agriculture, Food and Nutrition Service, "Food Stamp Program and Participation Costs," http://www.fns.usda.gov/pd/fssummar.htm.

86. For example, food stamps are available to individuals and families living in "households," an eligibility unit unlike that of any other welfare program. Also, the Food Stamp Program uses unique definitions of "counted monthly income" and "counted liquid assets" to determine financial eligibility. Simi-

larly, the program uses unique rules to determine categorical eligibility (for example, strikers need not apply). Moreover, hundreds of rules are intended to ensure that food stamp coupons are used to buy food but not alcohol, tobacco, and other nonfood items.

87. U.S. Department of Agriculture, Food and Nutrition Service, "Food Stamp Program and Participation Costs" (7.73 percent = $2,393.8 billion costs ÷ $30,961.5 billion total expenditures).

88. Unlike cash benefits, food stamp coupons are physically handled by over a dozen different entities in the course of their production, printing, issuance, redemption, clearance, and destruction. The electronic benefit program has reduced these costs, but it would still be cheaper to just distribute money instead.

Chapter 8. Making Social Security Work

1. See also Whitman and Purcell (2005), showing that Social Security provides 100 percent of income for 23.9 percent of *recipients* age 65 and older. Whitman and Purcell also show that Social Security provided 20.8 percent of the aggregate income of people age 65 and older in the highest quartile of income in 2004, 57.5 percent for those in the second quartile, 81.7 percent for those in the third quartile, and 85.6 percent for those in the lowest quartile.

2. See also Engelhardt and Gruber (2006), showing that the dramatic decline in elderly poverty can be attributed to the growth of Social Security.

3. This chapter builds on Forman (2004b).

4. See generally U.S. House Committee (2004), section 1.

5. For comparison, the earnings cap was $3,000 from 1937 to 1950 and only reached $7,800 in 1970 (U.S. House Committee 2004, table 1-1).

6. For example, the maximum nominal covered earnings for 1960 was $4,800, but indexing those earnings up to 1999 yields earnings of $34,572. The indexing year is the second year before the year in which the worker attains age 62, becomes disabled, or dies. Earnings after the indexing year are counted at their nominal value (U.S House Committee 2004, 1-17).

7. Social Security Administration, "Primary Insurance Amount" (updated October 14, 2005), http://www.ssa.gov/OACT/COLA/piaformula.html.

8. Social Security Administration, "Full Retirement Is Increasing," http://www.ssa.gov/retirechartred.htm.

9. Social Security Administration, "Examples of Benefit Computations for Workers Retiring in 2006" (updated January 11, 2006), Case A, http://www.ssa.gov/OACT/ProgData/retirebenefit2.html.

10. 42 U.S.C. § 402.

11. She would get her $300-a-month worker benefit and a $200-a-month spousal benefit. See, for example, *Code of Federal Regulations*, Title 20 § 404.403 (2000).

12. See, for example, U.S. House Committee (2004), 3-21–3-27.

13. 73.8 percent = ($603 a month × 12 months) ÷ $9,800; 82.2 percent = ($904 a month × 12 months) ÷ $13,200. See HHS (2006).

14. See also Forman (1994).

15. See, for example, Thompson (1998) and Seidman (1999).

16. The trustees also estimate that the unfunded liability over the infinite horizon is $13.6 trillion (Board of Trustees 2006, table IV.B6). That figure is an estimate of the maximum transition cost as of January 1, 2006, in connection

with replacing the current form of Social Security benefits with a new form of benefits. That maximum transition cost represents the cost for terminating the current Social Security program but continuing to pay benefits that have already been earned. See also Goss (1999).

17. See chapter 2.

18. The ratio of workers to beneficiaries has been declining for years. In 1950, there were 16.5 covered workers for each beneficiary; in 1975, there were about 3 workers per beneficiary; and by 2015, there will be about 2.7 workers per beneficiary. See, for example, Thompson (1997).

19. See, for example, Smith, Toder, and Iams (2003/04); GAO (2004); Leimer (1999, 2003); Forman (1992), 948–57; and Forman (2002).

20. For example, one might compare the expected value at age 65 of the OASI taxes a worker paid over a career, together with interest at a market rate on those tax payments, with the expected value at age 65 of the stream of OASI benefits the worker could expect to receive for life. The worker will receive her "money's worth" if the expected value of benefits received equals the expected value of all taxes paid. If the expected value of taxes paid exceeds the expected value of benefits, then the worker would, in effect, be paying other program participants. But if the expected value of benefits exceeds the expected value of the taxes paid, then the worker would be receiving extra benefits from other participants.

This lifetime perspective reflects a change in how Social Security benefits are viewed. They used to be viewed as social insurance, but now they are increasingly viewed as part of the employee's compensation package. Steven A. Sass describes this change as follows:

> Social Security had always functioned as an insurance program. It protected workers who grew old and were no longer able to find employment. By the early 1980s, however, Social Security had become something else. As a result of increased longevity and better health, essentially all workers now expected to claim a pension while still capable of finding employment, and then to live in retirement for an extended period of time. Social Security benefits thus were no longer seen as insurance, but as compensation—an income claimed in return for a lifetime's contribution to the system. (2003, 7)

21. See, for example, sources cited in Leimer (1999).

22. See also Social Security Administration, "The First Social Security Beneficiary," http://www.ssa.gov/history/imf.html.

23. See also SSA (2005a), table 3.

24. See, for example, Forman (1992), 937–43.

25. See, for example, Jon Forman, "Bill Gates and I Pay Equally—and This Is Supposed to Be a Fair System?" *Los Angeles Times*, 25 December 1998, B9. Along the same lines, David Cay Johnston argues that Social Security taxes on workers have actually subsidized income, estate, and gift tax cuts for the rich (Johnston 2003, 117–28).

26. See, for example, Duggan, Gillingham, and Greenlees (1995). See also Fullerton and Mast (2005) and Panis and Lillard (1996).

As noted in chapter 1, in 2001, 79.9 percent of households in the highest quintile of household income were married-couple families, but only 19.6 percent of households in the lowest quintile were married-couple families.

27. See generally Forman (1997c, 1998b, 1999b).

28. See Duncan Mansfield, "Civil War Widow Gertrude Janeway Dies at Age 93," (January 20, 2003), http://www.tennessean.com/obits/archives/03/01/27889583.shtml?Element_ID=27889583.

29. At this writing, the Civil War's last widow is still alive. She is Maudie Celia Hopkins of Arkansas. Thom Patterson, "Widow recalls marrying Civil War veteran" (June 17, 2004), http://www.cnn.com/2004/US/South/06/16/civilwar.widow/. See also David Lamb, "Civil War's Last Widow Shares Her Memories," *Los Angeles Times*, 3 February 2003, Part 1, 14 (about another Confederate widow, Alberta Martin, who died in 2004).

30. For survivor benefits, a surviving secondary earner will receive no additional benefits any time the worker benefit earned by the primary earner is more than the worker benefit earned by the secondary earner. See also Brien, Dickert-Conlin, and Weaver (2004), finding sizeable benefit losses when widow(er)s remarry.

31. See, for example, Powers and Neumark (2005); Neumark and Powers (1999, 2000, 2003/2004); and Baker et al. (2002), finding similar problems with Canada's Income Security programs for seniors. There is also evidence that the SSI asset test discourages low-income workers from saving for retirement (Neuberger, Greenstein, and Sweeney 2005).

32. See also figure 2.2 and accompanying text; and Purcell (2005a), 11. To be sure, older Americans stay busy. Eight out of 10 adults age 65 to 74 engage in at least one of four types of productive activity: paid work, formal or informal volunteering, or family caregiving (Zedlewski and Schaner 2005; U.S. House Committee 2004, table 1-14).

33. See also GAO (2006a), 6.

34. See, for example, Lahey (2005), 1, citing research suggesting "today's 70 year olds are comparable in health and mental function to 65 year olds from 30 years ago."

35. Workers in higher quintiles would see smaller increases: 12 and 71 percent for those in the second quintile, 10 and 61 percent for those in the third quintile, 8 and 52 percent for those in the fourth quintile, and 7 and 42 percent for those in the top quintile.

36. See, for example, President's Commission to Strengthen Social Security (2001) and Advisory Council on Social Security (1997).

37. See, for example, Social Security Advisory Board (2005b), discussing numerous options; Purcell (2005d); and Furman (2006), suggesting indexing payroll taxes and/or the benefit formula for demographic changes.

38. See, for example, Advisory Council on Social Security (1997); National Commission on Retirement Policy (1999); and Committee for Economic Development (1997, 2005a).

39. See also Advisory Council on Social Security (1997)—proponents of the Individual Accounts approach called for 2 percent add-on accounts, and proponents of the Personal Security Accounts approach called for a 5 percent carve-out; and Pensions Policy Institute (2006), recommending well-encouraged and regulated voluntary earnings-related pensions on top of a reformed state pension.

40. See, for example, Jeffrey Liebman, Maya MacGuineas, and Andrew Samwick, "Nonpartisan Social Security Reform Plan," http://www.nonpartisanssplan.com/pages/1/index.htm (coupling mandatory 3 percent individual accounts with concomitant Social Security benefit cuts); CBO (2006a); Forman (1995), 114–16; World Bank (1994), 74; and James and Vittas (1996).

41. This chapter makes little effort to resolve the current Social Security system's financial troubles, but see Forman (2001b), noting that the government has great flexibility about when to pay off the current Social Security system's unfunded liability.

42. To the same effect, see Feldstein (2005a).

43. See, for example, Geier (2002); Mitrusi and Poterba (2000); Forman (1992); and Jon Forman, "Bill Gates and I Pay Equally—and This Is Supposed to Be a Fair System?"

For example, under the current system, someone earning $94,200 in salary will pay $4,993 in Social Security retirement taxes in 2006, and her employer will pay a matching amount. A large portion of these taxes is redistributed to other workers and their families. But a rich heiress collecting $500,000 a year from her grandparent's trust fund will pay absolutely nothing to support those other workers and their families.

44. But see Munnell (2003), assuming that half the unfunded liability of the Social Security system will be made up with benefit cuts and half with unspecified tax increases, and also expressing concern about the relatively lower value of future benefits as a percentage of pre-retirement earnings.

45. It could also make sense to get rid of the disproportionately generous minimum benefits that are available to workers over age 62 who have worked for at least 10 years in covered employment.

46. If she had been ambitious enough to have worked while in high school, those earnings and the payroll taxes on them would also be ignored.

47. This high-35 rule also operates to subsidize the benefits of workers who have fewer than 35 years of covered earnings. For example, consider Carol, who from age 18 through age 61 works in the labor force just 30 years and spends the remaining 14 years caring for young children and elderly parents. In computing Carol's Social Security worker benefit, her career-average earnings are based on 35 years, not all 44 adult years from 18 through 61. The high-35 benefit computation formula will require her to average in 5 zero years, not the 14 zero years she actually had; as a result, she will get a relatively higher benefit than her career-average earnings should justify.

48. On the other hand, to increase worker benefits for women, some have suggested reducing the benefit computation period or giving individuals credit for years spent caring for their young children or elderly parents. See, for example, O'Connell (1993), 1494–95; and Staudt (1996). Such changes, however, would make the Social Security system even more redistributive and so exacerbate the system's work disincentives.

49. Similarly, to tighten the relationship between benefits and contributions, it could make sense to track the contributions of, and pay benefits to, workers with less than 10 years of covered service. Under current law, the payroll tax contributions made by those who work less than 10 years in covered employment yield no return. Those hurt by this rule include aliens who work in this country only a few years and homemakers who only occasionally participate in the paid workforce.

50. See also Gustman and Steinmeier (2002); GAO (2006a); and Munnell (2006).

51. The council wanted to raise the full retirement age to age 67 by 2011. Thereafter, the full retirement age would be indexed for increases in life expectancy at the rate of about one month every two years.

52. See, for example, Advisory Council on Social Security (1997), vol. 1, 31; Ippolito (1997), 192; and OECD (2005a), suggesting that the United States raise the early retirement age to 64 and speed up the transition from 65 to 67 for full retirement age. But see Moore (2001); and Munnell et al. (2004).

53. See, for example, Leonesio, Vaughn, and Wixon (2003), noting that about 25 percent of people age 62–64 who receive reduced Social Security benefits are estimated to have health problems that substantially impair their ability to work; Duggan, Singleton, and Song (2005), estimating that the gradual increase in the Social Security full retirement age will lead to a 1.6 percent increase in applications for disability benefits among 63- and 64-year-old men; and Clark et al. (2004), also raising the question of whether the SSI old-age eligibility at age 65 should be increased.

54. See, for example "Revenue Option 20: Tax Social Security and Railroad Retirement Benefits Like Private Pensions," in CBO (2005a); Advisory Council on Social Security (1997), vol. 1, 20–21 and vol. 2, 15–20; Committee for Economic Development (1997), 39–41; Forman (1992, 1998a); Seago (2003); and Ippolito (1997), 189–90.

55. Economists sometimes say that individuals have "a relatively high time preference rate." For example, according to Gustman and Steinmeier,

Individuals with a high time preference rate who are considering retiring at age 62 will see the loss of current benefits clearly, but they will devalue the increase in future benefits even though the increase is actuarially fair The loss of current benefits will be perceived as a reduction in net compensation and will create an incentive to retire at 62. (2002, 2)

56. See also Social Security Advisory Board (2005a), 41; and French (2005), estimating that the elimination of the earnings test for those older than 65 would cause them to delay retirement by almost one year. According to Steven A. Sass, Social Security (and employer plans) acted historically as "*severance* instruments encouraging retirement at age 65" (Sass 2003, 4). The retirement earnings test and reduced benefit accruals after reaching normal retirement age have "effectively slashed the incentive to work."

57. Recall, however, that up to 85 percent of those benefits may be subject to income taxation.

58. See, for example, Forman et al. (2002), 92–100 (remarks of Glenda Chambers).

59. To the same effect, see Chen (2002), 39:

The first-tier benefit should be integrated with the Supplemental Security Income program and funded with general revenue, not payroll taxes, because of its income redistributive and anti-poverty functions. The second-tier benefit should be financed by payroll taxes because contribution and benefit calculations are both based on earnings.

See also Cogan and Mitchell (2003); Schieber and Shoven (1999); Gramlich (1996); and Feldstein and Samwick (1998).

60. If we had the system of universal grants suggested in chapters 6 and 7, then only the excess over the monthly universal grant amount would have to be made up by the basic Social Security benefit. For example, with a system of $2,000 a year universal grants, just $650 a month would need to be made up by the first-tier benefit ($9,800 − $2,000 = $7,800; $7,800 ÷ 12 = $650).

61. To the same effect, Ackerman and Alstott (1999) suggest that each citizen get an entitlement to a basic retirement pension. See also Smeeding and Weaver (2002).

62. A cash balance plan is a defined benefit plan that looks like a defined contribution plan. The plan accumulates, with interest, a hypothetical account balance for each participant. The individual account balances are determined by the plan's benefit formula and consist of two components: an annual cash balance credit and an interest credit. For example, a simple cash balance plan might allocate 3 percent of salary to each participant's cash balance account each year, and credit the account with 7 percent interest on the balance.

In the private pension world, cash balance account statements are issued regularly to participants. Cash balance statements look like defined contribution plan statements and are generally easier for participants to understand than a traditional defined benefit plan formula. Cash balance plans may pay out account balances in a lump-sum distribution or as an annuity, but some sponsors encourage the selection of an annuity by specifying a favorable actuarial basis to convert accounts to annuities. See, generally, Forman and Nixon (2000) and references cited therein; and GAO (2000a, 2000b).

63. To be sure, creating and managing individual accounts for millions of American workers would be daunting (Forman 2001b). It would probably be easiest and cheapest to set up hypothetical individual accounts within the Social Security system and let Social Security handle all the investments.

64. As a yardstick, Carasso and Forman (2006) estimate that, in the long run, 3 percent add-on individual accounts could provide an annual retirement benefit equal to 14.5 percent of final wages for men and 13.3 percent of final wages for women.

Chapter 9. Making Pensions Work

1. This chapter builds on Forman (2000a, 2004a).
2. Public Law 93-406. See, generally, JCT (2005b) and Conison (2003).
3. I.R.C. §§ 72, 402. An annuity is a financial instrument that converts a lump sum of money into a stream of income payable for life. An individual receiving benefits under an annuity or pension usually excludes a fraction of those benefits from income. That fraction (the "exclusion ratio") is based on the amount of premiums or other after-tax contributions made by the individual. The exclusion ratio enables the individual to recover her own after-tax contributions tax free and to pay tax only on the remaining portion of benefits that represents income.
4. See also table 6.2 and CBO (2006b).
5. I.R.C. §§ 219, 408; IRS (2005c). Of note, IRAs are likely to become even more important retirement savings vehicles in the coming years. The maximum contribution amount is scheduled to increase to $5,000 in 2008 and thereafter (plus $1,000 for individuals over age 50). Therefore, the typical husband and wife will eventually be able to save $10,000 a year in their IRAs (or up to $12,000 a year if both are over age 50).
6. I.R.C. § 408A.
7. I.R.C. § 401(c).
8. See also table 2.10 and Purcell (2005b, 2005c).
9. See also Schwabish (2004).
10. When workers who participated in a current or previous job's plan are added to those who own an IRA or Keogh, the participation numbers improve modestly. In 2003, for example, 55.1 percent of workers age 16 or older had

some form of retirement plan, and 69.4 percent of workers age 51–60 had some form of plan (Copeland 2006b, 1).

11. Despite this rather regressive distribution of pension plan participation, employer contributions to pension plans contribute only modestly to the recent increases in wealth inequality. In fact, private pension wealth "smoothes the high end of the wealth distribution," and increases "wealth inequality only below the 20th percentile of the wealth distribution" (Slottje, Woodbury, and Anderson 2000, 375). See also Purcell (2006b).

12. Similarly, only about 12.4 percent of contingent workers participated in an employer-provided pension plan (BLS 2005c, table 9).

13. To help encourage small employers to start plans, Congress recently added a new tax credit that offsets part of the costs of starting a retirement plan (I.R.C. § 45E). The credit equals 50 percent of the cost to set up and administer the plan and to educate employees about the plan, up to $500 a year for each of the first three years of the plan. The employer can choose to start claiming the credit in the tax year before the tax year in which the plan becomes effective. The employer must have had 100 or fewer employees who received at least $5,000 in compensation for the preceding year, and at least one participant must be a non–highly compensated employee.

14. See also McDonnell (2005b).

15. See also GAO (2006a), 6.

16. See, for example, CBO (2003a); National Commission on Retirement Policy (1998); Committee for Economic Development (1995); Aaron et al. (1989); VanDerhei and Copeland (2003); Fore (2003); and Delorme, Munnell, and Webb (2006).

17. See also U.S. Census Bureau, "NP-T3-F, Projections of the Total Resident Population by 5-Year Age Groups, and Sex with Special Age Categories: Middle Series, 2025 to 2045," http://www.census.gov/population/projections/nation/summary/np-t3-f.pdf.

18. See Costo (2006); Buessing and Soto (2006); Rajnes (2002); McCourt (2006); Guzman and Sigalla (2004); Papke (1999); Council of Economic Advisers (1999a), 7, 131, 157–63; and GAO (2006a), noting that while the number of participants in defined benefit plans increased by 12 percent from 1978 to 1997, the number of participants in defined contribution plans tripled.

19. The shift from traditional defined benefit plans to defined contribution plans and cash balance plans may already be having a significant impact on the timing of retirement (Even and Macpherson 2003; Munnell, Cahill, and Jivan 2003).

20. See also VanDerhei (1999), noting that a survey of large U.S. employers that offer a defined benefit plan found that the percentage using a final-average-pay formula decreased from 85 percent to 72 percent from 1995 to 1999. That study also found that the share of large defined benefit plans using a career-average-pay formula declined from 15 percent in 1995 to 9 percent in 1999, and the use of cash balance plans increased from 6 to 16 percent. Career-average-pay plans pay benefits based on compensation averaged over a much greater number of years of service—say, 30, rather than three or five.

21. Nanette Byrnes, "The Rush to Shut Down Pensions," *Business Week Online* (January 9, 2006), quoting John Hotz, deputy director of the Pension Rights Center, a Washington consumer organization focused on retirement rights.

22. According to one definition, "phased retirement is any arrangement that enables employees approaching normal retirement age to reduce their work hours and job responsibilities for the purpose of gradually easing into full retirement" (Committee for Economic Development 1999, 3). See also Scahill and Forman (2002).

23. See, for example, Herz (1995) and Quinn (1999).

24. Also, according to a recent survey by Watson Wyatt, 16 percent of companies surveyed now offer phased retirement programs (1999).

25. An annuity converts a lump sum of money into a stream of income payable for life. Annuitization is the process of converting a lump sum into an annuity.

26. See also Copeland (2005c, 2006b) and Mitchell with Dykes (2003, 123).

27. See also VanDerhei and McDonnell (2000).

28. ERISA defines normal retirement age as the earlier of the time specified in the plan or the later of age 65 or the fifth anniversary of the time the employee commenced participation in the plan (ERISA § 3(24); I.R.C. § 411(a)(8)). Unless the participant elects otherwise, benefit payments must commence no later than the 60th day after the latest of the end of the plan year in which the participant reaches the earlier of 65 or normal retirement age, completes 10 years of service, or terminates service with the employer. If the plan provides for early retirement, participants who have met the service requirements but separated from service before satisfying the age requirement are entitled to actuarially reduced benefits upon reaching the early retirement age.

29. More specifically, employer contributions to pension plans are exempt from current income and payroll taxation. Elective contributions by employees to 401(k)-type plans are also exempt from income taxation, but these contributions are subject to payroll taxation. Similarly, IRA contributions tend to be deductible for income tax purposes but not for payroll tax purposes. Distributions from pension plans and IRAs are subject to income taxation but not payroll taxation. For international comparisons of the tax treatment of private pensions, see Yoo and de Serres (2004) and Forman (1997d).

30. For example, a single individual earning $60,000 in 2006 would face a marginal income tax rate of around 25 percent, pay 7.65 percent in payroll taxes, and see her employer pay another 7.65 percent in payroll taxes. On that last $10,000 she earned, she would pay $3,265 and keep $6,735, and she would also see her employer pay $765 in tax. She would be a lot better off if her employer contributed $10,765 to a pension plan for her. She would pay income and payroll taxes on just $50,000, and the $10,765 contributed to her pension would grow tax free until she retired. Eventually, she would have to pay income taxes on her pension distributions, but the net present cost of that future income taxation of her benefits would be quite low, say $1,000, rather than closer to $4,000 today. The deferral of income taxes and the complete avoidance of the payroll tax are both valuable economic benefits.

31. One study finds that "the income elasticity of worker contributions to a pension plan is approximately 1.5, indicating that if worker income increased by 10 percent, contributions to a pension plan would increase by 15 percent" (Fronstin 2000, 123).

32. Participating in a 401(k) plan may actually increase the lifetime tax burden on low-income workers. See, for example, Gokhale, Kotlikoff, and Neuman (2001).

33. Because the income and substitution effects often work in opposite directions, the net effect on work effort is ambiguous and will depend heavily on individual preferences (see chapter 3). Still, a fair amount of empirical evidence suggests that imposing high taxes on earned income tends to discourage work effort and reduce labor supply. See, for example, Richards (1999); Triest (1996b); Eissa (1996); and Hausman (1981).

34. See also Sass (2003), 3: "Retirement income systems let the elderly quit work and draw income over ever-lengthening lifetimes."

35. See also Whitman and Purcell (2005), showing that pensions accounted for 25.3 percent of the aggregate income of people age 65 and over in the highest quartile of income in 2004, 21.4 percent for those in the second quartile, 6.6 percent for those in the third quartile, and just 2.4 percent for those in the lowest quartile.

36. In short, "relative to defined contribution plans, defined benefit plans penalize early or late retirements" (Even and Macpherson 2003, 46).

37. See also Olsen and VanDerhei (1997).

38. See also Friedberg and Owyang (2004), finding that workers with defined benefit pensions have longer current and expected job tenure than workers without pensions and workers with defined contribution plans.

39. See, for example, Ippolito (1997), 133–50. According to the implicit contract theory, employers underpay their younger workers in exchange for overpayment later in their careers. The backloading of pension accruals encourages younger workers to stay with the company at least until early retirement age. At the same time, however, it gives employers a reason to discourage "late" retirement (Casey 1997; Wise 1991).

40. According to Dulitzky, the following features of defined benefit plans can be used to encourage workers to retire at a particular age: accrual rates that vary with age, earnings, or years of service; wage indexing rules to calculate pensions that vary with age of retirement or years of service; reduction in the normal retirement benefit for retiring early but by less than what would be actuarially fair; limits on the increase in pension accrual after a certain number of years in the firm; and explicit buyouts, offered from time to time, to some workers in the firm. (1999, 4)

41. At the same time, however, there is not much evidence about why some firms have early retirement incentives and others do not (Dorsey, Cornwell, and Macpherson 1998, 114–15).

42. One study of benefit accrual rates of defined benefit plans in 1983 and 1989 found that by the time workers in the study reached age 60, the median annual benefit accrual was already close to zero (Gustman and Steinmeier 1998). By age 62, many plans offered normal retirement benefits, and the average benefit accrual rate turned negative. At age 65, almost all the plans offered normal retirement benefits, and average benefit accruals were even more negative. This study also found that the average age for early retirement eligibility in these plans fell by about a year, from 54.2 in 1983 to 53.1 in 1989.

Similarly, a recent study found that, in 1997, 21 percent of participants in the defined benefit plans of medium and large firms were able to retire at age 62 with full (unreduced) benefits, up from 17 percent in 1981 (Mitchell with Dykes 2003). That study also found that early retirement was permitted by some 95 percent of defined benefits plans of those medium and large firms in 1997. More than 60 percent of participants were able to leave by age 55 (in some cases, depending upon having enough years of service). In addition, many of these plans provided significant subsidies for early retirement, such as providing less than actuarially neutral reductions in benefits.

43. Similarly, Social Security benefits are increased 8.3 percent a year from age 62 to 65, an amount generally thought to be actuarially fair for a person with average life expectancy (Council of Economic Advisers 1999a, 145).

44. When workers retire prior to normal retirement age, their benefits should be actuarially reduced to reflect that payments begin earlier and extend over a longer period. For example, the benefit payable at age 64 is about 90 percent of that payable at 65, and the benefit payable at 55 should be about 37 percent of that payable at 65 (Langbein and Wolk 2000, 447–48). However, plans often use more generous factors to compute early retirement benefits. For example, a plan might subsidize early retirement by allowing workers to retire at age 55 with 50 percent of their normal retirement benefits.

45. As already explained, the accrual rate for traditional final-average-pay plans increases rapidly as workers age. It also costs employers more to provide health insurance coverage for older workers than for younger workers. In fact, the cost of health insurance coverage is twice as high for working men over age 50 than for those under 50 (Committee for Economic Development 1999). The costs of life insurance coverage also naturally increase as workers age, as do the costs associated with work injury and disability. Moreover, many companies tie salaries and paid time off or vacation to age and tenure.

46. See, for example, Sholnn Freeman, "Historic Union Deal Will Pare Down GM," *Washington Post*, 23 March 2006, A1.

47. Of course, defined contribution plans and cash balance plans can be designed to influence the timing of retirement. Daniel Dulitzky summarizes the factors related to defined contribution plans that can influence the timing of retirement as follows: employer contribution rates that may change according to age or years of service, early retirement provisions (explicit buyouts), specific tax rules that may affect the timing of retirement (such as penalties for early withdrawal), and potential availability of a lump sum on the condition of leaving the firm (Dulitzky 1999, 5).

48. Instead, mobile employees can typically roll over their individual account accruals and accumulate large account balances to be used for retirement. Indeed, this portability is one of the most important advantages of defined contribution plans, especially for women, who typically have shorter job tenures because of greater child and dependent care responsibilities (National Economic Council Interagency Working Group on Social Security 1998; Teresa Heinz, Jeffrey Lewis, and Cindy Hounsell, "Women and Pensions: An Overview," http://www.wiser.heinz.org/pensions_overview.html).

49. See also Gale and Orszag (2003a).

50. On that topic, Dr. John C. Goodman recently noted:

In a free labor market, employees and employers would be able to strike any compensation bargain that both sides agree to.... But retirement plans involve something more than voluntary exchange. The ability to build up funds tax-free involves a taxpayer subsidy, and the social purpose of that subsidy is to encourage the private sector to make private provision for retirement income needs.

Employers who exact onerous vesting requirements are using a tax-subsidized vehicle created to achieve a socially desirable end in order to achieve a purely private, corporate end. . . . Vesting requirements not only undermine the social goal of encouraging people to have a reasonable retirement income, they also interfere with the labor market mobility that our modern economy requires. (Goodman 2004, 5–6)

In August 2006, the Pension Protection Act of 2006 reduced the cliff vesting period for defined contribution plans from five years to three years.

51. See, for example, Cavenaugh (2003); Iwry (2003); and Meulbroek (2005), suggesting that employees who invest one-quarter of their assets in company stock sacrifice 42 percent of the stock's market value relative to holding a well-diversified equity portfolio. On the other hand, there is some evidence that employee stock ownership can enhance firm productivity (Even and Macpherson 2003, 2004). That greater productivity could translate into greater expected investment returns on company stock than on alternative investments. Nevertheless, pension policy should encourage employees to diversify their retirement savings portfolios to minimize risk and so help ensure that they will have adequate retirement incomes.

52. See also BLS (2003), table 87, showing similar statistics for 2000.

53. I.R.C. § 72(t)(2).

54. See also Copeland (2005c); Purcell (2006a); Woods (1993); and Burman, Coe, and Gale (1999). But see Sabelhaus and Weiner (1999), finding that most lump-sum distributions are small, leading the authors to conclude that the leakage from the pension system is not significant relative to retirement income.

55. To be sure, the ability to borrow from a plan may encourage greater contributions and accumulations by some workers, leading to earlier retirement. But other workers may end up dissipating their retirement assets prematurely and find themselves needing to work longer in order to accumulate sufficient savings for retirement.

56. See, for example, Beshears et al. (2006); Choi, Laibson, and Madrian (2006); Madrian (2005); Madrian and Shea (2001); Thaler and Bernartzi (2004); Holden and VanDerhei (2005); and Iwry and John (2006).

57. I.R.C. § 25B.

58. Actually, recent research suggests that employer matching contributions may only modestly increase retirement saving and that alternative approaches may be needed. See, for example, Mitchell, Utkus, and Yang (2005).

59. See also Koenig and Harvey (2005); and Dickert-Conlin et al. (2005).

60. See, for example, IRS (2002), V-19; and JCT (2000), 119–20. See also Pension Rights Center (2005), proposing new retirement plans that would be attractive to employers that do not sponsor plans or plans that could be sponsored by banks and other financial institutions.

61. There are some 15 exceptions to this 10 percent penalty (Pratt and Bennett 1999). For example, there is an exception for distributions that take the form of a lifetime annuity. There are also exceptions for distributions because of disability or to cover high medical expenses; distributions from an IRA can even be used to purchase a residence or pay college tuition.

62. For example, pre-retirement distributions are not allowed under Canadian pension law (Dorsey 2000).

63. ERISA § 3(24); I.R.C. § 411(a)(8).

64. More specifically, distributions typically must begin no later than April 1 of the calendar year following the calendar year in which the employee

attains age 70½. Distributions after the death of a plan participant must also meet certain minimum distribution requirements.

65. I.R.C. § 4974.

66. See, for example, Warshawsky (1998a, 1998b) and Pratt and Bennett (1999). Warshawsky has been particularly forceful in arguing that the minimum distribution rules are outmoded in today's labor market and social conditions. Warshawsky contends that retirement plan participants need greater flexibility in how and when they draw down their pension assets. He also argues that the minimum distribution requirements are burdensome for plan sponsors and providers and that they are confusing for plan participants. Consequently, he suggests that Congress should repeal the minimum distribution rules or, at least, raise the required start age from 70½ to 76. But see Soled (2000).

67. Pertinent here, I.R.C. § 411(b)(1)(H) prohibits a defined benefit plan from ceasing accruals, or reducing the rate of benefit accruals, "because of the attainment of any age." Similarly, I.R.C. § 411(b)(2)(A) prohibits a defined contribution plan from ceasing allocations, or reducing the rate at which amounts are allocated, to a participant's account, "because of the attainment of any age." Parallel provisions are found in ERISA and in ADEA (ERISA §§ 204(b)(1)(H)(i) and (ii); 29 *United States Code* § 623(i)).

68. That study also found that 33 percent of participants faced a ceiling on the maximum dollar amount of benefits that could be paid to them.

69. Current law permits plan sponsors to subsidize early retirement in a whole range of ways that presumably would otherwise violate age discrimination laws. For example, the plan in the last example might give early retirees the full 60 percent of final average pay even if they have only 25 years of service. Alternatively, the plan might provide greater than actuarially fair subsidies for workers who have 30 years of service but who have not yet reached age 65. Or the plan might provide supplemental benefits to workers not yet eligible for Social Security. Each of these approaches is used to create financial incentives for older workers to retire, and some are even used to impose financial penalties on older workers who wish to remain on the job.

70. Of course, any time Congress adopts changes of this magnitude, it would be appropriate to provide plan sponsors with generous transition rules. The most generous transition rule would be to repeal the age discrimination exceptions only for new employees. Alternatively, the repeal could be made applicable only to workers then under the age of 40 or 50. Another approach would be to make the repeal effective only for benefit accruals after the date of enactment.

71. Consider, for example, a plan that makes early retirement benefits available at age 55 and unreduced normal benefits available at age 62 for workers with 25 years of service. The annual defined benefit limit (e.g., $175,000 in 2006) typically does not affect many plan participants. On the other hand, the early retirement reductions required by section I.R.C. § 415(b)(2)(C) can severely limit the benefits that can be paid to workers who retire early. In 1999, this early retirement reduction would have limited the maximum annual benefit payable to a worker who retired at age 55 to $53,931—less than 42 percent of the $130,000 benefit limit applicable in 1999. The example is from the remarks of Michael R. Fanning, in Wood (1999). Fanning views this outcome as "harsh and unfair." He and others argue that the solution is to significantly raise the normal retirement benefit amount and ease the limit on early retirement benefits.

72. On the other hand, if the government is interested in keeping older Americans in the workforce, then it makes little sense to relax the rule requiring actuarial reductions for early retirement (as some critics have suggested). Employers want to relax that rule because they want the freedom to use their tax-favored pensions for subsidies to encourage their costly older workers to retire early. But actuarially fair reductions are exactly what should be required if the government wants pension policy to be neutral on the timing of retirement.

Even actuarially fair reductions are unlikely to be sufficient to encourage elderly workers to postpone retirement. In the Social Security system, for example, the benefit reduction for taking benefits before age 65 is thought to be actuarially fair for the average worker—8.3 percent per year (Council of Economic Advisers 1999c, 145). Nevertheless, empirical research suggests that workers seem to undervalue higher future benefits relative to the loss of current benefits (see, for example, Aaron 1999a). Moreover, to the extent that individual workers may have insights into their own mortality risk, those who expect to die younger are given little motivation to delay benefits by an actuarial increase that is merely fair to the average worker.

In short, government policy that is, at least, ostensibly neutral on the timing of retirement should require actuarially fair reductions in benefits paid before normal retirement age. If the government wants to encourage workers to postpone retirement, then it might want to impose greater financial penalties on early retirement—for example, by toughening the I.R.C. § 72(t) penalty on premature distributions.

73. Treasury Regulation § 1.401-1(b)(1); ERISA § 205; I.R.C. §§ 410(a)(11), 417.

74. To be sure, plan provisions allowing lump-sum distributions may have mixed effects. Early eligibility for a lump-sum distribution may induce workers to retire early. Or the tendency to dissipate lump-sum distributions may result in workers having to work longer in order to accumulate sufficient savings for retirement.

75. In 2000, for example, only 7 percent of employees in private-sector defined benefit plans were in plans that provided for automatic cost-of-living increases (BLS 2003, table 60).

76. Most people think about retirement in current dollars. They look at the monthly benefits available to them from Social Security and their traditional defined benefit plans, and they look at the apparently large sums accumulated in their defined contribution plans (and generally available to them only if they retire). As a result, a kind of "money illusion" leads most older Americans to believe that they are better off than they really are.

77. See also He et al. (2005), table 4-9, showing that 9.0 percent of persons age 65 to 74 were poor in 2003, as well as 11.6 percent of those age 75 and over.

78. Similarly, distributions for married couples might be geared toward purchasing an indexed, joint and survivor annuity (i.e., paying $26,400 in 2006 [$26,400 = 2 × $13,200 poverty level for a married couple in 2006]) and appropriately inflation-adjusted amounts in future years.

79. Treasury Regulation § 1.401-1(b)(i). Starting in 2007, new I.R.C. § 401(a)(35) will allow defined benefit plans to make in-service distributions to workers who are age 62 or older.

80. For example, amounts may generally be withdrawn from profit-sharing and stock bonus plans after they have been in plan for two years, and earlier distributions are permitted in the event of retirement, death, disability, other

separation from service, or hardship. As for 401(k) plans, elective deferrals may be distributed on account of separation from service, death, disability, attainment of age 59½, or hardship.

81. See, for example, Scahill and Forman (2002). Along the same lines, it could make sense to allow employers to offer pro-rated fringe benefits for older employees who work reduced hours, rather than requiring them to provide the same fringe benefits to all employees who work more than 1,000 hours a year. ERISA's 1,000-hour requirement encourages employers to restrict part-time employees to working fewer than 1,000 hours a year. See Burtless and Quinn (2002); GAO (2006a), 11–14; and Chen and Scott (2006).

82. Defined contribution plans can certainly be designed to push older workers into retirement—for example, by having contributions cease after a specified number of years of service—but most defined contribution plans are designed to make them actuarially neutral on the timing of retirement.

83. The income and wealth effects of greater pension accumulations would still affect the timing of retirement. Consequently, proposals that expand pension coverage or increase and preserve pension accruals could result in earlier retirements by some individuals. But we should not object to policies that would promote additional retirement savings or encourage the preservation of benefits until retirement merely because such policies could result in earlier retirements. If the government is interested in ensuring that all elderly Americans have adequate retirement incomes, it should adopt policies that encourage retirement savings and the preservation of benefits. But it should also prohibit pension plan designs that push older workers into retirement.

84. In fact, it seems clear that nothing close to universal private pension coverage will occur under a voluntary private pension system (Halperin 1993).

85. Alternatively, this goal could be achieved by expanding the current Social Security system or SSI program.

86. See, for example, Morris (2006), 57; Prescott (2005); Albert B. Crenshaw, "Make 'em Provide Pensions," *Washington Post* 29 January 2006, F1; Morse (2006); and Pensions Policy Institute (2006), suggesting that a well-encouraged voluntary pension could meet the objectives of a mandatory pension.

Relatively few countries mandate private pension coverage of workers (World Bank 1994). Private pension coverage is mandatory in Australia and Switzerland, and industry-wide collective bargaining agreements make such coverage quasi-mandatory in Denmark and the Netherlands. Also, Chile requires its workers to contribute at least 10 percent of their wages to the privately managed individual retirement savings accounts that have replaced that country's social security system (see, for example, Forman 1995). But most private pension systems are voluntary.

87. A different approach would be for the government to mandate that employers provide a suitable pension plan for their employees. The government might authorize employers to use a central clearinghouse where employers could send pension contributions on behalf of their employees. Over the course of her career, each worker would earn entitlement to a benefit which, at retirement, would supplement Social Security.

Chapter 10. Making Health Care Work

1. See also National Center for Health Statistics, "Fast Stats," http://www.cdc.gov/nchs/fastats/hexpense.htm; and U.S. House Committee (2004), appendix C.

2. The percentages total more than 100 because some individuals have more than one source of coverage. For example, many elderly Americans have Medicare and private Medigap insurance.

3. See also Buckley and Van Glezen (2004); and Fronstin (2005d).

4. See also table 2.10, showing that, in 2005, 84 percent of workers in firms with 100 or more workers had health care benefits, compared with just 59 percent of those in smaller firms; and BLS (2005g), table 1, showing that 76 percent of workers in private industry had access to health care benefits in 2003.

5. See also table 2.10, showing that, in 2005, 87 percent of workers making $15 an hour or higher had health care benefits, while just 58 percent of those making less than $15 an hour had health care benefits; and Welcher (2006).

Of note, however, employer contributions to health plans "do not exacerbate inequalities of compensation and income" (Slottje et al. 2000, 374–75). Employer contributions for health insurance are far more unequally distributed than personal income generally, but employer contributions for health insurance are distributed in such a way that they have a "slightly equalizing effect on the distribution of income."

6. I.R.C. § 125.

7. Public Law 99-272; 29 *United States Code* §§ 1161 et seq.

8. See also The Kaiser Family Foundation and Hewitt Associates (2004); and Schieber (2004).

9. I.R.C. § 162(l).

10. Additional tax savings would result from the concomitant exclusion of employment-based health care coverage from the Social Security payroll tax.

11. The estimate includes employer contributions for medical care, health insurance and long-term care insurance premiums, and employer-provided health insurance purchased through cafeteria plans and health care spending through flexible spending accounts.

12. ERISA § 514(a), 29 *United States Code* § 1144(a).

13. See *New State Ice Co. v. Liebmann*, 285 U.S. 262, 311 (1932) (Justice Louis Brandeis, dissenting).

14. See also Bhandari and Gifford (2003); Robert Wood Johnson Foundation (2005); The Urban Institute (2002); and Dubay, Hill, and Kenney (2002), finding that about 27 percent of poor children were uninsured in 2002.

15. The estimated number of uninsured in the text is a cross-sectional estimate and so understates the number of people who experienced a spell without insurance that year. Longitudinal estimates that ask whether people had spells without insurance over a one- or two-year period produce higher counts. See, for example, Short (2004).

16. See also GAO (2002b), 5–8.

17. See also Blumberg and Nichols (2004), discussing how worker and employer choices combine to determine coverage levels.

18. See also BLS (2005g), 15–16, showing employer and employee monthly premiums in 2005.

19. See also GAO (2005c); Board of Trustees (2006); Boards of Trustees (2006); Shaviro (2004b); and CBO (2005d).

20. See also Hunt-McCool, McCool, and Dor (2000).

21. See, for example, Goldman, Sood, and Leibowitz (2005), finding that two-thirds of an employee premium increase was paid for with wages and the remaining third was paid for with a reduction in benefits.

22. See, for example, Wolaver, McBride, and Wolfe (2003), suggesting that policies that increase health care coverage among low-wage workers tend to decrease full-time employment for that group.

23. See also Fronstin (2003).

24. See also Fronstin (2005b); and Burtless and Quinn (2001).

25. See also Johnson, Davidoff, et al. (2003); and Gruber and Madrian (1995).

26. See also Committee for Economic Development (1999), 30–32, noting that the cost of health care coverage is twice as high for working men over age 50 than for those under 50; Munnell (2006), 14–15; and Holahan (2004), 20–21.

27. Moreover, many companies tie salaries and paid time off or vacation to age and tenure.

28. Similarly, employers that have promised retiree health benefits but did not pre-fund those promised benefits can be at a real competitive disadvantage in hiring workers and in selling their products. General Motors, for example, provides health insurance to some 1.1 million workers, retirees, and dependents; that coverage cost $5.2 billion in 2004 ($1,500 per car), with $4 billion going to retirees. Amy Joyce, "GM's UAW Retirees Face Health Care Costs: Deal Would End Free Coverage," *Washington Post*, 21 October 2005, D1.

29. See also Boushey et al. (2001), 49; and Hartmann and Spalter-Roth (2004), 77.

30. Public Law 107-210; 19 *United States Code* § 3801 note.

31. See, for example, "Beating Up on Wal-Mart," *Washington Post*, 12 January 2006, A12; and Matthew Mosk and Ylan Q. Mui, " 'Wal-Mart Law' in Md. Rejected by Court," *Washington Post*, 20 July 2006, A1.

32. It might also make sense to tax the insurance value of Medicare benefits (Forman 1994). In particular, as Medicare is not means-tested, many Medicare beneficiaries are relatively well off. In effect, Medicare payroll taxes collected from low-income working taxpayers are being used to pay for health care benefits for well-off retirees. That hardly seems fair. Taxing the insurance value of Medicare benefits could raise more than $30 billion a year (CBO 1996b).

33. See, for example, Himmelstein and Woolhandler (2003).

34. See, for example, Morone (2003).

35. The Health Security Act of 1993, H.R. 3600 and S. 1757, 103rd Cong., 1st sess.; White House Domestic Policy Council, *Health Security: The President's Report to the American People* (Washington, DC: U.S. Government Printing Office, 1993).

36. These mandates could be enforced, for example, by denying certain tax benefits unless the individual provides proof of coverage (JCT 2006b).

37. See also Haase (2005).

38. See, for example, "Health Care Access and Affordability Conference Committee Report," http://www.mhalink.org/public/news/2006/attach/news-04-07-2.pdf.

39. See, for example, Morris (2006).

40. Also, if some types of workers are exempt from the mandate—such as part-time and contingent workers—then employers are likely to convert full-time jobs with coverage to part-time or contingent positions without coverage.

41. Alternatively, those workers who value the coverage the least would have an incentive to move on to jobs that do not offer coverage (Baicker and Chandra 2005).

Chapter 11. Making Labor Markets Work

1. Discrimination results in a bimodal distribution of earnings in which the group that is discriminated against has much lower average earnings.

2. See, for example, McNamee and Miller (2004). Of note, some analysts believe that our antidiscrimination laws are too feeble to have much effect on economic inequality. For example, Baker and colleagues believe that the legal system has great potential to promote what they call "equality of condition" but that antidiscrimination laws are just too narrow to achieve that kind of result. In particular, they note:

Pay equity is narrowly construed and does not demand any reconsideration of how certain forms of work are devalued while others bring enormous financial reward; it is concerned only with correcting the wages of individual employers. (Baker et al. 2004, 129–30)

3. See, for example, table 2.1, the text following table 2.3, and figure 3.4.

4. See also Lahey (2005) and The Anti-Ageism Task Force (2006).

5. Equal Employment Opportunity Commission, "Charge Statistics," http://www.eeoc.gov/stats/charges.html. See also Nicholson (2003).

6. See also Robert J. Samuelson, "Retirement at 70 (Cont'd)," *Washington Post*, 24 August 2005, A15. Similarly, the average duration of an unemployment spell for workers age 55 to 64 was 23.9 weeks, compared with 18.6 weeks for workers age 25 to 34.

7. As more fully explained in chapter 9, it would also make sense to repeal the exceptions to ADEA that permit employers to provide early retirement incentives that tend to push older workers into premature retirement.

8. Equal Employment Opportunity Commission, "Charge Statistics."

9. Crime may also result as an externality of an unfair earnings distribution. If so, then reducing economic inequality should itself reduce the crime rate. See also Levitt and Dubner (2005).

10. Bureau of Justice Statistics, "Drugs and Crime Facts: Drug Law Violations: Enforcement," http://www.ojp.usdoj.gov/bjs/dcf/enforce.htm.

11. See, for example, sources cited on the National Center for State Courts "Probation and Alternatives to Incarceration: Resource Guide," http://www.ncsconline.org/WC/Education/ProAltGuide.htm.

12. For example, Freeman (2003) notes that "the ideal criminal justice system would release ex-offenders who would find work in the legitimate labor market and make a positive contribution to their families and communities rather than return to crime." See also Edelman et al. (2006).

13. See also Timothy Hughes and Doris James Wilson, "Reentry Trends in the United States," http://www.ojp.usdoj.gov/bjs/reentry/reentry.htm.

14. See, for example, Atkinson (2002); Reynolds (1997); and David Leonhardt, "As Prison Labor Grows, So Does the Debate," *New York Times*, 19 March 2000, A1.

15. Bureau of Justice Statistics, "Key Crime & Justice Facts at a Glance," Correctional populations trends, http://www.ojp.usdoj.gov/bjs/glance/tables/corr2tab.htm.

16. See, for example, McNamee and Miller (2004), 113, noting that "less privileged children are awarded fewer and lower-valued credentials, and inequality is largely reproduced across generations."

17. See, for example, Committee for Economic Development (2002) and Karoly and Bigelow (2005). See also Warren and Tyagi (2003), noting that

preschool costs are a growing burden on middle-class families. Warren and Tyagi also note that:

The decision about how old children should be when they start school was made more than a century ago, when views about the learning capacity of young children were very different. The absence of publicly funded preschool is an anachronism, one that could easily be remedied. (2003, 39)

18. See, for example, Levine (1998).

19. The term "high school dropouts" refers to those individuals age 16–19 that are not high school graduates and not currently enrolled in school. The 2000 dropout rate is down from 11.2 percent in 1990 (Day with Jamieson 2003).

20. In particular, we need to figure out ways to improve the motivation of disadvantaged boys and young men so they stay in school and improve their skills, and we need to increase funding for such proven programs as Job Corps, Youth Service Academies, and Career Academies (Edelman et al. 2006). See also Mishel and Roy (2006).

21. Most states require students to stay in school until they are 16, although a few require students to stay in school until they are 17, 18, or complete high school (National Center for Educational Statistics [NCES] 2005).

22. U.S. students also performed poorly on the science scale. See also Council of Economic Advisers (2006) and NCES (2005).

23. To be sure, compared to other industrialized countries, U.S. schools had relatively fewer instructional days (178) but relatively more hours of instruction each day (5.6). All in all, the average number of hours of instruction per year in U.S. schools (1,003) exceeded hours per year in most of the other countries sampled (NCES 1996, indicator 20: time in formal instruction).

24. Some 60 percent of new jobs require postsecondary education, but that level of education is currently held by just one-third of Americans (DOL 2004, 102).

25. See also JCT (2004b). The Hope credit is a nonrefundable credit of up to $1,500 per student a year for qualified tuition and related expenses paid for the first two years of the student's postsecondary education in a degree or certificate program. The Lifetime Learning credit is a nonrefundable tax credit for up to 20 percent of qualified tuition and related expenses incurred during the taxable year on behalf of the taxpayer, the taxpayer's spouse, or any dependents. Up to $10,000 of expenses per return are eligible for the Lifetime Learning credit (i.e., the maximum credit per return is $2,000).

26. See, for example, Pell Institute (2004), using census data to estimate that 31 percent of low-income students, compared with 79 percent of high-income students, were enrolled in college or had attended college in 2001; and Jencks (2002), noting that in the 1980s, college enrollment tended to rise more rapidly at the top of the income scale than at the bottom.

27. Although such tuition assistance programs provide employees with general skills that make the employees more marketable to other firms, these programs can also help firms hire better quality, more educated, more productive employees. These programs can also help reduce employee turnover as employees stay to continue using the benefit and gain loyalty to the firm along the way. See, for example, Cappelli (2002).

28. See, for example, Edelman et al. (2006); Shulman (2005); Galbraith (1998); Handler and Hasenfeld (1997); Boushey et al. (2001); Chapman and Ettlinger

(2004); Sawhill and Haskins (2002); National Economic Council (2000); and Hartmann and Spalter-Roth (2004).

29. See also Employment Policies Institute (2000), Figart (2004), and Quigley (2003).

30. See also Boushey et al. (2001).

31. Quigley suggests the following amendment: "Every person shall have the right to work and to receive a living wage for their work" (2003, 10).

32. The study did find that living wage laws had a positive effect on the income distribution. Adams and Neumark estimate that a 50 percent increase in the living wage would reduce the overall poverty rate by 1.7 percent.

33. Martin Feldstein (2005a), however, suggests that unemployment insurance does not, in fact, redistribute very much to the poor.

34. See also Vroman (2005), noting that low recipiency is typical of the program.

35. See also BLS (2005i), noting that 37 percent of the working poor had a bout of unemployment during 2003.

36. See also Bernhardt and Bailey (1998); and Bernstein et al. (2005).

37. If we do relax the rules on voluntary quits, we should be careful how we count those quits against the experience-rated premiums paid by their employers.

38. An alternative approach would be to redesign the unemployment insurance program around individual unemployment savings accounts backed up by a government line of credit. See, for example, Feldstein (2005a) and Feldstein and Altman (1998). Under this approach, individuals would be required to accumulate enough funds in individual unemployment savings accounts to pay their own unemployment benefits for two spells of unemployment. Individuals with inadequate balances would be able to borrow their benefits from the government and repay them when they return to work (although it is a little hard to imagine how low-skilled workers could ever afford to make those repayments). Any unused savings in these unemployment savings accounts would be made available for the individual to spend in retirement or bequeath to heirs. There is a fair amount of evidence that the current tax-and-transfer unemployment system leads to labor market distortions, including, for example, longer durations of unemployment. Theoretically, those labor market distortions could be reduced with an individual unemployment savings account system, as there would be a closer relationship between individual "contributions" to the system and benefits received.

39. 29 U.S.C. §§ 151–169. See, for example, U.S. Commission on the Future of Worker-Management Relations (1994), suggesting changes in collective bargaining rules to enhance cooperation and reduce conflict and delay.

40. See also Greenlees and Welcher (2005), showing that, on average, union employees in private industry contribute less for health care than nonunion employees; Buchmueller, DiNardo, and Valletta (2005), showing that union jobs tend to offer workers more vacation, fewer hours per week, and a greater likelihood of dental, health, maternity, retirement, and pension benefits; and Shulman (2005).

41. See also DOL (2004).

42. See, for example, Molly Moore, "French Students Hit Streets to Protest New Labor Law: Swelling Unrest Seen as Threat to Ruling Party," *Washington Post*, 17 March 2006, A13.

43. S. 842 sponsored by Sen. Edward Kennedy (D-MA) and Arlen Spector (R-PA) and H.R. 1696 sponsored by Rep. George Miller (D-CA) and Peter King (R-NY) (109th Cong., 1st sess.); AFL-CIO, "Employee Free Choice Act," http://www.aflcio.org/joinaunion/voiceatwork/efca.

44. See, for example, Handler and Hasenfeld (1997); Bell and Wray (2004); and Solow (1998).

See also Kaus (1995). Kaus would replace most welfare programs for the able-bodied poor "with a single, simple offer from the government—an offer of employment for every American citizen over eighteen who wants it, in a useful public job, at a wage slightly below the minimum wage for private-sector work." In addition, the government would supplement the wages of all low-income workers "to ensure that every American who works full-time has enough money to raise a normal-sized family with dignity, out of poverty" (1995, 125).

45. Hyman P. Minsky is credited with developing this terminology. See, for example, Bell and Wray (2004) and Minsky (1986).

46. To be sure, public employee unions have never been very supportive of guaranteed jobs programs. Public employee unions generally worry that a guaranteed jobs program could lead to a reduction in union jobs and downward pressure on union pay. (Similar concerns often lead public employee unions to oppose prison work programs and the privatization of prisons.)

47. See also Papadimitriou (1998).

48. I.R.C. §§ 162(m), 280G.

49. See also H.R. 3260 (109th Cong., 1st sess.), a bill introduced by Rep. Martin Olav Sabo (D-MN) that would deny employers a deduction for payments of excessive compensation, defined as salary, wages, bonuses, and certain noncash benefits that exceed "25 times the lowest compensation for services performed by any other full-time employee."

50. See U.S. Department of Labor, "Compliance Assistance–Fair Labor Standards Act (FLSA)" web page, http://www.dol.gov/esa/whd/flsa/.

51. Of note, the Department of Labor's recent overhaul of its overtime pay regulations set off a storm of controversy. Under the new rules, only workers earning less than $23,660 a year—or $455 a week—are guaranteed overtime protection ("DOL's FairPay Overtime Initiative," http://www.dol.gov/esa/regs/compliance/whd/fairpay/main.htm). Many observers expressed concern that the revisions would make millions of low-income workers ineligible for overtime pay and so reduce their incomes. See, for example, Eisenbrey and Bernstein (2003).

52. See, for example, Papadimitriou (1998); and Alesina et al. (2005), noting that the European labor market policies promoting shorter workweeks and longer vacations have not increased employment but may have tilted societal norms toward enjoying more leisure.

53. Immigration was transferred from the Treasury Department to the newly created Department of Commerce and Labor in 1903, stayed with the Department of Labor when the Department of Commerce and Labor divided into separate cabinet departments in 1913, shifted to the Department of Justice in 1940, and now resides in the new Department of Homeland Security. Consequently, many of the immigration papers for this author's Russian-born mother and maternal grandparents have Department of Labor headings on them. A brief visit to the Ellis Island Immigration Museum's exhibit on the "Peak

Immigration Years" from 1880 through the 1924 should convince almost anyone of the government desire to populate the country (and the goal of the railroads to sell as many tickets west as possible). See, for example, the National Park Service, "Statue of Liberty National Monument and Ellis Island," http://www.nps.gov/stli/serv02.htm.

54. PRWORA, Public Law 104-193.

55. See, for example, The White House, "Immigration: Fair and Secure Immigration Reform," http://www.whitehouse.gov/infocus/immigration/more-immigration.html; Orrenius (2003); and Wasem (2005).

56. Since September 11, 2001, however, security has also been a major concern of immigration policy, and since 2005, immigration reform has become a very important political issue.

57. See, for example, The Century Foundation (2000); OECD (2005a); and Council of Economic Advisers (2006), noting that immigrants make up a significant and increasing share of scientists and engineers in the United States.

REFERENCES

Aaron, Henry. 1969. "What Is a Comprehensive Tax Base Anyway?" *National Tax Journal* 22(4): 543–49.

———. 1982. "Discussion (following the paper 'A Simulation Analysis of the Economic Efficiency and Distributional Effects of Alternative Program Structures: Negative Income Tax Versus the Credit Income Tax')." In *Income-Tested Transfer Programs*, edited by Irwin Garfunkel (212–14). New York: Academic Press.

———. 1999a. "Retirement, Retirement Research, and Retirement Policy." In *Behavioral Dimensions of Retirement Economics*, edited by Henry J. Aaron (43–80). Washington, DC: Brookings Institution Press.

———. 1999b. "Should Policy Be Designed to Encourage Later Retirement?" Paper presented at the first annual Joint Conference for the Retirement Research Consortium, Washington, D.C., May 20.

———. 2004. "HSAs—The 'Sleeper' in the Drug Bill." *Tax Notes* (February 23): 1025–30.

Aaron, Henry J., Barry P. Bosworth, and Gary T. Burtless. 1989. *Can America Afford to Grow Old? Paying for Social Security*. Washington, DC: Brookings Institution Press.

Aaron, Henry J., Harvey Galper, and Joseph A. Pechman, eds. 1988. *Uneasy Compromise: Problems of a Hybrid Income-Consumption Tax*. Washington, DC: Brookings Institution Press.

Aaronson, Daniel, and Bhashkar Mazumber. 2005. "Intergenerational Economic Mobility in the United States, 1940 to 2000." Working Paper No. 2005-12. Chicago, IL: Federal Reserve Bank of Chicago.

Abraham, Katherine G., and Susan N. Houseman. 2004. "Work and Retirement Plans among Older Americans." Working Paper No. 2004-3. Philadelphia, PA: Pension Research Council.

Ackerman, Bruce, and Anne Alstott. 1999. *The Stakeholder Society*. New Haven and London: Yale University Press.

Acs, Gregory, and Pamela Loprest. 2005. "Who Are Low-Income Working Families?" Low-Income Working Families Paper No. 1. Washington, DC: The Urban Institute.

Adams, Gina, and Monica Rohacek. 2003. "Child Care and Welfare Reform." *Welfare Reform & Beyond* Policy Brief No. 14. Washington, DC: The Brookings Institution.

Adams, Scott, and David Neumark. 2005. "A Decade of Living Wages: What Have We Learned?" *California Economic Policy* Vol. 1, No. 3. San Francisco: Public Policy Institute of California.

Advisory Council on Social Security. 1997. *Report of the 1994–1996 Advisory Council on Social Security.* 2 vols. Washington, DC: Social Security Administration.

Advisory Council on Unemployment Compensation. 1996. *Collected Findings and Recommendations: 1994–1996.* Washington, DC: U.S. Government Printing Office.

Aizcorbe, Ana M., Arthur B. Kennickell, and Kevin B. Moore. 2003. "Recent Changes in U.S. Family Finances: Evidence from the 1998 and 2001 Survey of Consumer Finances." *Federal Reserve Bulletin* (January): 1–32.

Alesina, Alberto, and George-Marios Angeletos. 2005. "Fairness and Redistribution." *American Economic Review* 95(4): 960–80.

Alesina, Alberto, Edward Glaeser, and Bruce Sacerdote. 2005. "Work and Leisure in the U.S. and Europe: Why So Different?" Working Paper No. 11,278. Cambridge, MA: National Bureau of Economic Research.

Alger, Horatio, Jr. 1986. *Ragged Dick and Struggling Upward.* New York: Penguin Books.

Allgood, Sam. 2003. "Redistributing Income and Relative Efficiency." *Economic Inquiry* 41(3): 480–95.

Alstott, Anne L. 2004. *No Exit: What Parents Owe Their Children and What Society Owes Parents.* Oxford and New York: Oxford University Press.

Altig, David, and Charles T. Carlstrom. 1999. "Marginal Tax Rates and Income Inequality in a Life-Cycle Model." *American Economic Review* 89(5): 1197–1215.

American Assembly, The. 1999. *The Economy: Sustaining Growth with Opportunity: Final Report of the Ninety-Fifth American Assembly.* Uniting America Series. New York: The American Assembly.

American Bar Association. Section of Taxation. 1989. *Value-Added Tax: A Model Statute and Commentary.* Chicago, IL: American Bar Association.

American Enterprise Institute for Public Policy Research. 2000. "Income, Leisure, and Economic Well-Being." Conference Summary No. 11,858. Washington, DC: American Enterprise Institute for Public Policy Research.

American Law Institute. 1993. *Federal Income Tax Project: Integration of the Individual and Corporate Income Taxes: Reporter's Study of Corporate Tax Integration* (Alvin C. Warren, Jr., Reporter). Philadelphia, PA: The American Law Institute.

Anderson, Patricia M., and Bruce D. Meyer. 2003. "Unemployment Insurance Tax Burdens and Benefits: Funding Family Leave and Reforming the Payroll Tax." Working Paper No. 10,043. Cambridge, MA: National Bureau of Economic Research.

Anderson, Sarah, John Cavanagh, Scott Klinger, and Liz Stanton. 2005. *Executive Excess 2005: Defense Contractors Get More Bucks for the Bang. 12th Annual CEO Compensation Survey.* Boston, MA: United for a Fair Economy.

Anderson, Sarah, John Cavanagh, Ralph Estes, Chuck Collins, and Chris Hartman. 1999. *A Decade of Executive Excess: The 1990s. Sixth Annual Executive Compensation Survey.* Boston, MA: United for a Fair Economy.

Anderson, Sarah, John Cavanagh, Chris Hartman, Scott Klinger, and Stacey Chan. 2004. *Executive Excess 2004: Campaign Contributions, Outsourcing, Unexpensed Stock Options and Rising CEO Pay. 11th Annual Executive Compensation Survey.* Boston, MA: United for a Fair Economy.

Andrews, William D. 1967. "The Accessions Tax Proposal." *Tax Law Review* 22: 589–633.

————. 1974. "A Consumption-Type of Cash Flow Personal Income Tax." *Harvard Law Review* 87(6): 1113–88.

Anti-Ageism Task Force at the International Longevity Center, The. 2006. *Ageism in America.* New York: International Longevity Center.

Aronson, Stephanie. 2002. "The Rise in Lifetime Earnings Inequality among Men." Finance and Economics Discussion Series Paper No. 2002-21. Washington, DC: Federal Reserve Board.

Atkinson, Robert D. 2002. "Prison Labor: It's More than Breaking Rocks." Policy report. Washington, DC: Progressive Policy Institute.

Auerbach, Alan J., and Kevin A. Hassett. 2005. "Conclusion." In *Toward Fundamental Tax Reform,* edited by Alan J. Auerbach and Kevin A. Hassett (149–58). Washington, DC: AEI Press.

Auten, Gerald, and Robert Carroll. 1999. "The Effect of Income Taxes on Household Income." *Review of Economics and Statistics* 81(4): 681–93.

Autor, David H., Lawrence F. Katz, and Melissa S. Kearney. 2005. "Trends in U.S. Wage Inequality: Re-assessing the Revisionists." Working Paper No. 11,627. Cambridge, MA: National Bureau of Economic Research.

Avi-Yonah, Reuven S. 2005. "The Three Goals of Taxation." Ann Arbor: University of Michigan Law School.

Baicker, Katherine, and Amitabh Chandra. 2005. "The Labor Market Effects of Rising Health Insurance Premiums." Working Paper No. 11,160. Cambridge, MA: National Bureau of Economic Research.

Bailey, Deborah Smith. 2003. "Alternatives to Incarceration: Drug and Mental Health Courts Give Offenders What They Really Need: Treatment." *Monitor on Psychology* 34(7): 54.

Baker, John, Kathleen Lynch, Sara Cantillon, and Judy Walsh. 2004. *Equality: From Theory to Action.* Hampshire, U.K. and New York: Palgrave Macmillan.

Baker, Michael, Jonathan Gruber, and Kevin Milligan. 2005. "Universal Childcare, Maternal Labor Supply, and Family Well-Being." Working Paper No. 11,832. Cambridge, MA: National Bureau of Economic Research.

Bankman, Joseph, and Thomas Griffith. 1987. "Social Welfare and the Rate Structure: A New Look at Progressive Taxation." *California Law Review* 75(6): 1905–67.

Barnow, Burt S., and Christopher T. King. 1999. "Strategies for Improving the Odds." In *Improving the Odds: Increasing the Effectiveness of Publicly Funded Training,* edited by Burt S. Barnow and Christopher T. King (235–45). Washington, DC: Urban Institute Press.

Bartik, Timothy J. 2001. *Jobs for the Poor: Can Labor Demand Policies Help?* New York: Russell Sage Foundation.

Bassi, Laurie J. 1995. "Stimulating Employment and Increasing Opportunity for the Current Work Force." In *The Work Alternative: Welfare Reform and the Realities of the Job Market,* edited by Demetra Smith Nightingale and Robert Haveman (137–56). Washington, DC: Urban Institute Press.

Beatty, Phillip, Barry Holman, and Vincent Schiraldi. 2000. "Poor Prescription: The Costs of Imprisoning Drug Offenders in the United States." San Francisco, CA: Center on Juvenile and Criminal Justice.

Becker, Gary S. 1968. "Crime and Punishment: An Economic Approach." *Journal of Political Economy* 76: 169–217.

Bell, Stephanie A., and L. Randall Wray. 2004. "The War on Poverty after 40 Years: A Minskyan Assessment." Public Policy Brief No. 78. Annandale-on-Hudson, NY: Levy Economics Institute, Bard College.

Berman, Greg, and John Feinblatt. 2003. "Problem-Solving Justice: A Quiet Revolution." *Judicature* 86(4): 182–83.

Bernhardt, Annette, and Thomas Bailey. 1998. "Improving Worker Welfare in the Age of Flexibility." *Challenge* 41(5): 16–44.

Bernstein, Jared, and Dean Baker. 2003. *The Benefits of Full Employment: When Markets Work for People.* Washington, DC: Economic Policy Institute.

Bernstein, Jared, and Ellen Houston. 2000. *Crime and Work: What We Can Learn from the Low-Wage Labor Market.* Washington, DC: Economic Policy Institute.

Bernstein, Jared, and Isaac Shapiro. 2005. "Unhappy Anniversary: Federal Minimum Wage Remains Unchanged for Eighth Straight Year, Falls to 56-Year Low Relative to the Average Wage." Washington, DC: Center on Budget and Policy Priorities and Economic Policy Institute.

Bernstein, Jared, Elizabeth McNichol, and Karen Lyons. 2005. "Pulling Apart: A State-by-State Analysis of Income Trends." Washington, DC: Center on Budget and Policy Priorities.

Berube, Alan. 2003. *Rewarding Work through the Tax Code: The Power and Potential of the Earned Income Tax Credit in 27 Cities and Rural Areas.* Center on Urban and Metropolitan Policy, EITC Series. Washington, DC: The Brookings Institution.

Berube, Alan, William G. Gale, and Tracy Kornblatt. 2005. "Tax Policies to Help Working Families." Tax Policy Center Discussion Paper No. 24. Washington, DC: The Urban Institute.

Berube, Alan, Anne Kim, Benjamin Forman, and Megan Burns. 2002. *The Price of Paying Taxes: How Tax Preparation and Refund Loan Fees Erode the Benefits of the EITC.* Survey Series. Washington DC: The Brookings Institution and Progressive Policy Institute.

Beshears, John, James J. Choi, David Laibson, and Brigette C. Madrian. 2006. "The Importance of Default Options for Retirement Savings Outcomes: Evidence from the United States." Working Paper No. 2006-2. Philadelphia, PA: Pension Research Council.

Besl, John R., and Balkrishna D. Kale. 1996. "Older Workers in the 21st Century: Active and Educated, a Case Study." *Monthly Labor Review* 119(6): 18–28.

Bhandari, Shailesh, and Elizabeth Gifford. 2003. *Children with Health Insurance: 2001.* Current Population Report No. P60-224. Washington, DC: U.S. Bureau of the Census.

Bittker, Boris I. 1969a. "Accounting for Federal 'Tax Subsidies' in the National Budget." *National Tax Journal* 22: 244–61.

————. 1969b. "The Tax Expenditure Budget—A Reply to Professors Surrey and Hellmuth." *National Tax Journal* 22: 538–42.

————. 1975. "Federal Income Taxation and the Family." *Stanford Law Review* 27(6): 1389–1463.

Blakely, Stephen. 1999. "Executive Summary." In *Severing the Link Between Health Insurance and Employment*, edited by Dallas L. Salisbury (xviii–xxv). Washington, DC: Employee Benefit Research Institute.

Blank, Rebecca M. 1995. "Outlook for the U.S. Labor Market and Prospects for Low-Wage Entry Level Jobs." In *The Work Alternative: Welfare Reform and the Realities of the Job Market*, edited by Demetra Smith Nightingale and Robert H. Haveman (33–69). Washington, DC: Urban Institute Press.

————. 1997. *It Takes a Nation: A New Agenda for Fighting Poverty*. Princeton, NJ: Princeton University Press.

————. 2002a. "Can Equity and Efficiency Complement Each Other?" *Land Economics* 9(4): 451–68.

————. 2002b. "Evaluating Welfare Reform in the United States." *Journal of Economic Literature* 40(4): 1105–66.

Blank, Rebecca M., David Card, and Philip K. Robins. 1999. "Financial Incentives for Increasing Work and Income among Low-Income Families." Working Paper No. 69. Chicago, IL: Joint Center for Poverty Research, Northwestern University/University of Chicago.

Blassi, Laurie J. 1995. "Stimulating Employment and Increasing Opportunity for the Current Work Force." In *The Work Alternative: Welfare Reform and the Realities of the Job Market*, edited by Demetra Smith Nightingale and Robert Haveman (137–56). Washington, DC: Urban Institute Press.

Blau, Francine D., and Lawrence M. Kahn. 2000. "Gender Differences in Pay." *Journal of Economic Perspectives* 14(4): 75–99.

Blinder, Alan S. 1974. *Toward an Economic Theory of Income Distribution*. Cambridge, MA: MIT Press.

Bloom, Dan, and Charles Michalopoulos. 2001. "The Next Generation: How Welfare and Work Policies Affect Employment and Income. A Synthesis of Research." New York: Manpower Demonstration Research Corporation.

BLS. See U.S. Department of Labor, Bureau of Labor Statistics.

Blumberg, Linda J., and Len M. Nichols. 2004. "Why Are So Many Americans Uninsured?" In *Health Policy and the Uninsured*, edited by Catherine McLaughlin (35–95). Washington, DC: Urban Institute Press.

Blumenthal, Marsha, and Joel Slemrod. 1992. "The Compliance Cost of the U.S. Individual Income Tax System: A Second Look After Tax Reform." *National Tax Journal* 45(2): 185–202.

Board of Trustees of the Federal Old-Age and Survivors Insurance and Disability Insurance Trust Funds. 2006. *2006 Annual Report of the Board of Trustees of the Federal Old-Age and Survivors Insurance and Disability Insurance Trust Funds*. Washington, DC: Board of Trustees of the Federal Old-Age and Survivors Insurance and Disability Insurance Trust Funds.

Boards of Trustees of the Federal Hospital Insurance and Federal Supplementary Medical Insurance Trust Funds. 2006. *2006 Annual Report of the Boards of Trustees of the Federal Hospital Insurance and Federal Supplementary Medical Insurance Trust Funds*. Washington, DC: Boards of Trustees of the Federal Hospital Insurance and Federal Supplementary Medical Insurance Trust Funds.

Bok, Derek. 1993. *The Cost of Talent: How Executives Are Paid and How It Affects America.* New York: The Free Press.

Bonczar, Thomas P. 2003. "Prevalence of Imprisonment in the U.S. Population, 1974–2001." Publication NCJ 197976. Washington, DC: U.S. Department of Justice, Office of Justice Programs.

Book, Leslie. 2003. "The Poor and Tax Compliance: One Size Does Not Fit All." *University of Kansas Law Review* 51(5): 1145–95.

Boortz, Neil, and John Linder. 2005. *The Fair Tax Book: Saying Goodbye to the Income Tax and the IRS.* New York: Regan Books.

Borass, Stephanie, and William M. Rogers III. 2003. "How Does Gender Play a Role in the Earnings Gap? An Update." *Monthly Labor Review* 126(3): 9–15.

Borjas, George J. 2002. "The Wage Structure and the Sorting of Workers into the Public Sector." Working Paper No. 9,313. Cambridge, MA: National Bureau of Economic Research.

———. 2003. "The Labor Demand Curve Is Downward Sloping: Reexamining the Impact of Immigration on the Labor Market." Working Paper No. 9,755. Cambridge, MA: National Bureau of Economic Research.

Boushey, Heather. 2002. "Staying Employed after Welfare: Work Supports and Job Quality Vital to Employment Tenure and Wage Growth." Briefing Paper No. 128. Washington, DC: Economic Policy Institute.

Boushey, Heather, Chauna Brocht, Bethney Gundersen, and Jared Bernstein. 2001. *Hardship in America: The Real Story of Working Families.* Washington, DC: Economic Policy Institute.

Bowler, Mary. 1999. "Women's Earnings: An Overview." *Monthly Labor Review* 122(12): 13–21.

Bowles, Samuel, Herbert Gintis, and Melissa Osborne, eds. 2005. *Unequal Chances: Family Background and Economic Success.* Princeton, NJ: Princeton University Press.

Bradbury, Katherine, and Jane Katz. 2002. "Are Lifetime Incomes Growing More Unequal? Looking at New Evidence on Family Income Mobility." *Regional Review: The Federal Reserve Bank of Boston* 12(4): 2–5.

Bradford, David J. 2005. "A Tax System for the Twenty-first Century." In *Toward Fundamental Tax Reform,* edited by Alan J. Auerbach and Kevin A. Hassett (11–33). Washington, DC: AEI Press.

Bradford, David, and the U.S. Treasury Tax Policy Staff. 1984. *Blueprints for Tax Reform.* 2nd ed. Arlington, VA: Tax Analysts.

Brazer, Harvey E. 1969. "The Federal Income Tax and the Poor." *California Law Review* 57 (April): 422–49.

Brien, Michael J., Stacy Dickert-Conlin, and David A. Weaver. 2004. "Marriage Penalties in Public Programs: Social Security's Child-in-Care Widow(er) Benefits." *National Tax Journal* 57(4): 829–46.

Brooks, Sarah, and R. Kent Weaver. 2005. "Lashed to the Mast? The Politics of Notional Defined Contribution Pension Reforms." Working Paper No. 2005-04. Boston, MA: Center for Retirement Research at Boston College.

Browne, Jeffrey C. 2003. "Public Policy that Makes Work Pay: Releasing the Working Poor from the Tax Trap" Milwaukee, WI: Public Policy Forum.

Browning, Edgar K. 1977. "Commentaries (on papers in a section entitled, Where Do We Go from Here?)" In *Income Redistribution,* edited by Colin D. Campbell (207–10). Lanham, MD: Rowman and Littlefield.

———. 1987. "On the Marginal Welfare Cost of Taxation." *American Economic Review* 77(1): 11–23.

———. 1995. "Effects of the Earned Income Tax Credit on Income and Welfare." *National Tax Journal* 48(1): 23–43.

Buchmueller, Thomas C., and Robert G. Valletta. 1999. "The Effect of Health Insurance on Married Female Labor Supply." *Journal of Human Resources* 34(1): 42–70.

Buchmueller, Thomas C., John E. DiNardo, and Robert G. Valletta. 2005. "A Submerging Labor Market Institution? Unions and the Nonwage Aspects of Work." In *Emerging Labor Market Institutions for the Twenty-First Century*, edited by Richard B. Freeman, Joni Hersch, and Lawrence Mishel (211–63). Chicago, IL, and London: University of Chicago Press.

Buckley, John E. 2005. "Rankings of Full-Time Occupations, by Annual Earnings, July 2004." *Compensation and Working Conditions Online*, November 30.

Buckley, John E., and Robert W. Van Glezen. 2004. "Federal Statistics on Health Care Benefits and Cost Trends: An Overview." *Monthly Labor Review* 127(11): 43–56.

Budetti, Peter P., Richard V. Burkhauser, Janice M. Gregory, and H. Allan Hunt, eds. 2001. *Ensuring Health and Income Security for an Aging Workforce.* Kalamazoo, MI: W.E. Upjohn Institute for Employment Research.

Buessing, Marric, and Maurice Soto. 2006. "The State of Private Pensions: Current 5500 Data." Issue in Brief No. 42. Boston, MA: Center for Retirement Research at Boston College.

Burke, Thomas P. 2000. "Social Security Earnings Limit Removed." *Compensation and Working Conditions* (Summer): 44–46.

Burkhauser, Richard V., and Joseph F. Quinn. 1997. "Pro-Work Policy Proposals for Older Americans in the 21st Century." Policy Brief No. 9. Syracuse, NY: Syracuse University Maxwell School of Citizenship and Public Affairs, Center for Policy Research.

Burkhauser, Richard V., and David C. Stapleton. 2003. "Employing Those Not Expected to Work: The Stunning Changes in the Employment of Single Mothers and People with Disabilities in the United States in the 1990s." Ithaca, NY: Rehabilitation Research and Training Center for Economic Research on Employment Policy for Persons with Disabilities, Cornell University.

Burman, Leonard E. 2000. Testimony of Treasury Deputy Assistant Secretary Leonard E. Burman before the Senate Appropriations Subcommittee on Treasury and General Government, April 13.

———. 2003. "Is the Tax Expenditure Concept Still Relevant?" *National Tax Journal* 56(3): 613–27.

Burman, Leonard E., and Jonathan Gruber. 2005. "Tax Credits for Health Insurance." Tax Policy Issues and Options Brief 11. Washington, DC: The Urban Institute.

Burman, Leonard E., and Deborah I. Kobes. 2003. "EITC Reaches More Families than TANF, Food Stamps." *Tax Notes* (March 17): 1769.

Burman, Leonard E., and Troy Kravitz. 2004. "Lower-Income Households Spend Largest Share of Income." *Tax Notes* (November 8): 875.

Burman, Leonard, and Mohammed Adeel Saleem. 2003. "Hidden Taxes and Subsidies." *Tax Notes* (September 15): 1437.

Burman, Leonard E., Norma B. Coe, and William G. Gale. 1999. "Lump Sum Distributions from Pension Plans: Recent Evidence and Issues for Policy and Research." *National Tax Journal* 52(3): 553–91.

Burman, Leonard E., William G. Gale, and Jeffrey Rohaly. 2003. "The AMT: Projections and Problems." *Tax Notes* (July 7): 105–17.

Burman, Leonard E., Richard W. Johnson, and Deborah I. Kobes. 2004. "Pensions, Health Insurance, and Tax Incentives." Tax Policy Center Discussion Paper 14. Washington, DC: The Urban Institute.

Burman, Leonard E., Elaine Maag, and Jeffrey Rohaly. 2005. "Tax Credits to Help Low-Income Families Pay for Child Care." Tax Policy Issues and Options Brief 14. Washington, DC: The Urban Institute.

Burtless, Gary. 1990. "The Economist's Lament: Public Assistance in America." *Journal of Economic Perspectives* 4(1): 57–78.

———. 1995. "Employment Prospects of Welfare Recipients." In *The Work Alternative: Welfare Reform and the Realities of the Job Market,* edited by Demetra Smith Nightingale and Robert Haveman (71–106). Washington, DC: Urban Institute Press.

———. 1998. "Can the Labor Market Absorb Three Million Welfare Recipients?" *University of Wisconsin-Madison Institute for Research on Poverty Focus* 19(3): 1–6.

———. 1999. "An Economic View of Retirement." In *Behavioral Dimensions of Retirement Economics,* edited by Henry J. Aaron (7–42). Washington, DC: Brookings Institution Press.

Burtless, Gary, and David Greenberg. 1983. "Measuring the Impact of NIT Experiments on Work Effort." *Industrial and Labor Relations Review* 36(4): 592–605.

Burtless, Gary, and Christopher Jencks. 2003. "American Inequality and Its Consequences." In *Agenda for the Nation,* edited by Henry J. Aaron, James M. Lindsay, and Pietro S. Nivola (61–108). Washington, DC: Brookings Institution Press.

Burtless, Gary, and Joseph F. Quinn. 2001. "Retirement Trends and Policies to Encourage Work among Older Americans." In *Ensuring Health and Income Security for an Aging Workforce,* edited by Peter P. Budetti, Richard V. Burkhauser, Janice M. Gregory, and H. Allan Hunt (375–415). Kalamazoo, MI: W.E. Upjohn Institute for Employment Research.

———. 2002. "Is Working Longer the Answer for an Aging Workforce?" Issue in Brief No. 11. Boston, MA: Center for Retirement Research at Boston College.

Butrica, Barbara, Karen Smith, and Eugene Steuerle. 2006. "Working for a Good Retirement." Working Paper No. 2006-8. Boston, MA: Center for Retirement Research at Boston College.

Cagetti, Marco, and Mariacristina De Nardi. 2005. "Wealth Inequality: Data and Models." Working Paper No. 2005-10. Chicago, IL: Federal Reserve Bank of Chicago.

Calabrese, Michael, and Lauri Rubiner. 2004. "Universal Coverage, Universal Responsibility: A Roadmap to Make Coverage Affordable for All Americans" Working Paper No. 1. Washington, DC: New America Foundation.

Campbell, Sharyn. 1996. "Hybrid Retirement Plans: The Retirement Income System Continues to Evolve." Issue Brief No. 171. Washington, DC: Employee Benefit Research Institute.

Cancian, Maria, Robert Haveman, Thomas Kaplan, Daniel Meyer, and Barbara Wolfe. 1999. "Work, Earnings and Well-Being after Welfare: What Do We Know?" Working Paper No. 73. Chicago, IL: Joint Center for Poverty Research, Northwestern University/University of Chicago.

Caner, Asena, and Edward N. Wolff. 2004. "Asset Poverty in the United States: Its Persistence in an Expansionary Economy." Public Policy Brief No. 76. Annandale-on-Hudson, NY: Levy Economics Institute, Bard College.

Cappelli, Peter. 2002. "Why Do Employers Pay for College?" Working Paper No. 9,225. Cambridge, MA: National Bureau of Economic Research.

Capps, Randy, Michael Fix, Jeffrey S. Passel, Jason Ost, and Dan Perez-Lopez. 2003. "A Profile of the Low-Wage Immigrant Workforce." Immigrant Families and Workers Brief No. 4. Washington, DC: The Urban Institute.

Carasso, Adam, and Jonathan Barry Forman. 2006. "Tax Considerations in a Mandatory Universal Pension System." Working paper for the Society of Actuaries symposium on "Re-envisioning Work and Retirement in the 21st Century," May.

Carasso, Adam, and C. Eugene Steuerle. 2005. "The Hefty Penalty on Marriage Facing Many Households with Children." *Marriage and Child Wellbeing* 15(2): 157–75.

Carasso, Adam, Jeff Rohaly, and C. Eugene Steuerle. 2005. "A Unified Children's Tax Credit." *National Tax Association Proceedings, Ninety-Seventh Annual Conference 2004* (221–31). Washington, DC: National Tax Association.

Card, David, and Alan Krueger. 1995. *Myth and Measurement: The New Economics of the Minimum Wage.* Princeton, NJ: Princeton University Press.

Casey, Bernard. 1997. "Incentives and Disincentives to Early and Late Retirement." Ageing Working Paper No. AWP 3.3. Paris: Organisation for Economic Co-operation and Development.

Catts, Timothy. 2003. "Kucinich Launches Tax Plan for Capital Hill and Campaign Trail." *Tax Notes* (December 15): 1264–66.

Cauthen, Kenneth. 1987. *The Passion for Equality.* Lanham, MD: Rowman and Littlefield.

Cavenaugh, Maureen B. 2003. "Tax as Gatekeeper: Why Company Stock Is Not Worth the Money." *Virginia Tax Review* 23(2): 365–415.

CBO. See Congressional Budget Office.

Census Bureau. See U.S. Bureau of the Census.

Center for American Progress. 2005. "A Fair and Simple Tax System for Our Future." *Tax Notes* (May 9): 767–79.

Century Foundation, The. 2000. *Immigration Reform: The Basics.* New York: The Century Foundation.

———. 2002. *Bad Breaks All Around: The Report of the Century Foundation Working Group on Tax Expenditures.* New York: Century Foundation Press.

Chapman, Jeff, and Michael Ettlinger. 2004. "The Who and Why of the Minimum Wage: Raising the Wage Floor Is an Essential Part of a Strategy to Support Working Families." Issue Brief No. 201. Washington, DC: Economic Policy Institute.

Chen, Yung-Ping. 2002. "Social Security Reform: Assuring Solvency or Improving Benefits." *Journal of Financial Service Professionals* (July): 29–41.

Chen, Yung-Ping, and John C. Scott. 2006. "Phased Retirement: Who Opts for It and Toward What End?" Research Report No. 2006-1. Washington, DC: AARP Public Policy Institute.

Chester, C. Ronald. 1976. "Inheritance and Wealth Taxation in a Just Society." *Rutgers Law Review* 30: 62–101.

———. 1982. *Inheritance, Wealth, and Society.* Bloomington: Indiana University Press.

Chirelstein, Marvin A. 2002. *Federal Income Taxation.* 9th ed. New York: Foundation Press.

Choi, James J., David Laibson, and Brigette C. Madrian. 2006. "Reducing the Complexity Costs of 401(k) Participation through Quick Enrollment™." Working Paper No. 2006-3. Philadelphia, PA: Pension Research Council.

Citizens for Tax Justice. 2003. "Effects of First Three Bush Tax Cuts Charted." Washington, DC: Citizens for Tax Justice.

———. 2005. "International Tax Comparisons, 1965–2003 (federal, state & local)." Washington, DC: Citizens for Tax Justice.

Citro, Constance F., and Robert T. Michael, eds. 1995. *Measuring Poverty: A New Approach.* Washington, DC: National Academy Press.

Clark, Robert L., Richard Burkauser, Marilyn Moon, Joseph Quinn, and Timothy M. Smeeding. 2004. *The Economics of an Aging Society.* Malden, MA: Blackwell Publishing.

Clear, Todd R. 1996. "Backfire: When Incarceration Increases Crime." *Journal of the Oklahoma Criminal Justice Research Consortium,* vol. 3. Oklahoma City: Oklahoma Criminal Justice Research Consortium.

Cleveland, Robert W. 2005. "Alternative Income Estimates in the United States: 2003." Current Population Report No. P60-228. Washington, DC: U.S. Bureau of the Census.

Coe, Norma B., Gregory Acs, Robert I. Lerman, and Keith Watson. 1998. "Does Work Pay? A Summary of the Work Incentives under TANF." *Assessing the New Federalism* Policy Brief A-28. Washington, DC: The Urban Institute.

Cogan, John F., and Olivia S. Mitchell. 2003. "Perspectives from the President's Commission on Social Security Reform." *Journal of Economic Perspectives* 17(2): 149–72.

Cohen, Sheldon S. 1969. "Administrative Aspects of a Negative Income Tax." *University of Pennsylvania Law Review* 117(5): 678–730.

Committee for Economic Development. 1995. *Who Will Pay for Your Retirement? The Looming Crisis.* New York: Committee for Economic Development.

———. 1997. *Fixing Social Security.* New York: Committee for Economic Development.

———. 1999. *New Opportunities for Older Workers.* New York: Committee for Economic Development.

———. 2000. *Welfare Reform and Beyond: Making Work Work.* New York: Committee for Economic Development.

———. 2002. *Preschool for All: Investing in a Productive and Just Society.* New York: Committee for Economic Development.

———. 2005a. "Fixing Social Security: A CED Policy Update." New York: Committee for Economic Development.

———. 2005b. *A New Tax Framework: A Blueprint for Averting a Fiscal Crisis.* New York: Committee for Economic Development.

Conaway, Carrie. 2003. "Accidents Will Happen: So What Improves Workplace Safety?" *The Federal Reserve Bank of Boston Regional Review* 13(3): 11–19.

Congressional Budget Office. 1986. *Earnings Sharing Options for the Social Security System.* Washington, DC: Congressional Budget Office.

————. 1996a. "Labor Supply and Taxes." CBO Memorandum. Washington, DC: Congressional Budget Office.

————. 1996b. *Reducing the Deficit: Spending and Revenue Options.* Washington, DC: Congressional Budget Office.

————. 1997. *For Better or For Worse: Marriage and the Federal Income Tax.* Washington, DC: U.S. Government Printing Office.

————. 2003a. *Baby Boomers' Retirement Prospects: An Overview.* Washington, DC: Congressional Budget Office.

————. 2003b. *Effective Federal Tax Rates, 1997 to 2000.* CBO paper. Washington, DC: Congressional Budget Office.

————. 2004a. "CBO's Projections of the Labor Force." Background paper. Washington, DC: Congressional Budget Office.

————. 2004b. *Effective Tax Rates under Current Law, 2001 to 2014.* CBO paper. Washington, DC: Congressional Budget Office.

————. 2004c. *Estimating the Value of Subsidies for Federal Loans and Loan Guarantees.* CBO study. Washington, DC: Congressional Budget Office.

————. 2005a. *Budget Options.* CBO study. Washington, DC: Congressional Budget Office.

————. 2005b. *Effective Marginal Tax Rates on Labor Income.* CBO paper. Washington, DC: Congressional Budget Office.

————. 2005c. "Historical Effective Federal Tax Rates: 1979–2003." Washington, DC: Congressional Budget Office.

————. 2005d. *The Long-Term Budget Outlook.* CBO study. Washington, DC: Congressional Budget Office.

————. 2005e. *The Role of Immigrants in the U.S. Labor Market.* CBO paper. Washington, DC: Congressional Budget Office.

————. 2006a. "Long-Term Analysis of the Liebman-MacGuineas-Samwick Proposal." Washington, DC: Congressional Budget Office.

————. 2006b. *Utilization of Tax Incentives for Retirement Savings: An Update.* Background paper. Washington, DC: Congressional Budget Office.

Conison, Jay. 2003. *Employee Benefit Plans in a Nutshell.* 3rd ed. St. Paul, MN: Thomson/West.

Cooper, George. 1979. "Taking Wealth Taxation Seriously." *Record of the Association of the Bar of the City of New York* 34: 24–57.

Copeland, Craig. 2005a. "Employee Tenure: Stable Overall, But Male and Female Trends Differ." *Employee Benefit Research Institute Notes* 22(3): 2–10.

————. 2005b. "Employment-Based Retirement and Pension Plan Participation: Geographic Differences and Trends, 2004." Issue Brief No. 286. Washington, DC: Employee Benefit Research Institute.

————. 2005c. "Lump-Sum Distributions." *Employee Benefit Research Institute Notes* 26(12): 7–17.

————. 2006a. "IRA and Keogh Assets and Contributions." *Employee Benefit Research Institute Notes* 27(1): 2–9.

————. 2006b. "Retirement Plan Participation and Retirees' Perception of Their Standard of Living." Issue Brief No. 289. Washington, DC: Employee Benefit Research Institute.

Corak, Miles, Christine Lietz, and Holly Sutherland. 2005. "The Impact of Tax and Transfer Systems on Children in the European Union." Working Paper No. 2005-04. Florence, Italy: UNICEF Innocenti Research Center.

Costa, Dora. 1999. "Has the Trend Toward Early Retirement Reversed?" Paper presented at the First Annual Joint Conference for the Retirement Research Consortium, "New Developments in Retirement Research," Washington, D.C., May 20–21.

Costo, Stephanie L. 2006. "Trends in Retirement Plan Coverage over the Last Decade." *Monthly Labor Review* 129(2): 58–64.

Council of Economic Advisers. 1999a. *Economic Report of the President 1999.* Washington, DC: U.S. Government Printing Office.

———. 1999b. *Families and the Labor Market, 1969–1999: Analyzing the "Time Crunch."* Washington, DC: Council of Economic Advisers.

———. 1999c. "Technical Report: The Effects of Welfare Policy and the Economic Expansion on Welfare Caseloads: An Update." Washington, DC: Council of Economic Advisers.

———. 2005. *Economic Report of the President 2005.* Washington, DC: U.S. Government Printing Office.

———. 2006. *Economic Report of the President 2006.* Washington, DC: U.S. Government Printing Office.

Cremer, Helmuth, and Peter Pestieau. 2003. "Wealth Transfer Taxation: A Survey." Working Paper No. 393. Annandale-on-Hudson, NY: Levy Economics Institute, Bard College.

Crimmel, Beth Levin, and Jeffrey L. Schildkraut. 2001. "Stock Option Plans Surveyed by NCS." *Compensation and Working Conditions Online,* spring: 3–21.

Cunningham, Noel B., and Deborah H. Schenk. 1993. "Colloquium on Capital Gains: The Case for a Capital Gains Preference." *New York University Tax Law Review* 48 (Spring): 319–80.

Currie, Janet. 2001. "Early Childhood Education Programs." *Journal of Economic Perspectives* 15(2): 213–38.

———. 2006. "The Take-Up of Social Benefits." In *Public Policy and the Income Distribution,* edited by Alan J. Auerbach, David Card, and John M. Quigley (80–148). New York: Russell Sage Foundation.

Cushing, Matthew J. 2005. "Net Marginal Social Security Tax Rates over the Life Cycle." *National Tax Journal* 58(2): 227–45.

Cutler, David M. 1997. "Public Policy for Health Care." In *Fiscal Policy: Lessons from Economic Research,* edited by Alan J. Auerbach (159–98). Cambridge, MA: MIT Press.

Dalaker, Joe. 2005. *Alternative Poverty Estimates in the United States: 2003.* Current Population Report No. P60-227. Washington, DC: U.S. Bureau of the Census.

Daniels, Norman. 1978. "Merit and Meritocracy." *Philosophy and Public Affairs* 7(3): 206–23.

Danziger, Sheldon. 1987. "Tax Reform, Poverty and Inequality." Discussion Paper No. 829-87. Madison: University of Wisconsin Institute for Research on Poverty.

Danziger, Sheldon, and Deborah Reed. 1999. "Winners and Losers: The Era of Inequality Continues." *Brookings Review* 17(4): 14–17.

Danziger, Sheldon, Colleen M. Heflin, Mary E. Corcoran, Elizabeth Oltmans, and Hui-Chen Wang. 2002. "Does It Pay to Move from Welfare to Work?" Working Paper No. 254. Chicago, IL: Joint Center for Poverty Research, Northwestern University/University of Chicago.

Davies, John H. 1984. "Income-Plus-Wealth: In Search of a Better Tax Base." *Rutgers Law Review* 15(4): 849–96.

Davis, Steven J., and Magnus Henrekson. 2004. "Tax Effects on Work Activity, Industry Mix, and Shadow Economy Size: Evidence from Rich-Country Comparisons." Working Paper No. 10,509. Cambridge, MA: National Bureau of Economic Research.

Day, Jennifer Cheeseman, with Amie Jamieson. 2003. "School Enrollment: 2000." Census 2000 Brief No. C2KBR-26. Washington, DC: U.S. Bureau of the Census.

Day, Jennifer Cheeseman, and Eric C. Newburger. 2002. "The Big Payoff: Educational Attainment and Synthetic Estimates of Work-Life Earnings." Current Population Report No. P23-210. Washington, DC: U.S. Bureau of the Census.

Delorme, Luke, Alicia Munnell, and Anthony Webb. 2006. "Empirical Regularity Suggests Retirement Risks." Issue in Brief No. 41. Boston, MA: Center for Retirement Research at Boston College.

DeNavas-Walt, Carmen, and Robert W. Cleveland. 2002. *Money Income in the United States: 2001.* Current Population Report No. P60-218. Washington, DC: U.S. Government Printing Office.

DeNavas-Walt, Carmen, Bernadette D. Proctor, and Cheryl Hill Lee. 2005. *Income, Poverty, and Health Insurance Coverage in the United States: 2004.* Current Population Report No. P60-229. Washington, DC: U.S. Government Printing Office.

DeWitt, Larry. 1996. "Details of Ida May Fuller's Payroll Tax Contributions." Social Security Administration Historian's Office Research Note No. 3. Washington, DC: Social Security Administration.

Diamond, Peter A. 2005. "Pensions for an Aging Population." Working Paper No. 11,877. Cambridge, MA: National Bureau of Economic Research.

Dick, James C. 1975. "How to Justify a Distribution of Earnings." *Philosophy and Public Affairs* 4(3): 248–72.

Dickert-Conlin, Stacy, and Scott Houser. 1998. "Taxes and Transfers: A New Look at the Marriage Penalty." *National Tax Journal* 51(2): 175–218.

———. 2002. "EITC and Marriage." *National Tax Journal* 55(1): 25–39.

Dickert-Conlin, Stacy, Katie Fitzpatrick, and Andrew Hanson. 2005. "Utilization of Income Tax Credits by Low-Income Individuals." *National Tax Journal* 58(4): 743–85.

Dilley, Patricia E. 2004. "Hope We Die Before We Get Old: The Attack on Retirement." *Elder Law Journal* 12(2): 245–325.

Dodge, Joseph M. 1978. "Beyond Estate and Gift Reform: Including Gifts and Bequests in Income." *Harvard Law Review* 91: 1177–1211.

———. 1995. "A Democratic Tax Manifesto." *Tax Notes* (February 27): 1313–30.

DOL. See U.S. Department of Labor.

Domestic Policy Council, Low-Income Opportunity Working Group. 1986. "Up from Dependency: A New National Public Assistance Strategy. Report to the President by the Domestic Policy Council." Washington, DC: The White House.

Donaldson, Samuel A. 2003. "The Easy Case Against Tax Simplification." *Virginia Tax Review* 22(4): 645–746.

Dorn, Stan. 2004. "Towards Incremental Progress: Key Facts about Groups of Uninsured." Washington, DC: Economic and Social Policy Research.

Dorsey, Stuart. 2000. "Current Policy Issues towards Private Pensions in Canada and the United States." In *Employee Benefits and Labor Markets in Canada and the United States,* edited by William T. Alpert and Stephen A. Woodbury (413–50). Kalamazoo, MI: W.E. Upjohn Institute for Employment Research.

Dorsey, Stuart, Christopher Cornwell, and David Macpherson. 1998. *Pensions and Productivity.* Kalamazoo, MI: W.E. Upjohn Institute for Employment Research.

Dubay, Curtis S., and Scott A. Hodge. 2006. "State Business Tax Climate Index." Background Paper No. 51. Washington, DC: Tax Foundation.

Dubay, Lisa, Ian Hill, and Genevieve M. Kenney. 2002. "Five Things Everyone Should Know about SCHIP." *Assessing the New Federalism* Policy Brief A-55. Washington, DC: The Urban Institute.

Duggan, James E., Robert Gillingham, and John S. Greenlees. 1995. "Progressive Returns to Social Security? An Answer from Social Security Records." Research Paper No. 9,501. Washington, DC: U.S. Treasury Department, Office of the Assistant Secretary for Economic Policy.

Duggan, Mark, Perry Singleton, and Jae Song. 2005. "Aching to Retire? The Rise in the Full Retirement Age and Its Impact on the Disability Rolls." Working Paper No. 11,811. Cambridge, MA: National Bureau of Economic Research.

Dulitzky, Daniel. 1999. "Incentives for Early Retirement In Private and Health Insurance Plans." Retirement Project Series Paper No. 3. Washington, DC: The Urban Institute.

Dworkin, Ronald. 1981a. "What Is Equality? Part 1: Equality and Welfare." *Philosophy & Public Affairs* 10(3): 185–246.

———. 1981b. "What Is Equality? Part 2: Equality of Resources." *Philosophy & Public Affairs* 10(4): 283–345.

Dynarski, Susan M. 2004. "Who Benefits from the Education Savings Incentives? Income, Educational Expectations, and the Value of the 529 and Coverdell." Working Paper No. 10,470. Cambridge, MA: National Bureau of Economic Research.

Edelman, Peter, Harry J. Holzer, and Paul Offner. 2006. *Reconnecting Disadvantaged Young Men.* Washington, DC: Urban Institute Press.

Ehrenberg, Ronald G., and Robert S. Smith. 1996. *Modern Labor Economics: Theory and Public Policy.* 6th ed. Reading, MA: Addison-Wesly.

Ehrenreich, Barbara. 2001. *Nickel and Dimed: On (Not) Getting By in America.* New York: Metropolitan Books, Henry Holt and Company, LLC.

———. 2005a. *Bait and Switch: The (Futile) Pursuit of the American Dream.* New York: Metropolitan Books.

———. 2005b. "Earth to Wal-Mars." In *Inequality Matters: The Growing Economic Divide in America and Its Poisonous Consequences,* edited by James Lardner and David A. Smith (41–53). New York and London: The New Press.

Eisenbrey, Ross, and Jared Bernstein. 2003. "Eliminating the Right to Overtime Pay: Department of Labor Proposal Means Lower Pay, Longer Hours for Millions of Workers." Briefing paper. Washington, DC: Economic Policy Institute.

Eissa, Nada. 1996. "Tax Reforms and Labor Supply." In *Tax Policy and the Economy,* vol. 10, edited by James Poterba (119–51). Cambridge, MA: MIT Press.

Eissa, Nada, and Hilary Hoynes. 1999. "The Earned Income Tax Credit and the Labor Supply of Married Couples." Working Paper No. 6,856. Cambridge, MA: National Bureau of Economic Research.

———. 2005. "Behavioral Responses to Taxes: Lessons from the EITC and Labor Supply." Working Paper No. 11,729. Cambridge, MA: National Bureau of Economic Research.

Eissa, Nada, Henrik Jacobsen Kleven, and Claus Thustrup Kreiner. 2004. "Evaluation of Four Tax Reforms in the United States: Labor Supply and Welfare Effects for Single Mothers." Working Paper No. 10,935. Cambridge, MA: National Bureau of Economic Research.

Ellwood, David. 2000a. "Anti-Poverty Policy for Families in the Next Century: From Welfare to Work—and Worries." *Journal of Economic Perspectives* 14(1): 187 98.

———. 2000b. "The Impact of the Earned Income Tax Credit and Social Policy Reforms on Work, Marriage, and Living Arrangements." *National Tax Journal* 53(4): 1073–1106.

———. 2001. "The Sputtering Labor Force of the 21st Century: Can Social Policy Help?" Working Paper No. 8,321. Cambridge, MA: National Bureau of Economic Research.

Ellwood, David T., and Thomas Kane. 2000. "Who Is Getting a College Education? Family Background and the Growing Gaps in Enrollment." In *Securing the Future: Investing in Children from Birth to College*, edited by Sheldon Danziger and Jane Waldfogel (283–313). New York: Russell Sage Foundation.

Ellwood, David T., and Isabel V. Sawhill. 2000. "Fixing the Marriage Penalty in the EITC." Brookings Institution Economics Papers. Washington, DC: The Brookings Institution.

Ellwood, David T., Rebecca M. Blank, Joseph Blasi, Douglas Kruse, William A. Niskanen, and Karen Lynn-Dyson. 2000. *A Working Nation: Workers, Work, and Government in the New Economy*. New York: Russell Sage Foundation.

Emmons, David W., Eva Madly, and Stephen A. Woodbury. 2005. "Refundable Tax Credits for Health Insurance: The Sensitivity of Simulated Impacts to Assumed Behavior." Working Paper 05-119. Kalamazoo, MI: W.E. Upjohn Institute for Employment Research.

Employment Policies Institute. 2000. *Living Wage Policy: The Basics*. Washington, DC: Employment Policies Institute.

Engelhardt, Gary V., and Jonathan Gruber. 2006. "Social Security and the Evolution of Elderly Poverty." In *Public Policy and the Income Distribution*, edited by Alan J. Auerbach, David Card, and John M. Quigley (259–87). New York: Russell Sage Foundation.

Engels, Freidrich. 1881. "A Fair Day's Wages for a Fair Day's Work." *The Labour Standard* No. 1, May 7.

Engler, Mitchell L. 2003. "A Progressive Consumption Tax for Individuals: An Alternative Hybrid Approach." *Alabama Law Review* 54: 1205–49.

Esenwein, Gregg A., and Jane G. Gravelle. 2003. "The Taxation of Dividend Income: An Overview and Economic Analysis of the Issues." Report No. RL31597. Washington, DC: Congressional Research Service, Library of Congress.

Even, William E., and David A. Macpherson. 2003. "Benefits and Productivity." In *Benefits for the Workplace of the Future*, edited by Olivia S. Mitchell, David S. Blitzstein, Michael Gordon, and Judith F. Mazo (43–57). Philadelphia: University of Pennsylvania Press.

————. 2004. "Company Stock in Pension Funds." *National Tax Journal* 57(2, Part 2): 299–313.

Executive Office of the President. 2001. *A Blueprint for New Beginnings: A Responsible Budget for America's Priorities.* Washington, DC: Executive Office of the President.

Executive Office of the President and Office of Management and Budget. 2006a. *Analytical Perspectives, Budget of the United States Government, Fiscal Year 2007.* Washington, DC: U.S. Government Printing Office.

————. 2006b. *Historical Tables, Budget of the United States Government, Fiscal Year 2007.* Washington, DC: U.S. Government Printing Office.

Falivena, Michael. 1990. "Pension Portability: No Easy Solution." *Pensions & Investments,* Feb. 5, 1990. As reprinted in John H. Langbein and Bruce A. Wolk. 2000. *Pension and Employee Benefit Law.* 3rd ed. New York: Foundation Press.

Feenberg, Daniel R., and Harvey S. Rosen. 1994. "Recent Developments in the Marriage Tax." Working Paper No. 4,705. Cambridge, MA: National Bureau of Economic Research.

Fehr, Ernst, and Armin Falk. 2002. "Psychological Foundations of Incentives." Discussion Paper No. 507. Zurich, Switzerland: Institute for the Study of Labor.

Fehr, Hans, John C. Goodman, Sabine Jokisch, and Laurence J. Kotlikoff. 2005. "Tax and Social Security Reform: Thinking Outside the Box." NCPA Policy Report No. 275. Dallas, TX: National Center for Policy Analysis.

Feinberg, Joel. 1970. *Doing and Deserving.* Princeton, NJ: Princeton University Press.

————. 1973. *Social Philosophy.* Englewood Cliffs, NJ: Prentice Hall.

Feldman, Robin Cooper. 2002. "Consumption Taxes and the Theory of General and Individual Taxation." *Virginia Tax Review* 21(3): 293–360.

Feldstein, Martin. 1974. "Unemployment Compensation: Adverse Incentives and Distributional Anomalies." *National Tax Journal* 27 (June): 231–44.

————. 1995. "The Effect of Marginal Tax Rates on Taxable Income: A Panel Study of the 1986 Tax Reform Act." *Journal of Political Economy* 102(3): 551–72.

————. 1999. "Tax Avoidance and the Deadweight Loss of the Income Tax." *Review of Economics and Statistics* 81(4): 674–80.

————. 2005a. "Rethinking Social Insurance." *American Economic Review* 95(1): 1–24.

————. 2005b. "Structural Reform of Social Security." Working Paper No. 11,098. Cambridge, MA: National Bureau of Economic Research.

Feldstein, Martin S., and Daniel Altman. 1998. "Unemployment Insurance Savings Accounts." Working Paper No. 6,860. Cambridge, MA: National Bureau of Economic Research.

Feldstein, Martin S., and Andrew A. Samwick. 1998. "Potential Effects of Two Percent Personal Retirement Accounts." *Tax Notes* (May 4): 615–20.

Fennell, Lee Anne, and Kirk J. Stark. 2004. "Taxation Over Time." Law and Economics Research Paper 5-24. Los Angeles, CA: UCLA School of Law.

Ferrell, Warren. 2005. *Why Men Earn More: The Startling Truth Behind the Pay Gap—and What Women Can Do About It.* New York: AMACOM.

Field, Thomas F. 2003. "The Emperor Has No Clothes." *Tax Notes* (December 1): 1125–27.

Figart, Deborah M., ed. 2004. *Living Wage Movements: Global Perspectives*. London and New York: Routledge.

Fisher, Gordon M. 1992. "The Development and History of the Poverty Thresholds." *Social Security Bulletin* 55(4): 3–14.

———. 1996. "Relative or Absolute—New Light on the Behavior of Poverty Lines Over Time." *Joint Newsletter of the Government Statistics Section and the Social Statistics Section of the American Statistical Association* (July): 10–12.

Fishman, Mike. 2004. "Multiple Work Supports and Services May Help Low-Wage Workers Climb the Economic Ladder." *The Forum* (newsletter from the Research Forum, National Center for Children in Poverty, Columbia University Mailman School of Public Health) 7(3): 1–8.

Forbes, Steve. 2005. *Flat Tax Revolution: Using a Postcard to Abolish the IRS*. Washington, DC: Regnery Publishing, Inc.

Fore, Douglas. 2003. "Do We Have A Retirement Crisis in America?" Research Dialogue No. 77. New York: TIAA-CREF Institute.

Forman, Jonathan Barry. 1986. "The Origins of the Tax Expenditure Budget." *Tax Notes* (February 10): 537–45.

———. 1988. "Improving the Earned Income Credit: Transition to a Wage Subsidy Credit for the Working Poor." *Florida State University Law Review* 16(1): 41–101.

———. 1989. "Beyond President Bush's Child Tax Credit Proposal: Towards a Comprehensive System of Tax Credits to Help Low-income Families with Children." *Emory Law Journal* 38(3): 661–700.

———. 1992. "Promoting Fairness in the Social Security Retirement Program: Partial Integration and a Credit for Dual-Earner Couples." *Tax Lawyer* 45(4): 915–69.

———. 1993a. "Administrative Savings from Synchronizing Social Welfare Programs and Tax Provisions." *Journal of the National Association of Administrative Law Judges* 13(1): 5–76.

———. 1993b. "Time to Cash Out Food Stamps." *Legal Times: Law and Lobbying in the Nation's Capital*, Feb. 22, 36–37.

———. 1993c. "Would a Social Security Tax Expenditure Budget Make Sense?" *Public Budgeting and Financial Management* 5(2): 311–35.

———. 1994. "The Income Tax Treatment of Social Welfare Benefits." *University of Michigan Journal of Law Reform* 26(4): 785–816.

———. 1995. "Universal Pensions." *Chapman Law Review* 2: 95–131.

———. 1996a. "Simplification for Low-Income Taxpayers: Some Options." *Ohio State Law Journal* 57: 145–201.

———. 1996b. "What Can Be Done About Marriage Penalties?" *Family Law Quarterly* 30: 1–22.

———. 1997a. "The Impact of Moving to a Consumption Tax on Pension Plans and Their Beneficiaries." In *Comprehensive Tax Reform: Implications for Economic Security and Employee Benefits*, edited by Dallas L. Salisbury (51–64). Washington, DC: Employee Benefit Research Institute.

———. 1997b. "The Once and Future Social Security Tax Expenditure." *Benefits Quarterly* 13(3): 77–82.

———. 1997c. "Social Security: What Can Be Done About Marriage Penalties?" *Tax Notes* (April 14): 270–73.

———. 1997d. "The Tax Treatment of Public and Private Pensions Around the World." *American Journal of Tax Policy* 14: 299–333.

————. 1998a. "Reforming Social Security to Encourage the Elderly to Work." *Stanford Law and Policy Review* 9: 289–302.

————. 1998b. "Whose Pension Is It Anyway? Protecting Spousal Rights in a Privatized Social Security System." *North Caroline Law Review* 76(5): 1653–85.

————. 1999a. "Jeepers, Creepers, Where'd We Get Those Peepers." *Tax Notes* (December 6): 1335 (letter to the editor).

————. 1999b. "Making Social Security Work for Women and Men." *New York Law School Journal of Human Rights* 16(Part 1): 359–73.

————. 1999c. "Public Pensions: Choosing between Defined Benefit and Defined Contribution Plans." *Law Review of Michigan State University Detroit College of Law* 1999(1): 187–213.

————. 2000a. "How Federal Pension Laws Influence Individual Work and Retirement Decisions." *Tax Lawyer* 54(1): 143–84.

————. 2000b. "Rescue in the Balance: Here's a Plan to Save Social Security That Will Work." *Barron's* (December 18): 54.

————. 2001a. "Comparing Apples and Oranges: Perspectives on the Tax Expenditures Associated with Social Security and Private Pensions." *Employee Rights and Employment Policy Journal* 5(1): 297–326.

————. 2001b. "Saving Social Security with a Cash Balance Plan." In *New York University 59th Institute on Federal Taxation—Employee Benefits & Executive Compensation*, edited by Alvin D. Lurie (3-1–3-29). Newark, NJ: LexisNexis.

————. 2001c. "Simplification for Low-Income Taxpayers: 2001." In *Study of the Overall State of the Federal Tax System and Recommendations for Simplification, Pursuant to Section 8022(3)(B) of the Internal Revenue Code of 1986* by the Joint Committee on Taxation, vol. 3 (10–18). Washington, DC: Joint Committee on Taxation.

————. 2002. "The Social Security Cash Machine." In *Estate Planning Strategies: A Lawyer's Guide to Retirement and Lifetime Planning*, edited by Jay A. Soled (3–9). Chicago, IL: American Bar Association Publishing, Senior Lawyers Division.

————. 2004a. "Making Pensions Work." In *New York University Review of Employee Benefits & Executive Compensation*, edited by Alvin D. Lurie (5-1–5-60). Newark, NJ: LexisNexis.

————. 2004b. "Making Social Security Work." *Ohio State Law Journal* 65(1): 145–83.

Forman, Jonathan Barry, and Nina Jung. 2004. "Poverty Levels and Federal Tax Thresholds: 2004." *Community Tax Law Report* 7(2): 5–7, 19.

Forman, Jonathan Barry, and Amy Nixon. 2000. "Cash Balance Pension Plan Conversions." *Oklahoma City University Law Review* 25(1 and 2): 379–434.

Forman, Jonathan Barry, Adam Carasso, and Mohammed Adeel Saleem. 2005. "Designing a Work-Friendly Tax System: Options and Trade-Offs." Tax Policy Center Discussion Paper No. 20. Washington, DC: The Urban Institute.

Forman, Jonathan B., John Turner, Glenda Chambers, Steven L. Willborn, and Kathryn L. Moore. 2002. "State, Local and Foreign Pensions: Implications for Social Security and Pension Reform. Proceedings of the 2002 Annual Meeting of the Association of American Law Schools, Section on Employee Benefits." *Employee Rights and Employment Policy Journal* 6(1): 83–127.

Förster, Michael, and Marco Mira d'Ercole. 2005. "Income Distribution and Poverty in the OECD Countries in the Second Half of the 1990s." Social,

Employment and Migration Working Paper No. 22. Paris: Organisation for Economic Co-operation and Development.

Fortin, Nicole M., and Thomas Lemieux. 1997. "Institutional Changes and Rising Wage Inequality: Is There a Linkage?" *Journal of Economic Perspectives* 11(2): 75–96.

Fox, Aubrey, and Robert V. Wolf. 2004. "The Future of Drug Courts: How States Are Mainstreaming the Drug Court Model." New York: Center for Court Innovation.

Frank, Robert H., and Philip J. Cook. 1995. *The Winner-Take-All Society.* New York: The Free Press.

Freeman, Richard B. 1996. "Why Do So Many Young American Men Commit Crimes and What Might We Do About It?" Working Paper No. 5,451. Cambridge, MA: National Bureau of Economic Research.

———. 1997. "The Facts about Rising Economic Disparity." In *Fiscal Policy: Lessons from Economic Research,* edited by Alan J. Auerbach (19–33). Cambridge, MA: MIT Press.

———. 2003. "Can We Close the Revolving Door? Recidivism vs. Employment of Ex-Offenders in the U S " Paper presented at the Urban Institute Reentry Roundtable, New York University Law School, May 19–20.

French, Eric. 2005. "The Effects of Health, Wealth, and Wages on Labour Supply and Retirement Behaviour." *Review of Economic Studies* 72(2): 395–427.

Fried, Barbara. 1995. "Wilt Chamberlain Revisited: Nozick's 'Justice in Transfer' and the Problem of Market-Based Distribution." *Philosophy and Public Affairs* 24(3): 226–45.

———. 2002. "Why Proportionate Taxation?" In *Tax Justice: The Ongoing Debate,* edited by Joseph J. Thorndike and Dennis J. Ventry, Jr. (149–92). Washington, DC: Urban Institute Press.

Friedberg, Leora, and Michael Owyang. 2004. "Explaining the Evolution of Pension Structure and Job Tenure." Working Paper No. 10,714. Cambridge, MA: National Bureau of Economic Research.

Friedberg, Leora, and Anthony Webb. 2004. "Retirement and the Evolution of the Pension Structure." Working Paper No. 9,999. Cambridge, MA: National Bureau of Economic Research.

Friedman, Joel, and Katharine Richards. 2006. "Capital Gains and Dividend Tax Cuts: Data Make Clear that High-income Households Benefit the Most." Washington, DC: Center on Budget Priorities.

Friedman, Milton. 1962. *Capitalism and Freedom.* Chicago, IL: University of Chicago Press.

Fronstin, Paul. 1997. "Employee Benefits, Retirement Patterns, and Implications for Increased Work Life." Issue Brief No. 184. Washington, DC: Employee Benefit Research Institute.

———. 1999. "Employment-Based Health Insurance: A Look at Tax Issues and Public Opinion." In *Severing the Link between Health Insurance and Employment,* edited by Dallas Salisbury (1–18). Washington, DC: Employee Benefit Research Institute.

———. 2000. "An Economic Model of Employee Benefits and Labor Supply." In *Employee Benefits and Labor Markets in Canada and the United States,* edited by William T. Alpert and Stephen A. Woodbury (87–127). Kalamazoo, MI: W.E. Upjohn Institute for Employment Research.

———. 2001. "Defined Contribution Health Plans." Issue Brief No. 231. Washington, DC: Employee Benefit Research Institute.

————. 2003. "Retiree Health Benefits: Savings Needed to Fund Health Care in Retirement." Issue Brief No. 254. Washington, DC: Employee Benefit Research Institute.

————. 2004. "Health Savings Accounts and Other Account-Based Health Plans." Issue Brief No. 265. Washington, DC: Employee Benefit Research Institute.

————. 2005a. "Employment-Based Health Benefits: Trends in Access and Coverage." Issue Brief No. 284. Employee Benefit Research Institute.

————. 2005b. "The Impact of the Erosion of Retiree Health Benefits on Workers and Retirees." Issue Brief No. 279. Washington, DC: Employee Benefit Research Institute.

————. 2005c. "Sources of Health Insurance and Characteristics of the Uninsured: Analysis of the March 2005 Current Population Survey." Issue Brief No. 287. Washington, DC: Employee Benefit Research Institute.

————. 2005d. "Uninsured Unchanged in 2004, but Employment-Based Health Care Coverage Declined." *Employee Benefit Research Institute Notes* 26(10): 2–10.

————. 2006. "The Tax Treatment of Health Insurance and Employment-Based Health Benefits." Issue Brief No. 294. Washington, DC: Employee Benefit Research Institute.

Fronstin, Paul, and Sara R. Collins. 2005. "Early Experience with High-Deductible and Consumer-Driven Health Plans: Findings from the EBRI/Commonwealth Fund Consumerism in Health Care Survey." Issue Brief No. 288. Washington, DC: Employee Benefit Research Institute.

Fronstin, Paul, and Paul Yakoboski. 2005. "Options and Alternatives to Fund Retiree Health Care Expenditures." Policy Brief. New York: TIAA-CREF Institute.

Fullerton, Don, and Brent Mast. 2005. *Income Redistribution from Social Security.* Washington, DC: AEI Press.

Furman, Jason. 2006. "Coping with Demographic Uncertainty." Paper prepared for the New York University School of Law Colloquium on Tax Policy and Public Finance, spring. Available at http://taxprof.typepad.com/taxprof_blog/files/Furman.doc.

Gac, Edward J., and Sharon K. Brougham. 1988. " A Proposal for Restructuring the Taxation of Wealth Transfers: Tax Reform Redux." *Akron Tax Journal* 5: 75–105.

Galbraith, James K. 1998. *Created Unequal: The Crisis in American Pay.* New York: Free Press.

Gale, William G. 1999. "The Required Tax Rate in a National Retail Sales Tax." *National Tax Journal* 52(3). 443–57.

————. 2005. "The National Retail Sales Tax: What Would the Rate Have to Be?" *Tax Notes* (May 16): 889–911.

Gale, William G., and Peter R. Orszag. 2003a. "Private Pensions: Issues and Options." Tax Policy Center Discussion Paper No. 9. Washington, DC: The Urban Institute.

————. 2003b. "Sunsets in the Tax Code." *Tax Notes* (June 9): 1553–61.

Gale, William, and Jeffrey Rohaly. 2003. "Three-Quarters of Filers Pay More in Payroll Taxes than in Income Taxes (Tax Facts from the Tax Policy Center)." *Tax Notes* (January 6): 119.

Gale, William G., and Seth Stephens-Davidowitz. 2005. "Consumption Taxes in the United States and Abroad." *Tax Notes* (September 12): 1299.

Gale, William G., J. Mark Iwry, and Peter R. Orszag. 2005. "Improving Tax Incentives for Low-Income Savers: The Saver's Credit." Tax Policy Center Discussion Paper No. 22. Washington, DC: The Urban Institute.

Gale, William G., Peter R. Orszag, and Isaac Shapiro. 2004. "Distribution of the 2001 and 2003 Tax Cuts and Their Financing." *Tax Notes* (June 21): 1539–48.

Gann, Pamela. 1980. "Abandoning Marital Status as a Factor in Allocating Income Tax Burdens." *Texas Law Review* 59(1): 1 69.

GAO. See U.S. General Accounting Office, U.S. Government Accountability Office.

Garfinkel, Irwin, and Robert Haveman. 1983. "Income Transfer Policy in the United States." In *Handbook of Social Intervention*, edited by Edward Seidman (479–98). Beverly Hills, CA: SAGE Publications.

Garner, Thesia I., and Kathleen Short. 2005. "Economic Well-Being Based on Income, Consumer Expenditures, and Personal Assessments of Minimum Needs." Working Paper No. 381. Washington, DC: Bureau of Labor Statistics.

Garrett, A. Bowen, Len M. Nichols, and Emily K. Greenman. 2001. "Workers without Health Insurance. Who Are They and How Can Policy Reach Them?" Washington, DC: The Urban Institute.

Gebhardtsbauer, Ron 1999. "Hybrid Pension Plan Coverage: Retirement into the 21st Century." Testimony before the Senate Committee on Health, Education, Labor, and Pensions, September 21. Available at http://www.actuary.org/pdf/pension/retire99.pdf.

Geier, Deborah A. 2002. "Integrating the Tax Burdens of the Federal Income and Payroll Taxes on Labor Income." *Virginia Tax Review* 22 (Summer): 1–65.

———. 2003. "Incremental versus Fundamental Tax Reform and the Top One Percent." *SMU Law Review* 56(1): 99–169.

Geisler, Gregory G. 2003. "Current Year Tax Laws that Cause Low Visibility of an Individual's Effective Marginal Tax Rate." *Tax Notes* (November 3): 627–34.

Giannarelli, Linda, Sarah Adelman, and Stefanie Schmidt. 2003. *Getting Help with Child Care Expenses.* Washington, DC: The Urban Institute. *Assessing the New Federalism* Occasional Paper No. 62.

Giertz, Seth H. 2005. "The Taxable Income Elasticity Over the 1980s and 1990s." In *2004 Proceedings of the Ninety-Seventh Annual Conference on Taxation* (236–44). Washington, DC: National Tax Association.

Gilbert, Richard S. 1991. *How Much Do We Deserve? An Inquiry in Distributive Justice.* Lanham, MD: University Press of America.

Gokhale, Jagadeesh, Laurence J. Kotlikoff, and Todd Neuman. 2001. "Does Participating in a 401(k) Raise Your Lifetime Taxes?" Working Paper No. 8,341. Cambridge, MA: National Bureau of Economic Research.

Goldberg, Daniel S. 2003. "The U.S. Consumption Tax: Evolution, Not Revolution." *Tax Lawyer* 57(1): 1–31.

Goldman, Dana, Neeraj Sood, and Arleen Leibowitz. 2005. "Wage and Benefit Changes in Response to Rising Health Insurance Costs." Working Paper No. 11,063. Cambridge, MA: National Bureau of Economic Research.

Goodman, John C. 2004. "Statement on America's Private Retirement System: The Need for Reform." Testimony before the U.S. Senate Special Committee on Aging, January 27. Available at http://aging.senate.gov/_files/hr115jg.pdf.

Goss, Stephen C. 1999. "Measuring Solvency in the Social Security System." In *Prospects for Social Security Reform*, edited by Olivia S. Mitchell, Robert J. Myers, and Howard Young (16–36). Philadelphia, PA: Pension Research Council and University of Pennsylvania Press.

Gottschalk, Peter. 1997. "Inequality, Income Growth, and Mobility: The Basic Facts." *Journal of Economic Perspectives* 11(2): 21–40.

Gottschalk, Peter, and Sheldon Danziger. 2003. "Wage Inequality, Earnings Inequality, and Poverty in the U.S. Over the Last Quarter of the Twentieth Century." Working Paper in Economics No. 560. Chestnut Hill, MA: Boston College.

Graetz, Michael J. 1979. "Implementing a Progressive Consumption Tax." *Harvard Law Review* 92(8): 1575–1661.

———. 1983. "To Praise the Estate Tax, Not to Bury It." *Yale Law Journal* 93(2): 259–86.

———. 1997. *The Decline (and Fall?) of the Income Tax.* New York: W.W. Norton.

———. 2002. "100 Million Unnecessary Returns: A Fresh Start for the U.S. Tax System." *Yale Law Journal* 112(2): 261–310.

Graetz, Michael J., and Ian Shapiro. 2005. *Death by a Thousand Cuts: The Fight over Taxing Inherited Wealth.* Princeton and Oxford: Princeton University Press.

Gramlich, Edward M. 1996. "Different Approaches for Dealing with Social Security." *Journal of Economic Perspectives* 10(3): 55–66.

Greenlees, Elizabeth M., and Paul A. Welcher. 2005. "Employee Contributions to Employer-Provided Medical Plans by Bargaining Status, Private Industry, 2005." *Compensation and Working Conditions Online*, August 31.

Gregg, Paul. 2000. "The Use of Wage Floors as Policy Tools." *OECD Economic Studies* 31(2): 133–46.

Grogger, Jeffrey, Lynn A. Karoly, and Jacob Ale Klerman. 2002. *Consequences of Welfare Reform: A Research Synthesis.* DRU-2676-DHHS. Santa Monica, CA: RAND Corporation.

Gruber, Jonathan. 2005. "Tax Policy for Health Insurance." In *Tax Policy and the Economy*, vol. 19, edited by James M. Poterba (39–63). Cambridge, MA: MIT Press.

Gruber, Jonathan, and Brigitte C. Madrian. 1995. "Health-Insurance Availability and the Retirement Decision." *American Economic Review* 85(4): 938–48.

———. 2004. "Health Insurance, Labor Supply, and Job Mobility: A Critical Review of the Literature." In *Health Policy and the Uninsured*, edited by Catherine McLaughlin (97–177). Washington, DC: Urban Institute Press.

Gruber, Jonathan, and Emmanuel Saez. 2002. "The Elasticity of Taxable Income: Evidence and Implications." *Journal of Public Economics* 84(1): 1–32.

Gruber, Jonathan, and David Wise. 2003. "Social Security Programs and Retirement around the World: Micro Estimation." Working Paper No. 9,407. Cambridge, MA: National Bureau of Economic Research.

Gueron, Judith M. 1990. "Work and Welfare: Lessons on Employment Programs." *Journal of Economic Perspectives* 4(1): 79–98.

Gustman, Alan L., and Thomas L. Steinmeier. 1995. *Pension Incentives and Job Mobility.* Kalamazoo, MI: W.E. Upjohn Institute for Employment Research.

———. 1998. "Changing Pensions in Cross-Section and Panel Data: Analysis with Employer Provided Plan Descriptions." Working Paper No. 6,854. Cambridge, MA: National Bureau of Economic Research.

————. 2002. "The Social Security Early Entitlement Age in a Structural Model of Retirement and Wealth." Working Paper No. 9,183. Cambridge, MA: National Bureau of Economic Research.

————. 2004. "The Social Security Retirement Earnings Test, Retirement and Benefit Claiming." Michigan Retirement Research Center Working Paper 2004-90. Ann Arbor: University of Michigan.

————. 2005. "Retirement Effects of Proposals by the President's Commission to Strengthen Social Security." *National Tax Journal* 58(1): 27–49.

Guyton, John L., John F. O'Hare, Michael P. Stavrianos, and Eric J. Toder. 2003. "Estimating the Compliance Cost of the U.S. Individual Income Tax." *National Tax Journal* 56(3): 673–88.

Guzman, Mark G., and Fiona Sigalla. 2004. "Is the Pension System a Liability?" *Federal Reserve Bank of Dallas Southwest Economy* Issue 5: 1, 7–12.

Haase, Leif Wellington. 2005. *A New Deal for Health: How to Cover Everyone and Get Medical Costs under Control.* New York: Century Foundation Press.

Haider, Steven, and David Loughran. 2001. "Elderly Labor Supply: Work or Play?" Working Paper No. 2001-04. Boston, MA: Center for Retirement Research at Boston College.

Haig, Robert M. 1921. "The Concept of Income—Economic and Legal Aspects." In *The Federal Income Tax,* edited by Robert M. Haig (1–28). New York: Columbia University Press.

Hall, Robert E., and Alvin Rabushka. 1995. *The Flat Tax.* 2nd ed. Stanford, CA: Hoover Institution Press.

Halperin, Daniel I. 1993. "Special Tax Treatment for Employer-Based Retirement Programs: Is It 'Still' Viable as a Means of Increasing Retirement Income? Should It Continue?" *Tax Law Review* 49 (Fall): 1–51.

————. 2003. "Employer-Based Retirement Income—The Ideal, the Possible, and the Reality." *Elder Law Journal* 11(1): 37–76.

Hamermesh, Daniel S., and Albert Rees. 1988. *The Economics of Work and Pay.* 4th ed. New York: Harper & Row Publishers.

Hamersma, Sarah. 2003. "The Work Opportunity and Welfare-to-Work Tax Credits: Participation Rates among Eligible Workers." *National Tax Journal* 56(4): 725–38.

Handler, Joel F., and Yeheskel Hasenfeld. 1997. *We the Poor People: Work, Poverty, and Welfare* (Twentieth Century Fund). New Haven: Yale University Press.

Harrington, Michael. 1962. *The Other America.* New York: Macmillan.

Harrison, Paige M., and Jennifer C. Karberg. 2004. "Prison and Jail Inmates at Midyear 2003." Bureau of Justice Statistics Bulletin, Publication No. NCJ 203947. Washington, DC: U.S. Department of Justice, Office of Justice Programs.

Hartmann, Heidi, and Roberta Spalter-Roth, with Melissa Sills. 2004. *Survival at the Bottom: The Income Packages of Low-Income Families with Children.* Washington, DC: Institute for Women's Policy Research.

Hassett, Kevin A., and Anne Moore. 2005. "How Do Tax Policies Affect Low Income Workers?" Working Paper No. 05-16. Ann Arbor: National Poverty Center, University of Michigan.

Hausman, Jerry. 1981. "Labor Supply." In *How Taxes Affect Economic Behavior,* edited by Henry J. Aaron and Joseph A. Pechman (27–72). Washington, DC: Brookings Institution Press.

Hausman, Jerry A., and James M. Poterba. 1987. "Household Behavior and the Tax Reform Act of 1986." Working Paper No. 2,120. Cambridge, MA: National Bureau of Economic Research.

Haveman, Robert. 1988. *Starting Even: An Equal Opportunity Program to Combat the Nation's New Poverty.* New York: Simon and Schuster.

————. 1995. "The Clinton Alternative to 'Welfare as We Know It': Is It Feasible?" In *The Work Alternative: Welfare Reform and the Realities of the Job Market,* edited by Demetra Smith Nightingale and Robert Haveman (185–202). Washington, DC: Urban Institute Press.

Haveman, Robert, and Andrew Berkshadker. 1998. "Self-Reliance and Poverty." Public Policy Brief No. 46A. Annandale-on-Hudson, NY: Levy Economics Institute, Bard College.

Haveman, Robert H., and John L. Palmer, eds. 1982. *Jobs for Disadvantaged Workers.* Washington, DC: Brookings Institution Press.

Haveman, Robert H., Andrew Bershadker, and Jonathan A. Schwabish. 2003. *Human Capital in the United States from 1975 to 2000.* Kalamazoo, MI: W.E. Upjohn Institute for Employment Research.

He, Wan, Manisha Sengupta, Victoria A. Velkoff, and Kimberly A. DeBarros. 2005. *65+ in the United States: 2005.* Current Population Report No. P23-209. Washington, DC: U.S. Government Printing Office.

Heckman, James, and Pedro Carneiro. 2003. "Human Capital Policy." Working Paper No. 9,495. Cambridge, MA: National Bureau of Economic Research.

Heckman, James J., and Alan B. Krueger, eds. 2003. *Inequality in America: What Role for Human Capital Policies?* Cambridge, MA: MIT Press.

Heckman, James J., and Lance Lochner. 2000. "Rethinking Education and Training Policy: Understanding the Sources of Skill Formation in a Modern Economy." In *Securing the Future: Investing in Children from Birth to College,* edited by Sheldon Danziger and Jane Waldfogel (47–83). New York: Russell Sage Foundation.

Heckman, James J., Lance Lochner, and Christopher Taber. 1998. "Tax Policy and Human Capital Formation." Working Paper No. 6,462. Cambridge, MA: National Bureau of Economic Research.

Herrick, Devon. 2001. "Would National Health Insurance Benefit Physicians?" Brief Analysis No. 370. Dallas, TX: National Center for Policy Analysis.

Herz, Diane E. 1995. "Work after Early Retirement: An Increasing Trend among Men." *Monthly Labor Review* 11(4): 14–20.

HHS. See U.S. Department of Health and Human Services.

Hill, Kent, Dennis Hoffman, and Tom R. Rex. 2005. "The Value of Higher Education: Individual and Societal Benefits (with Special Consideration for the State of Arizona)." Tempe: W. P. Carey School of Business, Arizona State University.

Himmelstein, David U., and Steffie Woolhandler. 2003. "National Health Insurance or Incremental Reform: Aim High, or at Our Feet?" *American Journal of Public Health* 93(1): 102–105.

Hobbes, Thomas. 1887. *Leviathan.* 3rd ed. London: George Rutledge & Sons.

Hoffman, David. 2002. "Who Pays the Federal Individual Income Tax?" Special Report No. 118. Washington, DC: Tax Foundation.

Hoffman, Earl Dirk, Jr., Barbara S. Klees, and Catherine A. Curtis. 2005. "Brief Summaries of Medicare and Medicaid." Washington, DC: U.S. Department of Health and Human Services.

Hoffman, Saul D., and Lawrence S. Seidman. 2002. *Helping Working Families: The Earned Income Tax Credit*. Kalamazoo, MI: W.E. Upjohn Institute for Employment Research.

Holahan, John. 2004. "Health Insurance Coverage of the Near Elderly." Washington, DC: Henry J. Kaiser Family Foundation, Kaiser Commission on Medicaid and the Uninsured.

Holcomb, Pamela A., Karen Tumlin, Robin Koralek, Randy Capps, and Anita Zuberi. 2003. "The Application Process for TANF, Food Stamps, Medicaid and SCHIP: Issues for Agencies and Applicants, Including Immigrants and Limited English Speakers." Study for the U.S. Department of Health and Human Services, Office of the Assistant Secretary for Planning and Evaluation. Washington, DC: The Urban Institute.

Holden, Sarah, and Jack VanDerhei. 2005. "The Influence of Automatic Enrollment, Catch-Up, and IRA Contributions on 401(k) Accumulations at Retirement." Issue Brief No. 283. Washington, DC: Employee Benefit Research Institute.

Holt, Steven D. 2005. "Making Work *Really* Pay: Income Support and Marginal Effective Tax Rates among Low-Income Working Households." Paper presented to the American Tax Policy Institute, Washington, D.C., July 7.

Holtzblatt, Janet, and Janet McCubbin. 2004. "Tax Administrative Issues Affecting Low-Income Filers," In *The Crisis in Tax Administration*, edited by Henry J. Aaron and Joel Slemrod (148–200). Washington, DC: Brookings Institution Press.

Holtzblatt, Janet, and Robert Rebelein. 2001. "Measuring the Effect of the Earned Income Tax Credit on Marriage Penalties and Bonuses." In *Making Work Pay: The Earned Income Tax Credit and Its Impact on America's Families*, edited by Bruce D. Meyer and Douglas Holtz-Eakin (166–95). New York: Russell Sage Foundation.

Holzer, Harry J., Paul Offner, and Elaine Sorenson. 2004. "Declining Employment among Young Black Less-Educated Men: The Role of Incarceration and Child Support." Discussion Paper No. 1281-04. Madison: Institute for Research on Poverty, University of Wisconsin-Madison.

Homeland Security. See U.S. Department of Homeland Security.

Horn, Wade F. 2001. "Wedding Bell Blues: Marriage and Welfare Reform." *Brookings Review* 19(3): 39–42.

Hotz, V. Joseph, and John Karl Scholz. 2003. "The Earned Income Tax Credit." In *Means-Tested Transfer Programs in the United States*, edited by Robert A. Moffitt (141–97). Chicago, IL: University of Chicago Press.

Hotz, V. Joseph, Charles H. Mullin, and John Karl Scholz. 2001. "The EITC and Labor Market Participation of Families on Welfare." In *The Incentives of Government Programs and the Well-Being of Families*, edited by Bruce Meyer and Greg Duncan (97–143). Chicago, IL: Joint Center for Poverty Research, Northwestern University/University of Chicago.

Hoynes, Hilary Williamson. 1997. "Work, Welfare, and Family Structure: What Have We Learned?" In *Fiscal Policy: Lessons from Economic Research*, edited by Alan J. Auerbach (101–46). Cambridge, MA: MIT Press.

———. 2005. "The Earned Income Tax Credit." Presentation to the President's Advisory Panel on Federal Tax Reform, New Orleans, March 23.

Hoynes, Hilary Williamson, and Robert Moffitt. 1999. "Tax Rates and Work Incentives in the Social Security Disability Insurance Program: Current Law and Alternative Reforms." *National Tax Journal* 52(4): 623–54.

Hoynes, Hilary, Marianne Page, and Ann Stevens. 2006. "Poverty in America: Trends and Explanations." *Journal of Economic Perspectives* 20(1): 47–68.

Human Rights Watch. 2002. "Race and Incarceration in the United States." Press backgrounder, February 22. New York: Human Rights Watch.

Hunt-McCool, Janet, Thomas McCool, and Avi Dor. 2000. "Employer-Provided versus Publicly Provided Health Insurance." In *Employee Benefits and Labor Markets in Canada and the United States*, edited by William T. Alpert and Stephen A. Woodbury (325–48). Kalamazoo, MI: W.E. Upjohn Institute for Employment Research.

Institute for Fiscal Studies. 1978. *The Structure and Reform of Direct Taxation: Report of a Committee Chaired by Professor J. E. Meade.* London: George Allen & Unwin Ltd.

Internal Revenue Service. 1987. *Current Feasibility of a Return-Free Tax System.* Washington, DC: U.S. Government Printing Office.

———. 2002. "Report of the Employee Plans Small Business Access and Compliance Project Group." In *Advisory Committee on Tax Exempt and Government Entities (ACT), Public Meeting.* Washington, DC: Internal Revenue Service.

———. 2004a. "Distributions from a Pension Plan under a Phased Retirement Program." *Federal Register* 69 (2004): 65,108–117.

———. 2004b. *Tax Incentives for Distressed Communities.* Publication No. 954. Washington, DC: Internal Revenue Service.

———. 2004c. *Taxable and Nontaxable Income.* Publication No. 525. Washington, DC: Internal Revenue Service.

———. 2005a. *Child Tax Credit.* Publication No. 972. Washington, DC: Internal Revenue Service.

———. 2005b. *Individual Income Tax Returns 2003.* Publication No. 1304. Washington, DC: Internal Revenue Service.

———. 2005c. "Revenue Procedure 2005-70." *Internal Revenue Bulletin* 2005-47. Washington, DC: Internal Revenue Service.

———. 2005d. "Selected and Other Historical Data." *Statistics of Income Bulletin* 25(2): 279–365.

———. 2006. "IRS Updates Tax Gap Estimates." Press Release IR-2006-28. Washington, DC: Internal Revenue Service.

Ippolito, Richard A. 1986. *Pensions, Economics, and Public Policy.* Homewood, IL: Dow Jones-Irwin.

———. 1997. *Pension Plans and Economic Performance.* Chicago, IL: University of Chicago Press.

IRS. See Internal Revenue Service.

Isaacs, Barry L. 1977. "Do We Want a Wealth Tax in America?" *University of Miami Law Review* 32: 23–50.

Iwry, J. Mark. 2003. "Promoting 401(k) Security." Tax Policy Issues and Options Brief 7. Washington, DC: The Urban Institute.

Iwry, J. Mark, and David C. John. 2006. "Pursuing Universal Retirement Security through Automatic IRAs." Working Paper. Washington, DC: Retirement Security Project.

Jaeger, David A. 2003. "Estimating the Returns to Education using the Newest Current Population Survey Education Questions." *Economics Letters* 78(3): 385–94.

James, Estelle, and Dimitri Vittas. 1996. "Mandatory Saving Schemes: Are They the Answer to the Old Age Security Problems?" In *Securing Employer-Based Pensions: An International Perspective*, edited by Zvi Bodie, Olivia S. Mitchell, and John Turner (151–82) (Pension Research Council). Philadelphia: University of Pennsylvania Press.

JCT. See U.S. Congress, Joint Committee on Taxation.

Jencks, Christopher. 2002. "Does Inequality Matter?" *Daedalus* 131(1): 49–65.

Jencks, Christopher, Lauri Perman, and Lee Rainwater. 1988. "What Is a Good Job? A New Measure of Labor Market Success." *American Journal of Sociology* 93(6): 1322–57.

Johnson, David S., Timothy M. Smeeding, and Barbara Boyle Torrey. 2005. "Economic Inequality through the Prisms of Income and Consumption." *Monthly Labor Review* 128(4): 11–23.

Johnson, George E. 1997. "Changes in Earnings Inequality: The Role of Demand Shifts." *Journal of Economic Perspectives* 11(2): 41–54.

Johnson, Jennifer. 2002. *Getting By on the Minimum: The Lives of Working-Class Women.* New York and London: Routledge.

Johnson, Julia Overturf. 2005. "Who's Minding the Kids? Child Care Arrangements: Winter 2002." Census Household Economic Studies No. P70-101. Washington, DC: U.S. Bureau of the Census.

Johnson, Richard W. 2003. "When Should Medicare Coverage Begin?" Health and Income Security for an Aging Workforce Paper No. 6. Washington, DC: National Academy of Social Insurance.

Johnson, Richard W., and Eugene Steuerle. 2003. "Promoting Work at Older Ages: The Role of Hybrid Pension Plans in an Aging Population." Working Paper No. 2003-26. Philadelphia, PA: Pension Research Council.

Johnson, Richard W., Amy J. Davidoff, and Kevin Perese. 2003. "Health Insurance Costs and Early Retirement Decisions." *Industrial and Labor Relations Review* 56(4): 716–30.

Johnson, Richard W., Melissa M. Favreault, and Joshua Goldwyn. 2003. "Employment, Social Security, and Future Retirement Outcomes for Single Mothers." Working Paper No. 2003-14. Boston, MA: Center for Retirement Research at Boston College.

Johnston, David Cay. 2003. *Perfectly Legal: The Covert Campaign to Rig Our Tax System to Benefit the Super Rich—and Cheat Everybody Else.* New York: Portfolio.

Joint Economic Committee. See U.S. Congress, Joint Economic Committee.

The Kaiser Family Foundation and Health Research and Education Trust. 2005. *Employer Health Benefits: 2005 Annual Survey.* Menlo Park, CA: Kaiser Family Foundation.

The Kaiser Family Foundation and Hewitt Associates. 2004. "Current Trends and Future Outlook for Retiree Health Benefits." Menlo Park, CA: Henry J. Kaiser Foundation.

Kaplan, Richard L. 2002. "Crowding Out: Estate Tax Reform and the Elder Law Policy Agenda." *Elder Law Journal* 10(1): 15–46.

———. 2005. "Who's Afraid of Personal Responsibility: Health Savings Accounts and the Future of American Health Care." *McGeorge Law Review* 36(3): 535–68.

Kaplow, Louis. 2006. "Optimal Income Transfers." Working Paper No. 12,284. Cambridge, MA: National Bureau of Economic Research.

Karger, Howard J., and David Stoesz. 1992. "Options in Social Welfare Policy." In *Reconstructing the American Welfare State,* edited by David Stoesz and Howard J. Karger (119–60). Lanham, MD: Rowman and Littlefield.

Karoly, Lynn A. 1998. "Growing Economic Disparities in the U.S.: Assessing the Problem and Policy Options." In *The Inequality Paradox: Growth of Income Disparity,* edited by James A. Auerbach and Richard S. Belous (234–59). Washington, DC: National Policy Association.

Karoly, Lynn A., and James H. Bigelow. 2005. "The Economics of Investing in Universal Preschool Education in California." Santa Monica, CA: RAND Corporation.

Karoly, Lynn A. and Constantijn W.A. Panis. 2004. *The 21st Century at Work: Forces Shaping the Future Workforce and Workplace in the United States.* Santa Monica, CA: RAND Corporation.

Katz, Lawrence F., and Alan B. Krueger. 1999. "Unemployment? New Trend in the High-Pressure U.S. Labor Market of the 1990s." *Brookings Review* (Fall): 4–8.

Kaus, Mickey. 1995. *The End of Equality.* 2nd paperback ed. New York: Basic Books.

Kennickell, Arthur B. 2003. "A Rolling Tide: Changes in the Distribution of Wealth in the U.S., 1989–2001." Working Paper No. 393. Annandale-on-Hudson, NY: Levy Economics Institute, Bard College.

Kesselman, Jonathan. 1969. "Labor-Supply Effects of Income, Income-Work, and Wage Subsidies." *Journal of Human Resources* 4(3): 275–92.

King, Christopher T. 2004. "The Effectiveness of Publicly Financed Training in the United States: Implications for WIA and Related Programs." In *Job Training Policy in the United States,* edited by Christopher J. O'Leary, Robert A. Straits, and Stephen A. Wandner (57–99). Kalamazoo, MI: W.E. Upjohn Institute for Employment Research.

Kirshberg, Richard D. 1966. "The Accessions Tax: Administrative Bramblebush or Instrument of Social Policy." *University of California at Los Angeles Law Review* 14: 135–202.

Kochran, Thomas. 2004. "Education, Families, and Workplace Policies." *Challenge* 47(6): 69–81.

———. 2005. *Restoring the American Dream. A Working Families' Agenda for America.* Cambridge, MA: MIT Press.

Koenig, Gary, and Robert Harvey. 2005. "Utilization of the Saver's Credit: An Analysis of the First Year." *National Tax Journal* 58(4): 787–806.

Kopszuk, Wojciech, and Emmanuel Saez. 2004. "Top Wealth Shares in the United States, 1916–2000: Evidence from Estate Tax Returns." *National Tax Journal* 57(2, Part 2): 445–87.

Kornhauser, Marjorie M. 1992. "The Constitutional Meaning of Income and the Income Taxation of Gifts." *Connecticut Law Review* 25 (Fall): 1–55.

———. 1993. "Love, Money, and the IRS: Family, Income Sharing, and the Joint Return." *Hastings Law Journal* 45 (November): 63–111.

Kosters, Marvin H. 1998. *Wage Levels and Inequality: Measuring and Interpreting the Trends.* Washington, DC: AEI Press.

Kotlikoff, Lawrence, and Jagadeesh Gokhale. 1992. "Estimating a Firm's Age-Productivity Profile Using the Present Value of Worker's Earnings." *Quarterly Journal of Economics* 107(4): 1215–42.

Kotlikoff, Lawrence, and David Wise. 1985. "Labor Compensation and the Structure of Private Pension Plans: Evidence for Contractual versus Spot Labor Markets." In *Pensions, Labor, and Individual Choice*, edited by David A. Wise (55–87). Chicago, IL: University of Chicago Press.

———. 1987. "The Incentive Effects of Private Pension Plans." In *Issues in Pension Economics*, edited by Zvi Bodie, John B. Shoven, and David A. Wise (283–339). Chicago, IL: University of Chicago Press.

———. 1989. "Employee Retirement and a Firm's Pension Plans." In *The Economics of Aging*, edited by David A. Wise (279–330). Chicago, IL: University of Chicago Press.

Kranich, Laurence. 1994. "Equal Division, Efficiency, and the Sovereign Supply of Labor." *American Economic Review* 84(1): 178–89.

Krueger, Dirk, and Fabrizio Perri. 2002. "Does Income Inequality Lead to Consumption Inequality? Evidence and Theory." Working Paper No. 9,202. Cambridge, MA: National Bureau of Economic Research.

Labonte, Marc. 2004. "Job Loss: Causes and Policy Implications." CRS report, updated December 22. Washington, DC: Congressional Research Service, Library of Congress.

Lahey, Joann N. 2005. "Do Older Workers Face Discrimination?" Issue in Brief No. 33. Boston, MA: Center for Retirement Research at Boston College.

Lampman, Robert. 1965. "Approaches to the Reduction of Poverty." *American Economic Review* 55 (May): 521–29.

Langbein, John H., and Bruce A. Wolk. 2000. *Pension and Employee Benefit Law*. 3rd ed. New York: Foundation Press.

Lardner, James, and David A. Smith, eds. 2005. *Inequality Matters: The Growing Economic Divide in America and Its Poisonous Consequences*. New York and London: The New Press.

Larsen, Luke J. 2004. "The Foreign-Born Population in the United States: 2003." Current Population Report No. P20-551. Washington, DC: U.S. Bureau of the Census.

Lea, Stephen E. G., Roger M. Tarpy, and Paul Webley. 1987. *The Individual in the Economy: A Survey of Economic Psychology*. Cambridge: Cambridge University Press.

Ledbetter, Mark A. 2005. "Comparison of BEA Estimates of Personal Income and IRS Estimates of Adjusted Gross Income." *Survey of Current Business* 85(11): 30–35.

Lehner, Moris. 2000. "The European Experience with a Wealth Tax: A Comparative Discussion." *Tax Law Review* 53(4): 615–91.

Leibfritz, Willi. 2002. "Retiring Later Makes Sense." *OECD Observer* (No. 234, October).

Leimer, Dean A. 1999. "Lifetime Redistribution under the Social Security Program: A Literature Synopsis." *Social Security Bulletin* 62(2): 43–51.

———. 2003. "Historic Redistribution under the Social Security Old-Age and Survivors Insurance Program. Working Paper 101. Washington, DC: Social Security Administration, Office of Research, Evaluation and Statistics.

Leonesio, Michael V. 1993. "Social Security and Older Workers." *Social Security Bulletin* 56(2): 47–57.

———. 1996. "The Economics of Retirement: A Nontechnical Guide." *Social Security Bulletin* 59(4): 29–50.

Leonesio, Michael V., Denton R. Vaughn, and Bernard Wixon. 2003. "Increasing the Early Retirement Age under Social Security: Health, Work, and Financial Resources." Health and Income Security for an Aging Workforce Paper No. 7. Washington, DC: National Academy of Social Insurance.

Lerman, Robert I. 1985. "Separating Income Support from Income Supplementation." *Journal of the Institute for Socio-economic Studies* 10 (Autumn): 101–25.

Lerman, Robert I., and Michael Wiseman. 2002. "Restructuring Food Stamps for Working Families." Washington, DC: The Urban Institute.

Lerman, Robert I., Signe-Mary McKernan, and Stephanie Rigg. 2004. "The Scope of Employer-Provided Training in the United States," In *Job Training Policy in the United States,* edited by Christopher J. O'Leary, Robert A. Straits, and Stephen A. Wandner (211–43). Kalamazoo, MI: W.E. Upjohn Institute for Employment Research.

Lessnoff, M. H. 1978. "Capitalism, Socialism and Justice." In *Justice and Economic Distribution,* edited by John Arthur and William H. Shaw (137–49). Englewood Cliffs, NJ: Prentice Hall.

Levine, David I. 1998. *Working in the Twenty-First Century: Policies for Economic Growth through Training, Opportunity, and Education.* Armonk, NY: M.E. Sharpe.

Levitis, Jason A., and Nicholas Johnson. 2006. "The Impact of State Income Taxes on Low-income Families in 2005." Washington, DC: Center on Budget and Policy Priorities.

Levitt, Steven D., and Stephen J. Dubner. 2005. *Freakonomics: A Rogue Economist Explores the Hidden Side of Everything.* New York: Harper Collins.

Lipman, Francine J. 2003a. "Enabling Work for People with Disabilities: A Post-integrationist Revision of Underutilized Tax Incentives." *American University Law Review* 53(2) 393–458.

———. 2003b. "The Working Poor Are Paying for Government Benefits: Fixing the Hole in the Anti-Poverty Purse." *Wisconsin Law Review* 2003(2): 461–98.

Liu, Liqun, and Andrew J. Rettenmaier. 2002. "The Economic Cost of the Social Security Payroll Tax." NCPA Policy Report No. 252. Dallas, TX: National Center for Policy Analysis.

Lochner, Lance. 2004. "Education, Work, and Crime: A Human Capital Approach." Working Paper No. 10,478. Cambridge, MA: National Bureau of Economic Research.

Loughran, David, and Steven Haider. 2005. "Do the Elderly Respond to Taxes on Earnings?" Labor and Population Program Working Paper No. WR-223. Santa Monica, CA: RAND Corporation.

Louray, Glenn C. 1998. "Comment." In *Work and Welfare* by Robert Solow, edited by Amy Gutmann (45–54). Princeton, NJ: Princeton University Press.

Lugalia, Terry A. 2005. "Participation of Mothers in Government Assistance Programs: 2001." Census Household Economic Studies No. P70-102. Washington, DC: U.S. Bureau of the Census.

Lumsdaine, Robin L., James H. Stock, and David A. Wise. 1997. "Retirement Incentives: The Interaction between Employer-Provided Pensions, Social Security, and Retiree Health Benefits." In *The Economic Effects of Aging in the United States and Japan,* edited by Michael D. Hurd and Nashiro Yashiro (261–93). Chicago, IL: University of Chicago Press.

Lynch, Lisa M. 2005. "Developing Intermediaries and the Training of Low-Wage Workers." In *Emerging Labor Market Institutions for the Twenty-First Century,* edited by Richard B. Freeman, Joni Hersch, and Lawrence Mishel (293–314). Chicago, IL, and London: University of Chicago Press.

Lynch, Robert G. 2004. *Exceptional Returns: Economic, Fiscal, and Social Benefits of Investing in Early Childhood Development.* Washington, DC: Economic Policy Institute.

Maag, Elaine. 2003. "Recent Expansions to the Child and Dependent Care Credit." *Tax Notes* (October 27): 539.

———. 2005. "Paying the Price: Low-Income Parents and the Use of Paid Tax Preparers." *Assessing the New Federalism* Policy Brief B-64. Washington, DC: The Urban Institute.

MacDonald, John A. 2006. "Survey of Consumer-Driven Health Plans Raises Key Issues." *Employee Benefit Research Institute Notes* 27(2): 2–9.

MacGuineas, Maya. 2004. "Radical Tax Reform." *The Atlantic Monthly* 293(1): 148–51.

Macphearson, David A. 2004. "Living Wage Laws and the Case for a Targeted Wage Subsidy." In *Living Wage Movements: Global Perspectives,* edited by Deborah M. Figart (43–50). London and New York: Routledge.

Madrian, Brigette C. 2005. "Enhancing Retirement Savings Outcomes in Employer Sponsored Savings Plan, Part I—Increasing Participation." Institute Trends and Issues Paper. New York: TIAA-CREF.

Madrian, Brigitte C., and Dennis F. Shea. 2001. "The Power of Suggestion: Inertia in 401(k) Participation and Savings Behavior." *Quarterly Journal of Economics* 116(4): 1149–87.

Mann, Roberta F. 2000. "The (Not So) Little House on the Prairie: The Hidden Costs of the Home Mortgage Interest Deduction." *Arizona State Law Journal* 32 (Winter): 1347–97.

Marguerite Casey Foundation. 2005. "The Earned Income Tax Credit: Analysis and Proposals for Reform." *Tax Notes* (December 26): 1669–86.

Mashaw, Jerry L., and Virginia P. Reno. 1996. *Balancing Security and Opportunity: The Challenge of Disability Income Policy: Report of the Disability Policy Panel.* Washington, DC: National Academy of Social Insurance.

Mastromarco, Dan R. 1999. "What's So Fair about a Tax on Income?" *Tax Notes* (October 8): 217–41.

Mayer, Gerald. 2004. "The Distribution of Earnings of Wage and Salary Workers in the United States, 1994–2003." CRS report, updated December 2. Washington, DC: Congressional Research Service, Library of Congress.

Maynard, Rebecca A. 1995. "Subsidized Employment and Non-Labor Market Alternatives for Welfare Recipient." In *The Work Alternative: Welfare Reform and the Realities of the Job Market,* edited by Demetra Smith Nightingale and Robert Havemen (109–36). Washington, DC: Urban Institute Press.

Mazumder, Bhashkar. 2004. "What Similarities between Siblings Tell Us about Inequality in the U.S." *Chicago Fed Letter* No. 209, December.

———. 2005. "Fortunate Sons: New Estimates of Intergenerational Mobility in the United States Using Social Security Earnings Data." *The Review of Economics and Statistics* 87(2): 235–55.

McCaffery, Edward J. 1992. "Tax Policy under a Hybrid Income-Consumption Tax." *Texas Law Review* 70 (April): 1145–1218.

―――. 1994. "The Uneasy Case for Wealth Transfer Taxation." *Yale Law Journal* 104: 283–365.

―――. 2002a. *Fair Not Flat: How to Make the Tax System Simpler and Better.* Chicago, IL: University of Chicago Press.

―――. 2002b. "Women and Taxes." NCPA Policy Report No. 250. Dallas, TX: National Center for Policy Analysis.

―――. 2003. "The Fair Timing of Tax." Working Paper No. 17. Los Angeles: University of Southern California–Caltech Center for the Study of Law and Politics.

McClendon, Janice Kay. 2004. "Bringing the Bulls to Bear: Regulating Executive Compensation to Realign Management and Shareholders' Interests and Promote Corporate Long-Term Productivity." *Wake Forest Law Review* 39(4): 971–1031.

McCourt, Stephen P. 2006. "Defined Benefit and Defined Contribution Plans: A History, Market Overview and Comparative Analysis." *Benefits & Compensation Digest* 43(2), web exclusive.

McDonnell, Ken. 2005a. "Finances of Employee Benefits: Health Costs Drive Changing Trends." *Employee Benefits Research Institute Notes* 26(12): 2–7.

―――. 2005b. "Retirement Annuity and Employment-Based Pension Income." *Employee Benefits Research Institute Notes* 26(2): 7–14.

McMahon, Martin J., Jr. 2004. "The Matthew Effect and Federal Taxation." *Boston College Law Review* 45(5): 993–1128.

McMahon, Martin J., Jr., and Alice G. Abreu. 1999. "Winner Take All Markets: Easing the Case for Progressive Taxation." *Florida Tax Review* 4(1): 1–81.

McNamee, Stephen J., and Robert K. Miller Jr. 2004. *The Meritocracy Myth.* Lanham, MD: Rowman & Littlefield Publishers, Inc.

McNeil, Jack. 2001. "Americans with Disabilities: 1997." Census Household Economic Studies No. P70-73. Washington, DC: U.S. Bureau of the Census.

McVay, Doug, Vincent Schiraldi, and Jason Ziedenburg. 2004. "Treatment or Incarceration? National and State Findings on Efficiency and Cost Savings of Drug Treatment versus Imprisionment." Policy report. Washington, DC: Justice Policy Institute.

Meulbroek, Lisa. 2005. "Company Stock in Pension Plans: How Costly Is It?" *Journal of Law and Economics* 48(2): 443–74.

Meyer, Bruce, and Dan Rosenbaum. 2000. "Making Single Mothers Work: Recent Tax and Welfare Policy and Its Effects." *National Tax Journal* 53(4, part 2): 1027–62.

Meyers, Robert J. 1991. "Should Social Security's Age for First Benefits or for Full Benefits Be Increased? Robert J. Meyers: Yes, Changes Are Needed." In *Retirement and Public Policy: Proceedings of the Second Conference of the National Academy of Social Insurance,* edited by Alicia H. Munnell (223–30). Dubuque, IA: Kendall/Hunt Publishing.

Michalopoulous, Charles. 2005. "Does Making Work Pay *Still* Pay? An Update of Four Earnings Supplement Programs on Employment, Earnings, and Income." New York: MDRC.

Michalopoulos, Charles, and Gordon Berlin. 2001. "Financial Work Incentives for Low-Wage Workers: Encouraging Work, Reducing Poverty, and Benefiting Families." In *The Incentives of Government Programs and the Well-Being of Families,* edited by Bruce Meyer and Greg Duncan (144–59). Chicago,

IL: Joint Center for Poverty Research, Northwestern University/University of Chicago.

Miller, David. 1999. *Principles of Social Justice.* Cambridge, MA: Harvard University Press.

Miller, David S. 2005."A Progressive System of Mark-to-Market Taxation." *Tax Notes* (November 21): 1047–80.

Minda, Gary. 1994. "Opportunistic Downsizing of Aging Workers: The 1990s Version of Age and Pension Discrimination in Employment." *Hastings Law Journal* 48(3): 511–76.

Minsky, Hyman P. 1986. *Stabilizing an Unstable Economy.* New Haven, CT: Yale University Press.

Mirlees, James. 1971. "An Exploration into the Theory of Optimal Income Taxation." *Review of Economic Studies* 38(2): 175–208.

Mishel, Lawrence, and Joydeep Roy. 2006. *Rethinking High School Graduation Rates and Trends.* Washington, DC: Economic Policy Institute.

Mishel, Lawrence, and Matthew Walters. 2003. "How Unions Help All Workers." Briefing Paper No. 143. Washington, DC: Economic Policy Institute.

Mishel, Lawrence, Jared Bernstein, and Sylvia Allegretto. 2005. *The State of Working in America: 2004–2005.* Ithaca, NY: Cornell University Press.

Mishel, Lawrence, Jared Bernstein, and Heather Boushey. 2003. *The State of Working in America: 2002–2003.* Ithaca, NY: Cornell University Press.

Mitchell, Olivia S. 2003. "Introduction: Benefits for the Workplace of the Future." In *Benefits for the Workplace of the Future,* edited by Olivia S. Mitchell, David S. Blitzstein, Michael Gordon, and Judith F. Mazo (1–18). Philadelphia: University of Pennsylvania Press.

Mitchell, Olivia S., with Erica L. Dykes. 2003. "New Trends in Pension Benefit and Retirement Provisions." In *Benefits for the Workplace of the Future,* edited by Olivia S. Mitchell, David S. Blitzstein, Michael Gordon, and Judith F. Mazo (110–33). Philadelphia: University of Pennsylvania Press.

Mitchell, Olivia S., Stephen P. Utkus, and Tongxuan (Stella) Yang. 2005. "Turning Workers into Savers? Incentives, Liquidity, and Choice in 401(k) Plan Design." Working Paper No. 2005-18. Philadelphia, PA: Pension Research Council.

Mitrusi, Andrew, and James Poterba. 2000. "The Distribution of Payroll and Income Tax Burdens, 1979–1999." *National Tax Journal* 53(3): 765–94.

———. 2001. "The Changing Importance of Income and Payroll Taxes on U.S. Families." In *Tax Policy and the Economy,* vol. 15, edited by James Poterba (95–119). Cambridge, MA: MIT Press.

Modigliani, Franco, and Arun Muranlidhar. 2004. *Rethinking Pension Reform.* Cambridge and New York: Cambridge University Press.

Moffitt, Robert. 1992. "Incentive Effects of the U.S. Welfare System: A Review." *Journal of Economic Literature* 30(1): 1–61.

———. 2002. "Economic Effects of Means-tested Transfer Programs in the U.S." In *Tax Policy and the Economy,* vol. 16, edited by James Poterba (1–35). Cambridge, MA: MIT Press.

———. 2003. "The Negative Income Tax and the Evolution of U.S. Welfare Policy." *Journal of Economic Perspectives* 17(3): 119–40.

Monahan, Amy B. 2006. "The Promise and Peril of Ownership Society Health Care Policy." *Tulane Law Review* 80(3): 777–848.

Moore, Kathryn L. 2001. "Raising the Social Security Retirement Ages: Weighing the Costs and Benefits." *Arizona State Law Journal* 33 (Summer): 543–612.

Morris, Charles R. 2006. *Apart at the Seams: The Collapse of Private Pension and Health Care Protections*. New York: Century Foundation Press.

Morone, James A. "Medicare for All." In *Covering America: Real Remedies for the Uninsured*, vol. 2, edited by Jack A. Meyer and Elliot K. Wicks (63–74). Washington, DC: Economic & Social Research Institute.

Morse, David E. 2006. "From the Editor: Rethinking Employee Benefits, Part 3: Should Pensions Be Voluntary?" *Benefits Law Journal* 19(1): 1–4.

Mortensen, Dale T. 2003. *Wage Dispersion: Why Are Similar Workers Paid Differently?* Cambridge, MA: Massachusetts Institute of Technology.

Mosisa, Abraham T. 2002. "The Role of Foreign-Born Workers in the U.S. Economy." *Monthly Labor Review* 125(5): 3–14.

Moynihan, Daniel Patrick. 1973. *The Politics of a Guaranteed Income*. New York: Random House.

Munnell, Alicia H. 2003. "The Declining Role of Social Security." *Just the Facts on Retirement Issues* No. 6. Boston, MA: Center for Retirement Research at Boston College.

———. 2006. "Policies to Promote Labor Force Participation of Older People." Work Opportunities for Older Americans Working Paper No. 2. Boston, MA: Center for Retirement Research at Boston College.

Munnell, Alicia H., and Mauricio Soto. 2005. "Why Do Women Claim Social Security Benefits So Early?" Issue in Brief No. 35. Boston, MA: Center for Retirement Research at Boston College.

Munnell, Alicia H., Kevin E. Cahill, and Natalia A. Jivan. 2003. "How Has the Shift to 401(k)s Affected the Retirement Age?" Issue in Brief No. 13. Boston, MA: Center for Retirement Research at Boston College.

Munnell, Alicia H., Robert K. Triest, and Natalia A. Jivan. 2004. "How Do Pensions Affect Expected and Actual Retirement Ages." Working Paper No. 2004-27. Boston, MA: Center for Retirement Research at Boston College.

Munnell, Alicia H., Francesca Golub-Sass, Mauricio Soto, and Fraancis Vitagliano. 2006. "Why Are Healthy Employers Freezing Their Pensions?" Issue in Brief No. 44. Boston, MA: Center for Retirement Research at Boston College.

Munnell, Alicia H., Kevin B. Meme, Natalia A. Jivan, and Kevin E. Cahill. 2004. "Should We Raise Social Security's Earliest Eligibility Age?" Issue in Brief No. 18. Boston, MA: Center for Retirement Research at Boston College.

Murphy, Liam, and Thomas Nagel. 2002. *The Myth of Ownership: Taxes and Justice*. Oxford: Oxford University Press.

Murray, Charles. 2006. *In Our Hands: A Plan to Replace the Welfare State*. Washington, DC: AEI Press.

Nagle, Ami, and Nicholas Johnson. 2006. "A Hand Up: How State Earned Income Tax Credits Help Working Families Escape Poverty in 2005." Washington, DC: Center for Budget and Policy Priorities.

Nathanson, Stephen. 1998. *Economic Justice*. Upper Saddle River, NJ: Prentice Hall.

National Academy of Social Insurance. 2005a. "Social Security Finances: A Primer." Washington, DC: National Academy of Social Insurance.

————. 2005b. *Uncharted Waters: Paying Benefits from Individual Accounts in Federal Retirement Policy (Study Panel Final Report, Co-chairs Kenneth S. Apfel and Michael J. Graetz).* Washington, DC: National Academy of Social Insurance.

National Association of State Budget Officers. 2005. *2004 State Expenditure Report.* Washington, DC: National Association of State Budget Officers.

National Center for Educational Statistics. 1996. *Education in States and Nations: Indicators Comparing U.S. States with Other Industrialized Countries in 1991.* Publication No. 96-160. Washington, DC: U.S. Department of Education, National Center for Educational Statistics.

————. 2005. *Digest of Educational Statistics, 2004.* Publication No. 2006005. Washington, DC: U.S. Department of Education, National Center for Educational Statistics.

National Center for Health Statistics. 2005. *Health, United States, 2005.* Washington, DC: National Center for Health Statistics.

National Commission on Retirement Policy. 1998. *Can America Afford to Retire? The Retirement Security Challenge Facing You and the Nation.* Washington, DC: Center for Strategic and International Studies.

————. 1999. *The 21st Century Retirement Security Plan: Final Report of the National Commission on Retirement Policy.* Washington, DC: Center for Strategic & International Studies.

National Economic Council. 2000. "The Minimum Wage: Increasing the Reward for Work. A Report by the National Economic Council with the Assistance of the Council of Economic Advisors and the Office of the Chief Economist, U.S. Department of Labor." Washington, DC: National Economic Council.

National Economic Council Interagency Working Group on Social Security. 1998. "Women and Retirement Security." Washington, DC: National Economic Council Interagency Working Group on Social Security.

National Rehabilitation Hospital, Center for Health & Disability Policy Research. 2003. "Health and Employment among Adults with Disabilities." Health & Disability data brief. Washington, DC: NRH Center for Health & Disability Policy Research.

Neal, Derek, and Sherwin Rosen. 1998. "Theories of the Distribution of Labor Earnings." Working Paper No. 6,378. Cambridge, MA: National Bureau of Economic Research.

Neuberger, Zoe, Robert Greenstein, and Eileen Sweeney. 2005. "Protecting Low-Income Families' Savings: How Retirement Accounts Are Treated in Means-Tested Programs and Steps to Remove Barriers to Retirement Saving." Paper No. 2005-6. Washington, DC: Retirement Security Project.

Neumark, David, and Elizabeth T. Powers. 1999. "Means Testing Social Security." In *Prospects for Social Security Reform,* edited by Olivia S. Mitchell, Robert J. Myers, and Howard Young (243–67). Philadelphia: University of Pennsylvania Press.

————. 2000. "Welfare for the Elderly: The Effects of SSI on Pre-Retirement Labor Supply." *Journal of Public Economics* 78(1/2): 51–80.

————. 2003/04. "The Effect of the SSI Program on Labor Supply: Improved Evidence from Social Security Administrative Files." *Social Security Bulletin* 65(3): 45–60.

Neumark, David, Mark Schweitzer, and William Wascher. 2000. "The Effects of Minimum Wages Throughout the Wage Distribution." Working Paper No. 7,519. Cambridge, MA: National Bureau of Economic Research.

Nichols, Len M. 2001. "Policy Options for Filling Gaps in the Health Insurance Coverage of Older Workers and Retirees." In *Ensuring Health and Income Security for an Aging Workforce*, edited by Peter P. Budetti, Richard V. Burkhauser, Janice M. Gregory, and H. Allan Hunt (451–75). Kalamazoo, MI: W.E. Upjohn Institute for Employment Research.

Nichols, Orlo, Michael Clingman, and Alice Wade. 2005. "Internal Real Rates of Return under the OASDI Program for Hypothetical Workers." Actuarial Note No. 2004.5. Baltimore, MD: Social Security Administration, Office of the Chief Actuary.

Nicholson, Trish. 2003. "Boomers Discover Age Bias: Age Complaints Surge as Midlife Workers Find the Going Harder." *AARP Bulletin Online* (March).

Nicholson, Walter. 1978. *Microeconomic Theory: Basic Principles and Extensions.* 2nd ed. Hinsdale, IL: The Dryden Press.

Nightingale, Demetra Smith. 1995. "Welfare Reform: Historical Context and Current Issues." In *The Work Alternative: Welfare Reform and the Realities of the Job Market*, edited by Demetra Smith Nightingale and Robert Haveman (1–13). Washington, DC: Urban Institute Press.

O'Connell, Mary E. 1993. "On the Fringe: Rethinking the Link between Wages and Benefits." *Tulane Law Review* 67(5): 1421–1529.

O'Neill, June. 2003. "Catching Up: The Gender Gap in Wages, circa 2000." *American Economic Review* 93(2): 309–14.

OECD. See Organisation for Economic Co-operation and Development.

Okner, Benjamin A. 1975. "The Role of Demogrants as an Income Maintenance Alternative." In *Integrating Income Maintenance Programs*, edited by Irene Lurie (79–107). New York: Academic Press.

Okun, Arthur M. 1975. *Equality and Efficiency: The Big Tradeoff.* Washington, DC: The Brookings Institution.

Oliver, Pamela E. 2001. "Racial Disparities in Imprisonment: Some Basic Information." *University of Wisconsin–Madison Institute for Research on Poverty Focus* 21(3): 28–31.

Olsen, Kelly, and Jack VanDerhei. 1997. "Defined Contribution Plan Dominance Grows across Sectors and Employers Sizes, while Mega Defined Benefit Plans Remain Strong: Where We Are and Where We Are Going." Special Report No. 33 and Issue Brief No. 190. Washington, DC: Employee Benefit Research Institute.

Olson, Craig A. 2000. "Part-Time Work, Health Insurance Coverage, and the Wages of Married Women." In *Employee Benefits and Labor Markets in Canada and the United States*, edited by William T. Alpert and Stephen A. Woodbury (295–324). Kalamazoo, MI: W.E. Upjohn Institute for Employment Research.

Organisation for Economic Co-operation and Development (OECD). Council at Ministerial Level. 2004. "Strengthening Growth and Public Finances in an Era of Demographic Change." Paris: OECD.

———. 2005a. "Economic Survey of the United States: 2005." OECD Observer Policy Brief, October. Paris: OECD.

———. 2005b. "Taxing Working Families: A Distributional Analysis." Tax Policy Study No. 12. Paris: OECD.

———. 2006a. *Live Longer, Work Longer.* Paris: OECD.

———. 2006b. *OECD Factbook: Economic, Environmental, and Social Statistics.* Paris: OECD.

Orrenius, Pia M. 2003. "U.S. Immigration and Economic Growth: Putting Policy on Hold." *Federal Reserve Bank of Dallas Southwest Economy* Issue 5: 1–7.

———. 2004. "Immigrant Assimilation: Is the U.S. Still a Melting Pot?" *Federal Reserve Board of Dallas Southwest Economy* Issue 3: 1–5.

Orszag, Peter R., and Matthew G. Hall. 2003. "Tax Facts from the Tax Policy Center: The Saver's Credit." *Tax Notes* (June 9): 1541.

Paglin, Morton. 1975. "The Measurement and Trend of Inequality: A Basic Revision." *American Economic Review* 65(4): 598–609.

Panis, Constaintijn W.A., and Lee A. Lillard. 1996. "Socioeconomic Differentials in the Returns to Social Security." Labor and Population Program Working Paper Series 96-05, No. DRU-1327-NIA. Santa Monica, CA: RAND Corporation.

Papadimitriou, Dimitri B. 1998. "(Full) Employment Policy: Theory and Practice." Working Paper No. 258. Annandale-on-Hudson, NY: Levy Economics Institute, Bard College.

Papke, Leslie E. 1999. "Are 401(k) Plans Replacing Other Employer-Provided Pensions? Evidence from Panel Data." *Journal of Human Resources* 34(2): 346–68.

Parisi, Michael, and Scott Hollenbeck. 2005. "Individual Income Tax Returns, 2003." *Statistics of Income Bulletin* 25(2): 9–49.

Parisi, Michael, and Michael Strudler. 2003. "The 400 Individual Income Tax Returns Reporting the Highest Adjusted Gross Incomes Each Year, 1992–2000: Data Release." *Statistics of Income Bulletin* (Spring): 7–9.

Pavetti, LaDonna. 2004. "The Challenge of Achieving High Work Participation Rates in Welfare Programs." *Welfare Reform & Beyond* Policy Brief No. 31. Washington, DC: The Brookings Institution.

PBGC. See Pension Benefit Guaranty Corporation.

Pechman, Joseph A., ed. 1977. *Comprehensive Income Taxation.* Washington, DC: The Brookings Institution.

———. 1980. *What Should Be Taxed: Income or Expenditure?* Washington, DC: Brookings Institution Press.

Pell Institute for the Study of Opportunity in Higher Education, The. 2004. "Indicators of Opportunity in Higher Education: Fall 2004 Status Report." Washington, DC: The Pell Institute for the Study of Opportunity in Higher Education.

Penner, Rudolph. 2004. "Searching for a Just Tax System." Tax Policy Center Discussion Paper 13. Washington, DC: The Urban Institute.

Pension Benefit Guaranty Corporation. 2005. "PBGC Announces Maximum Insurance Benefit for 2006." Washington, DC: Pension Benefit Guaranty Corporation.

Pension Rights Center. 2005. Conversation on Coverage, "Covering the Uncovered: Common Ground Recommendations to Expand Retirement Savings for American Workers." Working Report. Washington, DC: Pension Rights Center.

Pensions Policy Institute. 2006. "Shaping a Stable Pensions Solution: How Pension Experts Would Reform U.K. Pensions." London: Pension Policy Institute.

Pesando, James E., and John A. Turner. 2000. "Labor-Market Effects of Canadian and U.S. Pension Tax Policy." In *Employee Benefits and Labor Markets in Canada and the United States,* edited by William T. Alpert and Stephen

A. Woodbury (451–73). Kalamazoo, MI: W.E. Upjohn Institute for Employment Research.

Pew Research Center for the People and the Press, The. 2003. "The 2004 Political Landscape: Evenly Divided and Increasingly Polarized." Washington, DC: The Pew Research Center for the People and the Press.

Phelps, Edmund S. 1997. *Rewarding Work: How to Restore Participation and Self-Support to Free Enterprise.* Cambridge, MA: Harvard University Press.

Phillips, Kevin. 2002. *Wealth and Democracy: A Political History of the American Rich.* New York: Broadway Books.

Pierce, Brooks. 1999. "Compensation Inequality." Working Paper No. 323. Washington, DC: U.S. Department of Labor.

Pigeon, Marc-Andre, and L. Randall Wray. 1999. "Down and Out in the United States." Public Policy Brief No. 54A. Annandale-on-Hudson, NY: Levy Economics Institute, Bard College.

Piketty, Thomas, and Emmanuel Saez. 2003. "Income Inequality in the United States, 1913–1998." *Quarterly Journal of Economics* 143(1): 1–39.

———. 2006. "The Evolution of Top Incomes: A Historical and International Perspective." *American Economics Association Papers and Proceedings* 96(2): 200–205.

Plato. 1901. *The Republic.* Trans. Benjamin Jowett. New York: P. F. Collier & Son.

Polapink, Paul S. 2006. "Pension Penchant." *Contingencies* (January/February): 12–14.

Pollack, Harold, and Karl Kronebusch. 2004. "Health Insurance and Vulnerable Populations." In *Health Policy and the Uninsured,* edited by Catherine McLaughlin (205–55). Washington, DC: Urban Institute Press.

Powers, Elizabeth T., and David Neumark. 2005. "The Supplemental Security Income Program and Incentives to Claim Social Security Retirement Early." *National Tax Journal* 58(1): 5–26.

Pratt, David A., and Dianne Bennett. 1999. "Simplifying Retirement Plan Distributions." In *Proceedings of the Fifty-Seventh New York University Institute on Federal Taxation—Employee Benefits and Executive Compensation,* edited by Alvin D. Lurie (5-1–5-54). New York: Matthew Bender & Company.

Prescott, Edward C. 2004. "Why Do Americans Work So Much More than Europeans?" *Federal Reserve Bank of Minneapolis Quarterly Review* 28(1): 2–13.

———. 2005. "The Elasticity of Labor Supply and the Consequences for Tax Policy." In *Toward Fundamental Tax Reform,* edited by Alan J. Auerbach and Kevin A. Hassett (123–34). Washington, DC: AEI Press.

President's Advisory Panel on Federal Tax Reform. 2005a. "America Needs a Better Tax System: Statement by the Members of the President's Advisory Panel on Federal Tax Reform." Washington, DC: President's Advisory Panel on Federal Tax Reform.

———. 2005b. *Simple, Fair & Pro-Growth: Proposals to Fix America's Tax System.* Washington, DC: President's Advisory Panel on Federal Tax Reform.

President's Commission on Income Maintenance. 1969. *Poverty amid Plenty: The Report of the President's Commission on Income Maintenance.* Washington, DC: U.S. Government Printing Office.

President's Commission on Pension Policy. 1981. *Coming of Age: Toward a National Retirement Income Policy.* Washington, DC: President's Commission on Pension Policy.

President's Commission to Strengthen Social Security. 2001. *Strengthening Social Security and Creating Personal Wealth for All Americans: Report of the President's Commission.* Washington, DC: President's Commission to Strengthen Social Security.

Presidential Task Force on Employment of Adults with Disabilities. 1998. *Recharting the Course: First Report of the Presidential Task Force on Employment of Adults with Disabilities.* Washington, DC: U.S. Department of Labor.

———. 2002. *People with Disabilities: Strengthening the 21st Century Workforce.* Washington, DC: U.S. Department of Labor.

Pressman, Steven. 2005. "Income Guarantees and the Equity-Efficiency Trade-off." *Journal of Socio-Economics* 34(1): 83–100.

Purcell, Patrick J. 2005a. "Older Workers: Employment and Retirement Trends." CRS report, updated September 14. Washington, DC: Congressional Research Service, Library of Congress.

———. 2005b. "Participation in Retirement Plans: Findings from the Survey of Income and Program Participation." CRS report, October 5. Washington, DC: Congressional Research Service, Library of Congress.

———. 2005c. "Pension Sponsorship and Participation: Summary of Recent Trends." CRS report, updated September 8. Washington, DC: Congressional Research Service, Library of Congress.

———. 2005d. "Progressive Indexing of Social Security: Effects on Future Benefits." *Journal of Pension Planning & Compliance* 31(3): 55–77.

———. 2006a. "Lump-Sum Distributions and Retirement Income Security." *Journal of Pension Planning & Compliance* 31(4): 52–74.

———. 2006b. "Retirement Savings and Household Wealth: Trends from 2001 to 2004." CRS report, updated May 22. Washington, DC: Congressional Research Service, Library of Congress.

Quigley, William P. 2003. *Ending Poverty as We Know It.* Philadelphia, PA: Temple University Press.

Quinn, Joseph F. 1999. "Retirement Patterns and Bridge Jobs in the 1990s." Issue Brief No. 206. Washington, DC: Employee Benefit Research Institute.

———. 2005. "Americans Can Work Longer." In *In Search of Retirement Security: The Changing Mix of Social Insurance, Employee Benefits, and Individual Responsibility,* edited by Teresa Ghilarducci, Van Doorn Ooms, John L. Palmer, and Catherine Hill (25–35). Washington, DC: Brookings Institution Press.

Quinn, Joseph F., Richard V. Burkhauser, and Daniel A. Myers. 1990. *Passing the Torch: the Influence of Economic Incentives on Work and Retirement.* Kalamazoo, MI: W.E. Upjohn Institute for Employment Research.

Rajnes, David. 2002. "An Evolving Pension System: Trends in Defined Benefit and Defined Contribution Plans." Issue Brief No. 249. Washington, DC: Employee Benefit Research Institute.

Raphael, Steven. 2006. "The Socioeconomic Status of Black Males: The Increasing Importance of Incarceration." In *Public Policy and the Income Distribution,* edited by Alan J. Auerbach, David Card, and John M. Quigley (319–58). New York: Russell Sage Foundation.

Rawls, John. 1971. *A Theory of Justice.* Cambridge, MA: Harvard University Press.

Reagan, Patricia B., and John A. Turner. 2000. "Did the Decline in Marginal Tax Rates during the 1980s Reduce Pension Coverage?" In *Employee Benefits and Labor Markets in Canada and the United States,* edited by William T.

Alpert and Stephen A. Woodbury (475–95). Kalamazoo, MI: W.E. Upjohn Institute for Employment Research.

Rees, Albert. 1974. "An Overview of the Labor-Supply Results." *Journal of Human Resources* 9(2): 158–80.

———. 1993. "The Role of Fairness in Wage Determination." *Journal of Labor Economics* 11(1, Part 1): 243–52.

Renshaw, Claude D., and Ken Milani. 2004. "Fixing the Marriage Penalty: Whatever Happened to the Lower Class?" *Tax Notes* (April 19): 356–57.

Reynolds, Morgan O. 1997. "The Economic Impact of Prison Labor." Brief Analysis No. 245. Dallas, TX: National Center for Policy Analysis.

Richards, Gordon. 1999. "The Effect of Lower FICA Taxes: A Retrospective Econometric Analysis." *Tax Notes* (January 11): 245–49.

Rivlin, Alice M. 2002. "Challenges of Modern Capitalism." *Regional Review: The Federal Reserve Bank of Boston* 12(3): 4–10.

Rix, Sara E. 2004. "Aging and Work—A View from the United States." Paper No. 2004-02. Washington, DC: AARP Public Policy Institute.

———. 2005. "Rethinking the Role of Older Workers: Promoting Older Worker Employment in Europe and Japan." Issue Brief No. 77. Washington, DC: AARP Public Policy Institute.

Robert Wood Johnson Foundation. 2005. "Going Without: America's Uninsured Children." Washington, DC: Robert Wood Johnson Foundation.

Robins, Philip K., and Charles Michalopoulos. 2001. "Using Financial Incentives to Encourage Welfare Recipients to Become Economically Self-Sufficient." *Federal Reserve Bank of New York Economic Policy Review* 7(2): 105–23.

Roddis, Suzanne and Zafiris Tzannatos. 1999. "Family Allowances." Social Protection Discussion Paper Series No. 9814. Washington, DC: The World Bank.

Rodríguez, Santiago Budría, Javier Díaz-Giménez, Vincenzo Quadrini, and José-Víctor Ríos-Rull. 2002. "Updated Facts on the U.S. Distributions of Earnings, Income, and Wealth." *Federal Reserve Bank of Minneapolis Quarterly Review* 26(3): 2–35.

Roemer, John E. 1996. *Theories of Distributive Justice*. Cambridge, MA: Harvard University Press.

———. 1998a. "Comment." In *Work and Welfare* by Robert Solow, edited by Amy Gutmann (63–76). Princeton, NJ: Princeton University Press.

———. 1998b. *Equality of Opportunity*. Cambridge, MA: Harvard University Press.

Romich, Jennifer L. 2006. "Difficult Calculations: Low-Income Workers and Marginal Tax Rates." *Social Service Review* 80(1): 27–66.

Rosen, Harvey S. 2002. *Public Finance*. 6th ed. Boston, MA: McGraw-Hill Irwin.

Rubin, Rose M., Shelley I. White-Means, and Luojia Mao Daniel. 2000. "Income Distribution of Older Americans." *Monthly Labor Review* 123(11): 19–30.

Rudnick, Harry J. 1945. "A Proposal for an Accessions Tax." *Tax Law Review* 1: 25–43.

———. 1950. "What Alternative to the Estate and Gift Taxes." *California Law Review* 38: 150–82.

Ryscavage, Paul. 1999. *Income Inequality in America: An Analysis of Trends*. Armonk, NY: M.E. Sharpe.

Sabelhaus, John, and David Weiner. 1999. "Disposition of Lump-Sum Pension Distributions: Evidence from Tax Returns." *National Tax Journal* 52(3): 593–613.

Saez, Emmanuel. 2006. "Income and Wealth Concentration in Historical Perspective." In *Public Policy and the Income Distribution*, edited by Alan J. Auerbach, David Card, and John M. Quigley (221–58). New York: Russell Sage Foundation.

Samuelson, Paul. 1980. *Economics*. New York: McGraw-Hill.

Samwick, Andrew A. 1998. "New Evidence on Pensions, Social Security, and the Timing of Retirement." *Journal of Public Economics* 70(2): 207–236.

Sanford, C. T. 1971. *Taxing Personal Wealth*. London: George Allen & Unwin Ltd.

Sass, Steven A. 2003. "Reforming the U.S. Retirement Income System: The Growing Role of Work." Global Issue in Brief No. I. Boston, MA: Center for Retirement Research at Boston College.

Saving, Jason L., and W. Michael Cox. 2000. "Some Pleasant Economic Side Effects." *Federal Reserve Board of Dallas Southwest Economy* Issue 4: 7–12.

Sawhill, Isabel. 1999. "From Welfare to Work: Toward a New Antipoverty Agenda." *Brookings Review* 17(4): 27–30.

Sawhill, Isabel, and Ron Haskins. 2002. "Welfare Reform and the Work Support System." *Welfare Reform & Beyond* Policy Brief No. 17. Washington, DC: The Brookings Institution.

Sawhill, Isabel, and Adam Thomas. 2001. "A Tax Proposal for Working Families with Children." *Welfare Reform & Beyond* Policy Brief No. 3. Washington, DC: The Brookings Institution.

Sawicky, Max B. 2003. "And Now for Something Completely Different: Doing a Fiscal U-Turn." *Tax Notes* (December 15): 1353–54.

Scahill, Patricia. 1999. "Twenty-Five Years of ERISA Leaves Defined Benefit Plans Battered and Bruised." *Benefits Quarterly* 15(4): 34–47.

Scahill, Patricia L., and Jonathan Barry Forman. 2002. "Protecting Participants and Beneficiaries in a Phased Retirement World." In *New York University Review of Employee Benefits and Executive Compensation–2002*, edited by Alvin D. Lurie (1-1–1-48). Newark, NJ: LexisNexis.

Schieber, Sylvester J. 2004. "The Outlook of Retiree Health Benefits." Research Dialogue No. 81. New York: TIAA-CREF Institute.

Schieber, Sylvester J., and John B. Shoven. 1999. *The Real Deal: The History and Future of Social Security*. New Haven, CT, and London: Yale University Press.

Schmalbeck, Richard, and Lawrence Zelenak. 2004. *Federal Income Taxation Teacher's Manual*. New York: Aspen Publishers.

Schmidt, Lucie, and Purvi Sevak. 2005. "Gender, Marriage, and Asset Accumulation in the United States." Working Paper No. 2005-109. Ann Arbor: University of Michigan Retirement Research Center.

Schneider, Friedrich, and Dominik Enste. 2002. "Hiding in the Shadows: The Growth of the Underground Economy." Economic Issues Paper No. 30. Washington, DC: International Monetary Fund.

Schroyen, Fred. 2003. "Redistributive Taxation and the Household: The Case for Individual Filings." *Journal of Public Economics* 87: 2527–47.

Schwabish, Jonathan A. 2004. "Accounting for Wages and Benefits Using ECI." *Monthly Labor Review* 127(9): 26–41.

Schwenk, Albert E., and Jordan N. Pfuntner. 2001. "Compensation in the Later Part of the Century." *Compensation and Working Conditions Online*, fall: 33–40.

Scott, Frank A., Mark C. Berger, and John E. Garen. 1995. "Do Health Insurance and Pensions Costs Reduce Job Opportunities of Older Workers." *Industrial and Labor Relations Review* 48(4): 775–91.

Seago, W. Eugene. 2003. "Taxing Social Security Receipts as Private Pensions." *Tax Notes* (November 10): 785–87.

Seidman, Laurence S. 1999. *Funding Social Security: A Strategic Alternative.* New York: Cambridge University Press.

———. 2004. "A Progressive Value Added Tax: Has Its Time Finally Come?" *Tax Notes* (June 7): 1255–63.

Shakow, David J. 1986. "Taxation without Realization: A Proposal for Accrual Taxation." *University of Pennsylvania Law Review* 134(5): 1111–1206.

Shakow, David, and Reed Schuldiner. 2000. "A Comprehensive Wealth Tax." *Tax Law Review* 53(4): 499–585.

Shapiro, Isaac, and Sharon Parrott, eds. 2003. "Are Policies that Assist Low-Income Workers Receiving Appropriate Priority?" Washington, DC: Center on Budget and Policy Priorities.

Shavell, Steven. 2004. *Foundations of Economic Analysis of Law.* Cambridge, MA, and London: Belknap Press of Harvard University Press.

Shaviro, Daniel N. 1997. "The Minimum Wage, the Earned Income Tax Credit, and Optimal Subsidy Policy." *University of Chicago Law Review* 64(2): 405–81.

———. 1999. "Effective Marginal Tax Rates on Low-Income Households." *Tax Notes* (August 23): 1191–1201.

———. 2000. "Inequality, Wealth, and Endowment." *Tax Law Review* 53 (Spring): 397–421.

———. 2004a. "Replacing the Income Tax with a Progressive Consumption Tax." *Tax Notes* (April 5): 91–113.

———. 2004b. *Who Should Pay for Medicare?* Chicago, IL, and London: University of Chicago Press.

Sher, George. 1987. *Desert.* Princeton, NJ: Princeton University Press.

Shipler, David K. 2004. *The Working Poor: Invisible in America.* New York: Alfred A. Knopf.

Short, Kathleen. 2001. *Experimental Poverty Measures: 1999.* Current Population Report No. P60-216. Washington, DC: U.S. Bureau of the Census.

Short, Pamela Farley. 2004. "Counting and Characterizing the Uninsured." In *Health Policy and the Uninsured,* edited by Catherine G. McLaughlin (1–34). Washington, DC: Urban Institute Press.

Shulman, Beth. 2005. *The Betrayal of Work.* New York: The New Press.

Sillamaa, M. A. 1999. "How Work Effort Responds to Wage Taxation: An Experimental Test of a Zero Top Marginal Tax Rate." *Journal of Public Economics* 73(1): 125–34.

Silverberg, Marsha, Elizabeth Warner, Michael Fong, and David Goodwin. 2004. *National Assessment of Vocational Education: Final Report to Congress.* Washington, DC: U.S. Department of Education, Office of the Undersecretary, Policy and Program Studies Service.

Simons, Henry C. 1938. *Personal Income Taxation: The Definition of Income as a Problem of Fiscal Policy.* Chicago, IL: University of Chicago Press.

Slemrod, Joel. 1996. "Which Is the Simplest Tax System of Them All?" In *Economic Effects of Fundamental Tax Reform,* edited by Henry J. Aaron and William G. Gale (355–91). Washington, DC: Brookings Institution Press.

————. 2003. "2002 Erwin N. Griswold Lecture before the American College of Tax Counsel: 'The Dynamic Tax Economist.' " *Tax Lawyer* 56(3): 611–23.

Slemrod, Joel B., ed. 2002. *Does Atlas Shrug? The Economic Consequences of Taxing the Rich.* Cambridge, MA: Harvard University Press.

Slemrod, Joel, and Jon Bakija. 2000. *Taxing Ourselves: A Citizens's Guide to the Great Debate Over Tax Reform.* 2nd ed. Cambridge, MA: Massachusetts Institute of Technology.

Slemrod, Joel, Shlomo Yitzhaki, Joram Mayshar, and Michael Lundholm. 1994. "The Optimal Two Bracket Linear Income Tax." *Journal of Public Economics* 53(2): 269–90.

Slottje, Daniel J., Stephen A. Woodbury, and Rod W. Anderson. 2000. "Employee Benefits and the Distribution of Income and Wealth." In *Employee Benefits and Labor Markets in Canada and the United States,* edited by William T. Alpert and Stephen A. Woodbury (349–78). Kalamazoo, MI: W.E. Upjohn Institute for Employment Research.

Smeeding, Timothy M. 2006a. "Government Programs and Social Outcomes: Comparison of the United States with Other Rich Nations." In *Public Policy and the Income Distribution,* edited by Alan J. Auerbach, David Card, and John M. Quigley (149–218). New York: Russell Sage Foundation.

————. 2006b. "Poor People in Rich Nations: The United States in Comparative Perspective." *Journal of Economic Perspectives* 20(1): 69–90.

Smeeding, Timothy M., and Peter Gottschalk. 1998. "Cross-National Income Inequality: How Great Is It and What Can We Learn from It?" *University of Wisconsin Madison Institute for Research on Poverty Focus* 19(3): 15–19.

Smeeding, Timothy M., and R. Kent Weaver. 2002. "The Senior Income Guarantee (SIG): A New Proposal to Reduce Poverty among the Elderly." Working Paper No. 2001-12. Boston, MA: Center for Retirement Research at Boston College.

Smith, Adam. 1986. *The Wealth of Nations, Books I–III.* London: Penguin Books, Penguin Classics.

Smith, James P. 2003. "Assimilation across the Latino Generations." *American Economic Review* 93(2): 315–19.

Smith, Karen, Eric Toder, and Howard Iams. 2003/04. "Lifetime Distributional Effects of Social Security Retirement Benefits." *Social Security Bulletin* 65(1): 33–41.

Smith, Marian L. 1998. "Overview of INS History." In *A Historical Guide to the U.S. Government,* edited by George T. Kurian. New York: Oxford University Press. Reprinted on the U.S. Citizenship and Immigration Services web site, http://uscis.gov/graphics/aboutus/history/articles/OVIEW.htm.

Snyder, Lester B. 1998. "Taxation with an Attitude: Can We Rationalize the Distinction between 'Earned' and 'Unearned' Income?" *Virginia Tax Review* 18(2): 241–300.

Social Security Administration. 2002. *Social Security Bulletin, Annual Statistical Supplement: 2001.* Washington, DC: Social Security Administration.

————. 2004a. *Income of the Aged Chartbook, 2002.* Washington, DC: Social Security Administration.

————. 2004b. *Performance and Accountability Report: Fiscal Year 2004.* Washington, DC: Social Security Administration.

————. 2005a. "The Distributional Consequences of a 'No-Action' Scenario: Updated Results." Policy Brief No. 2005-1. Washington, DC: Social Security Administration, Office of Retirement Policy.

————. 2005b. "Poverty-Level Annuitization Requirements in Social Security Proposals Incorporating Personal Retirement Accounts." Issue Paper No. 2005-01. Washington, DC: Social Security Administration.

————. 2005c. "2006 Social Security Changes." Fact sheet. Baltimore, MD: Social Security Administration press office.

————. 2006a. "Defined Contribution Pension Plans and the Supplemental Security Income Program." Policy Brief No. 2006-01. Washington, DC: Social Security Administration, Office of Policy.

————. 2006b. *Social Security Bulletin, Annual Statistical Supplement: 2005.* Washington, DC: Social Security Administration.

Social Security Advisory Board. 2003. *The Social Security Definition of Disability.* Washington, DC: Social Security Advisory Board.

————. 2005a. *Retirement Security: The Unfolding of a Predictable Surprise.* Washington, DC: Social Security Advisory Board.

————. 2005b. *Social Security: Why Action Should Be Taken Soon.* Washington, DC: Social Security Advisory Board.

Soled, Jay A. 2000. "When Will Congress Police the Minimum Distribution Rules?" *Tax Notes* (February 11): 1003–1009.

Solon, Gary. 1992. "Intergenerational Income Mobility in the United States." *American Economic Review* 82(3): 393–408.

Solow, Robert M. 1998. "Guess Who Pays for Workfare." In *Work and Welfare,* by Robert Solow, edited by Amy Gutmann (23–43). Princeton, NJ: Princeton University Press.

SSA. See Social Security Administration.

Stanfield, Rochelle, with Corinna Nicolaou. 2000. "Social Security: Out of Step with the Modern Family." Washington, DC: The Urban Institute.

Stark, Kirk J. 2004. "Fiscal Federalism and Tax Progressivity: Should the Federal Income Tax Encourage State and Local Redistribution?" *UCLA Law Review* 51(5): 1389–1435.

————. 2005. "Enslaving the Beachcomber: Some Thoughts on the Liberty Objections to Endowment Taxation." *Canadian Journal of Law and Jurisprudence* 43(1): 47–68.

Staudt, Nancy C. 1996. "Taxing Housework." *Georgetown Law Journal* 84: 1571–1647.

Steuerle, C. Eugene. 2003. "A Workable Social Insurance Approach to Expanding Health Insurance Coverage." In *Covering America: Real Remedies for the Uninsured,* vol. III, edited by Jack A. Meyer and Elliot K. Wicks (97–112). Washington, DC: Economic & Social Research Institute.

————. 2004. "Congress Spends More to Increase Number of Uninsured." *Tax Notes* (April 12): 237–38.

Steuerle, C. Eugene, and Jon M. Bakija. 1994. *Retooling Social Security for the 21st Century: Right & Wrong Approaches To Reform.* Washington, DC: Urban Institute Press.

Steuerle, C. Eugene, and Christopher Spiro. 1999. "Nonemployment: A Necessary Economic Indicator." Straight Talk on Social Security and Retirement Policy No. 2. Washington, DC: The Urban Institute.

Steuerle, C. Eugene, Christopher Spiro, and Adam Carasso. 1999a. "Does Social Security Treat Spouses Fairly?" Straight Talk on Social Security and Retirement Policy No. 12. Washington, DC: The Urban Institute.

———. 1999b. "Social Security's Cost-of-Living Adjustments: Can Reforms Protect the Most Vulnerable Recipients?" Straight Talk on Social Security and Retirement Policy No. 8. Washington, DC: The Urban Institute.

Stewart, Jay. 1995. "Do Older Workers Respond to Changes in Social Security Benefits? A Look at the Time Series Evidence." Working Paper No. 271. Washington, DC: U.S. Department of Labor, Bureau of Labor Statistics.

Stoker, Robert P., and Laura A. Wilson. 2006. *When Work Is Not Enough: State and Federal Policies to Support Needy Workers*. Washington, DC: Brookings Institution Press.

Stoops, Nicole. 2004. "Educational Attainment in the United States: 2003." Current Population Report No. P20-550. Washington, DC: U.S. Bureau of the Census.

Strnad, Jeff. 1990. "Periodicity and Accretion Taxation: Norms and Implementation." *Yale Law Journal* 99(8): 1817–1912.

Strudler, Michael, Tom Petska, and Ryan Petska. 2004. "Further Analysis of the Distribution of Income and Taxes, 1979–2002." Paper presented at the American Statistical Association Joint Statistical Meeting, Toronto, April 5–12.

Sullivan, Martin A. 2003. "Economic Analysis: Low-Income Stimulus: Why a Payroll Tax Cut is Unlikely." *Tax Notes* (January 6): 16–23.

Sunley, Emil M., Jr. 1977. "Employee Benefits and Transfer Payments." In *Comprehensive Income Taxation*, edited by Joseph A. Pechman (75–114). Washington, DC: Brookings Institution Press.

Surrey, Stanley S. 1950. "An Introduction to Revision of the Federal Estate and Gift Taxes." *California Law Review* 38(1): 1–27.

———. 1969. "Income Maintenance Programs." *Tax Law Review* 24(3): 305–35.

———. 1973. *Pathways to Tax Reform: The Concept of Tax Expenditures*. Cambridge, MA: Harvard University Press.

Surrey, Stanley S., and William F. Hellmuth. 1969. "The Tax Expenditure Budget—Response to Professor Bittker." *National Tax Journal* 22: 528–37.

Terkel, Studs. 1985. *Working: People Talk About What They Do All Day and How They Feel About What They Do*. New York: Ballantine Books.

Thaler, Richard H., and Shlomo Bernartzi. 2004. "Save More Tomorrow: Using Behavioral Economics to Increase Employee Saving." *Journal of Political Economics* 112(1): S164–87.

Thompson, Lawrence H. 1997. "Overview of Social Security Issues." In *Report of the 1994–1996 Advisory Council on Social Security* by Advisory Council on Social Security (vol. 2, 279). Washington, DC: Advisory Council on Social Security.

———. 1998. *Older & Wiser: The Economics of Public Pensions*. Washington, DC: Urban Institute Press.

Thompson, Tommy G. 2003. "Welfare Reform: Building on Success." Statement by Tommy G. Thompson, Secretary of Health and Human Services, before the Senate Committee on Finance, March 12.

Thoreau, Henry David. 1849/1906. "Civil Disobedience," originally published as "Resistance to Civil Government." In *The Writings of Henry David Thoreau*, vol. 4. New York: Houghton Mifflin.

Thuronyi, Victor. 2000. "Commentary: The European Experience with a Wealth Tax." *Tax Law Review* 53(4): 693–95.

Thurow, Lester C. 1972. "Net Worth Taxes." *National Tax Journal* 25(3): 417–23.

———. 1973. "Toward a Definition of Economic Justice." *Public Interest* 31 (Spring): 56–80.

———. 1975. *Generating Inequality: Mechanisms of Distribution in the U.S. Economy.* New York: Basic Books.

———. 1976. "The Pursuit of Equality." *Dissent* (Summer): 253–58.

———. 1998. "Wage Dispersion: 'Who Done It?'" *Journal of Post-Keynesian Economics* 21(1): 25–37.

Tobin, James. 1965. "On Improving the Economic Status of the Negro." *Daedalus* (4): 878–98.

———. 1977. "Considerations Regarding Taxation and Equity." In *Income Redistribution,* edited by Colin D. Campbell (127–33). Washington, DC: American Enterprise Institute for Public Policy Research.

Tobin, James, Joseph A. Pechman, and Peter M. Mieszkowski. 1967. "Is a Negative Income Tax Practical?" *Yale Law Review* 77: 1–77.

Toossi, Mitra. 2005. "Labor Force Projections to 2014: Retiring Boomers." *Monthly Labor Review* 128(11): 25–44.

Topel, Robert H. 1997. "Factor Proportions and Relative Wages: The Supply-Side Determinants of Wage Inequality." *Journal of Economic Perspectives* 11(2): 55–74.

Triest, Robert K. 1996a. "The Efficiency Cost of Increased Progressivity." In *Tax Progressivity and Income Inequality,* edited by Joel Slemrod (137–69). Cambridge: Cambridge University Press.

———. 1996b. "Fundamental Tax Reform and Labor Supply." In *Economic Effects of Fundamental Tax Reform,* edited by Henry J. Aaron and William G. Gale (247–78). Washington, DC: Brookings Institution Press.

Triest, Robert K., Margarita Sapozhnikov, and Steven A. Sass. 2006. "Population Aging and the Structure of Wages." Working Paper No. 2006-5. Boston, MA: Center for Retirement Research at Boston College.

Turner, Mark D., and Burt S. Barnow. 2003. "Living Wage and Earned Income Tax Credit: A Comparative Analysis." Washington, DC: Employment Policies Institute.

Turnier, William J. 2003. "PAYE as an Alternative to an Alternative Tax System." *Virginia Tax Review* 23(1): 205–74.

Uccello, Cori E. 1998. "Factors Influencing Retirement: Their Implications for Raising Retirement Age." Paper No. 9,810. Washington, DC: American Association of Retired Persons Public Policy Institute.

University of Wisconsin–Madison Institute for Research on Poverty. 2005. "Inequality in America: What Role for Human Capital Policies?" *Focus* 23(3): 1–10.

Urban, Julie A., and Pamela N. Olson. 2005. "A Comprehensive Employment Model for Low-Income Mothers." *Journal of Family and Economic Issues* 26(1): 101–22.

Urban Institute, The. 2002. "States Resist Cuts to Children's Health Insurance Program in Face of Growing Deficits." Press release, October 1. Washington, DC: The Urban Institute.

U.S. Bureau of the Census. 2000. "Table NP-T7-B. Projected Life Expectancy at Birth by Race and Hispanic Origin, 1999 to 2100." Washington, DC: U.S. Bureau of the Census. http://www.census.gov/population/projections/nation/summary/np-t7-b.pdf.

———. 2003. "Supplemental Measures of Material Well-Being: Expenditures, Consumption, and Poverty: 1998 and 2001." Current Population Report No. P23-201. Washington, DC: U.S. Bureau of the Census.

———. 2004a. *Current Population Survey Historical Income Tables—Experimental Measures*. Washington, DC: U.S. Bureau of the Census. http://www.census.gov/hhes/www/income/histinc/incexper.html.

———. 2004b. *Current Population Survey Historical Income Tables—Income Inequality*. Washington, DC: U.S. Bureau of the Census. http://www.census.gov/hhes/www/income/histinc/ineqtoc.html.

———. 2005a. "College Degree Nearly Doubles Annual Earnings, Census Bureau Reports." Press release CB 05-38. Washington, DC: U.S. Bureau of the Census.

———. 2005b. *Current Population Survey Historical Income Tables—Families*. Washington, DC: U.S. Bureau of the Census. http://www.census.gov/hhes/www/income/histinc/incfamdet.html.

———. 2005c. "Table HH-4. Households by Size: 1960 to Present." Washington, DC: U.S. Bureau of the Census. http://www.census.gov/population/socdemo/hh-fam/hh4.pdf.

. 2005d. "Supplemental Measures of Material Well-Being: Basic Needs, Consumer Durables, Energy, and Poverty, 1981 to 2002." Current Population Report No. P23-202. Washington, DC: U.S. Bureau of the Census.

———. 2006. "The Effects of Government Taxes and Transfers on Income and Poverty: 2004." Washington, DC: U.S. Bureau of the Census.

U.S. Commission on the Future of Worker-Management Relations. 1994. *The Dunlop Commission on the Future of Worker-Management Relations: Final Report*. Washington, DC: U.S. Department of Labor. http://digitalcommons.ilr.cornell.edu/cgi/viewcontent.cgi?article=1004&context=key_workplace.

U.S. Congress. Joint Committee on Taxation. 2000. *Description of Revenue Provisions Contained in the President's Fiscal Year 2001 Budget Proposal*. Publication No. JCS-2-00. Washington, DC: U.S. Government Printing Office.

———. 2001. *Study of the Overall State of the Federal Tax System*. Vol. 1 of *Study of the Overall State of the Federal Tax System, and Recommendations for Simplification, Pursuant to Section 8022(3)(B) of the Internal Revenue Code of 1986*. Washington, DC: U.S. Government Printing Office.

———. 2004a. "List of Expiring Tax Provisions." Document No. JCX-71-04. Washington, DC: Joint Committee on Taxation.

———. 2004b. "Present Law and Analysis Relating to Tax Benefits for Higher Education." Document No. JCX-52-04. Washington, DC: Joint Committee on Taxation.

———. 2005a. *Options to Improve Tax Compliance and Reform Tax Expenditures*. Document No. JCS-2-05. Washington, DC: Joint Committee on Taxation.

———. 2005b. "Present Law and Background Relating to Employer-Sponsored Defined Benefit Plans and the Pension Benefit Guaranty Corporation ("PBGC")." Document No. JCX-03-05. Washington, DC: Joint Committee on Taxation.

———. 2005c. "Present Law and Background Relating to the Individual Alternative Minimum Tax." Document No. JCX-37-05. Washington, DC: Joint Committee on Taxation.

———. 2006a. *Estimates of Federal Tax Expenditures for Fiscal Years 2006–2010*. Document No. JCS-2-06. Washington, DC: U.S. Government Printing Office.

————. 2006b. "Present Law and Analysis Relating to the Tax Treatment of Health Care Expenses." Document No. JCX-12-06. Washington, DC: Joint Committee on Taxation.

U.S. Congress. Joint Economic Committee. Subcommittee on Fiscal Policy. *Income Security for Americans: Recommendations of the Public Welfare Study.* 93rd Congress, 2nd sess., 1974. Committee Print.

————. Joint Economic Committee. 1997. "Payroll Taxes and the Redistribution of Income." Joint Economic Committee study. Washington, DC: Joint Economic Committee.

U.S. Department of Agriculture. 2005. "Making America Stronger: A Profile of the Food Stamp Program." Washington, DC: U.S. Department of Agriculture.

U.S. Department of Agriculture. Food and Nutrition Service. Office of Analysis, Nutrition, and Evaluation. 2003. "Food Stamp Participation Rates and Benefits: An Analysis of Variation within Demographic Groups." Washington, DC: U.S. Department of Agriculture.

U.S. Department of Health and Human Services. 1985. *Report of Earnings Sharing Implementation Study.* Washington, DC: U.S. Government Printing Office.

————. 2000. *Healthy People 2010.* 2nd ed. With *Understanding and Improving Health and Objectives for Improving Health.* 2 vols. Washington, DC: U.S. Government Printing Office.

————. 2005. "Medicare Premiums and Deductibles for 2006." Fact sheet, September 16. Washington, DC: U.S. Department of Health and Human Services.

————. 2006. "Annual Update of the HHS Poverty Guidelines." *Federal Register* 71 (2006): 3,848–49.

U.S. Department of Health and Human Services. Administration for Children and Families. 1999. *Access to Child Care for Low-Income Working Families.* Washington, DC: U.S. Department of Health and Human Services.

U.S. Department of Homeland Security. Office of Immigration Studies. 2003. *2002 Yearbook of Immigration Statistics.* Washington, DC: U.S. Government Printing Office.

————. 2005. *2004 Yearbook of Immigration Statistics.* Washington, DC: U.S. Government Printing Office.

U.S. Department of Justice. Bureau of Justice Statistics. 2003. "Census of State and Federal Correctional Facilities, 2000." Revised October 15. Washington, DC: U.S. Department of Justice.

U.S. Department of Labor. 2002. "Association Health Plans: Improving Access to Affordable Quality Health Care for Small Businesses." Washington, DC: U.S. Department of Labor.

————. 2004. *America's Dynamic Workforce.* Washington, DC: U.S. Department of Labor.

————. 2005. *A Chartbook of International Labor Comparisons.* Washington, DC: U.S. Department of Labor.

U.S. Department of Labor. Bureau of Labor Statistics. 1999. *Employee Benefits in Medium and Large Private Establishments 1997.* Bulletin No. 2517. Washington, DC: U.S. Department of Labor, Bureau of Labor Statistics.

————. 2001. *Consumer Expenditures in 1999.* Report No. 949. Washington, DC: U.S. Department of Labor, Bureau of Labor Statistics.

————. 2002. *Working in the 21st Century: Chartbook*. Washington, DC: U.S. Department of Labor, Bureau of Labor Statistics.

————. 2003. *National Compensation Survey: Employee Benefits in Private Industry in the United States, 2000*. Bulletin No. 2555. Washington, DC: U.S. Department of Labor, Bureau of Labor Statistics.

————. 2004a. "Employee Tenure Summary." News Release No. USDL 04-1829. Washington, DC: U.S. Department of Labor, Bureau of Labor Statistics.

————. 2004b. "Number of Jobs Held, Labor Market Activity, and Earnings Growth among Younger Baby Boomers: Recent Results from a Longitudinal Study." News Release No. USDL 04-1678. Washington, DC: U.S. Department of Labor, Bureau of Labor Statistics.

————. 2005a. "American Time Use Survey–2004 Results Announced by BLS." News Release No. 05-1766. Washington, DC: U.S. Department of Labor, Bureau of Labor Statistics.

————. 2005b. "Characteristics of Minimum Wage Workers: 2004." Washington, DC: Bureau of Labor Statistics.

————. 2005c. "Contingent and Alternative Employment Arrangements, February 2005." News Release No. USDL 05-1433. Washington, DC: U.S. Department of Labor, Bureau of Labor Statistics.

————. 2005d. "Employment Characteristics of Families in 2004." News Release No. 05-876. Washington, DC: U.S. Department of Labor, Bureau of Labor Statistics.

————. 2005e. *Highlights of Women's Earnings in 2004*. Report No. 987. Washington, DC: U.S. Department of Labor, Bureau of Labor Statistics.

————. 2005f. "Labor Force Characteristics of Foreign-Born Workers in 2004." News Release No. USDL 05-834. Washington, DC: U.S. Department of Labor, Bureau of Labor Statistics.

————. 2005g. *National Compensation Survey: Employee Benefits in Private Industry in the United States, 2003*. No. 2577. Washington, DC: U.S. Department of Labor, Bureau of Labor Statistics.

————. 2005h. *National Compensation Survey: Occupational Wages in the United States, July 2004*. Bulletin No. 2576. Washington, DC: U.S. Department of Labor, Bureau of Labor Statistics.

————. 2005i. *A Profile of the Working Poor, 2003*. Report No. 983. Washington, DC: U.S. Department of Labor, Bureau of Labor Statistics.

————. 2005j. "Union Members Summary." News Release No. USDL 05-1433. Washington, DC: U.S. Department of Labor, Bureau of Labor Statistics.

————. 2005k. *Women in the Labor Force: A Databook*. Report No. 985. Washington, DC: U.S. Department of Labor, Bureau of Labor Statistics.

————. 2005l. "Work Experience of the Population in 2004." News Release No. 05-2353. Washington, DC: U.S. Department of Labor, Bureau of Labor Statistics.

————. 2006a. "Comparative Civilian Labor Force Statistics, 10 Countries, 1960–2004." Washington, DC: U.S. Department of Labor, Bureau of Labor Statistics.

————. 2006b. *Consumer Expenditures in 2004*. Report No. 992. Washington, DC: U.S. Department of Labor, Bureau of Labor Statistics.

————. 2006c. "Current Labor Statistics." *Monthly Labor Review* 129(1): 53–130.

————. 2006d. "Employer Costs for Employee Compensation—December 2005." News Release No. 06-456. Washington, DC: U.S. Department of Labor, Bureau of Labor Statistics.

———. 2006e. "Employer Costs for Employee Compensation—March 2006." News Release No. 06-1049. Washington, DC: U.S. Department of Labor, Bureau of Labor Statistics.

———. 2006f. *Tables Created by BLS: Annual Averages—Household Data.* Washington, DC: Bureau of Labor Statistics.

———. 2006g. "Usual Weekly Earnings of Wage and Salary Workers: First Quarter 2006." News Release No. USDL 06-696. Washington, DC: U.S. Department of Labor, Bureau of Labor Statistics.

U.S. Department of the Treasury. 1984. *Tax Reform for Fairness, Simplicity, and Economic Growth: The Treasury Department Report to the President.* Washington, DC: U.S. Department of the Treasury.

———. 1992a. *Integration of the Individual and Corporate Tax Systems: Taxing Business Income Once.* Washington, DC: U.S. Government Printing Office.

———. 1992b. *A Recommendation for Integration of the Individual and Corporate Tax Systems: Taxing Business Income Once.* Washington, DC: U.S. Department of Treasury.

———. 2003. *Report to the Congress on Return-Free Tax Systems: Tax Simplification Is a Prerequisite.* Washington, DC: U.S. Department of Treasury.

U.S. Departments of Labor and Treasury. 1986. *The Use of Tax Subsidies for Employment.* Washington, DC: U.S. Government Printing Office.

U.S. General Accounting Office. 1992. *Internal Revenue Service Opportunities to Reduce Taxpayer Burdens through Return-Free Filing.* GAO/GGD-92-88BR. Washington, DC: U.S. General Accounting Office.

———. 1996. *Earned Income Credit: Profile of Tax Year 1994 Recipients.* GAO-GGD-96-122BR. Washington, DC: U.S. General Accounting Office.

———. 1997. *Retirement Income: Implications of Demographic Trends for Social Security and Pension Reform.* GAO/HEHS-97-81. Washington, DC: U.S. General Accounting Office.

———. 2000a. *Cash Balance Plans: Implications for Retirement Income.* GAO/HEHS-00-207. Washington, DC: U.S. General Accounting Office.

———. 2000b. *Private Pensions: Implications of Conversions to Cash Balance Plans.* GAO/HEHS-00-185. Washington, DC: U.S. General Accounting Office.

———. 2000c. *Unemployment Insurance: Role as a Safety Net for Low-wage Workers Is Limited.* GAO-01-181. Washington, DC: U.S. General Accounting Office.

———. 2001a. *Means-Tested Programs: Determining Financial Eligibility Is Cumbersome and Can Be Simplified.* GAO-02-58. Washington, DC: U.S. General Accounting Office.

———. 2001b. *Welfare Reform: Moving Hard-to-Employ Recipients into the Workforce.* GAO-01-368. Washington, DC: U.S. General Accounting Office.

———. 2002a. *Food Stamp Program: Implementation of Electronic Benefit Transfer Systems.* GAO-02-332. Washington, DC: U.S. General Accounting Office.

———. 2002b. *Medicaid: Transitional Coverage Can Help Families Move from Welfare to Work.* GAO-02-679T. Washington, DC: U.S. General Accounting Office.

———. 2002c. *Welfare Reform: States Provide TANF-Funded Work Support Services to Many Low-Income Families Who Do Not Receive Cash Assistance.* GAO-02-615T. Washington, DC: U.S. General Accounting Office.

———. 2003. *Medicaid and SCHIP: States Use Varying Approaches to Monitor Children's Access to Care.* GAO-03-222. Washington, DC: U.S. General Accounting Office.

———. 2004. *Social Security: Distribution of Benefits and Taxes Relative to Earnings Level.* GAO-04-747. Washington, DC: U.S. General Accounting Office.

U.S. Government Accountability Office. 2005a. *Child Care: Additional Information Is Needed on Working Families Receiving Subsidies.* GAO-05-667. Washington, DC: U.S. Government Accountability Office.

———. 2005b. *Government Performance and Accountability: Tax Expenditures Represent a Substantial Federal Commitment and Need to Be Reexamined.* GAO-05-690. Washington, DC: U.S. Government Accountability Office.

———. 2005c. *Highlights of a GAO Forum: The Long-Term Fiscal Challenge.* GAO-05-282SP. Washington, DC: U.S. Government Accountability Office.

———. 2005d. *Redefining Retirement: Options for Older Americans.* GAO-05-620T. Washington, DC: Government Accountability Office.

———. 2005e. *Student Aid and Postsecondary Tax Preferences: Limited Research Exists on Effectiveness of Tools to Assist Students and Families through Title IV Student Aid and Tax Preferences.* GAO-05-684. Washington, DC: U.S. Government Accountability Office.

———. 2005f. *Tax Compliance: Reducing the Tax Gap Can Contribute to Fiscal Sustainability but Will Require a Variety of Strategies* (statement of Comptroller David M. Walker before the Senate Finance Committee). GAO-05-527T. Washington, DC: U.S. Government Accountability Office.

———. 2005g. *Tax Policy: Summary of Estimates of the Cost of the Federal Tax System.* GAO-05-878. Washington, DC: U.S. Government Accountability Office.

———. 2005h. *Unemployment Insurance: Information on Benefit Receipt.* GAO-05-291. Washington, DC: U.S. Government Accountability Office.

———. 2006a. *Older Workers: Labor Can Help Employers and Employees Plan Better for the Future.* GAO-06-80. Washington, DC: U.S. Government Accountability Office.

———. 2006b. *Tax Gap: Making Significant Progress in Improving Tax Compliance Rests on Enhancing Current IRS Techniques and Adopting New Legislative Actions.* GAO-06-453T. Washington, DC: U.S. Government Accountability Office.

U.S. House of Representatives. Committee on Ways and Means. *Report on Earnings Sharing Implementation Study.* 99th Cong. 1st sess., 1985. Committee Print.

———. 2004. *2004 Green Book: Background Material and Data on Programs within the Jurisdiction of the Committee on Ways and Means.* Washington, DC: U.S. Government Printing Office.

U.S. Securities and Exchange Commission. 2006. "SEC Votes to Adopt Changes to Disclosure Requirements Concerning Executive Compensation and Related Matters." Press Release No. 2006-123. Washington, DC: U.S. Securities and Exchange Commission.

VanDerhei, Jack. 1999. Statement before the Senate Health, Education, Labor and Pensions Committee Hearing on Hybrid Pensions, September 21. Document T-121. Washington, DC: Employee Benefit Research Institute.

———. 2006. "Defined Benefit Plan Freezes: Who's Affected, How Much, and Replacing Lost Accruals." Issue Brief No. 291. Washington, DC: Employee Benefit Research Institute.

VanDerhei, Jack, and Craig Copeland. 2003. "Can America Afford Tomorrow's Retirees: Results from the EBRI-ERF Retirement Security Projection

Model." Issue Brief No. 263. Washington, DC: Employee Benefit Research Institute.

VanDerhei, Jack, and Ken McDonnell. 2000. "Current Provisions and Recent Trends in Qualified Single-Employer Defined Contribution Plans in the Private Sector." In *The Future of Private Retirement Plans*, edited by Dallas L. Salisbury (53–56). Washington, DC: Employee Benefit Research Institute.

Van Parijs, Philippe. 1995. *Real Freedom for All: What (If Anything) Can Justify Capitalism?* Oxford: Clarendon Press.

———. 2000. "A Basic Income for All." *Boston Review* 25(5): 4–8.

Ventry, Dennis J., Jr. 2001. "The Collision of Tax and Welfare Politics: The Political History of the Earned Income Tax Credit." In *Making Work Pay: The Earned Income Tax Credit and Its Impact on America's Families*, edited by Bruce D. Meyer and Douglas Holtz-Eakin (15–66). New York: Russell Sage Foundation.

Vickers, Douglas. 1997. *Economics and Ethics: An Introduction to Theory, Institutions, and Policy.* Westport, CT: Praeger.

Vickrey, William. 1992. "An Updated Agenda for Progressive Taxation." *American Economics Association Papers and Proceedings* 82(2): 257–62.

Voos, Paula B. 2004. "Democracy and Industrial Relations." In *Proceedings of the 56th Annual Meeting of the Industrial Relations Research Association* (1–9). Urbana-Champaign: Industrial Relations Research Association, University of Illinois at Urbana-Champaign.

Vroman, Wayne. 2003. "Extending Unemployment Insurance (UI) Protection." Washington, DC: The Urban Institute.

———. 2005. "An Introduction to Unemployment and Unemployment Insurance." Perspectives on Low-Income Working Families brief 1. Washington, DC: The Urban Institute.

Waldron, Tom, Brandon Roberts, and Andrew Reamer. 2004. "Working Hard, Falling Short: America's Working Families and the Pursuit of Economic Security." Baltimore, MD: Annie E. Casey Foundation.

Waldrop, Judith, and Sharon M. Stern. 2003. "Disability Status 2000." Census 2000 Brief No. C2KBR-17. Washington, DC: U.S. Bureau of the Census.

Walker, David M. 2005. Statement of the Honorable David M. Walker, Comptroller General, U.S. Government Accountability Office, before the House Committee on Ways and Means, March 9.

Warren, Elizabeth, and Amelia Warren Tyagi. 2003. *The Two-Income Trap: Why Middle-Class Mothers and Fathers Are Going Broke.* New York: Basic Books.

Warshawsky, Mark J. 1998a. "Distribution for Retirement Plans: Minimum Requirements, Current Options, and Future Directions." Research Dialogue No. 57. New York: TIAA-CREF Institute.

———. 1998b. "Minimum Distribution Requirements: Reform or Remove Them." *Tax Notes* (November 30): 1133–34.

Wasem, Ruth Ellen. 2005. "Immigration: Legislative Issues on Nonimmigrant Professional (H-1B) Workers." CRS report, updated May 5. Washington, DC: Congressional Research Service, Library of Congress.

Watson Wyatt Worldwide. 1999. *Demographics and Destiny: Winning the War for Talent.* Washington, DC: Watson Wyatt Worldwide.

Weaver, R. Kent. 2000. *Ending Welfare as We Know It.* Washington, DC: Brookings Institution Press.

Weber, Mark C. 1998. "Beyond the Americans with Disabilities Act: A National Employment Policy for People with Disabilities." *Buffalo Law Review* 46 (Winter): 123–74.

Weisbach, David A., and Jacob Nussim. 2003. "The Integration of Tax and Spending Programs." John M. Olin Program in Law & Economics Working Paper No. 194 (2nd series). Chicago, IL: University of Chicago Law School.

Weiss, Andrew. 1990. *Efficiency Wages: Models of Unemployment, Layoffs, and Wage Dispersion.* Princeton, NJ: Princeton University Press.

Welch, Finis. 1999. "Richard T. Ely Lecture: In Defense of Inequality." *American Economic Association Papers and Proceedings* 89(2): 1–17.

———. 2003. "Catching Up: Wages of Black Men." *American Economic Review* 93(2): 320–25.

Welcher, Paul A. 2006. "Access to and Participation in Employer-Provided Health Care Plans, Private Industry, 2005." *Compensation and Working Conditions Online*, January 25.

Western, Bruce. 2001. "Incarceration, Unemployment, and Inequality." *University of Wisconsin–Madison Institute for Research on Poverty Focus* 21(3): 32–35.

Westin, Richard A. 2004. "Modifying the Federal Tax Framework to Stimulate Employment without Violating GATT Principles." *Tax Notes* (April 19): 335–45.

Whitman, Debra, and Patrick Purcell. 2005. "Topics in Aging: Income and Poverty among Older Americans in 2004." CRS report, updated November 7. Washington, DC: Congressional Research Service, Library of Congress.

Wicks, Elliot K. 2003. "Coping with Risk Segmentation: Challenges and Policy Options." Issues in Coverage Expansion Design No. 2. Washington, DC: Economic and Social Research Institute.

Wiener, Joshua M. 2003. "Medicaid and Work Incentives for People with Disabilities: Background and Issues." Briefing paper for the Social Security Administration Ticket to Work and Work Incentives Advisory Panel. Washington, DC: The Urban Institute.

Williamson, John B. 2004. "Assessing the Notional Defined Contribution Model." Issue Brief No. 24. Boston, MA: Center for Retirement Research at Boston College.

Williamson, John B., and Tay K. McNamara. 2001. "Why Some Workers Remain in the Labor Force beyond the Typical Age of Retirement." Working Paper No. 2001-09. Boston, MA: Center for Retirement Research at Boston College.

Wilson, William J. 1996. *When Work Disappears: The World of the New Urban Poor.* New York: Knopf.

Wise, David A. 1991. "Living Longer, Saving Less, Retiring Sooner." In *Retirement and Public Policy: Proceedings of the Second Conference of the National Academy of Social Insurance,* edited by Alicia H. Munnell (209–23). Dubuque, IA: Kendall/Hunt Publishing Company.

Wittenburg, David, and Pamela Loprest. 2003. "Ability or Inability to Work: Challenges in Moving Towards a More Work-Focused Disability Definition for Social Security Administration (SSA) Disability Programs." Briefing paper for the Social Security Administration Ticket to Work and Work Incentives Advisory Panel. Washington, DC: The Urban Institute.

Wolaver, Amy, Timothy McBride, and Barbara Wolfe. 2003. "Mandating Insurance Offers for Low-Wage Workers: An Evaluation of Labor Market Effects." *Journal of Health Politics, Policy and Law* 28(5): 883–926.

Wolff, Edward N. 1999. *Top Heavy: The Increasing Inequality of Wealth in America and What Can Be Done About It.* New York: The New Press.

———. 2004. "Changes in Household Wealth in the 1980s and 1990s in the U.S." Working Paper No. 407. Annandale-on-Hudson, NY: Levy Economics Institute, Bard College.

Wolff, Edward N., and Ajit Zacharias. 2006. "Household Wealth and the Measurement of Economic Well-Being in the United States." Working Paper No. 447. Annandale-on-Hudson, NY: Levy Economics Institute, Bard College.

Wolff, Edward N., Ajit Zacharias, and Asena Caner. 2004. "Levy Institute Measure of Economic Well-Being. Concept, Measurement, and Findings: United States, 1989 and 2000." Levy Institute Measure of Economic Well-being Paper. Annandale-on-Hudson, NY: Levy Economics Institute, Bard College.

Wood, James O. 1999. "Revising ERISA for the Next 25 Years." *Benefits Quarterly* 15(4): 66–72.

Woods, John R. 1993. "Pension Vesting and Preretirement Lump Sums among Full-Time Private-Sector Employees." *Social Security Bulletin* 56(3): 3–21.

Wooten, James A. 1999. "The 'Original Intent' of the Federal Tax Treatment of Private Pension Plans." *Tax Notes* (December 6): 1305–19.

World Bank, The. 1994. *Averting the Old Age Crisis: Policies to Protect the Old and Promote Growth.* Oxford: Oxford University Press.

Wrcholik, Wendy P., J. Scott Moody, and Scott A. Hodge. 2006. "The Rising Cost of Complying with the Federal Income Tax." Washington, DC: Tax Foundation.

Yakoboski, Paul J. 1997. "Large Plan Lump Sums: Rollovers and Cashouts." Issue Brief No. 194. Washington, DC: Employee Benefit Research Institute.

Yellon, Janet L. 1998. "Trends in Income Inequality." In *The Inequality Paradox: Growth of Income Disparity*, edited by James A. Auerbach and Richard S. Belous (7–17). Washington, DC: National Policy Association.

Yin, George K. 1992. "Corporate Tax Integration and the Search for the Pragmatic Ideal." *Tax Law Review* 47 (Spring): 431–508.

Yin, George K., and Jonathan Barry Forman. 1993. "Redesigning the Earned Income Tax Credit Program to Provide More Effective Assistance for the Working Poor." *Tax Notes* (May 17): 951–60.

Yin, George K., John Karl Scholz, Jonathan Barry Forman, and Mark Mazur. 1994. "Improving the Delivery of Benefits to the Working Poor: Proposals to Reform the Earned Income Credit Program." *American Journal of Tax Policy* 11: 225–98.

Yoo, Kwang-Yeol, and Alain de Serres. 2004. "Tax Treatment of Private Pension Savings in OECD Countries and the Net Tax Cost Per Unit of Contribution to Tax-Favoured Schemes." Economic Department Paper No. ECO/WKP 29. Paris: OECD.

Young, Michael. 1958. *Rise of the Meritocracy.* London: Thames and Hudson.

Zedlewski, Sheila R., and Simone G. Schaner. 2005. "Older Adults Engagement Should Be Recognized and Encouraged." Perspectives on Productive Aging No. 1. Washington, DC: The Urban Institute.

Zedlewski, Sheila R., Linda Giannarelli, Joyce Morton, and Laura Wheaton. 2001. "Extreme Poverty Rising, Existing Government Programs Could Do

More." *Assessing the New Federalism* Policy Brief B-45. Washington, DC: The Urban Institute.

Zedlewski, Sheila R., Sandi Nelson, Kathryn Edin, Heather L. Koball, and Kate Roberts. 2003. *Families Coping without Earnings or Government Cash Assistance.* Washington, DC: The Urban Institute. *Assessing the New Federalism* Occasional Paper No. 64.

Zelenak, Lawrence. 1993. "Taxing Gains at Death." *Vanderbilt Law Review* 46: 361–441.

———. 1994. "Marriage and the Income Tax." *Southern California Law Review* 67(2): 339–405.

Zelinsky, Edward A. 1999. "ERISA and the Emergence of the Defined Contribution Society." In *Proceedings of the Fifty-Seventh New York University Institute on Federal Taxation, Employee Benefits and Executive Compensation,* edited by Alvin D. Lurie (6-1–6-29). New York: Matthew Bender & Company.

———. 2004. "The Defined Contribution Paradigm." *Yale Law Journal* 114(3): 451–534.

Zimmerman, David J. 1992. "Regression toward Mediocrity in Economic Stature." *American Economic Review* 82(3): 409–29.

ABOUT THE AUTHOR

Jonathan Barry Forman is the Alfred P. Murrah Professor of Law at the University of Oklahoma College of Law, where he teaches tax, pensions, and elder law. In addition to his dozens of scholarly publications, Professor Forman has a monthly column in the *Journal Record* newspaper of Oklahoma City. He has also published op-eds in *Barron's*, the *Dallas Morning News, Pensions & Investments*, the *Cleveland Plain Dealer*, the *Washington Times*, the *Daily Oklahoman*, and *Tax Notes*. Professor Forman has lectured around the world, testified before Congress, and served on numerous federal and state advisory committees. He is vice chair of the board of trustees of the Oklahoma Public Employees Retirement System, and he is active in the American Bar Association and the Association of American Law Professors.

Professor Forman earned his law degree from the University of Michigan in 1978. He holds master's degrees in economics (George Washington University, 1983) and psychology (University of Iowa, 1975). Before entering academia, it was his privilege to serve in all three branches of the federal government, most recently as tax counsel to Senator Daniel Patrick Moynihan (D-NY).

INDEX

THE URBAN INSTITUTE PRESS
WASHINGTON, DC

"The stagnation of real wages and the increased income risks faced by American families are not just economic problems; they threaten the long-standing social tenet that hard work should lead to a brighter future. *Making America Work* tackles these problems head on."

Peter Orszag, Joseph A. Pechman Senior Fellow, The Brookings Institution

"In clear, crisp prose, Jon Forman explains the government's many influences on the activities and needs of ordinary working Americans. In the process, he challenges the government to make work more rewarding and to improve the amount of economic justice in the country. Forman has studied these issues for many years and his analysis is both sophisticated and straightforward. This book will be an excellent resource for anyone interested in the government's policy toward work."

George K. Yin, Edwin S. Cohen Distinguished Professor of Law and Taxation, University of Virginia, and former Chief of Staff, Joint Committee on Taxation

"It is remarkable that Professor Forman has offered so many reform ideas in so many policy arenas. One hopes that the book will have an impact on agenda setting in the 2006 and 2008 elections, and beyond."

Yung-Ping (Bing) Chen, Frank J. Manning Eminent Scholar's Chair, Gerontology Institute, John W. McCormack Graduate School, University of Massachusetts Boston

"No one has ever put together ideas, recom mendations, and facts in quite this way before. Jon Forman has organized his mat als around the theme of getting America to work. His ideas are good, and his resea is solid."

Joel S. Newman, Professor of Law, Wake Forest University

"Jon Forman superbly manages two feats a single book. First, he presents a lively, w written introduction to a whole range of re policy issues: taxes, welfare, Social Secur pensions, health care, and labor markets. Second, he offers thoughtful policy recom mendations for each issue. Anyone intere in these policy issues should read Forman stimulating book."

Laurence Seidman, Chaplin Tyler Professor of Economics, University of Delaware

"Forman is a master at tapping American values and showing how government can help transform the way society rewards most widely held and cherished value: w This timely book comes just as our belie in pensions, health care, Social Security, minimum wages, and other 'work-related benefits are being questioned. Policy analysts, researchers, and students will a find something to think and write about in this clearheaded, comprehensive, and compelling volume."

Timothy M. Smeeding, Distinguished Professor of Economics Public Administration, The Maxwell Sc of Syracuse University

COVER: LISA CAREY DESIGN

ISBN 0-87766-731-4

9 780877 667315

ISBN 0-87766-731-4